European Commission

General Report
on the Activities of
the European Union
1995

Brussels • Luxembourg • 1996

Cataloguing data can be found at the end of this publication

Luxembourg: Office for Official Publications of the European Communities, 1996

ISBN 92-827-5897-4

The President and the Members of the European Commission to the President of the European Parliament

Sir,

We have the honour to present the General Report on the Activities of the European Union for 1995, which the Commission is required to publish by Article 156 of the EC Treaty, Article 17 of the ECSC Treaty and Article 125 of the EAEC Treaty.

In accordance with the procedure described in the Declaration on the system for fixing Community farm prices contained in the Accession Documents of 22 January 1972, the Commission will shortly be sending Parliament the 1995 Report on the Agricultural Situation in the Community.

And, in accordance with an undertaking given to Parliament on 7 June 1971, the Commission is preparing its twenty-fifth annual Report on Competition Policy.

Please accept, Sir, the expression of our highest consideration.

Brussels, 13 February 1996

Jacques SANTER
President

Leon BRITTAN
Vice-president

Manuel MARÍN
Vice-president

Martin BANGEMANN

Karel VAN MIERT

Hans VAN DEN BROEK

João de Deus PINHEIRO

Pádraig FLYNN

Marcelino OREJA

Anita GRADIN

Édith CRESSON

Ritt BJERREGAARD

Monika WULF-MATHIES

Neil KINNOCK

Mario MONTI

Franz FISCHLER

Emma BONINO

Yves-Thibault de SILGUY

Erkki LIIKANEN

Christos PAPOUTSIS

NOTE

Legislative instruments under the co-decision procedure are mentioned in the Report followed by '(Table I)'. Instruments under the consultation, cooperation or assent procedures are followed by '(Table II)'. International agreements are followed by '(Table III)'. No footnotes are given for these instruments, which are listed in three separate tables annexed to the Report. The relevant references (OJ, COM, Bull.) for all the stages of the legislative procedure concerning each instrument, together with the appropriate point numbers in text, are given in the tables.

As a rule, no references are given in text for intermediate stages of procedures which started before 1 January 1995 and were not completed at 31 December 1995. These references also appear in the tables.

Standardized abbreviations for the designation of certain monetary units in the different languages of the Community.

BFR	Belgische frank/franc belge
DKR	Dansk krone
DM	Deutsche Mark
DR	Greek drachma
ESC	Escudo
FF	Franc français
FMK	Suomen markka
HFL	Nederlandse gulden (Hollandse florijn)
IRL	Irish pound/punt
LFR	Franc luxembourgeois
LIT	Lira italiana
OS	Österreichischer Schilling
PTA	Peseta
SKR	Svensk Krona
UKL	Pound sterling
USD	United States dollar

Contents

THE EUROPEAN UNION IN 1995   1

CHAPTER I — UNION CITIZENSHIP   9

   Section 1 — Priority activities and objectives   9

   Section 2 — Citizens' rights   11
   Freedom of movement and right of residence   11
   Right to vote and stand in elections   12
   Right to protection in non-member countries   13
   Right to petition and right of access to the Ombudsman   13

   Section 3 — Openness, subsidiarity and simplification   14

CHAPTER II — HUMAN RIGHTS AND FUNDAMENTAL FREEDOMS   19

   Section 1 — Inside the European Union   19

   Section 2 — Outside the European Union   21

CHAPTER III — THE COMMUNITY ECONOMIC AND SOCIAL AREA   25

   Section 1 — Implementation of the White Paper on growth, competitiveness and employment   25

   Section 2 — Economic and monetary policy   28
   Priority activities and objectives   28
   Economic situation   28
   Economic and monetary union   29
   Growth initiative and financial activities   36
   International monetary and financial matters   40
   Economic dialogue with the associated countries of Central and Eastern Europe   41

European Monetary Institute (EMI)   41

European Investment Bank (EIB)   43

European Investment Fund (EIF)   46

Section 3 — Statistical system   47

Priority activities and objectives   47

Policy aspects   48

Publications   49

Section 4 — Internal market   50

Priority activities and objectives   50

Management of the internal market   51

Free movement of goods   53

Free movement of persons   59

Freedom to provide services   60

Free movement of capital   62

Taxation   63

Company law   63

Intellectual and industrial property   64

Data protection   65

Public procurement   65

Legal professions: Training and information concerning the application of Community law   66

Preparation for the integration of the countries of Central and Eastern Europe with associate status into the internal market   66

Section 5 — Competition   67

Priority activities and objectives   67

Competition rules applying to businesses   68

State aid   73

Public undertakings and national monopolies   74

International aspects   75

Section 6 — Industrial policy   77

Priority activities and objectives   77

Industrial competitiveness   77

Individual sectors   80

Section 7 — Enterprise policy, distributive trades, tourism and cooperatives 88

Priority activities and objectives 88

Improving the business environment 88

Support measures for businesses 90

Small businesses and the craft sector 91

Cooperatives, mutual societies, associations and foundations 91

The distributive trades 92

Tourism 92

Section 8 — Research and technology 94

Priority activities and objectives 94

Community R&TD policy 94

Implementation of specific programmes under the fourth framework programme 98

Section 9 — Education, vocational training and youth 107

Priority activities and objectives 107

Cooperation in the field of education 108

Vocational training 109

Foreign language teaching 110

Open and distance learning and technological innovation 111

Cooperation in the field of youth 111

Cooperation with non-member countries 112

European Training Foundation, Turin 113

European Centre for the Development of Vocational Training (Cedefop) 114

European University Institute, Florence 114

Section 10 — Economic and social cohesion 116

Priority activities and objectives 116

Community support frameworks and single programming documents 117

Community initiatives 125

Innovative schemes and other regional schemes 131

Cohesion Fund 132

ECSC conversion loans 133

EEA Financial Mechanism 134

Section 11 — Measures for the most remote regions 135

Priority activities and objectives 135

Agriculture   136

Fisheries   136

Customs, tariff and trade measures   136

Taxation   137

Other measures   137

Section 12 — Trans-European networks   138

Priority activities and objectives   138

Transport   139

Telematics and telecommunications   140

Energy   141

Environment   142

Section 13 — Energy   143

Priority activities and objectives   143

Community energy strategy   144

Internal energy market   147

Individual sectors   148

Relations with third countries   149

Euratom Supply Agency   151

State aid to the coal industry   152

Section 14 — Transport   153

Priority activities and objectives   153

Infrastructure and traffic management and navigation systems   154

Transport and the environment   154

Research and technological development   155

Inland transport   155

Sea transport   158

Air transport   159

State aid   161

International cooperation   162

Section 15 — Information society, telecommunications   164

Priority activities and objectives   164

Information society   164

Telecommunications policy   166

Telematics applications	169
Remote transmission of administrative data, information and documents	173
Advanced television services	174
Postal services	174
Data protection	175
International cooperation	175
Regional aspects	176
Section 16 — Environment	177
Priority activities and objectives	177
Fifth action programme on the environment — taking the environment into account in other policies	178
General	178
Industry and environment	182
Civil protection	185
Quality of the environment and natural resources	185
European Environment Agency	190
Section 17 — Nuclear safety	191
Priority activities and objectives	191
Radiation protection	191
Plant safety	192
Radioactive waste	193
International action	193
Section 18 — Euratom safeguards	195
Section 19 — Agricultural policy	197
Priority activities and objectives	197
Content of the common agricultural policy	198
Management of the common agricultural policy	201
Financing the common agricultural policy: the EAGGF	211
Section 20 — Fisheries	216
Priority activities and objectives	216
Fisheries policy	216
Internal resources and policy on conservation and monitoring	217
External resources	219

Market organization 223

Fisheries and the environment 224

Structural action 224

State aid schemes 224

Section 21 — Employment and social policy 225

Priority activities and objectives 225

Implementation of the White Paper on social policy 226

Implementation of the Protocol on social policy 227

Employment 229

Structural operations 232

Social security 232

Working conditions 233

Health and safety 234

Combating social exclusion 235

European Foundation for the Improvement of Living and Working Conditions 236

International cooperation 236

Section 22 — Equal opportunities 237

Section 23 — Solidarity 240

Measures to help the disabled 240

Measures to help older people 240

Measures to help disaster victims in the European Union 240

Section 24 — Public health 242

Priority activities and objectives 242

Cancer 243

AIDS and other communicable diseases 244

Drugs 244

International cooperation 245

Section 25 — Consumer policy 246

Priority activities and objectives 246

Consumer participation 246

Consumer information and education 246

Protection of consumer health and safety 248

Protection of consumers' economic and legal interests 248

Section 26 — Information, communication, audiovisual media and culture   250

Priority activities and objectives   250

Information and communication policy   251

Audiovisual policy   255

Cultural policy   257

CHAPTER IV — ROLE OF THE EUROPEAN UNION IN THE WORLD   261

Section 1 — Priority activities and objectives   261

Section 2 — Common foreign and security policy   267

General   267

Common foreign policy   268

Common security policy   269

EU statements and presidency press statements   271

Section 3 — International organizations and conferences   278

United Nations and UN specialized agencies   278

World Trade Organization   281

Organization for Security and Cooperation in Europe   282

Western European Union   283

Council of Europe   284

Organization for Economic Cooperation and Development   285

European Bank for Reconstruction and Development   286

Section 4 — Commercial policy   287

General matters   287

Individual sectors   293

Section 5 — Development policy   300

Overview and cooperation in the run-up to 2000   300

Generalized system of preferences   302

Cooperation through the United Nations   302

Cooperation through non-governmental organizations   303

Commodities and world agreements   304

EC Investment Partners   305

Protecting the environment   305

North-South cooperation against drug abuse   306

North-South cooperation on health issues and HIV/AIDS 307

Rehabilitation aid 307

Food aid 308

Refugee assistance 310

Support for democratization and human rights 310

Section 6 — Humanitarian aid 311

Overall strategy 311

Humanitarian aid operations 312

Section 7 — European Economic Area, relations with the EFTA countries 315

European Economic Area 315

Relations with the EFTA countries 316

Section 8 — Relations with Central and Eastern Europe and the Baltic States 318

Pre-accession strategy and structured dialogue 318

Europe Agreements and other accords 320

Assistance for Central and Eastern Europe 321

Bilateral relations 323

Section 9 — Relations with Mediterranean non-member countries and the Middle East 327

Mediterranean non-member countries 327

The Middle East (Gulf Cooperation Council countries, Iran, Iraq and Yemen) 336

Euro-Arab Dialogue and relations with the Economic Cooperation Organization (ECO) 338

Section 10 — Relations with the independent States of the former Soviet Union and Mongolia 339

Overview 339

Partnership and cooperation agreements and other agreements 339

Trade arrangements 340

Assistance for the independent States of the former Soviet Union 340

Bilateral relations 343

Section 11 — Relations with the United States, Japan and other industrialized countries 348

Western Economic Summit (G7) 348

United States 349

Japan	352
Australia	354
Canada	355
New Zealand	356
Section 12 — Relations with the countries of Asia	357
Overview and relations with regional groupings	357
Bilateral relations	358
Cooperation	361
Section 13 — Latin America	362
Relations with regional groupings	362
Bilateral relations	364
Aid activities	366
Section 14 — Relations with the African, Caribbean and Pacific (ACP) countries, South Africa and the overseas countries and territories (OCTs)	367
Relations with ACP countries	367
Relations with South Africa	374
Overseas countries and territories (OCTs)	375
CHAPTER V — COOPERATION IN THE FIELDS OF JUSTICE AND HOME AFFAIRS	379
Section 1 — Priority activities and objectives	379
Section 2 — Asylum, external frontiers and immigration	381
Section 3 — Judicial, customs and police cooperation	384
Section 4 — The fight against drugs	387
CHAPTER VI — FINANCING COMMUNITY ACTIVITIES	389
Section 1 — Priority activities and objectives	389
Section 2 — Budgets	392
General budget	392
ECSC budget	407
Financial Regulation	408

Section 3 — Financial control   410

Section 4 — Action to combat fraud   412

Section 5 — Borrowing and lending operations   415
Operations concerning the New Community Instrument   416
Macrofinancial assistance   416
Financing ECSC activities   417
Financing Euratom activities   418
European Investment Bank   418

Section 6 — General budget guarantee for borrowing and lending operations   419

CHAPTER VII — INSTITUTIONAL MATTERS   421

Section 1 — Preparations for 1996 Intergovernmental Conference   421

Section 2 — Voting in the Council   425

Section 3 — Involvement of Parliament in decision-making   427

Section 4 — Implementing powers conferred on the Commission   428

Section 5 — Interinstitutional collaboration   429

CHAPTER VIII — INSTITUTIONS   431

Section 1 — Composition and functioning   431
Parliament   431
Council   434
Commission   438
Court of Justice and Court of First Instance   440
Court of Auditors   443
Economic and Social Committee   445
Committee of the Regions   448
ECSC Consultative Committee   450
European Monetary Institute   452

Section 2 — Administration and management   453
Staff policy and Staff Regulations   453

Data processing 458

Language services 458

CHAPTER IX — COMMUNITY LAW 461

Section 1 — Monitoring the application of Community law 461

Section 2 — Decisions by the Court of Justice and the Court of First Instance 462

Free movement of goods and customs union 462

Free movement of workers 463

Freedom to provide services 466

Free movement of capital 467

Equal treatment 468

Common commercial policy and external relations 469

Institutional matters 469

Activities of the Court of Justice and the Court of First Instance 472

Section 3 — Computerization of Community law 476

THE YEAR IN BRIEF 477

ANNEXES 495

Annex I   — Table I: Legislation under the co-decision procedure 496

Annex II — Table II: Legislation under the consultation, cooperation and assent procedures 521

Annex III — Table III: Legislation regarding international agreements 565

INSTITUTIONS AND OTHER BODIES 589

LIST OF ABBREVIATIONS 591

PUBLICATIONS CITED IN THIS REPORT 599

INDEX 601

The European Union in 1995

With the accession of Austria, Finland and Sweden in 1995, the Union now has 15 Member States and nearly 370 million citizens. The new Commission chaired by Mr Jacques Santer began its five-year term of office; this was the first Commission in the history of the Communities to have been subjected to formal confirmation by the European Parliament.

The institutions' main concerns throughout the year were to prepare for the third stage of economic and monetary union and the changeover to the single currency, develop a job-creating economy and give priority to the fight against unemployment by means of social solidarity measures to accompany economic policy measures, prepare for the 1996 Intergovernmental Conference, take up the challenge of enlargement and reinforce the Union's role on the world scene, and, at the same time, remember the citizen's central place in the process of European integration.

The Madrid European Council on 15 and 16 December unequivocally confirmed that the third stage of economic and monetary union, which will then be an irreversible process, will begin on 1 January 1999 in full compliance with the convergence criteria, timing, protocols and procedures established by the EC Treaty. It also adopted the scenario for the introduction of the single currency, to be called the Euro, following a debate launched by the Commission's Green Paper of 31 May. The Commission was also at pains to boost public awareness of the fact that a strong and stable single currency will make a valuable contribution to long-term sustainable job creation.

Job creation and its companion, the fight against unemployment, were the main social, economic and political objective pursued by the Union and its Member States throughout the year. The Madrid European Council welcomed the cooperation between all concerned in implementing the medium-term employment strategy and monitoring procedure established and confirmed by earlier European Councils. It noted that the Member States had put into operation multiannual employment action programmes incorporating the five priority lines of action agreed at Essen and that the innovatory measures involved were already bearing fruit. Approving the joint report presented by the Commission and the Council, the European Council noted that for the first time there was a consensual analysis of the means of ensuring that the current economic recovery was accompanied by an improvement in the employment situation. The Commission had presented an initial annual report on employment trends in the Union and defined a European strategy to encourage local employment initiatives, which had been taken as the basis for the joint report. It also presented the European Council with a report on the role of small businesses as a source of job-creation, growth and competitiveness, stressing the need to improve their access to information, training and research, to the internal market and to capital markets, to remove tax discrimination and to boost the Community lending instrument for them set up by the Edinburgh European Council. The Madrid European Council approved most of these points in its conclusions. Education and vocational training are a vital tool for combating unemployment and boosting competitiveness, and there were major developments, notably with the adoption of the Socrates and 'Youth for Europe' programmes, the implementation of the Leonardo da Vinci programme (which has been the source of significant progress in vocational training) and the presentation of the Commission's White Paper on education and training. Major progress was also made with the information society.

The Commission continued work on the trans-European networks, the development of which is a key component of the European Union's strategy for growth, competitiveness and employment. On 18 September the Council adopted the financial regulation governing the granting of Community financial aid for trans-European networks. On the basis of the Commission's progress report, the Madrid European Council called on Member States to give top priority to actually implementing projects identified by the Essen European Council as being of special importance and called on the Council to provide additional financial resources.

In its concern to ensure that economic policy was underpinned by a bold, balanced social policy as a core feature of European integration, the Commission adopted a new medium-term social action programme (1995-97), a fourth programme of action to develop health and safety at the workplace (1996-2000) and a communication to stimulate debate on the future of social protection in Europe. The social dialogue was reinforced, and the social partners came to their first agreement, dealing with reconciliation of working life and family life, under the social protocol. The Commission opened new consultations under the protocol, on the burden of proof in sex discrimination cases, flexibility in working time and stability of employment, and information and consultation of workers.

The Madrid European Council stressed that enlargement to Central and Eastern Europe and the Mediterranean without jeopardizing the acquis communautaire *was both a political necessity and a historic opportunity for Europe, and it adopted a timetable and a preparation strategy. It confirmed that accession negotiations with Cyprus and Malta, with whom a structured dialogue had already commenced this year, would begin on the basis of Commission proposals six months after the conclusion of the Intergovernmental Conference. Regarding the countries of Central and Eastern Europe, it stated that after the conclusion of the Intergovernmental Conference, it would consider the results of the Conference and the opinions and reports to be produced by the Commission and then take the decisions needed to launch accession negotiations; the hope is that their opening will coincide with the start of negotiations with Cyprus and Malta. The Commission took initiatives to implement the pre-accession strategy for the associated countries in Central and Eastern Europe and the Baltic States defined by the Essen European Council; they included publication of a White Paper on their preparation for integration into the internal market and reports on the links between accession and the common policies, particularly the common agricultural policy. The structured dialogue provided for as part of the strategy became fully operational in 1995, and several countries deposited their formal applications for membership; the Cannes European Council established a stable medium-term framework for financing external policy in relation to Central and Eastern Europe for the period from 1995 to 2000, and the Madrid European Council confirmed the key role of the PHARE programme in this respect.*

There were significant developments in all fields of the European Union's external relations. The Union manifested its determination to tighten its links with its Mediterranean partners. The Commission fleshed out the broad lines of partnership and proposed a financial instrument (MEDA) comparable to PHARE and TACIS, and the Cannes European Council produced a financial framework for relations with these countries in June; the Euro-Mediterranean Conference in Barcelona adopted a declaration and a work programme, welcomed by the Madrid European Council as the starting point for a comprehensive association which will encourage peace, stability and prosperity in the region and the establishment, in the long term, of a free-trade area. Apart from the new agreements with Tunisia, Israel and Morocco, Parliament gave its assent to the completion of the customs union with Turkey.

The Union maintained its resolute support for the peace process in the Middle East and former Yugoslavia, being the world's leading donor to these regions. At the end of the year the agreement putting an end to the conflict in former Yugoslavia was concluded at Dayton, Ohio, and signed in Paris. The Commission built up a regional reconstruction strategy and proposed practical measures to improve the management and coordination of inter-

national aid, and the European Council confirmed the Union's determination to make a substantial contribution to the implementation of the peace agreement in a climate of international burden-sharing.

Under the common foreign and security policy, the Stability Pact for Europe was adopted in April; this was the concrete outcome of the European Union's first joint action and an unprecedented example of preventive diplomacy in Central Europe.

Progress was made in consolidating relations between the European Union and the independent States of the former Soviet Union, thanks to negotiation of a new generation of partnership and cooperation agreements, to intensification of the political dialogue, to more detailed definition of the Union's relations with some of these States and to intensification of technical assistance under the TACIS programme. The Madrid European Council reiterated support for Russia's efforts to secure stability, development, peace and democracy, and reaffirmed the Union's readiness to pursue the programme of technical assistance to the independent States of the former Soviet Union so as to support their economic and political reform processes.

The deepening of relations between the European Union and the United States continued with the adoption of a new transatlantic agenda and an associated joint action plan at the summit held on 3 December.

The Commission began implementing the new approach established in 1994 to take account of the growing weight of Asia in world affairs. A medium-term strategy for relations with Japan was proposed, based on stronger cooperation and dialogue, and a long-term policy on relations with China was devised. Cooperation agreements were signed with Nepal, Sri Lanka and Vietnam, and negotiations commenced with the Republic of Korea.

The Commission further proposed strengthening the partnership with Latin America for the period from 1996-2000 on the basis of closer political links, stronger economic integration and free trade and the focusing of cooperation on priority themes; the approach was favourably received by the Madrid European Council. Relations with the region were marked by the signing of an interregional framework agreement for economic and trade cooperation with Mercosur on the occasion of the Madrid European Council, the aim being to tighten links between the two regions and prepare for eventual association. The Commission proposed that the San José dialogue between the European Union and Central America be renewed and presented a strategy for closer relations with Mexico, with which a solemn joint declaration was signed. A joint declaration on political dialogue was signed with Chile, and the Commission proposed that dialogue and regular consultations be started with Cuba.

The main event in relation to the ACP countries was the signing of the revised Lomé Convention in Mauritius in November. This will reinforce the association between the European Union and the ACP countries, with a substantially increased financial allocation. Regarding development policy more generally, the Commission continued to assert its international role, notably by attending UN conferences such as the Copenhagen World Social Development Summit and the fourth World Conference on Women in Beijing. It also stepped up its policy of seeking universal respect for human rights, consolidation of democracy and the rule of law, notably by inserting a suspension clause in international agreements to apply in the event of violations of human rights. The Union also played a decisive role in the international defence of the environment, notably in controls of transfrontier shipments and disposal of hazardous waste (Basle Convention), biological diversity, substances that deplete the ozone layer (Montreal Protocol) and the adoption of a pan-European environmental strategy (Sofia Conference).

Within the Union, the integration of environmental concerns into other policies was one of the Commission's priorities. Improving the quality of life through initiatives relating to public health, encouraging solidarity with the elderly and the disabled, promoting equal opportunities, combating racism and xenophobia, boosting consumer protection, developing cultural action at European level — these were all at the centre of attention in Community business. Throughout the year the institutions sought to bring the Union closer to its citizens. Regarding justice and home affairs cooperation, there was further consolidation of the new framework for cooperation established by the Union Treaty, and some significant results were achieved. In March, for instance, the first convention under Title VI of the Treaty, concerning a simplified extradition procedure, was signed; it was followed in July by three more conventions, one of which was on Europol, a major element of police cooperation between Member States. In November agreement was reached on the first joint position, concerning the interpretation of the concept of refugee. The Council adopted a joint action to determine the Community financing procedures for justice and home affairs. But these steps forward did not suffice to allay concern at the operation of Title VI and the scale of the results. To flesh out the concept of Community citizenship and secure real freedom of movement within the Union, the Commission presented three proposals for Directives on the removal of border checks, travel rights for third-country nationals within the Union and the adjustment of secondary legislation relating to entry and residence. The Council enacted measures relating to visas for third-country nationals crossing the Union's external borders, and the Madrid European Council welcomed the adoption of two decisions on consular protection that will enable Union citizens to seek assistance from the consulates of all Member

States in non-member countries. On 12 July Parliament appointed the Union's first Ombudsman with power to hear complaints from Union citizens or residents about maladministration by the Community institutions.

The institutions adopted a number of measures by way of follow-up to the 1993 interinstitutional declaration on democracy, transparency and subsidiarity. The Commission improved public access to its documents, intensified consultations with interested circles prior to making proposals and pursued its dialogue with interest groups. It presented the Madrid European Council with a report on the application of the principles of subsidiarity and proportionality, simplification and consolidation, entitled 'Better law-making'. It studied the report by the group of independent experts on simplification of legislation and administration, and emphasized the importance of a comparable effort by Member States to simplify their own legislation and lighten the burden on business. It also took great trouble to answer questions from the general public, clarify what was at stake and what was to be gained from European integration in terms of everyday life and explain Community policies so as to remedy the lack of understanding and general unintelligibility.

In this spirit, the Commission, as announced by its President, Jacques Santer, when he presented the new work programme — 'Doing less but doing it better' — endeavoured to reduce the number of proposals for new legislation, scrutinizing them very carefully for compliance with the principles of subsidiarity and proportionality and engaging in extensive prior consultation so as to stimulate reflection and thus prompt framework action plans. It amplified this reorientation of its working methods by initiatives relating to administrative and financial management and the fight against fraud, its constant concern being sound and efficient management.

The Commission hopes consequently to be well placed to meet the challenges facing the Union in 1996, which will have to be tackled comprehensively — securing employment and solidarity, attaining economic and monetary union on the basis of the timetable set at Madrid, exploiting the possibilities offered by the internal market, preparing for enlargement in accordance with the process determined by the European Council, and making a success of the Intergovernmental Conference to review the Treaties.

Active preparations were made during the year for the 1996 Intergovernmental Conference. The Community institutions and other bodies presented their reports on the operation of the Treaty on European Union as input for the Reflection Group chaired by Mr Carlos Westendorp, which began work in June and reported to the Madrid European Council in December. The report aroused keen interest at the European Council, where it was felt that the Group's conclusions laid a valuable foundation for the Conference. It was decided that the Conference will open on 29 March 1996. The revision of the Treaty should strengthen the peace and prosperity that the process of European integration has consolidated since its inception nearly 50 years ago. The aim must be to conclude a new pact for Europe, on the basis of the acquis communautaire, *and prepare the Union for subsequent enlargements; this will mean giving thought to the functioning of the institutions, their composition, their working methods and their decision-making mechanisms, the overall concern being to maintain a single institutional framework and to respect the general institutional balance. The Intergovernmental Conference will also have to put the citizen back at the heart of the Union by enhancing democracy, openness and the effectiveness of the institutions and policies.*

Chapter I

Union citizenship

Priority activities and objectives

1.   *Two of the major concerns of the European institutions throughout the year were how to translate the concept of European citizenship into practical action and bring the Community closer to its citizens while making it more open and transparent. The Commission took further steps to give effect to European citizens' rights under Article 8 of the EC Treaty, particularly freedom of movement inside the frontier-free area, and on 12 July it put forward a set of three proposals for directives. On 29 May the Council adopted measures to introduce a uniform visa for nationals of non-Community countries, and on 25 September decided on the list of non-Community countries whose nationals must have a visa when crossing the Member States' external borders. The European Union's first Ombudsman was appointed by Parliament on 12 July.*

Following on from the interinstitutional declaration of 1993 on democracy, transparency and subsidiarity, the institutions took a number of steps to enhance transparency and bring Europe closer to its citizens. For example, the Commission afforded the public improved access to documents, stepped up prior consultations with interested circles and held further exchanges with special-interest groups. In February it adopted its 1995 programme, and then gave Parliament a progress report on it for the first time before the end of the year concerned; in December it presented its work programme for 1996 to Parliament.

The Commission also ensured that the principles of subsidiarity and proportionality were applied in everyday practice, while pressing ahead with the review of existing legislation. This included action to simplify and slim down legislation and a great deal of work on consolidation. It sent the

Madrid European Council a report, entitled 'Better law-making', on the application of the principles of subsidiarity and proportionality, simplification and consolidation, in which it restates its concern to apply the principle of 'less action, but better action'. It also responded to the report delivered by the group of independent experts on the simplification of legislation and administration by sending Parliament and the Council its detailed observations on the report, stressing the importance of comparable efforts to be made by the Member States to simplify their legislation and remove unnecessary burdens on firms.

Section 2

Citizens' rights

Freedom of movement and right of residence

2.   In order to create an area without internal frontiers in accordance with the objective set out in Article 7a of the EC Treaty, the Commission adopted a set of three proposals for Directives on 12 July. The first provides for the elimination of controls by 31 December 1996 (Table II) on all persons, whatever their nationality, crossing any internal frontier (by air, land and sea). It goes hand in hand with the application of essential accompanying measures, some of which have already been adopted, such as the Dublin Convention on the determination of the Member State responsible for examining applications for asylum lodged in a Member State of the European Communities,[1] Regulation (EC) No 1683/95 on the introduction of a uniform format for visas *(→ point 3)* and Regulation (EC) No 2317/95 on third countries whose nationals must be in possession of a visa *(→ point 3)* while the adoption of others, notably under Title VI of the Treaty on European Union, such as the External Frontiers Convention *(→ point 961)* and the European Information System is awaited. The proposal also includes a safeguard clause in case of a serious threat to public order or security in the Member States. The second proposal, on the right of third-country nationals to travel in the Community (Table II), stipulates that any holder of a residence permit or a visa issued by a Member State can travel throughout the Community without further formalities. The third proposal (Table I) seeks to amend Directive 68/360/EEC on the abolition of restrictions on movement and residence within the Community for workers of the Member States and their families and Directive 73/148/EEC on the abolition of restrictions on movement and residence within the Community for nationals of the Member States with regard to establishment and provision of services by deleting any provisions which make the crossing of internal borders subject to the production of a valid identity document.

3.   Under Article 100c of the EC Treaty, the Council, on 28 May, adopted Regulation (EC) No 1683/95 (Table II) laying down a uniform format for visas for nationals of third countries. This single, clearly identifiable visa will be issued by the Member States and will contain all the necessary informa-

---

[1]   Twenty-fourth General Report, point 896.

tion; it will meet the highest technical standards, notably as regards safe-guards against counterfeiting and falsification, and will guarantee protection of the personal data involved. On 25 September, the Council adopted Regulation (EC) No 2317/95 (Table II) determining the third countries whose nationals must be in possession of a visa[1] when crossing the external borders of the Member States. This Regulation does not prevent the Member States from maintaining national lists including other countries. The visas in question are only those issued for a stay of not more than three months. In a resolution passed on 26 October, Parliament expressed the view that the associated countries of Central and Eastern Europe should enjoy equal treatment in the matter of visas.[2]

Right to vote and stand in elections

4.   In a resolution passed on 5 April,[3] Parliament took the view that by failing to consult it before granting a derogation to Belgium in the provisions of Directive 94/80/EC laying down detailed arrangements for the exercise of the right to vote and to stand as a candidate in municipal elections by citizens of the Union residing in a Member State of which they are not nationals,[4] the Council had prevented it from legitimately exercising the function conferred on it by Article 8b(1) of the EC Treaty. Parliament also warned the Member States against any action under this provision which would conceal unjustified discrimination between citizens of the Union.

5.   On 10 July the Representatives of the Governments of the Member States adopted a supplementary resolution[5] to the resolutions of 23 June 1981,[6] 30 June 1982[7] and 14 July 1986[8] concerning the introduction of a passport of uniform pattern in order to make provision for the European passport to bear the words *European Union* and to make the necessary linguistic changes to take account of the accession of the new Member States.

---

[1]   The full list of countries and territorial entities whose nationals must be in possession of a visa in order to cross the external borders of the Member States is given in Bull. 9-1995, point 2.2.1.
[2]   OJ C 308, 20.11.1995; Bull. 10-1995, point 1.1.1.
[3]   OJ C 109, 1.5.1995; Bull. 4-1995, point 1.1.1.
[4]   OJ L 368, 31.12.1994; 1994 General Report, point 4.
[5]   OJ C 200, 4.8.1995; Bull. 6-1995, point 1.1.1; Bull. 7/8-1995, point 1.1.5.
[6]   OJ C 241, 19.9.1981.
[7]   OJ C 179, 16.7.1982.
[8]   OJ C 185, 24.7.1986.

Right to protection in non-member countries

6. On 19 December the Representatives of the Governments of the Member States meeting within the Council adopted Decision 95/553/EC[1] on the protection of citizens of the European Union by diplomatic missions and consulates and a Decision[2] on measures for the implementation of Decision 95/553/EC to enable any citizen of the European Union to enjoy the consular protection of any diplomatic mission or consulate of a Member State in territories where his own Member State or the State which permanently represents his Member State maintains no accessible, permanent mission or relevant consulate. In this way, citizens can obtain assistance in the event of death, illness or serious accident, arrest, detention or assault as well as help and repatriation in the event of difficulty. At its meeting in Madrid in December,[2] the European Council welcomed the progress made in this area.

Right to petition and right of access to the Ombudsman

7. Pursuant to Article 138e of the EC Treaty, Parliament appointed Jacob Söderman Ombudsman of the European Union on 12 July.[3] Before the appointment, Parliament adopted a Decision on 16 May amending Article 159 of its Rules of Procedure on appointment of the Ombudsman.[4] The regulations and general conditions governing the performance of the Ombudsman's duties were laid down in Decision 94/262/ECSC, EC, Euratom;[5] he is empowered to receive complaints from any citizen of the Union or any natural person residing in a Member State or legal person having its registered office there, in respect of cases of maladministration in the activities of Community institutions or bodies. In a resolution passed on 14 July[6] on the role of the Ombudsman, Parliament expressed the opinion that the combination of its Committee on Petitions and the Ombudsman constitutes an effective system for defending the interests of ordinary citizens and hence for improving the democratic functioning of the Community.

---

[1] OJ L 314, 28.12.1995; Bull. 12-1995.
[2] Bull. 12-1995.
[3] Decision 95/376/EC, Euratom, ECSC; OJ L 225, 22.9.1995; Bull. 7/8-1995, point 1.1.6.
[4] Bull. 5-1995, point 1.10.1.
[5] OJ L 113, 4.5.1994; 1994 General Report, point 6.
[6] OJ C 249, 25.9.1995; Bull. 7/8-1995, point 1.1.7.

Section 3

Openness, subsidiarity and simplification

8. In accordance with the Declaration annexed to the Treaty on European Union and the conclusions of the Birmingham,[1] Edinburgh[1] and Copenhagen[2] European Councils, the institutions[3] of the European Union have taken various measures to bring Europe closer to the people. These measures, which are designed to make the work of the Union institutions more transparent, were confirmed in the interinstitutional declaration of 25 October 1993.[4] The initiatives taken by the Commission focus on four particular areas: preparation of Commission decisions and proposals, dissemination of available information, public access to Commission documents and dialogue with interest groups.

In its drive to improve prior consultation and involvement of interested parties in the preparation of its decisions and proposals, the Commission published its work programme (→ *point 9*) in the Official Journal and produced a number of Green and White Papers. Moreover, in the legislative programme, it gave prominence to proposals likely to require extensive preliminary discussions and to proposals for consolidation of Community law. Lastly, the practice of publishing summaries of Commission initiatives in the Official Journal was extended.

The Commission strove further to improve the dissemination of available information. Its activities in this area included efforts to make databases more familiar and more accessible to the public, publish lists of documents on general subjects in the Official Journal, increase public access to documents of relevance to particular sectors and speed up the publication of Commission documents in all the Union languages.

One of the main ways of making the Commission's work more transparent and fostering open dialogue is to facilitate access to internal documents. This policy, which is based on a code of conduct defined jointly by the Commission and the Council and adopted by the Commission on 8 February 1994,[5] has proved to be very effective, with less than 20% of requests for access being refused.

---

[1]   Twenty-sixth General Report, point 10.
[2]   Twenty-seventh General Report, point 10
[3]   See Chapter VII, Section 2 (Voting in the Council) for information on transparency of the Council's work (→ *point 1030*).
[4]   Twenty-seventh General Report, point 12.
[5]   Decision 94/90/ECSC, EC, Euratom, OJ L 46, 18.2.1994; 1994 General Report, point 10.

Lastly, the Commission continued its dialogue with interest groups, setting up a database covering all non-profit-making pan-European interest groups, which will be accessible both to officials of the institutions and to the general public. Furthermore, in response to the Commission's invitation to interest groups to introduce a policy of self-regulation, one category of such groups ('public affairs' sector) adopted a code of conduct and another ('public relations' sector) was finalizing a code at the end of the year.

9.   On 8 February, the Commission issued its work programme for 1995,[1] which, in keeping with the terms of the interinstitutional declaration of 25 October 1993 on democracy, transparency and subsidiarity,[2] set out its legislative intentions regarding the implementation of the Union Treaty and the sound operation of the single market. The joint declaration adopted by the European Parliament and the Commission on 26 June[3] underlined the following priorities: contribution to the building of a strong, job-creating economy, the completion of economic and monetary union and solidarity and security within the Union; assertion of the Union's role as a strong and reliable international partner; and active preparation for the Intergovernmental Conference to review the Union Treaty. Furthermore, the Commission's work programme and the other acts supplementing the contents of the 1995 programme (European Parliament resolution of 15 March,[4] Council declaration of 4 April,[5] joint declaration of the European Parliament and the Commission of 26 June[6]) were published in the *Official Journal of the European Communities*,[5] which, in accordance with the practice established in response to the interinstitutional declaration of 1993, has helped to emphasize the democratic nature of the institutions and to increase the transparency of the Community decision-making process.

The Commission report on the implementation of the 1995 programme, announced by President Santer when presenting the work programme to Parliament on 15 February[7] and adopted by the Commission on 31 October,[8] was presented to Parliament at the part-session from 13 to 17 November (→ *point 1042*) along with the work programme for 1996, adopted on the same date.[9] In 1995 the Commission focused on a few key areas — economic and monetary union, employment, internal market, Intergovernmental Conference, and external relations. There were two salient features in

[1]   Bull. 1/2-1995, point 1.9.14; Supplement 1/95 – Bull.
[2]   Twenty-seventh General Report, point 12.
[3]   OJ C 225, 30.8.1995; Bull. 6-1995, point 1.10.19.
[4]   OJ C 89, 10.4.1995; Bull. 3-1995, point 1.10.15; Supplement 1/95 – Bull.
[5]   OJ C 225, 30.8.1995.
[6]   OJ C 225, 30.8.1995; Bull. 6-1995, point 1.10.19.
[7]   Bull. 1/2-1995, point 1.9.3; Supplement 1/95 – Bull.
[8]   COM(95) 513; Bull. 10-1995, point 1.10.12.
[9]   COM(95) 512; Bull. 12-1995.

Commission business. One of them was the rethinking of its working methods, with a deliberate tactic of reducing the number of new legislative proposals and the reform of internal management to achieve greater efficiency and clarity and a tougher fight against fraud. The other was the concern for openness: the Commission now devotes much of its time and effort to prompting public debate as the forerunner of framework programmes. These two features illustrate the Commission's avowed objective of concentrating more than previously on stimulating and inspiring action to be undertaken primarily by the Member States while ensuring compliance with the accumulated body of Community law.

Mr Santer presented the 1996 work programme to Parliament at the part-session from 11 to 15 December (→ *point 1042*).[1]

10. On 22 November the Commission adopted a report for the Madrid European Council entitled 'Better law-making' on the application of the subsidiarity and proportionality principles, simplification and consolidation.[2] It was the follow-up to the first annual report on application of the subsidiarity principle presented to the Essen European Council in 1994,[3] but this time covered all aspects of improving the law-making process. It takes stock of 1995 in terms both of new legislative proposals and of existing legislation, and places the accent on doing less but doing it better, by being more selective in making proposals and by establishing ongoing and open dialogue with the public at large, the Member States and all relevant circles (Green and White Papers and policy statements). In this spirit of clarity in the law-making process, the Commission withdrew 61 obsolete proposals still outstanding. As for existing legislation, the Commission reports that the programme of simplification and recasting presented to the Brussels European Council in December 1993 is now virtually complete. The measures taken include the consolidation of 140 families of Community law and the transmission to Parliament and the Council of consolidation proposals entailing the repeal of some 250 instruments. The Commission also states its intention of stepping up the process of assessment, adaptation and clarification of existing legislation. It reaffirms that this process may not be allowed to jeopardize any of the *acquis communautaire*. The Madrid European Council examined the report and welcomed the progress made.[1]

11. In response to the conclusions of the Corfu European Council,[4] a group of independent experts on legislative and administrative simplifica-

---

[1] Bull. 12-1995.
[2] COM(95) 580; Bull. 11-1995, point 1.9.2.
[3] COM(94) 533; 1994 General Report, point 13.
[4] Bull. 6-1994, point I.6.

tion chaired by Bernhard Molitor was set up by the Commission in September 1994[1] to examine the impact of Community and national rules on employment and competitiveness and, if need be, ways of alleviating and simplifying them. The group reported to the Commission on 13 June.[2] It focused on Community legislation and made specific recommendations in the following areas: standards for machines, food hygiene, employment and social policy, the environment, biotechnology, public procurement, building products, rules of origin and small businesses. It went on to make general recommendations for the implementation of a programme of simplification, the key points of which are consolidation, the techniques used for simplification, the transparency and efficiency of the drafting and assessment processes and better application of Community legislation at national level. The Commission presented the Cannes European Council with a summary of the report as well as its own overall assessment. The report was also submitted to Parliament, the Council, the Economic and Social Committee and the Committee of the Regions and was published. The European Council,[3] noting the result of the group's activities, called on the Commission to propose practical simplification measures. The Commission's report 'Better lawmaking' (→ point 10) sets out what it has done in this area and its plans for the future. On 29 November the Commission sent Parliament and the Council its detailed reactions to the Molitor group's recommendations.[4] It drew attention to the fact that a parallel major effort would have to be made by the Member States to simplify their rules and regulations, which place the heaviest burden on enterprises. The Madrid European Council in December[5] reaffirmed the need to avoid subjecting business activity to unnecessary burdens, and to engage in a process of simplification of legislation and administration that would preserve the *acquis communautaire* and be accompanied by comparable national measures.

---

[1]   1994 General Report, point 1178.
[2]   COM(95) 288; Bull. 6-1995, point 1.9.5.
[3]   Bull. 6-1995, point I.6.
[4]   Bull. 11-1995, point 1.9.3.
[5]   Bull. 12-1995.

Chapter II

Human rights and fundamental freedoms

12.   *Upholding and protecting human rights is a major concern of the European Union, as reflected in the many initiatives aimed at its own citizens and also in external relations policy, one objective of which is to develop and strengthen democracy, the rule of law and observance of human rights and fundamental freedoms.*

Section 1

Inside the European Union

13.   Stressing the importance of Union-wide efforts to combat racism and xenophobia, the Cannes European Council[1] welcomed the work carried out by Council bodies (notably the Council report of 10 March[2]) and by the Consultative Commission set up in 1994 by the Corfu European Council.[3] The Madrid European Council called on the Consultative Commission to extend its work on the basis of the interim report submitted to it in order to complete its study of the feasibility of setting up a monitoring centre on racism and xenophobia.[4] It also called for the adoption of a joint action on racism and xenophobia with a view to approximating Member States' laws in the matter and enhancing the scope for judicial cooperation between them.

A Council resolution on the fight against racism and xenophobia in employment and social matters was adopted on 5 October.[5] At a high-level meeting held on 21 October as part of the social dialogue *(→ point 603)*, representatives of management and labour adopted a joint statement on pre-

---

[1]   Bull. 6-1995, points 1.2.1 and I.23.
[2]   Bull. 3-1995, point 1.5.9; Bull. 6-1995, point 1.2.2.
[3]   1994 General Report, point 1194.
[4]   Bull. 12-1995.
[5]   OJ C 296, 10.11.1995; Bull. 10-1995, point 1.2.1.

venting racial discrimination and xenophobia at the workplace. On 23 October the Council adopted a resolution on action taken by education systems to tackle racism and xenophobia. [1]

In accordance with its medium-term social action programme for 1995-97 *(→ point 595)*, the Commission adopted on 13 December a communication setting out a comprehensive plan of action against racism, xenophobia and anti-semitism aimed at giving fresh impetus to the Union's overall strategy and including a proposal for a Council Decision (Table II) proclaiming 1997 the 'European Year against Racism'. [2]

On 27 April Parliament adopted a resolution[3] recommending that an interim body be set up pending incorporation into the Treaty, following the 1996 Intergovernmental Conference *(→ point 1025)*, of Community powers in the field of racism, xenophobia and anti-semitism. Parliament also issued statements on racially motivated acts,[4] terrorism,[5] the expulsion of Vietnamese immigrants,[6] and on a day to commemorate the Holocaust.[7] It expressed support for the proposed 'network of cities of asylum' for threatened or persecuted writers. [8]

14. Parliament and the Council adopted on 24 October Directive 95/46/EC on the protection of individuals with regard to the processing of personal data and on the free movement of such data *(→ point 135)* in order to ensure observance of the right to privacy recognized in Article 8 of the European Convention for the protection of human rights and fundamental freedoms and also by the general principles of Community law.

---

[1]   Bull. 10-1995, point 1.2.2.
[2]   COM(95) 653; Bull. 12-1995.
[3]   OJ C 126, 22.5.1995; Bull. 4-1995, point 1.2.1.
[4]   OJ C 56, 6.3.1995; Bull. 1/2-1995, point 1.2.1; OJ C 308, 20.11.1995; Bull. 10-1995, point 1.2.3.
[5]   OJ C 56, 6.3.1995; Bull. 1/2-1995, point 1.2.2; OJ C 151, 19.6.1995; Bull. 5-1995, point 1.5.2.
[6]   OJ C 109, 1.5.1995; Bull. 4-1995, point 1.2.2.
[7]   OJ C 166, 3.7.1995; Bull. 6-1995, point 1.2.3.
[8]   OJ C 269, 16.10.1995; Bull. 9-1995, point 1.2.1.

Section 2

Outside the European Union

15.   In line with the EC Treaty's development cooperation objectives and the provisions of the Treaty on European Union on the common foreign and security policy, the European Union continued to adhere to its policy of promoting universal respect for human rights, the consolidation of democracy and the rule of law.

16.   On 22 November the Commission adopted a communication entitled 'The European Union and human rights: from Rome to Maastricht and beyond'.[1] The communication breaks new ground in laying down the foundations and priorities for EU action, reviewing the instruments available, and mapping out a strategy aimed at boosting the consistency, impact and profile of the measures taken. It also contains guidelines to which the Commission intends to give effect in the near future.

17.   Against a background of unrelenting serious infringements of democratic principles and human rights in various countries, the European Union continued to put pressure on the countries concerned either through behind-the-scenes representations (around 70) or by issuing some 69 statements condemning such practices. In certain cases it took measures such as altering the content of aid programmes, withholding the signatures necessary for the implementation of aid, or even suspending it altogether, while taking care to avoid harming the people of the country concerned.

18.   This policy also had implications for the Community's contractual ties with non-member countries, with each agreement becoming an instrument in a comprehensive political, social and economic development strategy. On 23 May the Commission adopted a communication on the inclusion of respect for democratic principles and human rights in agreements between the Community and non-member countries,[2] thus giving formal shape to what has been achieved already and defining the main thrust of current Community policy. This paper proposes enhancing the legal force of the wording to be inserted into new draft negotiating directives for agreements with non-Community countries, namely the clause first introduced in 1992 stipulating that respect for democratic principles and human rights is an 'essential element' of contractual relations, by means of a provision suspending imple-

---

[1]   COM(95) 567; Bull. 11-1995, point 1.2.1; Supplement 3/1995 — Bull.
[2]   COM(95) 216; Bull. 5-1995, point 1.2.2.

mentation if this key element in the agreement is flouted. This suspension mechanism to be inserted into international agreements was approved by the Council on 29 May.[1] Parliament conducted a hearing on 20 and 21 November on the impact and potential of such clauses.

19. In a resolution on 26 April,[2] Parliament tabled proposals for the 1996 Intergovernmental Conference (→ *point 1025*) designed to bolster the external policy dimension of the EU as it affects human rights and democratization. It gave its backing to the promotion of equal opportunities, the basic rights of women and children, national, ethnic, religious and language minorities and the victims of marginalization or discrimination, the right not to be tortured, the fight against the death penalty and the right to education. It also expressed support for a follow-up to the World Human Rights Conference held in 1993.[3]

20. Parliament also condemned the human rights situation in a number of countries[4] and expressed its opinion on key issues such as the need to set up a permanent international tribunal to judge war crimes and crimes against humanity[5] and the establishment of a European Union study centre for the active prevention of crises.[6]

21. The Commission made use of the financial instruments of Chapter B7-52 of the Community budget ('European initiative for democracy and the protection of human rights'), to help strengthen the rule of law and ease the transition to democracy in developing countries, Central and Eastern Europe, the former Soviet Union and the former Yugoslavia. It adopted a report on the implementation of those measures,[7] which gives an overview of the objectives pursued in 1994 and sets out the principles underlying Community action in this field.

22. The importance the European Union attaches to democratic principles and human rights was also reflected in its contribution to the deliberations of international organizations and forums, particularly the World Conference on Women (→ *point 780*), the United Nations General Assembly and UN Human Rights Commission (→ *point 710*), the conference on the human dimension of the Organization for Security and Cooperation in Europe

---

[1] Bull. 5-1995, point 1.2.3.
[2] OJ C 126, 22.5.1995; Bull. 4-1995, point 1.2.3.
[3] Twenty-seventh General Report, point 992.
[4] These Parliament resolutions are to be found in the EU Bulletin under the external action section of the chapter on human rights.
[5] OJ C 249, 25.9.1995; Bull. 7/8-1995, point 1.2.9.
[6] OJ C 166, 3.7.1995; Bull. 6-1995, point 1.4.7.
[7] COM(95) 191; Bull. 7/8-1995, point 1.2.1.

(→ *point 726)* and the Council of Europe *(→ point 731).* With a view to improving coordination between UN and EU activities on the human rights front, Mr José Ayala-Lasso, UN High Commissioner for Human Rights, visited the Commission in May;[1] he underscored the need to extend the assignment of human rights observers in Rwanda *(→ point 948),* to send observers to Burundi *(→ point 948)* and to organize joint training courses for human rights observers.

23.   The Sakharov Prize for freedom of the spirit[2] will be awarded at the start of 1996 by the President of Parliament to Ms Leyla Zana, a member of the Turkish Parliament of Kurdish origin.

---

[1]   Bull. 5-1995, point 1.2.4.
[2]   1994 General Report, point 1102.

Chapter III

The Community economic and social area

Section 1

Implementation of the White Paper on growth, competitiveness and employment

24. Putting into practice the policies and objectives set out in the White Paper on growth, competitiveness and employment[1] remained one of the Commission's priorities in 1995, particularly as regards the fight against unemployment.

25. The sound macroeconomic results *(→ points 31 et seq.)* achieved by the Community in 1994 were maintained despite slower growth attributable, among other things, to a period of currency turmoil.

26. Where employment is concerned *(→ points 594 et seq.)*, substantial progress was made in implementing the five action points recommended by the Essen European Council, as indicated in the Commission communication of 8 March on the follow-up to the Essen European Council on employment. That Council also approved a procedure for monitoring employment aimed at integrating these action points into Member States' policies by means of multiannual programmes for employment. In this context, the Commission presented in October its first report, which, together with the Member States' multiannual programmes, constituted the basis of the joint Council and Commission report submitted to the Madrid European Council. Reaffirming the importance of the fight against unemployment and welcoming the way in which the medium-term strategy and the procedure for monitoring employment had been implemented by means of a strategy of cooperation between all those involved, the European Council identified a

---

[1] Supplement 6/93 — Bull.; Twenty-seventh General Report, point 16; 1994 General Report, point 17.

number of priority spheres of action in the multiannual employment programmes and requested the Commission and the Council to monitor the application of these programmes continuously. In July the Commission adopted a communication on a European strategy for encouraging local development and employment initiatives that was welcomed by the Cannes European Council. It also took the initiative of reviewing Community activities concerned with analysis, research and cooperation in the field of employment. In addition, at the end of the year, it adopted a White Paper on education and training, entitled 'Teaching and learning: towards the learning society' (→ point 266).

27.   The efforts undertaken with a view to making the most of the internal market (→ points 93 et seq.) and guaranteeing European businesses better conditions in which to operate and compete were pursued throughout the year. Where small and medium-sized enterprises are concerned (→ points 205 et seq.), the Commission, ahead of the Madrid European Council, adopted a report on their role as a dynamic source of employment, growth and competitiveness.

At the end of a year's work culminating in June, the group of independent experts on simplification of legislation and administration (→ point 11), set up by the Commission in 1994 and chaired by Dr Molitor, submitted to the European Council its final report, of which due note was taken. The Commission's action programme on industrial competitiveness (→ point 176) received the support of the Council, Parliament, the Committee of the Regions and the Economic and Social Committee.

On 15 February, at the request of the European Council, the Commission appointed a Competitiveness Advisory Group (→ point 176). The Group presented its first report on improving European competitiveness to the Cannes European Council and its second to the Madrid European Council.

28.   Progress was achieved in sectors that are of particular relevance to the future. Activities falling within the scope of the fourth framework programme in the field of research and technological development (→ point 231) were successfully accomplished. The Commission took the step of enhancing the coordination of Member States' efforts in the field of research and adopted a Green Paper on policies to promote innovation. In connection with the information society (→ points 419 et seq.), it presented some important initiatives aimed at liberalizing infrastructures and universal services and which will be added to the regulatory framework for telecommunications. In the audiovisual field (→ point 676 et seq.), it proposed an amendment to the 'television without frontiers' Directive and the setting-up of a guarantee fund for audiovisual production. Progress was also achieved

in the context of the G7 Ministerial Conference held in February on the development of a global information society. In the biotechnology field (→ *point 479*), the Commission proposed amending the Directive on the contained use of genetically modified micro-organisms.

29.   Numerous guidelines were adopted on the development of trans-European networks (→ *points 340 et seq.*). The Commission continued to play a key role by facilitating implementation of the priority projects defined by the Essen European Council. As regards the financing of these networks, the Council adopted the relevant rules on the granting of aid and the Cannes European Council decided to earmark 75% of the appropriations available under the 'networks' budget heading for the priority projects. The Commission undertook to examine the measures which could be taken to encourage the establishment of partnerships between the public and private sectors and set out a number of proposals in this connection in its annual report, which was presented to the Madrid European Council.

30.   The Commission pursued its examination of the relationship between economic growth and the environment in its 1995 report on employment in Europe and its report on employment trends and systems (→ *point 466*). In May it adopted an amended proposal for a Directive introducing a tax on carbon dioxide emissions and energy (→ *point 465*).

Section 2

Economic and monetary policy

Priority activities and objectives

31.   *Economic prospects remained broadly favourable in 1995. The recovery continued, paving the way for the medium-term non-inflationary growth necessary for reducing unemployment, achieving economic and monetary union (EMU) and continuing the catching-up process in the less-favoured countries and regions. However, with growth not yet sufficiently established, unemployment fell only very slowly and job creation remained the main priority of the Community, which continued to act in accordance with the guidelines laid down by the European Council in Essen in December 1994 and confirmed by it in Cannes and Madrid in June and December 1995.*

The recovery in 1995 also improved the prospects for nominal convergence. However, additional efforts are still needed, especially with regard to the deficits and debt positions of some Member States. Economic policy coordination continued to play a key role in the process of creating the conditions for the transition to the final stage of EMU. A new set of broad economic policy guidelines was adopted in July, and the Member States, including Austria, Finland and Sweden, presented or updated their convergence programmes. The Council also carried out its periodic review of budgetary developments and concluded that only three Member States (Germany, Ireland and Luxembourg) did not have excessive deficits. At its meeting in Madrid in December, the European Council adopted a scenario for the introduction of the single currency, confirming that the third stage of EMU would begin on 1 January 1999 at the latest. It also decided to call the single currency, the Euro.

Economic situation

32.   The Community economy enjoyed a growth rate of just under 2.7% (2.8% in 1994). The main factors which had underpinned the recovery in 1994 continued to exert a positive influence on the Community economy, albeit to differing degrees. The international environment remained favourable despite the nominal appreciation of Member States' currencies resulting from the dollar's weakness at the beginning of the year. However, exports gradually gave way to investment as the main engine of growth, which

also benefited from a resurgence in private consumption. The improvement in the outlook for demand, optimism among managements, the rise in the level of capacity utilization and the sound corporate financial situation led to an acceleration in investment in plant and machinery. Consumer spending gradually picked up in the wake of the more favourable trend in private disposable income, which was itself boosted by the rise in employment and some improvement in wages.

33.   Despite the strength of the economy and the increase in capacity utilization, inflation did not, on average, accelerate in the Community (the private consumption deflator rose by 3.1%). This was made possible by wage developments that remained broadly in line with the objective of price stability and by Member States' efforts at budgetary consolidation. As a result, official interest rates fell and monetary conditions eased somewhat. The improvement in the prospects for price stability was reflected in the halt in the rise in long-term interest rates which had taken place in 1994.

34.   After three consecutive years of decline, employment grew by about 0.75%. The average rate of unemployment fell somewhat to 10.7% of the labour force (11.3% in 1994) and the labour supply remained unchanged.

35.   With the recovery exerting a direct positive influence and offering scope for additional austerity measures, Member States' budgetary positions improved significantly. Member States' net borrowing requirement was equivalent to 4.7% of their GDP (5.5% in 1994). However, deficits were not reduced enough to prevent a further increase in the average debt ratio to some 71% of GDP (68.1% in 1994).[1]

Economic and monetary union

36.   At its meeting in Cannes, the European Council reaffirmed its resolve to prepare for the move to the single currency by 1 January 1999 at the latest in strict accordance with the convergence criteria, timetable, protocols and procedures laid down in the EC Treaty.[2] At its meeting in Madrid,[3] the European Council confirmed this date, adopted a precise and realistic sce-

---

[1]   This average increase for the Community as a whole is due to the fact that the Federal Republic of Germany took over the debt of the Treuhandanstalt; without this, the Community's debt ratio would have remained stable.
[2]   Bull. 6-1995, point I.11.
[3]   Bull. 12-1995.

nario for achieving this objective, and fixed the name of the single currency. Parliament also adopted a resolution on EMU on 29 November.[1]

37. As a result of the favourable economic developments, further progress was made in terms of nominal convergence, albeit to differing degrees. An improvement was recorded as regards the inflation criterion, with most Member States experiencing a lower price increase than in 1994. In the case of long-term interest rates, the convergence process slowed somewhat, although most Member States can still meet this criterion. The picture was less favourable in relation to public finances. While most Member States improved their budget balances, the reduction in borrowing was not sufficient to cut the overall debt ratio significantly. Finally, assessment of compliance with the exchange-rate criterion has become more difficult since the temporary widening of the fluctuation margins in the exchange-rate mechanism. Following the variations in the first few months of the year, however, exchange rates remained relatively stable.

Implementation of the second stage of EMU

38. The procedures for monitoring and strengthening the convergence process among Member States were applied in accordance with the arrangements laid down by the EC Treaty. On 31 May the Commission approved a recommendation to the Council for the broad guidelines for economic policies (→ point 45). On 16 March Parliament had adopted a resolution asking the Commission and the Council to involve it more closely in the drawing-up of the broad guidelines for economic policies, the recommendations concerning excessive deficits and the Annual Economic Report, and in the multilateral surveillance procedure.[2]

39. The procedure for assessing convergence programmes was extended to the new Member States. On the basis of an assessment provided by the Commission, the Council examined the programmes presented by Sweden[3] and Finland.[4]

40. The excessive-deficit procedure was continued in accordance with Council Regulation (EC) No 3605/93.[5] The Council recommendations designed to bring to an end the excessive deficits in 10 Member States had

---

[1]   OJ C 339, 18.12.1995; Bull. 11-1995, point 1.3.8.
[2]   OJ C 89, 10.4.1995; Bull. 3-1995, point 1.3.6.
[3]   Bull. 9-1995, point 1.3.3.
[4]   Bull. 10-1995, point 1.3.16.
[5]   OJ L 332, 31.12.1993; Twenty-seventh General Report, point 22.

been adopted in 1994[1] in accordance with Article 104c(6) of the EC Treaty. On 10 July the Council adopted a Decision[2] abrogating the Decision on the existence of an excessive deficit in Germany, this being the first practical application of Article 104c(12) of the EC Treaty, under which the Council abrogates its decision when an excessive deficit has been corrected. It also adopted Decisions on the existence of excessive deficits in Austria, Finland and Sweden[3] and, on 24 July, recommendations designed to bring to an end excessive government deficits in 12 countries.[4] Only three countries — Ireland, Luxembourg and Germany — were judged not to have excessive deficits.

Preparations for the third stage of EMU

41.   The work on the technical and legal preparations for the transition to the third stage of EMU and to a single monetary policy intensified within the relevant institutions and committees, including the Commission — with the adoption of a Green Paper on the arrangements for the introduction of the single currency (→ point 43) — and the European Monetary Institute (→ point 73). The Expert Group on the changeover to the single currency, chaired by Mr Maas[5] and set up at the Commission's initiative in April 1994,[6] also submitted a progress report on 10 May which was the subject of a Parliament resolution on 19 May.[7]

42.   At its meeting in Madrid, the European Council adopted the definitive scenario for achieving economic and monetary union and broadly followed the approach put foward by the Commission in its Green Paper on the arrangements for the introduction of the single currency, setting out the timetable for the changeover. It also decided on the name of the single currency, the Euro.

Arrangements for the introduction of the single currency

43.   In its Green Paper[8] of 31 May, the Commission sought to dispel uncertainty over the transition to the single currency, to draw up a list of the

---

[1]   1994 General Report, point 36.
[2]   Bull. 7/8-1995, point 1.3.8.
[3]   Bull. 7/8-1995, point 1.3.9.
[4]   Belgium, Denmark, Greece, Spain, France, Italy, the Netherlands, Austria, Portugal, Finland, Sweden and the United Kingdom — Bull. 7/8-1995, point 1.3.10.
[5]   OJ C 153, 6.6.1994.
[6]   1994 General Report, point 40.
[7]   OJ C 151, 19.6.1995; Bull. 5-1995, point 1.3.8.
[8]   COM(95) 333; Bull. 5-1995, point 1.3.7.

problems involved in that transition and to define a strategy for safeguarding the credibility of the process. It set out a sequence of events designed to lead to the smooth introduction of the single currency in accordance with the timetable laid down by the Union Treaty, analysing the sectoral impact on all the parties concerned (administrations, banks, private sector and consumers). This approach, which draws in particular on the 'critical mass' concept, is based on six key criteria: technical feasibility, compliance with the Treaty, credibility of the process, simplicity, flexibility and low cost. It comprises three phases: the launch of economic and monetary union (phase A), the effective start of EMU and the emergence of a critical mass of activities in the single currency (phase B), and the final changeover to the single currency (phase C). The content of the phases was confirmed by the European Council in Madrid.

Phase A will begin with the Council's decision to launch EMU, with the designation of the participating countries and the establishment of the European System of Central Banks. At its meeting in Madrid, the European Council stated that this decision will have to be taken as early as possible in 1998 to enable the European Central Bank to become fully operational as from 1 January 1999. The Council will also have to announce the final date for the full introduction of the single currency (at the latest four years after the start of phase A). The European Council agreed the date of 1 January 2002 in Madrid. Various measures will have to be taken then, such as the adoption of a legal framework laying down the relationships between the single currency and national currencies in phase B, the definition of the technical characteristics of notes and coins, and the introduction in each participating country of a national structure for supervising the move to the single currency and of a plan for establishing the technical arrangements necessary for the changeover (capital markets and their infrastructures, quotation systems, payment systems).

Phase B will begin at the latest 12 months after the start of phase A, and therefore no later than 1 January 1999 (date confirmed by the European Council in Madrid), with the actual launching of EMU, i.e. with the irrevocable fixing of the conversion rates of the participating currencies and the taking-over of responsibility for the single monetary and exchange-rate policy by the European System of Central Banks. In accordance with the European Council's decisions in Madrid, the ecu will then cease to exist and will be replaced by the Euro, a currency in its own right and not a basket of currencies like the ecu. From the start of this phase, a 'critical mass' of transactions denominated in the single currency will be built up, with the changeover to the single monetary and exchange-rate policy (and the corresponding markets and infrastructures), and new public-debt issues denominated in the single currency. During this phase, banks and other financial institutions will have to continue to denominate transactions in the single currency. The other private and public operators could do likewise if technical and legal circumstances permitted.

At its meeting in Madrid the European Council decided that phase C should begin no later than 1 January 2002 and that it should not exceed six months. This phase, with the spread of the single currency to all means of payment, will see the end of the transitional phase and will mark the completion of the process of introducing the single currency, which will then be the sole legal tender in the EMU area.

44. Before the European Council meeting in Madrid, the Green Paper was presented to the European Council in Cannes in June as the Commission's own contribution to meeting the request received by the Council to submit to the European Council in Madrid in December an exclusive scenario for the changeover to the single currency on the basis of the different work in progress, including that of the EMI. In July the Commission embarked on detailed consultations with the sectors concerned (banks, companies, the distributive trades and consumers). The results of these contacts were transmitted to the Council, to which the EMI had on 14 November presented its technical scenario for the changeover to the single currency. On 14 November Mr de Silguy, Member of the Commission, welcomed[1] this report on behalf of the Commission. The Commission's Green Paper had been favourably received by Parliament in a resolution[2] adopted on 26 October and by the Economic and Social Committee in an opinion[3] delivered on the same date. On 29 November the Commission also adopted an interim report[4] to the European Council on the exchange-rate relationships between the Member States participating in the third stage of EMU and the other Member States. These different contributions, based on common foundations, enabled the European Council in Madrid to adopt a single approach to the changeover to the single currency and to settle the question of its name, the 'Euro'. It further requested the Commission, working in conjunction with the EMI, to prepare the legislation necessary for adopting the framework for the use of the Euro, the legislative amendments in the various fields concerned and the technical arrangements relating to coins and banknotes. It recommended that the Member States and the Community institutions make *ad hoc* arrangements as soon as possible to involve all the parties affected by the change of currency unit (administrations, central banks, private

---

[1]   Bull. 11-1995, point 1.3.6.
[2]   OJ C 308, 20.11.1995; Bull 10-1995, point 1.3.18.
[3]   Bull. 10-1995, point 1.3.19.
[4]   Bull. 11-1995, point 1.3.7.

sector and consumers) and to take the communication measures necessary for ensuring that the single currency is acceptable.

Economic policy coordination

45.   Alongside the application of the excessive-deficit procedure (→ point 40) and the assessment of convergence programmes (→ point 39), economic policy coordination again centred on the new instrument created by Article 103 of the EC Treaty: the broad guidelines of the economic policies of the Member States and the Community. These guidelines, which were the subject of a Commission recommendation of 31 May, were examined by the Council, finalized by the European Council in Cannes and formally adopted on 10 July.[1] They provide indications of the best way to achieve price and exchange-rate stability, sound public finances, improved competitiveness and stronger employment growth. Parliament adopted a resolution on these guidelines on 14 July.[2]

46.   The possible options, set out by the Commission in December 1994 in its Annual Economic Report for 1995,[3] gave rise to wide-ranging discussions on economic policy. The Economic and Social Committee delivered its opinion on 30 March[4] and Parliament adopted a resolution on 7 April.[5] The Commission concluded that the economic situation was more favourable than expected and reviewed the progress made regarding convergence, the medium-term economic outlook and the economic measures necessary to strengthen growth. It stressed that, notwithstanding the recovery in 1994 and 1995, the major policy challenges remained the same: to reduce unemployment substantially and to achieve the degree of nominal convergence necessary to complete economic and monetary union.

47.   At its meeting in Essen in December 1994,[6] the European Council had called on Member States to implement measures to improve employment prospects and to prepare multiannual programmes setting out the pace and details of their implementation. It had also called on the Council and the Commission to report on their implementation. On 8 March the Commission adopted a communication (→ point 604) on the monitoring of progress in this area, undertaking to give greater prominence to employment issues in the 1995 broad guidelines of economic policies (→ point 45) and to adopt

[1]   OJ L 191, 12.8.1995; Bull. 7/8-1995, point 1.3.6 (set out in full at point 2.2.1).
[2]   OJ C 249, 25.9.1995; Bull. 7/8-1995, point 1.3.7.
[3]   COM(94) 615; 1994 General Report, point 43.
[4]   OJ C 133, 31.5.1995; Bull. 3-1995, point 1.3.8.
[5]   OJ C 109, 1.5.1995; Bull. 4-1995, point 1.3.5.
[6]   Bull. 12-1994, point I.3.

in October a summary report on employment trends and policies
(→ *point 605)*. At its meeting in Madrid, the European Council reiterated
the need to maintain a high degree of convergence between Member States'
economies on a durable basis in order both to create stable conditions for
the changeover to the single currency and to ensure smooth functioning of
the internal market. It reaffirmed that the fight against unemployment was
the priority task of the Community and its Member States. In this connection, it stressed that the medium-term strategy outlined in Essen and confirmed in Cannes provided the appropriate framework *(→ point 1049)*.

Thrust of economic policies in 1995

48.   The broad thrust and objectives of economic policy set out in the 1993
White Paper on growth, competitiveness and employment[1] and in the previous broad guidelines remained unchanged. Putting forward a strategy for
transforming the recovery into the sustained, medium-term, non-inflationary growth process necessary for a substantial reduction in unemployment,
the 1995 economic policy guidelines, adopted on 10 July *(→ point 45)*,
stressed the need for advantage to be taken of the recovery to implement
structural measures aimed at improving competitiveness and productivity.
Such measures and more effective labour-market policies had to be implemented in order to improve the functioning of employment systems along
the lines of the five priorities identified by the European Council in Essen.[2]

49.   Member States continued their efforts to consolidate budgetary positions, with the progress made varying from one Member State to another.
The major currency fluctuations at the beginning of the year, although
prompted by the dollar's weakness, revealed the extent of the outstanding
problems and the lack of credibility of the efforts made. Progress in reducing inflationary pressures and expectations paved the way for an easing of
monetary conditions and a fall in both short- and long-term interest rates.

50.   The exchange-rate fluctuations which occurred at the beginning of the
year caused Member States to modify their policy priorities. While inflation
prospects improved in those countries whose currencies appreciated, inflationary pressures increased in those experiencing depreciation. This demonstrated even more clearly the need for these countries to exercise vigilance
over wage trends and fiscal consolidation.

---

[1]   1994 General Report, point 17.
[2]   1994 General Report, point 1196; Bull. 12-1994, point I.3.

Operation of the European Monetary System (EMS)

51.   On 9 January the Austrian schilling joined the group of Union currencies participating in the exchange-rate mechanism of the EMS. Its central rate was set at ÖS 13.7167 for ECU 1. During the year the schilling was unaffected by the market turmoil, barely moving from its central rate against the German mark.

52.   Against a background of renewed dollar weakness and international market unrest, the exchange-rate mechanism remained under pressure in the first months of the year. On 5 March the bilateral central rates of the peseta and the escudo were reduced by 7% and 3.5% respectively in relation to the other currencies in the exchange-rate mechanism.[1] The foreign-exchange markets subsequently calmed down, and the EMS exchange-rate mechanism was very stable.

53.   In response to a request from the European Council in Cannes, the Commission adopted on 31 October a communication[2] assessing the impact of intra-Community currency fluctuations on economic growth and the internal market and concluded that the single currency was the essential complement to the single market.

Growth initiative and financial activities

Growth initiative

54.   The action taken at Community level under the growth initiative launched by the European Council in Edinburgh in 1992[3] and reinforced by it in Copenhagen in 1993[4] comprises a whole series of measures, including the following: (i) the activities of the European Investment Fund (EIF) (which guarantees loans for the trans-European networks and SMEs) (→ point 83); (ii) the Edinburgh facility (a temporary EIB lending arrangement for trans-European network projects, the resources of which were fully drawn down in commitment terms in December 1994); (iii) the SME facility (→ point 55).

---

[1]   Bull. 3-1995, point 1.3.7.
[2]   COM(95) 503; Bull. 10-1995, point 1.3.17.
[3]   Twenty-sixth General Report, point 20.
[4]   Twenty-seventh General Report, point 16.

Development of financing techniques

55.   The SME facility, which was set up on 19 April 1994,[1] provided for Community interest subsidies of two percentage points on a volume of EIB loans to job-creating SMEs of ECU 1 billion. The loans were granted through a network of EIB financial intermediaries in each Member State. Most were granted during the course of 1995 and the total resources had been used up by the end of December.[2] In its report on the role of SMEs presented to the European Council in November, the Commission recommended that this facility be reinforced (→ point 205).

56.   The Commission continued to develop the 'Eurotech Capital' scheme, which is designed to stimulate investment in high technology and in which 14 specialist financial institutions are participating. The JOP programme (Joint venture programme PHARE, TACIS), set up in 1991 under the PHARE programme (→ point 824), was also further developed. Since the beginning of the programme, in which 60 financial intermediaries are participating, 669 projects have received Community support totalling ECU 47.5 million. Faced with growing demand, the JOP programme has been extended to 1999. Close cooperation has been established with the EBRD.

57.   At Parliament's initiative, the Commission launched the 'growth and environment' pilot project,[3] which is designed to facilitate access by small firms to bank loans for investment projects contributing to environmental protection. This programme provides for a mechanism under which firms will benefit from loan guarantees provided in particular by the European Investment Fund.

Community borrowing and lending

58.   All the information relating to Community borrowing and lending can be found in Section 5 (Borrowing and lending operations) of Chapter VI (→ point 1012). On 18 July the Commission adopted the report on the rate of utilization of the New Community Instrument (NCI) and the annual report on the Community's borrowing and lending activities in 1994

---

[1]   1994 General Report, point 61.
[2]   For more detailed information on the operation of the facility and the use of the loans in Member States, see the Commission's second annual report, adopted on 30 October, on the implementation of Decision 94/217/EC (OJ L 107, 28.4.1994) regarding the provision of Community interest subsidies on loans for small and medium-sized enterprises extended by the EIB under its temporary lending facility — COM(95) 485; Bull. 10-1995, point 1.3.21.
[3]   OJ C 177, 12.7.1995.

(→ points 1013 and 1014). No use was made during the year of the mechanism for providing medium-term financial assistance for Member States' payments balances *(→ point 1015).*

59.   On 1 June the Council adopted Decision 95/207/EC providing Community guarantees for loans granted by the EIB for investment projects in South Africa, subject to an overall ceiling of ECU 300 million over a two-year period. On 29 June the Council also adopted Decision 95/250/EC providing an interest-rate subsidy, chargeable to the Community budget, of three percentage points per year for a maximum of 12 years on EIB loans not exceeding ECU 15.85 million in principal for financing investment projects in the regions devastated by the cyclone which hit Madeira (Portugal) in October 1993.

European Bank for Reconstruction and Development (EBRD)

60.   The year was characterized by sustained economic growth in the countries of Central and Eastern Europe and by a stabilization of activity in the largest independent States of the former Soviet Union (Russia and Ukraine). The reforms designed to adapt production structures to the market economy also continued. Within this general framework, the volume of the EBRD's operations increased: 96 new projects were financed at a total cost of ECU 2.855 billion (as against 91 projects in 1994 costing a total of ECU 1.775 billion), i.e. an increase of more than 7% in the total financed. The number of projects financed by the Bank since it was set up thus totals 295, at an overall cost of ECU 8.94 billion. The most striking development concerns disbursements, which more than tripled between 1994 and 1995. This expansion in the Bank's activities conceals a change in the nature of the projects implemented, the main characteristics of which are: a reduction in average project size; confirmation of the tendency for the private sector's share of the Bank's commitments to grow; diversification of activities (a relative decrease in the Bank's activities in those countries which are at an advanced stage of transition to the market economy, with a corresponding increase in activities in the less-advanced economies). The Bank also continued to develop its network of local representatives, which enables it to ascertain the needs of recipient countries more effectively, to prepare projects and to monitor their implementation. It also made greater use of local financial intermediaries.

61.   At its annual meeting held in London in April, the Board of Governors invited the Board of Directors to submit to it a recommendation regarding a possible increase in the Bank's capital.

62.   The European Community continued to make an active contribution to the development of the Bank's activities, providing a total of ECU 28.35 million, particularly through the financing of technical assistance under the PHARE programme *(→ point 824)* and the TACIS programme *(→ point 869)*.

Macrofinancial assistance for non-member countries

63.   The Commission's annual report on the implementation of Community macrofinancial assistance for non-member countries (1994) was adopted on 27 November.[1]

64.   The European Community continued to provide financial assistance for the countries of Central and Eastern Europe within the framework of the Group of 24 industrialized countries (G24) *(→ point 823)* and in the form of loans and — exceptionally in the case of Albania — a grant. In June the Commission disbursed the first tranche of ECU 15 million of the second assistance package (ECU 35 million) approved for Albania in 1994.[2] In August it paid out a further tranche of ECU 25 million to Lithuania *(→ point 1016)*. In November it disbursed the first tranche (ECU 55 million) *(→ point 1016)* of the loan facility of ECU 125 million made available to Romania in 1994.

65.   With regard to the former Soviet Union, the Commission paid over to Moldova in August *(→ point 1016)* the second tranche (ECU 20 million) of the macrofinancial assistance approved for that country in 1994. In December the Commission paid out to Ukraine in a single tranche macrofinancial assistance of ECU 85 million *(→ point 1016)* provided for in a 1994 decision. Consideration was also given to funding for Belarus and to further assistance for Ukraine: on 10 April the Council decided to grant Belarus macrofinancial assistance of up to ECU 75 million according to the country's needs (Table II); it was subsequently agreed, given the reduction in that country's external financing needs, that the Community's contribution would be limited to ECU 55 million, a first ECU 30 million tranche of which was paid out in December *(→ point 1016)*. On 23 October the Council adopted Decision 95/442/EC granting Ukraine further macrofinancial assistance of up to ECU 200 million (Table II).

---

[1]   COM(95) 572; Bull. 11-1995, point 1.3.9.
[2]   1994 General Report, point 66.

66. On the basis of the decision taken in 1994[1] to grant further macrofinancial assistance of up to ECU 200 million to Algeria *(→ point 1016)*, the Commission disbursed a first tranche of ECU 100 million in November.

International monetary and financial matters

67. At its 44th meeting, held in Washington in April and attended by Mr Alphandéry, President of the Council, and Mr de Silguy, Member of the Commission, the Interim Committee of the International Monetary Fund (IMF) noted that developments in the world economy had generally been favourable. It welcomed the entry into force of the Uruguay Round agreements and the formation of the World Trade Organization. It also reaffirmed its intention to participate more closely in the process of economic policy cooperation and coordination. In this context, the Committee considered that the Fund should reinforce its surveillance in the light of the lessons to be drawn from the Mexican crisis. In particular, it encouraged the Fund to establish a close and continuous dialogue with member countries. It stressed the importance of rapid and regular communication of economic data by member countries to the IMF and the risks associated with overreliance on easily reversible capital flows. The Committee also welcomed the application by Paris Club creditors of the terms advocated at the Naples Summit for low-income countries and agreed that continued Fund support for the poorest of these countries on ESAF (Enhanced Structural Adjustment Facility) terms was desirable.

At its 45th meeting,[2] held in Washington in October and attended by Mr de Silguy, Member of the Commission, and Mr Solbes Mira, the Spanish Minister for Economic Affairs and President of the Council, the Interim Committee noted that trends in the world economy were encouraging in many respects but that a number of difficulties remained. Under the circumstances, it endorsed proposals to reinforce surveillance procedures within the IMF as part of an early-warning mechanism. It also examined means of accelerating disbursements of assistance in cases where the financial crisis threatened to affect the system as a whole. In this connection, the Committee considered a possible increase in Fund resources and welcomed the progress made within the G10 and with other countries towards doubling the amount currently available under the general borrowing arrangements.

68. At their annual meeting in Halifax *(→ point 886)*, the Heads of State or Government of the G7 countries and the President of the Commission,

---

[1] 1994 General Report, point 68.
[2] Bull. 10-1995, point, 1.3.22.

Mr Santer, reaffirmed their commitment to maintain close cooperation in economic surveillance and foreign-exchange markets. They discussed the need for early-warning systems to prevent financial shocks and for instruments that would permit a rapid and coordinated response where appropriate. They also welcomed the decision of the Paris Club creditors to improve the treatment of the debt of the poorest countries.

Economic dialogue with the associated countries of Central and Eastern Europe

69.   At its meeting in Essen in December 1994, the European Council adopted a pre-accession strategy for the associated countries of Central and Eastern Europe (→ point 814). The two main instruments of that strategy are structured dialogue and the Europe Agreements. In the economic and financial field, a multilateral dialogue has been established within the framework of the first instrument. The Council met the Finance Ministers of the associated countries on 22 May and 23 October. Application of the Europe Agreements has entailed a bilateral dialogue: economic subcommittees have been set up under the respective association committees and, in several cases, it was agreed that technical cooperation would be established between the associated country and the Commission on such matters as economic forecasting.

European Monetary Institute (EMI)

70.   During the second year of its existence,[1] the EMI continued its tasks of strengthening coordination of Member States' monetary policies with a view to ensuring price stability and preparing for the third stage of EMU, concentrating in particular on the setting-up of the future European System of Central Banks.

71.   In the context of the strengthening of monetary policy coordination between Member States, the EMI continued to monitor economic and monetary developments and policies. The regular *ex ante* (autumn) and *ex post* (spring) exercises, in which economic, monetary and financial trends in the Member States are reviewed and analysed, form an integral part of this general monitoring framework. This regular monitoring involves reviewing developments on foreign-exchange markets and in respect of interest rates;

---

[1]   1994 General Report, point 38.

particular attention was paid to public finance trends and to their implications for monetary policy coordination.

72.   Progress was made in many fields: in defining an operational framework for implementing a single monetary policy; in organizing intervention operations and laying down guidelines for the management of the national central banks' reserves; in preparing a payment-system arrangement for a single monetary policy and large-value transactions (Target); in harmonizing the rules and practices governing the collection, compilation and distribution of statistical data; in selecting possible themes for the design of the European banknotes and in studying the institutional and logistical aspects of the issuing, sorting and handling of those notes; in preparing recommendations for the harmonization of accounting rules and standards in the European System of Central Banks; in considering issues relating to credit institutions' management of credit risk, their internal controls and the operation of central credit registers; and, finally, in assessing the feasibility of setting up an EMU-wide information system for these different purposes.

73.   During the year the EMI studied various possibilities for the changeover to the single currency *(→ point 44)*. In November it presented to the Council the scenario the European Council had requested it to prepare on this topic at its meeting in Cannes.[1]

74.   In addition, the EMI continued to monitor central banks' compliance with the prohibitions referred to in Articles 104 and 104a of the EC Treaty. It was also consulted on draft Community and national legislation within its sphere of competence as laid down in Article 109f(6) of the EC Treaty.

75.   In April the EMI published its first annual report[2] covering its activities in 1994 as well as those of the former Committee of Governors in 1993. This report outlined the economic, monetary and financial situation in the Community. It also included an assessment of the progress made regarding convergence and of the state of play in the preparatory work for the third stage and an analysis of the institutional features of national central banks. A report fully meeting the requirements of Article 7 of the EMI's Statute was published in November.[3] It can be regarded as preparation for the role the EMI will play in assessing progress towards convergence as required by Article 109j(1) of the EC Treaty.

---

[1]   Bull. 6-1995, point I.11.
[2]   Bull. 4-1995, point 1.10.20.
[3]   *Report on progress towards convergence.*

European Investment Bank (EIB)

76. With the addition of the three new Member States of the European Union, the European Investment Bank (EIB)[1] now counts 15 shareholder Member States. The Board of Governors therefore decided to increase from six to seven the number of vice-presidents sitting on the Bank's Management Committee.[2]

All in all, the EIB granted loans totalling ECU 21 408 million in 1995 (ECU 19 928 million in 1994), including ECU 2 805 million within the framework of Community cooperation with non-member countries.

77. In the European Union countries, in addition to its normal activities, the EIB continued to implement the measures adopted in connection with the European growth initiative (→ point 54). By the end of the year, nearly all the funds available under the temporary lending facility (Edinburgh facility) (→ point 54) designed to speed up the financing of trans-European networks and environmental protection infrastructures were committed. All the funds earmarked for the mechanism introduced to support small and medium-sized job-creating enterprises (→ point 55) were made available in 1995; on 26 July an agreement[3] was signed between the EIB and the Commission under which the deadline for granting the loans was postponed from 31 July to 15 December in order to enable the three new Member States to benefit fully from the scheme.

78. Within the framework of its participation in the work of the Christophersen Group,[4] the EIB stepped up that part of its funding of large-scale infrastructure projects channelled to the development of the trans-European networks, and particularly for the 24 projects given high priority by the European Council at its meeting in Essen in December 1994.[5] A total of 13 projects were financed at a cost of ECU 2 126 million, and 11 other projects were still being appraised at the end of the year. To that end, it implemented financing arrangements appropriate to the unusual scale of some of those projects and to their specific funding requirements. In order to support the development of the less-favoured regions, the EIB, in addition to its normal activities, helped to vet 25 projects for the Cohesion Fund and administered

---

[1] Copies of the EIB's annual report and of other publications relating to the Bank's work and its operations can be obtained from the main office (100, boulevard Konrad Adenauer, L-2950 Luxembourg, tel. (352) 4379-1) or from its external offices.
[2] Bull. 1/2-1995, point 1.9.31.
[3] Bull. 7/8-1995, point 1.10.16.
[4] 1994 General Report, point 73.
[5] 1994 General Report, point 321.

the interest subsidies and grants awarded under the financial assistance mechanism provided for in the EEA Agreement.[1]

79. Loans granted for projects in the 15 countries of the European Union totalled ECU 18 603 million, compared with ECU 17 682 million in 1994; this against the background of a still difficult economic situation (see Table 1).

80. In accordance with the task assigned to it, the EIB gave priority to channelling the savings it borrows on the financial markets to investment projects contributing to the development of the less-favoured regions. This assistance accounted for some 68% of its financings in the European Union. Loans for trans-European transport and energy infrastructures — another important area of its activity — amounted to ECU 6.6 billion; financing for environmental protection or improvements totalled ECU 6 billion and that for the energy-supply sector ECU 3.4 billion. In the industrial and services sectors, assistance totalled ECU 4.5 billion, a marked upturn in investment projects undertaken by small and medium-sized firms and financed in the form of global loans to a large number of partner banks (ECU 2.9 billion for some 11 000 credit allocations).

81. Operations outside the Union amounted to ECU 2 805 million (compared with ECU 2 246 million in 1994 and ECU 1 887 million in 1993). Assistance provided in the Central and East European countries, including for the first time Albania, amounted to ECU 1 005 million. In the Mediterranean area, financings rose sharply to ECU 1 038 million, including ECU 718 million within the framework of the non-protocol operations, which included the first projects financed in Gaza and the West Bank, as part of efforts to support the peace process in the Middle East, and in Turkey. In the ACP countries and the OCTs, where a loan was granted for the first time in Haiti, financings under the fourth Lomé Convention totalled ECU 430 million, including ECU 225 million of risk capital. In order to support the democratic transition process, initial loans amounting to ECU 45 million were signed with South Africa under the reconstruction and development programme (→ point 953). Lastly, the EIB continued its operations in various countries in Latin America (ECU 120 million) and Asia (ECU 168 million).

82. The EIB obtained the funds needed for its lending activities by borrowing a total of ECU 12 395 million on the capital markets; 87% was raised in Community currencies and in ecus.

---

[1]   Twenty-seventh General Report, point 55.

TABLE 1

Contracts signed in 1995 and from 1991-95

(million ECU)

	1995		1991-95	
	Amount	%	Amount	%
Belgium	665.3	3.6	2 164.4	2.6
Denmark	825.0	4.4	3 779.7	4.5
Germany	2 715.0	14.6	10 183.6	12.0
Greece	525.2	2.8	2 315.4	2.7
Spain	2 817.6	15.1	15 197.3	18.0
France	2 206.8	11.9	10 709.2	12.7
Ireland	327.3	1.8	1 547.0	1.8
Italy	3 434.9	18.5	17 694.0	20.9
Luxembourg	78.8	0.4	155.2	0.2
Netherlands	318.9	1.7	1 427.9	1.7
Austria	241.9	1.3	403.9	0.5
Portugal	1 231.5	6.6	6 062.6	7.2
Finland	179.1	1.0	239.3	0.3
Sweden	273.1	1.5	288.4	0.3
United Kingdom	2 243.9	12.1	11 179.9	13.2
Other[1]	518.5	2.8	1 278.0	1.5
Union total[2]	18 602.8	100	84 625.8	100
ACP-OCTs	474.9	16.9	1 807.7	20.7
Mediterranean	1 037.5	37.0	2 887.3	33.0
Central and Eastern Europe	1 005.0	35.8	3 449.0	39.4
Latin America	120.0	4.3	285.0	3.3
Asia	168.0	6.0	322.0	3.7
Non-Union total[3]	2 805.4	100	8 751.0	100
Overall total	21 408.2		93 376.8	

[1] Projects of Community interest located outside the territory of the Member States.
[2] Includes guarantees amounting to ECU 151.1 million from 1991 to 1995.
[3] Includes risk capital from budgetary resources:
   (i) ACP-OCTs: ECU 225.2 million in 1995 and ECU 788 million from 1991 to 1995;
   (ii) Mediterranean: ECU 23 million in 1995 and ECU 74 million from 1991 to 1995.

European Investment Fund (EIF)

83.   On 20 June the EIF,[1] which was set up in 1994,[2] held its first ordinary general meeting under the chairmanship of Mr de Silguy, Member of the Commission (which holds 30% of the subscribed capital; the EIB holds 40%). The meeting approved the first annual report, covering the period from 14 June (the date of the inaugural general meeting) to 31 December 1994, and the balance sheet and profit-and-loss account for that part of 1994. During these first six months of activity, approved operations totalled ECU 702.7 million, ECU 500 million of which were committed in 1994. The majority of the Fund's operations involved loans granted by the EIB: 85.3% of the total guarantees provided went to projects associated with the trans-European networks, while the remaining 14.7% covered loans to small and medium-sized firms.

84.   In 1995, the Fund's first full year of activity, three of the four project signings (54% of the total) were connected with EIB loans. Since the Fund's launch in June 1994, the mix between projects associated with the trans-European networks and those involving small and medium-sized firms was of the order of four to one, and the volume of new guarantees will amount to ECU 1 290 million, of which signings account for ECU 619.6 million. The main recipient sectors included telecommunications, energy distribution and transport infrastructure. With the addition of 18 new shareholders subscribing ECU 84 million, the subscribed capital stood at ECU 1.784 billion (out of a total authorized capital of ECU 2 billion); the balance may be subscribed by banks and other financial institutions from Member States. While its initial gearing ratio currently limits the total volume of the Fund's outstanding guarantees to ECU 5.1 billion, this total could reach ECU 16 billion in the longer term. In accordance with the Fund's Statutes, shareholders released two of the four annual tranches of 5% of the subscribed capital (ECU 89.2 million each), i.e. ECU 178.4 million, in 1994 and 1995. The balance has to be paid in 1996 and 1997.

---

[1]   Copies of the EIF's report can be obtained from its provisional offices (100, boulevard Konrad Adenauer, L-2950 Luxembourg, tel. (352) 4379-3277).
[2]   1994 General Report, points 79 and 80.

Section 3

Statistical system

Priority activities and objectives

85. In order to produce a 'Community statistical area' based on a set of standards, methods and organizational structures for producing comparable, reliable and relevant statistics throughout the Community, Eurostat continued to implement its framework programme for priority actions in the field of statistical information (1993-97).[1] The institutions laid particular emphasis, throughout the year, on drawing up provisions for efficient statistical support for all the decisions to be taken in connection with the creation of economic and monetary union. Accordingly, on 23 October, the Council adopted framework Regulation (EC) No 2494/95 (Table II) concerning harmonized consumer price indices, which is aimed at making the convergence criteria laid down in the Treaty on European Union more comparable. On 27 November it reached agreement on a Regulation (Table II) on the European system of integrated economic accounts. On 13 September the Commission adopted Recommendation 95/377/EC[2] to the Member States on breaking down net turnover by type of activity. Eurostat also signed an agreement with the European Environment Agency establishing the guidelines for cooperation between the two institutions. Externally, following the Euro-Mediterranean Conference in Barcelona, it organized a seminar to launch a Euro-Mediterranean cooperation programme to support 12 Mediterranean countries;[3] it also increased cooperation with the countries of Central and Eastern Europe and the independent States of the former Soviet Union, in particular by signing an agreement with the national statistical offices in the three Baltic countries. This agreement, which is aimed at developing their statistical systems with a view to producing comparable, reliable and relevant statistics, will help these States to make progress along the road to democracy and the market economy.

---

[1]   Twenty-sixth General Report, point 58.
[2]   OJ L 225, 22.9.1995; Bull. 9-1995, point 1.7.2.
[3]   Algeria, Cyprus, Egypt, Israel, Jordan, Lebanon, Malta, Morocco, the Palestinian Territories, Syria, Tunisia, Turkey.

Policy aspects

86. Work on drawing up reliable and comparable statistical indicators continued in the fields laid down in the 1993-97 framework programme.

87. In the field of transport, on 14 September the Commission adopted a proposal for a Council Regulation on air transport (Table II). On 7 December, the Council formally adopted a Directive (Table II) on statistical returns in respect of sea transport *(→ point 406)*.

88. The adoption by the Council on 23 November of Directive 95/57/EC (Table II) on tourism statistics *(→ point 217)* will make it possible to establish a comprehensive system of information covering the European Union. In addition, in a resolution of 20 November[1] the Council agreed to continue its work in the cultural field.

89. With regard to social statistics, on 27 November the Council adopted Regulation (EC) No 2744/95 (Table II) on statistics on the structure and distribution of earnings in the Member States. In addition, on 16 October the Commission adopted a proposal for a European Parliament and Council Decision adopting a Community action programme on health monitoring *(→ point 637)* .

90. The process of adjusting agricultural statistics to the reform of the common agricultural policy continued. Accordingly, on 16 October the Commission adopted a proposal for a Council Decision (Table II) on improving these statistics at Community level. It also proposed, on 15 September, to revise a Directive on milk statistics (Table II). In the field of fisheries statistics, on 23 October the Council adopted Regulation (EC) No 2597/95 on the submission of statistics on catches in certain areas other than those of the North Atlantic (Table II). On 20 September, the Commission adopted a proposal for a Council Regulation (Table II) on statistics on aquaculture.

91. Lastly, Council Regulation (EC) No 1172/95 (Table II) on the statistics relating to the trading of goods by the Community and its Member States with non-member countries was adopted on 22 May.

---

[1]   OJ C 327, 7.12.1995; Bull. 11-1995, point 1.7.5.

Publications[1]

92.   Among Eurostat's publications in 1995, particular mention should be made of the first Yearbook,[2] which deals with five major topics (men and women, the countryside and the environment, national income and expenditure, trade and industry, the European Union), *Europe in figures* (fourth edition), *Social portrait of Europe* (second edition), *Women and men in the European Union — A statistical portrait* and *Ecustat*, a new publication intended to provide those involved in the money markets with a statistical work of reference.

---

[1]   See the 'Statistical system' section of the monthly *Bulletin of the European Union*.
[2]   Bull. 9-1995, point 1.7.7.

Section 4

Internal market

Priority activities and objectives

93. Efforts to ensure the proper functioning and consolidation of the internal market, which are fundamental to a dynamic economy and thus to job creation, as was underlined by the Cannes European Council in June and the Madrid European Council in December,[1] continued in line with the 1993 strategic programme.[2] While there was a considerable reduction in the number of new legislative measures proposed in this area, non-legislative activity was stepped up, particularly as regards monitoring progress by Member States in the transposal of directives and as regards administrative cooperation, including through setting up a database comprising contact points in several areas of legislation. In order to make appropriate adaptations to the single market in the light of experience and against a background of rapid technological change, a major study on the programme's impact on the completion of the single market was launched and Green Papers published so as to elicit views on the problems encountered, particularly in the context of the information society. On 3 May the Commission adopted a White Paper on the preparation of the associated countries of Central and Eastern Europe for integration into the internal market of the Union.

Meeting in Madrid in December,[3] the European Council reaffirmed the need to make completion of the internal market compatible with the public administration's tasks of general economic interest, in particular equal treatment for citizens, quality and continuity of services, and balanced regional development.

A step towards completing the internal market was taken with regard to the free movement of persons through the Commission's adoption of three proposals for Directives aimed at abolishing checks on persons at internal frontiers, provided that essential safeguards were retained. The Council adopted a uniform format for visas and a Regulation stipulating the third countries whose nationals must be in possession of a visa when crossing the Community's external frontiers.

---

[1] Bull. 6-1995, point I.9; Bull. 12-1995.
[2] COM(93) 632; Twenty-seventh General Report, point 70.
[3] Bull. 12-1995.

The Commission continued to ensure that the principle of the free movement of goods was being applied. Its proposal concerning the introduction of an appropriate procedure for guaranteeing the transparency of national measures derogating from the principle of the free movement of goods was adopted on 13 December by the Council.

In the financial services sector, the Council and Parliament adopted a Directive designed to reinforce prudential supervision of financial institutions. The Council also adopted common positions on proposals for Directives on cross-border payments, monitoring of unofficial off-exchange derivatives instruments, and compensation arrangements for investors. The Commission presented proposals for Directives on the setting-up of a securities committee and on the supervision of insurance undertakings forming part of an insurance group.

Significant progress was made on industrial and intellectual property. For example, the Council adopted common positions on the protection of databases and on a supplementary protection certificate for plant-protection products. The Commission presented Green Papers on copyright and neighbouring rights in the information society and on the protection of utility models. Since Parliament had rejected the Directive on the legal protection of biotechnological inventions, the Commission presented a new proposal on 13 December.

The Council and Parliament adopted a Directive on the protection of individuals with regard to the processing of personal data, which aims to establish the free movement of data within the Community while ensuring that individuals are equally well protected in respect of such data in all the Member States.

Lastly, the Commission proposed to amend a number of directives in the light of the multilateral agreement on public procurement, and it set up pilot projects using a new information system.

Management of the internal market[1]

94.   The Commission continued to stress forcefully the importance of rapid and correct transposal of the directives relating to the completion of the single market. The overall rate of transposal for the 15 Member States was 93.2% at the end of the year. However, the level remained below that figure in a number of areas, such as public procurement, intellectual property and insurance.

---

[1]   For further information, see in particular the *Annual report on the single market (1995)*.

95.   As part of its policy to promote cooperation between the authorities responsible for implementing Community law in the Member States, the Commission set up, in accordance with the Council resolution of 16 June 1994,[1] a database containing, for each Member State, details of contacts for some 20 areas of activity.

96.   In order to ensure that the rules are properly applied, there is also a need for penalties that are effective, proportionate and dissuasive. On 3 May the Commission adopted a communication[2] on this matter in which it stressed the need for greater transparency with regard to the penalties applicable in the event of breaches of Community law in the Member States. This approach was supported by the Council in a resolution passed on 29 June.[3] The Cannes European Council also stressed the importance of effective and uniform application of Community legislation in boosting confidence on the part of industry and among the public.[4]

97.   On 13 December Parliament and the Council adopted a Decision (Table I) establishing a procedure for the exchange of information on national measures derogating from the principle of the free movement of goods, which is designed to enable the Community to manage in a transparent and pragmatic manner the mutual recognition of national laws that have not been harmonized at Community level.

98.   'Internal Market Weeks',[5] designed to permit an exchange of views on the single market between the Commission, on the one hand, and firms and consumers, on the other, were held in the three new Member States. The Commission also decided to launch in mid-1996 a major information campaign entitled 'Citizens First' and aimed at providing members of the public with detailed information on their rights in the single market and on how to exercise them.

99.   The Commission pressed ahead with its study on the business and economic implications of the internal market.[6]

100.   The second annual report on the single market (1994)[7] was adopted by the Commission on 15 June, and opinions on it were delivered in

---

[1]   OJ C 179, 1.7.1994; General Report 1994, point 95.
[2]   COM(95) 162; Bull. 5-1995, point 1.3.12.
[3]   OJ C 188, 22.7.1995; for the full text of the Resolution, see Bull. 6-1995, point 1.3.17.
[4]   Bull. 6-1995, point I.9.
[5]   General Report 1994, point 96.
[6]   General Report 1994, point 97.
[7]   COM(95) 238; Bull. 6-1995, point 1.3.16.

November by Parliament[1] and the Economic and Social Committee.[2] On 6 December the Commission adopted a summary report on the single market in 1995,[3] which it sent to the Madrid European Council.

Free movement of goods

Implementation of Articles 30 to 36 of the EC Treaty[4]

101. As part of the ongoing process of removing controls at internal frontiers and abolishing barriers to trade, extended since 1 January 1995 to the three new Member States, the Commission continued its monitoring of compliance by Member States with the principles of Articles 30, 34 and 36 of the EC Treaty. The number of cases under examination as at 31 December 1995 was 1 030, and 259 new complaints have been received, including 33 against the new Member States. The Commission also acted on its own initiative by conducting general enquiries to examine the state of Member States' legislation in a particular sector. This year it concerned itself in particular with the rules governing intra-Community trade in gold, the parallel importation of pesticides and plant-protection products, and the application of Articles 30 to 36 of the EC Treaty to foodstuffs.

102. As regards special arrangements relating to freedom of movement, the Council adopted on 6 June negotiating directives relating to the draft Unidroit Convention on the international return of stolen or illegally exported cultural objects (Table III), the aim being to negotiate the inclusion in the Convention of a specific clause permitting Member States to continue to apply, in respect of one another, Community law in areas covered by the Convention that are already the subject of Community law (Directive 93/7/EEC).[5] On 19 October, in order to resolve problems of interpretation arising from discrepancies between several language versions, the Commission adopted a proposal for a Regulation (Table II) amending the annex to Council Regulation (EEC) No 3911/92[6] on the export of cultural goods, together with a proposal for a European Parliament and Council Directive (Table I) amending the annex to Directive 93/7/EEC.

---

[1]   OJ C 323, 4.12.1995; Bull. 11-1995, point 1.3.10.
[2]   Bull. 11-1995, point 1.3.10.
[3]   Bull. 12-1995.
[4]   Further information is contained in the 13th annual report to Parliament on Commission monitoring of the application of Community law (1995) (→ *point 1124*) of this Report.
[5]   OJ L 74, 27.3.1993; Twenty-seventh General Report, point 96.
[6]   Twenty-sixth General Report, point 161.

Technical aspects

103. Pursuant to Directive 83/189/EEC,[1] which lays down a procedure for the provision of information in the field of technical standards and regulations, the Commission received 438 notifications of draft technical regulations. Since the information procedure came into force, the Commission has received a total of 3 328 notifications. Over the last four years the number of notifications received has remained stable. This year the Commission issued detailed opinions on account of the breaches of Community law to which draft regulations might give rise in 114 cases.[2] The Member States did so in 102 cases.[2]

104. The number of notifications under the procedure for the exchange of information in the field of technical regulations provided for in the Agreement on the European Economic Area rose from seven[3] in 1994 to eight in 1995. For its part, the Commission, acting on behalf of the Community, issued a total of 6 observations to the EFTA countries which are signatories to the EEA Agreement.[2] The same procedure also applies informally to Switzerland. The number of notifications by Switzerland went from 43 in 1994 to 16 in 1995. The Commission, acting on behalf of the Community, issued 600 observations to that country.[2]

105. Where foodstuffs are concerned, on 20 February the European Parliament and the Council adopted Directive 95/2/EC on food additives other than colours and sweeteners (Table I) which, as part of the harmonization of the basic rules concerning additives,[4] establishes the list of authorized additives and specifies the conditions for their use. The Council adopted three new proposals concerning additives: a proposal for a Decision on the maintenance of national laws prohibiting the use of certain additives in the production of certain foodstuffs (Table I) which allows Member States to derogate from the additives directives to enable special production methods to be maintained for traditional foods produced on their territory; a proposal for a Directive (Table I) amending Directive 95/2/EC to authorize the use of alternatively refined carrageenan as a food additive; and a proposal (Table I) to amend Directive 94/35/EC on sweeteners to adapt it to technical progress. The Commission also adopted directives laying down purity

---

[1]   OJ L 109, 26.4.1983; Seventeenth General Report, point 150.
[2]   Figures as at 1 January 1996. The time limit for issuing detailed opinions concerning drafts notified in 1995 is 31 March 1996.
[3]   This figure does not take account of notifications under the procedure applicable to the three new Member States. These notifications (53) are included in the figures for 1994 concerning notifications by Member States.
[4]   1994 General Report, point 106.

criteria for sweeteners[1] and colours.[2] On 23 October the Council adopted a common position on the proposal for a European Parliament and Council Regulation on novel foods and novel food ingredients which seeks to ensure a high level of consumer protection, particularly as regards safety and labelling, without impeding innovation (Table I).

On 22 December the Council adopted a common position on a proposal for a European Parliament and Council Directive (Table I) on mineral waters. On the same day it also adopted a common position on a proposal for a European Parliament and Council Regulation (Table I) on flavourings.

On 11 December the Commission adopted an amended proposal for a Directive (Table I) amending Directive 79/112/EEC[3] on the approximation of the laws of the Member States relating to the labelling and presentation of foodstuffs. On 23 November it also adopted a proposal for a Council Directive (Table I) amending Directive 94/54/EC concerning the compulsory indication on the labelling of certain foodstuffs of particulars other than those provided for in Council Directive 79/112/EEC[4] in order to provide consumers with information about the presence of sweeteners in foodstuffs.

On 4 December the Commission adopted an amended proposal for a European Parliament and Council Directive (Table I) on the approximation of the laws of the Member States relating to foodstuffs intended for particular nutritional uses. It also adopted three Directives: the first amending Directive 91/321/EEC[5] on infant formulae to adapt it technical and scientific developments; the second relating to cereals-based formulae and babyfoods; and the third relating to foodstuffs intended to be used in energy-restricted diets. The Commission also adopted Directive 95/3/EC[6] amending for the third time Directive 90/128/EEC[7] relating to plastic materials and articles intended to come into contact with foodstuffs. In the scientific cooperation field, it twice updated the 1994 inventory[8] of tasks requiring the involvement of specialist research institutes in the Member States. Lastly, Commission staff paid their first visit to the Member States under Directive 93/99/EEC[9] on additional measures concerning the official control of foodstuffs.

---

[1] OJ L 178, 28.7.1995 (Directive 95/31/EC).
[2] OJ L 226, 22.9.1995 (Directive 95/45/EC).
[3] Directive last amended by Directive 93/102/EC — OJ L 291, 25.11.1993.
[4] OJ L 33, 8.2.1979.
[5] OJ L 175, 4.7.1991.
[6] OJ L 41, 23.2.1995.
[7] OJ L 75, 21.3.1990.
[8] OJ L 253, 29.9.1994; 1994 General Report, point 106.
[9] OJ L 290, 24.11.1993; Twenty-seventh General Report, point 76.

106.   Turning to the chemicals sector, the legislative work again[1] concerned in particular the amendment of Directive 76/769/EEC on the marketing and use of certain dangerous substances and preparations (→ point 480). On 27 October the Commission adopted an amended proposal for a European Parliament and Council Directive (Table I) amending that Directive for the 16th time to extend its scope to include hexachloroethane. On 8 December it adopted a proposal for a European Parliament and Council Directive (Table I) amending for the eighth time Directive 67/548/EEC on the approximation of the provisions relating to the classification, packaging and labelling of dangerous substances. On 20 July it also adopted an amended proposal for a Council and Parliament Directive (Table I) concerning the placing of biocidal products on the market (pesticides for non-agricultural use). In the pharmaceuticals sector, on 10 February the Council adopted Regulation (EC) No 297/95 (Table II) establishing the fees payable to the European Agency for the Evaluation of Medicinal Products[2] to obtain and maintain Community marketing authorizations for medicinal products and for other services provided by the Agency (→ point 198). In addition, on 19 April the Commission adopted a proposal for a Directive (Table I) aimed at harmonizing the national laws on in vitro diagnostic medical devices, following the 'new approach'.

107.   In the motor vehicles sector,[3] on 2 February the European Parliament and the Council adopted Directive 95/1/EC (Table I) on the maximum engine power of two or three-wheeled motor vehicles. The proposal for a Directive concerning certain components of such vehicles (Table I) was the subject of a Council common position on 23 November. Where flammability is concerned, on 24 October the European Parliament and the Council adopted Directive 95/28/EC (Table I) relating to the nature of materials to be used in the fittings of coaches. At the Council's request, the Commission adopted Directive 95/56/EC on the adaptation to technical progress of Directive 74/61/EC on anti-theft devices for private cars.[4] On 27 November the Commission adopted an amended proposal for a European Parliament and Council Directive concerning front impact (Table I). On 23 November the Council adopted a common position on the proposal for a European Parliament and Council Directive concerning frontal collision (Table I). Lastly, on 20 December the Commission adopted a communication clarify-

---

[1]   1994 General Report, point 107.
[2]   Set up by Regulation (EEC) No 2309/93, OJ L 214, 24.8.1993; Twenty-seventh General Report, point 77.
[3]   Aspects concerning emissions of gaseous pollutants from vehicles are covered in Section 16 (Environment) of this chapter (→ point 500); aspects concerning maximum authorized weights and dimensions for road vehicles over 3.5 tonnes are covered in Section 14 (Transport) of this chapter (→ point 400).
[4]   OJ L 286, 29.11.1995.

ing the rules applicable to imports by private individuals of new or second-hand cars previously registered in another Member State.[1]

108. On 29 June the Council and the European Parliament signed Directive 95/16/EC (Table I) on the approximation of the laws of the Member States relating to lifts. On 16 November the Commission adopted an amended proposal for a Directive (Table II) on the safety of cableways. On 23 November the Council reached agreement on a common position on a proposal for a European Parliament and Council Directive on pressure equipment (Table I). On 17 November the Commission adopted a proposal for a European Parliament and Council Directive (Table I) on personal protective equipment.

Veterinary and plant-health fields

109. In the plant-health field, a number of 'protected areas' were recognized under Commission Directive 95/40/EC,[2] and Commission Directive 95/44/EC[3] set out various exemptions from the plant-health arrangements of the Community[4] with regard to trials and scientific and varietal selection work. In the area of seeds and reproductive material, the Council adopted two decisions which grant equivalent status to some non-member countries with repect to arable seed and seed potatoes. The Commission adopted Decision 95/232/EC[5] organizing a temporary trial under the terms of Directive 69/208/EEC with a view to laying down the conditions to be met by hybrid seed and varietal associations of swede rape and turnip rape. On 17 July, the Council adopted Directives 95/38/EC (Table II) and 95/39/EC (Table II) to adjust the regime for fixing maximum levels of pesticide residues in foodstuffs. On 25 October the Council adopted Regulation (EC) No 2506/95 amending Regulation (EC) No 2100/94 on Community plant variety rights (Table II). The Community Plant Variety Office, whose job is to supervise the protection of plant varieties in the Community, was set up in application of Regulation (EC) No 2100/94.[6]

110. Important decisions were adopted this year in the veterinary and zootechnical field. On 29 June the Council adopted Directive 95/29/EC (Table II) concerning the protection of animals during transport. On 15 De-

---

[1]   Bull. 12-1995.
[2]   OJ L 182, 2.8.1995.
[3]   OJ L 184, 3.8.1995.
[4]   1994 General Report, point 117.
[5]   OJ L 154, 5.7.1995.
[6]   OJ L 227, 1.9.1994.

cember the Commission adopted a communication on the welfare of calves. [1] The Council also adopted on 22 June Directive 95/23/EC amending Directive 64/433/EEC on conditions for the production and marketing of fresh meat (Table II), Directive 95/22/EC concerning the animal health conditions governing the placing on the market of aquaculture animals and products (Table II), and Decision 95/408/EC on provisional terms for the import of certain products of animal origin, fishery products and live bivalve molluscs (Table II). The Council also adopted Decisions 95/409/EC, 95/410/EC and 95/411/EC on tests for salmonella in connection with the shipping of certain animals and products of animal origin to Finland and Sweden. [2] The Commission, for its part, adopted several proposals particularly with regard to meat-based products. [3] It also adopted numerous decisions on Community financing of programmes for the eradication of animal diseases and designed to restrict their spread within the Community. On 7 June the Commission adopted a proposal for a Directive amending Directive 77/93/EEC on protective measures against the introduction into the Member States of harmful organisms of plants or plant products (Table II) and, on 23 October, for a Council Directive (Table II) amending Directive 92/117/EEC concerning measures for protection against specified zoonoses (animal diseases transmissible to man such as rabies). On 22 December the Council adopted a Directive (Table II) with a view to establishing measures to control diseases of bivalve molluscs. Parliament adopted on 22 September[4] a resolution concerning the conference on the use of growth promoters in livestock farming, following up its resolution of 16 March on combating the trafficking of hormones. [5] On 25 October the Council adopted Directive 95/52/EC (Table II) amending Directive 90/675/EEC in order to extend until the end of 1996 the transitional measures intended to facilite the harmonization of conditions for imports of livestock products originating in third countries.

111.   In the area of animal feedingstuffs, the Council adopted on 21 December, Directive (Table II) establishing the terms and conditions and detailed procedures for the approval of certain establishments and amending Directives 70/524/EEC, 74/63/EEC, 79/373/EEC and 82/471/EEC. On 25 October, the Council adopted Directive 95/53/EC (Table II) fixing the principles governing the organization of official inspections in the field of animal nutrition.

---

[1]   COM(95) 711; Bull. 12-1995.
[2]   OJ L 243, 11.10.1995; Bull. 6-1995, points 1.3.25-1.3.27.
[3]   OJ C 192, 26.7.1995.
[4]   OJ C 269, 16.10.1995.
[5]   OJ C 89, 10.4.1995; Bull. 3-1995, point 1.3.11.

112.   The Veterinary and Phytosanitary Office (French abbr. OICVP) organized inspections of establishments inside and outside the Community producing fresh meat and meat-based products, as well as visits to establishments producing poultrymeat in the Member States. Special missions were also organized in several Member States affected by outbreaks of animal diseases, and the health conditions governing imports of various products of animal origin from a number of non-member countries were laid down. Inspection visits in the fisheries sector were carried out in various non-member countries in order to establish the health requirements for the import of their fishery products. In the plant-health field, the inspection, monitoring and surveillance operations in the Member States mainly covered checks on the proper application of the Community rules, in particular with regard to the monitoring of 'protected areas' and the issuing of plant-health 'passports'.

113.   In December the Commission, in a desire to clarify Community law and make it more transparent, adopted a series of proposals for Directives designed to consolidate existing Directives in the veterinary and plant-health fields.[1]

114.   Finally, at international level, bilateral negotiations took place with a number of countries on the basis of negotiating instructions adopted on 20 February for the purposes of concluding an agreement in the veterinary and plant-health fields (Table III).

Free movement of persons

Abolition of controls at internal frontiers

115.   Information on the abolition of controls at internal frontiers is given in Section 2 (Citizens' rights) of Chapter I *(→ point 2).*

Right of entry and right of residence

116.   Information on the right of entry and the right of residence is given in Section 2 (Citizens' rights) of Chapter I *(→ point 2).*

---

[1]   COM(95) 598, COM(95) 622, COM(95) 628; Bull. 12-1995.

Right of establishment and mutual recognition of qualifications

117.   With a view to facilitating the free movement of doctors and the mutual recognition of their qualifications, the Commission on 27 November amended the proposal for a European Parliament and Council Directive (Table I). In connection with the general system for the recognition of diplomas (→ point 270) introduced by Council Directive 92/51/EEC,[1] the Commission adopted on 20 July Directive 95/43/EC,[2] which, in response to requests from Austria and the Netherlands, classifies a number of training courses at a higher level.

Free movement of workers

118.   Information on the free movement of workers is given in Section 21 (Employment and social policy) of this chapter (→ point 611).

Freedom to provide services

Financial services

119.   With a view to reinforcing prudential supervision, European Parliament and Council Directive 95/26/EC of 29 June 1995 (Table I) amended the Directives on credit institutions, insurance and investment firms, and undertakings for collective investment in transferable securities.

120.   On 6 September the Council adopted a common position (Table I) on the proposal for a Directive amending Directive 89/647/EEC with respect to the supervisory recognition of contracts for novation and netting agreements ('contractual netting'), in order to refine the prudential treatment of credit risks inherent in unofficial off-exchange derivative instruments. On 22 September Parliament adopted a resolution on financial derivatives,[3] and on 25 October the Economic and Social Committee adopted an own-initiative opinion on this question.[4]

121.   On 4 October the Commission adopted a proposal for a Directive (Table I) on the supervision of insurance undertakings forming part of a

---

[1]   OJ L 209, 24.7.1992; Twenty-sixth General Report, point 167.
[2]   OJ L 184, 3.8.1995.
[3]   OJ C 269, 16.10.1995; Bull. 9-1995, point 1.3.15.
[4]   Bull. 10-1995, point 1.3.47.

group, which is designed to facilitate the exercise of the right of establishment and the freedom to provide services.

122. On 4 December the Council adopted a common position (Table I) on the proposal for a European Parliament and Council Directive on cross-border transfers.[1] Among other things, the Directive requires banks to discharge their contractual obligations as regards the time-scale for transfers, makes double-charging illegal, requires lost payments to be reimbursed and enhances transparency. The Commission continued its extensive consultations on the application of the competition rules to cross-border credit transfers. On 13 September it adopted a communication designed to facilitate the establishment of the appropriate interbank systems *(→ point 145).*

123. On 23 October the Council adopted a common position on the proposal for a European Parliament and Council Directive (Table I) on investor compensation arrangements, which is modelled largely on Directive 94/19/EC on deposit-guarantee schemes.[2] On 17 July the Commission adopted a proposal for a Directive (Table I) amending Council Directive 93/6/EEC on the capital adequacy of investment firms and credit institutions and Council Directive 93/22/EEC on investment services in the securities field, one of the aims being to set up a securities committee.

124. On 3 March the Commission adopted the first report on the implementation of Directive 91/308/EEC concerning the fight against money laundering;[3] the report was endorsed by the Council on 20 March.[4]

125. On 31 October the Commission adopted a draft communication[5] on freedom to provide services and the interest of the general good in the Second Banking Directive (89/646/EEC) which will form the basis for an interpretative communication once consultations with interested parties have been completed.

Other services

126. As provided for in the 1994 Commission communication on the follow-up to the consultation process relating to the Green Paper on 'Pluralism and media concentration in the internal market — an assessment of the need

---

[1]   1994 General Report, point 134.
[2]   OJ L 135, 31.5.1994; 1994 General Report, point 129.
[3]   COM(95) 54; Bull. 3-1995, point 1.3.13.
[4]   Bull. 3-1995, point 1.3.13.
[5]   OJ C 291, 4.11.1995; Bull. 10-1995, point 1.3.46.

for Community action',[1] a second series of consultations was launched in January. The Economic and Social Committee,[2] the Committee of the Regions[3] and Parliament[4] have all given their opinions on the question. In addition, following its communication entitled 'Europe's way to the information society — An action plan'[5] (→ point 419), the Commission in March initiated consultations among the Member States and interested parties with a view to producing a Green Paper on the legal protection of encrypted services in the internal market.

Free movement of capital

127. Monitoring by the Commission of the free movement of capital and of payments within the Union (Article 73b of the EC Treaty) demonstrated that, in general, the situation in this field was satisfactory. Community law on capital movements has been transposed by all the Member States and the temporary derogations have expired. Capital is moving freely in the Union, in substantial amounts and in different forms. However, the Commission has identified a number of indirect obstacles and the continued presence of a number of restrictions that take the form of conditions imposed on access by foreign securities to capital markets, favourable tax arrangements applied to certain financial investments, and restrictions on the physical transfer of funds. Accordingly, it has tried to eliminate such obstacles that are incompatible with Community law. As regards the most appropriate policy for limiting the negative effects of speculative capital movements often associated with transactions on the derivatives markets, it has stressed the importance of creating an economic, financial and political environment conducive to strengthening confidence and reducing uncertainty. In this connection, it recalled in a communication published in April that the free movement of capital was guaranteed by the Treaty and was essential for the completion of the internal market, financial integration and movement towards monetary union. At international level, the Council on 10 April authorized the Commission to take part in the negotiations on the multinational agreement on investment under the auspices of the OECD (→ point 755).

---

[1] COM(94) 353; 1994 General Report, point 137.
[2] Bull. 1/2-1995, point 1.3.16.
[3] Bull. 7/8-1995, point 1.3.22.
[4] OJ C 166, 3.7.1995; Bull. 6-1995, point 1.3.39.
[5] COM(94) 347.

Taxation

Direct taxation

128. Following the judgments *(→ point 1129)* concerning the taxation of frontier workers handed down on 14 February[1] and 11 August,[2] in which the Court of Justice followed the guidelines set out in Commission recommendation 94/79/EC,[3] the Commission urged the Member States to make the necessary changes to their tax laws. On 21 December the Economic and Social Committee adopted an own-initiative opinion on direct and indirect taxation.[4]

Indirect taxation

129. On 10 April the Council adopted Directive 95/7/EC (Table II) amending Directive 77/388/EEC and introducing new simplification measures with regard to value-added tax. The Directive is designed to simplify the tax treatment of a number of operations for traders and for the tax administrations of the Member States, thereby ensuring smoother functioning of the internal market.

130. On 13 September the Commission adopted a report[5] on the application by the Member States since 1 January 1993[6] of minimum rates of excise duties to manufactured tobacco products, alcohol, alcoholic beverages and mineral oils. On 20 December it adopted a proposal for a Directive (Table II) on setting the minimum level for the standard rate of VAT.[4] On 27 November the Council adopted Directive 95/60/EC (Table II) on fiscal marking of gas oils and kerosene and Directive 95/59/EC on taxes other than turnover taxes which affect the consumption of manufactured tobacco (consolidated text) (Table II).

Company law

131. On 14 November the Commission adopted a communication setting out a new strategy *vis-à-vis* international harmonization in the field of ac-

---

[1] Case C-279/93 *Finanzamt Köln-Altstadt* v *R. Schumacker*; Bull. 1/2-1995, point 1.8.30.
[2] Case C-80/94 *Wielockx*.
[3] OJ L 39, 10.2.1994.
[4] Bull. 12-1995.
[5] COM(95) 285; Bull. 9-1995, point 1.3.17.
[6] Twenty-seventh General Report, point 124.

counting.[1] New guidelines for the Statute for a European Company are expected in 1996. Also on 14 November the Commission adopted a communication on informing and consulting employees (→ point 601) in which it suggested a broad approach instead of proposals for Directives specific to each entity concerned, such as the European company.

Intellectual and industrial property

132.   On 29 June the Council adopted a decision on the extension of the legal protection of topographies of semiconductor products to persons from the United States of America[2] provided for by Directive 87/54/EEC[3] until the TRIPs Agreement (outcome of the Uruguay Round negotiations) is implemented on 1 January 1996. On 10 July it adopted a common position (Table II) on the proposal for a Directive on the legal protection of databases. On 19 July the Commission adopted a Green Paper on 'Copyright and related rights in the information society'.[4] The Green Paper is part of the Commission's action plan on the information society (→ point 419) and examines the possible impact of the development of new technologies with a view to providing adequate protection for copyright and related rights.

133.   With regard to industrial property, the Commission adopted the three Regulations implementing Regulation (EC) No 40/94 on the Community trade mark,[5] these being essential for the functioning of the Office for Harmonization in the Internal Market (trade marks, designs and models). The first applications for the Community trade mark can be lodged from the beginning of 1996 and firms will be able to obtain, through a single application submitted to the Office, a trade mark covering all the Member States. On 27 November the Council adopted a common position on the proposal for a European Parliament and Council Regulation (Table I) concerning the creation of a supplementary protection certificate for plant protection products. On 1 March Parliament voted to reject the proposal for a Directive (Table I) on the legal protection of biotechnological inventions. As a result, the Commission had to undertake detailed discussions on the best strategy to pursue and, in particular, on the advisability of presenting a new legislative proposal. It presented such a proposal on 13 December (Table I). In the Green Paper on 'The protection of utility models in the single market',[6] which it adopted on 19 July, the Commission sets out to assess the need for

---

[1]   COM(95) 508; Bull. 11-1995, point 1.3.30.
[2]   OJ L 158, 8.7.1995; Bull. 6-1995, point 1.3.41.
[3]   OJ L 24, 27.1.1987; Twenty-first General Report, point 295.
[4]   COM(95) 382; Bull. 7/8-1995, point 1.3.24.
[5]   OJ L 11, 14.1.1994; 1994 General Report, point 153.
[6]   COM(95) 370; Bull. 7/8-1995, point 1.3.23.

Community action on utility models, a means of legal protection for industrial property that is often used for technical inventions.

134. At international level, the Commission on 3 May adopted a recommendation for a Council Decision (Table III) concerning approval of the European Convention relating to questions on copyright law and neighbouring rights in the framework of transfrontier broadcasting by satellite, which had been adopted by the Council of Europe on 16 February 1994. On 29 June the Council adopted a decision on the signing of the Trademark Law Treaty *(→ point 717).*

Data protection

135. On 24 October the Council and Parliament signed the Directive on the protection of individuals with regard to the processing of personal data and on the free movement of such data (Table I). The Directive is part of the moves to set up a European information area where processing of personal data is expected to develop significantly. It seeks to ensure the free movement of personal data in the Community and to remove distortions of competition and the resulting risks of relocation by affording individuals in all the Member States an equivalent, high level of protection of persons with regard to the processing of data *(→ point 14).*

Public procurement

136. The Commission continued its monitoring of the transposal of the public procurement directives. On the external front, the Commission adopted on 29 March two proposals amending Directives 92/50/EEC, 93/36/EEC and 93/37/EEC (Table I), and Directive 93/38/EEC respectively (Table I). Both proposals are designed to prevent certain consequences for intra-Community relations that might arise from the implementation of the multilateral Government Procurement Agreement[1] concluded on 15 April 1994 under the auspices of the WTO. On 29 May the Council adopted Decision 95/215/EC concerning the conclusion of an Agreement between the European Community and the United States of America on government procurement (Table III), and on 24 July it adopted Regulation (EC) No 1836/95 completing the Annex to Regulation (EEC) No 1461/93 concerning access to public contracts for tenderers from the United States of America (Table II). The Commission also pressed ahead with work on

---

[1]   1994 General Report, point 158.

developing an information system for public procurement, SIMAP,[1] the purpose of which is to improve the effectiveness of public procurement, in particular by making notification more efficient, improving the dissemination of information, perfecting the tools used for monitoring and analysis, and making it easier for economic operators to exchange information. The first pilot schemes began in October. On 16 November the Committee of the Regions adopted an own-initiative opinion on the procedures for awarding public service contracts.[2]

Legal professions: Training and information concerning the application of Community law

137.   In the context of the strategic programme for the internal market,[3] and following a survey launched in 1994 among lawyers, the Commission organized in March and October two meetings of legal experts (judges, lawyers and academics) from the Member States to discuss in detail possible ways of improving training of, and dissemination of information to, legal practitioners in the field of Community law.

Preparation for the integration of the countries of Central and Eastern Europe with associate status into the internal market

138.   Information concerning the preparations for the integration of countries of Central and Eastern Europe with associate status into the internal market is provided in Section 8 (Relations with the countries of Central and Eastern Europe and with the Baltic States) of Chapter IV *(→ point 816)*.

---

[1]   Twenty-seventh General Report, point 114.
[2]   Bull. 11-1995, point 1.3.33.
[3]   COM(93) 632; Twenty-seventh General Report, point 113.

Section 5

Competition[1]

Priority activities and objectives

139. *The Commission's activities in the competition policy field in 1995 can be divided into four main areas.*

Firstly, the Commission continued to apply the existing rules with vigilance in all areas of competition policy in the interests of the proper functioning of the single market and in order to ensure that effective competition is maintained and developed in the European Union. It is an essential consideration here that the Commission should have at its disposal a set of interdependent competition policy instruments. Secondly, the Commission was sufficiently pragmatic to lock on to the momentum of the process of globalization and innovation which characterizes the current economic environment, while safeguarding public services in areas where market forces are inadequate. In the information society context, telecommunications and the media proved to be a priority here.

Thirdly, the Commission continued its drive to increase the efficiency of its operations. It will thus concentrate more on essentials, being more selective when it comes to deciding which competition cases, and in particular which complaints, it should deal with. Fourthly, the Commission took steps to improve the transparency of competition policy. In particular, it started work on drawing up various Green Papers, including one on vertical restrictions of competition and another on the review of the Merger Regulation.

On 28 April, the Commission adopted the Twenty-fourth Report on Competition Policy,[2] *on which the Economic and Social Committee gave its opinion on 22 November.[3] On 16 March, Parliament delivered its opinion[4] on the* Twenty-third Report on Competition Policy.[5]

---

[1]   For further details, see the *Twenty-fifth Report on Competition Policy* (1995), to be published by the Office for Official Publications of the European Communities in 1996 in conjunction with this General Report. A report on the application of the competition rules in the European Union in 1995, prepared under the sole responsibility of the Directorate-General for Competition in conjunction with the *Twenty-fifth Report on Competition Policy*, is also available.

[2]   COM(95) 142; Bull. 4-1995, point 1.3.18.

[3]   Bull. 11-1995, point 1.3.34.

[4]   OJ C 89, 10.4.1995; Bull. 3-1995, point 1.3.20.

[5]   COM(94) 161; 1994 General Report, point 160.

Competition rules applying to businesses

140. New cases under Articles 85 and 86 of the EC Treaty totalled 559, comprising 368 notifications, 145 complaints and 46 cases where the Commission acted on its own initiative. New cases under Articles 65 and 66 of the ECSC Treaty totalled 36, comprising 34 notifications and two complaints. The Commission received 29 notifications under Article 66 of the ECSC Treaty. Of these, eight culminated in a decision, 17 in the sending of an exemption letter under High Authority Decision No 25/67, and four in no action being taken. The main decisions here were those concerning the privatization of Ilva Laminati Piani, Siderurgia Nacional-Planos and Siderurgia Nacional-Largos.

General rules

141. On 20 April, the Commission adopted Regulation (EC) No 870/95[1] on the application of Article 85(3) of the Treaty to certain categories of agreements, decisions and concerted practices between liner shipping companies (consortia) pursuant to Council Regulation (EEC) No 479/92.[2] This Regulation, which is the second block exemption Regulation to have been adopted in the liner shipping sector,[3] grants block exemption to liner shipping consortia set up with a view to establishing varying degrees of cooperation for the running of a joint service.

142. On 21 June, the Commission adopted Regulation (EC) No 1475/95 on the application of Article 85(3) of the Treaty to certain categories of motor vehicle distribution and servicing agreements.[4] The Regulation replaces Regulation (EEC) No 123/85,[5] which expired on 30 June, and introduces changes designed to boost competition in motor vehicle distribution by altering the balance between the various interests involved. The Economic and Social Committee and Parliament expressed their views on the subject on 29 March[6] and 7 April[7] respectively.

---

[1]   OJ L 89, 21.4.1995; Bull. 4-1995, point 1.3.21.
[2]   OJ L 55, 29.2.1992; Twenty-sixth General Report, point 197.
[3]   Since 1 July 1987, liner conferences have already qualified for block exemption under Council Regulation (EEC) No 4056/86 laying down detailed rules for the application of Articles 85 and 86 of the Treaty to maritime transport — OJ L 378, 31.12.1986.
[4]   OJ L 145, 29.6.1995; Bull. 6-1995, point 1.3.46.
[5]   OJ L 15, 18.1.1985; Eighteenth General Report, point 212.
[6]   OJ C 133, 31.5.1995; Bull. 3-1995, point 1.3.21.
[7]   OJ C 109, 1.5.1995; Bull. 4-1995, point 1.3.19.

143.   By adopting on 17 January Regulation (EC) No 70/95,[1] and then on 7 September Regulation (EC) No 2131/95,[2] the Commission extended until 31 December 1995 the term of validity of Regulation (EEC) No 2349/84 as regards certain categories of patent licensing agreements.

144.   On 30 October, the Commission adopted a preliminary draft Regulation with a view to the possible amendment of Regulation (EEC) No 1617/93 on the application of Article 85(3) of the Treaty to certain categories of agreement in air transport.[3] The possible amendment in question concerns the exclusion of tariff consultations on cargo transport from the scope of the Regulation.

145.   On 13 September, the Commission adopted a notice containing guidelines on the application of the competition rules to cross-border credit transfers.[4] The notice, which accompanies the proposal for a Directive on this type of transfer *(→ point 122)*, provides a framework within which banks can conclude cooperation agreements aimed at making cross-border credit transfers more effective without unduly restricting competition, in particular as regards market access and prices.

146.   On 19 December, the Commission published a draft communication to the Member States on the non-imposition or reduction of fines where firms furnish detailed information on the existence of unlawful agreements, provided certain conditions are met.[5]

Prohibited agreements

147.   Illustrating the fact that the professions do not fall outside the scope of the competition rules laid down in the Treaty, the Commission adopted on 30 January Decision 95/188/EC requiring the Colegio Oficial de Agentes de la Propiedad Industrial, the professional association of industrial property agents in Spain, to refrain from fixing compulsory minimum scales of fees for certain services rendered by its members.[6]

148.   The Decision of 12 July concerning *Glasurit*[7] reflects the Commission's resolve to take action against firms which seek to wall off national

---

[1]   OJ L 12, 18.1.1995; Bull. 1/2-1995, point 1.3.23.
[2]   OJ L 214, 8.9.1995; Bull. 9-1995, point 1.3.18.
[3]   Bull. 10-1995, point 1.3.53.
[4]   OJ C 251, 27.9.1995; Bull. 9-1995, point 1.3.19.
[5]   OJ C 341, 19.12.1995; Bull. 12-1995.
[6]   OJ L 122, 2.6.1995; Bull. 1/2-1995, point 1.3.22.
[7]   OJ L 272,15.11.1995; Bull. 7/8-1995, point 1.3.49.

markets by restricting parallel imports. The Commission imposed fines of ECU 2.7 million on BASF and ECU 10 000 on Accinauto, BASF's exclusive distributor in Belgium and Luxembourg of Glasurit car refinishing paints, on account of the obstacles the firms had placed in the way of exports of those products to the United Kingdom.

149. On 29 November, the Commission fined the FNK (Federatie van Nederlandse Kraanverhuurbedrijven) and SCK (Stichting Certificatie Kraanverhuurbedrijf) for concluding horizontal price fixing agreements and horizontal exclusive dealing agreements in the crane-hire sector.[1]

Authorizations

150. Many cases were settled by comfort letter. This reflects the Commission's favourable attitude towards forms of cooperation which enable firms to derive benefits which are necessary if they are to remain competitive, especially on markets which are becoming increasingly global, or which enable them to make their R&TD more effective or reduce their production or distribution costs.

Abuses of dominant positions

151. Acting on a request for interim measures made by the shipping company *Irish Continental Group* (ICG), which operates ferry transport services for passengers and vehicles and which complained against the conduct of the Chamber of Commerce and Industry of the town of Morlaix (CCI Morlaix) in Brittany, France, the Commission decided to impose interim measures.[2] On the basis of its preliminary examination of the case, it found that the conditions for applying interim measures were met: firstly, the Breton port of Roscoff was the only French port which had the facilities needed to run ferry services between Brittany and Ireland, so that, *prima facie*, CCI Morlaix held a dominant position; secondly, the refusal of CCI Morlaix to allow ICG services access to the facilities of the port of Roscoff was, *prima facie*, an abuse of a dominant position. Consequently, the Commission required CCI Morlaix to take the necessary steps to ensure that such access was afforded until the end of the summer season. Following the Commission's intervention, the parties concluded a five-year contract and ICG withdrew its complaint.

---

[1]   OJ L 312, 23.12.1995; Bull. 11-1995, point 1.3.42.
[2]   Bull. 5-1995, point 1.3.31.

Mergers

152. The Commission received 112 notifications in 1995. During the year, some 109 decisions were taken under Council Regulation (EEC) No 4064/89,[1] an increase of 25% over 1994. The great majority of the cases were cleared at the end of the first stage of examination. The Commission initiated the second stage of examination in seven cases, in two of which the notified operation was found to be incompatible with the common market. In three other cases, the Commission made the merger subject to requirements and conditions.

153. At the request of the Dutch Government under Article 22 of the Merger Regulation,[2] the Commission examined a Dutch television joint venture, *Holland Media Groep* (HMG),[3] although the Merger Regulation thresholds were not met. The Commission found that HMG could not be approved in its current form. The joint venture had a very high share of the Dutch television audience and was uniquely able to offer advertisers coordinated scheduling. Endemol already had a dominant position on the Dutch TV programming market and participation in HMG strengthened that position. Decisions taken under Article 22 are not suspensive, so HMG may continue its operations. The parties were invited by the Commission to propose appropriate amendments within three months of the date of the prohibition decision.

154. In the *NSD* case,[4] the Commission found that the proposed joint venture would strengthen or create a dominant position in three markets, namely the market for the provision of satellite television transponder capacity in the Nordic region, the market for Danish cable television networks, and the market for direct-to-home encrypted television channels, and that the resulting vertical integration would reinforce the anti-competitive effects foreclosing the Nordic satellite television market. The Commission invited the parties to present an amended proposal compatible with the common market and the EEA Agreement.

155. In the *Mercedes-Benz/Kässbohrer* case,[5] the Commission decided to declare the transaction compatible with the common market. Although Mercedes would have large market shares on the markets for buses in Germany, the Commission considered that the company would be adequately con-

---

[1]   OJ L 395, 30.12.1989; Twenty-third General Report, point 376.
[2]   As Regulation 4064/89 is more commonly known.
[3]   Bull. 5-1995, point 1.3.27.
[4]   Bull. 7/8-1995, point 1.3.34.
[5]   Bull. 1/2-1995, point 1.3.28.

strained by competition from other German and European suppliers. The latter would be aided by the EU Directives on public procurement, which would make EU-wide tenders obligatory for some 70% of German requirements. Furthermore, Mercedes gave an undertaking that it would allow non-German manufacturers access to Kässbohrer's sales and servicing network.

156.   To avoid a prohibition decision on the grounds that they were establishing a dominant position on the Norwegian beer market, the parties in *Orkla/Volvo*[1] agreed to sell the Hansa brewery as a going concern, thereby reducing the joint venture's market share for beer in Norway to acceptable levels. Commission action in this case was based on the EEA Agreement, and the Commission investigation was carried out in close liaison with the Norwegian competition authority and the EFTA Surveillance Authority.

157.   The Commission authorized the creation of a joint venture between *Siemens and Italtel*[2] although the combined market share for equipment for telecommunications networks was large and despite a degree of vertical integration. The Commission took into consideration the fact that technological developments, standardization and public procurement legislation would progressively enlarge and open national markets. In addition, STET, Italtel's parent company, gave undertakings not to intervene in Telecom Italia's purchasing policy and to separate the management of its supply and operating companies.

158.   The acquisition of *Carnaud Metalbox* by Crown, Cork & Seal,[3] a major US metal packaging and can manufacturer, was authorized subject to the divestiture en bloc of five firms which they control, accounting for almost 22% of the EEA tinplate aerosol can market. The merger of the two companies had caused the Commission serious concern specifically in the tinplate aerosol can market, since the two companies' combined market share was some 65% in 1994. The Commission considers that, as a result of the divestiture, the two companies will no longer have a dominant position on the aerosol can market.

159.   In the *ABB/Daimler-Benz* case,[4] the Commission authorized the formation of a rail transportation joint venture. To remedy competition problems in the German market for trams and metro systems, the parties agreed to sell Kiepe Elektrik GmbH, a firm specializing in electrical systems for

---

[1]   Bull. 9-1995, point 1.3.25.
[2]   Bull. 1/2-1995, point 1.3.29.
[3]   OJ C 161, 12.7.1995; Bull. 11-1995, point 1.3.37.
[4]   Bull. 10-1995, point 1.3.56.

local trains, which thus becomes an independent supplier free to cooperate with other manufacturers in the German market.

State aid

General policy

160.   During the year, the Commission received 674 notifications of new aid schemes or amendments to existing aid schemes, and registered 113 cases of unnotified aid schemes. In 460 cases it decided not to raise any objections; in 45 cases it decided to initiate proceedings under Article 93(2) of the EC Treaty or Article 6(4) of Decision No 3855/91/ECSC, as a result of which it took 19 positive final decisions, eight negative final decisions and five conditional final decisions. It decided to propose appropriate measures under Article 93(1) of the EC Treaty in respect of four existing aid schemes.

161.   Following a number of instances of Member States failing to fulfil their obligation to notify proposals to grant State aid, the Commission informed them[1] that it reserved the right to take a provisional decision requiring them to recover, with interest,[2] any aid paid unlawfully pending a final decision by it on the compatibility of the aid with the common market.

162.   On 19 July, the Commission adopted employment aid guidelines describing the approach it intends to follow when examining this type of aid.[3] In particular, it will give sympathetic consideration to aid for the creation of new jobs in SMEs located in regions eligible for regional aid and for the recruitment of certain categories of worker experiencing particular difficulties in entering or re-entering the labour market.

163.   On 20 December, the Commission adopted a new Community framework for State aid for research and development.[4]

164.   On 31 October, the Commission adopted a notice on cooperation between itself and national courts.[5]

---

[1]   OJ C 156, 27.6.1995; Bull. 5-1995, point 1.3.32.
[2]   Bull. 1/2-1995, point 1.3.34.
[3]   OJ C 334, 12.12. 1995; Bull. 7/8-1995, point 1.3.53.
[4]   Bull. 12-1995.
[5]   Bull. 10-1995, point 1.3.64.

165. The Commission published its fourth survey on State aid in the Community covering the period 1991-92.[1]

Industry schemes

166. The Commission again extended (until 31 March 1996) the validity of the code on aid to the synthetic fibres industry.[2] Following a judgment of the Court of Justice,[3] it also decided to extend, retroactively from 1 January 1995, the validity of the framework on State aid to the motor vehicle industry and proposed that the framework be reintroduced in a slightly modified form for a further period of two years from 1 January 1996.[4] In March it adopted, for presentation to the Council, a draft Decision amending the Steel Aid Code in respect of aid for environmental protection.[5] On 26 July, it adopted a proposal for a Council Regulation on aid to shipbuilding which it amended on 14 December so as to comply with the new OECD Agreement on normal competitive conditions (→ point 192). The Regulation, adopted on 21 December, will not enter into force until after the OECD Agreement has been ratified by all its signatories. On 7 April Parliament, for its part, adopted a resolution on prospects for the future development of the industry.[6]

Regional schemes

167. The Commission continued its review of assisted area maps. Decisions were adopted this year for the Netherlands,[7] Belgium,[8] Spain[9] and Italy.[10] The Commission also continued its examination, in the light of Articles 92 and 93 of the EC Treaty, of the compatibility with the competition rules of Structural Fund assistance for various objectives.

Public undertakings and national monopolies

168. In the course of the year, the Commission adopted three proposals for Directives on telecommunications which, by facilitating the generaliza-

---

[1] COM(95) 365.
[2] Bull. 4-1995, point 1.3.34; OJ C 186, 18.7.1991; Twenty-fifth General Report, point 253.
[3] Case C-135/93 Spain v Commission.
[4] Bull. 7/8-1995, point 1.3.52.
[5] Bull. 3-1995, point 1.3.35.
[6] OJ C 109, 1.5.1995; Bull. 4-1995, point 1.3.57.
[7] Bull. 3-1995, point 1.3.45.
[8] Bull. 7/8-1995, point 1.3.62.
[9] Bull. 7/8-1995, point 1.3.67.
[10] Bull. 3-1995, point 1.3.44.

tion of competition in telecommunications markets, seek to liberalize all telecommunications services and infrastructures and are milestones on the road leading to the information society (→ point 419).

169.   On 26 July, the Commission adopted a draft notice in which it examines the application of the competition rules to the postal sector (→ point 454).

170.   On 28 June, the Commission adopted Decision 95/364/EC in which it found that the system of discounts on landing fees at Brussels Airport produced discriminatory effects incompatible with Articles 90 and 86 of the EC Treaty, and required that the Belgian Government bring the infringement to an end.[1]

171.   On 4 October, the Commission adopted Decision 95/489/EC in which, finding that the conditions imposed on the second operator of GSM radiotelephony services in Italy distorted competition, it called upon the Italian Government to ensure that the two operators in Italy were placed on an equal footing.[2]

International aspects

172.   The Europe Association Agreements with the Czech Republic, Slovakia, Romania and Bulgaria (→ point 819), which entered into force on 1 February, contain competition provisions based on Community law. Work on finalizing implementation of the antitrust and State aid rules laid down has been speeded up. Work has also started on implementing the free trade agreements with the three Baltic States (→ point 819). These entered into force on 1 January and contain competition provisions that are identical to those set out in the abovementioned Europe Agreements. The association agreements that are being negotiated or concluded with the Mediterranean countries will contain similar provisions. Moreover, the Decision on a customs union with Turkey (→ point 844) provides for strict alignment of the Turkish competition system on that of the European Union.

173.   On 10 April, the Council and the Commission adopted Decision 95/145/EC, ECSC concerning the conclusion of the Cooperation Agreement between the European Communities and the United States of America regarding the application of their competition laws (Table III). The Agreement

---

[1]   OJ L 216, 12.9.1995.
[2]   OJ L 280, 23.11.1995.

was concluded by the Commission in 1991[1] but formed the subject-matter of a judgment of the Court of Justice in 1994 according to which the power to conclude such an agreement lay with the Council.[2] At the same time, both institutions approved the wording of an exchange of letters with the US authorities clarifying the interpretation of certain provisions of the agreement.[3] On 23 January, the Council adopted negotiating briefs with a view to concluding an agreement with Canada on the application of the competition rules (Table III).

174. On 12 July, the Commission authorized the publication, with a view to generating a wide-ranging discussion both within the Union and with its main trading partners, of a report by a group of independent experts entitled 'Competition policy in the new trade order'. The report calls for improved cooperation between the Commission and the competition authorities of third countries through the conclusion of bilateral agreements and, at the same time, the negotiation of a multilateral agreement based *inter alia* on a set of minimum common rules and a dispute-settlement procedure.

---

[1]   Twenty-fifth General Report, point 246.
[2]   Judgment of 9 August 1994 in Case C-327/91 *France v Commission*; OJ C 275, 1.10.1994; 1994 General Report, point 185.
[3]   OJ L 95, 27.4.1995; corrigendum: OJ L 131, 15.6.1995.

Section 6

Industrial policy

Priority activities and objectives

175. The Commission continued its efforts to improve the Union's industrial competitiveness, a key factor for economic growth, job creation and greater economic and social cohesion. These followed the general approach defined in the 1990 communication on industrial policy in an open and competitive environment,[1] in the 1993 White Paper on growth, competitiveness and employment[2] and in the 1994 communication on an industrial competitiveness policy for the European Union.[3] They were based on the principle of shared responsibility between the various economic circles involved and on the role of the public authorities in creating an environment favouring industrial activity, facilitating structural change and ensuring that the markets operate smoothly, by coordinating policies with an impact on industry.

Industrial competitiveness

176. As indicated in the 1995 edition of *Panorama of EU industry*, the competitiveness of European industry continued to improve as a result of a more favourable economic climate but also, above all, under the combined effect of the efforts made on restructuring, investment, productivity, research and greater involvement in high-growth markets. However, further efforts are still needed to overcome certain handicaps (insufficient penetration of fast-growing markets, lower productivity than the USA or Japan and inadequate research effort) highlighted in June in the first six-monthly report[4] by the Competitiveness Advisory Group,[5] a panel of independent experts set up at the request of the Essen European Council.[6] These handicaps had been identified in the 1994 communication from the Commission on an industrial competitiveness policy.[7] The Committee of the Regions,[8] Parlia-

---

[1] COM(90) 556; Twenty-fourth General Report, point 212.
[2] 1994 General Report, point 17.
[3] COM(94) 319; Supplement 3/94 — Bull.
[4] Bull. 6-1995, point 1.3.3.
[5] Bull. 3-1995, point 1.3.61.
[6] Bull. 12-1994, point I.8.
[7] 1994 General Report, point 203.
[8] Bull. 4-1995, point 1.3.59.

ment[1] and the Council[2] endorsed the measures announced by the Commission in this context. The Commission in turn proposed an action programme and a timetable for implementation of these measures on 22 March,[3] in a communication accompanied by a proposal for a Council Decision (Table II), which were endorsed by the Economic and Social Committee[4] and the Committee of the Regions[5] in November. The proposals included action to promote intangible investment, to develop industrial cooperation, to increase competition and to modernize the role of the public authorities. They include the establishment of a series of research/industry task forces (→ *point 226*) to establish closer links between all involved and to help to make the action taken by the Community more effective and increase the spin-offs from Europe's research for citizens, consumers and taxpayers. The Competitiveness Advisory Group, chaired by Mr Ciampi, submitted its second report to the Madrid European Council on 12 December.[6]

177. The Council also adopted conclusions on industrial competitiveness and competition policy[7] and on services to business on 6 November (→ *point 207*) and a resolution on the industrial aspects of the information society[8] on 27 November.

Industrial cooperation with non-member countries

178. The Commission continued to promote industrial cooperation with non-member countries, a driving force for fostering Europe's industrial competitiveness. On 6 November, the Council adopted conclusions[9] stressing the importance of creating a favourable environment and legal framework for industrial cooperation with third countries. The fourth R&TD framework programme (→ *point 231*) in turn provides for promoting scientific and technical cooperation with non-member countries, particularly on information technologies and the information society. Research centres in non-EU countries are also participating in the Esprit and INCO programmes.

179. As part of the pre-accession strategy for the associated countries in Central and Eastern Europe, the Commission adopted a further communi-

---

[1]   OJ C 183, 17.7.1995; Bull. 6-1995, point 1.3.76.
[2]   Bull. 4-1995, point 1.3.58.
[3]   COM(95) 87; Bull. 3-1995, point 1.3.59.
[4]   Bull. 11-1995, point 1.3.62.
[5]   Bull. 11-1995, point 1.3.63.
[6]   Bull. 12.1995.
[7]   Bull. 11-1995, point 1.3.60.
[8]   OJ C 341, 19.12.1995; Bull. 11-1995, point 1.3.61.
[9]   Bull. 11-1995, point 1.3.65.

cation[1] on industrial cooperation with these countries (→ point 828) and organized various information campaigns. In the Union's relations with its Mediterranean partners, particular attention was paid to industrial cooperation during the preparatory work for the Euro-Mediterranean conference in Barcelona (→ point 839). In Asia, the Commission intensified the dialogue and strengthened the prospects for cooperation, particularly with Japan, China and India. As part of the industrial cooperation with Latin America, alongside programmes such as Al-Invest[2] and ECIP[3] (→ point 788), various seminars were held.

Standardization

180.   A communication on broader use of standardization in Community policy was adopted by the Commission on 30 October.[4] Ten years after the introduction of the new approach, a turning point has been reached in the development of European standardization. The European standards bodies, particularly ETSI (European Telecommunications Standards Institute), started a strategic review of the priorities and the re-engineering of the standardization system. Finally, in the field of information and communication technologies, intensive debates were held on how standardization could meet the challenge of digital interoperability.

Quality policy

181.   The Commission kept up its work to coordinate the measures taken to implement its quality policy. On the technical regulations front, 1995 marked the entry into force of Directive 93/68/EEC[5] on the CE marking. Since 1 January 1995, Member States are therefore under an obligation to accept on their territory any product complying with the new harmonized regulations. In this area, the Commission placed the emphasis on consolidation of the existing measures rather than developing new instruments. Exchanges of experience on private conformity assessment continued, centred on the European Organization for Testing and Certification (EOTC). On 6 November, the Council approved the Commission's plan to submit a communication on a European quality policy. With the support of the Commission, the European Organization for Quality (EOQ) organized a series

---

[1]   COM(95) 70.
[2]   Action on the establishment of an industrial cooperation scheme as part of a multiannual programme of decentralized activities based on a dialogue via networks of intermediaries.
[3]   ECIP also applies to Asia, the Mediterranean countries and South Africa.
[4]   COM(95) 412; Bull. 10-1995, point 1.3.23.
[5]   OJ L 220, 31.8.1993.

of pilot schemes to launch European Quality Week, and the European Foundation for Quality Management (EFQM) organized the European Quality Prize.

Industry and the environment

182. The Commission continued to pay special attention to environmental protection in industry.[1] Industry's efforts to take account of the sustainable development concept have brought far-reaching changes to fundamental aspects of industrial life, by virtue of the obligation to take account of all aspects of environmental impact throughout the life cycle of processes and products. As the environment has become one of the factors making a difference to the competitive position of companies or industries, from now on industry will have to consider the environmental aspects as an integral component of business strategy.

Individual sectors

Basic industries (steel, chemicals, raw materials) and the construction industry

183. In line with the Council's conclusions of 8 November 1994,[2] and after finding the capacity-shedding proposed by the steel industry insufficient, the Commission decided to withdraw some of the measures to support the restructuring of the Community steel industry. Within the Union, the quarterly guidelines system was not extended beyond the fourth quarter of 1994.[3] On the external front, only the prior statistical monitoring of imports from Central and East European countries was maintained. As regards tariff quotas, agreement was reached with the Czech Republic and Slovakia to extend the quotas for 1995, after adjustments to take account of the enlargement of the Union. On the internal front, however, the Commission continued to monitor developments on the steel market, by adopting the forward programmes for steel for the first and second halves of 1995 on 22 March[4] and 20 July[5] respectively and the forward programme for the

---

[1]   Information on taking account of environmental considerations in industry is given in Section 16
       (Environment) of this chapter (→ *points 478 et seq.*).
[2]   1994 General Report, point 210.
[3]   OJ C 379, 31.12.1994.
[4]   OJ C 73, 25.3.1995; Bull. 3-1995, point 1.3.62.
[5]   OJ C 194, 28.7.1995; Bull. 7/8-1995, point 1.3.75.

first half of 1996[1] on 15 December. To maintain the social support measures for the steel industry, amounts were entered in the 1995 ECSC budget on an *ad hoc* basis.[2] As part of the programme to assist the restructuring of the steel industry in Central and Eastern Europe and the former Soviet Union, on 9 and 10 November the Commission organized a seminar with representatives of those countries on the impact of new technologies on the process and their economic, social and regional costs.

184.   As regards chemicals, the Council adopted a common position on the proposal for a Directive amending for the 16th time Directive 76/769/EEC (→ *point 106*). As regards fertilizers, the Commission adopted Directive 95/8/EC[3] relating to methods of analysis for trace elements.

185.   As regards raw materials, the Commission completed the bulk of the work to follow up the Council conclusions of 18 November 1993[4] on the competitiveness of the non-energy mining industry, particularly as regards information[5] and the environment. In the non-ferrous metals sector, to confirm the importance of industrial cooperation as an instrument for promoting competitiveness, a seminar between the EU and Russia was held in Moscow and an industrial meeting in China. Two seminars on East-West cooperation highlighted the growing importance of the timber and paper industries in the Union and the importance of trade with the Central and East European countries. The entry of Austria, Finland and Sweden has boosted the Union's self-sufficiency in forestry products from 55% to 90%.

186.   Good progress was made with the technical harmonization[6] provided for by Directive 89/106/EEC[7] to allow the free movement of construction (building and civil engineering) products.

Machinery

187.   To follow up the 1994 communication from the Commission on strengthening the competitiveness of the machinery construction industry,[8] on 21 September Parliament adopted a resolution[9] stressing the need to

---

[1]   Bull. 12-1995.
[2]   OJ L 335, 23.12.1994.
[3]   OJ L 86, 20.4.1995.
[4]   Twenty-seventh General Report, point 197.
[5]   Publication of the first edition of the *European Minerals Yearbook*.
[6]   OJ L 129, 14.6.1995; OJ L 268, 10.11.1995.
[7]   OJ L 40, 11.2.1989.
[8]   COM(94) 380; 1994 General Report, point 223.
[9]   OJ C 269, 16.10.1995; Bull. 9-1995, point 1.3.41.

revitalize demand and the importance of training. This was followed by a Council resolution on 27 November.[1]

Motor industry

188. The Commission pressed ahead with implementing the strategy mapped out in the 1994 communication on the future of the motor industry,[2] on which Parliament adopted a resolution on 21 September.[3] The task force on the car of tomorrow *(→ point 226)* coordinated the research efforts in Europe to speed up the development of cars with very low emissions. As regards social measures, a transnational network was set up to disseminate vocational training programmes and to help workers adapt to the structural changes in the industry. As one of the measures to complete the internal market *(→ point 107)*, wide use was made of the European type-approval system for vehicles, which is designed to help to lower makers' costs and to maintain identical technical specifications and a high level of protection throughout the European Union. With regard to competition, after substantial amendments the Commission extended the block exemption granted to certain categories of distribution, sales and after-sales agreements concerning motor vehicles *(→ point 142)*. Finally, as part of its foreign trade policy, the Commission provided further financing for the JAMA-CLEPA conferences to foster relations between Japanese vehicle makers and European component suppliers *(→ point 775)*. The Commission also pressed ahead with negotiating a series of bilateral and multilateral trade agreements opening up access to the motor vehicle markets in non-Union countries *(→ point 776)*.

Maritime industries

189. Talks continued between the Commission and the maritime industries, notably at the fourth meeting of the Maritime Industries Forum in Bremen in June. On 23 February, the Commission adopted its report on the state of the shipbuilding industry in the European Union in 1993,[4] which stressed the marked revival in demand for new vessels, both worldwide and within the Community, and the significant parallel increase in orders.

---

[1]   OJ C 341, 19.12.1995; Bull. 11-1995, point 1.3.64.
[2]   COM(94) 49; 1994 General Report, point 213.
[3]   OJ C 269, 16.10.1995; Bull. 9-1995, point 1.3.40.
[4]   COM(95) 38.

190. The Commission set up a task force on maritime systems of the future to coordinate the research programmes concerning the maritime industries.

191. To bring the information society to the maritime industries, the MARIS pilot project adopted within the G7 set an example as the only industrial-scale project on information technologies and applications of telematics. The Commission also coordinated the research efforts and developed, at European level, specific examples of applications of the information society in this industry.

192. The Directives on aid to the shipbuilding industry[1] expired on 31 December. To replace them, on 26 July the Commission adopted a proposal for a Regulation (Table II) implementing the provisions of the OECD Agreement on respecting normal competitive conditions in the commercial shipbuilding and repair industry,[2] an Agreement which should enter into force on 1 January 1996 (→ *point 166)*. This proposal for a Regulation was adopted by the Council on 21 December. After noting that it would not be possible for the OECD Agreement to enter into force on the date originally foreseen for lack of ratification by certain parties to the Agreement, the same Council meeting decided to extend the validity of the seventh Directive (90/684/EEC)[3] until 1 October 1996.

Aerospace

193. The difficult, uncertain phase in the civil aerospace industry in Europe persisted, particularly in the regional aircraft sector. However, after the downturn in 1991, air traffic has recovered and is expected to grow by over 5% a year until 2010. This should generate demand for over 17 000 jet aircraft over the next 20 years, a trend which will be paralleled on the engine and components markets. European aircraft builders must continue their rationalization and international cooperation activities and improve their research and development efforts. To this end, the Commission set up an 'Aeronautics' task force (→ *point 226)* to bring together in joint projects of interest to the entire industry the research being undertaken at Community or national level or in the context of specific applications of the information society.

---

[1]   Directive 90/684/EEC, as amended by Directive 94/73/EC.
[2]   OJ C 355, 30.12.1995.
[3]   OJ L 351, 31.12.1994.

194.   There were positive developments in the European space industry in 1995. However, the industry's long-term future will depend on whether it can become more competitive.

Railway industry

195.   The Commission began to consider the structural problems facing the railway industry.

Textiles and clothing

196.   On 10 April, the Council adopted Regulation (EC) No 852/95 on the granting of financial assistance to Portugal for a specific programme for the modernization of the Portuguese textile and clothing industry (→ point 319). Subsequently, on 5 October the Commission approved the programme submitted by Portugal. On 11 October the Commission also adopted a communication[1] on the impact of international developments on the textile and clothing sector in the Community to follow up the Council's conclusions of 22 April 1994.[2] Among other things, it proposed reinforcing the measures on exports, industrial cooperation, information technology and training. As part of the policy to improve the competitiveness of the industry, the Commission carried out a series of pilot projects on subcontracting.

Biotechnology

197.   As a further follow-up to its 1994 communication on biotechnology and to the White Paper on growth, competitiveness and employment,[3] the Commission sought to protect public health and the environment and to make European industry more competitive, as requested by the Heads of State or Government in Essen in December 1994.[4] Modern biotechnology spread further into industry and agriculture, although the main developments have been in the pharmaceuticals industry (with two thirds of the new products undergoing clinical trials derived from modern biotechnology) and enzyme production (with an estimated share of 70%). Several applications to market genetically modified agricultural crops were submitted in accordance with the legislation on the deliberate release of genetically modified

---

[1]   COM(95) 447; Bull. 10-1995, point 1.3.85.
[2]   1994 General Report, point 217.
[3]   COM(94) 219; 1994 General Report, point 218.
[4]   Bull. 12-1994, point I.8.

organisms. As regards regulatory measures, the Commission incorporated the scientific and technical experience acquired into the existing legislation and introduced effective procedures for marketing products derived from biotechnology. To this end, on 6 December the Commission adopted a proposal amending Directive 90/219/EEC[1] on the contained use of genetically modified micro-organisms (→ *point 479)*. Along the same lines as the system introduced for pharmaceuticals since 1 January 1995, the Commission's objective was to establish a sectoral regulation policy in order to include the environmental risk assessment provided for in Part C of Directive 90/220/EEC[1] in the legislation on evaluation of products on the basis of the traditional criteria of safety, efficacy and quality. Under the co-decision procedure, on 1 March Parliament rejected the draft proposal for a Directive on the legal protection of biotechnological inventions (→ *point 133)*. As regards the ethical aspects, the Commission took full account of the opinions of the Group of Advisers on the Ethical Implications of Biotechnology, particularly on gene therapy and on the labelling of food produced with the aid of modern biotechnology. Finally, international cooperation continued at both bilateral (particularly with the USA and Japan) and multilateral level.

Pharmaceutical industry

198.   Further work was done to follow up the 1994 Commission communication on an industrial policy for the pharmaceutical sector.[2] The new Community authorization system for medicinal products for human and veterinary use entered into force on 1 January, introducing two new procedures. Under the centralized procedure introduced by Council Regulation (EEC) No 2309/93,[3] applications for marketing authorizations are submitted to the European Agency for the Evaluation of Medicinal Products (→ *point 106)*, which conducts the scientific evaluation of the application and gives its opinion to the Commission, which adopts the decision, subject to endorsement by a committee of representatives of the Member States. The marketing authorization obtained at the end of this procedure is valid throughout the Community. On 23 October, the Commission issued the first Community marketing authorization under this procedure. Under the decentralized procedure, the pharmaceuticals company concerned asks one or more Member States to recognize the marketing authorization issued by another Member State. The Member States may refer the application to the Agency for arbitration.

---

[1]   OJ L 117, 8.5.1990.
[2]   COM(93) 718; 1994 General Report, point 220.
[3]   OJ L 214, 24.8.1993.

Information technologies

199. The Commission pressed ahead with the tasks outlined in its 1991 communication[1] and in the Council resolution of 18 November 1991.[2] A report on the centralized information system concerning global barriers to trade was submitted to the Council on 29 March.[3] The industrial cooperation pilot programme launched in 1993 to improve the component supply for the consumer electronics industry was completed.

200. The Commission implemented the specific programme in the field of information technologies, which was adopted in November 1994[4] under the fourth R&TD framework programme *(→ point 231)* with a budget of ECU 1 932 million for the period 1994 to 1998. The main objectives of the programme are to contribute to the establishment of information technology infrastructure in Europe, to improve the competitiveness of European industry and to give Europe a firmer scientific and technological base in the field of information technology, including pre-standardization work, fitting in fully with the efforts to develop the information society. In response to the first two calls for proposals,[5] 431 projects were selected to receive funding totalling approximately ECU 500 million. In the ESSI project to encourage better use of software some 142 proposals were granted a total of approximately ECU 33 million. In September roughly half of the 50 or so applications received for exploratory awards were accepted for funding.

201. On 10 March, the Council adopted negotiating directives with a view to an international cooperation agreement in the field of intelligent manufacturing systems with the USA, Japan, Australia, Canada, Norway and Switzerland (Table III). The Community's contribution will be financed from the specific programmes for information technologies and industrial and materials technologies under the fourth R&TD framework programme. To seize the opportunities opened up by the specific programme for information technologies, R&TD projects started in 1995 involving bodies established in non-Union countries. Finally, the international cooperation programme also included various specific activities with different countries, particularly the Central and East European countries and the independent States of the former Soviet Union.

---

[1]   Twenty-fifth General Report, point 278.
[2]   Bull. 11-1991, point 1.2.33.
[3]   COM(95) 78.
[4]   OJ L 334, 22.12.1994; 1994 General Report, point 237.
[5]   OJ C 357, 15.12.1994; OJ C 148, 15.6.1995.

202.   Various measures were taken in the field of communication networks. In addition to the scheme to provide a very high capacity (54 Mbit/s) intra-European network for research, a group of European industrialists and operators started to develop standards, while a network of users created new services as part of the international development work on the World Wide Web in conjunction with the MIT. In response to the call for proposals published on 15 June, a series of training schemes were started to disseminate the principal findings of the R&TD projects *(→ point 261)*. The European Information Technologies Conference (EITC) was held in Brussels in November on the theme of managing change. The 1995 Information Technology European Awards went to new products with an information technology content.

Telecommunications industry

203.   The conformance testing services (CTS) programme came to an end and the task of managing the remaining CTS projects was transferred to the European Organization for Testing and Certification (EOTC) which has been asked to investigate whether the experience gained in the telecommunications and information technology field is of interest and applicable to other sectors of industry. A start was made with revising the regulatory framework for telecommunications terminal equipment, following the new approach to standardization, testing and certification, with a view to ensuring greater consistency in the regulatory framework applicable to IT equipment of similar complexity. With the cooperation of the EOTC, efforts continued to promote the establishment of the principle of mutual recognition of certification and testing in the non-regulatory sphere. Finally, the Community provided further support for industrial validation and technological promotion of the latest generation of mobile digital terminal equipment.

Other activities

204.   To confirm the important role played by business services in boosting the competitiveness of European industry, on 6 November, the Council adopted conclusions[1] stressing the complementarity of industrial production and of services to business. On 7 April, the Council adopted conclusions[2] on specific measures to improve the competitiveness of high-tech industries and businesses.

---

[1]   Bull. 11-1995, point 1.3.59.
[2]   Bull. 4-1995, point 1.3.60.

Section 7

Enterprise policy, distributive trades, tourism and cooperatives

Priority activities and objectives

205.   In 1995, enterprise policy was the object of a new strategy confirming the role of small and medium-sized enterprises (SMEs) as a dynamic source of employment, growth and competitiveness. Accordingly, the Commission responded to the request of the European Council in Cannes,[1] which stressed the decisive role of SMEs in job creation, by presenting a report[2] on current policies to assist SMEs and ways of making these policies more effective. This report, which was favourably received by the Madrid European Council,[3] identified a number of priority measures, including reducing administrative constraints, ending fiscal discrimination between firms' equity capital and borrowed funds, and providing finance for SMEs, in particular by extending the Edinburgh facility.[4] The European Union continued to implement the integrated programme in favour of SMEs and the craft sector through a series of schemes aimed at improving the environment of SMEs and supporting their expansion. In addition, the report on the future operation of the information (Euro-Info Centres) and cooperation (BC-Net and BCC) networks was adopted by the Commission on 5 December.[5] Lastly, under the Community action plan to assist tourism, the Commission continued its efforts to promote cooperation and coordination and improve information, and also its discussions on the role of the Union in tourism as part of the preparations for the Intergovernmental Conference.

Improving the business environment

206.   The integrated programme in favour of SMEs and the craft sector,[6] which was adopted by the Council on 10 October 1994[7] and favourably received by the Committee of the Regions,[8] remained in 1995 the overall

---

[1]   Bull. 6-1995, point 1.3.79.
[2]   COM(95) 502; Bull. 11-1995, point 1.3.66.
[3]   Bull 12-1995.
[4]   1994 General Report, points 60 and 61.
[5]   COM(95) 435; Bull. 12-1995.
[6]   COM(94) 207; 1994 General Report, point 188.
[7]   OJ C 294, 22.10.1994; 1994 General Report, point 188.
[8]   Bull. 1/2-1995, point 1.3.62.

framework for steps to give substance to the objectives of the White Paper on growth, competitiveness and employment.[1] Under this programme, two forums were organized by the Commission to encourage the exchange of information on best practices for establishing and starting up companies — one concerned with simplifying administrative formalities and the other with support measures for setting up companies. The European Parliament[2] and the Economic and Social Committee[3] gave their opinions on the second annual report of the European Observatory for SMEs (1994), which was set up on the Commission's initiative in 1992,[4] while on 23 March the Commission received the annual report of the Observatory for 1995, which was the subject of a communication from the Commission of 8 November[5] and of an opinion of the Economic and Social Committee of 20 December.[6]

In addition, in order to reduce the burden which late payments impose on the liquidity of SMEs, on 12 May the Commission adopted a recommendation to the Member States on payment periods in commercial transactions.[7] Regarding the legislative process, the Commission continued to rely on the 'impact form' system, introducing a cost/benefit analysis to assess the effects of proposed Community legislation on enterprises, particularly on SMEs.

207.   On 6 November, the Council adopted conclusions on industrial competitiveness and business services (→ point 177), and, on 27 November, a resolution on SMEs and technological innovation.[8]

Improving access to finance and credit

208.   To give SMEs easier access to finance, the Commission revived the Round Table of leading representatives of the banking sector[9] ('Banks/SMEs Round Table') and gave the representatives of SME organizations a larger role. It continued to support financing mechanisms appropriate to SMEs, i.e. mutual guarantees and seed capital funds. It encouraged the setting-up of a European Association for Dealers in Securities (EASD) and also adopted, on 25 October, a communication[10] on the feasibility of the creation of a European capital market for smaller, entrepreneurially managed growing companies, which was favourably received by the Council on 6

[1]   1994 General Report, point 25.
[2]   OJ C 43, 20.2.1995; Bull. 1/2-1995, point 1.3.60.
[3]   OJ C 102, 24.4.1995; Bull. 1/2-1995, point 1.3.61.
[4]   Twenty-sixth General Report, point 243.
[5]   COM(95) 526; Bull. 11-1995, point 1.3.70.
[6]   Bull. 12-1995.
[7]   OJ C 144 and OJ L 127, 10.6.1995; Bull. 5-1995, point 1.3.45.
[8]   OJ C 341, 19.12.1995; Bull. 11-1995, point 1.3.68.
[9]   1994 General Report, point 193.
[10]   COM(95) 498; Bull. 10-1995, point 1.3.86.

November.[1] In addition, financial support from the European Union for SMEs took the form of loans at reduced rates of interest from the EIB (→ point 55) and the 'SMEs' Community initiative (→ point 55).

Support measures for businesses

Developing cooperation between businesses

209.   BC-Net, a confidential European network promoting cooperation and contact between businesses, had some 400 members in 1995, and the BCC, which endeavours to promote non-confidential contacts between businesses, was represented in 70 countries. Two 'Europartenariat' events were organized — in March in Dortmund (Germany) and in November in Lisbon (Portugal) — at which thousands of SMEs from some 50 countries were able to consolidate their contacts, while the 'Interprise' programme enabled some 40 regional events to be organized for contacts among businesses. Schemes to encourage subcontracting were also stepped up, in conjunction with the professional and trade organizations.

Supporting the adjustment of businesses and improving management quality

210.   Under 'Euromanagement — R&TD',[2] audit/counselling operations were carried out in 927 SMEs in order to encourage them to engage in transnational technological partnerships, in particular as part of the schemes under the fourth research and development framework programme (→ point 231). This type of operation, which enables SMEs to benefit from the services of specialist consultants, was extended to the field of environmental management and auditing. In addition, a final report was submitted on the 'Euromanagement — standardization, certification, quality and safety at the workplace' project, emphasizing the difficulties encountered by SMEs in these fields.

Improving information

211.   The Euro-Info Centre (EIC) network, which over the year was extended to Austria, Finland, Sweden and the European Economic Area, now

[1]   Bull. 11-1995, point 1.3.67.
[2]   OJ C 99, 8.4.1994; 1994 General Report, point 196.

has 232 members. In addition, 19 correspondent EICs became operational in the countries of Central and Eastern Europe and the Mediterranean basin. The EICs continued to carry out their task of supplying information on Community policies in order to help businesses tackle the single market more effectively.

Coordinating the involvement of SMEs in Community policies

212. In response to the Council's wishes,[1] on 8 September[2] the Commission adopted a report on the coordination of activities in favour of SMEs and the craft sector, which offers an overall picture of the European Union's measures to assist SMEs under both enterprise policy and other policies. This coordination both ensures that the SME dimension is incorporated into the drafting of European Union policies and increases the involvement of these businesses in the various Community programmes.

Small businesses and the craft sector

213. In response to a Council resolution,[3] on 26 October[4] the Commission adopted a communication, 'The craft sector and small enterprises — keys to growth and employment in Europe', based on the results of the second European conference on this topic, held in Berlin in 1994,[5] which presented monitoring measures and made recommendations to the Member States. In addition, it launched a pilot project for small and craft enterprises in border areas of the European Union and an experimental programme to assist transnational cooperation.

Cooperatives, mutual societies, associations and foundations

214. On 7 June, the Commission adopted an amended proposal for the Council Decision relating to a multiannual programme (1994-96) of work for cooperatives, mutual societies, associations and foundations[6] (Table II). The Council proceeded with its examination of this proposal and the Commission's proposals on draft European statutes for cooperatives, associations and mutual societies (Table I).

---

[1]   OJ L 161, 2.7.1993; Twenty-sixth General Report, point 164.
[2]   COM(95) 362; Bull. 9-1995, point 1.3.42.
[3]   OJ C 294, 22.10.1994; 1994 General Report, point 188.
[4]   COM(95) 502; Bull. 10-1995, point 1.3.87.
[5]   1994 General Report, point 188.
[6]   1994 General Report, point 199.

The distributive trades

215. The Commission continued to implement the projects for cooperation between commercial SMEs which were launched under the second
phase of the 'Commerce 2000' scheme,[1] and disseminated the results of the
completed pilot projects. Following a Council resolution,[2] the Commission
turned its attention to the relationship between trade cooperation structures
and Community rules on competition. At the same time, it continued to give
effect to the communication on a single market for distribution[3] and sent
cooperation missions to Russia, Ukraine and Hungary. Lastly, projects were
launched to draw up an assessment of the situation regarding the distributive trades and other services in the sparsely populated regions of Europe.

Tourism

216. The Commission stepped up discussions on the role of the Union in
the field of tourism with a view to the 1996 Intergovernmental Conference
(→ point 1025) by adopting, on 4 April, a Green Paper[4] on this topic in
which it identifies three centres of interest — the tourist industry, tourist
satisfaction and awareness of the cultural and natural heritage — and presents various options for the future development of the Union's role in this
field. This Green Paper was favourably received by the Economic and Social
Committee (ESC)[5] and the Committee of the Regions.[6] The European Parliament[7] and the Economic and Social Committee expressed the desire to
see a section on tourism included in the next revision of the Treaties. In addition, the Forum on European Tourism on 8 December was a particularly
good opportunity to assess the results of the discussions with a view to
defining the Union's role.

217. Under the Community action plan to assist tourism (1993-95),[8] the
Commission concentrated on the priority operations which had to be completed, and paid particular attention to increasing cooperation and coordination with tourism operators and improving knowledge of this sector. On
23 November, the Council adopted a Directive on collecting statistical information in the field of tourism (→ point 88). Efforts were made in the field

---

[1]   OJ C 277, 15.10.1993; Twenty-seventh General Report, point 179.
[2]   OJ C 294, 22.10.1994; 1994 General Report, point 188.
[3]   COM(91) 41 of 11.3.1991; Twenty-fifth General Report, point 303.
[4]   COM(95) 97; Bull. 4-1995, point 1.3.62.
[5]   OJ C 301, 13.11.1995; Bull 9-1995, point 1.3.43.
[6]   Bull. 11-1995, point 1.3.73.
[7]   OJ C 151, 19.6.1995; Bull. 5-1995, point 1.9.2.
[8]   OJ L 231, 13.8.1992; Twenty-sixth General Report, point 248.

of cooperation on tourism with non-Community countries and with regard to links between tourism and the environment, in particular by organizing a European Tourism Prize, which was awarded on 22 November.[1] On 2 February, the Committee of the Regions emphasized the importance of developing rural tourism.[2]

---

[1] Bull. 11-1995, point 1.3.72.
[2] Bull. 1/2-1995, point 1.3.63.

Section 8

Research and technology[1]

Priority activities and objectives

218.   The year 1995 saw a new departure in research and technological development (R&TD) strategy with a shift towards tighter coordination of the European research effort and a sharper focusing of Community R&TD activity on social problems. Against this background the Commission set up six task forces with the job of making the Union more competitive and producing results of immediate relevance to ordinary people.

The various specific programmes of the fourth R&TD framework programme, adopted in 1994, got under way this year. The first calls for proposals, launched on 15 December 1994,[2] closed on 15 March 1995, enabling the Commission to adopt the first research projects at the beginning of the summer.

Community R&TD policy

General developments

219.   The Commission adopted a much simplified standard contract to facilitate business — and especially SME *(→ point 231)* — participation in the fourth research and development framework programme.

220.   On 20 December, the Commission also adopted a new framework for State aid for research[3] *(→ point 163).*

221.   The accession to the Union of three new Member States had a marked impact on Community research activity, prompting the Council to increase the overall funding of the framework programmes by 6.87% *(→ point 231).*

---

[1]   For further details see the 1995 Annual R&TD Report adopted by the Commission on 28 September.
[2]   OJ C 357, 15.12.1994.
[3]   Bull. 12-1995.

222.   With the new political set-up came changes to the mandate of the Industrial Research and Development Advisory Committee (IRDAC), which advises the Commission on industrial research, to ensure a good balance between research expertise and industrial strategy and between the various industries represented (including SMEs).

223.   The European Science and Technology Assembly (ESTA), set up by the Commission in 1994,[1] held two plenary sessions and focused its work on evaluation of the fourth framework programme, coordination and cooperation,[2] relations between research and industry, the fifth framework programme, and trends in science and technology.

224.   In the area of science and culture, the third European Week of Scientific Culture took place from 20 to 24 November,[3] with the emphasis on applied industrial research and technology. Five new projects were launched through the European Science and Technology Forum.

Coordination of R&TD policies

225.   Having, on 9 June, adopted conclusions on the coordination of national and Community R&TD policies[4] and having noted the Commission's 1994 communication entitled 'Achieving coordination through cooperation',[5] the Council, on 28 September,[6] adopted a resolution advocating a greater role for the Scientific and Technical Research Committee (CREST) in laying down strategic guidelines for Community policy and coordinating Community and Member State R&TD activity. Parliament gave its opinion on the role of CREST and the coordination of R&TD policies in a resolution of 15 June,[7] and the Economic and Social Committee in an own-initiative opinion on 25 October.[8]

Joint projects of industrial interest

226.   On 1 June, the Commission set up six special research/industry task forces, their mandate being to develop joint projects of industrial interest, improve the long-term coordination of industrial research in the Union and

---

[1]   1994 General Report, point 231.
[2]   1994 General Report, point 232.
[3]   1994 General Report, point 234.
[4]   Bull. 6-1995, point 1.3.81.
[5]   COM(94) 438; 1994 General Report, point 232.
[6]   OJ C 264, 11.10.1995; Bull. 9-1995, point 1.3.44.
[7]   OJ C 166, 3.7.1995; Bull. 6-1995, point 1.3.82.
[8]   Bull. 10-1995, point 1.3.88.

make better use of the Union's technological potential in certain areas, producing results of immediate relevance to the general public. The six target areas are: car of tomorrow, multimedia educational software, new-generation aircraft, vaccines and viral diseases, train of the future and transport intermodality.

Joint Research Centre

227.   Two new Joint Research Centre (JRC) programmes (1995-98) got under way in 1995, one for the European Community and the other for the European Atomic Energy Community (EAEC).[1] On 15 November, the Commission adopted a proposal for a Council Decision (Table II) adopting a supplementary research programme to be carried out by the JRC for the EAEC, concerning the operation of the Petten reactor. The JRC pursued two types of activity: institutional research and scientific and technical support for Union policies, and activities carried out on a competitive basis, including participation in shared-cost research projects, support for Commission departments and work performed under contract for public and private sector outside bodies. The year 1995 also saw the Institute for Prospective Technological Studies come onstream in Seville.[2]

228.   Over the year, the eight JRC institutes helped implement various specific programmes under the framework programmes.

229.   Thanks to the marketing efforts of the institutes and the central administration, the JRC concluded contracts with outside bodies worth a total of ECU 13 million. Its expertise also benefited the R&TD task forces set up by the Commission (→ point 226).

Framework programme 1990-94 (third framework programme)

230.   The Commission monitored the final projects launched in 1994, for a total of more than ECU 2 000 million, under the 1990-94 framework programme.[3]

---

[1]   OJ L 361, 31.12.1994; 1994 General Report, point 242.
[2]   1994 General Report, point 243.
[3]   OJ L 117, 8.5.1990; Twenty-fourth General Report, point 247.

Framework programme 1994-98 (fourth framework programme)

231.   On 30 November, the Council adopted a common position on a proposal for a Decision concerning a 6.87% increase in the budgets for the framework programmes (Tables I and II). This increase is equivalent to what Austria, Finland and Sweden were already paying towards Community actions as member countries of the European Economic Area. It may also, for the benefit of the six task forces set up in 1995 *(→ point 226)*, be supplemented by a further ECU 700 million or so, a reserve amount provided for in the Decisions on the framework programmes (1994-98). Parliament and the Council are due to reach a decision on the supplementary funding in 1996 on the basis of the guidelines approved by the Commission on 18 October.[1]

232.   All the specific R&TD programmes under the EC and Euratom framework programmes (1994-98), adopted by the Council and Parliament in April 1994,[2] were adopted at the end of 1994[3] and the first calls for proposals went out in 1994 for some of them. Further calls have gone out in 1995. The specific programmes cover telematics applications of common interest *(→ point 234)*, advanced communication technologies and services *(→ point 235)*, information technologies *(→ point 235)*, industrial and materials technologies *(→ point 236)*, standardization, measurement and testing *(→ point 237)*, environment and climate *(→ point 238)*, marine science and technology *(→ point 241)*, biotechnology *(→ point 242)*, biomedicine and health *(→ point 244)*, agriculture and fisheries *(→ point 243)*, non-nuclear energy *(→ point 245)*, transport *(→ point 252)*, targeted socioeconomic research *(→ point 253)*, cooperation with third countries and international organizations *(→ point 254)*, dissemination and exploitation of the results of research activities *(→ point 261)*, training and mobility of researchers *(→ point 264)* and nuclear fission safety *(→ point 246)*. The two Joint Research Centre (JRC) programmes *(→ point 247)* and the controlled thermonuclear fusion programme *(→ point 248)* were also implemented.

233.   There was a very high rate of response to the first calls for proposals, with applications displaying both a high degree of cooperation (an average of more than six participants per project) and an increase in the number of industrial partners. Most programmes also included special measures for small businesses.

---

[1]   Bull. 10-1995, point 1.3.92.
[2]   OJ L 126, 18.5.1994; 1994 General Report, point 236; OJ L 115, 6.5.1994; 1994 General Report, point 236.
[3]   1994 General Report, points 237 and 238.

Implementation of specific programmes under the fourth framework programme

Telematics applications of common interest

234.   This area is covered in Section 15 (Information society, telecommunications) of this chapter *(→ point 437)*.

Information technologies

235.   This area is covered in Sections 15 (Information society, telecommunications) *(→ points 436 et seq.)* and 6 (Information technologies) *(→ point 199)* of this chapter.

Industrial and materials technologies

236.   Activity in 1995 focused mainly on monitoring the contracts signed under the second and third framework programmes[1] and launching the first call for proposals under the BRITE/EURAM III programme.[2] The call led to 209 research projects being adopted by the Commission, including 81 technology stimulation projects to help SMEs. The JRC's Institute for Advanced Materials carried out various research work, including studies of certain material properties (mechanical performance, corrosion, etc.) and the development of new alloys, ceramics and environmentally friendly materials.

237.   Under the specific programme on standardization, measurement and testing (1994-98),[3] the Commission launched two calls for proposals[4] covering the three programme areas (measurement of European quality products, standards-related research and technical support for trade and measurements concerned with social needs). The JRC's Institute for Reference Materials and Measurements continued its work on the harmonization and standardization of analytical measurement and also produced a series of reference materials for various Commission departments, notably in the areas of legal controls and the quality control of agricultural products.

---

[1]   OJ L 269, 25.9.1991; 1994 General Report, point 245.
[2]   OJ C 357, 15.12.1994; 1994 General Report, point 246.
[3]   OJ L 334, 22.12.1994; 1994 General Report, point 249.
[4]   OJ C 357, 15.12.1994; OJ C 148, 15.6.1995.

Environment

Environment and climate

238. Under the environment and climate programme adopted on 15 December 1994,[1] the Commission launched a call for proposals[2] which elicited 1 607 responses. Following evaluation, 318 projects were selected for Community funding totalling ECU 217 million. Three further calls were published in the area of space techniques applied to environmental monitoring and research.[3] Following two of these calls, the Commission selected 15 research projects and two education and training operations for funding of ECU 12.7 million. In addition, 22 grants were awarded in 1995, and the Commission earmarked ECU 19 million for the 'vegetation' spatial instrument.

239. The Commission continued to implement its space policy, with the support of an *ad hoc* group on space and in collaboration with the European Space Agency (ESA) and the Committee on Earth Observation Satellites (CEOS). A work programme was drafted for setting up the Centre for Earth Observation in 1996, in concert with the JRC.

240. In 1995 the JRC's Institute for Systems Engineering and Informatics developed innovative environmental technologies for industrial reliability, including for the transport of dangerous substances. It also ran the Community Documentation Centre for Industrial Risk (CDCIR) and the Documentation Centre on Biotechnology Safety and Regulations (Biosafe). The Institute for the Environment continued its studies of pollution of air, soil and water and in buildings (notably by radon), as well as its work on the role of natural and artificial aerosols in global warming. The work of the Institute for Remote Sensing Applications included the development of advanced Earth observation techniques, the setting-up of the Centre for Earth Observation and technical support for the European Environment Agency (→ *point 507*).

Marine science and technology

241. The Commission implemented the MAST III programme (1994-98) adopted in November 1994.[4] A call for proposals[5] attracted 335 research

---

[1]   OJ L 361, 31.12.1994; 1994 General Report, point 252.
[2]   OJ C 12, 17.1.1995.
[3]   OJ C 148, 15.6.1995; OJ C 271, 17.10.1995.
[4]   OJ L 334, 22.12.1994; 1994 General Report, point 257.
[5]   OJ C 357, 15.12.1994.

project applications, 63 of which were selected for Community funding totalling ECU 113 million, while three advanced training courses were organized and 17 grants awarded.

Life sciences and technologies

Biotechnology

242. An initial call for proposals had already been published under the biotechnology programme (1994-98)[1] covering the following areas: cell factories, functions research and comparative analysis in the field of genome analysis, genome mapping and improvement of farm animal selection, somatic gene therapy, immunological substances and horizontal infrastructures and activities. Following evaluation, 62 research projects involving 432 participants were selected. The second call for proposals was published on 15 September.[2] In addition, 49 grants were awarded this year.

Agriculture and fisheries

243. The new programme of agriculture and fisheries R&TD, including agro-industry, food technologies, forestry, aquaculture and rural development (1994-98),[3] got under way in 1995 with two calls for proposals.[4] The Commission also monitored the development of the 430 projects selected under the agriculture programme (including agro-industry and fisheries) under the third framework programme (1990-94). Lastly, the JRC's Institute for Remote Sensing Applications provided statistical data from satellite measurements, notably with a view to evaluating agricultural production (MARS STAT) and checking that cultivated surface areas correspond to the levels set under the common agricultural policy (MARS CAP).

Biomedicine and health

244. The new biomedicine and health programme (1994-98)[5] got under way with the publication of a call for proposals.[6] Of the 1 709 projects sent in, 308 were selected, involving more than 1 500 medical research teams

1   OJ C 12, 17.1.1995; 1994 General Report, point 259.
2   OJ C 240, 15.9.1995.
3   OJ L 334, 22.12.1994; 1994 General Report, point 261.
4   OJ C 357, 15.12.1994; OJ C 148, 15.6.1995.
5   OJ L 361, 31.12.1994; 1994 General Report, point 265.
6   OJ C 12, 17.1.1995.

around the Union, with funding totalling ECU 150 million. The Commission also monitored the 400 projects it is supporting through the Biomed I programme under the third framework programme (1990-94). [1]

Energy

Non-nuclear energy

245.   Following the call for proposals published in 1994, [2] 181 priority R&TD projects were selected under the new non-nuclear energies programme (1994-98). [3] The projects will receive Community funding of ECU 191.5 million and cover four areas: analysis of energy R&TD strategy, rational use of energy (including 21 projects contributing to the objectives of the task force on the car of tomorrow) (→ point 226), renewable energy sources and fossil fuels. The Commission also evaluated and disseminated the results of projects launched under or alongside the third framework programme (clean coal, renewable energy sources, advanced automobile technologies for electric vehicles). Lastly, the JRC's Institute for Advanced Materials carried out several projects on new materials with a view to developing clean technologies for the car industry and energy production.

Nuclear fission safety

246.   Following the call for proposals published in 1994, [2] 102 shared-cost projects and seven concerted actions were selected under the new programme on nuclear fission safety. [4] With Community funding of ECU 85.6 million, the projects cover five areas: exploration of innovative approaches, reactor safety, management and storage of radioactive waste and decommissioning, radiological impact on man and the environment, and historical liabilities. The Commission also evaluated and disseminated the results of completed R&TD projects.

247.   Several JRC institutes carried out research in the area of nuclear fission safety: the Institute for Reference Materials and Measurements (nuclear safety monitoring), the Institute for Transuranium Elements (nuclear fuel cycle safety and safety and management of fissile materials) and the Institute for Systems Engineering and Informatics (monitoring of fissile material

---

[1]   1994 General Report, point 264.
[2]   OJ C 357, 15.12.1994.
[3]   OJ L 334, 22.12.1994; 1994 General Report, point 267.
[4]   OJ L 361, 31.12.1994; 1994 General Report, point 269.

safety and development of mobile robots for work in difficult environments).

Controlled thermonuclear fusion

248.   In the Community programme of research and training in the field of controlled thermonuclear fusion (1994-98),[1] focusing on magnetic confinement, activities were stepped up with a view to establishing new association contracts, notably with Ireland, Austria and Finland.

249.   On 6 June, the Commission adopted a proposal for a Council Decision (Table II) extending the Joint European Torus (JET) up to the end of 1999, the aim being to supply additional data for the International Thermonuclear Experimental Reactor (ITER). The Council reached conclusions on ITER on 30 October.[2] In December the ITER Council adopted the interim report on the ITER engineering design and decided to continue with the technical work with a view to finalizing the design on the basis of recommendations by the parties (Euratom, United States, Russia and Japan).

250.   On 25 July, the Commission and Canada signed a Memorandum of Understanding (Table III) for cooperation in the field of controlled thermonuclear fusion and an Agreement on Canada's involvement in Euratom's contribution to ITER.[3]

251.   The JRC pursued its fusion activities through the Institute for Systems Engineering and Informatics (remote handling), the Institute for Advanced Materials (effects of irradiation and thermal fatigue of materials) and the Institute for Safety Technology (tritium handling laboratory, ETHEL).

Transport

252.   Under the transport R&TD specific programme,[4] the Commission launched two calls for proposals on 17 January[5] and on 15 December with the aim of helping to develop, integrate and manage a more efficient, safe and environmentally friendly transport system, while promoting sustainable mobility of persons and goods. The programme covers seven areas: strategic research, rail transport, integrated transport chains, air transport, urban

[1]   OJ L 331, 21.12.1994; Twenty-sixth General Report, point 272.
[2]   Bull. 10-1995, point 1.3.94.
[3]   OJ L 211, 6.9.1995.
[4]   OJ L 361, 31.12.1994; 1994 General Report, point 276.
[5]   OJ C 12, 17.1.1995.

transport, water-borne transport and road transport. In conclusions adopted on 19 June,[1] the Council welcomed the importance attached to this area of research. Following the first call for proposals, the Commission proposed that 111 projects be selected, involving Community funding totalling ECU 117 million.

Targeted socioeconomic research

253.   Under the specific programme adopted by the Council on 15 December 1994,[2] a call for proposals was published covering three areas:[3] evaluation of science policy options, research into education and training, and research into social integration and social exclusion in Europe. The call attracted 548 proposals.

Cooperation with non-member countries and international organizations

254.   The Commission began implementing the programme on cooperation with non-member countries and international organizations (1994-98),[4] which is a new feature of the fourth framework programme. On 13 November, it proposed modifying the specific programme (Table II) in the light of the Council's conclusions on INTAS (→ point 256). On 18 October, it adopted a communication on international cooperation[5] setting out eight priority courses of action to adapt the Union's scientific cooperation policy to changes on the international stage: increasing the role of industry, stepping up the external dimension of European R&TD policy, promoting non-member country cooperation on the specific programmes, promoting better knowledge of their scientific achievements, stepping up the research potential of the less-advanced countries, making use of other funds to support R&TD, launching special calls for proposals for the Mediterranean countries, and supporting the countries of Central and Eastern Europe and the associated Baltic countries during the pre-accession phase.

255.   Under the Agreement on the European Economic Area (EEA), Iceland and Norway, along with Liechtenstein (for which the EEA Agreement entered into force on 1 May), took part in the non-nuclear specific programmes of the fourth framework programme (1994-98). The Commission

---

[1]   Bull. 6-1995, point 1.3.120.
[2]   OJ L 361, 31.12.1994; 1994 General Report, point 277.
[3]   OJ C 64, 15.3.1995.
[4]   OJ L 334, 22.12.1994; 1994 General Report, point 285.
[5]   COM(95) 489; Bull. 10-1995, point 1.3.96.

continued its negotiations with Switzerland on a science and technology co-operation agreement (Table III).

256.   A call for proposals was published on 17 October[1] to help open up the specific programmes under the fourth framework programme to the countries of Central and Eastern Europe and the new independent States of the former Soviet Union. On 16 May, the Commission adopted a communication on prospects for cooperation in science and technology with the independent States of the former Soviet Union[2] concerning, among other things, the future of INTAS beyond 31 December. In 1995 the Community contributed ECU 8 million to cooperation activities administered by INTAS.[3] In a resolution of 27 October[4] Parliament hoped cooperation with INTAS would continue. On 30 October,[5] the Council decided the Community would continue to take part in INTAS up to 31 December 1998. The International Science and Technology Centre (ISTC) in Moscow, which aims to help redirect military research towards civil applications in the former Soviet Union, continued its work with active assistance from the Commission.

257.   Scientific and technical cooperation agreements were signed in 1995 with a number of non-European industrialized countries. An R&TD Cooperation Agreement on the monitoring of nuclear safety was signed by the European Atomic Energy Community and the United States (Table III) on 6 January, a general Nuclear Cooperation Agreement was signed on 7 November (→ point 895), and an Agreement on scientific and technical cooperation was signed by the European Community and Canada (Table III) on 17 June. On 13 July, the Commission approved a recommendation for a Council Decision authorizing it to negotiate an Agreement on scientific and technical cooperation between the European Community and the Republic of South Africa (Table III). Lastly, an Agreement on scientific and technical cooperation was initialled with Israel (Table III) on 31 October.

258.   The Commission also continued to step up its links with various European scientific organizations in order to make the European research effort more consistent. On 17 January an administrative arrangement was concluded between the Commission and the European Molecular Biology Laboratory (EMBL).[6] Cooperation with other organizations, including the

---

[1]   OJ C 271, 17.10.1995.
[2]   COM(95) 190; Bull. 5-1995, point 1.3.46.
[3]   COM(95) 52; Bull. 3-1995, point 1.3.67.
[4]   OJ C 308, 20.11.1995; Bull. 10-1995, point 1.3.97.
[5]   Bull. 10-1995, point 1.3.98.
[6]   Bull. 1/2-1995, point 1.3.65.

European Southern Observatory, the European Science Foundation and the European Space Agency (ESA), continued on the basis of existing contacts. The Commission also continued to cooperate with the Eureka and COST programmes.

259.   The first call for proposals was published for that part of the fourth framework programme covering R&TD cooperation with the developing countries.[1] In the fields of human vaccines and animal health, 33 joint projects and three concerted actions were selected for a total of ECU 12 million.

Dissemination and utilization of research results

260.   The dissemination and utilization activities implemented under Decision 92/272/EEC, adopted by the Council on 29 April 1992, were completed at the end of 1994. A group of independent experts evaluated the results in 1995.

261.   The Commission pursued and expanded research dissemination and utilization activities and innovation under the specific programme on the dissemination and utilization of R&TD results and demonstration adopted by the Council on 15 December 1994 in implementation of the third activity of the fourth framework programme.[2] Action under the new programme is based on a global and integrated approach focusing on three main objectives, namely promotion of an environment conducive to innovation and the take-up of technology, development of a European area open to the dissemination of knowledge and technology, and provision of appropriate technology within that area. In addition to the Relay Centres Network, which now covers the entire European Economic Area, and the Cordis Information Service, with 150 000 documents spread over nine databases, other instruments (→ point 263) have been introduced to promote innovation.

262.   Work to help utilize the results obtained by the Joint Research Centre and the specific programmes was pursued, and a coordination and planning instrument was set up to make this activity more effective. With regard to intellectual property, continued management of the Community trade mark and patent portfolios was supplemented by the launch of new pilot initiatives on training and the use of patents databases as a source of technology watch.

---

[1]   OJ C 64, 15.3.1995.
[2]   OJ L 361, 31.12.1994; 1994 General Report, points 286 and 426.

Promotion of innovation and technology transfer

263.   On 20 December,[1] the Commission adopted a Green Paper on innovation, the aim of which is to identify factors which encourage or hamper innovation in the European Union and to propose, at all decision-making levels, practical measures to step up the Union's overall innovation capacity, with special emphasis on SMEs. In addition, through Council Decision 94/917/EC,[2] the Commission set up several instruments to promote innovation and its economic, sociological and financial environment, including technology validation and transfer projects, regional operations in support of science parks, innovation management techniques and action to help finance innovation, all in close coordination with other related Community action, such as Eurotech Capital and the European Investment Fund.

Stimulation of training and mobility of researchers

264.   Under the specific programme on the training and mobility of researchers (1994-98),[3] the Commission launched four calls for proposals,[4] following which 91 research networks were proposed for funding, and the Commission decided to support 84 projects on large-scale facilities, 582 training grants and 55 Euroconferences, summer schools and practical courses. It continued to implement the research programme in the field of human capital and mobility (1992-94)[5] and selected 609 new grant-holders under the institutional grant projects set up between 1992 and 1994. It also organized the European Union Contest for Young Scientists in Newcastle upon Tyne.

Other activities (coal and steel technical research)

265.   Under Article 55 of the ECSC Treaty and in accordance with the guidelines on technical coal research (1994-99),[6] the Commission decided to grant financial aid of ECU 21 million to 35 projects.[7] It also decided to grant ECU 39.9 million to 57 technical steel research projects[8] and, on 3 November, adopted its medium-term guidelines (1996-2002) for this type of research.[9]

---

[1]   COM(95) 688; Bull. 12-1995.
[2]   OJ L 361, 31.12.1994.
[3]   OJ L 361, 31.12.1994; 1994 General Report, point 288.
[4]   OJ C 12, 17.1.1995; OJ C 148, 15.6.1995; OJ C 240, 15.9.1995; OJ C 337, 15.12.1995.
[5]   OJ L 107, 24.4.1992; Twenty-sixth General Report, point 313.
[6]   OJ C 67, 4.3.1994.
[7]   Bull. 10-1995, point 1.5.95.
[8]   Bull. 3-1995, point 1.3.65.
[9]   OJ C 294, 9.11.1995; Bull. 11-1995, point 1.3.77.

Section 9

Education, vocational training and youth

Priority activities and objectives

266.   Viewed as an essential component of moves to bring the European Union closer to its citizens and of the drive for jobs and improved business competitiveness in Europe, and conceived as a means of bringing people's knowledge into line with society's changing needs, of boosting continuing training arrangements, combating the phenomenon of failure at school and social exclusion, and developing the potential of the information society, the European Union's action on the education and training front took a great leap forward in 1995. The 14 March saw the adoption of the Socrates programme, covering the whole of the educational field and bringing together earlier education policy measures (e.g. Erasmus and Lingua) as well as developing new activities, and of the 'Youth for Europe III' programme, which deals with cooperation policy in the youth field, including exchanges with non-member countries, again taking in earlier measures (Youth for Europe and certain of the PETRA measures) as well as creating new ones. The year 1995 also saw the implementation of the Leonardo da Vinci programme in the field of vocational training (bringing together the Comett, FORCE and PETRA programmes). At the same time, there was enhanced cooperation with non-member countries, more particularly with the opening-up of Community programmes to the associated countries of Central and Eastern Europe along with Cyprus and Malta, and with the negotiation of bilateral agreements with the United States and Canada.

Parliament and Council Decision 95/2493/EC (Table I) proclaiming 1996 the 'European Year of Lifelong Learning' was adopted on 23 October. With a budget of ECU 8 million for 1995 and 1996, its aim is to promote the role of education and training in individual development, and to promote the integration of individuals in the world of work and society in general.

The White Paper entitled 'Teaching and learning: towards the knowledge-based society', which was adopted by the Commission on 29 November,[1] sets out possible Community approaches to the challenges of the 21st century on the education and training front which the Community and its Member States will have to address in the medium term. It will be the sub-

---

[1]   COM(95) 590; Bull. 11-1995, point 1.3.79.

ject of wide-ranging discussions throughout the European Year of Lifelong Learning. To assist it in this process, the Commission set up a high-level committee of experts on 21 June.[1]

Cooperation in the field of education

267.   The Community action programme 'Socrates' was adopted on 14 March by Parliament and Council Decision 95/819/EC (Table I). This is a five-year programme (1995-99) with ECU 850 million funding; it covers the 15 Member States of the European Union, along with Iceland, Liechtenstein and Norway, and is open to the countries of Central and Eastern Europe and to Malta and Cyprus, provided the additional funding is available. It lays down cooperation arrangements in six fields of action: higher education, school education, foreign language learning, open and distance learning, adult education and exchanges of information and experience. Targeting schoolchildren, students and adults alike, it forms part of a broadly conceived strategy for promoting lifelong learning in a changing world; it is coordinated with other Community programmes Leonardo da Vinci (→ *point 272)*, Youth for Europe III *(→ point 280)* and the fourth R&TD framework programme *(→ point 231)*. It incorporates the earlier programmes Lingua *(→ point 278)* and Erasmus *(→ point 268)*, as well as creating new measures such as Comenius *(→ point 269)*. With 1995 being a preparatory year prior to implementation of activities under Socrates, the Commission set up, in conjunction with the national authorities, an intensive information campaign to inform potential target groups about openings under the programme. On 23 October,[2] the Council adopted conclusions on social participation at the various levels of the education system.

268.   On the higher education front, Erasmus programme activities continued throughout 1995 under the Socrates programme. On 8 September, the Commission adopted the annual Erasmus report (1994),[3] establishing that financial assistance had been granted to 2 280 interuniversity cooperation programmes, that the total number of eligible students was 127 211 and that 9 753 teachers had taught abroad, these two figures representing a 20% increase over 1993.

269.   Regarding secondary education, and under the new Comenius measure, the Commission set up a number of activities in conjunction with the Member States: selection of 500 school partnerships; 800 teacher exchange

---

[1]   Bull. 6-1995, point 1.3.90.
[2]   Bull. 10-1995, point 1.3.101.
[3]   COM(95) 416; Bull. 9-1995, point 1.3.48.

schemes; 1 000 preparatory visits and 500 study visits for head teachers; development of transnational projects for migrants' children and in the interests of intercultural education; transnational projects for in-service teacher training. Finally, the Commission gave support to a wide range of projects connected with artistic education.

270.   The year 1995 also brought — in conjunction with the Member States — substantial progress in evaluating the quality of teaching and the recognition of qualifications for academic and professional purposes (→ point 117), with the Economic and Social Committee publishing its opinion on 27 April[1] and Parliament on 15 November.[2]

271.   Information on the Jean Monnet scheme is dealt with in Section 26 (Information, communication, audiovisual media and culture) of this chapter (→ point 662).

Vocational training

272.   The initial phase of implementation, with effect from 1 January, of the Leonardo da Vinci programme (1995-97)[3] was marked by the creation of the requisite structures and the adoption of the work programme, including the breakdown of the ECU 139.4 million allocated for the programme in 1995. At a second stage, launch conferences were organized in each of the participating countries, along with the introduction of transnational training programmes and the publication of calls for proposals at Community[4] and national levels, generating considerable interest. The third stage comprised the selection of 581 pilot projects, 121 transnational placement and exchange programmes and 47 surveys and analyses. In addition, preparatory work was done in respect of the participation of associated countries from Central and Eastern Europe and of Malta and Cyprus. With a budget of ECU 620 million, Leonardo da Vinci incorporates — and innovates — various Community initiatives in the field of vocational training, such as Comett (→ point 273), PETRA, FORCE (→ point 274), Eurotecnet (→ point 275) and Lingua (→ point 275), and addresses four objectives: enhancing the quality of vocational training in Europe; developing exchange schemes; acquiring a better understanding of the way training operates and of the real needs in terms of training; and making it easier to adapt to the

---

[1]   OJ C 155, 21.6.1995; Bull. 4-1995, point 1.3.64.
[2]   OJ C 323, 18.12.1995; Bull. 11-1995, point 1.3.78.
[3]   OJ L 340, 29.12.1994; 1994 General Report, point 300.
[4]   OJ C 128, 24.5.1995; OJ C 143, 9.6.1995; OJ C 141, 7.6.1995; OJ C 149, 16.6.1995; OJ C 201, 5.8.1995.

information society's range of instruments. The quality of vocational training was the subject of Council conclusions of 24 July.[1]

273. On 6 September,[2] the Commission adopted the report on the Comett II programme, which continued in 1995 under the Leonardo da Vinci banner. In its report, the Commission gives an appraisal of five years of Comett, which was funded to the tune of ECU 240 million and led to the creation of 200 university-enterprise training partnerships, the organization of almost 40 000 transnational placement schemes for students and young graduates and of staff exchanges between universities and business, 10 000 advanced training courses, involving 250 000 people, and the development of more than 4 500 items of teaching material.

274. The activities of the FORCE programme, which sought to promote continuing training for workers, were incorporated into the Leonardo programme. An appraisal of the 1992 and 1993 projects revealed that 720 projects were retained as a result of the various calls for proposals. These projects now constitute a network for the transfer of expertise and innovation on continuing vocational training, bringing in 5 000 enterprises, social partners, training providers and public authorities.

275. In the field of training and the new technologies, the Eurotecnet programme, which terminated in December 1994, presented details of the main achievements arising from its network of 300 innovative projects.

276. Following the Council resolution of 1992 on the transparency of qualifications,[3] collaborative work undertaken by the Commission, the Member States and the social partners led to the presentation in March of a standard vocational skills portfolio model. Projects concerned with the enhanced transparency of vocational qualifications are now incorporated in the Leonardo da Vinci programme (→ point 272).

Foreign language teaching

277. Reaffirming the principle of linguistic diversity and desirous of continuing the construction of a Europe without internal frontiers and of strengthening understanding between the peoples of the European Union, the Council adopted, on 31 March, a resolution[4] designed to improve the

---

[1]   OJ C 207, 12.8.1995; Bull. 7/8-1995, point 1.3.82.
[2]   COM(95) 409; Bull. 9-1995, point 1.3.47.
[3]   OJ C 49, 19.2.1993; Twenty-sixth General Report, point 421.
[4]   OJ C 207, 12.8.1995; Bull. 3-1995, point 1.3.70.

quality and diversification of language learning and teaching within the Member States' educational systems.

278. On 9 October, the Commission adopted the report on the Lingua programme (1994),[1] whose activities continued in 1995, partly under the Socrates programme and partly under the Leónardo da Vinci programme. What emerges from the report is that 6 800 in-service training schemes were run for foreign language teachers, 30 000 young people took part in exchanges, 1 357 partners were involved in 276 projects designed to develop cooperation in the field of in-service teacher training, teaching materials were produced and language courses were certified, and more than 10 000 students took part in language-related mobility schemes.

Open and distance learning and technological innovation

279. Activities in this field included the continuation of four projects (Telescopia, LOGOS, EOUN and Humanities) selected in 1994 for Community development and demonstration purposes in the field of open and distance learning. The results of these projects were presented in Berlin at Educa-on Line. On 30 May, Louvain hosted the symposium on open and distance learning activities, bringing together the people working on the four projects. In addition, a total of 60 projects (24 of which gave open and distance learning as their priority theme) were adopted under the Leonardo da Vinci programme and will receive Community funding. A further 33 projects were accepted under Socrates and will receive funding in the sum of ECU 4.084 million. Work also went on in the context of the 'Multimedia educational software' task force (→ point 226). Finally, in its opinion of 20 September,[2] the Committee of the Regions endorsed the Commission's approach as set out in its communication entitled 'Education and training in the face of technological, industrial and social challenges: first thoughts'.[3]

Cooperation in the field of youth

280. On 14 March, Parliament and the Council adopted Decision 95/818/EC establishing the third phase of the Youth for Europe programme (Table I), designed to operate outside the context of education and vocational training structures, principally by way of enhanced cooperation between the Member States. This programme, which has an overall budget of

---

[1]   COM(95) 458; Bull. 10-1995, point 1.3.102.
[2]   Bull. 9-1995, point 1.3.46.
[3]   COM(94) 528; 1994 General Report, point 292.

ECU 126 million and is scheduled to cover the period 1995-99, provides continuity for earlier Community initiatives for young people (i.e. Youth for Europe and part of PETRA), but extending their scope. It is addressed to the European Union's Member States and provides support for exchanges with young people from non-member countries, more especially from Central and Eastern Europe and from Cyprus and Malta. On 11 May, the Commission adopted the report on the Youth for Europe II programme, taking stock of work undertaken in 1993.[1] The Commission also adopted, on 27 March, a report on priority actions in 1993 in the youth field.[2]

281.   On 31 March, the Council approved a resolution on cooperation in the field of youth information.[3] It agreed to step up cooperation at European level in three areas: the training of information workers, socio-educational youth workers and educators; stepping up the networking of youth information structures; concentration of studies to obtain a better understanding of young people's needs in targeted areas. The creation of a European voluntary service scheme was the subject of a European Parliament resolution of 22 September.[4] On 5 October,[5] the Council adopted a resolution on stepping up cooperation with non-member countries on youth-related matters in the following areas: cooperation between governmental and non-governmental youth structures; training for youth workers; youth exchange schemes; voluntary service for young people.

Cooperation with non-member countries

282.   Since 1 January, the EFTA countries which are signatories to the EEA Agreement *(→ point 809)* have taken part in all Community cooperation activities in the fields of education, training and youth.

283.   Against the background of the gradual opening-up in 1996 and 1997 of Community programmes to the countries of Central and Eastern Europe, the Commission organized symposia in June and September, along with bilateral meetings with representatives of the countries concerned. This was also the central theme of the meeting of Education Ministers from the European Union and the countries of Central and Eastern Europe which was held in Luxembourg on 23 October[6]. On 20 September, the Committee of the Regions had already adopted an own-initiative opinion on the role of

---

[1]   OJ C 207, 12.8.1995; COM(95) 159; Bull. 5-1995, point 1.3.48.
[2]   COM(95) 90; Bull. 3-1995, point 1.3.73.
[3]   Bull. 3-1995, point 1.3.72.
[4]   OJ C 269, 16.10.1995; Bull. 9-1995, point 1.3.49.
[5]   OJ C 296, 10.11.1995; Bull. 10-1995, point 1.3.103.
[6]   Bull. 10-1995, point 1.4.62.

local and regional authorities in education and training provided by the European Union in the countries of Central and Eastern Europe.[1]

284.   On 21 December, the Commission adopted two decisions on cooperation with Cyprus (Table III) and Malta (Table III) in the fields of education, training and youth, with a view to commencing negotiations on bilateral agreements with these two countries.

285.   On 23 October, the Commission adopted the decision with a view to concluding an agreement between the European Community and the United States to establish a cooperation programme in the field of higher education and vocational training (Table III). On 27 November, the Commission adopted a similar decision on an agreement with Canada (Table III). These two programmes seek to encourage interaction between higher education establishments, training providers and undertakings in the European Union, the United States and Canada; they further seek to facilitate exchanges of knowledge and staff with a view to intensifying the transatlantic dialogue (→ point 895), while not losing sight of the European dimension. The agreement with the United States was signed on 21 December.

European Training Foundation, Turin

286.   The European Training Foundation, which was set up by the Council on 7 May 1990,[2] and whose headquarters are located in Turin,[3] commenced operations on 1 January. Its objective is to contribute to the development of vocational training systems in the countries of Central and Eastern Europe and in the independent States of the former Soviet Union. The Foundation's report for 1994 was adopted by the Commission on 21 September.[4]

287.   The Foundation also provides technical assistance to the Commission for measures under the Tempus programme. The report on activities under the Tempus programme (1993-94), the aim of which is to provide support for changes to the higher education systems in the countries of Central and Eastern Europe and certain independent States of the former Soviet Union,[5] was adopted by the Commission on 17 July.[6]

---

[1]   Bull. 9-1995, point 1.4.32.
[2]   OJ L 131, 23.5.1990; Twenty-fourth General Report, point 391.
[3]   Twenty-seventh General Report, point 268.
[4]   COM(95) 388.
[5]   Beneficiary countries under this programme are Albania, Bulgaria, Estonia, Hungary, Latvia, Lithuania, Poland, Slovenia, Romania, the Czech Republic, Slovakia, Russia, Belarus, Ukraine, Moldova, Kazakhstan, Uzbekistan and Kyrgyzstan.
[6]   COM(95) 344; Bull. 7/8-1995, point 1.3.85.

European Centre for the Development of Vocational Training (Cedefop)

288. On 6 February, the Council adopted Regulation (EC) No 251/95 amending Regulation (EEC) No 337/75 establishing Cedefop (Table II). All the necessary measures were taken — more particularly the signature of the agreement with the Greek Government — to enable Cedefop to commence operations in Thessaloniki on 1 September.

289. Cedefop activities in 1995 centred on three main elements: qualifications and changing occupations; analysis of vocational training systems in the Member States; communication and information.

290. As regards Cedefop's ongoing activities, the study visit programme was incorporated into the Leonardo da Vinci programme *(→ point 272).*

European University Institute, Florence

291. The Commission contributed ECU 4.532 million towards the Institute's 1995 budget,[1] most of which (ECU 3.605 million) went on support for certain scientific and research work, more specifically the research library and the European library (Eurolib programme), research data processing, research projects, the Robert Schuman Centre, the Jean Monnet Chair, the Jean Monnet scholarships, the European Forum and the European Law Academy. The other ECU 927 000 was spent on the historical archives of the European Communities, which are managed by the Institute *(→ point 672).*

292. At its meeting in December 1994, the Institute's governing board had appointed Mr E. Noël (whom Professor P. Masterson of University College Dublin succeeded as President of the Institute in January 1994) Honorary President. In June, the Institute played host to a delegation from the European Parliament's Committee on Culture, Youth, Education and the Media, led by the Committee Chair, Ms L. Castellina.

293. For the 1995/96 academic year, the Institute and its four departments (history, economics, law, political and social sciences) have 44 professorial posts, three of which are held jointly between a department and the Robert Schuman Centre, which devotes most of its work to a study of the construc-

---

[1]　The report of the Institute's President and copies of the information brochure on the work of the Institute are available from the Institute at Badia Fiesolana, via dei Roccettini, 9, I-50016 San Domenico di Fiesole (Firenze).

tion of Europe. There are 325 research students, 285 of whom come from the 15 Member States of the European Union. In the course of the 1994/95 academic year, 62 doctorates were awarded.

294.   The 1994/95 session of the European Forum, which each year brings together a group of academics and researchers from outside universities on a specific theme, addressed the subject ' "Gender" and the use of time', the 1995/96 session being devoted to 'Citizenship'.

295.   The annual Jean Monnet lecture was given on 20 October by Mr J. Santer, President of the Commission, on the subject 'The future of Europe: what role for the Commission? In praise of the Community method'. On the same day, Mr Santer inaugurated the European Centre for Industrial Relations in Florence. This Centre, set up by the social partners at European level with Commission support, is required to have close contact with the Institute on social-dialogue-related research topics (→ *point 603*), more particularly by creating a Chair dealing with the subject.

Section 10

Economic and social cohesion

Priority activities and objectives

296.   *The main features in 1995 were the adoption of a large number of programmes arising from the Community support frameworks approved the previous year, the approval of a large number of financing decisions under various Community initiatives adopted in 1994, the launching of the peace initiative for Northern Ireland, a decision allocating the financial reserve created for the Community initiatives, and the development of a number of innovative measures, in particular in urban renewal. In addition, following the accession of Austria, Finland and Sweden, the Commission settled the programming of Structural Fund resources for the regions in these new Member States: the areas eligible under Objectives 2 and 5b were defined, which allowed the adoption of the corresponding single programming documents (SPDs) and the Commission also adopted SPDs involving Objectives 3 and 4.*

The Commission adopted, on 20 March, the fifth annual report on the implementation of the reform of the Structural Funds (1993)[1] providing a first survey of implementation by Objective and by country in the first programming period (1989-93), which was the subject of an own-initiative opinion of the Economic and Social Committee on 25 October.[2] The Commission also adopted, on 14 December,[3] the sixth annual report on the Structural Funds (covering 1994). In it, the Commission also introduces the new programming for 1994-99 and examines the structural aspects of enlargement to include the three new Member States and looked at complementarity between the Structural Funds and various other Community policies.

On 31 October, the Commission adopted a communication on the integrated management of coastal zones[4] (→ point 499). In its communication on cohesion and the environment,[5] adopted on 22 November, the Commission analyses the relationship between cohesion policy and the priorities set for the Community's environmental policy. The communication lists ex-

---

¹   COM(95) 30; Bull. 3-1995, point 1.3.74.
²   Bull. 10-1995, point 1.3.109.
³   COM(95) 583; Bull. 12-1995.
⁴   COM(95) 511; Bull. 10-1995, point 1.3.107.
⁵   COM(95) 509; Bull. 11-1995, point 1.3.81.

amples of the contribution of the Structural Funds and the Cohesion Fund to investment to protect and improve the environment, and identifies options for taking more account of environmental concerns in cohesion policy. In the field of spatial development planning, the Commission's communication of 1994[1] continued to be the subject of a broad-based discussion in the context, in particular, of opinions of the European Parliament,[2] the Committee of the Regions[3] and the Economic and Social Committee[4] as well as informal consultation with the Member States. Finally, on 15 November the Committee of the Regions adopted an own-initiative opinion on the financial and administrative impact of European Union legislation on the local and regional authorities,[5] and on 15 October the Economic and Social Committee adopted an own-initiative opinion on local development initiatives and Community regional policy.[6]

Community support frameworks and single programming documents

Concept and guidelines

297.   On 29 March, the Commission adopted a communication on new regional programming under Objectives 1 and 2 of the Community structural policies.[7] In it, the Commission sets out the expected impact on the economic development of the recipient areas, the contribution to strengthening of other Community policies and the progress made in guaranteeing greater effectiveness in the use of Community funds.

298.   The Commission's fifth periodic report on the social and economic situation and development of the regions of the Community (1994)[8] was the subject in May of an opinion of the Economic and Social Committee[9] and of a resolution of the European Parliament in June.[10]

299.   The application of the principle of partnership in the Member States was the subject of an opinion of the Committee of the Regions on 20 July.[11]

---

[1]   COM(94) 354; 1994 General Report, point 433.
[2]   OJ C 183, 17.7.1995; Bull. 6-1995, point 1.3.92.
[3]   Bull. 7/8-1995, point 1.3.86.
[4]   OJ C 133, 31.5.1995; Bull. 3-1995, point 1.3.77; OJ C 301, 13.11.1995; Bull. 9-1995, point 1.3.51.-
[5]   Bull. 11-1995, point 1.3.82.
[6]   Bull. 10-1995, point 1.3.108.
[7]   COM(95) 111; Bull. 3-1995, point 1.3.75.
[8]   COM(94) 322; 1994 General Report, point 436.
[9]   OJ C 236, 11.9.1995; Bull. 5-1995, point 1.3.49.
[10]   OJ C 183, 17.7.1995; Bull. 6-1995, point 1.3.93.
[11]   Bull. 7/8-1995, point 1.3.88.

Financial assistance

300. In a communication adopted on 27 January,[1] the Commission fixed the distribution of financial resources between Objectives 2 to 5b for the new Member States in 1995-99; this covered 90% of the total funds available, 9% being devoted to the Community initiatives and 1% to innovative measures and pilot projects.

The Objectives

Regions lagging behind in their development (Objective 1)

301. Objective 1 is designed to help regions lagging behind in their development, as defined in Regulation (EEC) No 2052/88.[2] Negotiations for the second programming period (1994-99) had largely been completed in 1994,[3] but continued in 1995 with the adoption on 15 November[4] of the single programming document (SPD) for the region of Burgenland in Austria.

302. The breakdown of commitments under Objective 1 by Member State in 1995 is given in Table 2.

Regions suffering industrial decline (Objective 2)[5]

303. The list of the eligible areas in Austria and in Finland was adopted by the Commission on 22 February[6] and a list was approved on 22 March for Sweden.[7] The SPDs under Objective 2 for the new Member States were adopted on 11 July[8] in the case of Finland, 15 November[9] in the case of Austria and 23 November[10] in the case of Sweden. The guidelines call for a development strategy based in particular on the modernization and diversification of the regional economies concerned.

---

[1]   Bull. 1/2-1995, point 1.3.70.
[2]   Amended by Council Regulation (EEC) No 2081/93 (OJ L 193, 31.7.1993).
[3]   The breakdown of the financial contribution under Objective 1 for 1994-99 is indicated in Table 3 in point 445 of the 1994 General Report; the priorities given in CSFs and SPDs adopted in 1994 under Objective 1 are given in Table 4 in point 446 of the 1994 General Report.
[4]   Bull. 11-1995, point 1.3.83.
[5]   The breakdown of the Community contribution under Objective 2 for 1994-96 is given in Table 5 in point 448 of the 1994 General Report.
[6]   OJ L 51, 8.3.1995; Bull. 1/2-1995, point 1.3.71.
[7]   Bull. 3-1995, point 1.3.78.
[8]   OJ L 208, 5.9.1995; Bull. 7/8-1995, point 1.3.91.
[9]   Bull. 11-1995, point 1.3.84.
[10]   Bull. 11-1995, point 1.3.85.

TABLE 2

Objective 1 — Budget commitments in 1995

(million ECU)

Member State	ERDF	ESF	EAGGF (Guidance Section)	FIFG	Total
Belgium	1.970	—	7.000	—	8.970
Germany	921.899	606.054	482.601	12.000	2 022.554
Greece	1 812.992	368.563	452.189	19.300	2 653.044
Spain	3 202.104	837.746	571.120	167.930	4 778.900
France	96.219	115.640	9.498	1.113	222.470
Ireland	498.129	295.126	154.763	6.194	954.212
Italy	1 158.983	223.389	411.687	34.570	1 828.629
Netherlands	10.000	5.000	0.000	2.200	17.200
Austria	19.960	5.000	3.800	—	28.760
Portugal	709.832	370.861	275.102	23.926	1 379.721
United Kingdom	128.708	58.870	27.420	3.600	218.598
Total	8 560.796	2 886.249	2 395.180	270.833	14 113.058

304.   The breakdown of commitments under Objective 2 by Member State in 1995 is given in Table 3.

TABLE 3

Objective 2 — Budget commitments in 1995

(million ECU)

Member State	ERDF	ESF
Belgium	—	4.630
Denmark	6.000	—
Germany	20.330	17.683
Spain	545.101	114.106
France	261.897	51.191
Italy	—	—
Luxembourg		
Netherlands	0.090	9.056
Austria	38.912	15.237
Finland	24.800	6.300
Sweden	—	22.560
United Kingdom	352.262	165.993
Total	1 249.392	406.756

Combating long-term unemployment, and assisting the occupational integration of young people and people at risk of exclusion from the labour market (Objective 3)

305.   The Commission continued with the process of adopting programming documents which it started in 1994[1] by approving the SPDs under Objective 3 for the new Member States: on 21 June for Finland,[2] 19 July for Austria[3] and 26 July for Sweden.[4] These SPDs make provision for implementing specific activities in the fields of training and the integration of people at risk of unemployment and exclusion.

Adjustment of the workforce to industrial changes and changes in production systems (Objective 4)

306.   SPDs under Objective 4, as redefined during the review of the Regulations on the Structural Funds,[5] were approved for Austria,[6] Finland[7] and Sweden[8] on 19 July, 21 June and 6 December respectively. The priorities selected mainly cover the development of vocational training and schemes to take account of anticipated changes in working life and of trends in the labour market.

Adjustment of agricultural structures (Objective 5a)

307.   For horizontal structural measures,[9] the EAGGF Guidance Section committed ECU 889 million in 1995, including ECU 234 million in regions eligible under Objective 5b. The distribution of these commitments by Member State is given in Table 4.[10]

308.   As part of the implementation of measures to improve the conditions under which agricultural and forestry products are processed and marketed,

---

[1]   1994 General Report 1994, point 449. The breakdown of the Community contribution under Objectives 3 and 4 for 1994-99 is given in Table 6 in point 450 of the 1994 General Report.
[2]   Bull. 6-1995, point 1.3.95.
[3]   Bull. 7/8-1995, point 1.3.92.
[4]   Bull. 7/8-1995, point 1.3.93.
[5]   OJ L 193, 31.7.1993.
[6]   Bull. 7/8-1995, point 1.3.94.
[7]   Bull. 6-1995, point 1.3.96.
[8]   Bull. 12-1995.
[9]   These are measures applying throughout the Union, involving the improvement of production, processing and marketing conditions for agricultural and forestry products under Objective 5a of the Structural Funds; they are optional for the Member States.
[10]   The horizontal measures applying in Objective 1 regions are paid for out of appropriations for Objective 1.

TABLE 4

Objective 5a — Budget commitments in 1995

(million ECU)

Member State	Areas not in Objective 1 or 6
Belgium	33.0
Denmark	16.7
Germany	246.3
Spain	79.2
France	287.8
Italy	—
Luxembourg	5.5
Netherlands	9.3
Austria	92.8
Finland	73.0
Sweden	13.7
United Kingdom	31.4
Total	888.7

as provided for in Regulations (EEC) Nos 866/90 and 867/90,[1] the Commission, at the end of the year, approved 50 single programming documents[2] covering the German,[3] Belgian[4] and French[4] regions concerned. On 17 November, it adopted the SPD for Finland[5] and on 15 December the SPD for Austria.[6]

309.   As part of the measures accompanying the CAP reform, 160 agri-environment programmes were approved by the Commission under Regulation (EEC) No 2078/92[7] on agricultural production methods compatible with the requirements of the protection of the environment and the maintenance of the countryside. Programmes presented by Finland, Sweden and Austria were also adopted.

310.   In all, 10 Member States[8] have implemented, in the form of multiannual national or regional programmes, the Community regime of aid for

[1]   OJ L 91, 6.4.1990 (Regulation last amended by Regulation (EC) No 2843/94 to adapt it to the new programming period of the Structural Funds (1994-99)); 1994 General Report, point 454.
[2]   The breakdown of the Community contribution planned for the SPDs approved in 1994 under Objective 5a is given in Table 9 in point 456 of the 1994 General Report.
[3]   OJ L 77, 6.4.1995; Bull. 3-1995, point 1.3.81; OJ L 127, 10.6.1995; Bull. 5-1995, point 1.3.51; OJ L 161, 12.7.1995; Bull. 6-1995, point 1.3.98; OJ L 188, 9.8.1995; Bull. 7/8-1995, point 1.3.95.
[4]   OJ L 77, 6.4.1995; Bull. 3-1995, point 1.3.81.
[5]   OJ L 282, 24.11.1995; Bull. 11-1995, point 1.3.87.
[6]   Bull. 12-1995.I
[7]   OJ L 215, 30.7.1992; Twenty-sixth General Report, point 516.
[8]   The United Kingdom, the Netherlands and Luxembourg do not apply this measure, while among the new Member States only Finland is applying it.

early retirement schemes in farming under Regulation (EEC) No 2079/92.[1] Approximately 33 000 holdings have also received investment aid, which is now being gradually restricted to cut down on agricultural surpluses. The assistance for young farmers, including start-up premiums and supplementary investment aid, is designed to put farms into the hands of young people able to adapt to the new realities in agriculture.

311.   Turning to region-based structural measures in farming, more than 1.1 million holdings in mountain regions and other less-favoured farming areas have continued to receive compensatory allowances, to help sustain agricultural activity and maintain population levels. The Council designated the less-favoured areas for Finland[2] and Sweden[3] on the basis of criteria deriving from the *acquis communautaire* and from specific commitments entered into in the Act of Accession.[4]

Fisheries structures (Objective 5a — fisheries)

312.   On 26 and 28 July,[5] the Commission adopted SPDs in the fisheries sector for Austria and Finland and on 8 November[6] for Sweden.[7] On 20 February, 19 May and 13 June it adopted programmes under the Community's PESCA initiative *(→ point 322)* for the Netherlands, Italy, France and the United Kingdom. In 1995 the commitments per Member State for Objective 5a in the fisheries sector amounted to the following (in million ECU): Denmark: 23.28; Germany: 12.41; Spain: 19.90; France: 31.62; Italy: 22.37; Luxembourg: 0.89; Netherlands: 1.4; Austria: 2; Finland: 23; Sweden: 40.

313.   On 20 March, the Commission adopted a communication on socio-economic measures to accompany the restructuring of the fisheries sector,[8] after which the Council on 20 November adopted Regulation (EC) No 2719/95 (Table II) amending Regulation (EC) No 3699/93 laying down criteria and conditions for Community structural assistance in this sector with a view to defining new socioeconomic measures to support fishermen, particularly older fishermen. In addition, the Council adopted Regulation (EC)

---

[1]   OJ L 215, 30.7.1992.
[2]   OJ L 241, 10.10.1995; Bull. 9-1995, point 1.3.54.
[3]   OJ L 287, 30.11.1995; Bull. 11-1995, point 1.3.86.
[4]   Act of Accession of Austria, Finland and Sweden; OJ L 241, 29.8.1994, point 1.3.15; OJ L 1, 1.1.1995.
[5]   OJ L 192, 15.8.1995; Bull. 7/8-1995, point 1.3.96.
[6]   OJ L 275, 18.11.1995; Bull. 11-1995, point 1.3.90.
[7]   The indicative breakdown among Member States of the financial resources available under Objective 5a — fisheries — for 1994-99 is given in Table 14 in point 463 of the 1994 General Report.
[8]   COM(95) 55; Bull. 3-1995, point 1.3.82.

No 1614/95 (Table II) also amending Regulation (EC) No 3699/93.[1] This had the purpose of replacing 'gross registered tonnes' (GRT) by the unit 'gross tonnes' (GT) for calculating the tonnage of vessels eligible for structural assistance. The Commission, for its part, adopted on 5 December a proposal for a Council Regulation amending Regulation (EC) No 3699/93 to encourage the withdrawal of vessels over 30 years old (Table II). On 25 July, the Commission adopted Regulation (EC) No 1796/95 laying down detailed rules for the implementation of assistance granted by the Financial Instrument for Fisheries Guidance (FIFG) for schemes defined in Regulation (EC) No 3699/93. It also adopted Decisions 95/238/EC to 95/248/EC[2] amending Decisions 92/588/EEC to 92/598/EEC on multiannual guidance programmes for the fishing fleets of Member States. On 20 March, the Commission adopted a Decision[3] on implementing the Annex to Regulation (EEC) No 2930/86 defining the characteristics of fishing vessels so as to ensure by 1 January 2004 an accounting of the whole Community fleet in accordance with the London Convention of 1969. On 26 October, the Council adopted Decision 95/451/EC on a specific measure for the granting of an indemnity to Spanish and Portuguese fishermen who had to suspend their fishing activities in waters under the sovereignty or jurisdiction of Morocco.[4]

Rural development (Objective 5b)

314.   Objective 5b is concerned with the development of rural areas in difficult circumstances which are not located in Objective 1 regions; 12 Member States are involved. The Objective 5b areas designated for the period 1994-99[5] have a total population of approximately 32 745 000, i.e. 8.8% of the Community's population including the three new Member States, and a combined surface area of 840 876 km². The Commission drew up the list of areas for the new Member States on 17 February in the case of Austria and Finland[6] and on 18 April in the case of Sweden.[7]

315.   The majority of SPDs under Objective 5b were adopted in 1994.[8] In 1995 the Commission adopted those for a number of German, Belgian,

---

[1]   Twenty-seventh General Report, point 394.
[2]   OJ L 166, 15.7.1995.
[3]   Decision 95/84/EC; OJ L 67, 25.3.1995.
[4]   OJ L 264, 7.11.1995; Bull. 10-1995, point 1.3.118.
[5]   1995-99 in the case of the three new Member States.
[6]   OJ L 49, 4.3.1995; Bull. 1/2-1995, point 1.3.73.
[7]   OJ L 92, 25.4.1995; Bull. 4-1995, point 1.3.70.
[8]   1994 General Report, point 459. The breakdown of the Community contribution under Objective 5b (1994-99) is given in Table 11 in point 460 of the 1994 General Report.

French, Italian and UK regions.[1] The SPD for Finland[2] was adopted on 13 November, and that for Austria[3] was approved on 31 October.

316.   The breakdown of budget commitments for 1995 is given in Table 5.

TABLE 5

Objective 5b — Budget commitments in 1995

(million ECU)

Member State	EAGGF	ERDF	ESF
Belgium	2.8	4.824	1.548
Denmark	—	3.359	—
Germany	81.2	49.476	5.102
Greece	—	—	—
Spain	58.1	25.215	5.297
France	35.7	45.022	29.733
Ireland	—	—	—
Italy	15.8	12.405	3.272
Luxembourg	—	—	—
Netherlands	4.5	1.940	0.919
Austria	31.3	33.342	—
Portugal	—	—	13.683
Finland	11.6	16.029	5.180
Sweden	—	—	—
United Kingdom	8.6	36.776	29.238
Total	249.6	228.388	93.972

Regions with very low population density (Objective 6)

317.   As a result of the accession of Finland and Sweden, a new Objective has been created, to apply from 1 January 1995, for the development of regions in those countries with very low population density. These are defined in the Act of Accession as regions with a population density of eight or less per km². The north and east of Finland and the northern half of Sweden, except for certain coastal strips, have been classified as eligible for Community assistance under this Objective. As well as suffering from depopulation problems, these regions are also disadvantaged by their peripheral location and by the harsh arctic or subarctic climate.

---

[1]   Bull. 3-1995, point 1.3.84; Bull. 4-1995, point 1.3.73; Bull. 4-1995, point 1.3.72.
[2]   Bull. 11-1995, point 1.3.91.
[3]   Bull. 10-1995, point 1.3.115.

318.   The SPD for Finland, adopted by the Commission on 11 July,[1] will channel towards the region concerned a sum of ECU 460 million financed by the Union over the period 1995-99. Its main priorities are development of the local economy, human resources, agriculture, forestry, fisheries, farmland improvement and the environment. The SPD for Sweden, adopted by the Commission on 6 November,[2] will provide ECU 252 million in Community assistance over the period 1995-99 and will be focused on five priority sectors: development of commerce, the promotion of know-how, agriculture and natural resources, farmland improvement, and Community social projects and improvement of the situation of the Sami people.

Community initiatives

Concept and guidelines

319.   In 1994,[3] a total of 13 Community initiatives were adopted representing a volume of ECU 11.85 billion, to which a reserve of ECU 1.6 billion can be added which was allocated in principle among the Member States by a Commission Decision approved on 4 October.[4] A part of this Decision also proposed new guidelines to assist the control of floods and droughts, encourage transnational cooperation projects in spatial development and provide for various employment schemes. In the context of the Interreg, URBAN, ADAPT and Employment initiatives, the Commission adopted draft communications on 20 November[5] setting out the guidelines for Member States when preparing their forward programming documents. The 13 initiatives are:

(i)   Interreg II (cross-border cooperation and completion of energy networks);
(ii)   Leader II (innovation and rural development);
(iii)   REGIS II (integration of remoter regions);
(iv)   Employment and development of human resources (revival of employment, social solidarity, equal opportunities);
(v)   ADAPT (adaptation of the labour force to industrial changes);
(vi)   Rechar II (conversion of areas affected by the decline of the coalmining industry);
(vii)   Resider II (economic and social conversion of steelmaking areas);

---

[1]   OJ L 208, 5.9.1995; Bull. 7/8-1995, point 1.3.97.
[2]   Bull. 11-1995, point 1.3.92.
[3]   1994 General Report, point 466.
[4]   Bull. 10-1995, point 1.3.117.
[5]   Bull. 11-1995, point 1.3.93.

(viii) Konver (diversification of activities in areas dependent on the defence sector);

(ix)   RETEX (economic diversification in areas dependent on the textiles industry);

(x)   Modernization of the textiles and clothing sector in Portugal. On 10 April, the Council adopted Regulation (EC) No 852/95 (Table II) on the granting of financial assistance to Portugal for a specific programme for the modernization of the Portuguese textile and clothing industry;

(xi)   SMEs (to help small and medium-sized enterprises adjust to the single market and to international competition);

(xii) URBAN (tackling inner-city problems);

(xiii) PESCA (restructuring the fisheries sector).

320. Following enlargement of the Union to include three new Member States, the Commission adopted a communication on 4 April[1] on the allocation of funds and on the implementation of the Community initiatives in Austria, Finland and Sweden, taking into account the specific situation in these countries.

321. Following up the conclusions of the European Council in Essen[2] and its 1994 communication on the subject,[3] the Commission adopted a notice[4] to the Member States on 16 May setting out the guidelines for an initiative under the special aid programme for peace and reconciliation in Northern Ireland and in the counties of Ireland bordering on Northern Ireland. This envisages the following priorities: support for employment, urban and rural regeneration, the development of cross-border infrastructures, social integration through cooperation between the different communities, industrial development and the promotion of investment in production by small and medium-sized businesses. The European Parliament,[5] the Economic and Social Committee[6] and the Committee of the Regions[7] each gave an opinion on this initiative.

---

[1]   COM(95) 123; Bull. 4-1995, point 1.3.74.
[2]   Bull. 12-1994, point I.10; 1994 General Report, point 475.
[3]   COM(94) 607; 1994 General Report, point 475.
[4]   COM(95) 37; Bull. 5-1995, point 1.3.54.
[5]   OJ C 109, 1.5.1995; Bull. 4-1995, point 1.3.75.
[6]   OJ C 155, 21.6.1995; Bull. 4-1995, point 1.3.76; OJ C 236, 11.9.1995; Bull. 5-1995, point 1.3.55.
[7]   Bull. 4-1995, point 1.3.77.

Financial assistance

322. The financing allocated to the Community initiatives in 1995 is set
out in Table 6.

TABLE 6

Financing of Community initiatives in 1995

(million ECU at 1994 prices)

Initiative	Country/target of area	Total commitments
ADAPT	Belgium	5.694
	Denmark	5.310
	Germany	42.922
	Greece	6.286
	Spain	43.288
	France	42.557
	Ireland	3.899
	Italy	36.100
	Luxembourg	0.054
	Netherlands	11.510
	Austria	11.570
	Portugal	3.990
	Finland	19.700
	Sweden	11.250
	United Kingdom	53.490
Employment	Belgium	16.954
	Denmark	—
	Germany	—
	Greece	—
	Spain	1.643
	France	—
	Ireland	—
	Italy	—
	Luxembourg	0.255
	Netherlands	—
	Austria	23.010
	Portugal	—
	Finland	29.150
	Sweden	20.690
	United Kingdom	9.747
Interreg II	Spain/Portugal	220
	Ireland/Wales	82.9
	Ireland/Northern Ireland	157
	Spain/Portugal	
	• Natural gas	552

TABLE 6 (continued)

(million ECU at 1994 prices)

Initiative	Country/target of area	Total commitments
	Germany/Switzerland	
	• Bodensee/Upper Rhine	4.855
	Germany/Czech Republic/Poland	
	• Saxony	146.45
	Germany/Switzerland/France	
	• Upper Rhine/South Centre	24.58
	Germany/Netherlands	
	• Ems/Dollart	22.47
	Germany/Netherlands	
	• Euregio	22.01
	Germany/Netherlands	
	• Euregio Rhine/Waal	11.53
	Germany/Netherlands	
	• Euregio Rhine/Northern Maas	6.38
	Germany/Netherlands/Belgium	
	• Meuse-Maas/Rhine	35.705
	Germany/Poland	
	• Mecklenburg/Pomerania	63.1
	Germany	
	• Bavaria	16.8
	Germany/Poland	
	• Brandenburg	72.02
	Germany/Luxembourg	8
	Denmark/Germany	
	• South Jutland	11.1
	• Fyn/Kern	1.8
	• Storstrøm	5.2
	Greece	
	• Energy sypply	180
	• External borders	309.8
	France/Switzerland	
	• Franche-Comté	7
	• Rhône-Alpes	5.3
Konver	Belgium	
	• Wallonia	4.92
	Denmark	2.35
	Portugal	
	• Lisbon, Alentejo, Azores	7.89
SMEs	Germany	
	• Bremen	0.97
	• North Rhine-Westphalia	7.92
	Greece	82.2
	Ireland	28.78
	United Kingdom	
	• Northern Ireland	6.2

TABLE 6 (continued)

(million ECU at 1994 prices)

Initiative	Country/target of area	Total commitments
Leader II	Germany	
	• Berlin	0.24
	• Bavaria	43.05
	• Brandenburg	19.83
	• Hesse	6.20
	• Mecklenburg-Western Pomerania	15.56
	• Saxony-Anhalt	15.56
	• Saxony	18.01
	• Thuringia	13.92
	France	
	• Aquitaine	17.226
	• Auvergne	12.78
	• Lower Normandy	10.133
	• Burgundy	8.53
	• Corsica	3.05
	• Languedoc-Roussillon	14.40
	• Limousin	15.04
	Greece	148
	Spain	
	• Andalusia	68.81
	• Aragon	27.48
	• Asturias	13
	• Balearic Islands	3.13
	• Canary Islands	12.33
	• Cantabria	6.41
	• Castile-La Mancha	41
	• Castile-Leon	53.50
	• Catalonia	13.62
	• Extremadura	24
	• Galicia	43.80
	• Madrid	3.60
	• Murcia	9.52
	• Navarre	4.81
	• Basque Country	2.47
	• Rioja	3.68
	• Valencia	22.63
	Ireland	67.92
	Italy	
	• Abruzzi	15.97
	• Basilicata	19.55
	• Campania	25.82
	• Apulia	26.60
	• Sardinia	32.37

TABLE 6 (continued)

(million ECU at 1994 prices)

Initiative	Country/target of area	Total commitments
Rechar II	Belgium	
	• Wallonia	0.93
	• Limburg	14.75
	Germany	
	• North Rhine-Westphalia	66.45
	Greece	1.5
	Portugal	0.86
	United Kingdom	
	• North-East England	23.17
	• Wales	20.21
	• East of Scotland	9.99
	• East Midlands	41.64
	• Yorkshire	44.03
	• West of Scotland	3.03
REGIS II	Portugal	124
Resider II	Belgium	
	• Charleroi and Centre	11.9
	Germany	
	• Bremen	3.28
	• Saxony	14.88
	• Saxony-Anhalt	5
	• North Rhine-Westphalia	101.89
	• Lower Saxony	14.80
	Greece	4.63
	France	
	• Picardy	2.28
	Netherlands	18.1
	United Kingdom	
	• Wales	12.8
	• West of Scotland	10.23
RETEX II	Belgium	
	• Hainaut (part of)	3
	France	24.59
	Netherlands	1
	United Kingdom	
	• Northern Ireland	4.2
URBAN	Belgium	
	• Antwerp	4.57
	• Charleroi	5.6

TABLE 6 (continued)

(million ECU at 1994 prices)

Initiative	Country/target of area	Total commitments
	Germany	
	• Magdeburg	12.88
	• Erfurt	12.9
	• Chemnitz	9.2
	• Bremen	8
	• Berlin	16.1
	• Brandenburg	7.2
	Greece	45.2
	Spain	
	• Badalona, Badajoz, baracaldo, Cadiz, Cartagena, Huelva, Corunna, Langreo, Madrid, Malaga, Sabadell, Salamanca, Seville, Toledo, Valencia, Valladolid, Vigo	160.4
	Netherlands	
	• Amsterdam	4.65
	• The Hague	4.65
	Portugal	
	• Lisbon, Oporto	43.7
	United Kingdom	
	• Northern Ireland	16.9
Peace and reconciliation	Northern Ireland/Ireland	300
PESCA	France	18.781
	Italy	4.424935
	United Kingdom	5.071

Innovative schemes and other regional schemes

323. This year saw the presentation to Member States of guidelines for a new generation of pilot projects under Article 10 of Regulation (EEC) No 4254/88.[1] The schemes to be undertaken in 1995-99 will concentrate on four topics: interregional cooperation inside and outside the Community (ECU 180 million); innovation in regional and local economic development (ECU 90 million); spatial development planning (ECU 45 million); urban policies (ECU 80 million). The Committee of the Regions, in an own-initiative opinion of 21 September,[2] gave its conclusions on innovative schemes. Urban development in the Union had also been discussed in an opinion by the Committee of the Regions on 20 July.[3] The Commission has worked out

---

[1]   Twenty-seventh General Report, point 390.
[2]   Bull. 9-1995, point 1.3.53.
[3]   Bull. 7/8-1995, point 1.3.87.

details of how to institute transnational cooperation in the field of spatial development planning. Three types of measure are proposed, starting at the end of 1995: pilot cooperation projects involving major European transnational spatial planning areas (such as the Alps, the Mediterranean, the Baltic); a programme of pilot projects of an innovative nature involving specific kinds of area (mountain and coastal areas, river basins, etc.); and a scheme to disseminate know-how and develop cooperation on a series of topics in spatial planning, bringing in non-member countries of Europe and the Mediterranean.

324. In the field of interregional cooperation, the networks launched under the Recite (internal cooperation) and ECOS-Ouverture (external cooperation) programmes continued to be closely monitored.[1]

325. As regards support for regional SMEs, the pilot activities of the European business and innovation centres (EBICs) continued[2] with the adoption of six new integrated-services centres for SMEs, and two Europartenariat events were successfully held *(→ point 209).*

Cohesion Fund

Concept and guidelines

326. On 17 January,[3] the Commission adopted its first annual report on the activities of the cohesion financial instrument from its creation on 1 April 1993 until its replacement by the Cohesion Fund on 26 May 1994.[4] This report was supplemented on 14 June[5] by an additional report on the activities of the Cohesion Fund from 26 May to 31 December 1994, and was the subject of a resolution passed by the European Parliament on 29 June[6] and of an opinion from the Committee of the Regions on 21 September.[7]

---

[1]   1994 General Report, point 469.
[2]   1994 General Report, point 468.
[3]   COM(95) 1; Bull.1/2-1995, point 1.3.80.
[4]   Regulation (EC) No 1164/94 — OJ L 130, 25.5.1994; 1994 General Report, point 434.
[5]   COM(95) 222; Bull. 6-1995, point 1.3.105.
[6]   OJ C 183, 17.7.1995; Bull. 6-1995, point 1.3.93.
[7]   Bull. 9-1995, point 1.3.52.

Financial assistance

327. The appropriations allocated to the Cohesion Fund for the period covered by the financial perspective for 1993-99 come to ECU 15.15 billion at 1992 prices. Commitment appropriations approved for budget year 1995 totalled ECU 2.1517 billion. In 1995, the total amount of commitments to financing projects in Greece, Spain, Portugal and Ireland came to ECU 2 152.687999 million, of which ECU 1 042.238215 million was devoted to environmental projects and ECU 1 107.601380 million to projects in the field of transport; ECU 1.848404 million was committed in technical assistance for 1995.

The breakdown by country of all the commitments for these projects is given in Table 7. Altogether, 181 projects were financed by the Cohesion Fund in 1995, of which 45 were in Greece, 65 in Spain, 24 in Portugal and 47 in Ireland.

TABLE 7

Cohesion Fund — Commitment appropriations in 1995

	Environment		Transport		Total (million ECU)	Breakdown (%)
	Million ECU	%	Million ECU	%		
Greece	228.184658	58.9	159.729130	41.2	387.913788	18.02
Spain	574.225818	48.5	610.206854	51.5	1 184.432672	55.05
Ireland	93.179175	48.1	97.192548	50.1	190.371723	8.84
Portugal	146.648564	37.8	240.472848	62.0	387.121412	17.99
Technical assistance	—	—	—	—	1.848404	0.086
Total	1 042.238215	—	1 107.601380	—	2 151.687999	99.99

ECSC conversion loans

328. The total volume of the new ECSC conversion loans granted in 1995 (see Table 8) came to ECU 14.8[1] million (with the number of jobs created coming to 112). From the ECSC budget for 1995, ECU 11.45 million were committed to reducing interest on current loans.

---

[1]   To this can be added ECU 379.6 million in new global loans which the Council is expected to give assent early in 1996. The number of jobs arising from these loans should come to 26 968.

TABLE 8

ECSC conversion loans*

	1995	
	(a)	(b)
Spain	14.8	112
European Union	14.8	112

[1] (a) = total of loans granted in million ECU.
[2] (b) = number of jobs created/to be created.
*   The figures in the table do no include 12 new conversion loans in several Member States to which the Council is expected to give assent early in 1996.

EEA Financial Mechanism

329.   The financial mechanism set up under the EEA Agreement is the EFTA-EEA countries' contribution to the Community's internal cohesion effort. It provides for a total of ECU 900 million in grants and interest subsidies equal to 2 points over 10 years on European Investment Bank loans totalling ECU 1 500 million. This financial assistance is intended for projects in Greece, Ireland, Northern Ireland, Portugal and parts of Spain (Objective 1 regions under the Structural Fund system as designated in 1988 and 1993). Priority is to go to projects focused on the environment, transport, education and training. Special attention is given to small businesses (SMEs).

Section 11

Measures for the most remote regions

Priority activities and objectives

330.   Further progress was made in 1995 in pursuing and consolidating the efforts of the Union to assist the French overseas departments, the Canary Islands, the Azores and Madeira.

Necessary adjustments in pursuit of the objectives of the Poseidom,[1] Poseima[2] and Poseican[3] programmes, and amendments to Regulation (EEC) No 1911/91 on the application of the provisions of Community law to the Canary Islands,[2] were proposed and/or adopted. These measures are prepared within a framework of partnership between the Community, the Member State and the region which is organized by an interdepartmental group at the Commission responsible for the most remote regions; the aim is to ensure that, in the application of Community policies, proper account is taken of the constraints and specific characteristics of the regions concerned.

The adoption of operational programmes under the Structural Funds (→ points 301 et seq.) covering each of these regions and other measures in the context of the Regis II Community Initiative (→ point 319), which is specifically designed to help the most remote regions, were additional milestones in 1995.

The regions concerned made it clear that they would like to see a strengthening of the legal basis for the Union's policies with regard to them. For its part, the Commission declared itself ready to support any initiative likely to help clarify, reaffirm and deepen this approach. The question of introducing into the Treaty a provision for special treatment to support these regions was mentioned by several delegations participating in the Reflection Group preparing for the Intergovernmental Conference (→ point 1026).

---

[1]   OJ L 399, 30.12.1989; Twenty-third General Report, point 490.
[2]   OJ L 171, 29.6.1991; Twenty-fifth General Report, point 526.
[3]   OJ L 171, 29.6.1991; Twenty-fifth General Report, point 528.

Agriculture

331. On 30 October the Council adopted Regulation (EC) No 2598/95 (Table II) adjusting the agriculture part of the Poseidom programme and implementing new measures to encourage development of the agricultural sector in the French overseas departments. The Commission also adopted new implementing and management rules needed to apply specific measures covering a number of agricultural products contained in the framework Regulations (EEC) Nos 3763/91,[1] 1600/92 and 1601/92[2] on the Poseidom, Poseima and Poseican programmes.

332. On 6 October the Commission also decided[3] to allocate an exceptional additional quantity under the tariff quota for imported bananas, in the wake of tropical storms Iris, Luis and Marilyn in August and September, in order to make it possible for banana producers in Martinique and Guadeloupe to maintain activity and so safeguard their distribution and marketing networks.

Fisheries

333. On 30 October the Council adopted Regulation (EC) No 2337/95 (Table II) establishing for the period 1995-97 a system of compensation for the additional costs incurred in the marketing of certain fishery products (tuna, sardines, mackerel and Guiana shrimps).

Customs, tariff and trade measures

334. On 20 December, the Council adopted Regulation (EC) No 3012/95 (Table II) extending until 31 March 1996 the application of Regulation (EEC) No 1605/92. Concurrently, on 14 December the Commission adopted a proposal for a Council Regulation (Table II) setting out the details for the phased introduction in the Canary Islands of import duties on certain industrial products in accordance with the common customs tariff, aiming at full application by 31 December 2000 at the latest, and for maintaining the suspension of duties over the same period.

335. In connection with antidumping legislation, the Commission also adopted, on 11 December, a proposal for a Council Regulation (Table II)

---

[1]   OJ L 356, 24.12.1991; Twenty-fifth General Report, point 523.
[2]   OJ L 173, 27.6.1992; Twenty-sixth General Report, point 494.
[3]   Commission Regulation (EC) No 2358/95, OJ L 241, 10.10.1995.

amending Regulation (EEC) No 1602/95 to give Canary Islands importers one more year of exemption from antidumping duties.

336.   The Commission also adopted, on 6 November, a proposal for a Council Regulation (Table II) according favourable tariff treatment to imports of various goods into the free zones of Madeira and the Azores by reason of their specific destination. This measure supplements and reinforces the measures taken to develop the free zone in Madeira.[1]

Taxation

337.   On 20 December the Commission adopted a Decision on the recognition of special tax treatment for the Canary Islands, which maintains, for local products, the exemption from the regional tax (called APIM), which is to be gradually phased out between now and 31 December 2000.

338.   In connection with excise duties, the Council adopted on 30 October a decision permitting the French Republic to apply in its territory a reduced rate of excise duty on so-called 'traditional rums' produced in its overseas departments.

Other measures

339.   On 6 September[2] and 25 September,[3] the Commission approved two emergency aid packages worth ECU 500 000 and ECU 700 000 respectively (→ point 636) to assist sections of the population in Martinique and Guadeloupe who had suffered from the tropical storms Iris and Luis.

---

[1]   1994 General Report, point 479.
[2]   Bull. 9-1995, point 1.3.127.
[3]   Bull. 9-1995, point 1.3.128.

Section 12

Trans-European networks

Priority activities and objectives

340.   The development of trans-European networks (TENs) has long been a priority for the Union. Their importance was recognized in the Treaty on European Union, stressed in the Commission's White Paper on growth, competitiveness and employment (→ points 24 et seq.) and reiterated at several European Councils. Union action to develop the TENs is geared towards filling in the missing links in Europe's networks to make its economy more competitive, create jobs and reinforce cohesion.

1995 was mainly a year of consolidation in this area. Following the Commission's adoption of the essential legislative bases in 1994, proposals were adopted on 31 May for a general strategy on telecommunications networks. In addition, guidelines for digital telecommunications networks (ISDN) were adopted on 11 October, and the Regulation governing the granting of Community financial aid on 18 September. At the same time, work aimed at launching or speeding up the priority projects was stepped up.

At its June meeting in Cannes[1] the European Council turned its attention to the financing of the networks. In particular it agreed on guidelines for allocating the appropriations available in 1995 and 1996 between 'priority' and other projects. It also asked the Commission to re-examine the financial evaluation of the projects, to seek other types of funding and to take all necessary steps to allow the projects eligible under the forthcoming funding Regulation to be submitted as soon as possible. The Council's adoption, on 18 September, of Regulation (EC) No 2236/95 (Table II) laying down general rules for the granting of Community financial aid in the field of trans-European networks enabled the Commission to commit the available appropriations. A total of ECU 274 million was thus committed: ECU 240 million for transport, ECU 22 million for telecommunications and ECU 12 million for energy. Regarding other types of funding, the Commission conducted studies and continued its contacts with financial and industrial circles with a view to making recommendations to promote public/private sector partnerships. These recommendations were included in the report on trans-European networks[2] adopted by the Commission on 22 November and

---

[1]   Bull. 6-1995, point 1.3.107.
[2]   Bull. 11-1995, point 1.3.101.

submitted to the Madrid European Council. The report shows that there has been progress, especially on the priority TEN projects, but that too many problems persist and that further efforts are needed to solve them. The Member States need to give greater priority to TEN projects, especially as the likely 'Community benefit' is larger than originally anticipated. Several priority projects are facing financial problems, which means even more encouragement should be given to partnerships between the public and private sectors. These problems will also influence the decisions — requested at Essen — on supplementing TEN funding. At the same time the Commission adopted an annual report on the TENs,[1] detailing these issues. In December the European Council in Madrid[2] confirmed that the trans-European networks could make a fundamental contribution to competitiveness, job creation and cohesion in the Union. It took note with satisfaction of the Commission report and recent progress in this area. It called upon the Council and the European Parliament to complete the legislative framework as soon as possible and called upon the Member States to assign the highest priority to the effective implementation of projects and in particular those identified by the European Council as being of particular importance. Lastly, it called upon the Council to adopt, on a Commission proposal, the decisions needed in order to supplement the funding now available for trans-European networks.

Transport

341.   In February the Commission amended its proposal on Community guidelines for the development of the trans-European transport network (Table I) to include Austria, Finland and Sweden and to introduce a list of joint projects to be begun in the next five years, in accordance with the conclusions of the Essen European Council.[3] In June the Council reached agreement with a view to a common position, which was formalized on 28 September. Parliament delivered its opinion on second reading on 13 December, confirming its position on the need to give greater priority to environmental protection and to update the list of priority projects in accordance with the co-decision procedure.

342.   On 8 December the Council adopted a common position on the proposal for a Directive on the interoperability of the European high-speed train network (Table II).

---

[1]   COM(95) 571; Bull. 11-1995, point 1.3.102.
[2]   Bull. 12-1995.
[3]   1994 General Report, point 324.

343.   In the field of telematics applications in the transport sector *(→ point 439)*, the Council gave its assent in June[1] to a resolution, formally adopted on 28 September,[2] asking the Commission to take the necessary steps for the introduction of telematics tools in the road transport sector. In accordance with the resolution the Commission set up a high-level working party of representatives of the Member States, industry, users and the competent international organizations, which met for the first time in December. Following the Commission communication on satellite navigation services,[3] a high-level working party was set up to devise an action plan.

344.   The Commission endeavoured throughout the year to facilitate and accelerate the implementation of the priority projects adopted by the Essen European Council.[4] Encouraging progress was made, in particular the creation of a European Economic Interest Grouping (EEIG) for the high-speed train South and the high-speed train Lyon-Turin. Following the adoption of the funding Regulation the Commission was able to give concrete support to the priority projects by granting them ECU 182.5 million in financial aid, which in accordance with the conclusions of the Cannes European Council[5] accounts for 75% of the appropriations available in the transport sector.

Telematics and telecommunications

345.   The key event of the year, for trans-European telecommunications networks, was the adoption by the Commission on 31 May, at the request of the Council, of a proposal for a Decision on a set of guidelines (Table I), based on Article 129c of the EC Treaty. This is an overall or 'multimode' proposal covering all areas of telecommunications networks. The Commission's proposal points the way to coordinated action for optimum use of Community instruments and financial resources while developing new services and applications for the information society. Given the uncertain commercial viability of certain projects, it believes the Union should encourage certain initiatives. The proposed guidelines also aim to make European firms more competitive, improve economic and social cohesion, and hasten the development of activities in industries with job-creation potential. In particular, the Commission has identified a list of projects of common interest for the basic networks (ISDN and IBC (integrated broadband communica-

[1]   OJ C 183, 17.7.1995; Bulletin 6-1995, point 1.3.126.
[2]   OJ C 264, 11.10.1995; Bulletin 9-1995, point 1.3.74.
[3]   COM(94) 248; 1994 General Report, point 366.
[4]   Bull. 12-1994, points I.6 and I.35; 1994 General Report, point 324.
[5]   Bull. 6-1995, point 1.3.107.

tions)), generic services and some ten sectoral applications. The Council reached unanimous agreement on this proposal on 27 November.

346.   With regard to integrated services digital networks (ISDN), the Commission had already proposed guidelines in 1993 and this proposal continued its course through the legislative process during the year (Table I) with final adoption by the Council and Parliament on 9 November.

347.   In 1993 the Commission had also adopted proposals to create trans-European telematics networks between administrations (TNA) (Table I) and a Community multiannual operation supporting their introduction and the interchange of data between administrations (IDA) (Table II). At the end of 1994 the Council reached an agreement radically amending the Commission's original proposals, in particular eliminating the TNA proposal and changing the legal basis of the IDA proposal from Article 235 to Article 129d of the EC Treaty. Although Parliament, on 21 September, rejected the change of legal basis, the Council adopted Decision No 95/468/EC on 6 November.

348.   The Commission sought throughout the year to stimulate the introduction of basic networks, the deployment of generic services on a continental scale and the development of specific applications, in particular of public interest. To this end it stepped up contacts with public and private operators and granted more than ECU 70 million in financial aid for preparatory measures, pilot schemes and feasibility studies (IDA appropriations and TEN Regulation). Encouraging progress was made.

Energy

349.   The proposals adopted by the Commission in 1994 establishing a set of guidelines for the energy sector (Table I) and laying down a series of measures to create a more favourable context for the development of trans-European networks (Table II) were the subject of a Council common position on 29 June and a Parliamentary opinion at second reading on 26 October.

350.   At the same time as enacting the legislation, the Commission has endeavoured, through its contacts with the parties concerned, to facilitate and accelerate the implementation of the projects mentioned by the Essen European Council[1] and the larger number on the list of projects of common in-

---

[1]   1994 General Report, point 322.

terest[1] submitted to Parliament and the Council for adoption. Progress was made in particular on gas interconnection between Spain and Portugal and the gas network in Portugal. Thanks to the entry into force of the funding Regulation on trans-European networks, the Commission was able, for the first time, to give financial assistance, totalling ECU 12 million, to a number of feasibility studies.

Environment

351. In response to the Essen European Council's request regarding environmental networks, the Commission set up a high-level working party, which established criteria for joint environmental projects (JEPs) consisting of joint action by Member States to devise projects of common interest for protecting or improving the environment. Possible JEPs include waste management (processing and recycling) and water policy (flood prevention, drainage basin management, waste water treatment). The Commission also decided to develop a methodology for the strategic assessment of the environmental impact of trans-European networks in the field of transport.

---

[1]   1994 General Report, point 323.

Section 13

Energy

Priority activities and objectives

352.   *The year was marked by the adoption by the Commission of the Green Paper for a European Union energy policy on 11 January followed, on 13 December, by the adoption of a White Paper entitled 'An energy policy for the European Community'. This document, designed to provide the reference framework and instruments required for smooth operation of the internal energy market, proposed the principal lines of action for gradual convergence of the national policies around common objectives.*

The objectives of promoting energy efficiency and reducing CO_2 emissions will be pursued by the SAVE II programme, which is in the process of being adopted. Promotion of energy efficiency and the transfer of technological innovations are also amongst the central objectives of the draft Synergy multiannual programme on cooperation between the European Community and non-member countries in the energy sector. On the same topic of international relations, an Agreement between Euratom and the USA on cooperation on the peaceful uses of nuclear energy was signed on 7 November. Finally, at the Euro-Mediterranean Conference in Barcelona on 27 November the participants adopted a work programme in which energy features prominently.

In 1995 the Commission also conducted a review of Community energy legislation with a view to simplifying it and removing every provision which could create a barrier to economic competitiveness or job creation. In response to the Council conclusions of November 1994[1] and, in particular, on the basis of the work of the group of experts chaired by Mr Molitor (→ point 11), in a report dated 26 July[2] the Commission identified a number of legal acts to be repealed and submitted proposals to that effect to the Commission. Following this report on a review of Community energy legislation, on 23 November[3] the Commission repealed recommendations 88/285/EEC[4] and 80/823/EEC[5] on third-party financing and the rational use of energy in industrial enterprises, which were no longer applicable. In an

---

[1]   1994 General Report, point 334.
[2]   COM(95)391; Bull. 7/8-1995, point 1.3.102.
[3]   OJ L 290, 5.12.1995; Bull. 11-1995, point 1.3.107.
[4]   OJ L 122, 15.5.1988.
[5]   OJ L 239, 12.9.1980.

own-initiative opinion of 26 October[1] and a resolution of 15 December,[2] the Economic and Social Committee and the Eurpean Parliament endorsed the Commission's approach. On 26 July the Commission also adopted a proposal for a Regulation concerning investment projects of interest to the Community in the petroleum, natural gas and electricity sectors (Table II), with the objective of reformulating a number of Regulations in order to simplify the procedure for notifying the Commission and, hence, obtain a clear picture of the developments planned in capacity and equipment in the energy industry in the Community.

Community energy strategy

Community energy policy

353.   On 11 January the Commission adopted a Green Paper for a European Union Energy Policy,[3] which was drawn up following wide-ranging consultation with the Member States and the various economic operators. It identified four fundamental policy directions: stronger concerted action and cooperation between decision-makers and energy policy players, a comprehensive approach to national and Community energy policies, definition of the European Community's energy policy responsibilities and taking account of the environmental constraints. In response to all the reactions to the Green Paper, including a Council resolution,[4] an ECSC Consultative Committee resolution,[5] the opinion of the Economic and Social Committee, the opinion of the Committee of the Regions[6] and a European Parliament resolution,[7] on 13 December the Commission adopted a White Paper[8] on energy policy, which examined the general political context and market trends and proposed the broad lines of policy for the energy market, accompanied by a work programme and timetable.

354.   On 2 February the Committee of the Regions adopted an own-initiative opinion[9] on the 1994 Commission communication[10] on energy and economic and social cohesion.

---

[1]   Bull. 10-1995, point 1.3.126.
[2]   OJ C 17, 22.1.1996; Bull. 12-1995.
[3]   COM(94) 659; Bull. 1/2-1995, point 1.3.85.
[4]   Bull. 6-1995, point 1.3.113; OJ C 327, 7.12.1995; Bull. 11-1995, point 1.3.108.
[5]   OJ C 206, 11.8.1995; Bull. 6-1995, point 1.3.114.
[6]   Bull. 7/8-1995, points 1.3.104 and 1.3.105.
[7]   OJ C 287, 30.10.1995; Bull. 10-1995, point 1.3.128.
[8]   COM(95) 682; Bull. 12-1995.
[9]   Bull. 1/2-1995, point 1.3.86.
[10]   COM(93) 645; 1994 General Report, point 341.

Promotion of energy technology (Thermie) — technical coal research

355. Most of the activities covered by the Thermie programme continued under the fourth research and technological development (RTD) framework programme (1994-98) (→ point 235), notably under the specific programme on non-nuclear energy (JOULE-Thermie), which covers both the RTD (JOULE) and technological demonstration (Thermie II) sides. Following publication of the first call for proposals in December 1994, the Commission approved 151 demonstration projects involving a total of almost ECU 111 million, and 250 proposals for strategic and promotional activities amounting to ECU 26 million. The Commission also completed the action undertaken in the earlier Thermie programme,[1] produced various publications on the activities to promote energy technologies, and participated in the major events in Europe and non-Union countries, such as the Conference on Climate Change (→ point 504). The fifteenth Community Energy Centre, specializing in fossil fuels, was opened in Katowice (Poland). Finally, the Council continued its discussions on the proposal for a Regulation (Table II) providing further support for the promotion of European energy technology (1995-98) (Thermie II), on which Parliament adopted a resolution on 7 April.[2]

356. As the expiry of the ECSC Treaty approaches (→ point 1019), attention focused on continuing the coal research programme, in conjunction with the Community's other research programmes (→ point 231).

Promotion of energy efficiency (SAVE) and renewable energy sources (Altener)

357. On 20 September the Commission adopted a proposal for a Council Directive (Table II) to introduce rational planning techniques in the electricity and gas distribution sectors. The SAVE I programme,[3] which ended on 31 December, granted ECU 3.7 million to 44 projects in 1995, bringing the total financial support between 1991 and 1995 to ECU 25.1 million, shared between 250 projects. Under this programme, the aim of which is to promote the efficient use of electricity, on 20 December the Council agreed a common position on a draft Directive (Table II) on the development of energy efficiency standards for household refrigeration equipment.

---

[1] OJ L 185, 17.7.1990; Twenty-fourth General Report, point 608.
[2] OJ C 109, 1.5.1995; Bull. 4-1995, point 1.3.84.
[3] OJ L 307, 8.11.1991; Twenty-fifth General Report, point 781.

The SAVE II programme concerning the promotion of energy efficiency in the European Union was proposed by the Commission on 31 May (Table II). Under the Altener programme,[1] on 14 June the Commission granted ECU 7.9 million to 90 projects, bringing the total support over the period 1993-95 to ECU 19.1 million for 204 projects. In connection with energy consumption labelling, in May the Commission adopted two Directives on driers and washing machines respectively.

Regional and urban energy management (PERU)

358.   The Commission proposed that the pilot scheme on energy management at regional and urban level, started in 1989 with the objective of giving local authorities means of formulating and implementing energy policies close to citizens and targeted on rational use of energy and harnessing local resources, should be incorporated in the SAVE II programme as from 1996. This year the entire budget was allocated to supporting the establishment of over 40 urban or regional energy agencies.

Energy and environment

359.   In response to the Council's conclusions of December 1994,[2] the Commission proposed a set of options, at Community and national levels, for progressive limitation of emissions of greenhouse gases by 2005 and 2010. In 1995 the United Nations Framework Convention on Climate Change (→ point 504) enabled the European Union to play a mediating role between developed and developing countries on anthropogenic climate change. The Commission also continued to contribute to the fifth action programme on the environment (→ point 463), under which energy is one of the five target sectors.

Analyses and forecasts

360.   The Commission reviewed energy prospects up to 2020, backing up the White Paper on energy policy (→ point 353).

---

[1]   OJ L 235, 18.9.1993; Twenty-seventh General Report, point 292.
[2]   1994 General Report, point 1196.

Internal energy market

Natural gas and electricity

361. The proposals for Directives (Table I) on common rules for the internal market in electricity and natural gas were still under discussion at the end of the year.

362. As requested by the Council on 29 November 1994,[1] on 22 March the Commission adopted a working paper on the organization of the internal electricity market,[2] which paved the way for the conclusions adopted by the Council on 1 June,[3] in which the Council agreed with the Commission that the third-party access and single-buyer systems can co-exist only if certain essential requirements are met. Also, on 10 May the Commission adopted a working paper on small and very small electricity systems in the internal electricity market.[4]

Infrastructure and cohesion

363. The Commission continued its work on trans-European energy (gas and electricity) networks *(→ point 349).*

Standardization

364. Following the comprehensive approach to energy standardization, the Commission gave CEN-CENELEC independent mandates on photovoltaic solar energy systems and components, measurement standards for domestic light sources, domestic ovens and household water heater and hot water storage systems. In its communication of 30 October[5] on the broader use of standardization in Community policy, the Commission concluded that energy efficiency had to be an essential requirement of the new approach.

---

[1]   Bull. 11-1994, point 1.2.91; 1994 General Report, point 343.
[2]   Bull. 3-1995, point 1.3.90.
[3]   Bull. 6-1995, point 1.3.117.
[4]   Bull. 5-1995, point 1.3.64.
[5]   COM(95) 412.

Individual sectors

Oil

365.   On 20 December the Council adopted a Regulation (Table II) amending the registration system introduced for crude oil imports by Regulation (EEC) No 1893/79, which has already been extended several times.

Natural gas

366.   On 18 October the Commission adopted a communication[1] on gas supply and prospects in the Community which called for greater cooperation at Community level to enhance security of supply in the Community. The leading gas companies from Central and Eastern Europe were invited to a workshop on East-West gas interconnections held in June. A round-table discussion on the Yamal gas pipeline project in May was attended by gas companies from the Russian Federation, Germany and Poland, as well as by the EIB, the EBRD and the Commission. Information concerning the internal market in natural gas is provided in the 'Natural gas and electricity' (→ point 361) part of this section.

Solid fuels

367.   The Commission adopted a report[2] on the market in solid fuels in the Community in 1994 and the outlook for 1995. This was endorsed by the ECSC Consultative Committee.[3]

Electricity

368.   In addition to the projects carried out under the PHARE (→ point 824) and TACIS (→ point 869) programmes, considerable progress was made on interconnections between the electricity networks in the Middle East, as part of the peace process. Information concerning the internal market in electricity is provided in the 'Natural gas and electricity' (→ point 361) part of this section.

---

[1]   COM(95) 478; Bull. 10-1995, point 1.3.130.
[2]   Bull. 4-1995, point 1.3.86; Bull. 10-1995, point 1.3.131.
[3]   Bull. 7/8-1995, point 1.3.106; Bull. 10-1995, point 1.3.131.

Nuclear energy

369.   The Commission's standing working party on safe transport of radioactive materials approved its action plan up to the year 2000. Also, as
industrial cooperation in the nuclear energy field is a key component of the
global long-term approach to nuclear safety in Eastern Europe *(→ point
516)*, two forums were set up on this subject, one on nuclear training, the
other on in-service inspection of nuclear facilities.

Relations with third countries

European Energy Charter

370.   Following the signature of the European Energy Charter Treaty[1] by
the European Community and its Member States on 17 December 1994, on
20 September the Commission adopted a proposal for a Council and Commission Decision (ECSC, EC, Euratom) on the conclusion, by the European
Communities, of the Treaty (Table III) and of the Protocol on energy efficiency and related environmental aspects (Table III). The Economic and Social Committee adopted an own-initiative opinion on the European Energy
Charter Treaty on 25 October.[2]

371.   The Parties to the Agreement had decided to leave the Treaty open
for signature until 16 June. By then, 50 signatories of the European Energy
Charter, including all the European countries, the States of the former Soviet Union, Australia and Japan, had signed the Treaty and the Protocol.
On a joint proposal from the European Union and Russia, the Conference
decided to establish its Secretariat in Brussels. In this context, the European
Commission undertook to assist the Secretariat and to pre-fund its 1995 expenditure with an ECU 1 million loan, to be reimbursed in 1996. The Conference also designated a new Secretary-General, Mr Schütterle, who will
take office on 1 January 1996.

International cooperation

372.   International cooperation in the energy sector continued under the
Synergy and Thermie programmes and the energy sections of regional aid
and cooperation programmes such as PHARE *(→ point 824)* and TACIS

---

[1]   COM(94) 405; 1994 General Report, point 355.
[2]   Bull. 10-1995, point 1.3.132.

(→ point 869). On 23 May the Commission proposed converting the Synergy programme to promote international cooperation in the energy sector into a multiannual programme (Table II). On 17 December, an Energy Centre was inauguarated in Sofia.

373.   Energy was a key component in the White Paper to prepare for integration of the Central and Eastern European countries into the internal market (→ point 816). The Commission also proposed opening up the SAVE II programme to participants from these countries. Nuclear and non-nuclear energy account for some 6% of the annual budget for the PHARE programme.

374.   Under the TACIS programme (non-nuclear energy section), 27 projects involving a total cost of ECU 39 million were identified in the former Soviet Union as a whole, with the exception of Kazakhstan, Turkmenistan and Uzbekistan. In the nuclear field, ECU 56 million was shared between the Russian Federation and Ukraine, and a further ECU 37.5 million was granted to the action plan to close the Chernobyl power station. Discussions in the Council on proposed negotiating directives with a view to bilateral and nuclear cooperation agreements culminated in the adoption on 9 June of negotiating directives with a view to cooperation agreements on nuclear safety and fusion for Kazakhstan (Table III) and Ukraine (Table III). Cooperation agreements with Russia on thermonuclear fusion and nuclear safety were also negotiated.

375.   Projects in the Mediterranean region focused mainly on the regional, energy and urban environment action plan and on technical assistance to the Palestinian Energy Centre. Preparations were made for the Barcelona Conference (→ point 839) at a conference in Tunis on 27 and 28 March,[1] a follow-up meeting in Athens and a conference on private investment finance in Cairo.

376.   Activities in Latin America included training in modern energy management techniques, improved electricity-saving tools and improved demand forecasts in Brazil. On 4 December the Commission adopted negotiating directives with a view to a cooperation agreement between the European Atomic Energy Community and Argentina on the peaceful use of nuclear energy (Table III).

---

[1]   Bull. 3-1995, point 1.3.92.

377.   In Asia, training was given on modern energy management techniques in India and also in China, where two other schemes were organized, one on renewable sources, the other on nuclear safety.

378.   On 3 August the Council approved the conclusion, by the Commission, of a new Agreement on cooperation in the peaceful uses of nuclear energy with the USA to replace the 1960 Agreement which expired on 31 December (Table II). The approval procedure before the US Congress is now under way. This Agreement, which was signed on 7 November and is scheduled to enter into force at the beginning of 1996, aims at closer cooperation in fields such as the transfer of nuclear materials and equipment, research and development, and industrial and commercial activities. Parliament adopted a resolution on the same subject on 16 March.[1] A cooperation agreement with Canada on nuclear research and safety was signed on 17 June (→ point 908).

The Commission also sent the Council a proposal for a Decision with a view to accession by Euratom to the International Convention on the Management of Radioactive Wastes (→ point 516).

Dialogue between producers and consumers

379.   The Commission co-sponsored and took part in the fourth International Energy Conference in Puerto La Cruz (Venezuela) from 25 to 27 September.

Euratom Supply Agency

380.   In 1995 supplies of nuclear fuels to users in the Union followed the same pattern as in previous years.[2] Deliveries of both natural and enriched uranium continued primarily on the basis of multiannual contracts, with only a small proportion of requirements covered by spot contracts. As in the past, the Agency pursued a policy aiming at diversification of sources of supply and at prices reflecting production costs.

381.   Since 1 January the Euratom Treaty (particularly Chapter VI) has applied to supplies to users in Sweden and Finland, thus bringing a substantial increase in the average annual requirements for reactors in the Union for the period 1995 to 2004. Users in the new Member States communicated to

---

[1]   OJ C 89, 10.4.1995; Bull. 3-1995, point 1.3.91.
[2]   1994 General Report, point 361; Twenty-seventh General Report, point 298.

the Commission their nuclear supply contracts in force on 1 January with the result that, pursuant to the first paragraph of Article 105 of the Euratom Treaty, the provisions of the Treaty may not be invoked to prevent implementation of these contracts.

382.   As in 1994,[1] the former Soviet Union was the Union's chief external source of supplies of nuclear fuels. When exercising its right to conclude supply contracts, the Agency continued to apply, flexibly and pragmatically, the policy initiated in 1992 with the abovementioned general objectives of diversifying sources of supply and charging market prices.

383.   On 15 September[2] the Court of First Instance dismissed an action brought by a Portuguese natural uranium producer with the twin objectives of gaining recognition of preference for disposing of Community output, provided it is available at a reasonable price, and challenging the simplified procedure introduced by Article 5 bis of the Agency Regulation of 5 May 1960, as amended in 1975.[3] At the same time, the Court stressed that the Agency has the discretion to refuse to conclude supply contracts which could run counter to attainment of the objectives of the Euratom Treaty.

State aid to the coal industry

384.   In 1995 the Commission authorized State aid granted, under Decision 3632/93/ECSC,[4] by Germany[5] and France[6] in 1994 and 1995. Also, on 14 December it adopted its annual report on application of the Community rules on State aid to the coal industry in 1993.

---

[1]   1994 General Report, point 362.
[2]   Cases T-458/93 and T-523/93, *Empresa Nacional de Uranio* v *Commission*.
[3]   OJ 32, 11.5.1960; OJ L 193, 25.7.1975.
[4]   OJ L 329, 30.12.1993.
[5]   Bull. 4-1995, point 1.3.87; Bull. 7/8-1995, point 1.3.107.
[6]   Bull. 7/8-1995, points 1.3.108 and 1.3.109.

Section 14

Transport

Priority activities and objectives

385.   Substantial progress was made on the common transport policy in 1995, mainly as regards: integrating the trans-European transport networks and interoperability (in particular for the trans-European high-speed rail system) (→ point 342); promoting research and development applied to transport (the setting-up of task forces to determine priorities and to improve the targeting of efforts and the coordination of research activities (→ point 252);) improving safety (in particular in shipping and inland transport). Consolidation of the single market in transport also continued (inland waterways, rail transport).

On 12 July the Commission adopted an action programme[1] laying down the guidelines for a common approach to transport for the period 1995 to 2000 and following up the 1992 White Paper on the future development of the common transport policy.[2] The guidelines adopted cover the following areas: improving quality by developing integrated transport systems based on advanced technologies which also contribute to environmental and safety objectives; improving the functioning of the single market in order to promote efficiency, choice and the user-friendly provision of transport services while safeguarding social standards; broadening the external dimension by improving transport links between the European Union and third countries and the access of Community businesses to transport markets in other parts of the world. The programme was welcomed by the Economic and Social Committee on 22 November.[3]

The Commission also began a general study of the various options for the development of a range of quality public transport services and presented the results of its analysis in a Green Paper on passenger transport ('The citizens' network') (→ point 404). On 20 December it also adopted a Green Paper entitled 'Towards fair and efficient pricing in transport' (→ point 389).

In the field of external relations (→ points 415 et seq.), the European Union started negotiations with a number of countries to conclude agreements on

---

[1]   COM(95) 302; Bull. 7/8-1995, point 1.3.111.
[2]   COM(92) 494; Twenty-sixth General Report, point 643; Supplement 3/93 — Bull.
[3]   Bull. 11-1995, point 1.3.110.

land-based transport and air transport and strengthened its ties with the countries of Central and Eastern Europe in the context of the pre-accession strategy.

Infrastructure and traffic management and navigation systems

386.   As regards the trans-European networks *(→ points 341 et seq.)*, the Commission decided on 18 September to grant, under Regulation (EC) No 2236/95, financial support totalling ECU 240 million to projects of common interest and feasibility studies (1995 budget), more than half of it to rail and combined transport projects. Most of this support went to the 14 priority projects approved by the Essen European Council and to traffic management and interoperability schemes.

387.   The Commission set up a high-level working party to draw up an action plan for the deployment of a satellite navigation service for Europe. Parliament welcomed the Commission's approach[1] in a resolution of 19 January.[2]

388.   The use of telematics *(→ point 439)* in road transport was the subject of a resolution adopted by the Council on 28 September.[3] The European Parliament and the Economic and Social Committee also adopted a resolution[4] and an own-initiative opinion[5] on the communication from the Commission on telematics applications for transport in Europe.[6]

Transport and the environment

389.   On 20 December the Commission adopted a Green Paper entitled 'Towards fair and efficient pricing in transport' on the real costs of transport,[7] including external costs, emphasizing that, against the background of atmospheric pollution, congestion, accidents, noise and the infrastructure costs to which they give rise, the real costs of goods transport and personal mobility are not always taken into account in decisions taken by users.

---

[1]   COM(94) 248; 1994 General Report, point 366.
[2]   OJ C 43, 20.2.1995; Bull. 1/2-1995, point 1.3.88.
[3]   OJ C 264, 11.10.1995; Bull. 9-1995, point 1.3.74.
[4]   OJ C 183, 17.7.1995; Bull. 6-1995, point 1.3.121.
[5]   Bull. 10-1995, point 1.3.136.
[6]   COM(94) 469; 1994 General Report, point 414.
[7]   COM(95) 691; Bull. 12-1995.

390.   On 6 October the Council adopted a common position on the proposal for a Directive (Table II) on occupational qualifications for the carriage of dangerous goods by road *(→ point 398)*, rail *(→ point 394)* and inland waterway.

Research and technological development

391.   Apart from the specific programme of research and technological development, including demonstration, in the transport sector (1994-98), which is dealt with in Section 8 (Research and technology) of this chapter *(→ point 252)*, the Commission set up five of the eight task forces planned for transport. The task forces (new-generation aircraft, car of tomorrow, maritime systems of the future, railway systems of the future, transport intermodality) are intended to refocus research activities on priority areas so as to allow more effective coordination between transport policy, industrial policy and research policy.

Inland transport

Rail transport

392.   On 8 December the Council adopted a common position on the adoption of a Directive on the interoperability of the trans-European high-speed railway system *(→ point 342)*. On 19 June it adopted Directive 95/18/EC (Table II) on the licensing of railway undertakings, which lays down the broad lines of a Community licensing system setting out the criteria and procedures for granting licences, and Directive 95/19/EC (Table II) on the allocation of railway infrastructure capacities and the charging of infrastructure fees. On 19 June it also adopted a resolution on the development of rail transport and combined transport.[1]

393.   On 19 July the Commission adopted a communication on the development of the Community's railways[2] accompanied by a proposal for a Directive (Table II) amending Directive 91/440/EEC to open up access to railway infrastructure for all goods transport operations and for international passenger transport services.

---

[1]   OJ C 169, 5.7.1995; Bull. 6-1995, point 1.3.124.
[2]   OJ C 321, 1.12.1995, COM(95) 337; Bull. 7/8-1995, point 1.3.112.

394. With regard to the carriage of dangerous goods by rail (Table II), on 7 December the Council adopted a common position on the adoption of a Directive on the approximation of the laws of the Member States in this sector, providing for the uniform application of national and international railway transport safety standards.

Road transport

395. On 13 February the Commission adopted a proposal for a Council Directive (Table II) continuing the process of liberalizing and harmonizing the rules on the use of vehicles hired without drivers for the carriage of goods by road.

396. On 7 December the Council adopted a common position on a proposal for a Directive (Table II) on legislative consolidation of Community laws governing access to the profession of road haulage operator.

397. In the social field, the Commission continued its discussions with employer and labour representatives on the possibility of extending the common rules to cover the working/service time of road vehicle drivers and considered possible strengthening of the basic and further vocational training of drivers. The Council welcomed these activities in a resolution of 14 March. [1]

398. The Community regulations on the carriage of dangerous goods were significantly improved as a result of the adoption by the Council, on 6 October, of Directive 95/50/EC on uniform procedures for checks on the transport of dangerous goods by road (Table II).

399. On 7 December the Council reached political agreement on the adoption of a Directive amending Directive 91/439/EEC to introduce, from 1 July 1996, an optional Community model driving licence in credit card format (Table II). On 8 September the Commission also adopted a proposal for a Council Directive (Table II) on the approximation of the laws of the Member States on the technical inspection of motor vehicles and their trailers. On 25 October the Commission adopted Regulation (EC) No 2479/95 [2] (Table II) adapting to technical progress Council Regulation (EEC) No 3821/85 on recording equipment in road transport and, on 21 November,

---

[1] Bull. 3-1995, point 1.3.98.
[2] OJ L 256, 26.10.1995; Bull. 10-1995, point 1.3.135.

an amended proposal for a Regulation amending Regulation (EEC) No 3821/85 and Directive 85/599/EEC (Table II).

400.   With regard to technical harmonization, on 8 December the Council adopted a common position on a proposal for a Directive (Table II) laying down the maximum authorized weights and dimensions of certain road vehicles travelling in the Community.

401.   On 25 October the Economic and Social Committee delivered an own-initiative opinion on infrastructure costs for the carriage of goods by road.[1]

Inland waterway transport

402.   On 23 May the Commission adopted a communication on a common policy on the organization of the inland waterway transport market and supporting measures[2] in which it proposes a common overall approach to the future organization of the market and to scrapping which should allow more flexibility, create a better balance between supply and demand and enable prices to move in line with market rules. The communication is accompanied by a proposal for a Council Directive (Table II) on the systems of chartering and pricing in national and international inland waterway transport in the Community; a proposal for a Council Regulation (Table II) amending Council Regulation (EEC) No 1107/70 on State aid; and a proposal for a Council Regulation (Table II) amending Regulation (EEC) No 1101/89 on structural improvements in inland waterway transport to reduce capacity by 15% over the period 1996-98. On 7 December the Council approved the Commission's approach,[3] stressing the need to back up the liberalization of the market with an increase in measures to reduce overcapacity. On 5 December the Council adopted Regulation (EC) No 2819/95 (Table II) amending Regulation (EEC) No 1101/89 to create a legal basis to allow for a Community financial contribution to the national scrapping funds of the Member States concerned (ECU 5 million in 1995). On 8 December the Commission adopted Regulation (EC) No 2839/95[4] laying down rules for the allocation of the ECU 5 million.

403.   With a view to establishing freedom to provide services, on 10 May the Commission adopted a proposal for a Regulation (Table II) on common

---

[1]   Bull. 10-1995, point 1.3.137.
[2]   COM(95) 199; Bull. 5-1995, point 1.3.72.
[3]   Bull. 12-1995.
[4]   OJ L 296, 9.12.1995; Bull. 12-1995.

rules applicable to the transport of goods and passengers by inland waterway between Member States. On 8 December the Council adopted a Directive (Table II) on harmonization of the conditions for obtaining national boatmasters' certificates for inland waterway vessels for the carriage of goods and passengers.

Urban transport

404. On 29 November the Commission adopted a Green Paper on public passenger transport ('The citizens' network'),[1] the aim of which is to provoke broad discussion on the use of public transport as an alternative to cars. It proposes relevant areas of possible action for better integration of passenger transport systems.

Multimodal transport

405. On 19 July the Commission adopted a proposal for a Council Regulation (Table II) amending Regulation (EEC) No 1107/70 on the granting of aids for transport by rail, road and inland waterway to extend for two years the arrangement authorizing aid for combined transport and to simplify the procedure.

Sea transport

Implementation of the common policy

406. On 5 July the Commission adopted a communication on short sea shipping[2] which identifies three main areas of action: improving the quality and efficiency of this type of transport, improving port infrastructure and port efficiency, and including short sea shipping in the general framework of external relations. The Council approved the Commission's approach on 8 December.[3] In addition, the first report on the application of Regulation (EEC) No 3577/92[4] on the application of the principle to provide services to maritime transport within Member States was adopted by the Commission on 6 September.[5] Lastly, on 8 December the Council adopted a Direc-

---

[1] COM(95) 601; Bull. 11-1995, point 1.3.111.
[2] COM(95) 317; Bull. 7/8-1995, point 1.3.117.
[3] Bull. 12-1995.
[4] OJ L 364, 12.12.1992; Twenty-sixth General Report, point 670.
[5] COM(95) 383.

tive on statistical returns in respect of carriage of goods and passengers by sea (→ *point 87*).

Safety at sea

407. Under the action programme for a common policy on maritime safety,[1] on 21 June the Commission adopted a new proposal for a Directive (Table II) on marine equipment. On 8 December the Council adopted Regulation (EC) No 3015/95 (Table II) on the safety management of ro/ro passenger vessels to establish an efficient system of clear, detailed safety procedures. On 19 June it adopted Directive 95/21/EC (Table II) concerning the enforcement, in respect of shipping using Community ports and sailing in the waters under the jurisdiction of the Member States, of international standards for ship safety, pollution prevention and shipboard living and working conditions.

Social conditions

408. In April the Commission adopted a recommendation for a Council Decision on the negotiations for the revision of the 1978 IMO (International Maritime Organization) Convention on Standards of Training, Certification and Watchkeeping for Seafarers and the adoption of a new IMO Convention on Fishing Vessel Personnel. The two Conventions were concluded in July at the IMO Conference and signed by 68 countries. Most of the Commission's proposals were taken into consideration in the Conventions adopted.

Air transport

Implementation of the common policy

409. The Commission continued its activities under its action programme entitled 'The way forward for civil aviation in Europe',[2] which was the subject of a European Parliament resolution of 14 February[3] and an opinion of the Economic and Social Committee of 22 February.[4] It also continued to apply the rules contained in the third package of liberalization measures,

---

[1]   COM(93) 66; Twenty-seventh General Report, point 322.
[2]   COM(94) 218; 1994 General Report, point 384.
[3]   OJ C 56, 6.3.1995; Bull. 1/2-1995, point 1.3.93.
[4]   OJ C 110, 2.5.1995; Bull. 1/2-1995, point 1.3.94.

which entered into force on 1 January 1993.[1] On the protection of passengers' rights, on 20 December the Commission adopted a proposal for a Council Regulation (Table II) on the liability of air carriers in the event of an accident.

Air traffic management

410.   On 5 July the Commission adopted a communication on congestion and crisis in air traffic[2] proposing, as a short-term action plan, to reduce air traffic delays by making optimum use of the available air traffic control capacity. The communication was welcomed by the European Parliament on 16 November.[3] In a resolution[4] of 17 November, the Council called on the Member States and the Commission to coordinate their activities in the framework of the European Organization for the Safety of Air Navigation (Eurocontrol).

Air safety

411.   In order to facilitate implementation of the mutual recognition and free movement of aeronautical products and services, the Commission continued its work on the preparation of an overall regulatory framework for the safety of civil aviation on the basis of Regulation (EEC) No 3922/91[5] and cooperated closely with the Joint Aviation Authorities (JAAs). Similarly, on 20 June[6] the Council invited the Member States to expedite work on the joint certification of aeronautical products.

Social conditions

412.   In a resolution of 14 March[7] on relocation in air transport, the Council drew attention to the need to consider the social impact of recent developments in the air transport market.

---

[1]   OJ L 240, 24.8.1992; Twenty-sixth General Report, point 674.
[2]   COM(95) 318; Bull. 7/8-1995, point 1.3.118.
[3]   OJ C 323, 4.12.1995; Bull. 11-1995, point 1.3.120.
[4]   OJ C 317, 28.11.1995; Bull. 11-1995 1.3.121.
[5]   OJ L 373, 31.12.1991; Twenty-fifth General Report, point 726.
[6]   Bull. 6-1995, point 1.3.132.
[7]   Bull. 3-1995, point 1.3.101.

Airports

413. On 7 December the Council reached political agreement on a common position on a proposal for a Directive (Table II) on access to the ground-handling services market in Community airports. Furthermore, on 21 April[1] the Committee of the Regions adopted an own-initiative opinion on the guidelines for the trans-European airport network and stressed the importance of using regional airports' spare capacities and interconnecting with other modes of transport.

State aid

414. In the shipping sector, on 1 February the Commission approved the Danish Government's aid scheme for maritime training. On 7 June it decided to close the investigation procedure concerning the State aid granted by the Spanish authorities to the Golfo de Vizcaya Ferries company. With regard to inland transport, on 28 July[2] the Commission approved the Dutch Government's aid scheme for the promotion of telematics. On 20 September and 18 October[3] it also decided not to raise any objections to the aid granted by that government as aid for investment in combined transport equipment or to a development programme for inland waterways. It authorized French aid on 18 October[4] for the reorganization of road transport and on 14 November for inland waterways.[5] Lastly, it opened proceedings under Article 93(2) of the EC Treaty in respect of the Italian Government's aid scheme for the carriage of goods by road for hire or reward.[6] In the air transport sector, the Commission adopted two Decisions authorizing payments of the second instalment of aid to TAP[7] and Air France[8] following Decisions taken in 1994,[9] which demanded that the actual progress made in the restructuring programmes should be checked before successive instalments are granted. On 20 December[10] the Commission also decided to raise no objections to the payment of the third instalment of aid to Aer Lingus. In addition, on 19 July[11] the Commission authorized a capital increase for AOM and declared the aid granted to airlines by the region of Sardinia to

---

[1] Bull. 4-1995, point 1.3.83.
[2] Bull. 7/8-1995, point 1.3.121.
[3] Bull. 9-1995, point 1.3.80; Bull. 10-1995, point 1.3.141.
[4] Bull. 10-1995, point 1.3.142.
[5] Bull. 11-1995, point 1.3.125.
[6] Bull. 10-1995, point 1.3.140.
[7] OJ C 154, 21.6.1995; Bull. 4-1995, point 1.3.93.
[8] Bull. 6-1995, point 1.3.136.
[9] Decisions of 21.12.1993 (OJ L 54, 25.2.1994), 6.7.1994 (OJ L 279, 28.10.1994) and 27.7.1994 (OJ L 254, 30.9.1994) respectively.
[10] Bull. 12-1995.
[11] Bull. 7/8-1995, point 1.3.120.

be unlawful. On 26 July the Commission ordered the repayment of aid unlawfully granted to VLM.[1] With regard to Lufthansa's privatization programme, it considered that the German State had acted in the same way as a private investor and, on 10 March, decided to raise no objections. Similarly, on 19 July[2] the Commission adopted a Decision confirming Sabena as a Community carrier following the acquisition of holdings by Swissair, considering that the subscription of new shares in Sabena by the Belgian State was a normal commercial transaction since Swissair was making an equivalent investment under the same conditions. On 29 November the Commission took the view that the special depreciation scheme for aircraft registered in Germany was a specific and not a general fiscal measure and consequently called on the German authorities to cease applying it.

International cooperation

415.   On the basis of an amended recommendation taking account of the implementation by the Swiss authorities of the Alpine initiative,[3] on 14 March the Council authorized the Commission to open negotiations with Switzerland (→ point 813) on road, rail, air and combined transport (Table III).

416.   On 26 April the Commission adopted a recommendation for a Council Decision on the opening of negotiations with the USA on an Air Transport Agreement (Table III). On 20 June the Council adopted its conclusions on relations with the USA in this sector[4] in which it stressed in particular the need to strengthen the competitiveness of carriers. In a resolution of 7 April,[5] Parliament expressed its opinion on the bilateral Open Skies Agreements concluded between some Member States and the USA. The Commission also negotiated multilateral Agreements on the mutual recognition of aircraft and aeronautical products with the USA, Australia, Canada and New Zealand.

417.   On 10 April the Council authorized the Commission to open negotiations with the Republic of Croatia (Table III) on the conclusion of the same type of Transport Agreement as exists with Slovenia (Table III). On 29 June it authorized the Commission to negotiate an Additional Protocol to the Transport Agreement between the Community and the Republic of

---

[1]   OJ L 267, 9.11.1995.
[2]   OJ L 239, 7.10.1995.
[3]   1994 General Report, point 395.
[4]   Bull. 6-1995, point 1.3.135.
[5]   OJ C 109, 1.5.1995; Bull. 4-1995, point 1.3.91.

Slovenia (Table III) to ensure the non-discriminatory treatment of all lorries, regardless of their country of origin, in haulage operations through Austria. On 14 November the Commission adopted a recommendation for a Decision concerning an Agreement with the former Yugoslav Republic of Macedonia.

418.   With regard to the associated countries of Central Europe and the Baltic States, on 7 December the Council adopted negotiating directives authorizing the Commission to negotiate, firstly, an Agreement to facilitate occasional passenger transport services by bus and coach covering almost all the countries of Central and Eastern Europe (Table III) and, secondly, an Agreement on the carriage of goods concerning transit through Bulgaria, Hungary and Romania, the main aim of which is to facilitate transport between Greece and the rest of the Community (Table III). On 1 March the Commission also adopted a recommendation for a Council Decision to negotiate Air Transport Agreements with Bulgaria, the Czech Republic, Hungary, Poland, Romania and Slovakia *(→ point 820)* to create the conditions for the gradual liberalization of air transport services.

Section 15

Information society, telecommunications

Priority activities and objectives

419.   The information society and the telecommunications networks for bringing it about were presented in the Commission's White Paper on growth, competitiveness and employment (→ points 24 et seq.) as one of the main routes for leading Europe into the 21st century. The priority work in 1995 in this field was part of the implementation of the Commission's July 1994 action plan 'Europe's way to the information society'.[1] At international level, in February the Commission organized a G7 Ministerial Conference on the Information Society,[2] in the course of which certain projects were demonstrated, general principles were identified to govern the accelerated liberalization of worldwide telecommunications, and pilot programmes were launched in various fields. The European Council, meeting in Cannes on 26 and 27 June, emphasized the development potential of new growth sectors and the potential for job creation in promoting the information society and called for work to continue on establishing the regulatory framework that will enable it to develop, while taking care to maintain cultural diversity and bearing in mind the objective of equal access to these new services.[3] As regards telecommunications, the Commission accordingly adopted all the legislative instruments required for amending the regulatory framework with a view to the complete and rapid liberalization of all services and infrastructures by 1998. Several decisions were taken on initiatives in the field of trans-European networks (guidelines on developing ISDN networks, financial regulation, overall proposal on a methodology for meeting the needs of the information society) (→ points 345 et seq.).

Information society

420.   Under the Commission's 1994 action plan 'Europe's way to the information society',[4] several fields linked to the information society were tackled.

---

[1]   COM(94) 347; 1994 General Report, point 397.
[2]   Bull. 1/2-1995, point 1.3.97. The various topics discussed at this Conference led to the adoption of a declaration by the Presidency, which is given in full in point 2.2.1 of Bull. 1/2-1995.
[3]   Bull. 6-1995, points 1.3.137 and I.8.
[4]   COM(94) 347; 1994 General Report, point 397.

421. The Council and Parliament adopted a Directive on the protection of individuals with regard to the processing of personal data *(→ point 135).*

422. In connection with the information services market, on 30 June the Commission adopted a proposal for establishing a multiannual programme (1996-99) INFO 2000 (Table II), to stimulate the development of a European multimedia content industry and a multimedia information market, on which the Council reached agreement on 27 November.

423. Since the situation regarding educational multimedia in Europe is of particular importance, a specific task force was set up in March in the Commission to draw up a plan of action to stimulate this market and improve the efficiency of European research.

424. Because of the need to intensify the analysis of the economic and social aspects associated with developing information infrastructures, the Commission surrounded itself with think tanks and coordinating bodies. A group of high-level experts on the social and societal aspects of the information society held its first meeting in May. In addition, in order to raise the awareness of the general public and to inform it, an Information Society Project Office (ISPO) was established. It is intended to act as a single interface between the Commission and the parties which initiate projects in various areas in the information society. Its three main roles are: to provide information and raise awareness (in particular by updating catalogues of projects which are either planned or already being implemented), liaison between various sectors, and to act as a pointer towards sources of financial aid. At international level, the Commission organized the G7 Ministerial Conference in February, and also a series of conferences with the Central and East European countries, the Mediterranean basin and Latin America.

425. The Commission defined an approach to the legal framework for information society services, under which any regulations concerning the new services (tele-teaching, tele-purchasing, tele-medicine, etc.) must be embodied in the legal system of the single market, and projects must be designed to avoid any risk of refragmenting the area without borders, of over-regulating these services or of incompatibility in regulations which might prejudice the expansion of these services. In addition to the Green Paper on copyright *(→ point 132),* the Commission initiated analyses on certain regulatory aspects, such as the transparency and cohesion of future national draft legislation concerning the single market, legal protection of encoded signals, commercial communications and pluralism in the media. In addition, questions on encouraging the expansion of new audiovisual services, fostering cultural identities and linguistic diversity and on the implications for the protection of the public good will be studied in a Green Paper on the expansion of new audiovisual services.

426.   Following the February G7 meeting (→ point 456), some 15 pilot projects were selected, bearing on topics such as telematics applications in health and education, the citizen and information in the city and in the region, support for cooperation between enterprises, trade with the Central and East European countries and the non-Community countries in the Mediterranean basin, and Internet user networks. An information society forum, composed of 125 members representing the groups concerned, was established in February by the Commission. It constitutes a body in which the main topics concerning the information society are discussed, including the social, societal, cultural and linguistic aspects.

427.   In a communication adopted on 8 November,[1] accompanied by a proposal for a Council Decision (Table II), the Commission suggested that the linguistic dimension of the information society should be developed.

428.   Lastly, in the field of intellectual property, the Commission adopted a Green Paper on the possible effects of developing new technologies on copyright and related rights (→ point 132).

Telecommunications policy

Legislative aspects

429.   Following the Council's conclusions of 16 June[2] and 28 September 1994,[3] the Commission forwarded a Green Paper on the liberalization of the infrastructure for telecommunications and cable television networks. The first part of this Green Paper,[4] which had been adopted on 25 October 1994 and on which the Council had adopted a resolution on 29 June,[5] had established the general principle of free choice of infrastructure for the services which were already exposed to competition and laid down a timetable for liberalizing the infrastructure, which was adopted by the Council on 17 November 1994. In the second part, adopted on 25 January,[6] the Commission presented the regulatory questions relating to liberalizing the infrastruc-

---

[1]   COM(95) 486; Bull. 11-1995, point 1.3.126.
[2]   Twenty-seventh General Report, point 341.
[3]   1994 General Report, point 397.
[4]   COM(94) 440; 1994 General Report, point 399.
[5]   Bull. 6-1995, point 1.3.138.
[6]   COM(94) 682; Bull. 1/2-1995, point 1.3.101.

ture and initiated a public debate on these questions, the outcome of which it presented in a communication[1] dated 3 May. In a resolution dated 18 September[2] on the future regulatory framework for the infrastructure, the Council emphasized the importance of certain key elements of the regulatory framework, in particular the maintenance and development of the universal service, interconnection of the networks and the granting of licences.

430. In order to speed up liberalization, on 4 April the Commission adopted a communication[3] on the status and implementation of Directive 90/388/EEC on competition in the markets for telecommunications services.[4] It subsequently adopted three Directives, based on Article 90 of the EC Treaty, amending this Directive so as gradually to extend its field of application. The first,[5] which had been approved on 21 December 1994 and was formally adopted on 18 October 1995,[6] liberalizes the use of cable television networks for providing telecommunications services (other than voice telephony) from 1 January 1996.[7] The second, which was approved on 21 June[8] and formally adopted on 20 December,[9] concerns the liberalization on 1 January 1996 of mobile and personal communications. The third, which was approved on 19 July, provides for the complete liberalization of voice telephony and telecommunications infrastructures on 1 January 1998.[10] The Commission's Green Paper on a common approach in the field of mobile and personal communications, which was adopted in 1994,[11] was also the subject of a Parliament resolution dated 19 May[12] and a Council resolution of 29 June.[13]

431. With regard to harmonization, on 19 July the Commission adopted a proposal for a Directive on interconnection in telecommunications with regard to ensuring universal service and interoperability through application of the principles of open network provision (ONP) (Table I) *(→ point 429).*

---

[1]   COM(95) 158; Bull. 5-1995, point 1.3.79.
[2]   OJ C 258, 3.10.1995; Bull. 9-1995, point 1.3.82.
[3]   COM(95) 113; Bull. 4-1995, point 1.3.94.
[4]   OJ L 192, 24.7.1990; Twenty-fourth General Report, point 312.
[5]   OJ C 76, 28.3.1995; Bull. 12-1994, point 1.2.41.
[6]   OJ L 256, 26.10.1995; Bull. 10-1995, point 1.3.43.
[7]   Commission Directive amending Directive 90/388/EEC with regard to the abolition of the restrictions on the use of cable television networks for the provision of already liberalized telecommunications services.
[8]   OJ C 197, 1.8.1995.
[9]   Bull. 12-1995.
[10] OJ C 263, 10.10.1995; Bull. 7/8-1995, point 1.3.126.
[11] COM(94) 145; 1994 General Report, point 400.
[12] OJ C 151, 19.6.1995; Bull. 5-1995, point 1.3.82.
[13] OJ C 188, 22.7.1995; Bull. 6-1995, point 1.3.139.

432.   As regards personal communications by satellite, on 8 November the Commission adopted a proposal for a European Parliament and Council Decision (Table I) with the aim of establishing actions at Community level in this field. On 17 February,[1] Parliament adopted a resolution on the communication which the Commission had forwarded on 10 June 1994[2] on space segment capacity in satellite communications.

433.   In order to provide the general public with an affordable and high-quality telephone service when competition is introduced into this sector, on 13 December the Council and the European Parliament adopted Directive 95/62/EC relating to voice telephony in the ONP context (Table I). On 14 November the Commission proposed a Directive updating the existing ONP provisions and the Directives relating to leased lines. It also adopted, on 10 October,[3] a communication on the future development of the telephone directories market.

434.   On 14 November the Commission adopted a proposal for a European Parliament and Council Directive on a common framework for general authorizations and individual licences in the telecommunications services sector. On 6 December it adopted a proposal for a Directive on coding concerning satellite telecommunications terminal equipment, including mutual recognition of the conformity and applicability of such equipment. (Table I).

435.   Further progress was made in the field of trans-European networks in the telecommunications sector (→ point 345). A Decision proposing guidelines concerning the rapid deployment of Euro-ISDN (integrated services digital network)[4] and the provision of a number of basic services and applications was adopted by the European Parliament and the Council on 9 November (→ point 346). It lays down three priorities: to promote Euro-ISDN for SMEs and public bodies, to make test equipment available at reasonable prices, and to improve access to cheaper terminal equipment and applications software. In addition, on 18 September the Council adopted the Financial Regulation on trans-European networks (→ point 340), which lays down the general rules for the granting of Community financial aid, as from 1996, for projects of common interest which promote access, interconnection and interoperability of networks in order to meet users' needs. In addition, on 31 May the Commission forwarded a communication[5] on a

[1]   OJ C 56, 6.3.1995; Bull. 1/2-1995, point 1.3.103.
[2]   COM(94) 210; 1994 General Report, point 401.
[3]   COM(95) 431; Bull. 10-1995, point 1.3.144.
[4]   COM(93) 347; Twenty-seventh General Report, point 346.
[5]   COM(95) 224; Bull. 5-1995, point 1.3.78.

methodology for the implementation of information society applications (tele-working, health care, education, etc.), together with a proposal for a European Parliament and Council Decision (Table I) on a series of general guidelines for trans-European telecommunications networks (TEN-Telecom) (support networks, services and generic applications).

Technological aspects

436.   The implementation of the specific R&TD 'ACTS'[1] programme for advanced technologies and communications services involved a large number of tests, in particular on the basis of the high-speed server infrastructures provided by the public and private sectors at national level. ACTS is based on the work done under the RACE[2] programme, which was completed in 1995 and speeded up standardization and the coherent deployment of advanced digital communications and dissemination services. In addition, some special projects to assist the networking of small and medium-sized businesses in less-developed regions enabled such businesses to become more involved in the fourth R&TD framework programme (→ point 231). Similar support was given to Central and Eastern Europe under the 'Copernicus' programme. Special projects were also undertaken to encourage tele-working. Lastly, European cooperation in the field of telecommunications research remained a dominant theme of the COST programme .

Telematics applications

437.   The call for proposals in December 1994[3] for the new 'Telematics applications' programme (1994-98)[4] under the fourth R&TD framework programme (→ point 231), which aims to involve users in all stages of the projects and give priority to their requirements, aroused great interest and led to the selection of 304 projects and support operations calling for Community finance of ECU 424 million. Three further calls for proposals were issued in 1995[5] and led to the establishment of firm partnerships between users and suppliers, for example for urban, regional and rural networks. Telematics applications play a central role in the development of the information society. The programme consists of 12 sections (→ points 438 et seq.).

---

[1]   Decision 94/572/EC — OJ L 222, 26.8.1994; 1994 General Report, point 409.
[2]   OJ L 16, 21.1.1988; Twenty-second General Report, point 404.
[3]   OJ L 357, 15.12.1994; 1994 General Report, point 411.
[4]   1994 General Report, point 411; Twenty-seventh General Report, point 351.
[5]   OJ C 64, 15.3.1995; OJ C 240, 15.9.1995.

Public authorities

438. A series of accompanying measures initiated in 1994[1] made it possible in 1995 to publicize both the results of the projects and the experience acquired. At the same time, the first call for proposals for telematics for public authorities led to the selection of 16 projects and three assistance schemes calling for ECU 28 million of Community finance.

Transport

439. On 28 September the Council adopted a resolution on the use of telematics in the road transport sector *(→ point 343)* and on 29 June the European Parliament adopted a resolution on the use of telematics in all modes of transport.[2] Following the Council resolution and the communication from the Commission,[3] a high-level working party on 'global navigation satellite systems' was set up. Following the call for proposals in December 1994, 80 proposals were selected, involving Community finance of ECU 135 million. In addition, the 66 DRIVE II projects under the third R&TD framework programme were completed in 1995.

Research networks

440. Following the call for proposals in December 1994, 10 new projects were started. They cover various fields relating to 'computer-assisted teamwork' and their purpose is to set up a powerful communications network for research workers, based on Internet technologies. One of the most important projects is a joint scheme with the 'Information technology' programme to improve the interconnection of networks in universities and national research institutes.

Education and training

441. The 30 projects and 12 accompanying measures under the third R&TD framework programme were completed and the four trans-European demonstration projects begun in 1994 were on the way to completion at the end of the year.[4] The call for proposals of December 1994 led to the

---

[1]   1994 General Report, point 413.
[2]   Bull. 6-1995, point 1.3.121.
[3]   COM(94) 469; 1994 General Report, point 414.
[4]   1994 General Report, point 416.

selection of 23 research projects. In addition, substantial support was given to the task force on multimedia educational software (→ *point 226)*.

Libraries

442. In 1995, 14 new projects and six concerted actions were launched, covering internal library systems adapted for network use, telematics applications for interconnected integrated library services, and library services for access to networked information resources. The concerted actions concerned *inter alia* national libraries. Two new concerted programmes were launched in the fields of public libraries and multimedia for music. In addition, about a third of the 51 projects and studies started under the third R&TD framework programme were on the way to completion at the end of the year.

Urban and rural areas

443. Five accompanying measures were launched to investigate the impact of tele-working and tele-services in an urban environment, thus complementing the 'Rural areas' scheme under the third R&TD framework programme and providing further food for thought on employment. In addition, dissemination of the results of these studies and of the preceding action was assisted by the support of networks for cooperation between local authorities, such as 'Télérégions et Télécités', which covers 57 towns. Following the first call for proposals in the new sector (extended to urban areas in the fourth R&TD framework programme), 32 projects were selected.

Health

444. Most of the 42 projects resulting from the R&TD framework programme were completed. Following the call for proposals in December 1994, 70 new projects were launched, involving Community finance of ECU 77 million, relating to the development of regional networks to provide better integration and continuity of care, cooperation among staff specializing in fields of importance for public health and interoperability of tele-medicine services at the European level. In addition, work was started on feasibility studies and activities which contribute to the development of the information society and to G7 projects in this sector.

Integration of disabled and elderly people (TIDE)

445.   To give handicapped and elderly people better access to communications and information technologies, help them to cope with their environment and become more mobile, and to restore and improve their motor and cognitive functions, 55 projects were under way in 1995. These projects also cover integrated systems, including adapted intelligent houses and mobility systems for visually handicapped people. A call for proposals was issued in September, covering these various fields together with information and communications systems to improve the efficiency of support services for improved independence.

Environment

446.   Under the specific 'Telematics applications' programme, an exploratory operation was launched with a budget of ECU 20 million. In response to the first call, 17 proposals were selected involving finance of ECU 16 million. Work in this field was closely coordinated with work relating to the environment undertaken under other programmes and by institutions such as the European Environment Agency (→ *point 507*) and the Centre for Earth Observation.

Telematics engineering

447.   Five preparatory projects were completed in 1995. A further series of 11 proposals was given a positive assessment during the last quarter. The objectives of these projects cover most aspects of the work programme for this sector, including legal and socioeconomic questions relating to telematics applications.

Linguistic engineering

448.   The call for proposals dated 15 December 1994 in the linguistic engineering sector led to the selection of 25 projects requiring a contribution of ECU 31.5 million, in major socioeconomic sectors such as telebusiness, public administration, education and professional information services. Four other projects for the creation of large-scale linguistic databases received ECU 7.5 million. In the autumn, a new call for proposals was issued concerning *inter alia* documentary business management, language-learning and telematics translation services. Development work on the automatic translation system 'Systran' was put into the broader context of work on

the Euramis system (general multilingual services and reutilization of linguistic resources).

Information engineering

449. The 22 feasibility projects in the field of multimedia publishing and the eight associated studies launched in 1994 were completed. A new call for proposals issued in March led to the selection of nine large-scale pilot applications, four support measures and 10 new supplementary feasibility projects, requiring finance of ECU 21 million, in the following fields: newspapers, magazines and local electronic information services, networks for industrial or cultural multimedia resources, geographical information services, intelligent products and multimedia commercial catalogues, jobseeking services and scientific, technical and medical publications.

Remote transmission of administrative data, information and documents

Electronic transfer of commercial data (TEDIS)

450. Since 1987,[1] the TEDIS programme has encouraged the development of EDI (electronic data interchange), as a tool for improving the competitiveness of industry. ECU 25 million was allocated in 1995 to financing projects in seven key fields, namely: data security, telecommunications, legal aspects, multisectoral and European projects, standardization, studies on the economic and social impact of EDI, and awareness-raising campaigns. In addition, the Commission continued to take an active part in the United Nations initiatives connected with EDI and the G7 projects.

Telematics network for administration (TNA) and networks for the interchange of data between administrations (IDA)

451. The proposal for a European Parliament and Council Decision on a number of guidelines relating to trans-European telematics networks between administrations was replaced by a modified proposal on 27 September (→ *point 347)* as was the proposal for a Council Decision adopting a multiannual Community programme to support the implementation of trans-European networks for the interchange of data between administra-

---

[1]   Decision 87/499/EEC — OJ L 285, 8.10.1987.

tions (IDA) *(→ point 347)*. The Decision concerning the Community's contribution to the telematics system for the interchange of data between administrations (IDA) was adopted *(→ point 347)*.

452.   On the basis of a budget of ECU 60 million for 1995, the Commission continued to support the installation of trans-European telematics networks for the interchange of data between administrations, in order to ensure the smooth development of the internal market, and to provide public services which would be more efficient, more transparent, more receptive, more accessible to the general public and less expensive.

Advanced television services

453.   The action plan to introduce advanced television services, which is aimed at accelerating the market's adoption of the 16:9 large screen, which is the only parameter which has been adopted unanimously for future television systems,[1] moved into its second year. On 24 October, the European Parliament and the Council adopted a Directive (Table I) on the use of transmission standards for television *(→ point 430)*, thereby establishing the Community regulatory framework for advanced television services, including digital television.

Postal services

454.   Following the Council's conclusions of 13 June[2] and a Parliament resolution of 14 July,[3] on 26 July the Commission adopted a proposal for a Directive (Table I) establishing common rules for the development of Community postal services and improving the quality of the service. To complement these harmonization measures, on the same date it adopted a draft notice on the application of rules of competition to the postal sector, concerning in particular the assessment of certain State measures relating to postal services;[4] on 25 October[5] the European Parliament adopted a resolution calling for the withdrawal of this draft notice, and on 27 November the Council adopted its conclusions.[6]

---

[1]   1994 General Report, point 405.
[2]   Bull. 6-1995, point 1.3.145.
[3]   OJ C 249, 25.9.1995; Bull. 7/8-1995, point 1.3.134.
[4]   Bull. 7/8-1995, point 1.3.133.
[5]   OJ C 308, 20.11.1995; Bull. 10-1995, point 1.3.147.
[6]   Bull 11-1995, point 1.3.135.

Data protection

455. The first Infosec action plan was brought to a successful conclusion by a series of tests to explore the possibility of businesses using the digital signature and also the services of trusted third parties. A framework Directive on the protection of personal data was adopted by Parliament and the Council on 24 October *(→ point 135)* and work was continued with a view to drafting specific data-protection proposals for telecommunications networks. In addition, the principle was established, in particular in the conclusions of the G7 meeting in Brussels, of making personal data protection a component of the clear and stable legal framework which the development of the information society requires, as otherwise consumers would be reluctant to use the telematics services available to them.

International cooperation

456. The G7 Ministerial Conference on the Information Society, on which the European Parliament had previously adopted a resolution on 16 February,[1] was organized by the Commission in Brussels from 24 to 26 February.[2] The Conference led in particular to the launching of 11 pilot programmes on various topics. As a follow-up to this Conference, forums and bilateral discussions were organized and participation in the G7 pilot projects was opened up to a greater number of countries.

457. With regard to the countries of Central and Eastern Europe, a forum on the information society was organized in June and identified the following priority topics: liberalization and harmonization of information infrastructures to stimulate the competitiveness of these countries, increased cooperation in the field of R&TD and involvement in the G7 pilot projects. The dialogue between the Commission and these countries on regulatory aspects of telecommunications was stepped up, in particular by the adoption of a White Paper on incorporating the associated countries into the internal market *(→ point 816)*, one chapter of which deals with telecommunications, and through the PHARE programme. Provision has now been made for organizations in the countries of Central and Eastern Europe to take part in certain specific programmes under the fourth R&TD framework programme. A call for proposals for specific cooperation projects between the Union and the countries of Central and Eastern Europe was issued on 17 October.

---

[1]   OJ C 56, 6.3.1995; Bull. 1/2-1995, point 1.3.96.
[2]   Bull. 1/2-1995, point 1.3.97.

458.   As regards the Mediterranean basin, the Euro-Mediterranean Conference in Barcelona (→ point 839) and the civic society forum on 29 and 30 November included the information society and telecommunications among the themes for future cooperation. The Commission took part in the first Arab Telecommunications Symposium in Cairo from 3 to 6 April, where it established the principle of regular exchanges with the Arab League. Additional meetings were also held with Israel, Morocco and Turkey.

459.   In July a second bilateral meeting was held with the United States on the subject of the information society. Relations with Japan concerning telecommunications were further developed through a number of forums and bilateral discussions, in particular on deregulating telecommunications. Negotiations were also started with South Korea on opening up government procurement contracts for telecommunications equipment. The dialogue on the information society was also continued in Latin America, and extended to new regional partners in the Andean Pact. Lastly, international scientific cooperation with the developing countries in the fields of advanced communications technologies was included for the first time in the fourth R&TD framework programme (→ point 231).

460.   The Commission made an active contribution to the WTO negotiations on basic telecommunications with a view to opening up the world telecommunications services market. It also took part in the Telecom 95 world exhibition, organized by the ITU from 2 to 11 October in Geneva, and in the World Administrative Radio Conference (WARC 95) in Geneva from 15 October to 15 November. In February, the Commission had taken part in the OECD-APEC conference on the information society in Vancouver.

Regional aspects

461.   The Commission decided to assist six regions,[1] which had signed a declaration of intent at the end of 1994 expressing their common approach to creating the information society, in planning their interregional information society initiative (IRISI). It granted them financial aid for setting up regional partnerships, conducting awareness-raising campaigns, encouraging the creation of networks within the regions, and creating a European network. At a conference in October, these regions presented their action plans to other regions.

---

[1]   North-West England, Saxony, Nord-Pas-de-Calais, Valencia, Central Macedonia and Piedmont.

Section 16

Environment

Priority activities and objectives

*462.   The Union continued to implement the Community's fifth action pro-
gramme on the environment entitled 'Towards sustainability' and embarked
on a detailed review of the programme. Exchanges of views with numerous
groups at different levels put the Commission in a position to take stock of
implementation of the programme and to propose the broad lines of the
further action to be taken up to 2000. Consolidation and greater account of
environment policy in other policies[1] and activities, diversification of the
instruments used beyond the legislative approach and stronger emphasis on
information and awareness-raising to provide greater protection for the
environment were some of the main points to emerge from this review.*

*With regard to legislation, the Commission continued to put the emphasis
on framework directives and on developing the existing instruments. To follow up the environment sections of the White Paper on growth, competitiveness and employment (→ points 24 et seq.), numerous activities considered the economic and financial instruments. Revision of the financial
instrument for the environment (LIFE) likewise provided an opportunity to
take stock of implementation of the instrument and to propose the amendments necessary for it to continue supporting projects in the Union and in
the Mediterranean and Central and East European countries. Finally, the
European Council in Madrid[2] welcomed the fact that the European Union
remained committed to environmental protection and was actively involved
in international discussions and negotiations in various forums, particularly
with its Mediterranean and Central and East European neighbours and on
the control of transboundary movements of hazardous wastes and their disposal (Basle Convention), biological diversity, and substances that deplete
the ozone layer (Montreal Protocol). The Union's contributions to the Pan-
European Conference of Ministers of the Environment in Sofia and to the
Euro-Mediterranean Conference in Barcelona (→ point 839) were further
examples of this type of activity.*

---

[1]   Particularly on economic and social cohesion *(→ point 296).*
[2]   Bull. 12-1995.

Fifth action programme on the environment — taking the environment into account in other policies

463. The Commission conducted a review of the fifth action programme adopted in 1992[1] which provided for a review of the policy and strategy before the end of 1995. It focused on the latest scientific data, the results of the June 1992 Rio Conference on Environment and Development (particularly Agenda 21) and on the analyses conducted on the Community policies on industry, energy, transport, agriculture and the Structural Funds. On 25 October the Economic and Social Committee adopted an own-initiative opinion on an interim evaluation of the fifth action programme.[2]

General

Public awareness, information and education

464. As part of the openness policy introduced to pave the way for greater transparency, talks with the Commission's non-institutional partners (non-governmental organizations, regional and local authorities, small businesses, industry, research bodies, etc.) continued, mainly in the form of regular briefing sessions and jointly funded awareness-raising schemes. For example, on 8 December the Commission adopted a proposal for a Council Decision (Table II) on a Community action programme promoting non-governmental organizations primarily active in the field of environmental protection. The Commission also kept up its support for the European Blue Flag Campaign. In addition, it part-funded a project to set up a communications network with the national government departments responsible for information and communications concerning the environment. Finally, at a conference held in Valencia on 20 and 21 November to bring together regional environmental management authorities, a resolution and charter confirming the regional authorities' commitment to and responsibility for sustainable development were adopted. The Commission also continued its information schemes through publications, conferences and its environmental documentation centre. For the second year in succession,[3] the Commission published a call to submit proposals for environmental education schemes.[4]

---

[1] Twenty-sixth General Report, point 589.
[2] Bull. 10-1995, point 1.3.149.
[3] 1994 General Report, point 488.
[4] OJ C 66, 17.3.1995.

Economic, fiscal and legal instruments

465. On 10 May the Commission adopted an amendment to its proposal for a Council Directive (Table II) introducing a tax on carbon dioxide emissions and energy, to fulfil the commitment given at the Essen European Council[1] to submit guidelines to enable every Member State to apply a CO_2/energy tax on the basis of common parameters if it so desires. A degree of flexibility was proposed, notably a transition period until 1 January 2000, during which Member States will have a certain amount of latitude in deciding the tax rates, with the rates per product fixed in the original proposal taken as target rates towards which Member States will endeavour to make their domestic rates converge in the medium term. The other characteristics (tax base, chargeable event, chargeability and exemption for renewable energy sources), objectives (rational use of energy, reduction in greenhouse emissions) and fiscal neutrality of the tax remained unchanged. The Commission stated that before the end of the transition period it would submit a report on operation of the transitional arrangements, based, among other things, on the effectiveness of the measures taken to meet the targets set by the Council for CO_2 emissions, together with proposals for the switch to a harmonized system, which remains the medium-term objective.

466. The report submitted by the Commission *(→ points 24 et seq.)* to the Madrid European Council on the follow-up to the White Paper on growth, competitiveness and employment studied the relationship between economic growth and the environment, with a view to job creation in particular. It was based on the Commission's 1995 report on employment *(→ point 604)* and on the broad economic policy guidelines for 1995 *(→ point 45)*, which were based partly on the Commission communication on economic growth and the environment,[2] as endorsed by the Economic and Social Committee on 27 April[3] and on which Parliament adopted a resolution on 11 October.[4] The Commission also set up a high-level working party to determine the selection criteria for joint trans-European network projects in the field of the environment *(→ point 351)*.

467. In cooperation with the European Environment Agency *(→ point 507)*, the Commission continued its work to establish green national accounts combined with a series of environmental indicators to enable the Union to measure the progress made towards environmentally sustainable

---

[1]   COM(92) 226; OJ C 196, 3.8.1992; Bull. 5-1992, point 1.1.114.
[2]   COM(94) 465; 1994 General Report, point 489.
[3]   Bull. 4-1995, point 1.3.97.
[4]   OJ C 287, 30.10.1995; Bull. 10-1995, point 1.3.150.

development. On 11 October Parliament adopted a resolution[1] on the 1994 Commission communication on this subject.[2]

468.   Acting under Articles 92 and 93 of the EC Treaty, the Commission appraised several cases of State aid granted for environmental protection. The Community guidelines on State aid for environmental protection were applied with a view to striking a balance between competition policy and environmental considerations. The Community guidelines[3] are designed to ensure that State aid granted for environmental purposes complies with the 'polluter pays' principle and is consistent with the internal market and the Community's competition policy. So far the guidelines have proved to be a useful tool for the Commission and the Member States: during 1995 about 40 cases were dealt with without raising any particular problems.

469.   The Council agreed a common position on the Directive amending Directive 85/337/EEC on the assessment of the effects of certain public and private projects on the environment on 18 December (Table II).

Financial instruments

470.   With a view to extending the LIFE instrument[4] beyond 31 December, a progress report on implementation of the existing Regulation was adopted by the Commission on 12 April together with a proposal amending the Regulation (Table II) which was the subject of a Council common position on 18 December. The Regulation lays down the operating procedures for LIFE for the period from 1996 to 1999, with a budget of ECU 450 million. In 1995, the Community granted financial support to 135 demonstration schemes and technical assistance projects in the field of environmental protection and to 15[5] projects to provide technical assistance to the Mediterranean and Baltic regions.

471.   The Cohesion Fund (→ point 326) allocated ECU 1 042 238 215 for funding environmental infrastructure (water supply, sewage treatment, waste management and erosion control projects). As efforts were made to take the environment into account in the economic activities financed by the other Community funds (EAGGF, ERDF, etc.), greater importance was attached to the environmental infrastructure needed to implement the main

---

[1]   OJ C 287, 30.10.1995; Bull. 10-1995, point 1.3.151.
[2]   1994 General Report, point 490.
[3]   OJ C 72, 10.3.1994.
[4]   OJ L 206, 22.7.1992.
[5]   Including one project for 1994.

Directives on sewage and waste management. In the process, numerous projects were funded under the operational programmes adopted by the Commission, while other Community initiatives (URBAN, Interreg, Rechar, Resider, Konver, etc.) funded environmental protection and improvement projects (→ point 319). The Commission's communication on cohesion and the environment (→ point 296) proposed a number of measures to assess the environmental impact of the Structural Funds and the economic and social cohesion policy in general plus further action to generate greater synergy between cohesion and the environment.

International cooperation

472.   In preparation for the Euro-Mediterranean Conference in Barcelona (→ point 839), on 6 October[1] the Council adopted conclusions calling on the Commission to establish a short and medium-term priority action programme to concentrate the financial support essentially on such action and to provide a monitoring mechanism for its implementation, in particular regular dialogue.

473.   In the talks concerning the pre-accession strategy with the Central and East European countries (→ point 814), the Commission took measures to pave the way for closer cooperation with these countries on the environment, particularly on approximation of legislation.

474.   The Union participated in the third Pan-European Conference of Environment Ministers ('Environment for Europe'), which was held in Sofia from 23 to 25 October at the invitation of the Bulgarian Government, and brought together representatives of the United Nations Economic Commission for Europe, other OECD members and a large number of international organizations and institutions and NGOs. Parliament adopted a resolution[2] on the Conference and the Council adopted conclusions on the subject on 6 October.[3] The next Conference will be held in Denmark in 1998.

475.   The Union also participated in the third session of the Commission on Sustainable Development (→ point 789), the body responsible for the follow-up to the United Nations Conference on Environment and Development (UNCED), and in the other activities to build on UNCED. In preparation for this session, the Commission wrote a report on implementation

---

[1]   Bull. 10-1995, point 1.3.166.
[2]   OJ C 249, 25.9.1995; Bull. 7/8-1995, point 1.3.144.
[3]   Bull. 10-1995, point 1.3.164.

in the Community of Agenda 21, the action plan adopted at UNCED.[1] The Commission on Sustainable Development also set up an intergovernmental working party to examine the measures to be taken to combat the constant degradation of forests (→ point 713). The Union also participated in the 18th meeting of the Board of Administration of the United Nations Environment Programme (UNEP).

476. The Commission played an active part in the international meetings on trade and the environment within the WTO Committee on Trade and the Environment, OECD and Unctad.

477. The Commission was represented at the meeting of the G7 Ministers of the Environment in Hamilton on 30 April and 1 May, in preparation for the G7 Summit in Halifax (→ point 886). Parliament adopted a resolution[2] on taking the environment into account at the G7 Summit. The Commission also maintained its bilateral contacts with a number of industrialized countries, particularly the USA. The working party on the environment of the EU-China Joint Committee met for the first time in 1995.

Industry and environment

Environmental control of products, industrial installations and biotechnology

478.   Pursuant to Council Regulation (EEC) No 880/92[3] on a Community eco-label award scheme, on 25 July the Commission adopted a Decision establishing the ecological criteria for laundry detergents,[4] bringing the number of categories of manufactured products for which ecological criteria have been adopted at Community level to six.[5] This number was raised to eight in December with the adoption of Decisions establishing ecological criteria for single-ended light bulbs[6] and indoor paints and varnishes.[7]

479. Turning to biotechnology, on 6 December the Commission adopted a proposal (→ point 197) amending Directive 90/219/EEC on the contained use of genetically modified micro-organisms. On the basis of Directive

---

[1]   Twenty-sixth General Report, point 596.
[2]   OJ C 166, 3.7.1995; Bull. 6-1995, point 1.3.146.
[3]   OJ L 99, 11.4.1992; Twenty-sixth General Report, point 604.
[4]   OJ L 217, 13.9.1995.
[5]   Washing machines, dishwashers, soil improvers, toilet paper and kitchen rolls.
[6]   OJ L 302, 15.12.1995.
[7]   OJ L 4, 6.1.1996.

90/220/EEC[1] on the deliberate release into the environment of genetically modified organisms, on 29 November the Commission adopted a Decision authorizing the placing on the market of a genetically modified type of colza.

480. On dangerous chemicals (→ *point 106*), on 28 September[2] the Commission adopted a second list of priority chemical substances for which an environmental and health risk assessment must be made.

481. The Council adopted a common position on the proposal for a Parliament and Council Directive (Table I) concerning the disposal of polychlorinated biphenyls (PCBs) and polychlorinated terphenyls (PCTs) on 27 November.

Emissions from industrial installations and products

482. As part of the preparations for drafting a proposal on the reduction of emissions of pollutants from motor vehicles with effect from 2000 (Stage 2000 of the auto/oil programme), on the basis of a cost-effectiveness analysis of measures for meeting quantified environmental targets, the Commission started a series of preparatory activities, with the cooperation of the oil and motor industries and adopted, on 20 December, a communication on a strategy to reduce CO_2 emissions from cars.[3]

483. Under Council Regulation (EEC) No 1836/93[4] allowing voluntary participation by companies in the industrial sector in a Community eco-management and audit scheme (EMAS), which came fully into effect on 13 April 1995, the Commission actively encouraged collaboration between the Member States and started the procedure for recognition of national (British, Irish and Spanish) standards on environmental management systems.[5] It also gave the European Committee for Standardization (CEN) a mandate to develop standards for environmental management systems. Numerous pilot activities part-funded by the Commission are under way to encourage undertakings to participate in the system.

484. In June the Council agreed a common position on the proposal for a Directive (Table II) to improve and reinforce Directive 82/501/EEC (the Seveso Directive) on the major accident hazards of certain industrial activi-

---

[1] OJ L 117, 8.5.1990; Twenty-fourth General Report, point 523.
[2] OJ L 231, 28.9.1995.
[3] COM(95) 689; Bull. 12-1995.
[4] OJ L 168, 10.7.1993; Twenty-seventh General Report, point 470.
[5] COM(95) 422; Bull. 9-1995, point 1.3.86.

ties. Finally, on 27 November the Council agreed a common position on the proposal for a Directive (Table II) on integrated pollution prevention and control, with the objective of moving away from the earlier sectoral approach to industrial pollution towards an integrated approach.

Waste management

485. On 8 November the Commission adopted a report[1] on waste management policy outlining developments in the legislation on the subject since 1990.

486. At the third Conference of the Parties to the Basle Convention in September,[2] an amendment to the Convention was adopted, prohibiting exports of hazardous wastes to non-OECD countries immediately if they are intended for disposal and by 31 December 1997 in the case of waste intended for recovery. On 23 June[3] the Council had authorized the Commission to negotiate the incorporation of this amendment into the Convention.

487. On 8 February the Commission adopted a proposal for a Council Regulation (Table II) establishing common rules and procedures to apply to shipments of non-hazardous waste intended for recovery (green list) to non-OECD countries which have not agreed to accept this type of waste. The proposal is to apply the red list procedure (for hazardous recoverable waste), which, in practice, has the same effect as an export ban, while maintaining a degree of flexibility. On 26 April the Commission also adopted a proposal for a Regulation (Table II) amending Council Regulation (EEC) No 259/93 on the supervision and control of shipments of waste within, into and out of the European Community. The objective was to prohibit all exports of hazardous wastes from the Community to non-OECD countries for recycling with effect from 1 January 1998. Parliament had called for this on 5 April.[4]

488. On 6 October the Council formally adopted a common position on a proposal for a Directive on the landfill of waste (Table II).

---

[1] COM(95) 522; Bull. 11-1995, point 1.3.143.
[2] Bull. 9-1995, point 1.3.87.
[3] Bull. 6-1995, point 1.3.149.
[4] OJ C 109, 1.5.1995; Bull. 4-1995, point 1.3.99.

Civil protection

489. On 4 May the Commission adopted a proposal for a Council Decision (Table II) establishing a Community action programme in the field of civil protection, setting the priorities for action by the Community in the years ahead and giving details of the financing criteria and arrangements.

490. Following calls for proposals[1] for pilot projects, 54 civil protection projects and 21 marine pollution projects were selected to receive a financial contribution from the Community.

491. The civil protection authorities within the Commission, the Member States, Iceland and Norway held their first meeting in Nainville-les-Roches (France) on 29 June. They put the emphasis on flexibility as the key component in cooperation on civil protection at Community level and considered that efforts must be made to take account of civil protection aspects in other Community policies, particularly on training and education, information and public awareness.

Quality of the environment and natural resources

Protection of water, soil conservation, agriculture

492. On 4 January the Commission adopted a proposal for a Council Directive (Table II) concerning the quality of water intended for human consumption, with the objective of amending Directive 80/778/EEC in order to adapt it to the EC Treaty (particularly the subsidiarity principle) and scientific and technical progress and to enable the Member States to remedy cases of non-compliance with the various quality requirements.

493. In June the Commission published its 12th report on bathing water quality,[2] which found a slight improvement in sea water, but a deterioration in fresh water in the 1994 bathing season. It also published a summary report[3] containing the results of the measures taken to implement Directive 78/659/EEC on the quality of fresh waters needing protection or improvement in order to support fish life[4] and Directive 79/923/EEC on the

---

[1] OJ C 47, 24.2.1995.
[2] Bull. 6-1995, point 1.3.152.
[3] 'Quality of fresh water for fish and of shellfish water — Summary report on the state of application of Directives 78/659/EEC and 79/923/EEC' (text and maps).
[4] OJ L 222, 14.8.1978.

quality required of shellfish waters.[1] Also, on 20 February[2] the Council adopted a resolution on groundwater protection. Finally, the Committee of the Regions adopted an own-initiative opinion[3] and Parliament a resolution[4] on the drought in the European Union.

494. On 18 December[5] the Council adopted conclusions on water policy in the European Community and on acidification.

495. On the international scene, on 24 July the Council adopted Decision 95/308/EC on the conclusion of the Convention on the Protection and Use of Transboundary Watercourses and International Lakes (Table III), which was signed in 1992 to establish a framework for cooperation between the member countries of the United Nations Economic Commission for Europe on these subjects. On 6 January a proposal was submitted on conclusion of the Convention for the Protection of the Marine Environment of the North-East Atlantic (Table III). The Commission participated in the fourth International Conference on the Protection of the North Sea[6] on 8 and 9 June, at which a declaration was adopted setting new objectives for protection and for action to combat pollution.

Protection of nature, flora and fauna, and coastal zones

496. On 22 June the Council agreed a common position, subject to Parliament's opinion on the legal basis, which was delivered on 15 December, on the proposal for a Council Regulation (Table II) laying down provisions with regard to possession of and trade in species of wild fauna and flora (implementation of the CITES Convention). This had been under discussion within the Council since 1991.

497. On 29 May[7] the Commission adopted a communication on wise use and conservation of wetlands, which stressed the key functions played by these ecosystems and explained how to make protection of wetlands an integral part of the Union's principal policies. On 20 December the Council adopted Regulation (EC) No 3062/95 setting out the objectives and forms of action to ensure the conservation and sustainable management of tropical forests and of their biological diversity (Table II). Parliament in turn

[1] OJ L 281, 10.11.1979.
[2] OJ C 49, 28.2.1995; Bull. 1/2-1995, point 1.3.109.
[3] Bull. 7/8-1995, point 1.3.138.
[4] OJ C 249, 25.9.1995; Bull. 7/8-1995, point 1.3.139.
[5] Bull. 12-1995.
[6] Bull. 6-1995, point 1.3.154.
[7] COM(95) 189; Bull. 5-1995, point 1.3.90.

adopted a resolution on the depletion of Suriname's tropical forests on 12 October.[1] The Commission continued the preparations for implementation of the Natura 2000 European network of protected areas. It also granted support for the protection of natural habitats and endangered species, by part-financing 59 projects for a total of ECU 48.5 million from LIFE.

498.   On 24 July the Council adopted negotiating directives with a view to an Agreement on the conservation of African and Eurasian migratory waterbirds (Table III) to implement the Bonn Convention on the Conservation of Migratory Species of Wild Animals.[2] Under the same Convention, a draft Agreement was negotiated on the conservation of small cetaceans of the Mediterranean and the Black Seas (Table III). Whale hunting was the subject of a resolution adopted by Parliament on 18 May.[3] On 17 March the latter adopted a resolution on minimum standards for the keeping of animals in zoos.[4] On 12 December the Commission withdrew its proposal for a Directive and, in line with the subsidiarity principle, adopted instead a proposal for a recommendation to the Member States on the same subject.[5] On 18 December the Commission adopted a proposal for a Council Regulation (Table II) amending Council Regulation (EEC) No 3254/91[6] prohibiting the use of leghold traps in the Community and the introduction into the Community of pelts and manufactured goods of certain wild animal species. Among other things, this would allow an extra year (until 31 December 1996) before imposition of the embargo on non-Union countries which fail to comply with the Regulation, an embargo which Parliament opposed in a resolution adopted on 14 December.[7]

499.   The Commission communication adopted on 31 October[8] on the integrated management of coastal zones, on which the Council gave its opinion on 18 December[9] (→ point 296), announced a demonstration programme to promote implementation of sustainable development, in line with the principles of integration and subsidiarity. The revised Convention for the Protection of the Mediterranean Sea against Pollution (Barcelona Convention) (Table III) was signed on 10 June.[10] In particular, the aim was to extend the scope of the Convention to cover coastal zones, promote integrated management of such zones and introduce sustainable development

---

[1]   OJ C 287, 30.10.1995; Bull. 10-1995, point 1.3.161.
[2]   OJ L 210, 19.7.1982.
[3]   OJ C 151, 19.6.1995; Bull. 5-1995, point 1.3.92.
[4]   OJ C 89, 10.4.1995; Bull. 3-1995, point 1.3.108.
[5]   COM(95) 619; Bull. 12-1995.
[6]   OJ L 308, 9.11.1991; Bull. 11-1991, point 1.2.183.
[7]   OJ C 17, 22.1.1996; Bull. 12-1995.
[8]   COM(95) 511; Bull. 10-1995, point 1.3.107.
[9]   Bull. 12-1995.
[10] Bull. 6-1995, point 1.3.153.

objectives and principles such as the precautionary principle, the 'polluter pays' principle, use of the best available technologies and use of impact assessments.

Urban environment, air quality, transport and energy, noise

500.   On the urban environment, the Commission continued to examine implementation of the sustainable cities project in urban areas in the Community,[1] concentrating more on the social and economic aspects. On 6 September it adopted a proposal for a Directive (Table I) on the approximation of the laws of the Member States relating to the measures to be taken against the emission of gaseous and particulate pollutants from internal combustion engines to be installed in off-road mobile machinery (such as earthmoving equipment). The Parliament and the Council agreed common positions in December on the proposal for a Directive amending Directive 88/77/EEC on air pollution by diesel vehicles (Table I). On 22 December the Council adopted a common position on the proposal for a Directive amending Directive 70/220/EEC on air pollution by vehicles with positive ignition engines on 18 December (Table I).

501.   The report adopted by the Commission on 26 July[2] on ambient air quality took stock of implementation of the existing Directives up to 1992/93 and described the trends for the main pollutants in Europe's towns and cities. On 30 November the Council adopted a common position on a proposal for a framework Directive (Table II) on ambient air quality assessment and management. Parliament adopted a resolution on ozone smog on 13 July.[3]

502.   On 29 June Parliament and the Council adopted Directive 95/27/EC (Table I) amending Directive 86/662/EEC in order to reduce noise emitted by certain earthmoving equipment.

Global environment, climate change, geosphere and biosphere

503.   The Commission participated in the seventh Conference of the Contracting Parties to the Montreal Protocol on Substances that Deplete the Ozone Layer in Vienna from 28 November to 7 December,[4] which agreed

---

[1]   1994 General Report, point 531.
[2]   COM(95) 372.
[3]   OJ C 249, 25.9.1995; Bull. 7/8-1995, point 1.3.143.
[4]   Bull. 12-1995.

to tighten the controls on hydrochlorofluorocarbons and methyl bromide, and reached a number of accords enabling developing countries to keep closer control over substances that deplete the ozone layer.

504.   The first Conference of the Parties to the United Nations framework Convention on Climate Change was held in Berlin from 28 March to 7 April.[1] The Commission and a delegation of Members of the European Parliament attended. The principal outcome was the Berlin Mandate which stressed the inadequacy, for the industrialized countries, of the existing agreements on greenhouse gas emissions and the need to adopt a new Protocol or another legal instrument defining policies and measures with a view to a further reduction in emissions. In preparation for this Conference, on 1 March the Commission had adopted a working paper on EU climate change strategy.[2] Parliament[3] and the Council[4] had also adopted a resolution and conclusions, respectively, on this subject in March. In its conclusions of 23 June,[5] the Council welcomed the decision taken at the Conference to prepare a legal instrument for the period after the year 2000. It reaffirmed the determination of the Community to meet its commitments under the Convention and in particular to stabilize CO_2 emissions at 1990 levels by the year 2000. Another major event was the acceptance by the Intergovernmental Panel on Climate Change of the second situation report on climate change in December. This was welcomed by the Council on 18 December[6] in its conclusions on the Community strategy on climate change.

505.   Turning to action to protect the biosphere, the Community was actively involved in the second Conference of the Parties to the Convention on Biological Diversity[7] held in Jakarta from 6 to 17 November.[8] The principal result of this Conference was the adoption of the Jakarta Mandate to draft a biosafety Protocol. A resolution adopted by Parliament on 14 July[9] called for effective implementation of the Convention. In its conclusions of 18 December[6] the Council called on the Commission to propose a Community strategy on the subject.

---

[1]   Bull. 4-1995, point 1.3.101.
[2]   Bull. 3-1995, point 1.3.110.
[3]   OJ C 68, 20.3.1995; Bull. 3-1995, point 1.3.111.
[4]   Bull. 3-1995, point 1.3.112.
[5]   Bull. 6-1995, point 1.3.158.
[6]   Bull. 12-1995.
[7]   OJ L 309, 13.12.1993; Twenty-seventh General Report, point 487.
[8]   Bull. 11-1995, point 1.3.148.
[9]   OJ C 249, 25.9.1995; Bull. 7/8-1995, point 1.3.140.

506.   At the third session of the Commission for Sustainable Development (→ point 789) the Community actively supported the establishment of the Intergovernmental Panel on Forests.

European Environment Agency

507.   The Copenhagen-based European Environment Agency became fully operational in mid-year. The Commission contributed ECU 11.8 million to its budget, ECU 6.5 million of which was allocated to the Agency's work programme for 1994-95, the main areas of activity being data collection, analysis and dissemination and establishment of the Agency's network. In the course of the year, seven topic centres were set up to prepare projects on air quality, emissions into the air, inland water bodies, the coastal and marine environment, a catalogue of data sources, and soil. In September the Agency published a report on the state of the environment in Europe. Finally, in its conclusions of 9 November,[1] the Council decided to postpone until 30 October 1997 the decision on whether to give the Agency additional tasks, in order to leave it time to make a start on the tasks laid down in Regulation (EEC) No 1210/90 establishing the Agency.[2] Parliament adopted a resolution on this subject[3] on 13 October.

---

[1]   Bull. 11-1995, point 1.3.136.
[2]   OJ L 120, 11.5.1990; Twenty-fourth General Report, point 502.
[3]   Bull. 10-1995, point 1.3.148.

Section 17

Nuclear safety

Priority activities and objectives

508.   Nuclear plant safety and radioactive waste management in the former Soviet Union and Central and Eastern Europe again required the attention of the European Union and the G7. The participants at the G7 Summit in Halifax (→ point 516) accepted the Russian Federation's invitation to attend a meeting on nuclear safety matters in 1996.

The resumption by France of underground nuclear testing in Polynesia sparked off a debate about the role of the Union institutions in relation to the measures to protect the public and the environment against such testing. A verification mission in French Polynesia confirmed that the facilities established by the French authorities to carry out continuous monitoring of the level of radioactivity in the environment pursuant to Article 35 of the Euratom Treaty are operating efficiently. The French authorities refused access to the facilities monitoring the nuclear test sites. In addition, after evaluating the information provided by the French authorities in connection with the possibility that the nuclear tests were particularly dangerous (Article 34 of the Euratom Treaty), the Commission decided that Article 34 does not apply to the case in question, but recommended long-term monitoring of the level of radioactivity at the sites. It asked France for a firm assurance in this connection and for information concerning this monitoring.[1] The European Parliament reiterated its strong opposition to nuclear tests in resolutions adopted on 15 June,[2] 20 September[3] and 26 October (→ point 701).[4]

Radiation protection

509.   Radiation protection training and information courses were provided for representatives of the customs services of the Member States and certain non-member countries.

---

[1]   Bull. 10-1995, point 1.3.162.
[2]   OJ C 166, 3.7.1995; Bull. 6-1995, point 1.4.4.
[3]   OJ C 269, 16.10.1995; Bull. 9-1995, point 1.4.3.
[4]   OJ C 308, 20.11.1995; Bull. 10-1995, point 1.3.163.

510.   Pursuant to Article 33 of the Euratom Treaty, the Commission made 12 recommendations on draft national regulations. In accordance with Article 37 of the Treaty, it also delivered one opinion on a plan for the disposal of radioactive waste.[1] On 10 July it adopted a report on the application of that Article in the period July 1990 to June 1994.[2] In accordance with Article 35 of the Treaty, the Commission carried out two visits to verify the operation and efficiency of facilities for monitoring the level of radioactivity in Italy and French Polynesia. Pursuant to Article 36 of the Treaty, the Commission published the 24th report on radioactivity in the environment (1987-90).

511.   The proposal for a new Directive (Table II) laying down the basic safety standards for the protection of the health of the general public and workers against the dangers of ionizing radiation was still under discussion at the end of the year.

512.   On 24 November, acting pursuant to Article 31 of the Treaty, the Commission adopted on first reading a proposal for a Council Directive (Table II) on the protection of the health of the public against the dangers of ionizing radiation in connection with medical exposures, and revising Directive 84/466/Euratom. On 28 March the Council adopted Regulation (EC) No 686/95 (Table II) extending until the year 2000 Regulation (EEC) No 737/90 on conditions governing imports of agricultural products originating in third countries, which was adopted following the Chernobyl nuclear accident.

Plant safety

513.   The process of harmonization of safety criteria and practices in the Member States produced significant results, particularly with regard to the seismic re-evaluation of nuclear power stations, the consequences of the failure of a steam generator tube, the approval of electromechanical components of importance to safety, the evaluation of ultrasonic inspection methods for welded steel structures and the acceptance criteria for defects detected in such structures. The European Parliament adopted resolutions on the safety problems raised by the building of the Mochovce power station (Slovakia) on 16 February[3] and 16 March.[4]

---

[1]   OJ L 114, 20.5.1995.
[2]   COM(94) 328.
[3]   OJ C 56, 6.3.1995; Bull. 1/2-1995, point 1.3.116.
[4]   OJ C 89, 10.4.1995; Bull. 3-1995, point 1.3.114.

Radioactive waste

514. In implementation of the Council resolution[1] and the Commission communication[2] on a Community radioactive waste strategy in the European Union, efforts were made to harmonize the classification criteria for various types of waste, and work was carried out to improve the methods of determining equivalences between radioactive waste. Special attention was paid to the analysis of radiological risks arising from natural radionuclides. On 24 May the Commission adopted a report[3] on the application in the Member States of Directive 92/3/Euratom on the supervision and control of shipments of radioactive waste within, into and out of the European Community.[4]

515. In the context of cooperation with the independent States of the former Soviet Union, analyses were carried out of the waste storage situation and associated risks (study of the management possibilities for areas contaminated by the accident at the Chernobyl power station, and analysis of the facilities for storing and disposing of radioactive waste built up in north-west Russia). On 16 November Parliament adopted three resolutions on nuclear waste and pollution of the sea, the threat to the environment posed by nuclear submarines, and in particular Russian submarines, and the harassment of the Bellona Foundation (Norwegian environmental NGO) by the Russian security services.[5]

International action

516. At the Halifax Summit in June *(→ point 886)* the group of the seven most industrialized countries (G7) reacted favourably to the Russian initiative of holding a summit devoted exclusively to nuclear matters in Moscow in the spring of 1996. The Commission helped to prepare this summit, the main topics of which will be the safety of nuclear power stations of Soviet design, and radioactive waste management. Commissioner Van den Broek visited Ukraine on 13 April[6] in connection with the action plan decided upon by the G7 in July 1994.[7] During this visit Mr Koutchma, the President of Ukraine, announced the closure of the Chernobyl power station before the year 2000 *(→ point 881).* A Memorandum of Understanding on

[1]   OJ C 379, 31.12.1994; 1994 General Report, point 543.
[2]   COM(94) 66; 1994 General Report, point 543.
[3]   COM(95) 192.
[4]   OJ L 35, 12.2.1992; Twenty-sixth General report, point 731.
[5]   OJ C 323, 4.12.1995; Bull. 11-1995, points 1.3.150 to 1.3.152.
[6]   Bull. 4-1995, point 1.3.102.
[7]   1994 General Report, point 819.

this subject was signed on 20 December between the G7 and Ukraine. An Agreement in the form of an exchange of letters between the European Atomic Energy Community and Switzerland concerning the linking-up of the latter to the Ecurie (European Community urgent radiological exchange) system was concluded in December.[1] The Commission took part in the work of the International Atomic Energy Agency (IAEA) on the drawing-up of a Convention on the management of radioactive waste, the need for which was stressed in the preamble to the 1994 Convention on Nuclear Safety.[2] In the context of the Group of 24 (G24), the Commission continued to provide secretariat services for the international coordination of assistance on nuclear safety for the countries of Central and Eastern Europe and the former Soviet Union.

---

[1]   OJ C 335, 13.12.1995.
[2]   1994 General Report, point 545.

Section 18

Euratom safeguards[1]

517.   In 1995 the Euratom Safeguards Directorate conducted physical and accounting checks on average stocks of 406 tonnes of plutonium, 12 tonnes of highly-enriched uranium and 264 600 tonnes of (low-enrichment, natural and depleted) uranium, and 4 840 tonnes of thorium and heavy water. These materials were held in the 810 or so nuclear installations in the Community and gave rise to more than one million operator entries concerning physical movements and stocks. As in the past, the checks also covered equipment subject to external commitments under agreements concluded with non-member countries. The anomalies and irregularities detected by the Directorate were followed up rigorously by additional inspections.

518.   The number of man-days of inspection throughout the Union in 1995 increased slightly compared with 1994, from 8 723 to nearly 9 000. This increase represents the difference between the increase in the inspection effort in the major installations using plutonium and in the new Member States and the reduction in activities in Germany and Italy.

519.   The cooperation initiated in 1993 with the Central and East European countries and the former Soviet Union, in particular Russia, was stepped up in 1995, with activities taking place virtually every week, the main ones being seminars, lengthy training courses for Russian experts and three major projects in Russia concerning the inspection of nuclear materials. In addition, a high-level seminar on nuclear materials inspection and accounting, attended by Commissioner Papoutsis, Members of the European Parliament and various eminent persons from the European Union and the former Soviet Union, was held in St Petersburg in April. After the completion, at the end of 1994, of the first stage of cooperation during which the objectives were defined and a large number of experts were given basic training, the second stage started in 1995. Three major projects were defined in conjunction with the Russian authorities with a view to creating pilot modules for a modern, computerized nuclear materials inspection system in Russia. In addition to these major projects already in progress, five others were in preparation at the end of the year. One-off programmes continued along with intensive training courses for groups of two to five experts in Luxembourg.

---

[1]   Figures as at 31 October 1995.

520.   The year 1995 also saw the completion of the application of the principles underlying the new partnership approach (NPA), the framework for which had been set out by the Commission and the International Atomic Energy Agency (IAEA) in 1992.[1] Despite the difficulties encountered, new, coordinated practical inspection procedures were established and approved for most types of nuclear installations. Following the running-in period in 1994, the NPA is functioning, on the whole, to the satisfaction of the IAEA which wanted to make substantial savings by making greater use of Euratom's infrastructure. On the other hand, as far as the Commission is concerned the NPA has not reduced the financial or manpower requirements.

521.   The Euratom Safeguards Directorate completed its efforts to install and fine-tune highly-automated safeguards systems for the major plutonium processing plants (MELOX and UP2-800 in France; Thorp in the United Kingdom). Other projects concerned the Sellafield Mox Plant (United Kingdom) and Superphenix (Creys-Malville, France). In addition, work continued on the establishment of Euratom laboratories at the Sellafield and La Hague sites, an option entailing considerable initial investments but which represents the most effective, safest and most economic medium- and long-term solution.

522.   At international level, the Safeguards Directorate took part in negotiations on a new Agreement between the European Atomic Energy Community and the United States (→ point 378). The Safeguards Directorate also maintained bilateral contacts with non-member countries, in particular Australia, Canada, Japan and Russia.

523.   During the year the Safeguards Directorate also took action in relation to a number of cases of trafficking in nuclear materials from Eastern Europe. Given the importance of this problem, the Directorate played an active part in the warning system set up to ensure a rapid response. It also actively cooperated in the work of the groups of experts set up by the Commission on the one hand and by the IAEA, the G7 and certain Member States on the other.

524.   As part of the programme to step up the IAEA safeguards system, known as '93+2', the Directorate took steps, in compliance with the Treaty and national legislation, and with the assistance of the Joint Research Centre, in order to make a significant contribution to the development of novel approaches to safeguards using highly sophisticated new techniques so as to detect undeclared nuclear activities more effectively.

---

[1]   Twenty-sixth General Report, point 721.

Section 19

Agricultural policy[1]

Priority activities and objectives

525.   In 1995 Community activity in the field of agriculture was devoted principally to the implementation of the third and last stage of the reform of the common agricultural policy (CAP). This was facilitated by the satisfactory results of the last two years: production has been brought under control, internal cereal consumption has increased, public stocks have gone down, the level of farm incomes overall has improved and the use of fertilizers and plant-health products has been reduced. Various factors, primarily the weather (floods in the north of the Union and drought in the south), caused problems on a number of markets; a single set-aside rate reduced to 10% was therefore adopted for the 1996 marketing year.

The common organizations of the market were readjusted in the dried fodder, tobacco, sugar and cotton sectors, while reforms of the market organizations in wine and in fruit and vegetables were still under discussion at the end of the year. The reform of the rice sector was adopted by the Council on 22 December. The European Council, meeting in Madrid in December,[2] welcomed the progress achieved in this area. Market organizations were also established or adapted for many agricultural sectors following the agreement on agriculture within the framework of the Uruguay Round of multilateral trade negotiations.

On 1 January, Austria, Finland and Sweden became members of the European Union, accepting all the provisions of the Treaty as well as the totality of the acquis communautaire. *The CAP was therefore applied to them as from this date without a transitional period. In addition, at the invitation of the European Council in Essen, the Commission made a study of alternative development strategies for the future integration into the CAP of the agriculture sectors in the Central and East European countries (→ point 817).*

With regard to rural development, the Commission continued to implement Leader II and to approve Community support frameworks, single program-

---

[1]   For more details, see *The Agricultural Situation in the European Union — 1995 Report* published in association with this Report and available from the Publications Office.
[2]   Bull. 12-1995.

*ming documents and Objectives 1 and 5b operational programmes for
1994-99 (→ points 301, 314 and 319).*

Content of the common agricultural policy

526.   As well as implementing the reform of the CAP *(→ point 528)*, the
Commission followed up on political decisions going beyond the sphere of
agriculture proper (Uruguay Round agreements, future enlargement of the
Union, continuation of the trade agreements with EFTA and completion of
a new generalized preference scheme) and launched discussions in the following fields: relations with Central and East European countries with a
view to their accession in the future, start-up conditions for young farmers,
calf-rearing conditions in the Union, and the use of hormones.

527.   On 20 April the Commission adopted its annual report on the
agricultural situation in the European Union (1994).[1]

Implementation of the reform of the CAP

528.   The reform of the CAP reached its final phase in a number of sectors
(cereals, oilseeds, protein seeds, beef and veal, tobacco) *(→ points 535 to
547)*, while in others which were not originally included in the CAP reform
package (cotton, dehydrated fodder and potato starch) the market organization rules were adjusted. For other sectors (wine, fruit and vegetables and
rice), the Commission submitted draft amendments to the market organizations. The proposal for the rice sector has since been adopted. The Commission also continued its work in the field of bee-keeping,[2] which was the
subject of a resolution of Parliament on 20 January.[3]

Farm prices for the 1995/96 marketing year

529.   In keeping with the policy entailed by the reform of the CAP, the
Commission submitted a 'prices and related measures' package based primarily on continuing the implementation of the reform, freezing other prices
and amounts and controlling production in sectors not covered by the reform. This approach was facilitated by the buoyancy of the majority of agricultural markets. However, the settlement of a number of related issues

---

[1]   COM (95) 59; Bull. 4-1995, point 1.3.103.
[2]   1994 General Report, point 596.
[3]   OJ C 43, 20.2.1995; Bull. 1/2-1995, point 1.3.118.

delayed the final decision. It was necessary first of all to adapt the market organizations for cotton and tobacco, adopt a system to apply to sugar until 2000, solve the problem of Italian and Greek milk quotas and reach a political agreement on agrimonetary and set-aside policy, as well as legislating on the transport of animals, before a final decision on prices was reached on 29 June and established by Regulations (EC) Nos 1528/95 to 1551/95 (Table II). The main features of this decision were freezing prices and amounts, continuing implementation of the reform (except for the intervention price for milk, which was maintained at the same level), a slight reduction of the monthly increments and sugar storage levies and adjustments to the common organization of certain markets.[1]

Agricultural structures and rural development

530.   The EAGGF Guidance Section's operations are described in Section 10 of this chapter (Economic and social cohesion) (→ points 296 et seq.).

Forests, environment and agriculture

531.   In application of Regulation (EEC) No 2080/92[2] instituting a Community aid scheme for forestry measures in agriculture, national programmes for Austria and Finland and certain amendments to existing programmes were adopted by the Commission.

Several measures were also taken in the field of safeguarding European forests. In application of Regulation (EEC) No 2158/92[3] on the protection of the Community's forests against fires, the Commission approved lists of high- and medium-risk areas and issued a favourable opinion on protection plans. In parallel with this measure, in application of Regulation (EEC) No 3528/86[4] on the protection of the Community's forests against atmospheric pollution, it adopted Regulations (EC) Nos 690/95[5] and 1398/95[6] which provided for the establishment of a programme of intensive and continuous monitoring of European forest ecosystems.

532.   In addition, on 22 June the Council adopted Regulation (EC) No 1460/95 (Table II) amending Regulation (EEC) No 1765/92, whereby arable land withdrawn from production for environmental or afforestation

---

[1]   The prices adopted are listed in Bull. 6-1995, point 1.3.160.
[2]   OJ L 215, 30.7.1992; Twenty-sixth General Report, point 516.
[3]   OJ L 217, 31.7.1992; Twenty-sixth General Report, point 517.
[4]   OJ L 362, 17.11.1986; Twenty-sixth General Report, point 618.
[5]   OJ L 71, 31.3.1995.
[6]   OJ L 139, 22.6.1995.

purposes can be counted towards compulsory set-aside, and national aid may be granted to producers who use that land to plant fast-growing forest trees and shrubs for the production of biomass. On 21 August the Commission adopted Regulation (EC) No 2015/95[1] which includes under non-rotational set-aside all arable land withdrawn from production for environmental purposes or for afforestation.

Quality of agricultural products

533.   The Commission studied the proposals of the Member States concerning European protection of geographical indications and registered designations of origin recognized by the Member States, before the entry into force of the protection system[2] instituted by Regulation (EEC) No 2081/92, which was the subject of a resolution by Parliament on 26 October.[3] As regards the direction to be taken in policy on quality, the reflection focused on the general topic of raising consumer awareness of the producers' efforts to improve quality, whether or not involving traditional products. In addition, the Commission adopted, on 31 October, a proposal for a Council Regulation (Table II) drawing up special provisions for quality wines produced in specified regions. The Council adopted this Regulation on 18 December. Finally, on 13 December the Commission adopted a recommendation for a decision on a draft agreement with New Zealand on the marketing of wine (Table III).

Genetic resources

534.   Following a first call for proposals[4] under Regulation (EC) No 1467/94[5] on the conservation, characterization, collection and utilization of genetic resources in agriculture, 10 proposals were selected to receive a total of ECU 3.4 million in 1995.

---

[1]   OJ L 197, 22.8.1995.
[2]   OJ L 208, 24.7.1992; Twenty-sixth General Report, point 518.
[3]   OJ C 308, 20.11.1995; Bull. 10-1995, point 1.3.170.
[4]   OJ C 77, 29.3.1995.
[5]   OJ L 159, 28.6.1994; 1994 General Report, point 607.

Management of the common agricultural policy

Adjustment of the common organizations of markets

Crop products

535.   As part of the progressive implementation of the CAP reform over three marketing years from 1993/94, the single intervention price for cereals was adjusted for the last time in respect of the 1995 harvest. This reduction was offset by an increase in compensatory payments, which are paid on a per-hectare basis conditional on set-aside in the case of producers applying for compensation for a surface area representing a production volume of more than 92 tonnes of cereals. By way of derogation, the rotational set-aside rate was fixed at 12% for the 1995 harvest. Taking account of cereal stock trends in the Community and in the world, the Council adopted, on 26 September, Regulation (EC) No 2336/95 (Table II), which further reduced the compulsory set-aside rate to 10% for the 1996 harvest (for cereals, protein plants, oilseeds and fibre flax). On 4 April the Commission adopted a report on the purpose and methods of application of extraordinary set-aside,[1] i.e. unremunerated set-aside linked to overshoots of the basic area devoted to cereals, oilseeds and protein plants and conceived as a means of controlling cereal production. The Commission believes that this type of set-aside could cause undesirable side effects in future, such as reorientation of production leading to disturbances on the cereals market or even other markets. Following this report, on 26 July the Commission adopted a proposal for a Regulation (Table II) amending Council Regulation (EEC) No 1765/92. The Council adopted this Regulation on 19 December.

In addition, in order to stimulate the set-aside of arable land for afforestation under Regulation (EEC) No 2080/92 or to achieve specific environmental objectives under Regulation (EEC) No 2078/92, the Council accepted, by adopting Regulation (EC) No 1460/95 (→ point 532), that such set-aside should be counted as part of the annual set-aside obligation for producers applying for compensatory payments.

Following the accession of Austria, Sweden and Finland, the maximum guaranteed area for oilseeds was adjusted in accordance with international commitments.

---

[1]   COM(95) 122; Bull. 4-1995, point 1.3.106.

The International Grains Agreement, which extends the convention on wheat to all cereals, entered into force on 1 July. A declaration of provisional application was deposited on 30 June, pending adoption by the Council of a decision approving the Agreement on behalf of the Community. This decision was finally adopted on 19 December (Table III).

As regards the market organization in dried fodder, the Council adopted Regulation (EC) No 603/95 (Table II), amended by Regulations (EC) Nos 684/95 (Table II) and 1347/95 (Table II).

536. The Council adopted, on 20 February, Regulation (EC) No 636/95 (Table II) amending Regulation (EEC) No 2261/84 laying down general rules on the granting of aid for the production of olive oil and of aid to olive-oil producer organizations, and on 29 May, Regulation (EC) No 1267/95 (Table II) introducing specific measures in the table-olives sector.

537. Community sugar production and the Community sugar market remained subject to a production quota system, which was extended to 2000/2001 by Council Regulation (EC) No 1101/95 (Table II) of 24 April. The Council also introduced, for the same period, a specific arrangement for the supply of raw sugar to Community refineries in Finland, France, Portugal and the United Kingdom. Lastly, individual measures were introduced to enable the Community to honour commitments entered into under the agricultural agreement resulting from the multilateral negotiations of the Uruguay Round.

538. The proposal for a reform of the common organization of the market in wine (Table II) submitted by the Commission in May 1994 was the subject of a wide-ranging discussion within the Council and in trade circles. In order to honour the commitments made by the Union under the new multilateral agreements of the Uruguay Round, the system of minimum prices ('reference prices') for wines applied at the time of import and of the first reduction in the customs duties was abandoned with effect from 1 July. For grape juice and grape must, the reference-price system has been replaced since 1 September with an entry-price system, whereby a specific duty higher than the *ad valorem* customs duty is charged according to the level of import prices. In the case of export refunds, the Union has undertaken to decrease the quantities of wine products involved and expenditure on subsidized exports. On 23 November the Commission adopted a proposal for a Regulation (Table I) amending Regulation (EEC) No 1601/91 on wines and aromatized alcoholic drinks.

539.   In the fruit and vegetable sector, following the Commission's communication of 1994,[1] on which the Economic and Social Committee issued an opinion on 26 January,[2] as did Parliament on 17 February,[3] the Commission adopted on 4 October two proposals for Council Regulations on the reform of the common organization of the markets in fresh fruit and vegetables (Table II) and processed fruit and vegetables (Table II). This aims to consolidate the positive elements of the current arrangement (orientation towards market forces, decentralization, concentration of supply) through greater versatility and elimination of existing weaknesses (the operation of some producer organizations, subsidized withdrawals that have become structural, the poor reputation of the quality standards, gaps in statistics). Elsewhere, the results of the agreement concluded within the framework of the Uruguay Round modified the system of trade in fruit and vegetables with non-member countries. The reference-price system has been replaced by a system of decreasing entry prices; export refunds are subject to limits on value and quantity.

540.   In the banana sector, for which a common organization of the market has been functioning since 1 July 1993,[4] 1995 saw full implementation of the rules applying the agreement concluded for imports of 'third-country and ACP non-traditional' bananas within the framework of the Uruguay Round.[5] Following the accession of the three new Member States, a number of rules were adopted to allow satisfactory supplies to these markets under the best conditions, no decision having been taken by the Council to increase the tariff quota (Table II). In order to simplify the banana import system, the Commission adopted, on 4 April, a proposal for a Council Regulation (Table II) amending Regulations (EEC) Nos 404/93 and 1035/72 pertaining to the banana sector and fruit and vegetable sector respectively, and amending Regulation (EEC) No 2658/87 on the tariff and statistical nomenclature and on the Common Customs Tariff. The proposal provides for simplification of the system for allocating rights to importers; the possibility of a temporary transfer of quantities between ACP States belonging to the same geographical area; the right of ACP States to obtain supplies from other suppliers when, owing to exceptional circumstances, they are not in a position to deliver all or part of their quantities of traditional and non-traditional bananas; the exclusion of dwarf bananas from the scheme applicable to bananas and their inclusion on the same basis as other tropical fruit in the scheme applicable to fruit and vegetables. On 11 October the

[1]   COM(94) 360; 1994 General Report, point 616.
[2]   OJ C 102, 24.4.1995; Bull. 1/2-1995, point 1.3.126.
[3]   OJ C 56, 6.3.1995; Bull. 1/2-1995, point 1.3.127.
[4]   Regulation (EEC) No 404/93 — OJ L 47, 25.2.1993.
[5]   Regulation (EC) No 478/95 — OJ L 49, 4.3.1995.

Commission adopted a report[1] on the operation of the common organization of the market in bananas.

541. On 19 July the Commission adopted a communication on the reform of the Union's rice sector and the Uruguay Round agreement, accompanied by a proposal for a Council Regulation on the common organization of the market in rice (Table II). On the same day it adopted a proposal for a Council Regulation fixing the standard quality of rice (Table II). The Council arrived at a political agreement on these two proposals on 18 December and adopted them on 22 December.

542. Within the framework of the common organization of the market in seeds, the Commission adopted Regulation (EC) No 1589/95[2] concerning the fixing of reference prices and countervailing charges in that sector. Commission Regulation (EC) No 1588/95[2] specifies the different varieties of perennial rye-grass eligible for Community aid as from 1 July.

543. There is also an aid scheme for hops produced in the Union, and the level of aid is fixed each year by the Council. For the 1994 harvest this aid was fixed on 25 September at ECU 495/ha for aromatic varieties, ECU 532/ha for bitter varieties and ECU 368/ha for other varieties and experimental varieties (Table II).

544. Within the framework of the common organization of markets in raw tobacco, on 27 March the Council adopted Regulation (EC) No 711/95 (Table II) amending Regulation (EEC) No 2075/92 by adopting a production quota system for the 1995, 1996 and 1997 harvests; Commission Regulation (EC) No 1066/95[3] lays down the detailed rules for the implementation of this Regulation, including the 10% 'carry-over' and the possibility of paying premiums directly to producers from the 1994 harvest onwards. In accordance with the new system of production quotas, Regulation (EEC) No 3478/92 laying down detailed rules for the application of the premium system for raw tobacco was amended by Commission Regulation (EC) No 1067/95.[3] On 27 November the Commission adopted a new proposal for a Regulation (Table II) amending Regulation (EEC) No 2075/92 to fix guarantee thresholds for 1996 and 1997.

---

[1] Bull. 10-1995, point 1.3.178.
[2] OJ L 150, 1.7.1995.
[3] OJ L 108, 13.5.1995.

545.   In the field of textile fibres, the aid scheme for the production of un-ginned cotton was amended by Regulations (EC) Nos 1553/95 (Table II) and 1554/95 (Table II) with effect from the 1995/96 marketing year, in particular with a view to improving the operation of the stabilizer system.

Livestock products

546.   In the milk and milk products sector, the Commission adopted on 6 December a proposal for a Regulation on the common organization of the market in milk and milk products which consolidates Regulation (EEC) No 804/68 (Table II). The Council adopted, on 27 March, Regulation (EC) No 682/95[1] extending the 1994/95 milk year to 30 June 1995 and, on 29 May, Regulation (EC) No 1288/95 (Table II) extending to the period 1991-93 the increase adopted for the period 1993-95 in the total quantities fixed for Greece, Spain and Italy under the additional levy system. Within the framework of the annual price package, the Council adopted Regulation (EC) No 1538/95[2] amending Regulation (EEC) No 804/68 as regards fixing the eligibility criteria for benefiting from the intervention arrangement for skimmed-milk powder; Regulation (EC) No 1539/95[2] fixing the target price for milk and the intervention prices for butter and skimmed-milk powder for the period from 1 July 1995 to 30 June 1996, and Regulation (EC) No 1552/95 (Table II), which fixes the final increase for Italy and Greece in the guaranteed total quantity. The Commission also adopted, as part of the implementation of the Uruguay Round agreements, Regulations (EC) No 1466/95,[3] (EC) No 1600/95,[4] (EC) No 1598/95[4] and (EC) No 1629/95[5] which govern trade with third countries. Commission Regulation (EC) No 1585/95[6] extends the temporary reduction of the minimum proportion (i.e. 35%) of skimmed-milk powder incorporated in compound feedingstuffs until the end of 1995. The guaranteed overall quantities fixed in Article 3 of Council Regulation (EEC) No 3950/92[7] were adapted following the adoption of Regulation (EC) No 630/95[8] by the Commission.

---

[1]   OJ L 71, 31.3.1995.
[2]   OJ L 148, 30.6.1995.
[3]   OJ L 144, 28.6.1995.
[4]   OJ L 151, 1.7.1995.
[5]   OJ L 155, 6.7.1995.
[6]   OJ L 150, 1.7.1995.
[7]   OJ L 405, 31.12.1992.
[8]   OJ L 66, 24.3.1995.

547.   In the beef and veal sector, the Union opened new import tariff quotas[1] and raised the high-quality meat quota to 54 300 tonnes.[2] On 20 February the Council adopted Regulation (EC) No 424/95 on the deseasonalization premium (Table II). Under the terms of the agreements negotiated with various Central and East European countries, appropriate management measures were taken to limit imports of live bovine animals, other than pure-bred breeding stock and animals imported under specific quotas, to their traditional level compatible with the Community market's absorption capacity.[3] Lastly, to honour the commitments made in the agricultural section of the agreement resulting from the Uruguay Round negotiations, the machinery for issuing export licences was set up with a ceiling on subsidized exports.[4] In the sheepmeat and goatmeat sector, the Council adopted, on 29 May, Regulations (EC) Nos 1265/95[5] (Table II) and 1266/95. The Commission adopted Regulations (EC) Nos 1439/95[4] and 1440/95[4] to comply with Uruguay Round commitments. For the pigmeat sector, the Council adopted Regulation (EC) No 1541/95[6] which reduces the basic price for pig carcasses and adjusts the 'standard quality'.

Other work

Approximation of laws

548.   For the approximation of laws on animal health, public health, animal feed, plant-health products and seeds, see Section 4 (Internal market) of this chapter (→ points 109 to 114).

Agrimonetary measures

549.   The agrimonetary system for the single market was revised in order to allow for a degree of automatic adjustment of agricultural conversion rates to currency trends and to increase the possibilities of intervening. The mechanism that had de facto established a green ecu that could not be revalued was abolished, since its effects appeared to conflict with the objectives of the reform of the CAP. In view of the risks entailed since August 1993 by the widening of the margin of fluctuation to 15% under the EMS, the gaps authorized between the agricultural conversion rate and the mar-

---

[1]   OJ L 191, 12.8.1995; OJ L 144, 28.6.1995.
[2]   OJ L 119, 30.5.1995.
[3]   OJ L 150, 1.7.1995.
[4]   OJ L 143, 27.6.1995.
[5]   OJ L 123, 3.6.1995.
[6]   OJ L 148, 30.6.1995.

ket rate have been increased to a maximum of 5% instead of 4%. In the case of certain revaluations of particular magnitude, the Council must meet to decide what measures should be taken. These concern compensation to farmers and the scale of the reduction of the agricultural conversion rate, primarily to comply with the terms of the agreement resulting from the Uruguay Round and with budget discipline.

On 23 January, the Council adopted Regulation (EC) No 150/95 on the unit of account and the agricultural conversion rates to be applied for the purposes of the common agricultural policy, which confirmed the abandonment of the 'switchover' mechanism (Table II).

Following the deterioration of the monetary situation at the beginning of the year, the Council adopted, on 29 June, Regulation (EC) No 1527/95 (Table II) allowing the adjustments to the agricultural conversion rate provided for under the existing system to apply until 1 January 1996, while providing for *ad hoc* compensation measures. For the currencies in question which have revalued by between 2.2 and 3.2%, the conversion rate applicable before the revaluations continues to apply for the majority of direct aid to producers until 1 January 1999; a decreasing level of aid may be granted over three years with financing of half the maximum amounts by the Union. On 18 December the Council adopted Regulation (EC) No 2990/95 rolling forward for six months the provisions of Regulation (EC) No 1527/95 which apply in the event of marked revaluations of currencies (Table II).

On 19 September, Parliament stressed in a resolution[1] the potential risks that the agrimonetary system could generate in terms of distortion of competition and renationalization of the CAP.

550.   In addition, on 25 October the principle of authorizing national aid in cases where loss of income occurs as a result of monetary fluctuations in other Member States was approved by Regulation (EC) No 2611/95 (Table II). The aid must be authorized by the Commission before it is granted for a maximum period of three years, and the total amount of the aid may not exceed the losses actually caused by monetary fluctuations occurring before 1 January 1996.

---

[1]   OJ C 269, 16.10.1995; Bull. 9-1995, point 1.3.99.

Food aid for the needy in the Community

551. The Union continued its food-aid programme for the needy[1] under Regulation (EC) No 2535/95 (Table II) amending Regulation (EEC) No 3730/87. The programme's budget was increased by ECU 25 million, bringing it up to ECU 200 million. Since Germany again turned down its share of the programme, the amount concerned was distributed among the 11 other Member States.[2]

Food aid for non-member countries

552. On 4 August the Council adopted Regulation (EC) No 1975/95 (Table II) providing for an ECU 197 million aid budget, including 80 million from the EAGGF,[3] for the peoples of Armenia, Azerbaijan, Georgia, Kyrgyzstan and Tadjikistan.

State aid[4]

553. In 1995, 295 notifications of draft national aid programmes for agriculture and the food industry were submitted to the Commission for examination. The Commission also began examining 47 schemes which had not been notified in accordance with Article 93(3) of the EC Treaty and seven existing aid schemes. Following meetings with the representatives of the Member States concerned and receipt of additional information, the Commission had no objections to raise in the case of 213 schemes. At the same time, it proposed appropriate measures under Article 93(1) of the Treaty with regard to two existing aid schemes. The procedure provided for in Article 93(2) of the Treaty was initiated against several Member States in respect of 20 aid schemes. The Commission decided to close these procedures with regard to three schemes, but it sent a further three negative final decisions to Member States asking for the recovery of aid that had been paid out before the Commission had reached its final decision.

554. As regards national investment aid to improve processing and marketing conditions for agricultural products, the Commission adopted the principle of applying as from 1 January 1996 the new 'sectoral limits'

---

[1]   Twenty-first General Report, point 588.
[2]   The three new Member States have benefited from it since October, the beginning of the new programming period.
[3]   OJ L 191, 12.8.1995.
[4]   For detailed information, see the *Bulletin of the European Union* as well as the *XXVth Report on Competition Policy* (1995), publication of which is planned for spring 1996.

referred to in its Decision of 22 March 1994.[1] It also adopted the principle of reviewing its policy on subsidized management loans in the agricultural sector.[2]

Farm accountancy data network (FADN)

555.   The management committee responsible for the FADN network established by Regulation (EEC) No 79/65, which was amended on 29 November by Regulation (EC) No 2801/95 (Table II) in order to incorporate the changes arising from the reform of the CAP, held two meetings in 1995 and organized a working group on the treatment of income derived from woodland management and other non-agricultural activities. The economic situation of the milk, flower-growing and pigmeat sectors was analysed. Assistance was given to the new Member States in adjusting their national FADNs to the requirements of the Union FADN.

Advisory committees and relations with professional organizations

556.   During the 90 meetings of advisory committees and working groups organized in 1995, the Commission informed the representatives of producers, manufacturers, traders, consumers and workers about the application, development and future of the CAP.

The agricultural management and regulatory committees

557.   The activities of the agricultural management and regulatory committees are shown in Table 9.

---

[1]   OJ L 79, 23.3.1994; letter to the Member States dated 20 October 1995.
[2]   Letter to the Member States dated 20 October 1995.

TABLE 9

The agricultural management and regulatory committees

Committee	From 1 January to 31 December 1995			
	Meetings[1]	Favour-able opinions	No opinion	Unfavour-able opinion
Management Committee for Cereals	49	735	148	0
Management Committee for Pigmeat	17	42	4	0
Management Committee for Poultrymeat and Eggs	17	56	13	0
Management Committee for Fruit and Vegetables	18	44	11	0
Management Committee for Wine	20	71	2	0
Management Committee for Milk and Milk Products	27	125	44	0
Management Committee for Beef and Veal	28	76	8	0
Management Committee for Sheep and Goats	16	26	7	0
Management Committee for Oils and Fats	22	54	5	0
Management Committee for Sugar	50	160	1	0
Management Committee for Live Plants and Floricultural Products	2	2	0	0
Management Committee for Products Processed from Fruit and Vegetables	16	28	8	0
Management Committee for Tobacco	11	13	0	0
Management Committee for Hops	4	9	0	0
Management Committee for Flax and Hemp	6	8	0	0
Management Committee for Seed	4	7	0	0
Management Committee for Dried Fodder	1	1	0	0
Management Committee for Agricultural Income Aid	0	0	0	0
Implementation Committee for Spirit Drinks	6	3	1	0
Implementation Committee for Aromatized Wine-based Drinks	2	0	0	0
Management Committee for Bananas	20	8	25	0
Joint meetings of Management Committees[1]	44	37	10	0
Committee for Loans to the ex-USSR and its Republics	0	0	0	0
EAGGF Committee	20	21	2	0
Standing Committee on Feedingstuffs	12	7	1	0
Standing Veterinary Committee	28	250	0	0
Standing Committee on Seeds and Propagating Material for Agriculture, Horticulture and Forestry	18	14	0	0
Committee on Agricultural Structures and Rural Development	11	180	0	0
Community Committee on the Farm Accountancy Data Network	4	1	0	0
Standing Committee on Agricultural Research	2	0	0	0
Standing Committee on Plant Health	33	29	0	0
Standing Committe on Zootechnics	1	3	0	0
Standing Forestry Committee	11	4	0	0

TABLE 9 (continued)

Committee	From 1 January to 31 December 1995			
	Meetings[1]	Favour-able opinions	No opinions	Unfavour-able opinion
Standing Committee on Organic Farming	3	5	0	0
Standing Committee on Propagating Material and Ornamental Plants	1	0	0	0
Standing Committee on Propagating Material and Plants of Fruit Genera and Species	0	0	0	0
Committee on Geographical Indications and Designations of Origin[2]	5	0	0	0
Committee on Certificates of Specific Character[2]	0	0	0	0
Committee on the Conservation, Characterization, Collection and Utilization of Genetic Resources in Agriculture	3	1	0	0
Standing Committee on Plant Variety Rights	7	3	0	0
Ad Hoc Committee on the Supplementary Trade Mechanism	0	0	0	0

[1] Except for those relating to trade mechanisms (14 meetings) and agrimonetary matters (12 meetings).
[2] For agricultural and food products.

Financing the common agricultural policy: the EAGGF

Guarantee Section

558.   The (initial) 1995 budget, adopted on 15 December 1994,[1] provided for a total of ECU 37 925.5 million under the Guarantee Section of the EAGGF (apart from a monetary reserve of ECU 500 million), broken down as follows (in million ECU):

EAGGF, Guarantee Section (subsection B1) of which:	36 927.0
• Fisheries Guarantee Fund (Chapter B1-26) 39	
• Income aid (Chapter B1-40) 44	
• Accompanying measures (Chapter B1-50) 1 372	
Provisional appropriations (Chapter B0-40)	998.5
Guarantee Section total	37 925.5

[1]   OJ L 369, 31.12.1994; 1994 General Report, point 634.

Since supplementary and amending budget No 1/95 reduced the initial budget by ECU 1 028.5 million, appropriations for the EAGGF Guarantee Section for 1995 come to ECU 36 897 million (excluding the monetary reserve), leaving a margin of ECU 1 047 million below the guideline, which was fixed for 1995 at ECU 37 944 million.

559. In the 1996 preliminary draft budget 1996 *(→ point 980)*, total appropriations allocated to the EAGGF Guarantee Section amounted initially to ECU 40 797 million (excluding the monetary reserve of ECU 500 million); the Council maintained this level when it adopted the 1996 draft budget *(→ point 981)*. In its letter of amendment No 1, the Commission took account of the financial consequences of the Council Decisions on the 1995/96 price package, the reform of the cotton system and the new provisions on the agrimonetary system and proposed a budget in accordance with the guideline, i.e. ECU 40 828 million. When the budget *(→ point 986)* was adopted in December, the appropriations allocated to the EAGGF, Guarantee Section, were fixed at ECU 40 828 million.

560. In order to step up the combating of fraud, on 22 June the Council adopted Regulation (EC) No 1469/95 (Table II), known as the 'black list', intended to create a legal framework making it possible to identify unreliable economic operators in the field of export refunds and of sales at reduced prices of products held in public storage and to make them known to the national authorities concerned.

561. With a view to implementing the reform of the clearance of accounts procedure, the current rules were supplemented by the adoption by the Council, on 22 May, of Regulation (EC) No 1287/95 (Table II) and by the Commission, on 7 July, of Regulation (EC) No 1663/95[1] establishing detailed rules for the application of Regulation (EEC) No 729/70 and repealing Regulation (EEC) No 1723/72 with effect from 16 October. Lastly, the Commission adopted, on 23 October, the 24th financial statement (budget year 1994) of the EAGGF Guarantee Section.[2]

562. Table 10 shows 1993 to 1995 expenditure by chapter and the appropriations allocated in the 1996 budget.

---

[1] OJ L 158, 8.7.1995.
[2] COM(95) 483; Bull. 10-1995, point 1.3.180.

TABLE 10

EAGGF Guarantee Section appropriations, by sector

(million ECU)

Sector or type of measure	Expenditure 1993	Expenditure 1994	Expenditure 1995[1]	Appropriations 1996[2]
Arable crops[3]	10 610.7	12 652.3	15 048.1	17 185.0
Sugar	2 188.6	2 061.5	1 831.1	1 942.0
Olive oil	2 468.1	1 819.5	812.9	1 781.0
Dried fodder and dry vegetables	532.0	378.4	342.0	386.0
Fibre plants and silkworms	860.6	863.5	876.0	894.0
Fruit and vegetables	1 663.9	1 556.8	1 833.4	1 729.0
Wine products	1 509.6	1 176.2	849.0	1 113.0
Tobacco	1 165.1	1 057.4	993.0	1 106.0
Other crop products	259.5	287.1	372.1	314.0
Milk and milk products	5 211.3	4 248.8	4 031.6	4 214.0
Beef and veal	3 986.3	3 466.6	4 036.4	5 458.0
Sheepmeat and goatmeat	1 800.4	1 279.8	1 782.9	1 353.0
Pigmeat	200.9	416.3	143.4	168.0
Eggs and poultry	290.9	239.6	200.5	150.0
Other livestock product measures	134.8	117.3	114.7	146.0
Fisheries	32.4	35.5	39.0	48.0
Produce not covered by Annex II	743.5	631.4	573.3	616.0
ACAs and MCAs	143.5	4.7	0.7	0.0
Refunds on food aid	160.4	86.0	77.9	83.0
Interest following financial reform	100.3	83.3	80.9	0.0
Distribution to the needy	130.2	136.4	270.7	200.0
Fraud control	80.1	76.9	62.5	44.0
Clearance of accounts for previous financial years	– 384.8	– 612.0	– 1 146.4	– 1 090.0
Differentiation of market mechanisms	444.7	339.7	512.3	520.0
Other measures	0.0	47.1	21.3	194.0
Income aid	35.8	30.0	36.5	20.0
Accompanying measures	221.7	490.1[4]	830.8	2 254.0
Total	34 590.4	32 970.4	34 526.6	40 828.0[4]
Guideline	36 657.0	36 465.0	37 944.0	40 828.0
Margin	2 066.6	3 494.6	3 417.4	0.0

[1]   Provisional figures.
[2]   Commitment appropriations allocated under the 1996 preliminary draft budget.
[3]   Cereals, oilseeds, protein seeds and land withdrawal.
[4]   Not including appropriations allocated to the monetary reserve (ECU 500 million).

Guidance Section

563.   Financing from the EAGGF Guidance Section, like the other Structural Funds, is broken down by the Structural Fund Objectives assigned to it: adjustment of regions whose development is lagging behind (Objective 1), adjustment of agricultural structures (Objective 5a) and the development of rural areas (Objective 5b). The use to which the appropriations were put under the 1994 budget is shown in Table 11.

Commitment appropriations under the 1995 budget amount to ECU 3 769.3 million, including ECU 361.2 million for Community initiatives, and payment appropriations amount to ECU 3 137.9 million, including ECU 131.1 million for Community initiatives. These figures take account of appropriations for the new Member States. As for the previous year,[1] these amounts include that part of the appropriations allocated to implementation of structural measures on the territory of the former German Democratic Republic. The commitment appropriations do not, on the other hand, include appropriations allocated to measures in the fisheries sector (however, payment appropriations have been reserved for expenditure on a number of projects for which funds were committed before 1 January 1990). Finally, the amounts intended for implementing programmes in the most remote regions have again been incorporated in the 'Structural Funds' chapter of the budget.

564. While the budget for 1994, the first year of the new programming period (1994-99), was amended in line with the budgetary profile established for that period, and with the results of the negotiations of the new Community support frameworks and the single programming documents drawn up for the years 1994 to 1999, it was necessary to amend the 1995 budget to take account of the accession of three new Member States. The preliminary draft budget for 1996 provides for ECU 3 825 million in commitment appropriations and ECU 3 983 million in payment appropriations.

---

[1] OJ L 353, 17.12.1990; 1994 General Report, point 638.

TABLE 11

EAGGF Guidance Section, Agriculture — Summary of 1994 budget implementation
(Commitment appropriations)

(ECU)

	Total	CSF			Leader	Interreg	REGIS	Invireg	Article 8, Regulation (EEC) No 4256/88 and Article 22, Regulation (EEC) No 797/85	Transitional
		Objective 1	Objective 5a	Objective 5b						
Belgium	58 592 406	7 000 000	45 730 000	—	2 666 686	—	—	—	3 195 720	—
Denmark	42 491 470	—	39 920 470	2 571 000	—	—	—	—	—	—
Germany	679 187 015	379 000 000	244 804 000	54 052 015	—	—	—	—	—	1 331 000
Greece	266 287 820	266 287 820	—	—	—	—	—	—	—	—
Spain	544 770 010	408 548 749	84 587 843	46 086 814	—	—	5 418	5 483 893	57 293	4 665 678
France	619 763 579	59 708 000	439 650 462	115 703 618	—	—	—	—	35 821	558 454
Ireland	178 317 345	177 758 891	—	—	—	—	—	—	—	10 490 691
Italy	263 186 501	66 088 000	153 470 610	38 909 474	—	180 200	—	—	—	—
Luxembourg	9 801 840	—	9 496 872	304 968	—	—	—	—	—	—
Netherlands	32 067 716	1 900 000	25 251 516	4 916 200	—	—	—	—	—	—
Austria	—	—	—	—	—	—	—	—	—	—
Portugal	510 490 350	504 161 191	—	—	—	4 069 000	—	365 000	1 895 159	—
Finland	—	—	—	—	—	—	—	—	—	—
Sweden	—	—	—	—	—	—	—	—	—	—
United Kingdom	130 469 675	32 490 000	88 687 675	9 292 000	—	—	—	—	—	—
Total	3 335 425 727									

Section 20

Fisheries

Priority activities and objectives

565.   One of the main activities in the fisheries sector in 1995 was the work carried out in the various international organizations, in particular the agreement adopted at the United Nations Conference on Straddling Stocks and Highly Migratory Species (→ point 577), the agreement on the Greenland halibut fishery in the North-West Atlantic Fisheries Organization (NAFO) area adopted at that Organization's annual meeting (→ point 578), and the drafting within FAO (→ point 785) of a code of conduct for responsible fishing which covers all sea areas and fisheries but which is not binding. On the internal side, several important regulations were adopted as part of the implementation of the new instruments of the common fisheries policy (→ point 572) establishing the criteria, procedures, management system and control measures applicable to the management and regulation of fishing effort.

Fisheries policy

566.   On 27 March, the Council adopted Regulation (EC) No 685/95 (Table II) concerning certain Community fishing areas and resources, which establishes the criteria and procedures for the introduction of a system for the management of fishing effort aimed at bringing fleet capacities and catches under control. This new element of the common fisheries policy, which complements the traditional policy of resource management based on a quantitative limitation of catches, covers Community waters in the Atlantic and is aimed at a spatial distribution of fishing effort which preserves the existing balances between different areas. Under that Regulation, on 15 June, the Council adopted Regulation (EC) No 2027/95 (Table II) establishing a system for the management of fishing effort relating to certain Community fishing areas and resources. This system, which is to apply from 1 January 1996, marks the application for the first time in the common fisheries policy of a new management instrument (the regulation of fishing effort), fixing the maximum annual level of fishing effort for each Member State and fishery. It also completes the process of fully integrating Spain and Portugal into the common fisheries policy. This was approved by the Council in two stages, the first in May 1994 in Regulation (EC) No 1275/94[1] on adjustments to the arrangements in the fisheries chapters of the Act of Accession of 1985, and the second in March 1995, when the basis for the system of fishing effort management was laid down in Regulation (EC) No 685/95. On 8 December, the Council adopted a Regulation (Table II) to ensure equitable and non-discriminatory enforcement of this new system for managing fishing effort.

567. On 6 July, the Commission adopted a proposal for a Regulation (Table II) establishing the lists of species to be recorded in fishing logbooks and landing declarations.

568. The Commission also adopted, on 23 May, a proposal for a Council Decision (Table II) on restructuring of the fisheries sector in Sweden and Finland over the period from 1 January 1995 to 31 December 1996 with a view to achieving a sustainable balance between resources and their exploitation. The Council adopted this proposal on 21 December.[2]

569. Finally, on 6 October, the Commission presented a report on cooperation and coordination of the use of heavy equipment for fisheries research.[3] The Economic and Social Committee expressed a wish to see research stepped up in an own-initiative opinion of 22 November.[4]

Internal resources and policy on conservation and monitoring

Community measures

570. On 22 December, the Council adopted a Regulation (Table II) fixing the TACs (total allowable catches) and quotas for 1996. On 21 December, the Council adopted a Regulation laying down, for 1996, various technical conservation measures and fishery resource management measures within the 200-mile zone off the coast of the French department of Guiana.[2]

571. Regulation (EC) No 3362/94 fixing the TACs and quotas for 1995 was amended for the first time on 31 March by Regulation (EC) No 746/95 (Table II) to take account of the results of the discussions with Norway on mutual fishing rights, for the second time on 23 November by Regulation

---

[1] OJ L 140, 3.6.1994; 1994 General Report, point 644.
[2] Bull. 12-1995.
[3] COM(95) 392; Bull. 9-1995, point 1.3.105.
[4] Bull. 11-1995, point 1.3.170.

(EC) No 2726/95 (Table II) to allocate the additional quota of cod obtained by the Community in the Baltic Sea among Member States, and for the third time on 30 November by Regulation (EC) No 2780/95 (Table II) to provide for an increase in the TACs for fish stocks subject to precautionary TACs.

572.   On 22 May, the Council adopted Regulation (EC) No 1173/95 (Table II) amending, for the 16th time, Regulation (EEC) No 3094/86 laying down certain technical measures for the conservation of fishery resources, in order to ensure compliance with the criterion of restrictions on vessels' engine power in the flatfish protected area. On 24 July, the Council also adopted Regulation (EC) No 1909/95 (Table II) amending, for the 17th time, Regulation (EEC) No 3094/86 in order to incorporate definitively certain annual derogations. On 18 September, it adopted Regulation (EC) No 2251/95 (Table II) amending this Regulation for the 18th time in order to ban the use of drift-nets for tuna fishing in certain waters, and on 21 December it adopted Regulation (EC) No 3071/95 (Table II) amending the same Regulation for the 19th time in order to introduce technical measures applying to passive gear. The use of drift-nets was the subject of a Parliament resolution of 12 July.[1] On 6 December, the Commission adopted a proposal for a Regulation to consolidate Regulation (EEC) No 3094/86 (Table II) and a proposal for a Council Regulation[2] amending Regulation (EC) No 1626/94 laying down certain technical measures for the conservation of fishery resources in the Mediterranean.[3] The Commission also adopted a communication on the application of technical measures for the conservation of resources within the common fisheries policy on 15 December.[4]

573.   The Commission continued to monitor compliance with TACs and quotas and the technical conservation measures in Community waters and certain international waters. As a result of these controls, 67 fisheries were closed in 1995, while infringement proceedings relating to overfishing in previous years continued. The Commission monitored compliance with conservation measures, agreements with third countries and international agreements, and continued monitoring fisheries in the NAFO regulatory area.

574.   In the context of applying the Community rules on the use of drift-nets, the Commission chartered an inspection vessel for the period from 1 June to 30 September which was used in international waters in the northeast Atlantic and the Mediterranean.

---

[1]   OJ C 249, 25.9.1995; Bull. 7/8-1995, point 1.3.164.
[2]   COM(95) 635; Bull. 12-1995.
[3]   OJ L 171, 6.7.1994; 1994 General Report, point 640.
[4]   COM(95) 669; Bull. 12-1995.

575.   Under Council Decision 89/631/EEC,[1] the Community continued to contribute to the financing of programmes submitted by the Member States for acquiring and improving the means of monitoring and control. Since this Decision was to expire at the end of 1995, the Commission adopted a proposal for a Decision on 9 June (Table II) which was formally adopted by the Council on 8 December, together with a report on the Community's financial contribution towards expenditure on controls incurred by Member States for the period from 1 January 1996 to 31 December 2000. On 5 December, the Council adopted a Decision changing the time-limit for implementing certain pilot projects involving the continuous position-monitoring of fishing vessels and on the Community's contribution to the expenditure incurred in their implementation.

National measures

576.   The Commission was notified by the Member States of 173 national conservation measures, of which 106 were either the subject of comments or approved and 67 are still under review.

External resources

577.   At its sixth meeting in August,[2] the United Nations Conference on Straddling Stocks and Highly Migratory Species adopted an agreement by consensus on the implementation of the Convention on the Law of the Sea of 1982 as regards the conservation and management of straddling stocks and highly migratory species. The agreement was available for signature by future contracting parties from December onwards. The Community had a major influence on the final text of the agreement, submitting proposals to ensure a balance between the rights and obligations of coastal States and countries fishing on the high seas. More particularly, the Community helped gain acceptance for the principle of the biological unity of stocks and for the open character of regional fisheries organizations. The agreement provides for an inspection scheme to ensure compliance with international conservation and management measures relating to the stocks in question on the high seas, and for dispute-settlement procedures, measures to assist developing countries and international cooperation mechanisms for the conservation and management of straddling stocks and highly migratory species such as tuna and swordfish. The allocation of responsibilities for

---

[1]   OJ L 364, 14.12.1989; Decision as last amended by Decision 94/207/EC — OJ L 101, 20.4.1994; 1994 General Report, point 643.
[2]   Bull. 7/8-1995, point 1.3.173.

implementing this agreement was the subject of Council conclusions on 26 October.[1]

578.   Within the framework of the North-West Atlantic Fisheries Organization (NAFO), the Council — following up its decision objecting to the allocation of the 1995 TAC for Greenland halibut established by the NAFO Fisheries Commission for its regulatory area,[2] which was also criticized by Parliament on 16 February[3] — adopted a statement on fishing in that area on 6 March.[4] In this statement the Council drew attention to the procedure which had been initiated objecting to the allocation, confirmed its commitment to rational and responsible use of fishery resources and repudiated the unilateral action taken by the Canadian authorities in controlling the fishing activities of non-Canadian vessels beyond the 200-mile limit in contravention of the United Nations Convention on the Law of the Sea. In view of this objection procedure, the Council on 6 April[5] adopted Regulation (EC) No 850/95 fixing, as a precautionary measure, an autonomous quota of Greenland halibut for the Community fleet in NAFO subareas 2 and 3. Furthermore, as a result of the agreement initialled on 16 April between the Community and Canada on fisheries in the context of the NAFO Convention, the Council adopted on 17 April a decision on the signature and provisional application of that agreement; the latter was signed in Brussels on 20 April and concluded on 21 December (Table III). The agreement provides for new controls on fishing activities and allocates the total allowable catches for Greenland halibut in the NAFO area. It also provides that Canada is to return the fine imposed on the Spanish vessel *Estai* after it was stopped on 9 March and to restore the value of the confiscated cargo (the impounding of the vessel was condemned by Parliament[6]) and to repeal its rules on the monitoring of Spanish and Portuguese vessels beyond the 200-mile zone, which it adopted in contravention of international maritime law. In a communication of 5 May,[7] the Commission informed the Member States of the provisions of the EC-Canada agreement which are directly applicable to them. At the annual meeting of NAFO in Dartmouth from 11 to 15 September,[8] the participants placed this agreement on a multilateral footing.

---

[1]   Bull. 10-1995, point 1.3.206.
[2]   Bull. 1/2-1995, point 1.3.151.
[3]   OJ C 56, 6.3.1995; Bull 1/2-1995, point 1.3.150.
[4]   Bull. 3-1995, point 1.3.138.
[5]   OJ L 86, 20.4.1995; Bull. 4-1995, point 1.3.120.
[6]   OJ C 89, 10.4.1995; Bull. 3-1995, point 1.3.139.
[7]   OJ C 118, 13.5.1995; Bull. 5-1995, point 1.3.118.
[8]   Bull. 9-1995, point 1.3.114.

579. On 21 December, the Council adopted a Regulation (Table II) establishing a European Community observer scheme applicable to Community fishing vessels operating in the regulatory area of the North-West Atlantic Fisheries Organization; a Regulation (Table II) on the establishment of a pilot project on satellite tracking in the NAFO regulatory area; a Regulation (Table II) amending Regulation (EEC) No 1956/88 adopting provisions for the application of the scheme of joint international inspection adopted by the North-West Atlantic Fisheries Organization; and a Regulation (Table II) amending Regulation (EEC) No 189/92 adopting provisions for the application of certain control measures adopted by the North-West Atlantic Fisheries Organization. The Council also adopted on 21 December a Regulation (Table II) laying down for 1996 certain conservation and management measures for fishery resources in the NAFO regulatory area.

580. The Commission took up negotiations on fisheries agreements with Namibia (Table III) and South Africa (Table III), and adopted a recommendation for a Council Decision authorizing the negotiation of fisheries agreements with Estonia, Latvia, Lithuania, Poland and the Russian Federation; this Decision was adopted by the Council on 22 December (Table II). On 21 December, the Council authorized Spain and Portugal to extend by one year the agreement with South Africa on mutual fishing relations.[1]

581. The Council adopted protocols laying down the fishing opportunities and financial compensation provided for in the fisheries agreements with Guinea (Table III), Equatorial Guinea (Table III), Cape Verde (Table III), the Comoros (Table III), Côte d'Ivoire (Table III) and Senegal (Table III) respectively. It also adopted a decision on the provisional application of the protocols to the fisheries agreements with Senegal (Table III), Guinea-Bissau (Table III) and Madagascar (Table III). A third joint meeting on the agreement with Argentina was held by the Commission in Brussels on 4 December during which a total of 17 new joint ventures and joint enterprises were recommended.

582. In the context of relations with Morocco, a new fisheries agreement (Table III) was initialled on 13 November in Brussels and entered into force on 1 December for a period of four years. This is the most significant agreement between the Community and a non-member country, in particular in terms of the volume of fishing rights involved. Parliament expressed its views on this subject in July,[2] September[3] and October.[4] Mr A. Filali, the

---

[1]   OJ L 329, 30.12.1995; COM(95) 674; COM(95) 677; Bull. 12-1995.
[2]   OJ C 249, 25.9.1995; Bull. 7/8-1995, point 1.3.70.
[3]   OJ C 269, 16.10.1995; Bull. 9-1995, point 1.3.110.
[4]   OJ C 308, 20.11.1995; Bull. 10-1995, point 1.3.204.

Moroccan Prime Minister and Minister of State for Foreign Affairs and Cooperation, visited the Commission on 6 July to discuss the fisheries agreement in particular.[1] On 26 October, the Council adopted Decision 95/451/EC on a specific measure for the granting of an indemnity to fishermen from certain Member States who had had to suspend their fishing activities in Moroccan waters.

583.   The Council adopted regulations[2] definitively fixing the catch quotas for 1995 in the fishing areas of Greenland (Table II), the Faeroes (Table II) and Norway (Table II), and in the case of the Faeroes and Norway it also adopted regulations laying down various resource conservation and management measures applying to their fishing vessels. On 22 December, it also adopted regulations[3] laying down technical conservation and resource management measures as well as catch quotas in the fishing area of Norway, the area around Jan Mayen, and the fishing areas of the Faeroes, Latvia, Estonia, Lithuania and Poland. On the same day it also adopted regulations[3] fixing new catch quotas for 1996 for Greenland and Iceland.

584.   The Community participated in the work of several international fisheries organizations, attending in particular the annual meetings of the North Atlantic Salmon Conservation Organization (NASCO), NAFO, the International Baltic Sea Fishery Commission (IBSFC), the North-East Atlantic Fisheries Commission (NEAFC) and the International Whaling Commission (IWC), and the annual meeting of the Commission for the Conservation of Antarctic Marine Living Resources (CCAMLR).

585.   On 18 September, the Council adopted Decision 95/399/EC on the accession of the Community to the Agreement for the establishment of the Indian Ocean Tuna Commission (Table II).

586.   New technical measures adopted by the International Baltic Sea Fishery Commission were incorporated into Community legislation by Council Regulation (EC) No 2250/95 (Table II). The Commission also proposed the incorporation of various control measures adopted by that Organization into Community legislation (Table II). On 17 October, it adopted a proposal consolidating in a single regulation all the conservation and control measures adopted pursuant to Commission decisions on the conservation of Antarctic marine living resources (Table II).

---

[1]   Bull. 7/8-1995, point 1.3.171.
[2]   OJ L 74, 1.4.1995; Bull. 3-1995, points 1.3.134 to 1.3.136.
[3]   Bull. 12-1995.

Market organization

587.   On 30 November, the Council adopted Regulations (EC) Nos 2816/
95, 2817/95 and 2818/95 fixing guide prices for fishery products for the
1996 marketing year.[1]

588.   Work in 1995 was mainly devoted to the consequences of the enlargement of the Community, together with implementation of the reform of the
common organization of markets in fishery products which came into effect
at the end of 1994.[2] For example, the Council laid down common marketing standards for shrimps (Table II) and the guide price for them, and
amended the guide price for herring (Table II). In this context, the Commission made various amendments to regulations concerning carry-over aid, the
list of representative ports and markets, withdrawal prices, standard values
and reference prices. Under the new measures intended to help counter the
market slump in fishery products, the Commission amended Regulations
(EEC) No 3190/82[3] (extension of producer organizations' disciplinary rules)
and (EEC) No 3902/92[4] (financial compensation for the crisis). As regards
the tuna market, compensatory allowances were granted to producer
organizations for tuna delivered to the canning industry for the periods
1 October to 31 December 1993, 1 January to 31 March 1994 and 1 April
to 30 June 1994 respectively. The Commission adopted Regulation (EC)
No 2567/95[5] which grants private storage aid for the squid *Loligo
patagonica* offered for sale between 1 March and 31 May 1995. As regards
the situation and prospects of the sardine market, on 10 July the Commission adopted a report on the market in this product[6] on the basis of which
the Council agreed, in its conclusions of 26 October,[7] not to extend the
compensatory allowance scheme provided for in the Act of Accession of
Spain and Portugal.[8] In the same context, the Commission adopted implementing rules laying down conditions for the granting of specific recognition and financial aid to producers' organizations in the fisheries sector in
order to improve the quality of their products.[9] Finally, on 15 December
Parliament adopted a resolution on the slump in the salmon sector.[10]

---

[1]   OJ L 292, 7.12.1995; Bull. 11-1995, point 1.3.182.
[2]   Council Regulation (EC) No 3318/94 — OJ L 350, 31.12.1994; 1994 General Report, point 665.
[3]   OJ L 338, 30.11.1982.
[4]   OJ L 392, 23.12.1992.
[5]   OJ L 262, 1.11.1995.
[6]   COM(95) 320; Bull 7/8-1995, point 1.3.174.
[7]   Bull. 10-1995, point 1.3.210.
[8]   OJ L 302, 15.11.1985.
[9]   Regulation (EC) No 2636/95 — OJ L 271, 14.11.1995.
[10] OJ C 17, 22.1.1996; Bull. 12-1995.

Fisheries and the environment

589. The sustainable development of resources was fully integrated into the common fisheries policy by means of measures taken to conserve resources, preserve marine biodiversity and rationalize fishing. The environmental impact of fisheries was taken into account, in particular, by the systematic consultation of scientific experts when legislative measures on the exploitation of resources were drafted.

590. On 5 May, the Commission adopted a communication on the evaluation of the biological impact of fisheries,[1] in which it recommends concentrating research effort on a number of priority areas, in particular the effects of fishing on certain species (cetaceans, seals, reptiles, birds and benthic communities).

591. At the fourth North Sea Conference, held in Esbjerg on 8 and 9 September, the Commission helped to draw up the declarations ratified by the Conference, in particular those on scientific research programmes and fisheries management measures to protect marine ecosystems.

Structural action

592. Structural action is now covered in Section 10 (Economic and social cohesion) of this chapter *(→ point 312).*

State aid schemes[2]

593. Under Articles 92 and 93 of the EC Treaty, Member States notified 37 proposed aid schemes for fisheries and aquaculture. The Commission also examined 20 that had not been notified. The Commission raised no objection to implementation of 22 of these aid schemes. It decided to terminate the procedure under Article 93(2) of the EC Treaty in respect of one proposed scheme and adopted a final negative decision on one unnotified aid scheme.

---

[1]   COM(95) 40; Bull. 5-1995, point 1.3.122.
[2]   For further details, please refer to the *Bulletin of the European Union* and the *XXVth Report on Competition Policy* (1995), which is due to be published in the spring of 1996.

Section 21

Employment and social policy

Priority activities and objectives

594.　Tackling unemployment was — along with the equal opportunities drive — one of the European Union institutions' priorities in 1995, following on from the White Paper on growth, competitiveness and employment and the Essen European Council conclusions of December 1994,[1] which pinpointed five major issues to be addressed: improvement of workers' employment prospects by promoting investment in vocational training; improving the employment intensity of growth through more flexible organization of the labour market and a wages policy favouring job-creating investment and encouraging initiatives, particularly at regional and local levels, paving the way for job creation in line with new requirements, for example in the environmental field and in social services; reducing non-wage labour costs; more effective labour-market policies (e.g. employment services, geographical and occupational mobility, encouragement to return to work); and strengthening of measures to help those who are particularly vulnerable to unemployment (e.g. young people, the long-term unemployed, older workers and women). The Council also called on the Member States to incorporate these recommendations into their national policies by drawing up multiannual programmes commensurate with their economic and social situation. The European Council called on the Council and the Commission to keep a close watch on employment trends, to examine the Member States' policies and to report each year on progress made in respect of the jobs market.

Responding to the challenge of stimulating employment-intensive growth, the Commission's communication of 8 March described how the process initiated by the Essen European Council could be put into practice. On 13 June, the Commission adopted a communication on a European strategy for encouraging local development and employment initiatives, the importance of which had been underscored by the European Council meeting in Cannes in June, and a communication and a proposal for a Council Decision on analysis, research, cooperation and action in the field of employment. Still within the context of the employment strategy spelt out by the Essen European Council, and which provided for joint action by the Commission and the Member States, the Commission adopted, on 26 July, a

---

[1]　Bull. 12-1994, point I.3; 1994 General Report, point 562.

report on employment in Europe in 1995, as well as, on 11 October, a communication on trends and developments in employment systems in the European Union. This latter communication served as back-up for the report which the Commission presented, in conjunction with the Council, to the Madrid European Council in December.

Reaffirming the priority status of job creation and equal opportunities at European Union level, the Madrid European Council welcomed the joint Commission and Council report and the Member States' multiannual employment programmes. It noted the momentum which had built up under the strategy mapped out in Essen, taking the form more especially of Member States' multiannual employment programmes, and called on the Member States and the social partners to maintain and step up their efforts to put the Essen process into effect. It also highlighted a number of areas for action which it regarded as having priority status in the multiannual employment programmes.

Seeking to implement its 1994 White Paper on social policy, the Commission proposed, in April, a medium-term social action programme which sets out to define a framework for future action in the social policy field. It also presented, in October, a report on social protection in Europe, and a communication on the future of social protection. The Commission continued to apply the provisions of the Protocol on social policy and the annexed Agreement on social policy, more especially in respect of reconciling work and family life, gender discrimination (reversal of the burden of proof), flexible working time and job stability. It also continued the fight against social exclusion and helped strengthen European-level social dialogue, encouraging active participation by the social partners in implementing the Protocol on social policy. Finally, progress was made on the freedom of movement of workers (the EURES network) and on living and working conditions, with special reference to the adoption of a Community programme in the field of safety, hygiene and health at work.

Implementation of the White Paper on social policy

595. On 12 April,[1] the Commission adopted a communication on a medium-term social action programme (1995-97), which seeks to build on and take forward the achievements of the previous action programme[2] (implementing the Community Charter of the Fundamental Social Rights of Workers), and embraces the strategy set out by the Commission in its White

---

[1] COM(95) 134; Bull. 4-1995, point 1.3.126.
[2] Twenty-third General Report, point 394.

Paper[1] on social policy, in order to meet the new needs and challenges. The Commission's proposals focus on presenting new legislative proposals, having regard to the principles of subsidiarity and proportionality; launching studies on specific subjects; giving fresh impetus to proposals before the Council and withdrawing proposals which have been superseded; and continuing its efforts to ensure the effective transposal and implementation of adopted legislation. This flexible programme, which will be updated annually by the Commission, focuses on a number of major issues: employment, education and training, consolidation and development of social legislation, equal opportunities for women and men, an active society for all, and medium-term analysis and research. It was endorsed by the Committee of the Regions on 20 September.[2]

596. On 19 January, the European Parliament adopted a resolution[3] on the White Paper on European social policy, in which it confirmed its commitment to the European social model, considering that a basis of binding legislative provisions applicable throughout the Union constituted a suitable instrument for the achievement of a social union in parallel with economic and monetary union. It called in particular for further legislative measures in respect of equal opportunities, the organization of working time and cross-border employment, calling for the Community Charter of the Fundamental Social Rights of Workers to be included in the Treaty when that was revised in 1996, and for qualified majority voting and the co-decision procedure to be extended to the social sphere.

597. In a resolution adopted on 27 March,[4] the Council emphasized the importance of the transposition and application of Community social legislation to make it a tangible reality for citizens.

Implementation of the Protocol on social policy

598. In the light of the failure to reach unanimous agreement among the Member States on the proposal for a Directive of 1984,[5] which is opposed by the United Kingdom, the Commission decided to consult the social partners, on 22 February,[6] on the possible direction of Community action on the question of reconciling family and working life and, on 21 June,[7] on the

---

[1]   COM(95) 333; 1994 General Report, point 554.
[2]   Bull. 9-1995, point 1.3.116.
[3]   OJ C 43, 20.2.1995; Bull. 1/2-1995, point 1.3.156.
[4]   OJ C 168, 4.7.1995; Bull. 3-1995, point 1.3.143.
[5]   COM(84) 631; OJ C 316, 27.11.1984.
[6]   Bull. 1/2-1995, point 1.3.159.
[7]   Bull. 6-1995, point 1.3.205.

nature of such action with special reference to parental leave. On 7 July,[1] UNICE (European Employers' Organization), CEEP (Public Enterprises) and ETUC (European Trade Union Confederation) expressed a desire to enter into negotiations, whereupon the Commission suspended its legislative initiative, as of 20 July, for the set period of nine months at most. On 14 December,[2] the social partners signed an agreement on parental leave — the first of its kind — and called on the Commission to submit it to the Council so that the Council could adopt a decision and make the minimum requirements in the agreement binding in all the Member States apart from the United Kingdom.

599.   In the absence of unanimous agreement on a proposal for a Directive dating from 1988,[3] the Commission initiated, on 5 July, the first stage in the consultation of the social partners on the possible direction of Community action on the burden of proof in cases of discrimination on grounds of sex (→ point 631).

600.   In the absence of the required majority for the adoption of two proposals for Council Directives of 1990[4] relating to working conditions and distortions of competition, the Commission also decided, on 27 September,[5] to initiate the first stage in the consultation of the social partners on a Community initiative concerning the flexibility of working time and job security.

601.   On 14 November,[6] the Commission adopted a communication on the information and consultation of employees which follows on from the undertaking given in the 1995 medium-term social action programme to initiate consultations with the social partners on the expediency and possible direction of Community action in respect of the information and consultation of employees in national companies. The aim is to relaunch debate in the Community institutions on what approach should be adopted to unblock the current impasse in the Council on a series of proposals concerning worker participation.

602.   Pursuant to Article 7 of the Agreement on social policy, the Commission adopted its annual report on the Community Charter of the Fundamental Social Rights of Workers and on the Protocol on social policy.[7]

---

[1]   Bull. 7/8-1995, point 1.3.185.
[2]   Bull. 12-1995.
[3]   COM(88) 269; OJ C 176, 5.7.1988.
[4]   COM(90) 228; OJ C 224, 8.9.1990.
[5]   Bull. 9-1995, point 1.3.121.
[6]   COM(95) 547; Bull. 11-1995, point 1.3.189.
[7]   COM(95) 184; Bull. 5-1995, point 1.3.123.

Employment

Social dialogue

603. Within the context of the social dialogue, the importance of which was underlined by the Cannes European Council,[1] the Commission adopted, on 25 September,[2] a communication concerning the establishment of a European Centre for Industrial Relations (ECIR), the inauguration of which coincided with the social dialogue summit held in Florence on 21 October. At the summit,[3] the social partners adopted two joint resolutions, one on racial discrimination and xenophobia, the other on equal treatment at work (→ *point 13*), along with a resolution on employment. The latter resolution constituted the social partners' contribution, with a view to the Madrid European Council, to the follow-up to the employment strategy spelt out at the Essen European Council.

Employment and the labour market

604. On 8 March,[4] the Commission adopted a communication on the follow-up to the Essen European Council on employment, in which it describes how this strategy could be put into practice. The European Council, meeting in Cannes[5] on 26 and 27 June, confirmed the need to promote employment-intensive growth, reiterated that the fight against unemployment remained a high priority for the European Union and its Member States, and called on the Member States once again to come up with multiannual programmes. It also stressed the importance of local employment initiatives, in particular in the field of services linked to the environment and living standards, crafts and traditional products. On 13 June, the Commission presented a communication setting out a European strategy for encouraging local development and employment initiatives, and identified a number of fields with potential for meeting the new needs and offering substantial employment prospects. Also on 13 June,[6] the Commission adopted a communication and a proposal for a Council Decision on Commission activities of analysis, research, cooperation and action in the field of employment, the aim here being to foster a closer partnership between the Member States and the Commission and with all those involved in employment

---

[1]   Bull. 6-1995, points I.4 and I.5.
[2]   COM(95) 445; Bull. 9-1995, point 1.3.118.
[3]   Bull. 10-1995, point 1.3.220.
[4]   COM(95) 74; Bull. 3-1995, point 1.3.144.
[5]   Bull. 6-1995, points I.4 et seq.
[6]   OJ C 235, 9.9.1995; COM(95) 250; Bull. 6-1995, point 1.3.199.

policy, and to develop a new approach for such initiatives with a view to identifying and transferring examples of good practice.

In its annual report on employment in Europe of 26 July,[1] on which Parliament gave its views on 28 November,[2] the Commission presented a detailed analysis of developments and prospects in employment and the labour market in the Community, followed by a detailed description of the measures taken by the Member States in each of the five main areas pinpointed by the Essen European Council, along with an analysis of two specific issues identified by the European Council: firstly, the relationship between employment, social protection systems and labour costs; secondly, the scope for job creation in connection with environmental protection.

605.   With a view to the forthcoming Madrid European Council, the Commission also presented, on 11 October, a communication on trends and developments in employment systems in the European Union,[3] in the form of a critical evaluation of progress made in implementing the Essen and Cannes European Council conclusions, along with analyses of the macroeconomic situation with special reference to employment, the mutual benefits likely to result from closer coordination of economic and structural measures in the European Union, and the role of small and medium-sized businesses in creating jobs.

606.   The communication of 11 October, along with the employment reports prepared by the Council, formed the basis for a joint report on employment[4] by the Council and the Commission which was transmitted to the Madrid European Council as requested.[5] Approving the report and noting that the cooperation of all parties involved had enabled new steps to be taken towards identifying the obstacles in the way of reducing unemployment, above all in connection with the macroeconomic and structural aspects which substantially favour the creation of new jobs, the Council, meeting in Madrid in December, decided on the priority spheres of action in Member States' multiannual employment programmes: stepping up training programmes; rendering business strategies more flexible in areas such as the organization of work and of working time; ensuring a pattern of non-wage labour costs appropriate to unemployment-reducing objectives; continuing the present wage restraint by linking it to productivity; obtaining the maximum level of efficiency in social protection systems; pressing for greater conversion of passive policies to protect the unemployed into active

---

[1]   COM(95) 396; Bull. 7/8-1995, point 1.3.177.
[2]   OJ C 339, 18.12.1995; Bull. 11-1995, point 1.3.183.
[3]   COM(95) 465; Bull. 10-1995, point 1.3.211.
[4]   Bull. 12-1995.
[5]   Bull. 12-1994, point I.3; Bull. 6-1995, point I.4.

job-creation measures; improving the machinery for information between those providing and those seeking employment; promoting local employment initiatives. The European Council further emphasized that special attention should be paid to young people seeking their first job, the long-term unemployed and unemployed women.

607.   The Standing Committee on Employment, meeting in Brussels on 19 June[1] for its 48th session and on 28 November[2] for its 49th, was concerned essentially with the preparation and follow-up of European Council initiatives on employment.

608.   At its October session, the Economic and Social Committee adopted a number of own-initiative opinions on employment, concerned more specifically with the economic situation in 1995 and employment in Europe,[3] working time,[4] unemployment among young people,[5] and the repercussions of the common agricultural policy on employment.[6] On 13 July, the European Parliament adopted a resolution[7] on a coherent employment strategy for the European Union, followed on 14 July by a resolution[8] on the Commission's annual report[9] on employment (1994).

609.   The social consequences of business relocations in the European Union were also the subject of a number of Parliament resolutions[10] and a Committee of the Regions opinion.[11]

610.   European Employment Week took place in Brussels in November.

Freedom of movement for workers

611.   The EURES (European Employment Services) network, which was set up under Commission Regulation (EEC) No 2434/92[12] with a view to providing better information to European citizens looking for a job in another Member State, comprises 500 Euroadvisers, who work within the partner

---

[1]   Bull. 6-1995, point 1.3.201.
[2]   Bull. 11-1995, point 1.3.185.
[3]   Bull. 10-1995, point 1.3.213.
[4]   Bull. 10-1995, point 1.3.214.
[5]   Bull. 10-1995, point 1.3.215.
[6]   Bull. 10-1995, point 1.3.216.
[7]   OJ C 249, 25.9.1995; Bull. 7/8-1995, point 1.3.178.
[8]   OJ C 249, 25.9.1995; Bull. 7/8-1995, point 1.3.179.
[9]   COM(94) 381; 1994 General Report, point 564.
[10] OJ C 56, 6.3.1995; Bull. 1/2-1995, point 1.3.157; OJ C 249, 25.9.1995; Bull. 7/8-1995, point 1.3.180; OJ C 269, 16.10.1995; Bull. 9-1995, point 1.3.117.
[11] Bull. 7/8-1995, point 1.3.181.
[12] OJ L 245, 26.8.1992.

organizations and are trained to provide information, advice and placement services. Work this year has focused on developing the database on job vacancies and applications by integrating national public employment service systems; developing the database on living and working conditions; training the Euroadvisers; promoting the EURES network, providing back-up at national and transfrontier levels; running a university pilot project; seeking points of contact with other Community programmes; and conducting studies on transfrontier movements and employment prospects in the regional markets.

Structural operations

612. European Social Fund operations are dealt with in Section 10 (Economic and social cohesion) of this chapter (→ points 296 et seq.).

Social security

Social security and social action

613. On 31 October, the Commission adopted a report on social protection,[1] a companion to the Commission's report on employment in Europe (→ point 604). The social protection report examines the links between social protection and employment and focuses analysis on the rates of unemployment benefit paid in the European Union; access for the self-employed to health insurance and social assistance; social protection facilities for all persons — mainly women — who have to leave their jobs or work shorter hours to take care of children or handicapped or elderly people. Also on 31 October, the Commission adopted a communication on the future of social protection[2] in which it fixed the framework for a European debate on the subject.

614. On 16 May, the Commission proposed an amendment to Directive 86/378/EEC on the implementation of the principle of equal treatment for men and women in occupational social security schemes (→ point 632). On 11 September, it adopted a report on the application, in Spain and Portugal, of Directive 79/7/EEC on equal treatment for men and women in statutory social security schemes.[3]

---

[1]   COM(95) 457; Bull. 10-1995, point 1.3.218.
[2]   COM(95) 466; Bull. 10-1995, point 1.3.219.
[3]   COM(95) 418.

Social security for migrant workers

615. With a view to extending to all insured persons, regardless of nationality, the provision of immediate health care to a person insured in a Member State and temporarily resident in another Member State, the Commission amended, on 26 June (Table II), its proposal for a Council Regulation amending Regulation (EEC) No 1408/71. On 14 July, the Commission also presented a proposal (Table II) amending the same Regulation with a view to bringing it into line with changes in national social security legislation. These two proposals were adopted by the Council on 21 December.

Working conditions

Measures for workers in the ECSC industries

616. In 1995, ECU 123.8 million was granted in readaptation aid, pursuant to Article 56(1)(c) and (2)(b) of the ECSC Treaty, to 44 313 ECSC industry workers ('traditional aid'). The traditional form of aid programmes was supplemented in 1995 by aid (ECU 3.66 million of it complementing the 1994 provision) under the steel industry social measures totalling ECU 41.28 million and, under the coal industry social measures, totalling ECU 40 million (again, ECU 11.32 million of it complementing the 1994 provision). A breakdown of the total sum granted in readaptation aid in 1995, by Member State and sector, is given in Table 12.

TABLE 12

Readaptation aid — Appropriations committed (1995 programmes)

Member State	Steel making and iron-ore mining				Coalmining			
	Traditional aid		Social measures		Traditional aid		Social measures	
	Workers	Amount (ECU)	Workers	Amount (ECU)	Workers	Amount (ECU)	Workers	Amount (ECU)
Belgium	1 315	3 945 000	1 088	4 106 042	324	972 000	324	1 216 000
Germany	7 441	22 323 000	2 528	6 928 832	10 410	31 230 000	3 907	15 628 000
Greece	106	318 000						
Spain	1 477	4 431 000	1 097	4 911 732	2 376	7 128 000	2 376	8 107 695
France	1 299	3 897 000	724	2 440 629	888	1 835 705	503	1 790 000
Ireland	194	376 806						
Italy	7 017	21 051 000	4 392	16 531 666	2	6 000		
Luxembourg	378	1 134 000	301	1 505 000				
Netherlands	312	936 000						
Portugal	349	1 047 000	349	1 103 000	126	378 000	16	64 000
United Kingdom	24	72 000	22	96 000	10 275	22 702 000	850	1 870 000
Total	19 912	59 530 806	10 501	37 622 901	24 401	64 251 705	7 976	28 675 695

617.   As regards ECSC subsidized housing loans, the Commission approved, on 3 July, the financial package (ECU 38 million) for the final three years (1995-97) of the 12th and last programme of ECSC social housing loans. On 6 November, the Council gave its assent,[1] as required by Article 54(2) of the ECSC Treaty.

Health and safety

Health and safety at work

618.   On 29 June, the Council adopted Regulation (EC) No 1643/95[2] amending Regulation (EC) No 2062/94 setting up the European Agency for Health and Safety at Work to take into account the accession of Austria, Finland and Sweden.

619.   On 12 July,[3] the Commission adopted a Community programme concerning safety, hygiene and health at work (1996-2000) with a view to improving Member States' implementation of Community legislation, the consolidation and revision of existing Community legislation, the presentation of new proposals on high-risk activities and categories of workers, improved coherence of Union activities, the establishment of relations with non-member countries covered by an association agreement with the European Union, improved cooperation within the Union, and a range of non-legislative measures (Table II) covered by a proposal for a Council Decision. These measures include the preparation of information material to ensure the correct application of Community legislation; initiatives designed to enhance information, education and training; the investigation of key problem areas such as violence at the workplace and stress; and a new SAFE programme (Safety action for Europe) aimed at providing support for projects designed to improve working conditions, with special reference to SMEs, and to improve the organization of work and influence attitudes to health and safety at work so as to reduce the number of occupational accidents and diseases.

620.   On 12 July, the Commission decided to set up a Scientific Committee for Occupational Exposure Limits to Chemical Agents.[4] On 30 June, the Commission adopted Directive 95/30/EC[5] adapting to technical progress Council Directive 90/679/EEC on the protection of workers from the risks

---

[1]   OJ C 310, 22.11.1995.
[2]   OJ L 156, 7.7.1995.
[3]   COM(95) 282; Bull. 7/8-1995, point 1.3.182.
[4]   Decision 95/320/EC — OJ L 188, 9.9.1995.
[5]   OJ L 155, 6.7.1995.

related to exposure to biological agents at work. It also adopted, on 13 September, a proposal for a Directive (Table II), this being the first amendment of Directive 90/394/EEC on the protection of workers from the risks related to exposure to carcinogens at work and, on 18 September (Table II), a proposal for a Directive on minimum requirements for improving the safety and health protection of workers potentially at risk from explosive atmospheres, the aim here being to create, for industry in general, a protective framework such as already exists for the mineral-extracting industries. The Council, for its part, adopted, on 5 December, a Directive (Table II) amending Directive 89/655/EEC on the minimum safety and health requirements for work equipment.

Health and safety in the ECSC industries

621.   Ongoing projects in the programmes dealing with ergonomics, pollution and safety in the mining and steel industries were the subject of an evaluation exercise.

622.   On 28 June,[1] the ECSC Consultative Committee adopted a resolution on ECSC social research.

Combating social exclusion

623.   In the course of 1995, the Commission initiated a number of measures designed to combat social exclusion, for example a European initiative for the prevention of urban delinquency and the social reintegration of ex-offenders, and funding for various social exclusion action projects. It also adopted, on 27 March,[2] the final report on the Community programme 'Poverty 3' (1989-94) concerning the economic and social integration of the less privileged groups in society.

624.   Information on measures to combat racism and xenophobia are dealt with in Section 1 of Chapter II (→ point 13).

---

[1]   OJ C 206, 11.8.1995; Bull. 6-1995, point 1.3.204.
[2]   COM(95) 94; Bull. 3-1995, point 1.3.146.

European Foundation for the Improvement of Living and Working Conditions

625.   The Dublin-based European Foundation for the Improvement of Living and Working Conditions continued work under its four-year programme (1993-96), covering six main subject areas: social cohesion; access to employment; innovation and organization of work; human relations in businesses, social dialogue and industrial relations; health and safety; socioeconomic aspects of the environment; equal opportunities for women and men. During the year, a series of conferences, seminars and workshops, along with a wide range of publications, complemented the Foundation's research programme. The Foundation also developed its collaborative links with the European institutions and publicized its work among various target groups in the Member States.

International cooperation

626.   The Commission played its part in the UN World Summit for Social Development (→ point 779) and in the UN World Conference on Women (→ point 633). The annual tripartite conference on social affairs, organized within the context of cooperation between the European Union and Japan, was held in Brussels in December and focused on the question of structural change. On 25 January, the Economic and Social Committee adopted an own-initiative opinion on relations between the European Union and the International Labour Organization (ILO).

Section 22

Equal opportunities

627. *Throughout the year, the Commission and the other institutions upheld their firm commitment to promoting equal opportunities for women and men, and to promoting women's rights in general. Being the final year of the third action programme on equal opportunities for women and men (1991-95),[1] 1995 also saw consideration being given to, and adoption of, the fourth action programme and to the run-up to September's fourth World Conference on Women in Beijing. The group of Commissioners responsible for monitoring the development of equal opportunities at the Commission, set up at the start of the year and chaired by Mr J. Santer, concentrated on integrating the 'equal opportunities' element into the full range of Community policies. In December, the Madrid European Council[2] reiterated the importance of the equal opportunities issue and called for continued action in favour of women with a view to achieving fully equal treatment.*

628. Following a wide-ranging consultation exercise among the relevant organizations and authorities, the Commission adopted, on 19 July, a communication,[3] accompanied by a proposal for a Council Decision (Table II) on the fourth medium-term Community action programme on equal opportunities for women and men (1996-2000). This proposal was adopted by the Council on 22 December with a funding package of ECU 30 million. The programme sets out to ensure that equal opportunities are taken more into consideration in defining and implementing the relevant policies at all levels — Community, national and regional. Seeking to establish partnership arrangements between all concerned at all levels, the programme focuses on six objectives: to mobilize all the actors in economic and social life to promote equal opportunities; to promote equal opportunities in a changing economy; to reconcile family life and work; to promote a gender balance in decision-making; to make conditions more conducive to exercising equality rights; to implement, monitor and assess equal opportunities measures.

629. On 13 June,[4] the Commission adopted a report on the implementation of Council Recommendation 84/635/EEC[5] on the promotion of positive action for women, and of a mid-term report on the third action pro-

---

[1]   Twenty-fifth General Report, point 442.
[2]   Bull. 12-1995.
[3]   COM(95) 381; Bull. 7/8-1995, point 1.3.187.
[4]   COM(95) 247; Bull. 6-1995, point 1.3.207.
[5]   OJ L 331, 19.12.1984.

gramme on equal opportunities for women and men.[1] Meanwhile, the European Parliament adopted, on 16 March, a resolution on equal treatment and equal opportunities for men and women[2] followed, on 14 June, by a resolution on the evaluation of the third Community action programme on equal opportunities for women and men and proposals for the fourth Community action programme.[3] The Commission also adopted, on 18 September, a communication on the integration of gender issues in development cooperation (→ point 780), followed by a Council resolution in November (→ point 780).

630. The Council, for its part, adopted, on 27 March, a resolution[4] on balanced participation by men and women in decision-making, following which the Commission adopted, on 29 November, a proposal for a Council recommendation on the same subject.[5] On 5 October, the Council adopted a resolution on the portrayal of women and men in advertising and the media.[6]

631. Under the procedure provided for by the Social Protocol, the social partners were consulted on the possible direction of Community action in respect of reconciling work and family life (→ point 598) and the burden of proof in the event of sex discrimination.[7]

632. In the social security field, the Commission adopted, on 16 May, a proposal for a Council Directive (Table II) seeking to bring Directive 86/378/EEC on the implementation of the principle of equal treatment for men and women in occupational social security schemes into line with Article 119 of the EC Treaty as interpreted by the Court of Justice in the Barber judgment of 17 May 1990[8] and subsequent judgments. The Commission also consulted the social partners on the content of, and arrangements for, a code of good practice on the means of redress and procedures for the application of Article 119 of the EC Treaty on the principle of equal pay.

633. On the international scene, the Commission made an active contribution, more especially by way of a communication,[9] to the run-up to the fourth UN World Conference on Women. In Beijing, from 4 to 15

---

[1] COM(95) 246; Bull. 6-1995, point 1.3.206.
[2] OJ C 89, 10.4.1995; Bull. 3-1995, point 1.3.147.
[3] OJ C 166, 3.7.1995; Bull. 6-1995, point 1.3.208.
[4] OJ C 168, 4.7.1995; Bull. 3-1995, point 1.3.148.
[5] COM(95) 593; Bull. 11-1995, point 1.3.191.
[6] OJ C 296, 10.11.1995; Bull. 10-1995, point 1.3.221.
[7] Bull. 7/8-1995, point 1.3.188.
[8] OJ C 146, 15.6.1990; Twenty-fourth General Report, point 1056.
[9] COM(95) 221; Bull. 5-1995, point 1.3.126.

September,[1] the European Union, represented by Ms C. Alberdi, the Spanish Minister for Social Affairs and President-in-Office of the Council, and by Mr P. Flynn, Member of the Commission, was a driving force at the Conference itself and in the adoption of the final declaration and the platform for action. The platform is aimed at achieving equality, development and peace, and is intended as an instrument for encouraging and legitimizing measures taken for women in a variety of fields. It stresses women's rights, making implicit mention of sexual rights, the importance of women's economic independence and the integration of equal opportunities into all relevant policies. The Conference also generated resolutions from the European Parliament[2] and an own-initiative opinion from the Economic and Social Committee.[3]

---

[1]   Bull. 9-1995, point 1.3.122.
[2]   OJ C 166, 3.7.1995; Bull. 6-1995, point 1.3.209; OJ C 269, 16.10.1995; Bull. 9-1995, point 1.3.123.
[3]   OJ C 256, 2.10.1995; Bull. 7/8-1995, point 1.3.189.

Section 23

Solidarity[1]

Measures to help the disabled

634.   The Commission continued to implement the Helios II Community action programme to assist disabled people (1993–96),[2] which now also covers the EEA countries. The Helios II awards for best practice in the European Union concerning the integration of the disabled were made on 5 December in Brussels to a total of 18 projects. Under its medium-term social action programme *(→ point 595)* the Commission initiated consultations on the possibility of a new European cooperation programme concerning equal opportunities for the disabled. In the context of the third European Day for Disabled People, a report on non-discrimination was submitted on 7 December to the European Parliament and to the Commission. Finally, on 15 December,[3] the Commission adopted a proposal for a Council recommendation on the mutual recognition by the Member States of parking cards for disabled people. The European Parliament, for its part, adopted, on 14 December,[4] a resolution on disabled persons' human rights.

Measures to help older people

635.   To help Member States tackle the problem of population ageing, a proposal for a Council Decision (Table II) on Community support for actions in favour of older people was adopted by the Commission on 1 March. The question of jobs for older workers was the subject of a Council resolution of 29 June.[5]

Measures to help disaster victims in the European Union

636.   The purpose of emergency Community aid within the European Union is to relieve the suffering of people affected by sudden and major disasters. Intended as a symbol of solidarity between citizens, it is designed

---

[1]   Information on the drive to combat social exclusion can be found in Section 21 (Employment and social policy) of this chapter *(→ point 623).*
[2]   Twenty-seventh General Report, point 602.
[3]   COM(95) 696; Bull. 12-1995.
[4]   OJ C 17, 22.1.1996; Bull. 12-1995.
[5]   Bull. 6-1995, point 1.3.200.

to provide emergency aid in the face of disasters of exceptional seriousness and scale and cannot be considered as compensation for damage suffered by victims of disasters or caused to economic infrastructure. This year, the Commission granted emergency aid to victims of disasters in seven cases in 11 Member States of the European Union (Belgium, Germany, Greece, Spain, France, Ireland, Italy, Luxembourg, the Netherlands, Austria and the United Kingdom), totalling ECU 4.95 million.[1] Parliament also asked the Commission on several occasions to grant aid to victims of specific disasters, particularly drought, fires, floods, storms and earthquakes.[2]

---

[1] Bull. 1/2-1995, point 1.3.162; Bull. 3-1995, point 1.3.150; Bull. 5-1995, point 1.3.130; Bull. 6-1995, point 1.3.211; Bull. 9-1995, points 1.3.125, 1.3.127 and 1.3.128.
[2] OJ C 56, 6.3.1995; Bull. 1/2-1995, points 1.3.163 and 1.3.164; OJ C 89, 10.4.1995; Bull. 3-1995, point 1.3.151; OJ C 151, 19.6.1995; Bull. 5-1995, points 1.3.128 and 1.3.129; OJ C 249, 25.9.1995; Bull. 7/8-1995, points 1.3.190 to 1.3.192; OJ C 269, 16.10.1995; Bull. 9-1995, points 1.3.126, 1.3.129 to 1.3.132; OJ C 287, 30.10.1995; Bull. 10-1995, points 1.3.224 to 1.3.226; OJ C 323, 4.12.1995; Bull. 11-1995, point 1.3.192.

Section 24

Public health

Priority activities and objectives

637.   Activities in the area of public health pursuant to Articles 3(o) and 129 of the EC Treaty continued in 1995 on the basis of the broad lines set out in the framework for action in the field of public health adopted in 1993,[1] which provided for the designation by the Commission of five-year programmes of action in eight priority areas. Following a meeting of the Conciliation Committee, a joint text was adopted in December on the proposals for programmes concerning cancer (→ point 638), AIDS and other communicable diseases (→ point 640) and health promotion (Table I). This latter proposal is concerned with setting up a Community programme for health promotion, information, education and training for the period 1 January 1996 to 31 December 2000, more particularly by underpinning certain collaborative measures, encouraging the adoption of healthy lifestyles and increasing knowledge of risk factors. An action programme on health monitoring was the subject of a proposal for a Parliament and Council Decision (Table I) which was adopted by the Commission on 16 October, with a view to supporting the development of health indicators and the collection of health data to help in the planning, evaluation and implementation of policies and measures in health-related fields. The Council adopted a common position on the proposal for a programme concerning drugs (→ point 641). Blood safety and self-sufficiency in blood supplies, subjects on which the Commission[2] had already adopted a communication, were the subject of Council[3] and Parliament[4] resolutions and of Commission support for cooperation and coordination between Member States. Finally, human medicaments were the subject of four Council resolutions on 20 December.[5]

A first report on the state of health in the European Community,[6] produced with the help of the Regional Office for Europe of the World Health Organization (WHO), was adopted by the Commission on 19 July and was the subject of Council conclusions on 30 November[7] and of the Madrid

---

[1]   COM(93) 559; Twenty-seventh General Report, point 593.
[2]   COM(94) 652; 1994 General Report, point 683.
[3]   OJ C 164, 30.6.1995; Bull. 6-1995, point 1.3.216.
[4]   OJ C 249, 25.9.1995; Bull. 7/8-1995, point 1.3.195.
[5]   Bull. 11-1995, point 1.3.195; Bull. 12-1995.
[6]   COM(95) 357; Bull. 7/8-1995, point 1.3.193.
[7]   Bull. 11–1995, point 1.3.196.

European Council conclusions in December.[1] This report sets out the main demographic trends and patterns of mortality and morbidity and includes a discussion on major determinants of health. It shows that, while health in the Community is improving, there are still remarkable disparities, and important health problems remain which need to be overcome.

The integration into Community policies of health protection requirements (paragraph 3 of Article 129(1) of the EC Treaty) was the subject of a first annual Commission report adopted on 29 May[2] and of a Council resolution on 20 December.[3]

The Commission continued to provide support towards the coordination of Member States' activities on a variety of other health issues, such as fundamental health choices, health reforms, new health technologies and public health aspects of pharmaceuticals.

Cancer

638.   The proposal for a Parliament and Council Decision (Table I) with a view to the adoption of a third action plan (1995-2000) to combat cancer within the framework for action in the field of public health was the subject of a Council common position on 2 June. Subsequently, following the second reading in the European Parliament, the Conciliation Committee produced a 'joint text' in December. Seeking to encourage cooperation between the Member States, the programme's objectives are to reduce mortality and morbidity due to cancer, and to promote the general well-being of the population and the quality of life, as well as research into the possible causes of cancer and methods of prevention, and the dissemination of information and exchange of experience, particularly by intensifying the prevention drive and minimizing the economic and social consequences of cancer.

639.   As part of the implementation in 1995 of the 'Europe against cancer' programme, 96 projects were selected. On 18 July,[4] the Commission adopted a report on the implementation of the previous programme (1990-94). The European Week against Cancer, featuring the launch of the revised Code against Cancer, took place in October. Various meetings and other events were organized and supported by the Commission, such as a European seminar on nutrition and cancer and a European conference on in-service training in oncology.

---

[1]   Bull. 12-1995.
[2]   COM(95) 196; Bull. 5-1995, point 1.3.132.
[3]   Bull. 11-1995, point 1.3.194; Bull. 12-1995.
[4]   COM(95) 356; Bull. 7/8-1995, point 1.3.194.

AIDS and other communicable diseases

640. The Community action programme on the prevention of AIDS and certain communicable diseases (1996-2000) (Table I) was the subject of a Council common position on 2 June. Subsequent to the European Parliament second reading, the Conciliation Committee produced a 'joint text' in December. Laying the stress on prevention, the programme seeks to reduce mortality and morbidity, to contribute to the prevention drive and prioritize social and psychological assistance for AIDS victims, and to combat discrimination. The 'Europe against AIDS' programme (1991-93), meanwhile, had been extended to the end of the year by Parliament and Council Decision 95/1729/EC (Table I). In addition, the Commission adopted, on 7 November, the report[1] on the implementation of the programme in 1994.

Drugs

641. The proposal for a Parliament and Council Decision (Table I) establishing a Community action programme on the prevention of drug dependence (1996-2000) within the framework for Community action in the field of public health was the subject of a common position on 20 December. The programme is concerned essentially with heightening awareness of drug dependence, the consequences and methods of prevention, and information and education, with special reference to young people and other particularly vulnerable target groups. In the transitional period preceding adoption of the programme, the Commission continued to lend support to European cooperation on the prevention of drug dependence. On the basis of the guidelines set out in its communication on Community action in this field,[2] the Commission provided funding for 24 projects involving non-governmental organizations in the Member States, 14 of which came from transnational or regional transfrontier networks, concerning the development of partnership arrangements in public awareness-raising, health education, training, risk reduction, early detection, data collection and research. The drug dependence preventive strategy was the subject of an own-initiative opinion from the Economic and Social Committee on 25 January.[3]

642. The information on the follow-up to the European Union action plan to combat drugs (1995-99)[4] is contained in Section 4 (The fight against drugs) in Chapter V *(→ point 974).*

[1]   COM(95) 521; Bull. 11-1995, point 1.3.199.
[2]   COM(94) 223; 1994 General Report, point 687.
[3]   OJ C 102, 24.4.1995; Bull. 1/2-1995, point 1.3.167.
[4]   COM(94) 234; 1994 General Report, point 1081.

International cooperation

643.   In May, the Commission had observer status at the World Health Conference in Geneva, and also attended the September meeting of the Regional Committee for Europe, held in Tel Aviv. On 12 June, Dr Nakajima, the Director-General of the WHO, visited the Commission to discuss cooperation matters. The Commission also participated in the work of the Council of Europe's European Health Committee and, more particularly, in discussions concerning the exchange of therapeutic substances of human origin and the draft convention on bioethics.

Section 25

Consumer policy

Priority activities and objectives

644.   *Under the second three-year action plan in favour of European con-*
sumers (1993-95),[1] *the Commission pressed on with measures designed to*
complete the legislative armoury for consumer protection, adopting a pro-
posal for a Directive on price indication. On 21 October,[2] *the Commission*
presented a new consumer policy action plan (1996-98), which stresses the
need to address the problems which really affect consumers and to antici-
pate the changes generated by technological developments and the changing
face of the European Union. Attention is focused on 10 priority areas, cov-
ering a range of subjects such as financial services, food products, public
utility services and more openness vis-à-vis the countries of Central and
Eastern Europe and the developing countries. All this will lead to moves by
the Commission to integrate consumer policy more firmly into other
Community policies.[3]

Consumer participation

645.   On 13 June, the Commission adopted Decision 95/260/EC[4] setting
up a Consumer Committee to replace the Consumers' Consultative Council,[5] in the interest of more effective dialogue with consumers and with a
view to ensuring that consumers' requirements are taken into account when
Community policies are being formulated.

Consumer information and education

646.   Following on from the publication of the *European consumer guide*
to the single market in 1994,[6] a radio consumer information campaign was

---

[1]   COM(93) 378; Twenty-seventh General Report, point 372.
[2]   COM(95) 519; Bull. 10-1995, point 1.3.231.
[3]   More especially on the question of voice telephony *(→ point 430)* and postal services *(→ point 454).*
[4]   OJ L 162, 13.7.1995.
[5]   Commission Decision 90/55/EEC setting up a Consumers' Consultative Council — OJ L 38,
      10.2.1990, as last amended by Decision 95/13/EC; OJ L 21, 18.1.1995; 1994 General Report, point
      670.
[6]   1994 General Report, point 671.

run in November on limited subjects of significance for the development of consumer rights under European policy. The television company 'Euronews' produced and broadcast, between 1 January and 30 June, 26 brief items and three more in-depth items under the title 'Label Europe', dealing with a variety of subjects ranging from timeshares through slimming products to portable phones. The Commission also continued to provide financial support for information activities run by consumers' organizations. The Council, for its part, adopted, on 9 November,[1] a resolution on consumer education and information.

647.   The final of the second European Young Consumer Competition,[2] designed to encourage young people to become aware of consumer issues, was held in Brussels on 30 May, with the first prize going to a Spanish group. More than 800 groups of schoolchildren from the Member States took part in the competition, the theme of which was 'Young people and advertising — How to promote a healthy food product through advertising'.

648.   On 12 July, the Commission presented a proposal for a new Directive (Table I) with a view to improving consumer information on product price indication and to simplify the old system. In expectation of the new provisions, the old system was extended by two years by virtue of Directive 95/58/EC (Table I) of 29 November amending Directives 79/581/EEC and 88/314/EEC. The proposed new provisions, which give an enhanced role to the Member States in terms of practical application, should produce a significant improvement in the transparency of product pricing arrangements and make it easier for consumers to compare prices. Not only the selling price will in future have to be indicated, but also the unit price wherever products are comparable.

649.   The 'Coline' system,[3] which creates a computerized link between the national consumer information centres, and which was being expanded to take in five new member countries in 1995,[4] should shortly become accessible via the Internet and eventually cover the whole of the Community.

---

[1]   Bull. 11-1995, point 1.3.204.
[2]   1994 General Report, point 672.
[3]   1994 General Report, point 671.
[4]   Belgium, Greece, Ireland, Italy and Austria.

Protection of consumer health and safety

650. Decision 94/3092/EC,[1] establishing a Community system of information on home and leisure accidents (Ehlass), was amended by Decision 95/184/EC (Table II) to make the necessary changes brought about by enlargement of the Community. Additionally, in July the Commission convened a meeting of experts responsible for toy safety in the national administrations responsible for market surveillance, with a view to assessing the implementation of Directive 88/378/EEC.[2] 'Miracle' health products were the subject of a Council resolution of 9 November.[3]

651. With a view to maintaining the trade secrecy of certain cosmetics ingredients, but without prejudicing consumer safety, the Commission adopted, on 19 June, Directive 95/17/EC[4] laying down detailed rules for the application of Council Directive 76/768/EEC[5] as regards the non-inclusion of ingredients on the list used for the labelling of cosmetic products. On 7 July, the Commission adopted the sixth Directive[6] concerning checks on the composition of cosmetic products, followed, on 10 July, by the 18th Directive[7] adapting to technical progress Directive 76/768/EEC (lists of substances which are banned, subject to restrictions or authorized).

Protection of consumers' economic and legal interests

652. On the question of consumer credit, the Commission adopted, on 11 May,[8] a report on the operation of Directive 87/102/EEC on the approximation of Member States' national provisions. The report was welcomed by the Council in its resolution of 9 November.[9]

653. The proposal for a Parliament and Council Directive concerning consumer protection in respect of contracts negotiated at a distance was the subject of a Council common position on 29 June; Parliament gave its opinion on 13 December (Table I). It lays down minimum consumer protection rules concerning distance selling regardless of the technology used (e.g. mail-order sales by post, telephone, minitel, television, etc.).

---

[1] 1994 General Report, point 674.
[2] OJ L 187, 16.7.1988; Twenty-second General Report, point 602.
[3] Bull. 11-1995, point 1.3.202.
[4] OJ L 140, 23.6.1995; Bull. 6-1995, point 1.3.221.
[5] OJ L 262, 27.9.1976.
[6] Directive 95/32/EC — OJ L 178, 28.7.1995.
[7] Directive 95/34/EC — OJ L 167, 18.7.1995.
[8] COM(95) 117; Bull. 5-1995, point 1.3.136.
[9] Bull. 11-1995, point 1.3.206.

654. On 9 November, the Council reached agreement on a common position on a Parliament and Council Directive (Table I) on comparative advertising and the harmonized application thereof.

655. Finally, on 22 November, the Economic and Social Committee adopted an own-initiative opinion on the single market and consumer protection[1].

---

[1]   Bull. 11-1995, point 1.3.201.

Section 26

Information, communication, audiovisual media and culture

Priority activities and objectives

656.   *Bringing Europe's citizens closer to the Union and its institutions is one of the priorities which the new Commission set itself as soon as it took office.[1] The activities carried out as part of the information and communication policy were an attempt to answer the questions that citizens are asking about the Union, to clarify the issues at stake in European integration and to highlight the Union's practical achievements and their effects on people's day-to-day lives. To meet these objectives, and in line with the approach adopted by the Commission in 1993,[2] the emphasis was on greater decentralization and transparency. Greater importance was also attached to the use of modern means of communication such as satellite television and the Internet, so as to make information accessible in real-time to as many people as possible. Targeted operations were carried out to provide a more effective response to the special information needs of particular groups. The Commission continued its efforts to supply information to non-Community countries (→ point 689).*

A significant step forward for the audiovisual sector was taken with the adoption by the Commission of a proposal for a Directive amending the television without frontiers Directive, a communication designed to create an environment favourable to dynamic growth in the European programme industry (MEDIA II — training, MEDIA II — development and distribution), the first annual report on the action plan for the introduction of advanced television services in Europe, and a proposal for a Decision establishing a European Guarantee Fund to promote cinema and television production.

In the cultural field, as announced in its 1994 communication,[3] the Commission took further steps to implement Article 128 of the EC Treaty and, on 29 March, proposed the setting-up of a Community action programme on cultural heritage, the Raphael programme. The Madrid European

---

[1]   Bull. 1/2-1995, point I.1; Supplement 1/95 — Bull.
[2]   Twenty-seventh General Report, point 609.
[3]   1994 General Report, point 716.

Council restated the importance of cultural action to promote the Community dimension of Member States' cultures.[1]

Information and communication policy

Information and communication

657. Work to decentralize communication operations continued, in particular through the Commission's offices in the Member States and their regional suboffices, as well as the networks of relay organizations at the regional and local levels. Following the establishment of the 'Sources d'Europe' centre in Paris, a new European information and documentation centre known as the Jacques Delors Centre was inaugurated in Lisbon in March. On 9 May, with support from the Community institutions, some 1 500 events were organized in the Member States to mark Europe Day, which this year celebrated the 45th anniversary of the Robert Schuman Declaration.

658. In the audiovisual media field, the 'Europe by satellite' operation launched experimentally at the beginning of the year reached cruising speed in September, with an average of 130 hours' broadcasting a month. The service provides a means of sending pictures of Community news events to television stations in the European Union, Central and Eastern Europe and the Mediterranean basin. It also keeps the Commission in touch with its offices and delegations, the other institutions and interested bodies in the Member States, and provides a facility for interactive conferencing. Similarly, the Commission has responded to the development of new forms of information and telecommunications technology by opening a server called 'Europa' on the global Internet network which thousands of Internet users throughout the world can use to obtain information on the European Union's activities. By the end of 1995, Europa was receiving some 20 000 access requests each day.

659. The Commission also made use of more traditional methods of information, including updating the series of brochures describing the contribution the Union makes to the regions. Nearly 30 000 people visited the Commission to ask for information, and with its 743 'Team Europe' speakers it was able to communicate directly with the public in 19 countries. Exhibitions were used both as a medium for using state-of-the-art electronic

---

[1]   Bull. 12-1995.

information techniques and as a way of illustrating the Union's activities in visual form. Sport remained one of the Commission's priority areas, with support going to certain sports events (through the Eurathlon programme) and information being supplied to sports circles on the effects of the Community's activities on sport (the European Sports Forum).

660.   These exercises entail monitoring public opinion with instruments such as *Eurobarometer*[1] and *Europinion*. To keep abreast of short-term shifts in public opinion, an ongoing telephone survey was launched in September. New instruments were also set up to evaluate trends in the press and the audiovisual media.

661.   The Commission continued to devise targeted operations for specific groups such as young people, women, trade unions, economic interests and the press, through the Stendhal[2] and Natali Prizes,[3] and on 21 October it presented the 'gold stars of town-twinning' to 46 towns and communities.[4]

662.   In academic circles, the Commission took further steps to encourage teaching and thinking on the subject of European integration. As part of the Jean Monnet Project 1995,[5] which universities in the new Member States joined, the Commission supported the establishment of 63 new Jean Monnet 'chairs', bringing the total for the Community to 252. In addition, 73 full-time courses, 78 European modules, 22 research aids and 18 additional initiatives associated with these 'chairs' were also given Commission support. Since it was set up in 1990,[6] the Jean Monnet Project has supported a total of 1 140 academic initiatives related to the teaching of European integration. Under the Jean Monnet Project in Poland and Hungary, which was set up in 1993, 39 new schemes were supported in 1995. At the same time, the Commission supported associations of teachers and researchers specializing in European integration (ECSA-Europe). Projects were launched with partner associations in Eastern Europe (ECSA-Est) and on the northern shores of the Mediterranean (ECSA-MED). With the ECSA-NET communication network on the Internet, integrated into the Europa server, it will be possible to exchange information on university teaching and research into European integration. The Euristote database will be incorporated into it.

---

[1]   Bull. 1/2-1995, point 1.3.169; Bull. 3-1995, point 1.3.157; Bull. 7/8-1995, point 1.3.206.
[2]   Bull. 10-1995, point 1.3.235.
[3]   Bull. 9-1995, point 1.3.137.
[4]   Bull. 10-1995, point 1.3.234.
[5]   Bull. 5-1995, point 1.3.138; Bull. 7/8-1995, points 1.3.204 and 1.3.205.
[6]   Twenty-fourth General Report, point 963.

663.   Lastly, the Users' Advisory Council,[1] now known as the 'Information Users' Council', met three times and supplied the Commission with the opinions of experts in information and communication matters.

Press and broadcasting activities

664.   As in previous years, the number of correspondents in Brussels accredited to the Commission remained high, with 770 journalists from 61 countries, including some 616 writing for the press and 154 representing radio and television. This total includes the representatives of 75 international and national news agencies.

665.   The Spokesman's Service held 260 press meetings and briefings on decisions, proposals and reactions by the Commission, and there were 31 spokesman's news conferences on Commission meetings. The President and Members of the Commission gave 95 news conferences on particularly important subjects, several of them held jointly with guests of the Commission. The Spokesman's Service also gave the press the Commission's position on the occasion of Council and European Council meetings as well as during part-sessions of Parliament. Other special operations were also mounted during international events at which the Community was represented, such as the Western Economic Summit in Halifax (→ point 886).

666.   Over 3 000 briefing notes and documents were supplied to accredited journalists, while the offices in the Member States and the delegations outside the Community received 500 telegraphed instructions and commentaries designed exclusively for them, for the purpose of supplying their press contacts with day-to-day information.

Activities of the Office for Official Publications of the European Communities (OOPEC)

667.   For the Publications Office, the enlargement of the European Union meant bringing out 50 000 pages of secondary Community law in Swedish and Finnish and a new 12-language edition of the Treaties incorporating the provisions relating to the accession of Austria, Finland and Sweden. With the addition of two new official languages, the Office's annual output exceeded 1.65 million original pages.

---

[1]   1994 General Report, point 702.

668. The Office continued its work on the consolidation of Community legislation, as its contribution to the endeavour to ensure the transparency of Community law (→ point 10) called for by the Edinburgh European Council.[1] In addition to its everyday work as a publisher, the Office supplied the institutions with a new computerized system for producing budget documents; there are also plans to use it for other types of publication.

669. The Office set up a new archiving service for the distribution of electronic documents. This service, which is being marketed as EUDOR (European Document Repository), may be regarded as the European Union's electronic document library from which anyone may obtain a copy of the information stocked in it. Bridges are at present being built between this electronic records repository and documentary search systems such as CATEL (the Publications Office's electronic cataloguing system) and CELEX (→ point 1139).

670. The Office is now actively represented on world information networks, not only through the dissemination via the Europa server (→ point 658) of a document describing the Office's work and products, but also because it is now possible to connect to the Eurobases databases from the EuropaNET (the pan-European academic network) and the Internet. The Office's Managing Board also decided, on an experimental basis, to put IDEA (Interinstitutional directory of European administration) out on the Internet.

671. The circle of European Union bodies which avail themselves of OOPEC's vast range of services widened considerably. The Committee of the Regions was asked to take part in the work of the Office's Managing Board, and a great many of the agencies set up in October 1993[2] have already decided to have their publications brought out by the Office. To smooth the flow of text along the author-translator-publisher chain, the Office confirmed its willingness to work closely with the Translation Centre (→ point 1116).

Historical archives

672. The Commission released the archives of the ECSC High Authority, the EEC Commission and the Euratom Commission for consultation[3] un-

---

[1]   Twenty-sixth General Report, point 10.
[2]   OJ C 323, 30.11.1993; Twenty-seventh General Report, point 1019.
[3]   The historical archive files are kept in Florence at the European University Institute (→ point 291).

der the 30-year rule,[1] thereby adding more than 2 500 files to the 25 000 already made accessible to the public since 1952 in the case of the ECSC and 1958 in the case of the EEC and Euratom.

673.   The Commission also published the first volume[2] of a series of structured inventories of the files of the ECSC High Authority (1952 to July 1967) and the second revised and enlarged edition of the *Guide to the archives of Member States' Foreign Ministries and European Union institutions.*[2]

674.   Following the conclusions adopted by the Council in June 1994[3] and the report on archives in the European Union,[3] the Commission earmarked four priority measures which could be implemented in consultation with the Member States: the holding of a multidisciplinary forum on the problems of managing, storing, conserving and retrieving machine-readable data (MRD); the production of a publication containing archive-related news from across the European Union; the drafting of a practical guide to the access to archives in the Member States and the Community institutions; and the admission of archive students and archivists to the Community's education and vocational training programmes (Socrates *(→ point 267)* and Leonardo da Vinci *(→ point 272)*).

675.   The Commission confirmed its readiness to continue taking part in the work of transferring and salvaging archives in the context of the succession problems of the former Yugoslavia.[4]

Audiovisual policy

676.   In the area of rules, on 31 May the Commission adopted a proposal for a Council Directive (Table II) amending the television without frontiers Directive, 89/552/EEC, to create a clearer, more certain and more effective legal basis which would encourage the development of television broadcasting in the European audiovisual area. The proposal clarifies the rules of law applicable to broadcasting companies, protection for minors and the promotion of European productions. It caters for the new economic realities in the sector by laying down special rules for teleshopping, enabling special-subject broadcasting stations to contribute to efforts to promote the European programme industry by investing in European productions, introdu-

[1]   OJ L 43, 15.2.1983; Seventeenth General Report, point 54.
[2]   Available from the Office for Official Publications of the European Communities.
[3]   1994 General Report, point 710.
[4]   1994 General Report, point 711.

cing a limited 10-year period for the application of the rules on promoting European productions, and laying down provisions which allow for more advertising slots and sponsorship. The scope of the Directive remains unchanged: it will still apply to point-to-multipoint broadcasting services including pay-per-view, near-video-on-demand and teleshopping, but not to the new point-to-point services such as video-on-demand.

677.   As regards the programme industry, the Commission pressed ahead with the implementation of the MEDIA programme (1991-95),[1] which consists of activities divided up into three areas: training for professionals in the audiovisual industry, the development of production projects and the distribution of European material. After consultations with professional interests as a follow-up to the Green Paper on strategy options to strengthen the European programme industry in the context of the audiovisual policy in the European Union,[2] which was well received by the European Parliament,[3] and following the European audiovisual conference,[4] the Commission on 8 May adopted a communication on stimulating the dynamic growth of undertakings in the European programme industry.[5] With the communication were two proposals for Council Decisions on a training programme for professionals in the European audiovisual programme industry (MEDIA II — training) (Table II) and a programme to promote the development and distribution of European audiovisual works (MEDIA II — development and distribution) (Table II). The programmes are to run for five years from 1 January 1996. The Cannes European Council welcomed these proposals.[6] On 10 July, the Council adopted the Decision on the development and distribution aspects of the programme, which will be allocated a budget of ECU 265 million spread over five years, and on 22 December the Decision on the training aspects of the programme, which have a budget of ECU 45 million spread over five years. To supplement the MEDIA II programmes, on 14 November the Commission adopted a proposal for a Decision establishing a European Guarantee Fund to promote cinema and television production (Table II), to be administered as part of the structures of the European Investment Fund (EIF) *(→ point 83)*.

678.   On technological aspects, on 16 June the Commission approved the first annual report[7] on implementing the action plan for the introduction of

---

[1]   OJ L 380, 31.12.1990.
[2]   COM(94) 96; 1994 General Report, point 712.
[3]   OJ C 249, 25.9.1995; Bull. 7/8-1995, point 1.3.209.
[4]   1994 General Report, point 712.
[5]   COM(94) 523; Bull. 1/2-1995, point 1.3.170.
[6]   Bull. 6-1995, point I.26.
[7]   COM(95) 263.

advanced television services in Europe,[1] the aims of which are to create favourable conditions for the emergence of a quantity of advanced 16:9-format television services and to encourage adequate and increasing scheduling of 16:9-format broadcasts of a high technical standard. According to the report, the action plan is proving increasingly successful with the audiovisual industry. In 1995 a joint call for proposals covering both aspects, broadcasting and production, was published, followed by two separate calls.

679.   On 3 April, the Commission adopted the list of projects selected for assistance as part of its support for audiovisual festivals and for projects to mark the centenary of the cinema:[2] 93 events were selected[3] to share funding of ECU 1.695 million, the object being to encourage the circulation of European works in the Member States and enhance public awareness of the wealth of Europe's film heritage.

Cultural policy

680.   On 29 March, the Commission adopted a proposal for a Decision establishing a Community action programme in the field of cultural heritage, the Raphael programme (Table I). The object of this programme, which complements the cultural activities already being pursued under the Kaleidoscope 2000 and Ariane programmes, is to upgrade and conserve the fixed and movable heritage, ensure public access to it and encourage European initiatives in that field.

681.   The proposals for Decisions establishing the Ariane programme (Table I) (support for activities in the field of books and reading) and the Kaleidoscope 2000 programme (support for artistic and cultural activities having a European dimension) were well received by the Committee of the Regions. In the case of the Kaleidoscope programme (Table I), the conciliation procedure on 4 December failed to lead to the adoption of a joint text, and on 14 December the Commission issued an opinion containing an amended proposal.

682.   The Commission prepared a report on taking the cultural dimension into account in the Community's other policies, which is a key aspect of the development of the Union's cultural activity and specifically provided for in Article 128(4) of the EC Treaty.

---

[1]   OJ L 196, 5.8.1993.
[2]   Bull. 4-1995, point 1.3.135.
[3]   OJ C 258, 15.9.1994.

683.   On the question of access to culture, the Commission, in collaboration with the international ATD Quart Monde movement, organized a conference in Brussels on the subject of the contribution made by culture to combating social exclusion.

684.   Pending adoption of the new programmes proposed on the basis of Article 128 of the EC Treaty, the existing pilot measures were continued. In the field of safeguarding the architectural heritage, under the pilot project[1] for the restoration of religious monuments, funding totalling ECU 4.7 million was awarded to 100 projects. The Commission also contributed to schemes for the restoration of monuments of exceptional historical value (Mount Athos, the Acropolis, the Chiado, Coimbra, Santiago de Compostela) and further training schemes in conservation and restoration. It also launched an operation to support twinning programmes between European museums, and, as part of its cultural cooperation with non-member countries, gave its support to 23 projects to restore the architectural heritage.

685.   In the field of books and reading, the Commission gave assistance for the translation of 85 works by European authors, priority being given to the less-widely-spoken languages.[2] The European literary prize and the European translation prize (the Aristeion Prizes)[3] were presented in Luxembourg in December at the official closing ceremony for the European City of Culture celebrations. The Commission also awarded scholarships to translation colleges and set up consultations between experts from the Member States in the field of books. At the request of the Council, the Commission looked into the problems of book pricing, particularly in areas sharing the same language, from the point of view both of the cultural and economic context of books and the Community aspects (free movement of goods, competition, etc.).

686.   As part of its activities to encourage artistic and cultural exchanges and cooperation in Europe, the Kaleidoscope 1995 programme[4] gave assistance totalling ECU 4 055 900 to 144 projects. The Commission also supported a number of high-profile activities, including the European City of Culture (Luxembourg), the European Cultural Month (Nicosia in 1995, Valletta and Linz in 1998)[5] and the activities of the Youth Orchestra and

1   OJ C 283, 11.10.1994; Bull. 7/8-1995, point 1.3.203.
2   Bull. 9-1995, point 1.3.136.
3   OJ C 100, 22.4.1992.
4   OJ C 227, 17.8.1994; Bull. 5-1995, point 1.3.137; Bull. 7/8-1995, point 1.3.200.
5   Bull. 11-1995, point 1.3.209.

the Baroque Orchestra of the European Union. On 20 November, nine cities were declared European Cities of Culture for the year 2000.[1]

687.   Under the head of cultural cooperation with non-Community countries, support went to 75 cultural projects, mainly from the countries of Central and Eastern Europe and certain Latin American countries with which the Community has signed agreements containing a special clause on culture. In the former Yugoslavia, the Commission gave assistance for the Sarajevo winter festival. On 3 April, the Council adopted a resolution on cooperation with the associated countries of Central and Eastern Europe in the cultural domain,[2] following on from the conclusions of the Essen European Council.[3]

688.   On 3 April, the Council adopted a resolution on culture and multimedia[4] highlighting the importance of giving thought to the development of multimedia as a means of promoting and conserving Europe's heritage and cultures. On 12 June, it also adopted conclusions in which it emphasized the importance of multilingualism[5] (→ point 427) and on 20 November it adopted a resolution on the promotion of statistics on culture and economic growth.[6]

[1]   Avignon, Bergen, Bologna, Brussels, Helsinki, Krakow, Prague, Reykjavik, Santiago de Compostela. Bull. 11-1995, point 1.3.209.
[2]   OJ C 247, 23.9.1995; Bull. 4-1995, point 1.4.61.
[3]   1994 General Report, point 1196.
[4]   OJ C 247, 23.9.1995; Bull. 4-1995, point 1.3.132.
[5]   Bull. 6-1995, point 1.3.223.
[6]   Bull. 11-1995, point 1.7.5.

Chapter IV

Role of the European Union in the world

Section 1

Priority activities and objectives

689.   *Following enlargement of the European Union on 1 January to bring
Austria, Finland and Sweden into the fold, Heads of State or Government
gathering in Madrid in December devoted a large part of their deliberations
to the next enlargement, which is to embrace Central and Eastern Europe,
Cyprus and Malta. They underscored the political necessity of that process,
regarding it as an historic opportunity for Europe that would strengthen
European integration while upholding the* acquis communautaire *and the
common policies.*

*The Commission took the requisite steps to implement the pre-accession
strategy for the associated countries of Central and Eastern Europe, including the Baltic States. The strategy was mapped out in December 1994 at the
Essen European Council and reaffirmed at the European Council in Madrid.
The measures taken included publication of a white paper on preparing
those countries for integration into the internal market and an assessment
of the possible impact of accession on the common policies. A structured
dialogue is now fully operational, and several countries — Romania, Slovakia, Latvia, Estonia, Lithuania and Bulgaria — have lodged membership
applications. The Europe Agreements with Bulgaria, the Czech Republic,
Romania and Slovakia entered into force in February and like agreements
were signed in June with the Baltic States. A Europe Agreement was initialled with Slovenia. The Cannes European Council set up a stable medium-
term framework for financing the Union's policy on Central and Eastern
Europe, including the Baltic States, over the period 1995-99. The Madrid
European Council confirmed the pivotal role in the pre-accession strategy
played by the PHARE programme as a financial instrument to help Central
and East European countries restructure their economies, boost growth and*

align their laws on the acquis communautaire. *In addition, the ground was prepared for those countries' participation in various Community programmes. It was announced at December's European Council that the necessary decisions for inaugurating the accession negotiations with the associated countries of Central and Eastern Europe would be taken after the 1996 Intergovernmental Conference (IGC) in the light of its outcome and of opinions and reports tabled by the Commission, while the hope was also expressed that the initial stage of those negotiations could coincide with the start of negotiations with Cyprus and Malta.*

The EU has also drawn up a pre-accession strategy for Cyprus and Malta and initiated a structured dialogue with them. The Madrid European Council confirmed that accession talks would start six months after the IGC in the light of its outcome and the Commission's proposals.

Throughout the year the European Union made plain its intention to strengthen the ties binding it to its partners on the southern and eastern shores of the Mediterranean, its goal being to turn the Mediterranean into an area in which countries cooperate in fostering peace, security, stability and prosperity. The Euro-Mediterranean partnership proposed by the Commission in October 1994 was fleshed out this year and will take the shape of Euro-Mediterranean association agreements encompassing three major areas of cooperation: economic transition, a more equitable socioeconomic balance and regional integration. Underpinned by regular political dialogue, and with substantial financial aid, the partnership is intended to lead eventually to the creation of a free trade area. The Commission has accordingly proposed that cooperation be developed with the Mediterranean countries through the MEDA programme, modelled on the PHARE and TACIS programmes. Meanwhile, negotiations for Euro-Mediterranean association agreements went ahead: such accords were concluded with Israel, Morocco and Tunisia and are in the process of being negotiated with Egypt, Jordan and Lebanon, while the Madrid European Council stated that the EU was willing to negotiate similar agreements with Algeria and Syria as soon as possible. Funds were earmarked in June at the Cannes European Council for the Mediterranean countries to cover the period up to turn of the century. The impetus behind this preparatory work on the Euro-Mediterranean partnership culminated in November in the Barcelona Euro-Mediterranean Conference which, at the EU's initiative, brought together representatives from all Member States and all the Mediterranean partners. At the end of the conference, the participants adopted a declaration and a work programme inaugurating an ongoing dialogue and cooperation to foster peace, stability and prosperity in the region. The EC-Turkey Association Council reached agreement in March on the completion of the customs union between the EU and Turkey, an accord which Parliament endorsed in Decem-

ber, thereby paving the way for entry into force of the customs union on 1 January 1996. To help Turkey make the necessary economic adjustments, the Commission also adopted a proposal for a Council Regulation designed to put in place special cooperation measures.

As the chief aid donor in the region, the European Union gave stout backing to the Middle East peace process on both the political and economic fronts, among other things setting priorities for aid to the West Bank and Gaza. The signing of a Euro-Mediterranean association agreement with Israel will also help bring about a new state of equilibrium in the region. Furthermore, the Council asked for exploratory discussions to be started with the Palestinian Authority in order to negotiate a similar agreement at the earliest opportunity. This move was welcomed at the Madrid European Council.

In the former Yugoslavia, the European Union was an active player in the diplomacy designed to bring about a settlement of the conflict. The Dayton peace agreement was signed in Paris on 14 December, with the Commission again proving itself to be crucial to the aid effort in a region in which the EU is the world's foremost donor. The Commission also drew up a reconstruction strategy for the former Yugoslavia which involves practical measures to enhance EU aid management and the coordination of global aid, notably in tandem with the World Bank. Following the signing of the peace agreement, the EU reiterated its resolve, in Madrid, to contribute substantially to the implementation process as part of an equitable international burden-sharing arrangement. It also decided to suspend the sanctions in force against Serbia and Montenegro and declared its intention to forge contractual links with the Republics of the former Yugoslavia by negotiating an association agreement with Slovenia and issuing negotiating directives for cooperation and transport accords with Croatia and the former Yugoslav Republic of Macedonia.

On the humanitarian aid front, ECHO activities continued throughout the year, with the Commission focusing its efforts in Africa on the Great Lakes region in an effort to tackle the aftermath of the Rwanda tragedy, and in Europe assigning priority to the former Yugoslavia. The Commission's aim in the wake of the signing of the Dayton peace agreement was to coordinate global aid for that country and help pave the way for reconstruction whilst continuing to ensure that basic humanitarian needs were being met. It also continued its discussion of the role of humanitarian aid in preventing conflicts and natural disasters.

Turning to the ACP countries, this year saw the signing in Mauritius, in November, of the revised Lomé IV Convention. The mid-term review of Lomé IV has strengthened the political and institutional facets of the Con-

*vention, defined the development of trade as the engine of ACP-EC coop-
eration and streamlined implementation of financial and technical cooperation. The revamped Lomé IV contains a clause allowing for the total or
partial suspension of the Convention in the event of any breach of human
rights or democratic principles. It also earmarks funds for the eighth EDF
in keeping with the financial perspectives adopted at the Cannes European
Council: the new Financial Protocol for the period 1995-2000 represents an
increase of almost 22% in the EU's financial contribution compared with
the previous five years.*

*The European Union also displayed its readiness to participate in rebuilding
Angola, adopting a common position to that end. Deploring the flagrant
violations of human rights in Nigeria, the EU adopted two common
positions aimed at downgrading its ties with Nigeria.*

*The EU continued to flesh out its policy on South Africa, with the Council
adopting negotiating directives for a trade and cooperation agreement with
that country and a protocol on its future accession to the Lomé Convention. With the Commission having adopted a proposal on additional negotiating directives, the trade and cooperation accord should — building on
existing economic, trade, financial and technical cooperation over a wide
range of fields of mutual interest — culminate in the setting-up of a free
trade area between the European Union and South Africa.*

*In an effort to boost the consistency and effectiveness of the Community's
development policy, the Commission adopted proposals for regulations
aimed at endowing all the relevant budget headings with a legal basis. It
continued to raise its profile on the world stage, in particular by participating in UN-sponsored conferences such as the World Development Summit
in Copenhagen and the fourth World Conference on Women in Beijing.*

*Ties between the European Union and the independent States of the former
Soviet Union were strengthened further with the negotiation of a new generation of partnership and cooperation agreements to replace the 1989 accord with the former Soviet Union; political dialogue was stepped up, relations between the EU and some of the newly independent States were given
sharper focus and technical assistance was bolstered through the TACIS
programme. The Commission exercised its right of initiative by adopting
several draft common positions setting out objectives and priorities for the
EU vis-à-vis Russia, the Trans-Caucasian republics and the new independent
States of Central Asia. The Madrid European Council reiterated its support
for efforts in Russia to achieve stability, development, peace and democracy,
reaffirming that the European Union would continue its technical assistance
programme for the independent States with a view to backing their
economic and political reform process.*

The EEA Agreement with Liechtenstein entered into force on 1 May. The European Union's EFTA partners within the EEA fold are Iceland, Norway and Liechtenstein. Negotiations on sectoral agreements with Switzerland took place throughout the year.

Relations between the United States and the European Union were strengthened by the adoption, at the 3 December summit, of a new transatlantic agenda, which goes hand in hand with a plan of action to foster closer relations between the two sides. It provides a framework for four common goals: the promotion of peace, stability, democracy and development in the world; an appropriate response to the various global challenges; a genuine contribution to the development of world trade and the strengthening of bilateral economic ties; and the establishment of closer links between the two parties. The Commission had previously adopted a memorandum laying down the foundations for a substantial strengthening of transatlantic ties. It also proposed a medium-term strategy for relations with Japan founded chiefly on enhanced cooperation and political dialogue with that country.

The Commission proposed a strengthening of the partnership with Latin America over the period 1996-2000 on the basis of closer political links, greater economic integration and freer trade, and the focusing of cooperation on certain priority areas. This initiative received the backing of the Council and was endorsed by the Madrid European Council. On 15 December the EU signed a framework interregional economic and trade cooperation agreement with Mercosur intended to strengthen ties between the two sides and pave the way for eventual association. The Commission has proposed renewing the San José dialogue between the EU and Central America and has also set out objectives for closer ties with Mexico, with which a formal joint declaration was signed. A joint declaration on political dialogue was also signed with Chile, and the Commission proposed instigating a dialogue with Cuba involving regular consultations. The framework cooperation agreement with Brazil was formally concluded in October.

In a move designed to reflect Asia's growing importance on the world stage, the Commission launched the new strategy it had drawn up in 1994, defining a long-term policy for relations with China, while cooperation agreements were signed with Nepal, Vietnam and Sri Lanka, and negotiations started with the Republic of Korea.

The World Trade Organization (WTO), set up at the end of the Uruguay Round multilateral trade negotiations, came into being according to schedule on 1 January. The follow-up negotiations on financial services were wound up this year, and the WTO played an important role overall, particularly in the settlement of disputes. On the common commercial policy front, the Commission proposed an action programme (Customs 2000) to tighten customs controls at the EU's external frontiers; the Council gave Customs 2000 the green light at the end of the year. The Commission has also adopted a communication on the global harmonization of the rules governing direct investment. In shipbuilding, it proposed a special anti-dumping regulation.

In pursuance of its common foreign and security policy, the EU continued to adopt common positions and joint actions in both areas. On foreign policy, it signalled support for the diplomatic moves to halt the fighting in the former Yugoslavia, increased backing for the Middle East peace process and adopted common positions on Burundi, Angola and Nigeria; the Commission availed itself of its right of initiative to adopt several draft common positions defining the Union's objectives and priorities vis-à-vis certain countries. On security policy, a stability pact for Europe was adopted in April, the fruit of the first joint action by the European Union in this field and an unprecedented exercise in preventive diplomacy in Central Europe. Joint actions on the outlawing or limitation of the use of anti-personnel mines and blinding lasers and on the Nuclear Non-Proliferation Treaty and participation in international conferences on such issues represented major advances in the field of security policy. The Madrid European Council also appealed vigorously for negotiations on the Treaty for a blanket nuclear test ban treaty to be concluded by June 1996.

Austria, Finland and Sweden have been members of the European Union since 1 January. They have now converted their missions to the European Communities into Permanent Representations. Elsewhere, the heads of mission of Saint Kitts and Nevis and the Principality of Andorra became the first ambassadors of those countries to be accredited to the European Communities. The number of diplomatic missions from non-Community countries accredited to the Communities thus totalled 162 in 1995, as against 163 in 1994.

Diplomatic relations between the European Communities and the former Yugoslav Republic of Macedonia were established at the end of December. The Commission for its part opened delegations in Bratislava (Slovakia), Asmara (Eritrea), La Paz (Bolivia) and Colombo (Sri Lanka). Agreements were also signed with Lithuania, Latvia and Estonia to set up delegations in their respective capital cities, and similar agreements are being negotiated with Vietnam, Nicaragua and Guatemala, bringing the number of the Commission's diplomatic missions to 126. Representations of international organizations and bodies to the Commission now number 19.

The Commission has also extended its information activities in non-Community countries, particularly in Central and Eastern Europe and in the independent States of the former Soviet Union, the United States and Japan.

Section 2

Common foreign and security policy

General

690.   Implementation of the common foreign and security policy in 1995 saw the adoption by the Council of four joint actions under Article J.3 of the Treaty on European Union. Two concerned the continuation of the European Union's support for the administration of the city of Mostar (→ *point 695*), a third concerned the EU's involvement in the arrangements for implementing the peace agreement in Bosnia-Herzegovina (→ *point 695*) and a fourth the export of certain types of anti-personnel mines (→ *point 700*). The Council also made full use of Article J.2 of the Treaty, under which it adopted 12 common positions. Six of these concerned restrictions on trade with the Federal Republic of Yugoslavia (Serbia and Montenegro) (→ *point 695*), two concerned Burundi (→ *point 695*), two Nigeria (→ *point 695*) one Angola (→ *point 695*) and one blinding lasers (→ *point 700*). On 15 December, on the basis of Article J.7 of the Treaty on European Union, Parliament adopted a recommendation on the election of the Council and the President of the Palestinian Authority (→ *point 850*).

691.   On the security front, the EU continued to apply its system of controls on dual-use goods (→ *point 697*). The possible options for a European arms policy are being examined by an *ad hoc* group set up by the Council (→ *point 698*). Following the joint action adopted in July 1994 on the extension of the Treaty on the Non-Proliferation of Nuclear Weapons, the Council continued to promote the universality of the Treaty, particularly during the Review and Extension Conference (→ *point 699*). The Madrid European Council endorsed this approach.[1]

692.   With regard to active crisis prevention, in a resolution adopted on 14 June Parliament proposed the establishment of a policy analysis centre to diagnose potential crisis situations and prepare preventive diplomacy and any public or humanitarian action that might be required.[2]

693.   Article C of the Treaty on European Union establishes the principle of a single institutional framework designed to ensure the consistency and

---

[1]   Bull. 12-1995.
[2]   OJ C 166, 3.7.1995; Bull. 6-1995, point 1.4.7.

continuity of the activities carried out, while respecting the *acquis communautaire* and the Union's external relations, security, economic and development policies. The Council and the Commission have ensured such consistency.

694.   Implementation of the common foreign and security policy from November 1993 to December 1994 was the subject of a Parliament resolution on 18 May, in which it noted that the potential of Title V of the Treaty on European Union had not been sufficiently exploited and that the shortcomings which had become apparent were due largely to the intergovernmental nature of the policy.[1] It therefore suggested developing the 'security interest of the European Union' concept.

Common foreign policy[2]

695.   Under Decisions 95/23/CFSP, 95/517/CFSP and 95/552/CFSP, the European Union continued joint action 94/790/CFSP on the administration of Mostar *(→ point 845)* in ex-Yugoslavia. Decision 95/545/CFSP concerned EU participation in the arrangements for implementing the Bosnia-Herzegovina peace agreement *(→ point 845)*. The EU applied the UN resolutions on the embargo on the Federal Republic of Yugoslavia, Serbia and Montenegro *(→ point 845)* until their suspension following signing of the Dayton peace agreement in Paris in December, through the adoption of six common positions on restrictions on trade with the Federal Republic of Yugoslavia (Serbia and Montenegro) *(→ point 845)*: Decision 95/11/CFSP on 23 January, Decision 95/150/CFSP on 28 April, Decision 95/213/CFSP on 12 June, Decision 95/254/CFSP on 7 July, Decision 95/378/CFSP on 19 September and Decision 95/511/CFSP on 4 December. The EU also adopted common positions 95/91/CFSP and 95/206/CFSP (23 March and 6 June) concerning Burundi *(→ point 948)*, common position 95/413/CFSP (2 October) on Angola *(→ point 950)* and common positions 95/515/CFSP and 95/544/CFSP (20 November and 4 December) on Nigeria *(→ point 949)*, and Decisions 95/205/CFSP and 95/403/CFSP supplementing joint action 94/276/CFSP on support for the Middle East peace process *(→ point 850)*. The Commission, exercising the right of initiative enshrined in Article J.8 of the Treaty on European Union, adopted three draft common positions on the objectives of the European Union in respect of Russia *(→ point 880)*, the Caucasus Republics *(→ point 884)* and the independent States of Central Asia *(→ point 885)*.

---

[1]   OJ C 151, 19.6.1995; Bull. 5-1995, point 1.4.1.
[2]   Joint actions and common positions regarding a specific geographical area are mentioned here for the record and are described more fully under the geographical headings.

Common security policy

696.   At the final conference held in Paris on 20 and 21 March the participants signed a stability pact,[1] designed to foster peace and stability in Europe, strengthening the development of democracy and regional cooperation in Central and Eastern Europe with a view to resolving the problem of minorities and reinforcing the inviolability of frontiers. This represented the culmination of a European initiative launched by the Brussels European Council on 29 October 1993.[2] Seven regional round tables were chaired by the EU in the course of the year. These dealt with regional policy issues, identification of the bilateral agreements to be included in the pact and proposals for projects designed to promote the objectives of the initiative. The stability pact, which consists of a policy statement and a list of around 100 bilateral agreements and arrangements, was transmitted to the OSCE at the conference. A list of back-up measures supported by the European Union was also attached to the pact. On 19 May Parliament adopted a recommendation based on Article J.7 of the Treaty on European Union on the outcome of the stability pact and action to be taken.[3] On 25 July the OSCE (→ point 724) adopted a decision undertaking to monitor implementation of the pact.

697.   The European Union's system for controlling exports of dual-use goods is governed by Regulation (EC) No 3381/94[4] (→ point 738) and by joint action 94/942/CFSP.[5] The purpose of this integrated system is to ensure effective control of goods which can be used for both civil and military purposes. Decision 94/942/CFSP was amended by Decisions 95/127/CFSP[6] and 95/128/CFSP[7] which were adopted by the Council on 10 April in order to postpone application of the system until 1 July and take account of the EU enlargement and New Zealand's accession to the nuclear suppliers' group, and on 4 December the Council reached agreement on a further amendment to Decision 94/942/CFSP in order to update the system.[8] The need for European controls on the export or transfer of arms was the subject of a Parliament resolution on 19 January.[9]

---

[1]   Bull. 3-1995, point 1.4.4.
[2]   Twenty-seventh General Report, No 924.
[3]   OJ C 151, 19.6.1995; Bull. 5-1995, point 1.4.3.
[4]   1994 General Report, point 1004.
[5]   1994 General Report, point 745.
[6]   OJ L 90, 21.4.1995; Bull 4-1995, point 1.4.2.
[7]   OJ L 90, 21.4.1995; Bull. 4-1995, point 1.4.3.
[8]   Bull. 12-1995.
[9]   OJ C 43, 20.2.1995; Bull. 1/2-1995, point 1.4.3.

698.   On 27 July the Council set up an *ad hoc* group which met for the first time on 18 September to analyse the report drawn up by the informal group of EU and WEU experts who had been given the task of examining the options of a European arms policy, and to put forward recommendations for possible action in the Community framework or on the basis of Title V of the Treaty on European Union.

699.   The outcome of the Non-Proliferation Treaty (NPT) Review and Extension Conference, held from 17 April to 12 May,[1] was very satisfactory for the European Union. After the adoption by the Council on 25 July 1994 of joint action 94/509/CFSP,[2] the aim of which was to encourage the indefinite and unconditional extension of the NPT and promote its general objectives, an in-depth dialogue was organized with non-member countries before and during the conference. Parliament expressed its support for the joint action in its resolution of 5 April.[3] On 12 April the Commission approved a memorandum on Euratom's activities connected with the objectives of Articles III and IV of the NPT for this conference.[4] A dialogue intended to promote the NPT's universality is one of the measures taken by the EU to monitor the Treaty's implementation.

700.   On 12 May the Council adopted Decision 95/170/CFSP concerning a joint action introducing a European Union moratorium on the export of certain types of anti-personnel mines.[5] The EU undertook to endeavour to secure major amendments to the United Nations 1980 Convention on weapons and to make a voluntary contribution of ECU 3 million to the United Nations mine-clearance fund and ECU 160 000 to the organization of the UN international conference on mine clearance which was held in Geneva in July.[6] At the same time the Commission continued its mine-clearance activities in countries such as Afghanistan, Cambodia, Mozambique and northern Iraq and also its research projects on mine detection at its Joint Research Centre. On 29 June Parliament adopted a resolution on land mines and blinding weapons and on anti-personnel mines in which it called for the enlargement of the scope of the joint action.[7]

701.   The review conference of the States party to the 1980 United Nations Convention on inhuman weapons was held in Vienna from 25 September to

---

[1]   Bull. 5-1995, point 1.4.4.
[2]   OJ L 205, 8.8.1994; 1994 General Report, point 744.
[3]   OJ C 109, 1.5.1995; Bull. 4-1995, point 1.4.6.
[4]   COM(95) 127.
[5]   OJ L 115, 22.5.1995; Bull. 5-1995, point 1.4.2.
[6]   Bull. 7/8-1995, point 1.4.2.
[7]   OJ C 166, 3.7.1995; Bull. 6-1995, point 1.4.6.

13 October.[1] The Conference saw the adoption of a fourth protocol to the Convention banning the use or sale of blinding lasers. The Madrid European Council[2] in December welcomed the adoption of the protocol, which had been the subject of common position 95/379/CFSP adopted by the Council on 18 December.[3] The participants failed, however, to reach agreement on a review of the Protocol on anti-personnel mines. On 16 November Parliament adopted a resolution on these issues[4] and on the ratification of the Convention on the destruction of chemical weapons.[5] Its views were endorsed by the Madrid European Council.[2] It also adopted resolutions on nuclear testing[6] (→ point 508). The Madrid European Council expressed its sincere hope that negotiations for a comprehensive test ban treaty would be concluded by June 1996.

EU statements and presidency press statements[7]

702. In the former Soviet Union the European Union followed the upsurge of fighting in Chechnya with concern.[8] In response to the crisis undermining the democratic institutions of Kazakhstan, it called for free multiparty elections to be held soon under the surveillance of international observers[9] and expressed its deep regret that a referendum was being organized on the extension of the President's term of office to the year 2000.[10] The EU expressed its readiness to provide assistance to Russia following the earthquake in Sakhalin[11] and supported a fresh examination of Russia's application to join the Council of Europe.[12] It applauded the smooth running of the general elections on 17 December[2] and the holding of elections in Azerbaijan.[2]

703. The European Union continued to strive for a peaceful solution to the conflict in the former Yugoslavia, calling on the parties to implement the provisions of the 31 December 1994 agreement on the cessation of hostilities in Bosnia-Herzegovina. It expressed its commitment to the sover-

---

[1]   Bull. 10-1995, point 1.4.3.
[2]   Bull. 12-1995.
[3]   OJ L 277, 22.9.1995; Bull. 9-1995, point 1.4.2.
[4]   OJ C 323, 4.12.1995; Bull. 11-1995, point 1.4.3.
[5]   OJ C 323, 4.12.1995; Bull. 11-1995, point 1.4.2.
[6]   OJ C 166, 3.7.1995; Bull. 6-1995, point 1.4.4; OJ C 269, 16.10.1995; Bull. 9-1995, point 1.4.3; OJ C 308, 20.11.1995; Bull. 10-1995, point 1.4.2.
[7]   The following is a summary of the positions adopted in the EU's statements and in press statements issued by the Presidency on behalf of the Union in the field of international policy.
[8]   Bull. 1/2-1995, points 1.4.20 to 1.4.22; Bull. 4-1995, points 1.4.14 and 1.4.15; Bull. 6-1995, point 1.4.15.
[9]   Bull. 3-1995, point 1.4.9.
[10] Bull. 4-1995, point 1.4.11.
[11] Bull. 5-1995, point 1.4.11.
[12] Bull. 10-1995, point 1.4.9.

eignty and territorial integrity of Croatia within its internationally recognized borders. As regards the areas under United Nations protection, the EU expressed concern in January at the implications of the Croatian Government's decision not to accept the renewal of the mandate of Unprofor (United Nations Protection Force in Yugoslavia) for the overall peace process in the former Yugoslavia.[1] In February it endorsed the plan to hold a meeting of the former Yugoslav Republics with a view to their mutual recognition.[2] In May it expressed its concern at the persistence of considerable tensions in Croatia despite the conclusion of a ceasefire agreement[3] and voiced its indignation at the shelling of the civilian population and the taking of United Nations soldiers and observers in Bosnia-Herzegovina as hostages.[4] In June the EU noted the intention expressed by the 'parliaments' in Knin and Pale to merge the self-proclaimed Serb 'republics' of Krajina and Bosnia-Herzegovina, pointing out that this would be contrary to the UN resolutions and therefore null and void.[5] The Union supported the UN's efforts to give Unprofor a rapid reaction capacity enabling it to boost its security and perform its task more effectively.[6] The offensive by the Croatian armed forces in Krajina led the EU to suspend negotiations on a trade and cooperation agreement with Croatia and the implementation of the PHARE programme (→ point 845). In August it condemned the Krajina Serbs' involvement in the attacks on the Bihac pocket.[7] The deterioration of the situation in Dubrovnik and the neighbouring area of Bosnia prompted an appeal by the European Union for all parties to seek a negotiated solution to the crisis.[8] In November the Presidency expressed its satisfaction at the successful conclusion of the Dayton peace talks and its hope that the agreement would pave the way for future peace and stability in the former Yugoslavia. It reiterated the EU's willingness to help implement the civilian aspects of the peace agreement and participate in international efforts to support reconstruction and the restoration of stability in the region.

704.   The European Union condemned the attacks in Algeria and appealed to those involved to seek a peaceful solution to the crisis.[9] It took a keen interest in developments which enabled a number of individuals to come together to ponder the future of their country.[10] In November it welcomed the holding of presidential elections and expressed the hope that they would

---

[1] Bull. 1/2-1995, point 1.4.25.
[2] Bull. 1/2-1995, point 1.4.26.
[3] Bull. 5-1995, point 1.4.8.
[4] Bull. 5-1995, point 1.4.6.
[5] Bull. 6-1995, point 1.4.16.
[6] Bull. 6-1995, point 1.4.17.
[7] Bull. 7/8-1995, point 1.4.6.
[8] Bull. 7/8-1995, point 1.4.7; Bull. 9-1995, point 1.4.4.
[9] Bull. 1/2-1995, point 1.4.7.
[10] Bull. 1/2-1995, point 1.4.6.

be followed by general and local elections so that Algeria could resume normal political life through peaceful dialogue and free and fair elections.[1] It also welcomed the fact that on 12 January Algeria had deposited its instrument of accession to the NPT and invited it to commence negotiations with the IAEA without delay.[2] The Turkish intervention in northern Iraq prompted the EU to call for the withdrawal of Turkish troops and reaffirm the need for strict observance of human rights and international humanitarian law.[3] It roundly condemned the terrorist attacks in Saudi Arabia.[4]

705.   Throughout the year the European Union reaffirmed the need to push ahead with the Middle East peace process (→ *point 850*). In January it expressed its concern at the difficulties that had arisen in Gaza and the West Bank in implementing the Declaration of Principles of 13 September 1993 and at the incidents connected with continued Israeli settlement in the Occupied Territories.[5] Following the criminal attack in Netanya, it renewed its support for all the leaders in the Middle East who had chosen the way of dialogue and peace.[6] In May the EU expressed its concern at the decision of the Israeli authorities to authorize the expropriation of 53 hectares of land in East Jerusalem.[7] The Cairo Summit on 2 February, which brought together the Heads of State or Government of Egypt, Israel and Jordan as well as the Chairman of the Palestinian Authority, was seen by the EU as a sign of hope in a critical period of the peace process.[8] The EU expressed deep satisfaction at the conclusion of the Interim Agreement initialled by Israel and the PLO on 24 September, which paved the way for the second phase of Palestinian autonomy as envisaged in the Declaration of Principles.[9] It expressed its concern at the announcement of the expulsion of Palestinian citizens residing in Libya.[10]

706.   The European Union reaffirmed its commitment to all African countries and its readiness to assist them in their economic and political reforms. The kidnapping of an aid worker in Somalia prompted the European Union to demand his release and to review the guarantees which could be obtained for the safety of those working for humanitarian organizations in Somalia.[11] Further arrests and executions of prominent figures by the Nigerian authori-

---

[1]   Bull. 11-1995, point 1.4.4.
[2]   Bull. 1/2-1995, point 1.4.23.
[3]   Bull. 4-95, point 1.4.17; Bull. 5-1995, point 1.4.15.
[4]   Bull. 11-1995, point 1.4.5.
[5]   Bull. 1/2-1995, point 1.4.14.
[6]   Bull. 1/2-1995, point 1.4.15.
[7]   Bull. 5-1995, point 1.4.10.
[8]   Bull. 1/2-1995, point 1.4.16.
[9]   Bull. 9-1995, point 1.4.11.
[10]   Bull. 9-1995, point 1.4.9.
[11]   Bull. 1/2-1995, point 1.4.18.

ties prompted expressions of serious concern by the European Union,[1] followed by the expression of shock at the death sentence and execution of Ken Saro-Wiwa and others.[2] While noting with satisfaction that the period for transition towards a civil government in Gambia had been reduced, the EU was still concerned that a military government would remain in place until 1996.[3]

Recalling that its objectives regarding Burundi were to consolidate the process of national reconciliation and a return to normal democratic life,[4] the EU voiced concern at the proliferation of acts of violence and the destabilizing activities of extremists on all sides, but commended the efforts made by the country's leaders to restore confidence. It reaffirmed that the situation could return to normal only if there was respect for the government Convention of 10 September 1994 establishing the conditions for power-sharing, as pointed out by the President of the Republic and the Prime Minister in their joint statement on 30 March. In this connection it took note of the special measures announced on 18 June which showed the authorities' resolve to restore order, while hoping that they would be implemented in strict compliance with human rights.[5] It condemned the murder on 30 September of three Italian nationals in Burundi.[6] The European Union condemned the violence in Rwanda which had led to several thousand civilian deaths in the Kibeho camp on 22 April and urged the Rwandan authorities to identify and punish those responsible for the massacre. It pointed out that its development aid for Rwanda was conditional on respect for human rights and progress towards national reconciliation.[7]

The European Union noted with satisfaction the progress towards peace and national reconciliation in Angola. Expressing its unreserved support for this process, it decided to make a practical contribution to the consolidation of lasting peace, and to look favourably at requests for assistance with mine-clearance operations, while continuing to provide Angola with the necessary humanitarian and food aid.[8] It also welcomed the meeting between President José Eduardo Dos Santos and Mr Jonas Savimbi in Lusaka on 6 May.[9] The EU welcomed the signing of the peace agreement between the Government of Niger and the Armed Resistance Organization.[10] It deplored the

---

[1] Bull. 3-1995, point 1.4.11; Bull. 10-1995, points 1.4.7 and 1.4.8;
     Bull. 11-1995, point 1.4.6.
[2] Bull. 11-1995, point 1.4.7.
[3] Bull. 3-1995, point 1.4.8.
[4] Bull. 3-1995, point 1.4.6.
[5] Bull. 6-1995, point 1.4.9.
[6] Bull. 10-1995, point 1.4.4.
[7] Bull. 4-1995, point 1.4.12.
[8] Bull. 1/2-1995, point 1.4.8.
[9] Bull. 5-1995, point 1.4.5.
[10] Bull. 5-1995, point 1.4.9.

continuation of the conflict in Sierra Leone, calling on all parties to work towards national reconciliation, and welcomed the statement made by the government proposing a ceasefire and unconditional peace talks.[1] The EU welcomed the outcome of the constitutional referendum held in Gabon on 23 July.[2] It roundly condemned the military coup in São Tomé and Príncipe on 15 August,[3] and subsequently welcomed the restoration of constitutional legality and the reinstatement of the democratically elected President and the National Assembly.[4] It welcomed the decision by President Bashir of Sudan to release 32 political prisoners and persons already sentenced for political crimes.[5] The EU condemned the coup d'état in Moroni (Comoros)[6] and welcomed the democratic election of the President and Prime Minister in Ethiopia.[7] It expressed satisfaction at the peace agreement in Liberia between the main factions.[8] It also expressed satisfaction regarding the first parliamentary and presidential elections to be held in Tanzania despite certain difficulties.[9] It took note of the verdict of the Constitutional Court in South Africa judging the death penalty to be incompatible with the new constitution and giving expression to South Africa's commitment to the rule of law.[10]

707.   The European Union deeply regretted the standoff between Ecuador and Peru. Recalling its commitment to closer relations with Latin America, it expressed its support for any initiative aimed at reaching a peaceful solution to this frontier conflict.[11] It welcomed the deposit by Argentina of its instrument of accession to the NPT[12] and the accession of Chile.[13] The EU also expressed its satisfaction at the orderly operation of the judicial system with the verdict of the Supreme Court of Chile in the Letelier case and the confirmation of the prison sentences against Generals Contreras and Espinoza.[14] The European Union once again drew the attention of the United States authorities to its serious concern regarding the possible adoption by Congress of the Bill on Liberty and Democratic Solidarity with Cuba, recalling its opposition to the adoption of any measure having extra-territorial

---

[1]   Bull. 5-1995, point 1.4.12.
[2]   Bull. 7/8-1995, point 1.4.8.
[3]   Bull. 7/8-1995, point 1.4.14
[4]   Bull. 7/8-1995, point 1.4.13.
[5]   Bull. 9-1995, point 1.4.10.
[6]   Bull. 9-1995, point 1.4.5.
[7]   Bull. 9-1995, point 1.4.6.
[8]   Bull. 9-1995, point 1.4.8.
[9]   Bull. 12-1995.
[10] Bull. 6-1995, point 1.4.8.
[11] Bull. 1/2-1995, point 1.4.9.
[12] Bull. 1/2-1995, point 1.4.24.
[13] Bull. 6-1995, point 1.4.19.
[14] Bull. 6-1995, point 1.4.10.

application and in breach of WTO rules.[1] It applauded the successful action by the Colombian authorities in arresting the alleged head of the Cali cartel and reiterated its support for the fight against drug trafficking.[2] The European Union welcomed the smooth running of the ballot on 25 June in Haiti but deplored the fact that the elections had been accompanied by acts of violence.[3] It welcomed the undertaking entered into by Guatemala's political parties to respect the agreements signed under the peace process[4] and strongly condemned the massacre perpetrated by members of the army on 5 October.[5]

708.   The European Union followed the situation in Afghanistan particularly closely and expressed its support for the peace process initiated by the United Nations.[6] Following the entry into force on 8 January of an agreement on the cessation of hostilities signed by the Sri Lankan authorities and the LTTE (Liberation Tigers of Tamil Eelam), the EU expressed the hope that this step forward would be followed by the speedy opening of negotiations to find a political solution to the conflict and expressed its readiness to collaborate in the work of economic reconstruction.[7] It condemned the various attacks and massacres[8] and urgently called on the LTTE to enter into political negotiations with the Sri Lankan authorities.[9] In August it welcomed the government's efforts to draw up a set of devolution proposals aimed at satisfying the aspirations of all Sri Lankans.[10] The European Union followed with the greatest disquiet the development of the situation on the border between Myanmar (formerly Burma) and Thailand.[11] It also expressed concern at Myanmar's domestic political situation and the absence of democratic dialogue.[12] It deeply deplored the expulsion on 23 February by the North Korean authorities of the Polish officers belonging to the Neutral Nations Commission[13] and welcomed the fact that appeal proceedings in Pakistan had resulted in a verdict of not guilty for Rahmat and Salamat Massih, who had been sentenced to death by a lower court.[14] It noted with concern the latest developments in the South China Sea,[15] and expressed its

---

[1]   Bull. 4-1995, point 1.4.9; Bull. 10-1995, point 1.4.5.
[2]   Bull. 6-1995, point 1.4.12.
[3]   Bull. 6-1995, point 1.4.13.
[4]   Bull. 9-1995, point 1.4.7.
[5]   Bull. 10-1995, point 1.4.6.
[6]   Bull. 1/2-1995, point 1.4.4.
[7]   Bull. 1/2-1995, point 1.4.19; Bull. 3-995, point 1.4.12.
[8]   Bull. 4-1995, point 1.4.13; Bull.11-1995, point 1.4.9.
[9]   Bull. 5-1995, point 1.4.13.
[10]   Bull. 7/8-1995, point 1.4.15.
[11]   Bull. 3-1995, point 1.4.5.
[12]   Bull. 12-1995.
[13]   Bull. 3-1995, point 1.4.7.
[14]   Bull. 1/2-1995, point 1.4.13.
[15]   Bull. 3-1995, point 1.4.10.

concern about the human rights situation in China, deploring the fact that many dissidents and intellectuals had been arrested.[1] It expressed support for the peace talks between the Government of the Philippines and the Moro National Liberation Front.[2]

709.   A statement was issued on 20 October concerning the financial situation of the United Nations (→ point 711).[3]

---

[1]   Bull. 6-1995, point 1.4.11; Bull 12.1995.
[2]   Bull. 11-1995, point 1.4.8.
[3]   Bull. 10-1995, point 1.4.10.

Section 3

International organizations and conferences

United Nations and UN specialized agencies

General Assembly

710.   The 50th session of the United Nations General Assembly opened in New York on 19 September with the election of Mr Diogo Freitas do Amaral (Portugal) as president.[1] During the second week of the session, conducted at ministerial level, the European Union was represented by Mr Javier Solana Madariaga, the Spanish Foreign Minister, in his capacity as President of the Council, who spoke on behalf of the European Union on 26 September,[2] and also by Mr Marín and Mr Van den Broek, who both also took part during the week in a series of meetings with a number of countries and regional groupings and in several rounds of bilateral discussions. The main topics of discussion for the General Assembly were the situation in the former Yugoslavia, human rights, disarmament and nuclear non-proliferation, developments in Africa, the Middle East peace process, the major UN conferences held during 1995, work on the 'Agenda for development', the question of reforming the composition of the Security Council, and also the celebration of the 50th anniversary of the signing of the United Nations Charter.

711.   The General Assembly met in special session in New York from 22 to 24 October at Head of State or Government level, to commemorate the entry into force of the United Nations Charter on 24 October 1945. At this unprecedented gathering many participants mentioned the achievements of the UN, but also stressed the need for adjustment and reform to enable it to meet current and future challenges. A major point of concern in this context was the serious financial crisis *(→ point 709)* currently gripping the United Nations. At this special session, Mr Felipe González, Spanish Prime Minister and President of the Council, made a statement on behalf of the European Union; Mr Van den Broek, representing the European Community, which was present in an observer capacity at the session, also spoke. The European Union also circulated a statement on the United Nations' finan-

---

[1]   Bull. 9-1995, point 1.4.12.
[2]   The full text of the speech is given in point 2.3.1 of Bull. 9-1995.

cial situation at the opening of the commemorative special session. In a resolution adopted on 12 October Parliament stressed the need for greater financial and organizational support for the United Nations,[1] an approach endorsed at the Madrid European Council in December.[2]

United Nations Economic and Social Council, Commission on Sustainable Development, United Nations Economic Commission for Europe

712.   At its July session the Economic and Social Council addressed the issue of the implementation and follow-up of the major UN conferences devoted to human-centred sustainable development, in which the Community had taken an active part.

713.   At its third session, held in April, the Commission on Sustainable Development set up an Intergovernmental Panel on Forests (→ point 475), with the Community and the Member States playing a leading role, and adopted decisions on sustainable agriculture and the links between trade and the environment — to which the Community again made a crucial contribution — and also on technology transfer, financial resources for sustainable development and environmental indicators.

714.   The 50th annual session of the United Nations Economic Commission for Europe was held in Geneva from 3 to 11 April. The emphasis was again on the need to concentrate resources on the priority areas of activity in supporting the countries in transition to a market economy. A round-table discussion was held on promoting the expansion of these countries' trade. At a meeting involving a number of regional groupings possible synergies with the work of the ECE were explored. The Commission played its part in the proceedings, delivering statements on the development of the European Union's relations with countries in transition, the economic situation in the Union and trade facilitation. Mr Yves Berthelot, Executive Secretary of the ECE, had meetings with Mr Van den Broek, Mrs Bjerregaard and Mr Kinnock during his visit to the Commission on 24 and 26 April.[3]

---

[1]   OJ C 287, 30.10.1995; Bull. 10-1995, point 1.4.11.
[2]   Bull. 12-1995.
[3]   Bull. 4-1995, point 1.4.20.

Convention on the Law of the Sea

715. As a member of the International Seabed Authority, the Community took part in the meetings of the Assembly held in Kingston, Jamaica, from 27 February to 17 March and from 7 to 18 August. At this preliminary stage the Assembly examined procedural arrangements for the election of the Authority's Council at the meeting to be held in March 1996. The States party to the Convention on the Law of the Sea, which had entered into force in November 1994,[1] met in New York from 15 to 19 May and from 27 November to 1 December. Four Member States of the European Union (Germany, Greece, Italy and Austria) had deposited their instruments of ratification and participated in their own right. The meetings were concerned mainly with the measures to be adopted for establishing the Tribunal for the Law of the Sea.

International Monetary Fund and the World Bank

716. The IMF and the World Bank held a number of meetings in Washington in October in conjunction with the general assembly of the Bretton Woods institutions. The European Union was represented by Mr Pedro Solbes, Spain's Minister for the Economy and Finance, in his capacity as President of the Council, and by Mr de Silguy. Commission representatives also took part as observers at meetings of the Group of Ten, the Interim Committee (→ point 67) and the Development Committee.

World Intellectual Property Organization

717. The Commission contributed to the discussions on copyright (→ point 134) with a view to the possible adoption of an additional protocol to the Berne Convention and a new instrument on the rights of phonogram producers and performing artists.[2] It was also involved in negotiations on a draft treaty on dispute settlement in intellectual property matters. In the industrial property sphere (→ point 133), following authorization given by the Council on 29 June, the Treaty on trade mark law which had been adopted in October 1994[2] was signed on behalf of the Communities at WIPO headquarters in Geneva on 30 June (Table III). The Commission also continued to be involved in the work of the various WIPO working parties of experts.

---

[1] 1994 General Report, point 1056.
[2] 1994 General Report, point 1058.

World Trade Organization

718. The World Trade Organization, which emerged as one of the results of the Uruguay Round of multilateral trade negotiations, began its work on 1 January as scheduled, just nine months after the signing of the Uruguay Round agreements in Marrakesh on 15 April 1994.[1] The European Community and all the Member States have been members of the WTO from the beginning. On 16 May the Commission proposed a code of conduct for participation by the Community and its Member States in areas of shared powers, with the aim of defending their respective trade interests as effectively as possible.[2]

719. The WTO brings together under a single decision-making and administrative body the three agreements resulting from the Uruguay Round: the General Agreement on Tariffs and Trade (GATT), the General Agreement on Trade in Services (GATS) and the Agreement on trade-related aspects of intellectual property rights (TRIPs). The single structure has an important part to play both in dispute settlement, which has been unified from the standpoint of time-limits and procedures into an integrated system, and in decision-making.

720. The WTO also, by general consent, achieved an initial success with the conclusion of the Uruguay Round follow-up negotiations on financial services. On the initiative of the Community, following a three-month extension of the negotiations,[3] an interim agreement providing better market access based on the most-favoured-nation (MFN) principle was concluded by all WTO members on 28 July to run for 18 months until 1 November 1997.[4] The United States joined in the agreement, but only for the national treatment part (their offer does not guarantee access to the US market on an MFN basis). In putting to a practical test the effectiveness and economic advantage of a multilateral agreement on liberalizing financial services, the signatories to the interim agreement intend to safeguard the market access improvements obtained during the negotiations and also to persuade the United States in particular of the advantages of multilateralism. On 6 March the Council adopted negotiating directives (Table III) for agreements between the Community and the WTO member countries on financial and other services.

---

[1]   1994 General Report, point 986.
[2]   Bull. 5-1995, point 1.4.16.
[3]   Bull. 6-1995, point 1.4.21.
[4]   Bull. 7/8-1995, point 1.4.20.

721. The dispute-settlement body was established. It has been called on to deal with a number of contentious matters arising out of the implementation of the Uruguay Round agreements.

722. The Committee on Trade and Environment,[1] set up by the Marrakesh ministerial conference in April 1994, continued to look at ways of balancing the needs of environmental protection and the requirements of international trade.

723. Implementation of the tariff aspects of the Uruguay Round began, with the first stages in the dismantling of duties on industrial products[2] and agricultural products[3] incorporated into the Common Customs Tariff with effect from 1 January and 1 July respectively. The World Customs Organization recommendation on amendments to the nomenclature annexed to the Convention on the Harmonized Commodity Description and Coding System was given effect in the Common Customs Tariff scheduled to enter into force on 1 January 1996.[4]

Organization for Security and Cooperation in Europe

724. The principal matters occupying the OSCE (previously the CSCE until the end of 1994)[5] during the year were the security model for Europe in the 21st century, regional crises (notably in Chechnya and Nagorno-Karabakh), integration of the economic and human dimensions in the OSCE's political consultations and its monitoring of the stability pact in Europe (→ point 696). The Organization considered what contribution it might make to international efforts to restore democracy and civil society in the former Yugoslavia. The Commission was involved in all these activities throughout the year, particularly the work on the security model. The Madrid European Council reiterated the European Union's intention to play an active part in strengthening the OSCE.

725. As part of its preventive diplomacy and peacekeeping activities, the OSCE continued to monitor developments in current crises and their impact on regional stability, especially in the former Yugoslavia (through its missions to Skopje and Sarajevo) and in Georgia, Moldova and Tadjikistan. In Chechnya it set up an assistance group to help find a peaceful solution. It

---

[1] 1994 General Report, point 987.
[2] Commission Regulation (EC) No 3115/94 — OJ L 345, 31.12.1994.
[3] Commission Regulation (EC) No 1359/95 — OJ L 142, 26.6.1995.
[4] Commission Regulation (EC) No 3009/95 — OJ L 319, 31.12.1995.
[5] 1994 General Report, point 1068.

continued to be involved in the negotiations on Nagorno-Karabakh through the Minsk Group, and in preventive diplomacy missions in Estonia and Latvia. It also set up a mission in Ukraine.

726. The Committee of Senior Officials met in March and October. The March meeting concentrated on the follow-up to the decisions taken at the Budapest Summit in 1994[1] and on the crises in Chechnya and Nagorno-Karabakh. On 26 and 27 October the Committee met in Prague to pursue work on the security model, prepare for the Council of Ministers meeting in Budapest and consider the OSCE's contribution to settling the conflict in the former Yugoslavia.

When it met in Budapest on 7 and 8 December[2] the Council of Ministers decided to establish an OSCE mission for peace, democracy and stability in Bosnia-Herzegovina, in the framework of the Dayton peace agreement (→ point 850) relating to elections, human rights monitoring, arms control and confidence-building and security measures in the former Yugoslavia.

The Permanent Committee pursued its role as a political consultation and decision-making forum with weekly meetings in Vienna. The third meeting of the Economic Forum, held in Prague in June, was attended by representatives of 11 international organizations and regional groupings and was concerned mainly with regional economic cooperation. The Office for Democratic Institutions and Human Rights in Warsaw organized a number of seminars, including one on freedom of association and NGOs in civil society and one on tolerance. The second OSCE meeting on the implementation of human dimension commitments, held in Warsaw from 2 to 19 October, was attended by a large number of NGOs, drawn in particular from Central and Eastern Europe and the former Soviet Union, and a number of international organizations (Council of Europe, UNDP, Unesco, UNHCR and ICRC). The meeting reviewed implementation in practical terms and considered ways of improving adherence to commitments, in the light of the significant shortcomings observed. Also discussed were the possible OSCE role in the rehabilitation of the former Yugoslavia, and the issue of election monitoring.

Western European Union

727. The Western European Union (WEU) devoted much effort during the year to building up its operational capacity, giving its associated partners

---

[1] 1994 General Report, point 1068.
[2] Bull. 12-1995.

and its associate members and observers the possibility of becoming more closely involved in its activities, developing relations with Russia and Ukraine, and examining the nature of its relations with the European Union.

728.   On 7 March the WEU's Permanent Council approved measures to be taken to develop dialogue and the exchange of information on matters of mutual interest between the WEU and Russia, on the one hand, and Ukraine, on the other. Greece was welcomed as the 10th full member of the WEU at the Lisbon meeting on 15 May of the Foreign and Defence Ministers of the WEU member countries. At this meeting the role of the WEU as the future military arm of the European Union and the European pillar of the Atlantic alliance came in for discussion. The ministers agreed to improve the decision-making machinery by setting up a political and military group, a 'situation centre', and also an intelligence section within the planning cell. Lastly, at their meeting in Madrid on 14 November the ministers approved the WEU contribution to the 1996 Intergovernmental Conference (→ point 1025), a move welcomed by the European Council meeting in Madrid in December,[1] and also the publication of a joint study paper entitled 'European security: a common concept of the 27 WEU countries'. They also adopted decisions on a range of measures to strengthen further the WEU's operational capacity. The ministers welcomed the results achieved by the WEU's involvement in the administration of the city of Mostar (→ point 850) and in operations along the Danube and in the Adriatic; they approved the establishment of procedures for setting up a WEU force to carry out 'Petersberg'-type missions and also the arrangements to be made for putting into effect operations by the WEU humanitarian intervention force.

Council of Europe

729.   Membership of the Council of Europe continued to increase and cooperation with Central and Eastern Europe was strengthened further. The accession of Latvia on 10 February, Albania and Moldova on 10 July and Ukraine and the former Yugoslav Republic of Macedonia on 9 November brought the number of member countries to 38. New cooperation and assistance programmes for future member countries, notably Russia and Ukraine, were adopted, while cooperation continued with countries that had recently joined the organization.

730.   Community cooperation with the Council of Europe was extended to take in new areas. Under the institutional arrangements agreed on 16 June

---

[1]   Bull. 12-1995.

1987[1] the Community continued to be involved in the major political events which punctuated the activities of the Council of Europe throughout the year. These included the 96th and 97th meetings of the Committee of Ministers and also conferences of specialized ministers on family law, sport and social security. The President of the Commission, Mr Jacques Santer, had a meeting with the Council of Europe Secretary-General, Mr Daniel Tarschys, in Brussels on 6 March. Quadripartite meetings, normally an annual event, were held on two occasions, in Paris on 7 April, when the Commission was represented by Mr Van den Broek, and in Madrid on 6 November, when Mr Oreja was present.[2]

731.   Meetings were held between the Commission and the Council of Europe on a wide range of subjects, including legal matters (cultural cooperation, mass media, sports development, equality between the sexes, youth, social security, social policy, migration, bioethics, legal cooperation, conservation of European wildlife and natural habitats, work connected with the Convention on transfrontier television and the eighth international symposium on the European Convention on human rights).

732.   Cooperation with the Central and East European countries passed a new milestone with the signing in November of the joint programme for the reform of the legal system and local authorities and the recasting of arrangements for implementing legislation in Ukraine.

Organization for Economic Cooperation and Development

733.   In March South Korea made a formal application for OECD membership. The negotiations with four countries from Central and Eastern Europe continued;[3] the Czech Republic became an OECD member on completion of the negotiations in December. Discussions also continued on the future of the Organization. Contacts with non-member countries were stepped up and a forum was set up for dialogue with emerging market economy countries.

734.   At the annual ministerial meeting held in Paris on 23 and 24 May,[4] ministers adopted a study on employment, made up of a set of national studies on the topic, and called on the OECD to assist members in implementing recommendations on a country-by-country basis. The ministers also

---

[1]   OJ L 273, 26.9.1987; Twenty-first General Report, point 902.
[2]   Bull. 4-1995, point 1.4.21; Bull. 11-1995, point 1.4.10.
[3]   Czech Republic, Slovakia, Hungary and Poland.
[4]   Bull. 5-1995, point 1.4.18.

decided that negotiations should take place on a multilateral agreement on international investment, under which there would be close cooperation with the WTO *(→ point 755)*. On 22 May the Council of the European Union adopted a decision authorizing the Commission to take part in the negotiations in areas falling within the scope of Community powers (Table III); this was followed by the adoption of negotiating directives on 27 November. The Council had previously adopted, on 10 April, conclusions on trade and investment,[1] in response to the Commission communication on direct investment *(→ point 755)*, and Parliament adopted a resolution on the subject on 14 December.[2] Negotiations began in September. The OECD agreement on shipbuilding was ratified by the European Community on 11 December *(→ point 192)*.

735. Work was intensified on the multidisciplinary study on new trade issues (environment, competition, labour standards and technology) with a view to the WTO ministerial conference to be held in Singapore in December 1996. Lastly, special efforts were made within the Organization to ensure coordination on stabilizing public finances and on a study of population ageing and growing health care needs.

European Bank for Reconstruction and Development

736. Details of the activities of the EBRD are contained in Chapter III, Section 2, (Economic and monetary policy) *(→ point 60)*.

---

[1]   Bull. 4-1995, point 1.4.22.
[2]   OJ C 17, 22.1.1196; Bull. 12-1995.

Section 4

Commercial policy

General matters

Operation of the customs union and customs cooperation

737.   On 22 December the Council agreed a common position on the proposal for a Parliament and Council Decision (Table I) introducing a Community customs action programme (Customs 2000) to tighten up customs
procedures and controls at the European Union's external border. On 14
July the Commission adopted a proposal for a Regulation (Table I) amending Regulation (EEC) No 2913/92 establishing the Community Customs
Code to allow the Community to meet its commitments *vis-à-vis* the World
Customs Organization as regards binding information on origin. It also
adopted implementing provisions on customs value (successive sales) along
the same lines as the United States. On 13 January the Commission adopted
a proposal for a Council Regulation (Table II) laying down transitional customs measures following Finland's and Sweden's accession concerning its
relations with Norway. This proposal was amended on 2 May.

738.   In the form of Regulation (EC) No 1367/95,[1] the Commission
adopted the implementing provisions for Council Regulation (EC) No 3295/
94[2] on imports of counterfeit and pirated goods. It also adopted a proposal
for a Regulation amending Council Regulation (EEC) No 3911/92[3] on the
export of cultural goods to define the treatment for watercolours and
gouaches. On 10 April the Council adopted Regulation (EC) No 837/95
(Table II) amending Regulation (EC) No 3381/94 and Decisions 95/127/
CFSP and 95/128/CFSP *(→ point 697)* amending Decision 94/942/CFSP on
the control of exports of dual-use military/civilian goods to take account of
EU enlargement and New Zealand's accession to the nuclear suppliers group
and to set the entry into force of this control procedure at 1 July.

739.   On 11 April the Commission signed a Convention on customs
treatment of pool containers used in international transport (Table III).

---

[1]   OJ L 133, 17.6.1995.
[2]   OJ L 341, 30.12.1994; 1994 General Report, point 1004.
[3]   OJ L 395, 31.12.1992.

740.   On 6 February the Council adopted negotiating directives (Table III) for an agreement on the harmonization of non-preferential rules of origin under the auspices of the World Customs Organization and the World Trade Organization.

Anti-dumping and anti-subsidy activities

741.   On 4 July the Commission adopted its 13th annual report on the Community's anti-dumping and anti-subsidy activities (1994).[1] The 12th report (1993) was adopted on 15 February.[2]

742.   The Uruguay Round Agreement contains new and detailed rules on almost every aspect of anti-dumping and anti-subsidy activity and these were transposed into Community legislation[3] by Regulations (EC) Nos 3283/94 (anti-dumping) and 3284/94 (anti-subsidy). These introduced new time-limits for the anti-dumping and anti-subsidy procedures which came into force on 1 September following adoption by the Council, on 29 May, of Regulations (EC) Nos 1251/95 (Table II) and 1252/95 (Table II). In future, provisional measures must be introduced within nine months from the initiation of the proceedings and the final conclusions must be adopted within a further six or four months in the case of anti-subsidy investigations. On 20 February the Council adopted Regulation (EC) No 355/95 (Table II) amending for the first time Regulation (EC) No 3283/94 to clarify how it should be applied to the proceedings already pending when it entered into force. On 22 December the Council adopted a Regulation (Table II) which is a revised and consolidated version of Regulation (EC) No 3283/94.[4]

743.   As regards anti-dumping the Commission undertook 33 anti-dumping investigations and 26 reviews, imposed provisional anti-dumping duties in 24 cases (four of which after a review), terminated eight investigations without introducing any measures and temporarily suspended anti-dumping measures in three cases. The Council imposed definitive anti-dumping duties in 13 cases.

The main anti-dumping cases in 1995 were the following definitive measures: imports of disodium carbonate originating in the United States,[5] colour television receivers originating in Malaysia, the People's Republic of

---

[1]   COM(95) 309; Bull. 7/8-1995, point 1.4.23.
[2]   COM(95) 16; Bull. 1/2-1995, point 1.4.43.
[3]   OJ L 349, 31.12.1994; 1994 General Report, point 1008.
[4]   For more details of specific cases, see the 14th annual report on the Community's anti-dumping and anti-subsidy activities (1995) which will be published this year.
[5]   OJ L 244, 12.10.1995.

China, the Republic of Korea, Singapore and Thailand,[1] ammonium nitrate originating in Russia and Lithuania,[2] ferro-silico-manganese originating in Brazil, Russia, South Africa and Ukraine,[3] and photocopiers originating in Japan (review),[4] plus the following provisional measures: imports of microwave ovens originating in the People's Republic of China, the Republic of Korea, Thailand and Malaysia,[5] bicycles originating in Indonesia, Malaysia and Thailand,[3] and magnetic microdisks originating in Malaysia, Mexico and the United States.[6]

The two panels set up in 1994 by the GATT Anti-dumping Committee (matters covered by rules predating those of the WTO) to examine the compatibility with the anti-dumping code of two Community measures, one concerning imports of Japanese audio cassettes and the other imports of Brazilian cotton fibres, presented their reports in 1995. In the first case the panel concluded that the Community had fully complied with GATT rules and the report was adopted by the GATT Anti-dumping Committee. In the case of the audio cassettes the panel found that virtually all the objections raised were groundless. The Commission is considering what action to take on the report's conclusions regarding the only issue still in dispute.

744.   As far as anti-subsidy policy is concerned, the Community did not initiate any new proceedings this year under Regulation (EC) No 3284/94[7] but closely followed the proceedings initiated by a growing number of non-member countries against products originating in EC Member States. In almost all of these cases the Community held talks with the investigating authorities in the countries concerned in order to ensure that the relevant provisions of the GATT anti-subsidy code were being respected. Anti-subsidy investigations were initiated by the United States, Canada and Israel on pasta, by Canada on Community-subsidized sugar, by Israel on pastry products and by Argentina on tinned peaches. A proceeding initiated in September 1994 on olive oil was also continued. Mexico imposed countervailing duty on beef from the Community and on pork from Denmark. Jamaica continued its investigation of skimmed-milk powder imports and Bolivia terminated an investigation concerning wheat from Germany and Denmark without introducing any measures.

At the Community's request, the GATT Subsidies Committee adopted the report submitted in October 1994 by the GATT panel investigating the

---

[1]   OJ L 73, 1.4.1995.
[2]   OJ L 198, 23.8.1995.
[3]   OJ L 248, 14.10.1995.
[4]   OJ L 244, 12.10.1995.
[5]   OJ L 156, 7.7.1995.
[6]   OJ L 249, 17.10.1995.
[7]   OJ L 349, 31.12.1994.

countervailing duty imposed by the United States on hot-rolled carbon steel, lead and bismuth products from France, Germany and the United Kingdom. The United States opposed its adoption.

Obstacles to trade

745. In the wake of the Uruguay Round the Council had adopted, on 22 December 1994, Regulation (EC) No 3286/94 (obstacles to trade Regulation)[1] laying down Community commercial policy procedures to ensure the exercise of the rights conferred on the Community by international trade rules, in particular those established under the auspices of the World Trade Organization (WTO). This Regulation, which entered into force on 1 January, replaced Regulation (EEC) No 2641/84 concerning protection against illicit trade practices by third countries. It was amended by Council Regulation (EC) No 356/95 (Table II) of 20 February defining how long it would apply.

746. The two proceedings initiated under Regulation (EEC) No 2641/84, which were still pending on 31 December 1994[2] and concern the pirating of Community sound recordings in Thailand and measures affecting Community polyester fibre exports to Turkey, will in future be governed by Regulation (EC) No 3286/94. Although the first proceeding was suspended on 20 December, the Commission will continue to keep a watchful eye on the new Thai copyright law to see what practical implications it will have.

Import arrangements, including safeguards and other measures affecting exports to non-member countries

747. Regulation (EC) No 519/94 on the rules applying to imports from State-trading countries was amended for the first time by Regulation (EC) No 538/95 (Table II) of 6 March, which changed the system of non-textile quotas applying to imports from the People's Republic of China to take account of the European Union's enlargement, and for the second time by Regulation (EC) No 839/95 (Table II) of 10 April, which removed the Baltic States from the Regulation's scope. The Commission proposed a third amendment to the Regulation (Table II) on 13 October. This extends the Regulation to ECSC products.

---

[1] OJ L 349, 31.12.1994.
[2] 1994 General Report, point 1015.

748.   On 22 December the Council adopted a Regulation (Table II) amending Regulations (EC) Nos 3285/94 and 519/94 concerning a uniform Community surveillance document.

749.   On 6 October the Commission approved (Table II) a proposal amending Regulation (EC) No 520/94 on the administration of quantitative quotas to make the rules governing the redistribution of unused quantities more flexible.

Export arrangements

750.   Information on embargoes is given in the relevant geographical sections. Details of the control of dual-use exports are given in the section on the operation of the customs union and customs cooperation (→ point 738).

Treaties, trade agreements and mutual recognition agreements

751.   On 19 April the Council adopted Decision 95/133/EC (Table II) authorizing the tacit renewal or maintenance in force until 30 April 1996 of certain trade agreements concluded by the Member States with non-member countries.

752.   Acting on the conclusions of the Essen European Council[1] the Commission began work on collating, into a single system, preferential origin rules for all Central and East European countries with which the Community has concluded Europe Agreements.

753.   Pursuant to the Council Decision of 21 September 1992[2] authorizing it to negotiate agreements with non-member countries on mutual recognition in the field of conformity assessment, the Commission held negotiations in 1995 with the United States, Canada, Australia and New Zealand, and initiated negotiations with Japan.

754.   Under the Council Decision of 14 November 1989, negotiations were opened in 1995 with Israel on an agreement for the recognition of good laboratory practices in the field of chemicals.

---

[1]   Bull. 12-1994, point I.41.
[2]   Twenty-sixth General Report, point 983.

Foreign direct investment

755. On 1 March the Commission adopted a communication on a level playing-field for direct investment worldwide,[1] in which it underlined the crucial role played by foreign direct investment which has mushroomed over the last 15 years and is now seen, together with trade, as one of the key factors in the world economy. The Commission pinpointed obstacles to investment and proposed that the Council commence negotiations on multilateral rules on investment within the OECD and start work in the same area under the auspices of the WTO. The Council endorsed this approach on 10 April. On 22 May the Council gave the go-ahead for the Community to take part in the OECD negotiations on a multilateral agreement on investment which were launched by OECD ministers on 24 May and which are expected to continue into 1997 *(→ point 734)*. The Commission also began to canvass WTO members for support with a view to persuading the WTO ministerial meeting in 1996 to authorize the opening of negotiations on multilateral investment rules.

Export credits

756. On 26 June[2] the Commission adopted a proposal for a Council Decision amending the Decision of 4 April 1978 applying the 1977 OECD guidelines for officially supported export credits which was last amended in 1993.[3] These amendments concern the interest rate to be used when calculating the net present value of a credit lent to a borrower on concessional terms, commercial interest reference rates and the classification of purchasing countries. Future work will cover credit insurance premiums, market windows, the untying of aid and export credits for agricultural products.

On 12 July[4] the Commission adopted a second proposal amending the 1978 Decision laying down specific guidelines for exports of used aircraft. On 7 September it adopted a recommendation for a Council Decision authorizing it to negotiate, within the OECD, guidelines on export credits for agricultural and forestry products.

---

[1]   COM(95) 42; Bull. 3-1995, point 1.4.13.
[2]   Bull. 6-1995, point 1.4.31.
[3]   OJ L 44, 22.2.1993; Twenty-seventh General Report, point 875.
[4]   Bull. 7/8-1995, point 1.4.48.

Export promotion

757.   The Commission's export promotion programme followed the guidelines adopted in 1993[1] which gave priority to the Asian and Gulf countries, capital goods, striking a balance between fairs and trade forums and coordination with Community programmes and with Member States' export promotion programmes. Trade forums[2] again provided an opportunity to foster close cooperation with industry through the direct involvement of trade federations and provided an auspicious climate for parallel negotiations with local authorities and industry.

758.   China was again given priority because of the keen interest generated by its sustained economic growth, market potential and problems of access. Five events were successfully organized in China giving EU companies in key sectors such as the motor and components industry, building and environment industries an opportunity to gain a foothold in the market and raising European industry's profile in China through their combined presence. Other Community trade events were held in the Republic of Korea and the United Arab Emirates. With the Commission's backing, EU companies and trade organizations took part in trade fairs in Hong Kong, Singapore, China, Japan, Russia and Hungary in the textile, clothing, footwear and leather sectors.

759.   The Commission also mounted a specific programme to promote exports to Japan (→ point 903), under which groups of European companies took part in several events included JETRO (Japan External Trade Organization), the Health Care Fair, the Total Construction Trade Fair and the Japan Pack Trade Fair.

Individual sectors

Steel

Multilateral steel agreement

760.   The Commission continued its efforts[3] to seek a multilateral steel agreement although no bilateral discussions were held in 1995. It held a

---

[1]   Twenty-seventh General Report, point 877.
[2]   1994 General Report, point 1026.
[3]   1994 General Report, point 1027.

number of bilateral meetings with the United States in an attempt to breathe fresh life into the negotiation process.

Autonomous ECSC arrangements

761. Statistical surveillance of imports from all countries under automatic licensing arrangements continued in 1995.[1]

Relations with non-member countries

762. Following the annual review, the EC-Czech Republic[2] and EC-Slovak Republic[2] Joint Committees amended the tariff quota system set up in 1993[3] to take account of the accession of the new Member States to the Community. These amendments were implemented in the Community by Decision 1001/95/ECSC[2] and Regulation (EC) No 1005/95.[2] Following the bilateral talks initiated by Bulgaria and Romania under their respective agreements with the European Union a system of dual-licensing without quantitative restrictions was set up on a trial basis for one year. Under this system, imports of certain steel products into the Community will require an export licence from the appropriate Bulgarian or Romanian authorities.

763. On 7 and 15 December the Commission signed agreements with Russia and Ukraine (Table III) concerning imports into the Community in 1995 and 1996 of the same range of steel products as those previously covered by the quota system. Quotas for 1995 were set at 309 000 tonnes for Russia and at 131 000 tonnes for Ukraine. In addition, Member States set the tonnages for 1995 of zero-rated imports of steel products for the new German *Länder* (450 000 tonnes from Russia and 50 000 tonnes from Ukraine). Since it proved impossible to negotiate an agreement with Kazakhstan under the negotiating directives, an autonomous quotas system was again applied in 1995 to imports of certain steel products.

764. On 22 December the Council approved the conclusion of an agreement establishing a free trade area between the Community and Turkey (→ *point 844)* for ECSC products (Table III) to complete the customs union. Under the agreement, virtually all tariffs for ECSC products will be abolished and Turkey will apply Community State aid and competition disciplines in the steel sector.

---

[1] OJ L 330, 21.12.1994.
[2] OJ L 101, 4.5.1995.
[3] Twenty-seventh General Report, point 879.

Shipbuilding

765.   The OECD agreement on shipbuilding signed in Paris on 21 December 1994[1] by the European Community, Norway, South Korea, the United States and Japan was ratified by the European Community, Norway and South Korea on 11 December *(→ point 192)*. Japan and the United States undertook to do so by 15 June 1996. On 18 October the Commission adopted a proposal for a Regulation (Table II) on protection against price dumping in the shipbuilding sector. This Regulation introduces a specific anti-dumping instrument for the shipbuilding sector. On 22 December the Council adopted a Regulation on authorized aid *(→ point 166)*.

Textiles

Relations with non-member countries (bilateral agreements and preferential arrangements)

766.   The Council authorized the provisional implementation of the protocols to the bilateral agreements (Table III) negotiated by the Commission with 44 supplier countries to adjust the quantitative ceilings for textile imports to take account of the accession of Austria, Finland and Sweden to the European Union.

767.   In recent years China has become the European Union's main supplier (in value terms) of textiles and clothing from Asia. On 13 June the Council adopted a Decision concluding a new bilateral agreement (Table III) with China on textiles (silk, linen and ramie) not covered by the existing MFA-based agreement which still came under Council Regulation (EC) No 517/94.[2] This agreement was implemented provisionally by Council Decision 95/155/EC of 10 April. The Commission also negotiated, on the basis of the negotiating directives of 30 October (Table III), and initialled on 13 December, the renewal, subject to certain amendments, of the EC-China bilateral agreement on trade in textiles previously covered by the MFA which expired at the end of 1995. The Council adopted the Decision provisionally implementing this agreement on 22 December. Quantitative restrictions (basket extractor mechanism) were applied from 1 January to three categories of products imported from China which had not been subject to any restriction in the past but had grown dangerously in volume. The autonomous arrangements covering trade in textiles with Taiwan, which also ex-

---

[1]   1994 General Report, point 1032.
[2]   OJ L 67, 10.3.1994; 1994 General Report, point 1041.

pired at the end of 1995, were renewed for three years by Council Regulation (EC) No 3060/95 of 22 December (Table II). On 1 August the Commission initialled an agreement in the form of an exchange of letters making a number of amendments to the textile agreement with Vietnam (Table III). The Council decided on 22 December to provisionally implement this agreement.

768.   In line with the commitments entered into by the Copenhagen European Council,[1] the Council adopted, on 12 June, negotiating directives for the scheduled revision of the additional protocols on textiles to the Europe Agreements with Central and East European countries (Bulgaria, the Czech Republic, Hungary, Poland, Romania and the Slovak Republic). The additional protocols were amended by means of an exchange of letters with each of these countries. The Council Decision provisionally implementing the revised protocols was adopted on 22 December. A protocol on trade in textiles with Slovenia was initialled on 24 November. Under this protocol all quantitative restrictions will be abolished by 1 January 1998 and Slovenia will gradually dismantle all duties on textiles by 1 January 2001. On 22 December the Council adopted the Decision provisionally implementing the protocol.

769.   As regards the Mediterranean and Middle East, the Council adopted, on 12 June, negotiating directives for the conclusion of a protocol (Table III) with Croatia under the draft cooperation agreement with this country (→ point 845). An arrangement with Turkey (Table III) renewing the existing agreement and introducing quantitative restrictions for products imported directly or reimported after outward processing, which was initialled on 23 February and concluded by the Council on 18 September, was suspended as a result of the establishment of the customs union between the EU and Turkey (→ point 844). Agreements with Egypt, Malta, Morocco and Tunisia which expired at the end of 1995 were renewed for two years. The Council adopted the Decision to provisionally apply these agreements on 22 December. On 13 June the Council authorized the Commission to open negotiations with the countries in question. Negotiations were conducted with the United Arab Emirates on a bilateral textile and clothing agreement (Table III). An agreement was initialled on 11 December. The Council adopted, on 13 November, Regulation (EC) No 2635/95[2] introducing a system of surveillance of imports of certain textile products from the United Arab Emirates pending conclusion of the negotiations and implementation of the agreement.

---

[1]   Twenty-seventh General Report, point 1018.
[2]   OJ L 271, 14.11.1995; Bull. 11-1995, point 1.4.28.

770.   The agreements concluded with the 12 States of the former Soviet Union expired at the end of 1995 and the Council adopted fresh negotiating directives on 30 October. The agreement with Russia, which was renewed for one year, was initialled on 19 December. The agreements with Belarus, Ukraine, Uzbekistan, Kyrgyzstan, Moldova, Azerbaijan and Kazakhstan were extended for three years with tacit renewal for a further year. They were initialled on 7 and 9 November, and on 4, 11, 15, 18 and 20 December respectively. On 22 December the Council authorized the agreements negotiated with Russia, Belarus, Ukraine and Uzbekistan to be provisionally implemented. On 13 June the Council adopted a decision concluding the textile agreement with Mongolia (Table III) introducing arrangements which will apply until 31 December 1997.

Consequences of the Uruguay Round

771.   Following the agreement emerging from the Uruguay Round the Commission initialled administrative arrangements with 16 members of the World Trade Organization maintaining a number of administrative provisions in bilateral agreements had become void when the Textile and Clothing Agreement entered into force. The Textile Monitoring Body (TMB) met regularly throughout the year to oversee the Agreement's implementation by WTO members.

772.   Council Regulation (EC) No 517/94 on common rules applying to imports of textile products from certain third countries was amended by Regulation (EC) No 1325/95 of 6 June (Table II) to take account of the quotas amended as a result of the accession of Austria, Finland and Sweden to the European Union.

773.   The Commission set up a database on restrictive commercial practices in non-member countries to help improve market access for EU textile and clothing exporters. Studies were also undertaken to identify restrictive commercial practices in the leather and footwear sectors still prevalent on some non-Community markets.

Anti-fraud measures in the textile sector

774.   On 12 June the Council and Commission adopted a joint declaration on the fight against fraud in trade in textiles between the Community and non-member countries (→ point 1009).[1] They stressed the seriousness of the

---

[1]   OJ L 128, 13.6.1995; Bull. 6-1995, point 1.4.35.

problem and the need for urgent action, suggesting new ways of combating fraud in this sector. The Commission also reorganized its anti-fraud units to ensure more effective implementation of the textile anti-fraud initiative (TAFI) which was launched in 1993. Several operations, including investigations, publications and studies, were undertaken in 1995 under the budget heading for this programme to tighten up the monitoring of textiles and to combat fraud in this sector.

Motor industry

775.   In March the Commission extended the arrangements concluded in 1994 with Japan on the motor industry[1] to the new Member States in its efforts to achieve its objective of gradually opening up protected markets[2] to Japanese exports by the end of the transitional period (31 December 1999). The MITI[3] and the Commission approved overall levels of exports to the European Union and expected levels for 1995 for the five protected markets. In June the Commission negotiated with Japan the abolition of a number of technical barriers to imports of vehicles and automobile components (abolition of specific Japanese standards and simplification of type-approval of foreign vehicles in Japan). It also requested under the global economic deregulation programme adopted by Japan in 1995 that the remaining barriers be removed and expressed a wish to play a role in monitoring the US-Japan agreement on vehicle and components to ensure there was no discrimination against European interests. The first workshop organized by the Japanese Automotive Manufacturers' Association (JAMA) and the Liaison Committee for the Manufacture of Automobile Equipment and Spare Parts (CLEPA) in Paris on 6 and 7 March with the backing of the Commission and French and Japanese Governments was designed to foster trade between Japanese car manufacturers and European components suppliers.

776.   In 1995 the Commission and the European motor industry continued to work together to identify the greatest barriers to access to non-Community markets for vehicles and spare parts manufactured in the European Union. The spotlight focused on countries in which Community exports were still marginal (South Korea) and markets with a significant growth potential (China). In June the Commission started talks on standards and certification with China and Taiwan and continued its negotiations with South Korea on further deregulation of the Korean market. It also called, at

---

[1]   Twenty-fifth General Report, point 1060.
[2]   France, Spain, Italy, Portugal and the United Kingdom.
[3]   Japanese Ministry of International Trade and Industry.

both bilateral level and within the WTO, for the withdrawal of a Brazilian decree introducing quantitative restrictions and other investment-related measures aimed at protecting and promoting the Brazilian motor industry. It also called on the Brazilian authorities to take steps to create a trading environment which was both transparent and free. The Commission also pursued its efforts to promote international technical harmonization under the 1958 Geneva Agreement and continued its deliberations with a view to the Community's accession to the Agreement.

Other products

777. In the footwear and leather sectors, the Commission held talks with Poland, Romania and Bulgaria on the restrictions which they had imposed on exports of raw hide and skins.

Section 5

Development policy

Overview and cooperation in the run-up to 2000

778.   In the general context outlined in its communication of May 1992 on development cooperation in the run-up to 2000[1] and the resolutions and conclusions adopted by the Council in 1993 and 1994,[2] the Commission pursued its efforts to improve coordination between the Community and the Member States in certain development cooperation sectors, with particular emphasis on health care, education and the fight against poverty. On 3 May it adopted a communication on complementarity between the Community's development cooperation policy and the policies of Member States.[3] The Council continued to look for ways of translating complementarity into action, in particular through its resolution of 1 June,[4] and of ensuring consistency between the various Community policies. On 15 December the Commission adopted a report[5] on the pilot operational coordination schemes conducted in a number of countries since 1994.[6] It suggested extending the experience to other countries and proposed guidelines to overcome the difficulties encountered in strengthening coordination. The Council also adopted resolutions on structural adjustment[7] and regional integration.[8] On the subject of structural adjustment, it endorsed the key areas for dialogue with the Union's partners (the alleviation of poverty, the regional dimension and long-term development objectives), sought to enhance effectiveness by gearing the use of the various instruments more closely to the specific needs of the recipient countries, and addressed ways of legitimizing the Commission's sustained efforts in the field of adjustment, while pursuing dialogue with its partners on public finance and review of conditionality. Regional integration was welcomed by the Council as a major step towards integrating the developing countries into the world economy and one of the fundamental objectives of European development policy. The Council noted that an effective integration strategy should include elements intended to assist governments in reviewing their policy, facilitating the restructuring of

---

[1]   Twenty-sixth General Report, point 925.
[2]   Twenty-seventh General Report, point 807; 1994 General Report, point 944.
[3]   COM(95) 160; Bull. 5-1995, point 1.4.44.
[4]   Bull. 6-1995, point 1.4.41.
[5]   COM(95) 700; Bull. 12-1995.
[6]   1994 General Report, point 944.
[7]   Bull. 6-1995, point 1.4.40.
[8]   Bull. 6-1995, point 1.4.43.

the private sector and developing the necessary capabilities. The Commission set out its own views on this subject in a communication of 16 June.[1] Evaluation of the EU's development cooperation work continued at the same sustained pace as in previous years, through official and unofficial discussions, seminars organized with the Commission, and training initiatives and project and programme planning activities. On 8 September the Commission adopted a proposal for a Council Regulation on aid for population policies and programmes to provide budget heading B7-5050 with a legal basis (Table II). On 10 July it adopted a proposal for a Regulation (Table II) to provide a legal basis for budget heading B7-5077 on decentralized cooperation. On 1 June the Council adopted a declaration setting out a number of principles which should guide the implementation of development research programmes.[2] In October Parliament gave its opinion on coordination between the Community and the Member States in the field of education and training initiatives in relation to development.[3]

779.   At international level, the World Summit for Social Development,[4] held in Copenhagen from 6 to 12 March, addressed three main issues: eliminating poverty, creating jobs and reducing unemployment, and social integration. Mr Santer and Mr Flynn both spoke at the Summit, the outcome of which was the adoption of a political statement and a plan of action based on a common approach to social development objectives, highlighting the interdependence between economic, social and environmental aspects of sustainable development, and reaffirming the complementarity of national and international policies. On 22 February the Economic and Social Committee had contributed an own-initiative opinion[5] to the preparatory work, while on 2 March Parliament passed a resolution[6] in response to a Commission communication.[7]

780.   The fourth UN Conference on Women, which was held in Beijing from 4 to 15 September *(→ point 626)*, was a significant step forward in the emancipation of women. The political declaration and the plan of action to which the Conference contributed stated for the first time the need for the full integration of women's needs and interests in the drawing-up and evaluation of the various policies, not only domestic ones, but also those governing development aid. The Conference highlighted the importance of women in development and in particular the link between education,

---

[1]   COM(95) 219; Bull. 6-1995, point 1.4.44.
[2]   Bull. 6-1995, point 1.4.45.
[3]   OJ C 287, 30.10.1995; Bull. 10-1995, point 1.4.43.
[4]   Bull. 3-1995, point 1.4.42.
[5]   OJ C 110, 2.5.1995; Bull. 1/2-1995, point 1.4.64
[6]   OJ C 68, 20.3.1995; Bull. 3-1995, point 1.4.41.
[7]   1994 General Report, point 946.

women's health and people-centred sustainable development. On 18 September the Commission adopted a communication on the inclusion of gender issues in development cooperation.[1] The communication incorporated the most important points from the preparatory work for the Beijing Conference. It stressed the need to take into account the differences between women's and men's roles and positions throughout development work and put forward proposals aimed at strengthening collaboration and cooperation between the Community and the Member States in this sector. On 20 December the Council adopted a resolution on this subject.[2]

Generalized system of preferences

781. On 23 October the Council adopted Regulation (EC) No 2651/95 amending Regulation (EC) No 3283/94,[3] extending tariff preferences to agricultural imports from South Africa.[4] On 22 December the Council also adopted Regulation (EC) No 3058/95 (Table II) aimed at carrying over the existing agricultural arrangements until 30 June 1996 by extending the validity of Regulations (EEC) Nos 3833/90, 3835/90 and 3900/91 and (EC) No 2651/95 for 1996 and amending Regulation (EC) No 3282/94.

Cooperation through the United Nations

United Nations Conference on Trade and Development

782. The Commission took part in all Unctad's intergovernmental meetings this year. The Trade and Development Board held two regular meetings, in March/April and September, during which it reviewed structural adjustment policies in developed countries and their impact, sustainable development, the advancement of the least-developed countries, links between worldwide financial and trade flows and levels of economic activity and employment. The Community was granted participation rights similar to those held by the Conference's Member States (with the exception of voting rights) in Unctad's Special Committee on Preferences. A special board meeting held in December began work on the ninth conference.

---

[1]   COM(95) 423; Bull. 9-1995, point 1.4.23.
[2]   Bull. 12-1995.
[3]   OJ L 348, 31.12.1994.
[4]   1994 General Report, point 947.

United Nations Industrial Development Organization

783. Under the 1993 agreement between the Community and UNIDO,[1] Mr Mauricio del María y Campos, UNIDO's Director-General, met Mr de Deus Pinheiro on 9 and 10 November. During the meetings views were exchanged on a wide range of topics, in particular the satisfactory functioning of cooperation in Latin America.

World Food Programme

784. The European Union's allocations of food products to the WFP went chiefly to Afghanistan, Algeria, Angola, Benin, Cambodia, Cape Verde, Chad, China, Cuba, Ethiopia, Ghana, Guatemala, Haiti, India, Iraq, Jordan, Kenya, Lesotho, Malawi, Mozambique, Nepal, Nicaragua, Pakistan, Rwanda, Somalia, Sudan, Swaziland, Tanzania, Togo, Tunisia, Uganda and Yemen.

United Nations Food and Agriculture Organization

785. The Community, which became a full member of the FAO in 1991,[2] took an active part in the year's numerous meetings to voice its concern on agriculture, forestry, fisheries and food security. It made a significant contribution to the negotiations on the 'code of conduct for responsible fisheries' adopted at the Organization's 28th conference in October *(→ point 565)* and began preparations for the forthcoming World Food Summit (to be held in Rome in November 1996). On 15 May the FAO's Director-General, Mr Jacques Diouf, paid a visit to the new members of the Commission.[3]

Cooperation through non-governmental organizations

786. Cooperation with NGOs showed encouraging progress. The resources made available by the EU for NGO activities again rose substantially, chiefly for the co-financing of NGO initiatives, humanitarian operations, rehabilitation and food security projects. On 10 July the Commission adopted a proposal for a Regulation (TableII) aimed at providing a legal basis for budget heading B7-5010 which covers the co-financing of projects

---

[1]   Twenty-seventh General Report, point 811.
[2]   Twenty-fifth General Report, point 994.
[3]   Bull. 5-1995, point 1.4.48.

with NGOs. A total of ECU 174 million was allocated for development co-operation in conjunction with European development NGOs, which held their annual General Assembly in Brussels in April.[1] Some ECU 16 million was transferred to other budget headings to finance NGO projects, and the bulk of the remainder went to co-finance 601 development projects in 104 countries in Africa, Asia and Latin America, focusing on rural development, education and health care, at a total cost of ECU 140.1 million. The Community spent a further ECU 16 million on co-financing 174 public-awareness initiatives in Europe. In addition, NGOs continued to attract funds from a number of budget headings open to them for operations in specific countries (Vietnam, Cambodia and South Africa among others) and on specific issues (including human rights, the environment, drug abuse and rehabilitation). Under the decentralized approach introduced by the fourth Lomé Convention and the proposal for the MEDA Regulation and the Regulations on developing countries in Latin America and Asia, and funded under budget heading B7-5077, a number of experimental projects were launched in partnership with NGOs and other bodies and/or local public authorities to support local organizations, develop partnership schemes and start pilot economic and social development programmes.

Commodities and world agreements

787.   Following the entry into force in 1994 of the International Coffee Agreement,[2] the International Coffee Council, which met in January,[3] May[4] and September,[5] adopted a work programme aimed at establishing intergovernmental consultation machinery for international coffee trade issues and promoting growth of the trade through the publication of statistics and studies. The International Cocoa Agreement also entered into force in 1994,[6] and the International Cocoa Council's production and consumption committees were active, and the Council also took part in the planning of projects eligible for backing by the Common Fund for Commodities. The winding-down of the buffer stock continued as planned. An International Cocoa Conference was held in Abidjan in March,[7] and the Cocoa Consultative Group met in Yaoundé in June. The Commission was represented at both events. Following the conclusion of the Unctad-sponsored negotiations

---

[1]   Bull. 4-1995, point 1.4.55.
[2]   1994 General Report, point 954.
[3]   Bull. 1/2-1995, point 1.4.65.
[4]   Bull. 5-1995, point 1.4.46.
[5]   Bull. 9-1995, point 1.4.25.
[6]   1994 General Report, point 955.
[7]   Bull. 3-1995, point 1.4.43.

for a second International Tropical Timber Agreement in 1994,[1] the Community continued the in-depth scrutiny of the new Agreement. The procedures for the signing and provisional application of the Agreement by the Community and its Member States were also initiated. In May the International Tropical Timber Council held its 18th meeting in Ghana,[2] while the 19th meeting was held at the organization's headquarters in Yokohama in November. The International Jute Organization Council, which met in April at the Organization's headquarters in Dhaka, decided to extend for another two years the agreement in force. On 22 December the Council and the representatives of the Member States meeting within the Council decided to proceed with the signing and notification of provisional application of the 1995 International Natural Rubber Agreement.

EC Investment Partners

788. On 22 May the Council adopted a common position on the proposal for a Regulation (Table II) implementing the EC Investment Partners' Scheme. ECIP is a financial instrument designed to channel funds to Latin American, Asian and Mediterranean countries and South Africa. The Regulation would extend the enhanced facility for the period 1995-99 with the aim essentially of promoting joint initiatives which offer mutual benefits for Community operators and local industry in the eligible countries concerned, and expand it to include South Africa.

Protecting the environment

789. This year again efforts to integrate the environmental dimension in development cooperation followed up the recommendations of the UN Conference on the Environment and Development held in Rio de Janeiro in 1992.[3] Preparation for the adoption of a Council Regulation on cooperation initiatives in the field of tropical forests, launched in 1992, were virtually completed by the end of the year. In all, ECU 13.2 million of budget appropriations specifically earmarked for the environment in developing countries and ECU 50 million intended for initiatives to protect the tropical forest were allocated to operations concerned with forest conservation, the protection of biodiversity, urban and rural environment, land management, coastal resource management, and the preservation of the living conditions of the indigenous population in the commercial management of forestry

---

[1] 1994 General Report, point 957.
[2] Bull. 5-1995, point 1.4.45
[3] Twenty-sixth General Report, point 596.

resources. The Commission also continued to study the environmental impact of development and structural adjustment programmes, and conducted
awareness-raising and in-service training programmes to promote the inclusion of environmental considerations. It was also active at the third meeting
of the Commission for Sustainable Development *(→ point 475)*. On 27 June
it adopted a proposal for a Council Regulation (Table II) to provide a legal
basis for budget heading B7-5040, which deals with the environment in the
developing countries. On 13 July Parliament issued a statement on the
inclusion of population and environmental policies and programmes.[1]

790.   Studies on the integration of environmental considerations in the
implementation of the fourth Lomé Convention have shown that only a
limited number of ACP countries included environmental protection as an
underlying issue in their cooperation programmes with the European Union,
but that the environment had been integrated in a more systematic fashion
in rural development programmes. Accordingly, guidelines informed by the
strategic principles of the fifth action programme on the environment
(→ point 463) were drawn up for the programming of the second Lomé IV
Financial Protocol. A new protocol on sustainable management of forestry
resources was adopted as part of the mid-term review of the fourth Lomé
Convention.

North-South cooperation against drug abuse

791.   The Commission continued to cooperate actively with governments,
international organizations and other partners to implement the UN global
programme of action to control drug abuse and the relevant UN conventions, using a variety of instruments, including trade preferences, financial
assistance and technical and administrative assistance aimed at controlling
trade in precursors and preventing money laundering. This year the Community committed ECU 11.2 million for projects to combat drugs and drug
addiction in developing countries. Activities funded from budget heading
B7-5080, which covers North-South cooperation in the campaign against
drug abuse, were designed to help the countries concerned draw up policies
and strategies to control drug abuse, and on 30 June the Commission
adopted a proposal for a Regulation (Table II) to provide a legal basis for
the heading. In addition, the situation both at national and regional level
was being assessed in connection with the programming of the second Lomé
IV financial protocol *(→ point 936)*, with a view to including drug abuse
control projects.

---

[1]   OJ C 249, 25.9.1995; Bull. 7/8-1995, point 1.4.50.

North-South cooperation on health issues and HIV/AIDS

792.   Community activities in the health and HIV/AIDS sectors were stepped up in 1995, reflecting the growing importance attached to social and health issues as essential development factors in developing countries. By the end of 1995 some ECU 300 million had been spent on projects under the seventh EDF. An additional ECU 450 million from counterpart funds from structural adjustment programmes was allocated as budget support in the health sector. In addition to these contributions, intended to protect priority budget expenditure on the health sector, the Commission continued to fund a number of projects concerned in particular with the improvement of primary health care and the reform of the pharmaceutical sector. An important meeting on pharmaceuticals was held in Brussels in April, co-funded by the Community. It brought together the Health Ministers from 20 sub-Saharan countries with the aim of speeding up reform of essential-drugs policies in the franc zone and associated countries following the devaluation of the CFA franc, and ensuring better local access to vital medicines.

793.   HIV/AIDS assistance focused on regional and national strategies, including better treatment for sexually-transmitted diseases. Substantial programmes were adopted this year for Tanzania and Mozambique. A number of other countries received generous funding, including the Philippines and Thailand, Bolivia, Peru and Honduras, and several Mediterranean countries, notably for awareness and education campaigns aimed at high-risk groups.

On 10 July the Commission adopted a proposal for a Council Regulation (Table II) to provide a legal basis for budget heading B7-5046 on HIV/AIDS-related operations. On 15 November[1] Parliament adopted a resolution on the Commission communication on the Union's HIV/AIDS policy in the developing world.[2]

Rehabilitation aid

794.   On 20 December the Council approved a common position on a proposal for a Regulation (Table II) to provide a legal basis for budget heading B7-5076, which was introduced in 1994 to fund rehabilitation measures in developing countries. The Commission for its part continued with rehabilitation operations totalling ECU 78.3 million on the basis of the Council conclusions of 2 December 1993,[3] mainly working through the NGOs, with

---

[1]   OJ C 323, 4.12.1995; Bull. 11-1995, point 1.4.29.
[2]   1994 General Report, point 965.
[3]   Twenty-seventh General Report, point 783.

health, basic infrastructure, the resumption of agricultural production and economic and social rehabilitation once again the priority areas. For the eight countries covered by the 'Special initiative for Africa' launched in May 1993, some ECU 210 million was granted as rehabilitation aid. On 10 May the Commission adopted a proposal for a Council Regulation (Table II) laying down the amount of financial resources allocated by the Community to rehabilitation programmes in southern Africa. This year rehabilitation programmes were extended to Rwanda and neighbouring countries and Haiti, at a total cost of ECU 140.5 million.

Food aid

795.   Budget allocations for food aid to developing countries rose to ECU 646.3 million, of which ECU 413 million was spent on food and ECU 233 million on logistics: in 1994 the total was ECU 589.1 million. Table 13 below gives a breakdown of direct and indirect food aid for the year.

796.   Greater emphasis was placed on food aid as a long-term structural instrument, the aim being not only to promote long-term food security for the poor in areas with a food deficit but to contribute to the overall social and economic development of the countries concerned. The European Union now provides 53% of all international food aid. On 14 July the Commission adopted a proposal (Table II) for a basic Regulation on food-aid policy and food-aid management and special measures to boost food security on which the Council approved a common position on 20 December. The proposal serves three main aims: to enshrine food aid as a fundamental element in long-term food security policy; to update the list of potential recipient countries; and to consolidate all existing legal instruments into a single instrument.

797.   The year confirmed two trends already apparent in 1994:[1] the increase in the number of direct operations involving the establishment of counterpart funds to finance initiatives with direct impact on food security in the country concerned, and a significant rise in the number of triangular initiatives, which give a valuable boost to the development of interregional trade. Both kinds of operation are a powerful incentive for agricultural production and thus help reduce the risk of future food shortages. As regards the product breakdown, deliveries of cereals registered a record increase to 1 775 600 tonnes (up from 1 451 400 tonnes in 1994), whereas the supply of milk powder and butter oil continued to shrink. The fall in the category

---

[1]   1994 General Report, point 967.

TABLE 13

Allocation of food aid, 1995

Region or organization	Cereals (tonnes)	Milk powder (tonnes)	Butter oil (tonnes)	Vegetable oil (tonnes)	Sugar (tonnes)	Pulses (tonnes)	Other products (ECU)	Tools (ECU)
Direct aid								
• Africa	402 873	845	50	8 049	177	7 000	1 535 975	—
• Latin America	36 262	1 000	—	3 800	—	2 250	1 957 000	—
• Asia	180 000	—	—	—	—	—	—	—
• Mediterranean	46 000	—	—	—	—	—	1 020 000	—
Total direct aid	665 135	1 845	50	11 849	177	9 250	4 512 975	—
Indirect aid								
• ICRC	50 000	—	—	4 000	350	—	5 200 000	400 000
• Euronaid	321 000	7 800	—	20 250	3 445	41 164	18 970 000	1 500 000
• FAO	1 500	—	—	—	—	—	—	—
• UNHCR	9 648	2 675	—	128	—	—	3 770 000	—
• UNRWA	2 789	1 122	—	1 080	1 648	583	3 360 000	—
• WFP	318 236	5 000	500	20 650	6 050	14 813	7 500 000	—
• Rwanda Burundi	20 000	—	—	1 000	—	9 000	1 000 000	—
• Other NGOs	4 000	1 300	—	150	600	900	960 000	—
Total indirect aid	723 173	17 897	500	47 258	12 129	66 460	40 760 000	1 900 000
Grand total	1 392 308	19 742	550	59 107	12 306	75 710	45 272 975	1 900 000

'other products' is explained by the introduction of a separate heading for pulses, an increasingly popular form of Community food aid.

Refugee assistance

798. Fifty-three operations to assist refugees, returnees and displaced persons were approved, at a total cost of ECU 59.8 million, towards measures to support self-sufficiency among refugees in Asia and Latin America. On 26 June the Commission adopted a proposal for a Council Regulation (Table II) to provide a legal basis for budget heading B7-302, intended to cover measures to assist displaced groups in Asian and Latin American countries.

Nine operations in seven ACP countries[1] were approved at a total cost of ECU 13.6 million. In addition, a grant of the ECU 95 000 was approved for the Cayman Islands under Article 165 of Council Decision of 25 July 1991 on the association of OCTs with the European Economic Community. Since the entry into force of Lomé IV, 68 operations have been approved under Article 225, totalling ECU 81.65 million, out of ECU 100 million of available funds. The thrust of operations under this Article, and in particular the contribution to comprehensive rehabilitation programmes, as in Mozambique, and reliance on the work of NGOs and the UNHCR in the field, remained unchanged, as did the target sectors: health and agricultural production. The coordination of operations to assist refugees, returnees and displaced persons was boosted with the implementation of Permanent Interservice Group procedures involving consultations and meetings. On 6 October the Council adopted negotiating directives (Table III) with a view to concluding a Convention with the UNRWA for the period 1996-98. Mrs Sadako Ogata, UN High Commissioner for Refugees, paid a visit to the Commission on 22 May.[2]

Support for democratization and human rights

799. Information concerning support for democratization and human rights is given in Section 2 of Chapter II (→ point 21).

---

[1]   Angola, Côte d'Ivoire, Djibouti, Kenya, Malawi, Mozambique and Uganda.
[2]   Bull, 5-1995, point 1.4.54.

Section 6

Humanitarian aid

Overall strategy

800.   In order to give the budget headings relating to humanitarian aid a
legal basis, the Council, on 20 December, approved a common position on
the proposal for a Regulation (Table II) defining the types of situation in
which humanitarian aid may be provided and the types of assistance that
may be financed. Operations are financed or conducted by the European
Community Humanitarian Office (ECHO) in the light of this Regulation.

801.   The year 1995 saw the Commission look more closely at the need
for humanitarian aid and its limitations. Upon examination, emergencies
often proved to be structural in origin. Economic weakness, poverty and a
lack of public health structures are exacerbated by latent ethnic or political
tensions that can easily explode. This year man-made disasters accounted
for 96% of ECHO's activities, with the remaining 4% taken up by natural
disasters and their prevention, and epidemics. Where there is open warfare,
the role of the relief organization should be to calm tensions and reduce suffering so as to encourage the opening of peace negotiations and limit the
scale of the disaster. This may also involve short-term reconstruction work.
Where conflict is smouldering or there are glaring weaknesses in economic
and health structures, preventive humanitarian action may be considered as
a way of avoiding renewed outbreaks of violence or the spread of epidemics
and reducing the vulnerability of the weakest sections of the population.
Because ECHO's resources are limited, this type of assistance is reserved for
the most serious situations. Political negotiations must take over and the
normal cooperation process be strengthened or resumed as soon as possible.
Though the EU needs an efficient humanitarian relief arm for emergencies,
this is not in itself sufficient to keep or restore peace and bring about development. This is why the importance of coordination — both between
different departments of the Commission and with Member States, other
donors (especially the United States), international organizations and NGOs
— is becoming more obvious every day. In the course of the year,
Ms Bonino made field visits to many operations[1] and had meetings with the
heads of UN agencies and the UN Secretary-General and with the ICRC and

---

[1]   Bull. 1/2-1995, point 1.4.69; Bull. 3-1995, point 1.4.47; Bull. 5-1995, points 1.4.57, 1.4.58 and
1.4.103; Bull. 7/8-1995, point 1.4.60; Bull. 12-1995.

its president. ECHO was involved in setting up a working party to look at the safety needs in the vicinity of nuclear power stations in Central and Eastern Europe (→ point 516). It also continued to develop the NOHA humanitarian aid diploma as part of the Erasmus programme (→ point 268).[1] To improve coordination and increase the efficiency and impact of assistance programmes, ECHO has also given effect to the recommendations of the standing interdepartmental working party on refugees set up in 1994, and has held quarterly meetings with the Member States, attended high-level meetings in Geneva with the UNHCR, and maintained contacts with the United States Agency for International Development (USAID).

802.   On the evaluation side, ECHO refined its methodology and drew on a study of Member State NGOs specializing in humanitarian aid to improve its knowledge of its partners. ECHO also pressed on with its policy of openness and visibility aimed at encouraging the mobilization of equipment and human resources and keeping the public informed. Since *Eurobarometer 42* of 15 March had shown the Union's citizens' wish to know more about its activities, ECHO brought out a number of publications and audiovisual products in the course of the year and helped organize visits for journalists to the sites of humanitarian operations. During the French and Spanish Presidencies, the Member States took an active part in events organized in Paris and Madrid. On 14 December, Ms Bonino was present in Madrid for the first humanitarian summit, which resulted in the adoption of a declaration signed by all taking part.[2] The 1994 annual report on humanitarian aid was approved by the Commission on 22 February.[3]

Humanitarian aid operations[4]

803.   In the former Yugoslavia, ECHO's spending on humanitarian assistance in 1995 totalled ECU 229.7 million. In response to events leading to a considerable increase in population movements, it stepped up assistance to refugees and displaced persons. On 17 November, the Commission adopted a communication on prospects for humanitarian aid to the former Yugoslavia.[5]

804.   In Africa, the grave crises in Rwanda and Burundi continued to make themselves felt in the Great Lakes region through the presence in neighbour-

---

[1]   Network on Humanitarian Assistance — 1994 General Report, point 982.
[2]   Bull. 12-1995.
[3]   COM(95) 47; Bull. 1/2-1995, point 1.4.68.
[4]   For further details see the tables in the monthly *Bulletin of the European Union* (under 'Humanitarian aid') and the 1995 annual report on humanitarian aid (out soon).
[5]   COM(95) 564; Bull. 11-1995, point 1.4.35.

ing countries (Zaire, Uganda and Tanzania) of 2 million refugees; continuing tensions inside Rwanda and Burundi prevented the organization of any significant return of refugees, and relief operations for refugees still accounted for ECU 107 million of a total programme of ECU 211.4 million for the region. With its partners (the UNHCR, the International Committee of the Red Cross and NGOs), ECHO sought to get the repatriation process moving. In Angola, the end of the civil war marked by the November 1994 peace agreement did not lead to any reduction in the level of assistance, which this year amounted to ECU 21.4 million. Indeed, at September's round-table meeting organized in conjunction with the United Nations, the Commission pledged to increase its humanitarian assistance to Angola (→ *point 950*). Sudan continued to be ravaged by civil war in spite of several ceasefires, with the needs of 3.5 million victims of the fighting increasing as access by air worsened. ECHO financing totalled ECU 17 million. In Somalia, the withdrawal of UN forces led to a reduction in the activities of both UN agencies and NGOs. Humanitarian aid continued despite the dangerous conditions, with organizations attempting to cope with rising malnutrition. ECHO spent ECU 6 million, most of it on medical, nutritional and water programmes. Liberia's political situation, in spite of the August peace agreement, did not become noticeably more stable. As well as providing medical and food aid inside the country, ECHO also backed programmes aimed at helping Liberian refugees in Guinea and Côte d'Ivoire. Its aid to Liberia totalled ECU 6.125 million. In Sierra Leone humanitarian assistance continued to be hampered by the climate of insecurity caused by the civil war. ECHO funded programmes totalling ECU 6.4 million aimed at preventing a deterioration in the living conditions of displaced persons and the inhabitants of major towns dependent on outside help. There was an increase in ECHO-financed operations in Haiti following the return of President Aristide, aimed at underpinning the democratic process in this Caribbean ACP State. Some 20 medical, nutritional and water-treatment programmes were under way, at a cost of ECU 11.58 million compared with ECU 18 million in 1994.

805.   The year saw a further increase in humanitarian aid to the independent States of the former Soviet Union, which rose to ECU 138 million. The bulk of this aid went to Chechnya following the fighting which left over a million people in need. Besides the usual aid in the form of medicines, shelter and food, energy programmes were set up in Armenia and Georgia. For the second year running, these countries and Azerbaijan, Kyrgyzstan and Tadjikistan were the recipients of a special food aid programme (→ *point 877*), accompanied in the latter two countries by a limited amount of medical assistance. Aid operations for the three countries affected by the Chernobyl disaster — Belarus, Russia and Ukraine — continued; social and medi-

cal assistance was also provided for the destitute in Moscow and St Petersburg. To combat the resurgence of diphtheria in the former Soviet Union, ECHO pledged a contribution to a campaign launched by Unicef and the Red Cross. The Baltic States were also eligible for this Community aid, while other countries of Central and Eastern Europe, namely Albania and Romania, received basic medical and logistical assistance.

806.   In the Middle East, ECU 24.9 million was granted for Iraq, where the Turkish invasion and factional strife had greatly increased needs in the north of the country. Aid was also granted, on certain conditions, to areas controlled by the Iraqi authorities. In Algeria, Sahrawi refugees again received aid (ECU 5 million) and a further ECU 5.9 million worth of emergency food aid was shared between the Sahrawis and the Tuaregs fleeing Mali and Niger. Aid continued to Palestinians in the Occupied and Autonomous Territories (ECU 5.3 million) and in Lebanon.

807.   In Asia, Afghanistan was granted ECU 12.6 million in response to an upsurge in fighting. Aid to Cambodia continued, with an emphasis on the need to link it to food aid. Natural disasters in Bangladesh and Pakistan attracted grants, and refugees fleeing Myanmar, China and Bhutan for ethnic reasons also received help. In Latin America, humanitarian activities again centred on Cuba, where European NGOs independent of the Cuban authorities delivered ECU 15 million of aid, most of it in the form of food and medicines. Assistance was granted to Guatemala, Mexico, Nicaragua and Peru following civil disorder, while Bolivia, Ecuador and Peru received grants to cope with natural disasters.

808.   The European Parliament voted in favour of humanitarian aid for a number of countries.[1]

---

[1]   OJ C 269, 16.10.1995; Bull. 9-1995, point 1.4.29; OJ C 287, 30.10.1995; Bull. 10-1995, points 1.4.51 to 1.4.55; OJ C 323, 4.12.1995; Bull. 11-1995, points 1.4.37 and 1.4.38.

Section 7

European Economic Area, relations with the EFTA countries

European Economic Area

809. The Agreement between the European Union and Austria, Finland, Iceland, Norway and Sweden creating the EEA[1] entered into force on 1 January 1994, thereby establishing the world's largest integrated trading area, extending the geographical reach of the single market's four freedoms (free movement of goods, services, people and capital) and greatly enhancing the scope for cooperation in many sectors. Following enlargement of the European Union on 1 January to include Austria, Finland and Sweden, the Union's EFTA partners in the EEA are now Iceland, Norway and Liechtenstein.[2] On 1 May, following the 'yes' vote in Liechtenstein's referendum of 9 April,[3] the EEA Agreement entered into force there, too, subject to a few amendments required by EEA Council Decision 1/95 of 10 March,[4] which noted that, since the customs union agreement between Liechtenstein and Switzerland had been amended, the smooth functioning of the EEA Agreement was not impaired by that regional union.

810. The EEA Council, comprising members of the Council of the European Union, members of the Commission and one member of the government of each EFTA member of the EEA, met twice in 1995. On 30 May, it adopted a Joint Declaration on political dialogue[5] which intensifies cooperation on the common foreign and security policy. At the second meeting on 21 November,[6] the EEA Council confirmed that the EEA Agreement was functioning well. Various trade policy issues were discussed, including origin rules and processed agricultural products. A solution was also found to the problem of forwarding statements made by the Council and/or the Commission when Community acts of relevance to the EEA were adopted. At its monthly meetings the EEA Joint Committee, which is made up of representatives of the contracting parties, continued to update the Agreement by incorporating in it the most recent additions to the corpus of Community leg-

---

[1]   1994 General Report, point 778.
[2]   1994 General Report, point 780.
[3]   OJ L 140, 23.6.1995; Bull. 4-1995, point 1.4.59.
[4]   OJ L 86, 20.4.1995; Bull. 3-1995, point 1.4.49.
[5]   Bull. 5-1995, point 1.4.61.
[6]   Bull. 11-1995, point 1.4.40.

islation. Towards the end of the year several decisions were taken, including one to extend cooperation on accompanying policies in the social and cultural fields. The EEA Joint Parliamentary Committee, at its meetings of 29 May and 20 November, examined the Joint Committee's 1994 annual report and adopted resolutions on competition and State aid, the free movement of people and the environment. In a resolution dated 15 February[1] the European Parliament had invited the EEA contracting parties to examine the possibility of organizing EEA decision-making in a more efficient way.

Relations with the EFTA countries

811. On 6 March, the Council adopted negotiating directives (Table III) with a view to concluding protocols to the trade agreements with Norway, Switzerland and Iceland to take account of EU enlargement on 1 January (Table III).

812. Bilateral relations between the European Union and Norway and Iceland centred on the functioning and implementation of the EEA Agreement. Matters of common interest not fully covered by the Agreement were the establishing of a single set of rules of origin for the whole of Europe, the trans-European networks and cooperation on fisheries and the Barents Sea. Other important issues were discussed on 30 June when Mrs Gro Harlem Brundtland, the Norwegian Prime Minister, came to see Mr Santer.[2] Iceland and Norway were kept abreast of preparations for the 1996 Intergovernmental Conference.

813. On 6 December 1992, Switzerland had decided not to join the European Economic Area;[3] in January 1993, it had requested the opening of bilateral negotiations on a wide range of topics. Negotiations began on 12 December 1994, based on a Commission communication on the development of relations with Switzerland in the wake of the referendum of 20 February 1994 on Alpine transit[4] and the Council's subsequent conclusions and negotiating directives of 31 October 1994 (Table III), covering the free movement of people, cooperation in the field of scientific research, public procurement, mutual recognition of product evaluation and standards, and market access for farm products.[4] On 14 March, the Council added air and inland transport to this list *(→ point 415).*[5] The aim of the negotiations is

---

[1] OJ C 56, 6.3.1995; Bull. 1/2-1995, point 1.4.71.
[2] Bull. 6-1995, point 1.4.55.
[3] Twenty-sixth General Report, point 789.
[4] 1994 General Report, point 784.
[5] Bull. 3-1995, point 1.3.102.

to achieve an overall balance of mutual advantage within each agreement and among them so as to ensure an appropriate level of parallelism between the various sectoral agreements concerned. On 4 December, the Council underscored the importance of these negotiations for the future of EU-Switzerland relations. It asked the Commission to pursue them actively in line with the principles contained in the negotiating directives and hoped for early signs of progress.

Section 8

Relations with Central and Eastern Europe and the Baltic States

Pre-accession strategy and structured dialogue

814.   The Essen European Council in December 1994[1] adopted a pre-accession strategy for associated countries which had signed Europe Agreements with the Union,[2] *(→ point 819)*. It is based on those Agreements and on a new, structured relationship, and incorporates a number of specific measures.

The structured dialogue became fully operational in 1995, following agreement at the Essen European Council on the type and frequency of meetings between the Heads of State or Government and at ministerial level.[1] During the year, the associated countries, including the Baltic States, were invited to meet the Heads of State or Government at the Cannes European Council.[3] The second such meeting took place at the Madrid European Council.[4] There were also meetings at ministerial level on foreign affairs, the internal market, economics and finance, agriculture, transport, research, culture, education, justice and home affairs.[5] Mr Van den Broek and Ms Bjerregaard met Environment Ministers from the associated countries, including the Baltic States, in Brussels on 18 September. In addition, two key meetings took place between the President of the European Parliament and the Presidents of the Parliaments of the associated countries on 5 April and 5 December, in Strasbourg and Warsaw respectively. The Cannes and Madrid European Councils reviewed this structured dialogue, and the progress made in implementing the pre-accession strategy. Noting the various reports presented by the Commission *(→ point 817)*, the Madrid European Council in December signalled that it would take the necessary decisions to launch accession negotiations with the Central and East European countries at the earliest opportunity once the Intergovernmental Conference was over, in the light of the Commission's opinions and reports, and hoped that the initial stage of

---

[1]   1994 General Report, point 785.
[2]   Bulgaria, the Czech Republic, Estonia, Hungary, Latvia, Lithuania, Poland, Romania and Slovakia.
[3]   Bull. 6-1995, point 1.4.56.
[4]   Bull. 12-1995.
[5]   Bull. 1/2-1995, point 1.4.78; Bull. 4-1995, point 1.4.60; Bull. 5-1995, point 1.4.64; Bull. 6-1995, points 1.4.59 to 1.4.61; Bull. 9-1995, points 1.4.33 to 1.4.35; Bull. 10-1995, points 1.4.61 to 1.4.63; Bull. 11-1995, point 1.4.49.

those talks could coincide with the start of initial negotiations with Cyprus and Malta.

815. Six countries presented formal applications for EU membership to the President of the Council: Romania on 22 June,[1] Slovakia on 27 June,[2] Latvia on 27 October,[3] Estonia on 28 November,[4] Lithuania on 8 December,[5] and Bulgaria on 16 December.[5] The Council adopted Decisions initiating accession procedures under Article O of the Treaty on European Union for Romania,[6] Slovakia,[6] Latvia[3] and Estonia.[5]

816. Meanwhile, in response to the Essen European Council's request in December, on 3 May the Commission adopted a White Paper on preparing the associated countries for integration into the internal market, a key element of the pre-accession strategy.[7] For each market sector, the White Paper set out the main measures that Central and East European countries which had signed Europe Agreements should take to prepare their economies to operate within the rules of the Union's internal market and suggested the sequence in which domestic law should be brought into line with European law, without imposing a specific timetable. The Cannes European Council welcomed the White Paper and asked the Commission to provide progress reports, consulting associated countries on their national programmes to bring their legislation into line with the internal market. On 5 July, the Commission adopted a communication on the follow-up to the White Paper with regard to technical assistance.[8]

817. In addition to the White Paper, there were a number of trade measures with immediate effect: anti-dumping procedures and safeguard measures, adjustments to the Europe Agreements, and the alignment of the Romanian and Bulgarian Agreements on those with other associated countries in respect of customs duties and tariff quotas as of 1 January. Discussions were held with all the countries concerned with a view to offering Romania and Bulgaria the same scope for diagonal cumulation of origin of goods enjoyed by Poland, Hungary, the Czech Republic and Slovakia so as to harmonize rules of origin in trade preferences between the Community, Central and East European countries and EFTA.

---

[1]   Bull. 6-1995, point 1.4.57.
[2]   Bull. 6-1995, point 1.4.58.
[3]   Bull. 10-1995, point 1.4.60.
[4]   Bull. 11-1995, point 1.4.42.
[5]   Bull. 12-1995.
[6]   Bull. 7/8-1995, point 1.4.62.
[7]   COM(95) 163; Bull. 5-1995, point 1.4.63.
[8]   Bull. 7/8-1995, point 1.4.63.

Acting on another request by the Essen European Council, the Commission adopted three reports on relations with the associated countries in the run-up to accession: a progress report on the implementation of the pre-accession strategy,[1] a study of alternative strategies for developing agricultural relations between the European Union and the associated countries with a view to their future accession,[2] adopted on 29 November, and an interim report on the implications of enlargement for the Union's current policies and their future development,[3] adopted on 6 December. These reports were presented to the Madrid European Council in December.

818. With regard to the Baltic Sea region, the Council called on the Commission to present a report on the state of political and economic cooperation in the region and prospects for such cooperation in practice.[4] The report was adopted on 29 November.[5] Parliament adopted a resolution on 14 July[6] demonstrating its interest in the subject, which was shared by the Madrid European Council.[7]

Europe Agreements and other accords

819. The Europe Agreements with Bulgaria (→ point 833), the Czech Republic (→ point 835), Romania (→ point 834) and Slovakia (→ point 836), aimed at building closer political and economic relations to prepare the way for accession, entered into force on 1 February.[8] Further Europe Agreements were signed with the Baltic States on 12 June (→ point 830) and a draft Europe Agreement with Slovenia was initialled on 15 June (→ point 837).

820. In the wake of the enlargement of the European Union and the outcome of the Uruguay Round negotiations, the EU opened negotiations with the associated countries with the aim of adjusting the Europe Agreements and free trade agreements accordingly. On 19 June, the Council adopted general negotiating directives covering the fields concerned with a view to concluding a protocol to the Europe Agreements, the free trade agreements and other agreements laying down a number of tariff quotas for wines following enlargement (Table III). Specific negotiating directives for adjustments relating to agricultural products, accommodating both enlargement

---

[1]   COM(95) 606; Bull. 11-1995, point 1.4.46.
[2]   COM(95) 607; Bull. 11-1995, point 1.4.48.
[3]   COM(95) 605; Bull. 11-1995, point 1.4.47; Bull.12-1995.
[4]   Bull. 5-1995, point 1.4.70.
[5]   COM(95) 609; Bull. 11-1995, point 1.4.43.
[6]   Bull. 7/8-1995, point 1.4.71.
[7]   Bull. 12-1995.
[8]   Bull. 1/2-1995, points 1.4.73 to 1.4.77.

and the Uruguay Round conclusions and offering further potential concessions, had already been adopted on 6 March (Table III). A number of enlargement-related measures on textiles, applied provisionally, were introduced by means of an exchange of letters.[1] On 12 July, the Council adopted negotiating directives for an agreement on amending the Additional Protocols on trade in textile products attached to the Europe Agreements (Table III). There were also negotiations on adapting the Europe Agreements regarding ECSC products to take account of enlargement and the Uruguay Round. Air transport agreements were also concluded (→ point 418).

821.   On 15 November, Parliament gave its assent to Additional Protocols to the Europe Agreements with Bulgaria, the Czech Republic, Hungary, Poland, Romania and Slovakia aimed at enabling the associated countries to participate in Community programmes in a number of fields (Table III). The Council adopted a Decision on the conclusion of the Protocols on 4 December.

Assistance for Central and Eastern Europe

822.   The Cannes European Council in June[2] agreed a total allocation of ECU 6 693 million for aid to the countries of Central and Eastern Europe over the period 1995-99.

G24 and bilateral coordination

823.   The Commission continued to coordinate aid to Central and Eastern Europe from the G24 and the international institutions. At a high-level G24 meeting on 10 March, it was decided to boost on-the-spot coordination by holding regular meetings of the various donors in conjunction with the national authorities. The sectoral approach was further developed. The G24 working parties on transport and customs pushed ahead with the development of the 'corridors' identified in the context of trans-European networks. The Commission developed bilateral coordination with the main donors. Meetings were held with the United States in Poland, Albania and Romania, and there were frequent contacts with the World Bank, the European Bank for Reconstruction and Development and the European Investment Bank to exchange information with a view to co-financing projects, particularly infrastructure projects.

---

[1]   Decision 95/131/EC of 20.2.1995 — OJ L 94, 26.4.1995.
[2]   Bull. 6-1995, point I.57.

PHARE programme

824.   As the Madrid European Council acknowledged,[1] the PHARE programme has a key role to play in the Union's pre-accession strategy as a financial aid instrument to the associated countries, helping them in restructuring their economies and adapting their legislation to the *acquis communautaire*, so as to create favourable conditions for future membership of the Union. The Commission stepped up efforts to streamline and improve programming, with assistance incorporated into a country strategy and a multiannual programme setting out not only objectives and priorities but the means necessary to achieve those objectives, in operational terms. In addition, PHARE's performance has been enhanced by the introduction of programme conditionality and the abolition of fixed annual country allocations.

825.   The budget was increased by 15% over the previous year to ECU 1 146.23 million. On 12 June, it was decided to include Croatia in the list of countries eligible for assistance under PHARE.[2] However, following the offensive by the Croatian armed forces in Krajina, the EU decided on 4 August to suspend PHARE operations in Croatia.[3] On 20 December, the Commission proposed extending PHARE to include Bosnia-Herzegovina (→ point 845); the inclusion of the former Yugoslav Republic of Macedonia (→ point 845) was approved by the Council on 30 October.

826.   The year 1995 saw a greater emphasis on investment support, notably for infrastructure, the environment and private sector development. The Commission promoted intraregional cooperation and 'good neighbour' policies between the associated countries by financing a number of multi-country programmes, a cross-border cooperation programme and other schemes aimed at institution-building, developing civil society, promoting trade in the region and expediting the movement of goods and passengers across borders.

827.   A Technical Assistance Information Exchange Office was set up to cover the associated countries' collective needs for technical assistance with regard to the single market. It is due to open in January 1996. The Commission stepped up efforts to improve and streamline procedures for implementing PHARE, by further decentralizing responsibility, consolidating, simplifying and standardizing documents and implementation requirements, and delegating more management tasks to EU delegations. It also improved

---

[1]   Bull. 12-1995.
[2]   OJ L 133, 17.6.1995; Bull. 6-1995, point 1.4.77.
[3]   Bull. 7/8-1995, point 1.4.6.

its monitoring and evaluation systems and financial audits. Considerable effort was also devoted to making PHARE more transparent. On 20 February[1] and 20 July,[2] the Commission adopted the annual reports on the programme's implementation for 1992, 1993 and 1994; the Economic and Social Committee adopted an opinion on programme evaluation on 25 October.[3]

Other forms of cooperation

828.   On 14 March, the Commission adopted a communication on industrial cooperation with Central and East European countries,[4] and the Council adopted conclusions on the matter in April.[5]

829.   At a joint meeting of Justice and Home Affairs Ministers from the EU and associated Central and East European countries in Luxembourg on 20 June,[6] Ms Gradin presented the Commission's position on widening the PHARE programme to cover cooperation on justice and home affairs issues, in line with the conclusions of the Essen European Council.[7] At a second such joint meeting in Brussels on 25 September, ministers agreed on a joint action programme of cooperation on judicial matters to combat international organized crime.[8]

Bilateral relations

830.   The integration process for the three Baltic States of Estonia, Latvia and Lithuania gained considerable momentum in 1995, with three free trade agreements entering into force on 1 January. These accords form an integral part of the Europe Agreements subsequently negotiated with the Baltic States and signed on 12 June (Table III), which enabled them to enter fully into the Union's pre-accession strategy, and to which Parliament gave its assent on 15 November. The three countries formally requested membership of the European Union (→ point 815). In June, the Commission decided to set up delegations in each country. Mr Van den Broek paid his first official

---

[1]   COM(95) 13; Bull. 1/2-1995, point 1.4.82.
[2]   COM(95) 366; Bull. 7/8-1995, point 1.4.65.
[3]   Bull. 10-1995, point 1.4.66.
[4]   Bull. 3-1995, point 1.4.51.
[5]   Bull. 4-1995, point 1.4.62.
[6]   Bull. 6-1995, point 1.4.61.
[7]   Bull. 12-1994, point I.13; 1994 General Report, point 785.
[8]   Bull. 9-1995, point 1.4.33.

visit in February, meeting Heads of State or Government and Members of Parliament in all three countries.[1]

831.   Under the terms of the Europe Agreement with Poland,[2] the Association Council held its second meeting in Brussels on 17 July,[3] while the Association Committee met for the third time on 29 and 30 June in Warsaw. The Parliamentary Association Committee met on 30 January and 1 February in Warsaw, and again on 5 and 6 September in Brussels; a special session on agriculture was held in Strasbourg on 15 June. Mr Santer met the Polish Prime Minister, Mr Jozef Oleksy, in Brussels on 6 April and visited Warsaw on 25 and 26 September, where he met the President, Mr Lech Walesa, the Prime Minister and other members of the government.[4] Mr Van den Broek visited Poland on 18 May[5] for talks with Mr Walesa. He also met Poland's Foreign Minister, Mr Wladyslaw Bartoszewski, when the latter visited Brussels on 18 July.[6] On his visit to Poland on 2 and 3 October, Mr Monti met the Finance Minister, Mr Grzegorz Kolodko, and other members of the government.[7]

832.   Following the entry into force of the Europe Agreement with Hungary in 1994,[2] the Association Council held its second meeting on 17 July.[8] The Association Committee held its third meeting in Budapest on 1 and 2 June, while the Parliamentary Association Committee met twice. The Prime Minister of Hungary, Mr Gyula Horn, paid an official visit to the European institutions in Brussels on 9 and 10 February,[9] meeting Mr Santer and Mr Klaus Hänsch, President of the European Parliament, with whom he discussed preparations for Hungary's entry into the European Union. Mr Van den Broek visited Hungary on 7 and 8 December for the OSCE conference, where he met Mr Horn. He also had talks with Hungary's President, Mr Árpád Göncz, on 23 November in The Hague, and with the Foreign Minister, Mr László Kovács, at the UN General Assembly on 25 September.

833.   Following the entry into force of the Europe Agreement with Bulgaria on 1 February (Table III), the Association Council held its inaugural meeting in Brussels on 29 May,[10] while the Association Committee met for the

---

[1]   Bull. 1/2-1995, point 1.4.81.
[2]   1994 General Report, point 786.
[3]   Bull. 7/8-1995, point 1.4.67.
[4]   Bull. 9-1995, point 1.4.37.
[5]   Bull. 5-1995, point 1.4.68.
[6]   Bull. 7/8-1995, point 1.4.68.
[7]   Bull. 10-1995, point 1.4.67.
[8]   Bull. 7/8-1995, point 1.4.66.
[9]   Bull. 1/2-1995, point 1.4.80.
[10]   Bull. 5-1995, point 1.4.67.

first time on 9 and 10 November in Sofia. The Parliamentary Association Council met on 6 and 7 September in Sofia. On 7 February, Mr Guéorgui Pirinski, the Foreign Minister, visited Brussels for talks with Mr Van den Broek,[1] who in turn visited Bulgaria on 4 and 5 May.[2] The Prime Minister, Mr Jan Videnov, visited Brussels for talks with Mr Santer on 25 April. On 16 December, he presented Bulgaria's formal request for membership of the Union to Mr Felipe González, the Prime Minister of Spain and President of the Council.[3]

834.   Mr Nicolae Vacaroiu, Prime Minister of Romania, presented Mr Alain Juppé, President of the Council, with Romania's formal request for accession to the European Union on 22 June.[4] After the Europe Agreement with Romania (Table III) entered into force on 1 February, the Association Council held its first meeting in Luxembourg on 10 April.[5] The first Association Committee meeting was held in Bucharest on 12 and 13 October. Two Joint Parliamentary Committee meetings were held during the year. Mr Ion Iliescu, the President of Romania, visited Brussels for talks with Mr Santer on 10 March.[6]

835.   Following the entry into force 'on 1 February of the Europe Agreement with the Czech Republic (Table III), the Association Council met in Luxembourg on 10 April.[7] The first Association Committee meeting was held in Prague on 14 and 15 September, while the Joint Parliamentary Committee met twice, from 29 to 31 May and on 18 and 19 December. Mr Yves-Thibault de Silguy visited Prague on 21 March, primarily for talks with Mr Vaclav Klaus, the Prime Minister.[8] Ms Gradin held talks in April with several members of the government and the President of the Court of Auditors. On a visit to the Czech Republic on 7 July, Mr Van den Broek also met Mr Klaus and the President of Parliament, among others.[9] Mr Monti visited Prague on 2 and 3 October,[10] and Ms Wulf-Mathies attended a conference on cross-border cooperation on 16 and 17 October.[11]

836.   The first Association Council meeting with Slovakia following the entry into force of the Europe Agreement (Table III) on 1 February was held

---

[1]   Bull. 1/2-1995, point 1.4.79.
[2]   Bull. 5-1995, point 1.4.66.
[3]   Bull. 12-1995.
[4]   Bull. 6-1995, point 1.4.57.
[5]   Bull. 4-1995, point 1.4.67.
[6]   Bull. 3-1995, point 1.4.55.
[7]   Bull. 4-1995, point 1.4.66.
[8]   Bull. 3-1995, point 1.4.54.
[9]   Bull. 7/8-1995, point 1.4.69.
[10]   Bull. 10-1995, point 1.4.68.
[11]   Bull. 10-1995, point 1.4.69.

in Brussels on 29 May.[1] Slovakia presented a formal request for membership of the Union on 27 June.[2] On 10 November, Mr Santer met the President of Slovakia, Mr Vladimir Meciar, when they both attended the European Forum in Berlin.[3]

837.   Slovenia and the Community initialled a draft Europe Agreement (Table III) on 15 June in Brussels, the Council having approved the negotiating directives on 6 March. In a resolution on 30 November, Parliament expressed the hope that the Agreement would be signed at the earliest opportunity.[4] On 6 September, the Commission adopted a recommendation for a Decision on a draft Agreement on early implementation of the trade and trade-related measures provided for in the Agreement (Table III). Mr Van den Broek visited Slovenia from 3 to 5 March for talks with the Prime Minister, Mr Janez Drnvosek. Ms Gradin and Mr Fischler both visited Slovenia in July.[5] The President of Slovenia, Mr Milan Kuçan, met Mr Santer in Brussels on 30 November.[6]

838.   On Albania, the Commission adopted a report on democratization, human rights and conditions for minorities on 31 March.[7] The Council adopted a declaration on continuing macrofinancial aid to support the country's economic and political reforms.[8] Mr Van den Broek visited Albania on 27 and 28 April to discuss prospects for bilateral relations.[9] The third interparliamentary meeting between the European and Albanian Parliaments was held in Brussels on 23 and 24 February. In an own-initiative opinion of 31 May, the Economic and Social Committee urged the Union to step up aid and speed up the association procedure.[10]

[1]   Bull. 5-1995, point 1.4.69.
[2]   Bull. 6-1995, point 1.4.58.
[3]   Bull. 11-1995 point 1.4.54.
[4]   OJ C 339, 18.12.1995; Bull. 11-1995 1.4.51.
[5]   Bull. 7/8-1995, point 1.4.70.
[6]   Bull. 11-1995 1.4.55.
[7]   Bull. 3-1995, point 1.4.56.
[8]   Bull. 4-1995, point 1.4.69.
[9]   Bull. 4-1995, point 1.4.63.
[10]   Bull. 5-1995, point 1.4.65.

Section 9

Relations with Mediterranean non-member countries and the Middle East

Mediterranean non-member countries

Overall strategy

839.   The Barcelona Euro-Mediterranean ministerial conference took place on 27 and 28 November.[1] The European Union and its 12 Mediterranean partners[2] adopted, at the end of the proceedings, a Declaration[3] in which they decided to put their relations on a multilateral and durable footing based on a spirit of partnership and on a work programme. Reinforced and regular political dialogue, enhanced economic and financial cooperation in support of the creation of a free trade area and a further strengthening of the social, cultural and human dimension are the partnerships's three key components. It was agreed that implementation of the Declaration would be monitored through periodic meetings of the Foreign Ministers and *ad hoc* meetings. On 14 December, Parliament adopted a resolution on the Barcelona conference.[4] In December the Madrid European Council welcomed the Barcelona Declaration, which it considered the beginning of a broad new Euro-Mediterranean association.[5]

840.   In October 1994, the Commission proposed the establishment of a Euro-Mediterranean partnership, with a view to strengthening the European Union's policy for the peace, security and welfare of the Mediterranean.[6] The long-term goal of the proposed strategy is the creation of an extensive free trade area, backed up by substantial financial aid. Following the endorsement of this strategy by the Essen European Council[7] in December 1994, the Commission set out in a new communication, on 8 March, the main priorities for a future Euro-Mediterranean partnership: backing for

---

[1]   Bull. 11-1995, point 1.4.56; Supplement 2/95 — Bull.
[2]   Algeria, Cyprus, Egypt, Israel, Jordan, Lebanon, Malta, Morocco, Syria, Tunisia, Turkey, Palestinian Authority.
[3]   The full texts of the Barcelona Declaration and the work programme can be found in point 2.3.1 of Bull. 11-1995.
[4]   OJ C 17, 22.1.1996; Bull. 12-1995.
[5]   Bull. 12-1995.
[6]   COM(94) 427; 1994 General Report, point 845.
[7]   Bull. 12-1994, point I.14; 1994 General Report, point 845.

economic transition, a more equitable socioeconomic balance and regional integration.[1] The Cannes European Council in June endorsed this approach and set out the position to be adopted *vis-à-vis* the Mediterranean partners at the Barcelona conference.[2] The partnership should be based on Euro-Mediterranean association agreements embodying a political and security component, an economic and financial component and a social and human component. The European Council also fixed the budget appropriations to be set aside over the period 1995-99 for financial cooperation with the Mediterranean countries at ECU 4.685 billion.[3] On 7 June, the Commission adopted a proposal for a Regulation (Table II) for a new MEDA budget heading, which would be the single instrument for all cooperation with the countries concerned (in the manner of the PHARE *(→ point 824)* and TACIS *(→ point 869)* Regulations) and replace the system of bilateral financial protocols. On 14 September and 15 November, the Economic and Social Committee and the Committee of the Regions adopted own-initiative opinions on the Euro-Mediterranean partnership.[4] On 11 October and 17 November, Parliament welcomed the Commission's approach and stressed the importance of multilateral cooperation.[5] On 27 and 28 March, a conference was held in Tunis on Euro-Mediterranean cooperation on energy *(→ point 375)*;[6] on 9 March, looking ahead to the Barcelona ministerial conference, the Council had reiterated, in its conclusions, the importance of multilateral regional Mediterranean cooperation for the environment, outlining the broad priorities *(→ point 472)*;[7] its approach was fleshed out in new conclusions issued in October.[8]

841. The special nature of the EU's relations with its northern Mediterranean partners should be underscored. Relations with Cyprus and Malta reflect these two countries' envisaged membership of the European Union: a pre-accession strategy has been drawn up and a structured dialogue put in place. In March the EC-Turkey Association Council reached agreement on the completion of a customs union between the European Union and Turkey, to which Parliament gave its assent in December, and regarding which the Commission proposed to implement special financial cooperation arrangements.

---

[1]   COM(95) 72; Bull. 3-1995, point 1.4.57.
[2]   Bull. 6-1995, point I.13.
[3]   Bull. 6-1995, points 1.4.68 and I.19.
[4]   Bull. 9-1995, point 1.4.38; Bull. 11-1995, point 1.4.58.
[5]   OJ C 287, 30.10.1994; Bull. 10-1995, point 1.4.70; OJ C 323, 4.12.1995; Bull. 11-1995, point 1.4.57.
[6]   Bull. 3-1995, point 1.3.92.
[7]   Bull. 3-1995, point 1.4.58.
[8]   Bull. 10-1995, point 1.3.166.

842.   On 6 March (Table III), the Council adopted negotiating directives for protocols with a view to adapting the agreements concluded with the various Mediterranean partners to take account of the enlargement of the European Union.

Northern Mediterranean countries (Cyprus, Malta, Turkey, Andorra and San Marino)

843.   The Council adopted, on 6 March[1] and 10 April[2] respectively, time-tables for the opening of negotiations for the accession of Cyprus and Malta to the European Union and established the principle of a structured dialogue with these two countries. In December, the Madrid European Council confirmed its wish for accession negotiations to begin six months after the conclusion of the 1996 Intergovernmental Conference in the light of its outcome.[3] In the case of Malta, the Commission in response to a request by the Essen European Council[4] sent the Council a report on 1 March concerning the implementation of economic reforms.[5] On 12 June, at meetings of the Association Councils with Cyprus and Malta,[6] the EU and each of the countries concerned adopted a joint resolution on the establishment of a structured dialogue and signed new financial protocols (Table III), the Council having adopted the decisions on their conclusion on 30 October. On 17 July the Council adopted detailed procedures for implementing the structured dialogue and certain aspects of the pre-accession strategy.[7] On 25 September, the first joint ministerial meeting took place in Brussels between the European Union and Cyprus and Malta concerning cooperation in the fields of justice and home affairs.[8] Within the same framework, ministerial meetings in which the participants discussed questions relating to the internal market took place in Cyprus on 18 October[9] and in Malta on 16 October.[10] A second joint ministerial meeting, focusing on economic aspects of the structural dialogue, was held in Brussels on 21 November.[11] Mr Dinos Michaelides, the Cypriot Prime Minister, visited the Commission on 23 November.[12] Parliament, for its part, adopted resolutions on the acces-

---

[1]   Bull. 3-1995, point 1.4.60a.
[2]   Bull. 4-1995, point 1.4.72.
[3]   Bull. 12-1995.
[4]   1994 General Report, point 847.
[5]   Bull. 3-1995, point 1.4.63.
[6]   Bull. 6-1995, points 1.4.70 and 1.4.72.
[7]   Bull. 7/8-1995, points 1.4.72 and 1.4.75.
[8]   Bull. 9-1995, point 1.4.39.
[9]   Bull. 10-1995, point 1.4.72.
[10]   Bull. 10-1995, point 1.4.73.
[11]   Bull. 11-1995, point 1.4.59.
[12]   Bull. 11-1995, point 1.4.60.

sion of Cyprus and Malta in July.[1] The EU-Cyprus and EU-Malta Joint Parliamentary Committees met twice each during the year.

844. The EC-Turkey Association Council, which met in Brussels on 6 March,[2] reached agreement on a customs union between the European Union and Turkey. The two parties adopted the implementing procedures and agreed that the implementing decision would enter into force on 1 January 1996. The Association Council, which met on 30 October,[3] concentrated on issues to do with implementation of the customs union and produced a favourable assessment of the way in which the prior technical conditions had been fulfilled. It also adopted a resolution on political dialogue and institutional cooperation providing for regular meetings between the two parties. On 16 February, Parliament adopted a resolution stressing that the establishment of a customs union should hinge on an improvement in the human rights situation and called on the Commission to report on developments in this regard.[4] Parliament gave its assent on 13 December,[5] at the same time adopting a resolution on the human rights situation in Turkey.[5] The Madrid European Council welcomed Parliament's assent,[6] which enabled the final stage of the customs union to enter into force. On 22 December, the Council approved two draft decisions concerning the definitive entry into force of the customs union.

The Commission had adopted a proposal on 26 July for a Regulation regarding the implementation of special financial cooperation arrangements for Turkey (Table II). The adoption of this proposal follows the statement made by the Community at the Association Council meeting on 6 March,[2] in which the Commission undertook to resume financial aid to Turkey prior to the entry into force of the customs union and to adopt detailed implementing rules during the first half of 1995. On 12 December, the Commission adopted a draft ECSC decision concerning the conclusion of a free trade agreement on ECSC products *(→ point 764).* The troika and Mr Van den Broek visited Turkey on 23 and 24 March[7] while Mr Erdal Inönü, Turkey's Foreign Minister, met Mr Van den Broek in Brussels on 7 June.[8]

845. In the former Yugoslavia, following the peace agreement concluded in Dayton on 21 November and signed in Paris on 14 December, Mr Santer

---

[1]   OJ C 249, 25.9.1995; Bull. 7/8-1995, points 1.4.73, 1.4.74 and 1.4.76.
[2]   Bull. 3-1995, point 1.4.65.
[3]   Bull. 10-1995, point 1.4.76.
[4]   OJ C 56, 6.3.1995; Bull. 1/2-1995, point 1.4.87.
[5]   OJ C 17, 22.1.1996; Bull. 12-1995.
[6]   Bull. 12-1995.
[7]   Bull. 3-1995, point 1.4.66.
[8]   Bull. 6-1995, point 1.4.75.

and Mr Van den Broek issued a statement on behalf of the Commission.[1] On 27 September, the Commission sent the Council a broad outline of the aid that the EU could contribute to rebuilding the former Yugoslavia, stressing the need for a coordinated international effort,[2] an approach set out in a fresh Commission communication on the management and coordination of the aid on 20 November.[3] On the humanitarian aid front, the Commission also adopted a communication on humanitarian assistance in the former Yugoslavia (→ point 803). On 30 October the Council adopted conclusions[4] defining the EU's position on all the civilian issues, notably the process of reconstruction in the former Yugoslavia. In the wake of the peace agreement, an initial meeting of the donor countries and organizations helping to rebuild Bosnia-Herzegovina was held in Brussels on 20 and 21 December under the co-chairmanship of Mr Van den Broek and Mr Kemal Dervis, Vice-President of the World Bank.[5] On 4 December, the Council adopted Decision 95/516/CFSP[6] on support for supplying humanitarian aid to Bosnia-Herzegovina and extending joint action 93/603/CFSP up to the end of 1996. On 18 December the Commission adopted a communication on the financial aspects of reconstruction.[7] On 11 December, the Council adopted joint action 95/545/CFSP[8] on the EU's involvement in the structures implementing the peace agreement for Bosnia-Herzegovina. On 20 December, the Commission adopted a decision aimed at implementing the Council's decision.[5] The same day, it also adopted a proposal for a Council Regulation (Table II) amending Regulation (EEC) No 3906/89 (PHARE Regulation (→ point 825)) in order to extend its application to Bosnia-Herzegovina, along with a decision[5] on an urgent import programme for Bosnia-Herzegovina under the PHARE programme worth ECU 62.5 million.

The EU had played an active part under the common foreign policy in the diplomatic process aimed at producing a peaceful solution to the conflict. Decision 95/23/CFSP of 6 February[9] supplementing joint action 94/790/CFSP brought the EU's overall contribution to the administration of the city of Mostar to ECU 80 million (released in several instalments).[10] On 4 and 19 December, the Council adopted Decision 95/517/CFSP[6] and joint

[1]   Bull. 11-1995, point 1.4.61.
[2]   Bull. 9-1995, point 1.4.40.
[3]   COM(95) 582; Bull. 11-1995, point 1.4.62.
[4]   Bull. 10-1995, point 1.4.78.
[5]   Bull. 12-1995.
[6]   OJ L 298, 11.12.1995; Bull. 12-1995.
[7]   COM(95) 581; Bull. 12-1995.
[8]   OJ L 309, 21.12.1995; Bull. 12-1995.
[9]   OJ L 33, 13.2.1995; Bull. 1/2-1995, point 1.4.83.
[10]   Bull. 6-1995, point 1.4.76; Bull. 7/8-1995, point 1.4.80.

action 95/552/CFSP[1] aimed at extending administration of the city up to 22 July 1996 and earmarking ECU 32 million for that purpose. The EU also provided substantial humanitarian aid (→ point 803), notably to Bosnia-Herzegovina and the former Yugoslav Republic of Macedonia. Economic sanctions taken in 1994 against regions of Bosnia-Herzegovina controlled by the Bosnian Serbs remained in force.[2] Those applying to Serbia and Montenegro were suspended from 4 December (Table II).[3] On 27 December, the Council adopted Regulation (EC) No 3032/95 aimed at maintaining (Table II) the preferential import arrangements applied by the Community in 1995 to products originating in the republics of Bosnia-Herzegovina, Croatia and the former Yugoslav Republic of Macedonia.[4] The Commission played a key role in coordinating the Sanctions, Assistance, Missions in the neighbouring countries. It also sent 20 EU observers to help monitor the border between Serbia-Montenegro and Bosnia. A budget of ECU 6.69 million was earmarked for these operations. The Union also made a financial contribution to operations to foster independent media, democratization and the process of restoring peace in the former Yugoslav republics and the rebuilding of infrastructure in Bosnia-Herzegovina damaged in the war. On 26 January, Mr Van den Broek received Mr Haris Silajdzic, the Bosnian Prime Minister,[5] and, on 12 September, Mr Muhammed Sacirbey, the Foreign Minister.[6]

On 6 March, the Council adopted negotiating directives for an economic and trade cooperation agreement, including provisions on ECSC products, and a financial protocol with Croatia (Table III). The negotiations, which commenced on 19 June, were suspended on 1 August following Croatia's intervention in Krajina. On 12 June, by Regulation (EC) No 1366/95 (Table II), the Council decided to include Croatia in the PHARE programme (→ point 825), but this process also had to be suspended on 1 August. Parliament dealt with this subject in a resolution of 16 March[7] and expressed its views on the gamut of problems in the former Yugoslavia in six resolutions.[8] The Council adopted conclusions on these issues on several occasions.[9]

---

[1]   OJ L 313, 27.12.1995; Bull. 12-1995.
[2]   1994 General Report, point 850.
[3]   Decisions 95/511/CFSP and 95/510/ECSC — OJ L 297, 9.12.1995; Bull. 12-1995.
[4]   1994 General Report, point 854.
[5]   Bull. 1/2-1995, point 1.4.84.
[6]   Bull. 9-1995, point 1.4.42.
[7]   OJ C 89, 10.4.1995; Bull. 3-1995, point 1.4.62.
[8]   OJ C 109, 1.5.1995; Bull. 4-1995, points 1.4.74 and 1.4.79; OJ C 151, 19.6.1995; Bull. 5-1995, point 1.4.72; OJ C 249, 25.9.1995; Bull. 7/8-1995, point 1.4.78; OJ C 269, 16.10.1995; Bull. 9-1995, point 1.4.41; OJ C 17, 22.1.1996; Bull. 12-1995.
[9]   Bull. 4-1995, point 1.4.73; Bull. 6-1995, point 1.4.78; Bull. 7/8-1995, point 1.4.79.

To strengthen relations between the European Union and the former Yugo-slav Republic of Macedonia, the Commission adopted, on 14 November, a recommendation for a decision on a trade and cooperation agreement (Table III), accompanied by a financial protocol (Table III). Negotiating directives were adopted by the Council on 22 December. In addition, on 30 October, the Council confirmed the Republic's eligibility for the PHARE programme (→ point 825).

Information on Slovenia is given in Section 8 (Relations with Central and Eastern Europe and the Baltic States) of this chapter (→ point 837).

Maghreb (Algeria, Morocco, Tunisia and Libya)

846.   Financial cooperation under the fourth generation of financial protocols concluded with Algeria, Morocco and Tunisia continued satisfac-torily. Financing decisions were taken amounting to ECU 1 058 billion out of an overall total of ECU 1 247 billion made up of grants financed from the EC budget and EIB loans.

847.   The Commission held exploratory talks with Algeria with a view to the negotiation of a Euro-Mediterranean Association Agreement and the Madrid European Council asked it to present a proposal for negotiating di-rectives. This question was discussed at the EC-Algeria Cooperation Coun-cil meeting on 2 October.[1] This meeting also provided an opportunity to review the economic reforms undertaken by Algeria. On 19 January, Parlia-ment adopted a resolution condemning the terrorist attacks in Algeria and endorsing any attempt to reach a democratic political solution.[2] On 23 January, the Presidency published a statement in which the European Union expressed its concern over the situation in Algeria and reaffirmed its willingness to support a policy of democratic development and economic restructuring.[3]

848.   Negotiations were completed with Morocco on the conclusion of a Euro-Mediterranean Association Agreement (Table III) and a fisheries agree-ment to replace the 1992 agreement (→ point 825). These negotiations brought Mr Abdellatif Filali, Prime Minister and Minister for Foreign Affairs and Cooperation of Morocco, to the Commission on 6 July.[4] The Association Agreement, which was initialled on 16 November and will be signed at the beginning of 1996, is essentially the same as that signed with

[1]   Bull. 10-1995, point 1.4.81.
[2]   OJ C 43, 20.2.1995; Bull. 1/2-1995, point 1.4.90.
[3]   OJ C 43, 20.2.1995; Bull. 1/2-1995, point 1.4.6.
[4]   Bull. 7/8-1995, point 1.4.83.

Tunisia. On 5 September, the Commission adopted a statement on the European Union's relations with Morocco.[1] Parliament adopted a resolution on 16 March in which it called on the Moroccan authorities to comply with their undertakings regarding Western Sahara so that the peace plan could be implemented.[2]

849. The Euro-Mediterranean Agreement establishing an association between the European Communities, their Member States and the Tunisian Republic (Table III) was signed in Brussels on 17 July and received Parliament's assent on 14 December. It is the first of a series of new agreements to be concluded under the Euro-Mediterranean partnership (→ *point 840*). The principal components of the Agreement are: regular political dialogue, the step-by-step establishment of a free trade area, provisions on the right of establishment, services, free movement of capital and competition rules, strengthening of economic cooperation on the broadest possible front, and social, cultural and financial cooperation.

Mashreq (Egypt, Jordan, Lebanon and Syria), Israel and the Palestinian Territories, and support for the peace process

850. The European Union has maintained its support for the Middle East peace process. Mr Alain Juppé, French Foreign Minister and President of the Council, and Mr Marín visited Israel, the Palestinian Territories, Syria and Lebanon from 7 to 10 February in order to reaffirm the EU's support for the peace process.[3] The troika paid a further visit to the region from 25 to 29 October.[4] It also participated in the opening of the Amman Economic Summit. In the framework of the common foreign policy, the Council adopted, on 1 June,[5] Decision 95/205/CFSP supplementing Decision 94/276/CFSP[6] on a joint action in support of the peace process. Based on Article J.3 of the Treaty on European Union, this Decision provides for a contribution of ECU 10 million from the Community budget for the preparation, supervision and coordination of the international mission sent to observe the Palestinian elections (these funds were granted by a Commission Decision of 25 July).[7] On 25 September, the Council adopted Decision 95/403/CFSP concerning the observation of elections to the Palestinian Council, by sending a team of 300 observers, and the coordination of the international

---

[1] Bull. 9-1995, point 1.4.44.
[2] OJ C 89, 10.4.1995; Bull. 3-1995, point 1.4.67.
[3] Bull. 1/2-1995, point 1.4.92.
[4] Bull. 10-1995, point 1.4.86.
[5] OJ L 130, 14.6.1995; Bull. 6-1995, point 1.4.85.
[6] OJ L 119, 7.5.1994; 1994 General Report, point 743.
[7] Bull. 7/8-1995, point 1.4.2.

operation for observing the elections.[1] Parliament adopted two resolutions, on 16 February[2] and 19 May[3] respectively, the first calling on the Palestinian authorities to step up action against terrorism and on Israel to refrain from political and economic measures that could jeopardize the peace process, and the second stressing the need to implement rapidly the Declaration of Principles signed in 1993 by Israel and the PLO and, in particular, to hold elections in the Palestinian Territories. On 14 September, the Economic and Social Committee adopted an own-initiative opinion analysing the economic and social implications of the peace process and the new opportunities for regional cooperation.[4]

On 28 September, an agreement was signed in Washington, in the presence of Mr Felipe González, Spanish Prime Minister and President of the Council, and Mr Santer on extension of self-rule to the whole of the West Bank, the successful achievement of which was welcomed by the Madrid European Council.[5] The Council, too, welcomed the agreement, adopting on 2 October conclusions[6] in which it resolved to strengthen EU cooperation with the Palestinian Territories, affirmed the need to prepare a ministerial conference on economic assistance for the Palestinian people and invited the Commission to begin exploratory talks with the Palestinian Authority on the conclusion of a Euro-Mediterranean Association Agreement. On 23 October, the Commission adopted a communication[7] setting out the key facets of the European Union's strategy on aid to the Palestinians, which was endorsed by the Council on 21 December.[6] On 15 December, Parliament sent to the Council, under Article J.7 of the Treaty on European Union, a recommendation concerning elections to the Council and Presidency of the Palestinian Authority.[8]

851. Negotiations with Israel for a Euro-Mediterranean Association Agreement (Table III) were completed on 28 September and the Agreement signed on 20 November. The new accord, within the framework of the Euro-Mediterranean partnership, introduces the principle of a permanent political dialogue, provides for further reciprocal concessions on agricultural trade and extends the scope of economic cooperation. An interim agreement (Table III) was concluded in December enabling early implementation of the provisions of the Euro-Mediterranean agreement on trade and customs cooperation. The parallel negotiations for a separate agreement on science and

---

[1]   OJ L 238, 6.10.1995; Bull. 9-1995, point 1.4.47.
[2]   OJ C 56, 6.3.1995; Bull. 1/2-1995, point 1.4.93.
[3]   OJ C 151, 19.6.1995; Bull. 5-1995, point 1.4.77.
[4]   OJ C 301, 31.11.1995; Bull. 9-1995, point 1.4.48.
[5]   Bull. 12-1995.
[6]   Bull. 10-1995, point 1.4.84.
[7]   COM(95) 505; Bull. 10-1995, point 1.4.85.
[8]   OJ C 17, 22.1.1996; Bull. 12-1995.

technology through which Israel will be associated with the Community's fourth framework programme *(→ point 257)* were also concluded and the agreement was initialled on 31 October. In a statement on 4 November, Mr Santer expressed his deep shock at the assassination of the Prime Minister, Mr Yitzhak Rabin,[1] a feeling echoed by the Madrid European Council in December.[2]

852.   On 23 January, the European Union opened negotiations for a new Euro-Mediterranean Association Agreement with Egypt (Table III); negotiations continued throughout the year.

853.   On 12 June, the Council adopted negotiating directives (Table III) for a Euro-Mediterranean Association Agreement with Jordan similar to those being negotiated with other countries in the region. Negotiations got under way on 18 July.

854.   During the second meeting of the EC-Lebanon Cooperation Council held in Brussels on 6 March,[3] the Lebanese authorities stressed their wish to open negotiations for a Euro-Mediterranean Association Agreement. Mr Juppé, French Foreign Minister and President of the Council, and Mr Marín reaffirmed recognition of Lebanon's independence, sovereignty and territorial integrity. The Council approved negotiating directives for the new Agreement (Table III) on 2 October and negotiations started on 9 October.

855.   As regards financial cooperation with the countries of the region, ECU 830 million was committed by 31 December out of a total of ECU 1 088 billion, made up of grants from the Community budget and EIB loans.

The Middle East (Gulf Cooperation Council countries, Iran, Iraq and Yemen)

856.   The troika and the Gulf Cooperation Council (GCC) met in Granada on 20 July.[4] The ministers identified three areas in which cooperation between the two regions should be strengthened (economic relations, scientific and cultural cooperation and political dialogue) and agreed to propose setting up a group of experts to examine the scope for the conclusion of a free trade agreement and to draw up procedures for the participation of GCC countries in the decentralized cooperation programme as well as the organ-

---

[1] Bull. 11-1995, point 1.4.68.
[2] Bull. 12-1995.
[3] Bull. 3-1995, point 1.4.68.
[4] Bull. 7/8-1995, point 1.4.85.

ization of meetings of senior officials to strengthen political dialogue. The proposals, endorsed by the EU-GCC ministerial meeting in New York on 29 September, will ensure the desired qualitative improvement in relations between both sides. The third industrial conference between the European Union and the GCC was held in Muscat from 16 to 18 October with the aim of strengthening economic cooperation and promoting investment in both directions. On 22 November[1] the Commission adopted a communication to the Council on relations between the European Union and the GCC countries with a view to revitalizing the dialogue and the negotiations on the free trade agreement.

857.   The 'critical dialogue' between the European Union and Iran, instituted at the 1992 Edinburgh European Council,[2] continued throughout the year. The issue of human rights, particularly with regard to the situation of minorities in Iran and the case of Mr Salman Rushdie, the British author sentenced to death by Iran, was one of the principal matters discussed. Other questions of EU concern, notably Iran's attitude to the Middle East peace process, international terrorism and arms, were also broached. This approach was confirmed at the Madrid European Council in December.

858.   The European Union and its Member States continued to apply the embargo on Iraq decreed by the UN Security Council resolutions. For the time being, there are neither contractual relations nor official contacts between the European Union and Iraq. The Union takes an active interest in the humanitarian situation in Iraq and has continued to provide assistance to the population (→ point 806).

859.   Mr Yusuf A. Abdullah, Minister of State for Foreign Affairs of Oman, visited the Commission on 29 June to discuss with Mr Marín plans, as part of the Middle East peace process, to set up an international water desalination centre in Oman.[3]

860.   In Yemen, projects financed by the European Community were able to resume following the stabilization of the internal situation and the establishment of a new government in October 1994. On 6 March, the Council adopted a decision on the conclusion of an agreement (Table III) amending the existing cooperation agreement (1984), thus extending it to the whole of the territory of the unified Republic of Yemen (composed of the former Yemen Arab Republic and the former People's Democratic Republic of

---

[1]   COM(95) 541; Bull. 11-1995, point 1.4.71.
[2]   Twenty-sixth General Report, point 858.
[3]   Bull. 6-1995, point 1.4.83.

Yemen). The sixth meeting of the EU-Yemen Joint Cooperation Committee was held in Brussels on 29 March.

Euro-Arab Dialogue and relations with the Economic Cooperation Organization (ECO)

861.   In the context of the Euro-Arab Dialogue between the Commission and the Secretariat of the Arab League, cooperation activities took place in the fields of environment, banking and finance, standards, civil aviation, education and telecommunications. The Commission pursued its objective of establishing a Euro-Arab management school in Granada.[1]

862.   Following discussions in May 1994 between the Commission and the enlarged Economic Cooperation Organization,[2] which has its headquarters in Tehran, the Commission and the ECO exchanged information and experience, particularly in the energy and transport sectors. Cooperation continued with ECO on the prevention of drug trafficking, following the adoption by the 10 ECO member States in Islamabad, in March, of a masterplan for controlling drugs.

---

[1]   1994 General Report, point 873.
[2]   Members are: Afghanistan, Azerbaijan, Iran, Kazakhstan, Kyrgyzstan, Pakistan, Tadjikistan, Turkey, Turkmenistan and Uzbekistan.

Section 10

Relations with the independent States of the former Soviet Union and Mongolia

Overview

863.   Further strides were made towards consolidating ties between the European Union and the independent States of the former Soviet Union in keeping with the goals set in 1994[1] despite the occasional hitch such as the suspension of relations following Russia's intervention in Chechnya *(→ point 880)*. Negotiations continued throughout the year for a new generation of partnership and cooperation agreements to replace the trade and commercial and economic cooperation agreement signed with the former Soviet Union in 1989,[2] while political dialogue was stepped up in various bodies. With Russia, the EU's principal partner in the region, this dialogue was conducted in meetings at various levels: presidency, government, political directors and working parties. The European Parliament, for its part, had contacts with the members of the State Duma and of the Federation Council.

864.   The development of relations at international level, events in Russia and the pre-accession strategy for the Central and East European countries *(→ point 814)* required the Union's relations with the new independent States to be more clearly defined. The Commission accordingly adopted a communication on future relations between the European Union and Russia *(→ point 880)* spelling out political, security and economic objectives and priorities; it adopted similar communications on the Trans-Caucasian republics *(→ point 884)* and on Central Asia[3] *(→ point 885)*. Closer relations were also forged with Ukraine *(→ point 881)*.

Partnership and cooperation agreements and other agreements

865.   In addition to the partnership and cooperation agreements signed in 1994[4] with Russia, Ukraine and Moldova, like agreements were signed this

---

[1]   1994 General Report, point 806.
[2]   OJ L 68, 15.3.1990; Twenty-third General Report, point 797.
[3]   Bull. 10-1995, point 1.4.87.
[4]   1994 General Report, point 807.

year with Kyrgyzstan (→ *point 885)*, Belarus (→ *point 883)* and Kazakhstan (→ *point 885)* and initialled with Georgia (→ *point 884)*, Armenia
(→ *point 884)* and Azerbaijan (→ *point 884)*; exploratory contacts were
made with Uzbekistan (→ *point 885)*.

866.   Pending ratification of these partnership and cooperation agreements,
interim agreements covering trade-related matters were signed with Russia
(→ *point 880)*, Ukraine (→ *point 881)* and Moldova (→ *point 882)*. Others
were negotiated with Kyrgyzstan (→ *point 885)* and Belarus (→ *point 883)*.
The signing of an interim agreement with Kazakhstan (→ *point 885)* was
made contingent on the holding of democratic elections.

867.   In a resolution of 7 April,[1] Parliament pressed for the agreements
with the new independent States to be ratified but highlighted the need to
uphold the provisions on democratic principles, human rights and minorities. It gave its assent to several of the agreements on 30 November.

Trade arrangements

868.   Information on trade arrangements is to be found in Section 4 (Common commercial policy) of this chapter (→ *point 750)*.

Assistance for the independent States of the former Soviet Union

TACIS

869.   The TACIS programme continued to be implemented effectively and
new management techniques were devised.[2] TACIS has enabled the Commission to continue allocating substantial sums of aid to the independent
States with a view to underpinning the transition to a market economy in
those countries and entrenching democracy. To that end it committed ECU
511.19 million, notably in Armenia (6 million), Azerbaijan (6 million),
Belarus (12 million), Georgia (6 million), Kazakhstan (15 million), Kyrgyzstan (8 million), Moldova (9 million), Russia (161.19 million), Tadjikistan (4 million), Turkmenistan (4 million), Ukraine (35 million) and Uzbekistan (10 million); it also adopted the 1995 inter-State programme (ECU 66
million), a nuclear safety action plan (ECU 58.5 million), a programme for
the Chernobyl nuclear power station (ECU 37.5 million) and a programme

---

[1]   OJ C 109, 1.5.1995; Bull. 4-1995, point 1.4.81.
[2]   OJ L 187, 29.7.1993; Twenty-seventh General Report, point 675.

for the International Science and Technology Centre (ECU 10 million). Furthermore, the Commission approved programmes to disseminate information (ECU 5 million) and promote the coordination units (ECU 8 million), the partnership and cooperation programme (ECU 10 million), the TACIS programme to bolster democracy (ECU 10 million), and two multidisciplinary technical assistance programmes (ECU 30 million).

870.   Over these final 12 months of the first round of multiannual TACIS programming, the bulk of the commitments were implemented at a relatively early stage. The volume of contract awards went up again, reaching some ECU 560 million. Payments amounted to some ECU 370 million, around 25% up on 1994.

871.   On 22 February the Commission adopted a proposal for a new Regulation for the TACIS programme (Table II) as the current one expires in December.[1] The scope of TACIS has been extended to cover investment in infrastructure, cross-border cooperation and the environment. The Madrid European Council called for the Regulation to be adopted swiftly.[2] On 23 March[3] and 18 July[4] the Commission adopted the annual reports on the implementation of the programme in 1993 and 1994.

872.   The Commission took measures to improve coordination between those providing technical assistance, in particular the EBRD, the World Bank and other donors, among them the United States. Multilaterally, the Commission took part in meetings of the advisory groups set up by the World Bank for Uzbekistan, Moldova, Ukraine, Kazakhstan, Azerbaijan and Kyrgyzstan. The Bangkok agreement, which envisages the granting of EU technical assistance for EBRD operations, was revised, while the Commission took fresh common initiatives with the EBRD, in particular as regards support for the environment and aid for small and medium-sized businesses. A new monitoring and evaluation system was set up, with teams located in Moscow, Almaty and Kiev being assigned the task of monitoring and evaluating all TACIS-funded activities.

873.   A new programme to improve the environment was introduced for the former Soviet Union as a whole. TACIS also had a hand in helping the Central Asian countries improve the management of their water resources in order to remedy the shrinking of the Aral Sea, declining agricultural productivity and serious risks for human health. The environment was also the

---

[1]   OJ L 187, 29.7.1993; Twenty-seventh General Report, point 675.
[2]   Bull. 12-1995.
[3]   COM(95) 57; Bull. 3-1995, point 1.4.77.
[4]   COM(95) 349; Bull. 7/8-1995, point 1.4.91.

focus of attention in the Lake Baikal region and is one of the priority areas of the 1995 TACIS inter-State programme.

874.   The Commission decided to raise from ECU 20 to ECU 30 million its financial contribution to the International Centre for Science and Technology (ISTC),[1] the fruit of a multilateral initiative by the United States, Japan, the European Union and the Russian Federation to enable scientists and engineers from the former Soviet Union to apply their knowledge to peaceful ends. In September, 180 projects were accepted for an amount of ECU 75 million. By then, Armenia, Georgia, Belarus, Kazakhstan and Kyrgyzstan had joined the ISTC.

875.   At their Munich Summit in July 1992,[2] the G7 countries endorsed an urgent nuclear safety action programme for the independent States of the former Soviet Union and the Central and East European countries. As the foremost contributor to this programme, the European Union this year allocated ECU 123 million, bringing its overall contribution to ECU 515 million, including a contribution to the EU-G7 action plan in Ukraine.

876.   The second stage of the partnership and cooperation programme was successfully completed, with around 40 projects — part-financed by TACIS — launched in partnerships between EU firms and public and private bodies in the independent States of the former Soviet Union. The 1995 TACIS programme to foster democracy was adopted by the Commission on 20 October, running in tandem with the PHARE programme (→ point 824). Preparations for monitoring the Russian general elections got off the ground, along with cooperation with the Council of Europe with a view to the eventual accession of Ukraine and Russia to that body. A town-twinning programme was launched in September.

Other forms of assistance

877.   In the field of food and medical aid, the Commission granted a loan of ECU 1.25 billion to the republics of the former Soviet Union in 1991[3] (→ point 1017). Azerbaijan and Uzbekistan, which signed loan agreements after the other republics, received ECU 68 and ECU 59 million respectively. The food-aid programme approved by the Council on 27 July 1994 continued,[4] with Armenia, Georgia, Azerbaijan, Moldova, Kyrgyzstan and

---

[1]   Twenty-sixth General Report, point 786.
[2]   Twenty-sixth General Report, point 799.
[3]   OJ L 362, 31.12.1991; Twenty-fifth General Report, point 844.
[4]   OJ L 201, 4.8.1994; 1994 General Report, point 814.

Tadjikistan receiving deliveries totalling ECU 204 million, including ECU 35 million in emergency aid granted by ECHO (→ point 805) to particularly vulnerable sections of the population. The Council decided, on 17 July, to allocate them an additional ECU 197 million for a new food and agricultural support programme, including ECU 17 million in technical assistance to promote agricultural reform.

878.   On 16 May the Commission adopted a communication on prospects for cooperation in science and technology with the new independent States of the former Soviet Union,[1] in which it set priorities in a variety of fields such as environmental protection, nuclear safety and technologies, the information society, energy and space technology. It also underscored the importance of ensuring greater consistency with the TACIS programme and better coordination with the EBRD, the World Bank and EU Member States.

879.   Macro-financial assistance is covered below in the section on bilateral relations (→ points 880 et seq.).

Bilateral relations

880.   In order to implement the trade components of the 1994 partnership and cooperation agreement with Russia (Table III) — which received Parliament's assent and formed the subject of a resolution on 30 November[2] — an interim agreement on trade and trade-related measures was signed on 17 July (Table III) and will enter into force on 1 February 1996. The European Union had suspended the procedure owing to the war in Chechnya and the violation of human rights which were denounced in particular by Parliament in a recommendation to the Council adopted on 15 June.[3] At an informal meeting in March, EU Foreign Ministers had laid down the criteria for signing the accord, which included a ceasefire, unfettered access for humanitarian aid and the creation of an OSCE assistance group on the ground in Chechnya. As sufficient headway had been made along those lines, the interim agreement was signed on 17 July.

On 31 May, with a view to forging closer ties between the European Union and the Russian Federation, the Commission adopted a communication on the future of relations between the EU and Russia mapping out the Union's objectives and priorities vis-à-vis that country in the spheres of politics,

---

[1]   COM(95) 190; Bull. 5-1995, point 1.3.46.
[2]   OJ C 339, 18.12.1995; Bull. 11-1995, point 1.4.82.
[3]   OJ C 166, 3.7.1995; Bull. 6-1995, point 1.4.91.

security and energy.[1] It also adopted a draft common position under Title V of the Treaty on European Union. In its conclusions of 20 November,[2] the Council proposed that the EU, in striving to build a solid partnership with Russia founded on the partnership and cooperation agreement, take action in the following fields: support for democratic reforms in Russia; economic cooperation; cooperation in the fields of justice and home affairs; security issues; and foreign policy. The Madrid European Council confirmed these conclusions.[3]

Within the framework of political dialogue, the troika, comprising the Foreign Ministers of Germany, France and Spain, accompanied by Mr Van den Broek, met Mr Boris Yeltsin, President of the Russian Federation, and Mr Andrei Kozyrev, Foreign Minister, in Moscow on 9 March.[4] On 7 September a summit meeting took place between President Yeltsin, accompanied by the Prime Minister, Mr Viktor Chernomyrdin and other ministers, Mr Felipe González, President of the Council and Spanish Prime Minister, accompanied by Mr Javier Solana, Spanish Minister for Foreign Affairs, and Mr Santer, President of the Commission, accompanied by Mr Van den Broek, to discuss, among other things, EU-Russia relations, the situation in the former Yugoslavia, trade relations and security arrangements in Europe.

The Russian authorities invited Community observers to monitor the general elections, a joint operation by the OSCE, the Council of Europe, the European Parliament and the Member States, with the support of the Commission. This operation proved to be a resounding success. The Madrid European Council confirmed its support for that country's early accession to the Council of Europe and its backing for Russia's membership of the WTO and other international bodies. On 1 June,[5] Mr Van den Broek received Mr Oleg Davydov, Russian Deputy Prime Minister responsible for external economic affairs, to examine outstanding bilateral trade problems.

881. Political relations with Ukraine, with which a partnership and cooperation agreement was signed in 1994 (Table III), received Parliament's assent and was the subject of a resolution on 30 November,[6] were bolstered by a series of high-level contacts (the visit to Kiev of the troika of political directors on 5 and 6 January, first meeting of the Joint Committee on 24 March, high-level G7 mission to Chernobyl in April, visit of the President of the Republic, Mr Leonid Kuchma, to the Commission on 1 June[7] and

---

[1]   COM(95) 223; Bull. 5-1995, point 1.4.78.
[2]   Bull. 11-1995, points 1.4.81 and 2.2.1, which reproduces the conclusions in full.
[3]   Bull. 12-1995.
[4]   Bull. 3-1995, point 1.4.73.
[5]   Bull. 6-1995, point 1.4.92.
[6]   OJ C 339, 18.12.1995; Bull. 11-1995, point 1.4.84.
[7]   Bull. 6-1995, point 1.4.94.

visit of the ministerial troika and Mr Van den Broek to Kiev on 26 June). Prime Minister Yevhenii Marchuk paid a visit to the Commission on 24 November.[1] The settlement of the dispute on maritime agencies ended the discrimination against European companies in Ukraine, paving the way for the signing of the interim agreement (Table III) on 1 June during President Kuchma's visit to Brussels and for its conclusion in December.

As for macro-financial assistance, the Council decided on 23 October, by Decision 95/442/EC, to grant balance-of-payments assistance amounting to ECU 200 million (→ point 65) supplementing the ECU 85 million granted in December 1994.[2] This aid hinges on adherence to the timetable agreed upon for the closure of the nuclear power station at Chernobyl in keeping with arrangements adopted by the G7 and the European Union. President Kuchma's decision to close the Chernobyl nuclear power station between 1997 and 2000, the political importance of which was underlined at the G7 Summit (→ point 516) in Halifax in June and at the Madrid European Council,[3] enabled the EU and the G7 to put together with the Ukrainian authorities a memorandum of understanding on implementing practical support measures. Technical studies and preparatory work have gone ahead, with the TACIS contribution amounting this year to ECU 37.5 million. The Madrid European Council welcomed Ukraine's accession to the Council of Europe.[3]

882.   After the signing of the partnership and cooperation agreement (Table III) with Moldova on 28 November 1994,[4] to which Parliament gave its assent, adopting a resolution on the subject on 30 November,[5] an interim agreement (Table III) was signed on 2 October and endorsed by Parliament on 30 November. As part of the macro-financial support granted to Moldova, the European Union paid the second and last instalment, i.e. ECU 20 million, of the ECU 45 million loan approved in June 1994[6] (→ point 65). On 8 November the Commission adopted a proposal for a Decision granting a new macro-financial loan of ECU 15 million (Table II). Allocation of ECU 27 million granted in 1994 as part of the ECU 204 million food aid operation continued in 1995.

883.   A partnership and cooperation agreement was signed with Belarus on 6 March (Table III). During his visits to the Commission on 2 June[7] and 5

---

[1]   Bull 11.1995, point 1.4.88.
[2]   OJ L 366, 31.12.1994; 1994 General Report, point 67.
[3]   Bull. 12-1995.
[4]   1994 General Report, point 807.
[5]   OJ C 339, 18.12.1995; Bull. 11-1995, point 1.4.78.
[6]   OJ L 155, 22.6.1994; 1994 General Report, point 67.
[7]   Bull. 6-1995, point 1.4.88.

December,[1] Mr Uladzimir Syanko, Foreign Minister, stressed the importance for his country of a rapid signing of the interim agreement (Table III) initialled on 7 April. The textile quotas opened for Belarus were doubled in 1995. In line with its macro-financial support policy, the Council decided, on 10 April, to grant Belarus a long-term loan of ECU 55 million to help it over its balance-of-payments difficulties; it will be paid in two instalments, subject to implementation of certain economic reforms (→ point 65).

884. On 31 May the Commission adopted a communication on EU relations with the Trans-Caucasian republics (Georgia, Armenia and Azerbaijan).[2] It proposes an overall strategy to help these three republics, affected by fighting notably in Nagorno-Karabakh and Abkhazia, to cope with a difficult economic situation and to create the conditions for lasting development. It considers that this strategy could be underpinned by the negotiation, according to appropriate arrangements, of a cooperation and partnership agreement with each one of them, supplemented by food and humanitarian aid measures and, where necessary, by technical assistance for postwar reconstruction. Such a strategy would be contingent on progress towards finding solutions to the conflicts, with all parties accepting the sovereignty and territorial integrity of each republic, the promotion of human rights and democratic institutions and the resumption of regional cooperation and economic reform. In a draft common position adopted pursuant to Article J.2 of the Treaty on European Union, the Commission proposed defining, under the CFSP, the EU's objectives and priorities with respect to these three republics. The Council concluded, on 17 July, that negotiations for a partnership and cooperation agreement should be started with the three Caucasus republics. The talks culminated in the initialling, on 15 December, of agreements with Georgia (Table III) and, on 19 December, with Azerbaijan (Table III). The Commission made initial contacts with each of them in October. Mr Eduard Shevardnadze, President of Georgia, Mr Heydar Aliyev, President of Azerbaijan, and Mr Punsalmaagiin Ochirbat, President of Mongolia, met Mr Santer on 17 February, 18 April and 27 September respectively.[3] Mr Vahan Papazian, Foreign Minister of Armenia, was received by Mr Van den Broek on 1 June. On 20 June,[4] Mr Van den Broek saw the Deputy Prime Minister of Georgia, and the Prime Ministers of Azerbaijan and Georgia, and, on 22 September, the Deputy Prime Minister of Armenia on the occasion of the negotiation of a memorandum of agreement setting out arrangements for the granting of ECU 197 million in food aid.

---

[1] Bull. 12-1995.
[2] COM(95) 205; Bull. 5-1995, point 1.4.79.
[3] Bull. 4-1995, point 1.4.82.
[4] Bull. 6-1995, point 1.4.89.

Mr Van den Broek went to the Trans-Caucasus from 3 to 7 October,[1] where he saw the three presidents and their governments.

885. The Commission proposed, in a communication of 9 June,[2] accompanied by a draft Council common position under Article J.2 of the Treaty on European Union, an overall strategy for the Union's relations with the new independent States of Central Asia (Kazakhstan, Kyrgyzstan, Uzbekistan, Tadjikistan and Turkmenistan), where the European Union has key geopolitical and economic interests, especially in the energy sector. It states that the principal objective of the European Union is to preserve stability in the region, by fostering broadly representative democratic institutions and continuing to support economic reforms. The Commission recommends, subject to the upholding of human rights and the democratic process, negotiating partnership and cooperation agreements with Uzbekistan and Turkmenistan. The instruments of such a policy would include economic cooperation and assistance through partnership and cooperation agreements and sectoral agreements, combined with TACIS operations, humanitarian relief from ECHO, and a strengthening of political and diplomatic relations with the region. In the wake of this communication, exploratory contacts for partnership and cooperation agreements were made in July with Uzbekistan — which confirmed its readiness to embark on political dialogue with the Community and welcomed technical assistance under the TACIS programme in support of democracy — and with Turkmenistan. Partnership and cooperation agreements with Kazakhstan (Table III) and Kyrgyzstan (Table III) were signed on 23 January and 9 February respectively. Interim agreements were negotiated with the two countries (Table III), that with Kazakhstan being signed on 5 December. Having given its assent to the agreement with Kyrgyzstan, Parliament adopted, on 30 November, a resolution on the economic and commercial aspects of the agreement.[3] Mr Van den Broek received the Tajik Prime Minister, Mr Jamshed Karimov,[4] and the deputy premiers of Uzbekistan, Mr Utkar Sultanov,[4] and Kazakhstan, Mr Amangeldy Tasmagambetov.

---

[1]   Bull. 10-1995, point 1.4.94.
[2]   COM(95) 206, Bull. 6-1995, point 1.4.87; Bull. 10-1995, point 1.4.87.
[3]   OJ C 339, 18.12.1995; Bull. 11-1995, point 1.4.76.
[4]   Bull. 11-1995, point 1.4.89.

Section 11

Relations with the United States, Japan and other industrialized countries

Western Economic Summit (G7)

886. The 21st Western Economic Summit,[1] attended by the Heads of State or Government of the seven major industrialized countries (Canada, United States, Japan, Germany, France, Italy and the United Kingdom) along with the Commission President, Mr Santer, took place in Halifax (Canada) in June. The Russian President, Mr Boris Yeltsin, took part in the political discussions.

On the economic front, the priorities were identified as being to create quality jobs and cut unemployment in a climate of non-inflationary growth. It was decided that a meeting of Finance and Employment Ministers would be held prior to the next Summit in order to assess progress in job creation. Welcoming the outcome of February's Conference on the Information Society *(→ point 426)*, and advocating a dialogue on this subject with the developing countries and those in economic transition, the participants also backed the idea of a follow-up conference in South Africa in 1996. Underlining the importance of the role of international institutions in helping the world economy run smoothly, the Summit recommended improvements to the IMF's early-warning and surveillance system for economic policies and financial markets, the creation of an emergency financing mechanism, the consolidation of the WTO and the development of activities by the various multilateral institutions to promote sustainable development, combat poverty and provide humanitarian and emergency aid. The need to honour undertakings made at the Rio Conference on Environment and Development was also stressed.[2] The participants also reiterated their support for countries undergoing economic transition and their commitment to helping Ukraine restructure its energy sector in readiness for the closure of the Chernobyl nuclear power station.

Political discussion focused on the role of the UN, arms control and the extension of the Nuclear Non-Proliferation Treaty, and the fight against ter-

---

[1] Bull. 6-1995, point 1.4.97. The different subjects dealt with at this Summit led to the adoption of a communiqué and a Chairman's statement, the full texts of which are contained in Bull. 6-1995, point 2.2.1.

[2] Twenty-sixth General Report, point 596.

rorism and organized crime. The participants supported the European Union's contribution to stability and cooperation in Europe and expressed their views on the state of various parts of the world.

887.   At the Quad meetings in Whistler (May) and Ripley (October),[1] US Trade Representative Mickey Kantor, Japan's Minister for Trade and Industry, Mr Ryutaro Hashimoto, Canada's Minister for International Trade, Mr Roy MacLaren, and Sir Leon Brittan discussed the outlook for strengthening the role of the WTO and ways of sustaining the momentum behind trade liberalization generated by the conclusion of the Uruguay Round negotiations.

United States

Transatlantic Declaration

888.   Two EU-US summits were held this year in the framework of the 1990 Transatlantic Declaration:[2] in Washington on 14 June[3] and in Madrid on 3 December.[4] At the June summit, a group of high-level representatives was instructed to draw up a report for the next summit, to evaluate progress to date and to examine proposals aimed at strengthening the partnership between the European Union and the United States. The Cannes European Council welcomed this initiative.[5] The December summit approved a new transatlantic agenda and joint action plan, the importance of which was underlined by the Madrid European Council,[4] heralding new areas of cooperation between the two partners and completing the Transatlantic Declaration which had put the dialogue between the two partners on a formal footing. The four new pillars of cooperation were: to promote peace, stability, democracy and development throughout the world, to respond to global challenges, to contribute to the expansion of world trade and closer economic relations, and to establish closer ties between the partners. Other topics covered included the situation in Bosnia, relations with Turkey, Iran, Russia and the countries of Central and Eastern Europe, and the Middle East peace process.

---

[1]   Bull. 5-1995, point 1.4.89; Bull. 10-1995, point 1.4.96.
[2]   Twenty-fourth General Report, point 693.
[3]   Bull. 6-1995, point 1.4.99.
[4]   Bull. 12-1995.
[5]   Bull. 6-1995, point I.15.

889. The European Commission adopted a communication to the Council[1] on 26 July, outlining the framework for strengthening relations between the European Union and the United States, based both on a reinforcement of the key elements of the relationship (security, foreign policy, economic and trade relations and macroeconomic cooperation) and on the development of cooperation in new areas such as the environment, the information society, social policy, research, education and training. The various aspects of relations between the European Union and the United States were also examined in an Economic and Social Committee information report published on 14 September.[2]

890. At the ministerial meeting on 26 January,[3] Sir Leon Brittan and Mr Alain Juppé, France's Minister for Foreign Affairs and President of the Council, met the US Secretary of State, Mr Warren Christopher, to discuss the European security framework, nuclear cooperation and common concerns on a number of regional issues. The ministerial meeting held in July,[4] attended by Sir Leon, Spain's Minister for Foreign Affairs and President of the Council, Mr Javier Solana Madariaga, and Mr Christopher, focused on the prospects for developing and strengthening the transatlantic partnership.

Political dialogue

891. On 27 September, the Foreign Ministers of the Member States and Mr Van den Broek met Mr Warren Christopher during the United Nations General Assembly. The meeting focused on the situation in the former Yugoslavia, relations with Russia and Turkey, the Middle East peace process, United Nations peacekeeping and the future of transatlantic relations. On 25 February, Mr Santer, Sir Leon Brittan and Mr Van den Broek met US Vice-President, Mr Al Gore, at the Conference on the Information Society (→ point 426). They discussed nuclear cooperation, audiovisual media, the Berlin Conference on Climatic Change (→ point 504), the G7 action plan for Chernobyl and the prospects for expanding the European Union to the East.

892. At the beginning of July, at the Madrid meeting between the troika political directors and US Deputy-Secretary of State Richard Holbrooke, the two parties agreed that they should concentrate their efforts on the areas

---

[1] COM(95) 411; Bull. 7/8-1995, point 1.4.95.
[2] Bull. 9-1995, point 1.4.53.
[3] Bull. 1/2-1995, point 1.4.103.
[4] Bull. 7/8-1995, point 1.4.97.

identified at the June summit,[1] and on other regional questions of common interest. The first meeting of high-level representatives took place in July, with further meetings on 29 September in Washington and on 27 October in Madrid.

Economic and trade relations

893.   On 4 May, on the fringes of the Quad meeting, Sir Leon Brittan held talks with US Trade Representative Mickey Kantor on a number of bilateral trade issues (→ point 887). On 22 May[2] Mr Kantor visited the Commission for talks with Sir Leon and Mr Franz Fischler, a visit the latter returned in June.[3]

894.   The transatlantic trade dialogue, intended to provide a framework within which European and American firms could make joint recommendations to political decision-makers and so facilitate transatlantic trade and investment, was a joint initiative launched by the European Commission and the US Trade Department at the beginning of the year and inaugurated in Seville on 10 and 11 November.[4] This development was applauded by the Madrid European Council.[5]

895.   A decision concluding the new Euratom-United States Agreement on nuclear cooperation was adopted by the Council on 3 August (→ point 257). On 21 December an agreement was signed inaugurating a cooperation programme with the United States in the areas of basic and higher education and vocational training (→ point 285). April saw exploratory talks with the US administration on a possible agreement on scientific and technological cooperation. Negotiations continued on a mutual recognition agreement on the evaluation of conformity of certificates and trade marks (→ point 753). July saw the second round of bilateral meetings with the United States on the information society. The fourth round of official bilateral consultations in the framework of the agreement on civil aircraft took place in Brussels on 11 May (→ point 416). Consultations also took place on aid programmes targeted on unemployment and poverty. On 10 April the Council reached agreement on the conclusion of the EC-United States competition agreement (→ point 173). In the field of agriculture, consultations took place between the United States and the EU, chiefly on trade in canned fruit, the prospects

[1]   Bull. 6-1995, point 1.4.99.
[2]   Bull. 5-1995, point 1.4.90.
[3]   Bull. 6-1995, point 1.3.180.
[4]   Bull. 11-1995, point 1.4.90.
[5]   Bull. 12-1995.

for the conclusion of a veterinary agreement and an agreement on wine and the results of the special GATT panel which in 1994 had examined the effects of US tobacco legislation on European exports and found against the United States.[1] Consultations also took place pursuant to Article XXIII of the GATT on the European Union reference price system for cereals and rice, and arrangements for importing bananas into the European Union.

896. On 6 July the Commission published its 11th annual report on US barriers to trade and investment,[2] pointing out that major progress had been made due largely to the implementation of the results of the Uruguay Round. Furthermore, the European Union and the United States were once again each other's main trade and investment partners: bilateral trade totalled ECU 190 billion in 1994 and the aggregate amount of direct investment in both directions was ECU 410 billion (at historic prices).

Japan

General strategy

897. The Commission defined its new strategy in a communication of 29 May,[3] embraced by the Council, entitled 'Europe and Japan: the next steps'.[4] It confirmed its policy of securing greater access to the Japanese market in order to reduce the European Union's trade deficit and, in the longer term, to promote structural changes by emphasizing dialogue and cooperation with the Japanese and, in particular, by broadening the scope of a dialogue between the Union and Japan hitherto largely confined to the economic sphere.

898. A summit meeting took place in Paris on 19 June,[5] attended by the Japanese Prime Minister, Mr Tomiichi Murayama, President Chirac and Mr Santer. The main items on the agenda were bilateral trade, the WTO, the development of cooperation and the political dialogue between the European Union and Japan. Both parties confirmed their intention to hold annual summit meetings, attesting to the strengthening of the framework for dialogue between the European Union and Japan. Sir Leon Brittan was received by Emperor Akihito on 6 June.[6]

---

[1] 1994 General Report, point 824.
[2] Bull. 7/8-1995, point 1.4.96.
[3] Bull. 5-1995, point 1.4.91.
[4] COM(95) 73; Bull. 3-1995, point 1.4.80.
[5] Bull. 6-1995, point 1.4.101.
[6] Bull. 6-1995, point 1.4.100.

Political dialogue

899.   The troika of political directors, including the Commission representative, held two meetings with their Japanese counterparts, first in Tokyo on
30 June and then in Madrid on 20 December. In addition to relations between the EU and Japan and the possibilities of stepping up the political
dialogue, the participants broached a series of other issues such as regional
concerns in Europe and Asia, overall relations between the EU, Japan and
the United States, and the United Nations.

Economic and trade relations

900.   During his visit to Tokyo from 4 to 7 June,[1] Sir Leon Brittan met the
Japanese Prime Minister, Mr Tomiichi Murayama, the Foreign Minister, Mr
Yohei Kono, and the Minister for International Trade and Industry, Mr
Ryutaro Hashimoto. Their discussions centred on the development of relations between the European Union and Japan, the opening-up of Japan's financial services market and access to the country's car market. During this
visit, Sir Leon was accompanied by representatives of major European industries, who participated in a number of fruitful meetings with representatives of government and industry. In order to maintain the momentum
achieved, Sir Leon also visited Japan from 17 to 20 September for a series
of bilateral meetings with members of the government.

901.   A high-level meeting was held on 9 and 10 February to examine the
Japanese Government's latest deregulation plan, drafted in May and set to
run for five years. Although the individual measures announced were slightly
disappointing, the programme was welcomed by the Commission as a step
in the right direction. The duration of the programme was subsequently reduced to three years by the Japanese authorities. At the high-level consultations held on 7 November as part of the ongoing review of this programme,
the European Union presented the Japanese Government with a revised list
of deregulation requests.

902.   The third meeting in the framework of the dialogue on industrial
policy and cooperation held in Brussels on 19 June led to an increase in the
number of sectors covered. On their visit to Europe in November and
December, representatives of the Japanese employers' association, Keidan-
ren, held meetings with Mr Santer, Sir Leon Brittan and Mrs Cresson. In the
framework of the annual consultations provided for by the arrangements

---

[1]   Bull. 6-1995, point 1.4.100.

for trade in motor vehicles signed by the Community and Japan in July 1991,[1] the Japanese Government and the Commission set export forecasts for 1995 taking into account the accession of the new Member States. In contrast, consultations in the framework of Article XXII of the GATT on the divergent levels of taxes on spirituous drinks having failed to bear fruit, the European Union called for the establishment of a special WTO group. The opening round of negotiations to pave the way for mutual recognition agreements in the field of testing and certification (→ point 753) took place in Tokyo from 16 to 19 May. These talks were followed by a further meeting in Brussels from 11 to 13 December. In the social sphere, the dialogue launched in 1990 was followed by annual meetings of high-ranking officials in Brussels and Japan. There were also high-level meetings in other sectors, particularly finance, telecommunications and competition.

903.   On 23 May the Commission adopted a proposal for a Council Regulation (Table II) on measures to promote exports to Japan. The second meeting of the Committee on Trade Cooperation took place on 3 July, after links had been established between Community export promotion programmes (→ point 759) and the Japanese import promotion programme.

904.   The Commission monitored developments in relations between the United States and Japan in a number of areas, particularly cars and car parts, mobile telephones, semiconductors, medical equipment and financial services. The US-Japan trade dispute in the motor vehicle sector featured in the Council conclusions of 29 May.[2]

Australia

905.   There was a shift in emphasis in relations between the European Union and Australia: the agricultural problems that had hitherto dominated relations diminished in importance following the entry into force of the WTO agreement on agriculture. Australia is eager to deepen its relations with the European Union — its major economic partner — if account is taken of trade in goods and services and investments as a whole. Mr Santer and Australian Prime Minister Paul Keating both favoured a more formal, more structured relationship. The two parties underlined their common desire to avoid letting the dispute between France and Australia on nuclear testing affect Australia's relations with the European Union. Sir Leon Brittan met a parliamentary delegation led by Australia's Minister for Develop-

---

[1]   Twenty-fifth General Report, point 863.
[2]   Bull. 5-1995, point 1.4.92.

ment Cooperation and Pacific Island Affairs, Mr Gordon Bilney, which included Mr Alexander Downer, the opposition Foreign Affairs Spokesman, who was touring major European capitals to put across Australia's views on French nuclear testing. At a political dialogue meeting with Australian Foreign Minister Gareth Evans in Madrid on 5 October,[1] the Presidency and the Commission were represented respectively by Spain's Foreign Minister, Mr Javier Solana Madariaga, and Sir Leon Brittan. Mr Evans confirmed his government's wish to negotiate a framework agreement with the European Union. The prospects for the IGC (→ point 1025) and the enlargement of the European Union were also on the agenda, along with issues relating to the Asia-Pacific region.

906.   Sir Leon Brittan and Mr Fischler met Mr Bob McMullan, Australian Minister for Trade, in Brussels on 15 May[2] at the 12th EC-Australia ministerial meeting. Discussions centred on the strengthening of bilateral cooperation in areas such as employment, science and technology, mutual recognition of standards, industry, the environment and development cooperation, and the extension of cooperation to new fields such as competition, education and training, customs and the information society. Talks on agriculture focused on market access arrangements for certain products and cooperation on veterinary matters. More generally, European Union relations with the Asia-Pacific region were discussed, as was the need to ensure the success of the WTO.

Canada

907.   The key event in relations between the European Union and Canada in 1995 was the fishing dispute concerning Greenland halibut in the restricted area of the North-West Atlantic Fisheries Organization (NAFO), which was resolved by a bilateral agreement signed on 20 April and endorsed by all parties to NAFO in September (→ point 578).

908.   Two meetings were held in June in the framework of the 1990 EEC-Canada Transatlantic Declaration.[3] On 17 June,[4] on the sidelines of the G7 Summit in Halifax, Mr Santer and Sir Leon Brittan, Mr Jacques Chirac, President of France and President of the Council, accompanied by several French ministers, met Canadian Prime Minister Jean Chrétien and members of his government. The strengthening of transatlantic relations, the fisheries

---

[1]   Bull. 10-1995, point 1.4.97.
[2]   Bull. 5-1995, point 1.4.96.
[3]   Twenty-fourth General Report, point 712.
[4]   Bull. 6-1995, point 1.4.102.

agreement *(→ point 578)* and problems connected with the fur trade were tackled and an agreement signed on science and technology *(→ point 257)*. These discussions followed on from the meeting in Paris on 1 June at which Sir Leon and Mr Hervé de Charette, French Foreign Minister, had met Canada's Foreign Minister, Mr André Ouellet. Despite the problems concerning fisheries, the European Union and Canada continued to see eye to eye on international politics, jointly supporting the peace efforts in the former Yugoslavia and backing the reforms in the former Soviet Union. In the field of cooperation, agreements were concluded on science and technology and on higher education and vocational training *(→ point 285)*. In the nuclear field *(→ point 378)*, two memoranda of understanding were signed on cooperation in the area of controlled fusion and on participation in the ITER programme. Finally, the Council adopted negotiating directives with a view to concluding an agreement on the application of competition rules *(→ point 173)*.

New Zealand

909.   As part of the political dialogue, an EU-New Zealand meeting was held on 29 September during the United Nations General Assembly in New York, the main topics of discussion being bilateral relations, relations between the European Union and the Asia-Pacific region, and the situation in the former Yugoslavia. Mrs Bjerregaard met a New Zealand parliamentary delegation in Brussels on 6 September to discuss the French nuclear tests. The two parties pledged to avoid letting the dispute affect relations with the European Union. With trade disputes increasingly being dealt with by the World Trade Organization and New Zealand seeking to broaden its international relations, progress was made towards a more structured relationship.

Section 12

Relations with the countries of Asia

Overview and relations with regional groupings

910. In the light of Asia's growing economic and political importance in the world, the Commission's main concern in 1995 was to implement the new strategy for Asia which it set out in its 1994 communication,[1] and which was approved by the Essen European Council,[2] and by Parliament in its resolution of 14 June.[3] The Commission also launched studies for communications in the energy and information technology sectors. It played an active role with the Council Presidency in preparing the Euro-Asian Summit to be held in March 1996 which will bring together for the first time the Heads of State or Government of the European Union, ASEAN countries, China, Japan and the Republic of Korea. The Cannes and Madrid European Councils underlined the importance of this initiative.[4] On 4 December[5] the Council approved a report on the European Union position.

911. The ASEAN[6] regional forum met in Brunei on 1 August. The European Union was represented by the President of the Council, Mr Javier Solana Madariaga, Spanish Foreign Minister, and Mr Marín. Political problems in the Pacific region were discussed. The post-ministerial conference was held in Brunei on 2 and 3 August and was attended by the European troika. The inaugural meeting of ASEAN-EU senior officials was held in Singapore in May following the 11th EU-ASEAN ministerial meeting in 1994.[7]

---

[1]   COM(94) 314; 1994 General Report, point 875.
[2]   Bull. 12-1994, point I.18.
[3]   OJ C 166, 3.7.1995; Bull. 6-1995, point 1.4.103.
[4]   Bull. 6-1995, point I.16; Bull. 12-1995.
[5]   Bull 12-1995.
[6]   ASEAN comprises Brunei, Indonesia, Malaysia, Philippines, Singapore, Thailand and Vietnam.
[7]   1994 General Report, point 891.

Bilateral relations

South Asia

912. The European troika met the Indian Foreign Minister, Mr Prenab Mukherjee, in Paris on 6 April.[1] Both sides welcomed the start of the political dialogue institutionalized in 1994 and the achievements of economic cooperation since the entry into force of the agreement concluded in the same year.[2] Mr Marín visited New Delhi from 27 to 29 March,[3] where he met the Indian President, Mr Shankar Dayal Sharma, and several members of the Indian Government.

913. The cooperation agreement between the European Community and Nepal (Table III) was signed on 20 November. The agreement is based on respect for human rights and democracy. This first agreement between the Community and Nepal is a third-generation non-preferential agreement and does not contain a financial protocol. Its aim is to develop all forms of economic cooperation, with particular emphasis on trade and investment, and to foster environmental protection, regional cooperation and a better quality of life.

914. On 27 March the Council adopted the decision concerning the conclusion of the cooperation agreement between the European Community and the Democratic Socialist Republic of Sri Lanka on partnership and development (Table III). The agreement, based on respect for human rights and democratic principles, is non-preferential and does not contain a financial protocol. Its objective is to promote all forms of economic cooperation, and a joint declaration adopted when the agreement was signed calls for the establishment of political dialogue. At its meeting in Brussels in June the Joint Committee on Trade and Cooperation underlined the significance of the peace process for Sri Lanka's economic development. Parliament expressed the same view on 18 May[4] and 16 November.[5]

South-East Asia

915. The cooperation agreement between the European Community and Vietnam (Table III) was signed on 17 July. This third-generation non-pref-

---

[1] Bull. 4-1995, point 1.4.87.
[2] 1994 General Report, point 877.
[3] Bull. 3-1995, point 1.4.83.
[4] OJ C 151, 19.6.1995; Bull. 5-1995, point 1.4.97.
[5] OJ C 323, 4.12.1995; Bull 11-1995, point 1.4.93.

erential agreement, which is based on respect for human rights and democratic principles, contains provisions on the diversification of trade, greater
market access, closer cooperation in various sectors and environmental protection. Mr Marín paid a visit to Vietnam in September[1] and the Vietnamese Foreign Minister, Nguyen Manh Cam, visited the Commission on
18 July.[2] Mr Marín also paid a visit to Manila in the Philippines from 23 to
26 March.

China

916. On 5 July the Commission adopted a communication on a long-term
policy for China-Europe relations.[3] In the communication, which forms part
of the Commission's new strategy for Asia *(→ point 910)*, the Commission
underlines China's importance for Europe and the many areas of joint interest where closer relations are required in the future. It also calls for China
to play a more constructive role in the international community on political
and human rights issues, and stresses the importance of a smooth transfer
of sovereignty for Hong Kong and Macao. On economic and trade relations,
the Commission notes that there has been a huge increase in trade over the
last few years and points out the basic reforms which have already been undertaken. It does, however, recognize that the Chinese economy does not yet
comply with accepted international rules in a number of areas and that
China will have to remedy this situation if it is to be accepted into the World
Trade Organization. It calls for dialogue in various areas to promote mutual understanding and identify common interests, and for a closer cooperation programme focusing on human resources, continuing reform, measures
to alleviate poverty, environmental protection, business cooperation and
closer links on research. The Commission closes by stressing the need to
improve coordination of activities within the European Union and to raise
Europe's profile in China. This strategy was approved by the Council in its
conclusions of 4 December[4] and by the Madrid European Council.[4]

917. Sir Leon Brittan paid a visit to China in April[5] where he met representatives of the National People's Congress for discussions on various aspects of the European Union's relations with China. As part of the structured political dialogue established in 1994[6] the troika of EU Foreign Ministers and Mr Van den Broek met the Chinese Foreign Affairs Minister, Qian

---

[1]   Bull. 9-1995, point 1.4.54.
[2]   Bull. 7/8-1995, point 1.4.101.
[3]   COM(95) 279; Bull. 7/8-1995, point 1.4.98.
[4]   Bull. 12-1995.
[5]   Bull. 4-1995, point 1.4.85.
[6]   1994 General Report, point 887.

Qichen, at the United Nations General Assembly on 25 September. A new human rights organization held its first meeting in January.

918.   The Joint Committee held its annual meeting from 6 to 9 October,[1] chaired by Sir Leon Brittan and Wu Yi, Foreign Trade and Economic Cooperation Minister. The 20th anniversary of the establishment of bilateral relations and the 10th anniversary of the signing of the EC-China trade and economic cooperation agreement provided an opportunity to assess the progress made in trade and economic relations. Discussions ranged from China's accession to the WTO to the European Union's long-term policy and its strategy for Asia. An EC-China economic forum was also held and an EC-China working party on environmental cooperation met for the first time on 9 October.[1]

Republic of Korea

919.   On 6 March the Council adopted negotiating directives for a framework trade and cooperation agreement with the Republic of Korea (Table III). The aim of this non-preferential agreement is to provide a framework for closer bilateral economic relations between the European Community and the Republic of Korea, and to promote exchanges of information and mutually beneficial investment. The agreement will be based on respect for democratic principles and human rights. It will provide for a joint committee and will contain general provisions covering trade, economic and industrial cooperation, scientific and technological cooperation, and cultural and environmental cooperation. Negotiations began on 11 May in Brussels. A joint declaration on a political dialogue was also under negotiation.

920.   On 14 March[2] President Kim Young-Sam paid an official visit to the Commission to meet President Santer, the first visit of a Korean president to the Commission since 1986. The two sides reaffirmed their determination to forge closer links and quickly complete the negotiations on a framework agreement. President Kim Young-Sam had met the President of the Council in Paris on 2 March.

921.   On 28 November[3] the 11th EC-Republic of Korea ministerial meeting was held in Seoul. The Community delegation was led by Sir Leon Brittan and the Korean delegation by the Foreign Minister, Gong Ro Myung. Both sides called for closer economic and trade relations which they would

---

[1]   Bull. 10-1995, point 1.4.98.
[2]   Bull. 3-1995, point 1.4.82.
[3]   Bull. 11-1995, point 1.4.91.

like to see eventually extend to political matters (particular emphasis was put on the European Union's participation in the Korean Peninsula Energy Development Organization). They also discussed ways of promoting Korean participation in world affairs and a greater EU presence in Asia. The talks were held in a spirit of mutual confidence that the framework agreement would be concluded shortly.

922.   Preparatory talks were held on sectoral negotiations for an agreement on mutual recognition of conformity assessment. Negotiations on public procurement were started and the negotiations on a customs cooperation agreement continued.

Other countries (Hong Kong)

923.   Hong Kong's Chief Secretary, Anson Chan, met Mr Santer and Sir Leon Brittan on 24 April.[1] This meeting provided an opportunity to discuss EU-Hong Kong relations and future cooperation, in particular on trade.

Cooperation

924.   New horizontal programmes were drawn up under the new strategy for Asia based on partnership and decentralized cooperation and cultural cooperation. Financial and technical cooperation with Asia accounted for ECU 376 million (compared with ECU 280 million in 1994) and economic cooperation for ECU 91.54 million (compared with ECU 59 million in 1994). Operations focused on a variety of sectors ranging from rural development, education and training to health, environmental protection and regional cooperation.

---

[1]   Bull. 4-1995, point 1.4.86.

Section 13

Latin America

925. On 23 October the Commission adopted a communication on strengthening relations between the European Union and Latin America entitled 'The European Union and Latin America: the present situation and prospects for closer partnership 1996-2000'[1] in which it suggested that the strategy for strengthening these relations be based on the tightening of political ties, the stepping-up of economic integration and free trade and the focusing of cooperation on priority areas. The communication was the subject of Council conclusions of 4 December,[2] with the Madrid European Council calling for swift progress in boosting cooperation.[2]

Relations with regional groupings

926. In the light of the conclusions of the Corfu and Essen European Councils[3] and the Solemn Joint Declaration between the European Union and Mercosur,[4] the Commission negotiated an interregional framework commercial and economic cooperation Agreement with Mercosur[5] aimed at strengthening existing ties and preparing for eventual association (Table III). The Agreement, signed in Madrid on 15 December, provides for cooperation in the economic, trade, industrial, scientific, institutional and cultural fields and the promotion of wider political dialogue on issues of mutual interest. On 20 November the Council decided to put the Agreement's trade component into effect on a provisional basis. Both Parliament, in a resolution on 16 May,[6] and the Economic and Social Committee, in an own-initiative opinion of 25 October,[7] welcomed the Solemn Joint Declaration made in December 1994 and supported the strategy adopted at the same time for achieving an interregional political and economic association.

927. The 11th San José ministerial conference between the European Union and Central America[8] — part of the dialogue launched in San José in

---

[1]   COM(95) 495; Bull. 10-1995, point 1.4.102.
[2]   Bull. 12-1995.
[3]   Bull. 6-1994, point I.20; Bull. 12-1994, point I.19; 1994 General Report, point 896.
[4]   OJ C 377, 31.12.1994; 1994 General Report, point 896.
[5]   Mercosur: the Southern Cone Common Market (Argentina, Brazil, Paraguay and Uruguay).
[6]   OJ C 151, 9.6.1995; Bull. 5-1995, point 1.4.101.
[7]   Bull. 10-1995, point 1.4.104.
[8]   Costa Rica, El Salvador, Guatemala, Honduras, Nicaragua and Panama.

1984[1] — was held in Panama on 23 and 24 February.[2] The meeting was attended by ministerial representatives of the European Union and the countries of Central America, with Colombia, Mexico and Venezuela as cooperating countries and Belize in the role of observer. Mr Marín represented the Commission. The conference closed with the adoption of a declaration on strengthening relations between the two parties and continuing initiatives to promote peace, human rights and democracy. It also announced closer cooperation on reducing social injustice, modernizing the State and combating organized crime and drug trafficking. On 29 November the Commission adopted a recommendation for a Council Decision (Table III) on recasting the basic objectives of the San José dialogue (making the peace process and democratization in Central America irreversible by consolidating the rule of law, creating social stability, reducing inequalities and integrating the region into the world economy), adjusting its mechanisms and shifting the focus of cooperation between the partners in the dialogue to its new objectives. The recommendation was received with interest by the Madrid European Council.[3]

928.   As part of the political and economic dialogue institutionalized by the declaration adopted in Rome in December 1990,[4] a meeting took place in Paris on 17 March[5] involving the Foreign Ministers of the permanent members of the Rio Group,[6] together with Nicaragua and Trinidad and Tobago, designated as observers for Central America and the Caribbean respectively, and the Foreign Ministers of the European Union. Mr Marín also attended. The declaration adopted at the end of the meeting chiefly concerned the implementation of the action programme approved at the World Summit on Social Development (→ point 779), dealing with regional integration and improving trade and investment between the two regions.

929.   Following negotiations opened by the Commission on accords covering drug precursors and chemical substances, agreements were signed on 18 December with five Andean countries: Bolivia, Colombia, Ecuador, Peru and Venezuela (→ point 975).

---

[1]   Eighteenth General Report, point 707.
[2]   Bull. 1/2-1995, point 1.4.105.
[3]   Bull. 12-1995.
[4]   Twenty-seventh General Report, point 769.
[5]   Bull. 3-1995, point 1.4.86.
[6]   Argentina, Bolivia, Brazil, Chile, Colombia, Ecuador, Mexico, Panama, Paraguay, Peru, Uruguay and Venezuela.

Bilateral relations

930.   In the wake of the conclusions of the Corfu[1] and Essen[2] European Councils, the Commission tabled a communication on 8 February setting out a strategy for strengthening the Union's policy *vis-à-vis* Mexico.[3] Given Mexico's economic and political development and the strategic importance of EU-Mexico relations, the Commission proposed basing its strategy on an economic partnership and political consultation agreement. The Council and the Commission signed a Solemn Joint Declaration with Mexico in Paris on 2 May relating to the two parties' shared objectives, the content of a new agreement and preparations for its negotiation.[4] It was against this background that Mr Marín visited Mexico in February[5] where he met President Ernesto Zedillo, Mr José Angel Gurría, Foreign Minister, and Mr Herminio Blanco, Minister for Trade. Mr Gurría and Mr Blanco also visited the Commission during the year.[6] In a resolution on 17 November, Parliament expressed its support for the strategy proposed.[7] The Economic and Social Committee adopted an own-initiative opinion on relations between the European Union and Mexico on 21 December.[8]

931.   On 31 May the Commission, in response to a request from the Essen European Council,[2] presented an assessment of the economic situation and external relations of Chile[9] and defined strategic options at regional level (in the Mercosur framework) and bilateral level in response to Chile's desire for closer ties with the European Union. On 8 November the Commission, acting on a request from the Council on 17 July,[10] presented a recommendation for a decision on a new agreement between the European Union and Chile (Table III) providing for increased cooperation and the eventual establishment of a political and economic association. A joint declaration on political dialogue was signed in Madrid on 18 December.[8] Chile's President, Mr Eduardo Frei, visited the Commission on 8 March,[11] while Mr Marín visited Chile on 17 and 18 October.[12]

---

[1]   Bull. 6-1994, point I.20; 1994 General Report, point 906.
[2]   Bull. 12-1994, point I.19.
[3]   COM(95) 3; Bull. 1/2-1995, point 1.4.107.
[4]   Bull. 5-1995, point 1.4.104 (full text of the Declaration).
[5]   Bull. 1/2-1995, point 1.4.108.
[6]   Bull. 3-1995, point 1.4.90; Bull.9-1995, point 1.4.57.
[7]   OJ C 323, 4.12.1995; Bull. 11-1995, point 1.4.98.
[8]   Bull. 12-1995.
[9]   Twenty-fifth General Report, point 943; Bull. 5-1995, point 1.4.102.
[10]   Bull. 7/8-1995, point 1.4.104.
[11]   Bull. 3-1995, point 1.4.87.
[12]   Bull. 10-1995, point 1.4.107.

932.   In a communication on 28 June, the Commission proposed the initiation of a dialogue with Cuba[1] based on regular consultations, the principal aim being to determine a framework for future relations, taking into account the economic and institutional changes under way in that country. In its conclusions of 2 October,[2] the Council confirmed the Union's desire to strengthen relations with Cuba, a view endorsed by the Madrid European Council in December.[3] It was against this background that the EU troika paid its first visit to Cuba. Ms Bonino also met President Fidel Castro there in May (→ point 807).[4]

933.   The President of Brazil, Mr Fernando Henrique Cardoso, paid a visit to the Commission on 14 September[5] and met Mr Santer. This was the first visit to the Commission by a Brazilian president since the country's return to democracy. Mr Cardoso expressed Brazil's desire to extend and strengthen relations with the European Union. On 30 October the Council adopted Decision 95/445/EC on the conclusion of a framework cooperation agreement with Brazil (Table III).

934.   Mr Ernesto Samper, President of Colombia, visited the Commission in March[6] for discussions on the development of bilateral relations, the functioning of the Andean Pact (Colombia held the presidency of the Pact in 1995) and the Colombian Government's efforts on drug abuse control. On the latter point, the Commission announced its intention of studying ways of setting up a multilateral regional cooperation framework to combat drugs. During his visit to Costa Rica on 21 and 22 June,[7] Mr Marín held talks with President José-Maria Figueres Olsen and Mr Fernando Naranjo, the Foreign Minister; bilateral relations and relations between the Union and Central America in the San José context were the main issues broached (→ point 927). Mr Ramiro de León Carpio, President of Guatemala,[8] paid a visit to the Commission on 1 March and held talks on all facets of his country's relations with the European Union, measures to alleviate poverty, and the EU's support for reconciliation and economic progress in Guatemala. Mr Marín met Mr Rafael Caldera Rodriguez, the Venezuelan President, and Mr Miguel Angel Burelli Rivas, Foreign Minister,[9] in Venezuela in June for talks on bilateral relations, the generalized scheme of preferences

---

[1]   COM(95) 306; Bull. 6-1995, point 1.4.110.
[2]   Bull. 10-1995, point 1.4.108.
[3]   Bull. 12-1995.
[4]   Bull. 5-1995, point 1.4.103.
[5]   Bull. 9-1995, point 1.4.56.
[6]   Bull. 3-1995, point 1.4.88.
[7]   Bull. 6-1995, point 1.4.109.
[8]   Bull. 3-1995, point 1.4.89.
[9]   Bull. 6-1995, point 1.4.111.

and the prospects for a bilateral fisheries agreement. President Gonzalo Sanchez de Lozada of Bolivia visited the Commission on 13 October.[1] On 17 November, Dr Julio Maria Sanguinetti, President of Uruguay, called on the Commission.[2] In his capacity as acting President of the Mercosur Council he underlined the importance of the entry into force of the framework EU-Mercosur Agreement in 1996. Parliament adopted a resolution on 16 February on the border dispute between Peru and Ecuador and the safety of the indigenous communities.[3] The joint committee meetings between the Union and various countries of Latin America provided the opportunity to highlight developments in their relations and examine cooperation in depth.[4]

Aid activities

935.   Financial and technical assistance for the countries of Latin America, the main instrument for dispensing aid to the region, amounted in 1995 to ECU 205 million, while economic assistance totalled ECU 56 million. Other aid schemes implemented at a cost of around ECU 80 million concerned democratization, drug abuse control, rehabilitation and aid for refugees and displaced persons. Programmes covering food aid, NGOs, energy, research, science and technology, the environment and tropical forests accounted for ECU 180 million. The total aid granted to Latin America in 1995 amounted to ECU 520 million.

---

[1]   Bull. 10-1995, point 1.4.105.
[2]   Bull. 11-1995, point 1.4.99.
[3]   OJ C 56, 6.3.1995; Bull. 1/2-1995, point 1.4.106.
[4]   Paraguay and Uruguay in June, Chile and Argentina in September.

Section 14

Relations with the African, Caribbean and Pacific (ACP) countries, South Africa and the overseas countries and territories (OCTs)

Relations with ACP countries

Lomé IV Convention

Mid-term review

936.   Launched on 20 May last year,[1] talks on the mid-term review of the Lomé IV Convention and renewal of its financial protocol were wound up at the ACP-EC ministerial conference on 30 June this year,[2] after some problems in finalizing the EU's financial package for the second period of the Convention's lifetime (1995-2000). These difficulties, which cut short the ACP-EC ministerial conference on 16 February *(→ point 946)*, were finally overcome at the Cannes European Council.[3] The agreement amending the fourth ACP-EC Convention (Table III) was signed in Mauritius on 4 November at the 22nd meeting of the ACP-EC Council. The European Council meeting in Madrid in December welcomed the signing. With total funding for the ACP countries[4] over the next five-year period set at ECU 14 625 billion, of which ECU 12 967 billion comes from the eighth EDF and ECU 1 658 billion from EIB operations, the EU contribution (which is mainly in the form of grants) was up 21.6% on the previous five-year period. This reflects a desire to maintain aid levels in real terms to the ACP at a time when bilateral aid is stagnating or falling and other parts of the world are making demands on Community assistance. Renewal of the EDF was the subject of a Parliament resolution on 2 March.[5]

In addition to renewal of the financial protocol, the mid-term review opened the way for new additions to Lomé IV, tailoring ACP-EC cooperation to changes since 1989, when the Convention was signed, and making its vari-

---

[1]   1994 General Report, point 918.
[2]   Bull. 6-1995, point 1.4.115.
[3]   Bull. 6-1995, points 1.19 and 1.58.
[4]   In addition to the total of ECU 14 625 billion made available to the ACP countries, a further ECU 200 million is made available to the OCT (EDF = ECU 165 million, EIB = ECU 35 million).
[5]   OJ C 68, 20.3.1995; Bull. 3-1995, point 1.4.93.

ous aid instruments more effective. The main additions were: an emphasis on the protection of human rights and support for the democratic process; enhanced political dialogue; development of trade and greater access for ACP farm produce to the Community market; improvements to aid instruments in specific areas of cooperation; greater flexibility in financial and technical cooperation, particularly in connection with the programming of aid.

Implementation

937.   While the second financial protocol for Lomé IV was being negotiated, the Commission launched the financial and technical aid programming round, taking advantage of the time before ratification of the protocol to finalize indicative programmes, the cornerstone of Community cooperation with the ACP, and speed up implementation of the revised Convention. In accordance with new Lomé IV rules aimed at more effective use of resources, funding was programmed in two instalments, with the second tranche only being released if a mid-term assessment showed that resources had been used properly during the first. On 3 November, on a proposal from the Commission, the ACP-EC Council adopted a decision to ensure that Sysmin, Stabex, structural adjustment, emergency assistance and refugee aid operations under the seventh EDF could continue beyond 1 March.[1] On 18 December the Council adopted transitional measures provisionally applying certain clauses of the revised convention.[2]

Trade cooperation

938.   Over the year, ACP-EC cooperation activities were thoroughly reviewed in a bid to boost trade. The pilot ACP-EC trade development project got under way. National and subregional trade development programmes were drawn up for the Caribbean, the Indian Ocean, West Africa, Kenya, Namibia and South Africa (→ point 953). Cooperation through trade federations bodies such as Aproma and Coleacp was stepped up, with particular emphasis on the creation of national and regional associations for those involved in the commodity and fruit and vegetable sectors. Collaboration with Member States was boosted through the forum for national import promotion bodies. Cooperation with Unctad (→ point 782) also developed under the effective trade programme launched last year. In the tourism sec-

---

[1]   Bull. 11-1995, point 1.4.103.
[2]   Bull. 12-1995.

tor, new support programmes were prepared for the Caribbean and for a number of southern African countries.

Stabex

939. On 24 July[1] the Commission approved the Stabex transfers for 1994 and on 31 October adopted a report on the subject for the ACP-EU Committee of Ambassadors.[2] 26 ACP states were eligible for 30 transfers to the tune of ECU 138 089 469. For the first time since Lomé IV came into force, it was possible to cover all ACP earnings losses. In October the Commission adopted a report on the operation of Stabex in 1994.[3]

Sysmin

940. The last of the eight projects from Lomé II, all now completed, were closed at a cost of ECU 191 million. Commitments under Lomé III totalled ECU 159 million for 10 projects. Over ECU 100 million had been spent by the end of the year. The Togo phosphates programme was suspended because of the political situation. From a total package of ECU 480 million under Lomé IV, financing decisions worth ECU 292 million were taken and ECU 74 million paid out. Three financing decisions were taken: ECU 58 million to help Mauritania restart iron-ore production; ECU 11 million for repairs to a gold mine in Burkina Faso and ECU 15 million for geological mapping work. A number of countries applied for Sysmin aid. By the end of the year, eligibility and project evaluation studies were under way for Surinam, Botswana, Guinea, Jamaica, New Caledonia and Zimbabwe.

Support for ACP banana producers

941. In order to help traditional ACP banana suppliers maintain their position on the Community market, Regulation (EC) No 2686/94 introduced a special assistance system to accommodate changes arising from the new common organization of the banana market in July 1993.[4] The Regulation made provision for two types of assistance: earnings support to supplement Stabex payments (calculated retrospectively), and technical and financial assistance for projects to improve quality and competitiveness. This year, earnings support was calculated for 1994. However, no aid was paid out since

[1]   Bull. 7/8-1995, point 1.4.109.
[2]   Bull. 10-1995, point 1.4.118.
[3]   COM(95) 501; Bull. 10-1995, point 1.4.117.
[4]   1994 General Report, point 914.

Stabex payments covered losses in full. A number of projects were launched to take advantage of the ECU 30 million of technical and financial assistance still available.

Sugar protocol

942. On 17 July, the Council adopted a decision on the conclusion of agreements with ACP sugar suppliers and India on a special annual preferential import quota for unrefined cane sugar for the period 1 July 1995 to 30 June 2001. (Table III). The new quota comes on top of the quantities fixed in the sugar protocol and will be set annually on the basis of the Community's refining needs. On 22 May, the Council also approved Zambian membership of the sugar protocol annexed to the Lomé IV Convention as from 1 January 1995 (Table III). On 24 October the Council adopted the negotiating directives for an agreement on the guaranteed prices of sugar cane from ACP countries for the 1995-96 delivery period. (Table III). On 29 November it adopted Decision 95/518/EC concluding the agreement setting the price guarantees for the period 1994-95 (Table III).

Industrial cooperation

943. Industrial cooperation continued, with a number of private sector support programmes and projects under consideration, approved or under way in Barbados, Burkina Faso, Burundi, Cameroon, Comoros, Côte d'Ivoire, the Dominican Republic, Ethiopia, Ghana, Guyana, Jamaica, Mauritius, Namibia, Niger, Seychelles, Swaziland, Tanzania, Togo, Trinidad and Tobago and Zimbabwe. The third meeting of the Advisory Council to the Committee on Industrial Cooperation reviewed progress in this area and looked at investment flows between the Community and ACP countries. The Commission organized an industrial forum on building materials for Central Africa in Libreville and another for the West-African agro-industrial sector in Dakar.

Financial and technical cooperation

944. At the start of the year, funding for eligible countries was reapportioned (see Table 14). Financing decisions were adopted for 18 countries, with ECU 141 million coming from specific structural adjustment funds and ECU 98 million from the programmable resources for the individual countries. In addition, a resolution was adopted by the Council on 1 June, laying down the EC guidelines for structural adjustment support, on the basis of a communication from the Commission *(→ point 778).*

TABLE 14

Annual breakdown of financing decisions for ACP countries

(million ECU)

Sector	1991	1992	1993	1994	1995[1]
Trade promotion	18.270	40.833	85.054	30.008	57.143
Social and cultural development	29.693	209.535	340.891	151.826	129.456
• Education and training	2.589	73.548	94.241	101.217	36.604
• Water engineering, urban infrastructure	21.190	54.351	140.353	36.946	35.835
• Health	5.914	81.636	38.526	13.663	57.016
Economic infrastructure	254.741	310.105	181.714	319.303	188.930
• Transport and communications	254.741	310.105	181.714	319.303	188.930
Development of production	213.433	811.651	876.226	578.203	462.614
• Rural production	95.154	209.941	227.925	169.731	93.203
• Industrialization	66.835	149.871	190.609	256.837	277.731
• Campaigns on specific themes[2]	51.444	451.839	457.692	151.635	91.679
Exceptional aid, Stabex	570.153	497.328	140.584	1 115.698	285.084
• Rehabilitation	(1.516)	9.828	(0.072)	221.289	105.954
• Disasters	43.495	58.858	110.094	249.810	32.678
• AIDS	4.000	0.320	1.700	3.752	9.625
• Refugees and returnees	7.905	31.295	25.640	25.675	−1.266
• Stabex	515.819	397.027	3.222	615.172	138.093
Other[3]	148.064	187.088	55.675	250.422	255.968
Total	1 234.354	2 056.540	1 680.144	2 445.460	1 379.197

[1] Provisional figures.
[2] Including desertification and drought, disasters, major endemic and epidemic diseases, hygiene and basic health, endemic cattle diseases, energy saving research, sectoral import programmes and long-term schemes.
[3] Including information and documentation, seminars, programmes and general technical cooperation, general studies, multi-sectoral programmes, delegations, administrative and financial costs, improvements to public buildings, project-linked multisectoral technical cooperation (all projects).

Regional cooperation

945.   The role of the private sector in successful regional integration was a key topic for the Commission. A wide range of activities included support for West African economic and monetary union and the start of the cross-border initiative to facilitate trade in eastern and southern Africa and the Indian Ocean. On 1 June the Council adopted a resolution (→ *point 778*) on EC support for regional integration efforts in developing countries and on 16 June the Commission adopted a communication on this subject (→ *point 778*). The Madrid European Council[1] welcomed the establishment of political dialogue between the European Union and the OAU, and in particular the Council conclusions of 4 December on preventive diplomacy, conflict settlement and peacekeeping in Africa.[1] A meeting between EU and OAU representatives took place on 7 December.[1]

Institutional relations

946. The 21st meeting of the ACP-EC Council of Ministers was held in Brussels on 16 February,[2] when the mid-term review of Lomé IV was discussed, particularly the level of funding for the eighth EDF. The 22nd meeting in Mauritius on 3 and 4 November[3] was taken up mainly with the signing of the revised Convention (→ *point 936*) and the protocol of accession to the Convention of Austria, Finland and Sweden, following the enlargement of the Union on 1 January (TableIII ACCA95.100). Discussions focused on trade cooperation (bananas and rum), Stabex (particularly transfers to Sudan and the addition of pumpkin to the list of qualifying products), and commodities (inclusion of fat other than cocoa butter in chocolate production). The Council also adopted a resolution on the implementation of financial and technical cooperation, and a decision concerning amendments to the list of least developed ACP countries. The ACP-EC Council devolved to the ACP-EC Committee of Ambassadors the power to adopt transitional measures to implement the revised Convention, and discussed such topics as rehabilitation, debt, South Africa and Somalia.

947. As usual the ACP-EC Joint Assembly held two sessions, one in Dakar from 30 January to 3 February and one in Brussels from 25 to 29 September.[4] At the Dakar session the Assembly discussed the progress of negotiations on the mid-term review of Lomé IV, looked ahead to its implementation and considered the specific problems of West Africa and the situation in a number of other ACP regions and countries, including the Great Lakes. At the September session in Brussels the Joint Assembly adopted the general report on infrastructures in the context of ACP-EC cooperation, and discussed the revision of Lomé IV, the second financial protocol, industrial and

---

[1]   Bull. 12-1995.
[2]   Bull. 1/2-1995, point 1.4.111.
[3]   Bull. 11-1995, point 1.4.106.
[4]   Bull. 1/2-1995, point 1.4.110; Bull. 9-1995, point 1.4.59.

urban development and the refugee situation in ACP countries. It debated in depth the future of relations between South Africa, the ACP countries and the EC, and went on to look at the current situation in Sudan, Eritrea, Mali, Rwanda, Burundi, Liberia and Somalia. Time was also spent examining the outcome of the Beijing Conference on Women *(→ point 633)*, the problems of climate change for small island nations and the resumption of nuclear testing in the Pacific. On 19 January Parliament adopted a resolution on the work of the Joint Assembly in 1994.[1]

Bilateral relations

948.   Following the Presidency's statement on 19 March that the EU's priority for Burundi was to consolidate the process of national reconciliation and the return to normal democracy,[2] the troika met a number of Burundian leaders on 24 March.[3] The same day the Council adopted common position 95/91/CFSP under Article J.2 of the Union Treaty,[4] pledging assistance for the government of Burundi. On 6 June the Council adopted Decision 95/206/CFSP on implementation of the common position and allocated ECU 1.5 million to support efforts by the Organization of African Unity (OAU) to send observers to the country,[5] for which a financing decision was adopted by the Commission on 25 July.[6] In response to the massacre at Kibeho in Rwanda, the Council and Commission adopted a declaration on 12 May temporarily suspending Community development aid programmes for the country.[7] This did not, however, affect humanitarian and emergency aid, assistance for the health and education sectors or measures to promote human rights and the rule of law. On 1 June, in the light of favourable messages from the Rwandan government, the Council and Commission adopted a declaration looking forward to a fresh political and technical dialogue and the resumption of all types of EC aid.[8] On 12 July, the Commission therefore approved the resumption of economic cooperation with Rwanda, first informing the Member States.[9] Parliament spoke out on Burundi and Rwanda on a number of occasions.[10] On 18 May, it adopted a resolution on the ebola epidemic in Zaire.[11] In December the Madrid European Coun-

---

[1]   OJ C 43, 20.2.1995; Bull. 1/2-1995, point 1.4.109.
[2]   Bull. 3-1995, point 1.4.6.
[3]   Bull. 3-1995, point 1.4.95.
[4]   OJ L 72, 1.4.1995; Bull. 3-1995, 1.4.94.
[5]   OJ L 130, 14.6.1995; Bull. 6-1995, point 1.4.116.
[6]   Bull. 7/8-1995, point 1.4.2.
[7]   Bull. 5-1995, point 1.4.108.
[8]   Bull. 6-1995, point 1.4.117.
[9]   Bull. 7/8-1995, point 1.4.113.
[10]   OJ C 43, 20.2.1995; Bull. 1/2-1995, point 1.4.113; OJ C 89, 10.4.1995; Bull. 3-1995, point 1.4.96; OJ C 109, 1.5.1995; Bull. 4-1995, point 1.4.92; OJ C 269, 16.10.1995; Bull. 9-1995, point 1.4.62.
[11]   OJ C 151, 19.6.1995; Bull. 5-1995, point 1.4.109.

cil stressed the importance of national reconciliation and stability in the Great Lakes region.[1]

949.   On 20 November the Council adopted common position 95/515/ CFSP on Nigeria,[2] followed on 4 December by Common position 95/544/ CFSP aimed at implementing restrictive measures against Nigeria and suspending development cooperation.[3] On 12 November the Commission adopted a declaration denouncing the acts of the Nigerian regime and announcing the suspension of cooperation with that country,[4] and on 16 November Parliament adopted a resolution on the issue.[5] In its conclusions the Madrid European Council voiced concern about the situation in Nigeria, confirmed the sanctions already adopted and threatened further measures if the situation failed to improve.[6]

950.   On the initiative of the UNDP and with the support of the Commission, a round table was held in Brussels on 25 and 26 September for donors contributing to the reconstruction effort in Angola.[7] On 2 October, the Council adopted common position 95/143/CFSP, in which it set out the EU's goals for Angola and the cooperation activities in which the it was willing to become involved.[8]

951.   In line with its policy of support for democratic government, the EU roundly condemned the military coup d'état on 15 August in São Tomé and Príncipe (→ point 706). The Commission confirmed its support for the democratically elected authorities on a visit to Brussels by President Trovoada on 27 September.[9]

Relations with South Africa

952.   Having supported the transition to democratic government in South Africa since 1986,[10] the EU entered into negotiations with a view to providing a framework for long-term cooperation with the country.

---

[1]   Bull. 12-1995.
[2]   OJ L 298, 11.12.1995; Bull. 11-1995, point 1.4.111.
[3]   OJ L 309, 21.12.1995; Bull. 12-1995.
[4]   OJ C 323, 4.12.1995; Bull. 11-1995, point 1.4.112.
[5]   Bull. 11-1995, point 1.4.110.
[6]   Bull. 12-1995.
[7]   Bull. 7/8-1995, point 1.4.61.
[8]   OJ L 245, 12.10.1995; Bull. 10-1995, point 1.4.121.
[9]   Bull. 9-1995, point 1.4.63.
[10]   1994 General Report, point 843.

953.   On 19 June, the Council adopted negotiating directives (Table III) with a view to concluding a trade and cooperation agreement with South Africa and a protocol on South African accession to the Lomé Convention. Negotiations opened in Brussels on 30 June and the Madrid European Council expressed its hopes for a speedy conclusion.[1] On 23 October, the Commission adopted a recommendation for a Council decision to supplement the trade provisions contained in the negotiating directives. The cooperation agreement should lead to a free trade area and would govern all economic and trading ties between the Community and South Africa as well as financial and technical cooperation. It would also contain a clause on human rights and democratic principles. In this connection, the South African Vice-President, Mr Thabo Mbeki, paid a visit to the Commission in February[2] and Mr de Deus Pinheiro visited South Africa in May.[3] Pending the conclusion of the agreement, scheduled for 1996, on 10 May the Commission adopted a proposal for a Council Regulation (Table II) to set up a European programme for reconstruction and development in South Africa with the aim of contributing to the sustainable social and economic development of the country and consolidating the foundations of a democratic society. This would to provide a legal basis for budget heading B-5070 (special programme for South Africa), introduced in 1986. The Council adopted a common position on the regulation on 20 December, and on the same day, the Economic and Social Committee adopted an own-initiative opinion on relations between the European Union and South Africa.[1]

954.   On 1 June, the Council adopted conclusions reaffirming its continuing commitment to development cooperation with South Africa aimed at contributing to sustainable economic and social development and consolidating a democratic society, while taking account of the country's specific social and economic features.[4] Parliament also spoke on relations with South Africa in June and October,[5] and on 23 October the Council adopted a Regulation extending generalized tariff preferences to agricultural products originating in South Africa (→ point 781).

Overseas countries and territories (OCTs)

955.   Implementation of the seventh EDF was stepped up in the overseas countries and territories whose indicative Community cooperation pro-

---

[1]   Bull. 12-1995.
[2]   Bull. 1/2-1995, point 1.4.114.
[3]   Bull. 5-1995, point 1.4.112.
[4]   Bull. 6-1995, point 1.4.119.
[5]   OJ C 166, 3.7.1995; Bull. 6-1995, point 1.4.120; OJ C 287, 30.10.1995; Bull. 10-1995, point 1.4.128.

grammes were signed last year,[1] with EDF commitment rates running at satisfactory levels. On 14 July, the Commission adopted a proposal for a Council decision (Table II) to ensure that Sysmin and Stabex operations for the OCT under the seventh EDF would continue.

956.   Much of the year was given over to the mid-term review of Decision 91/482/EEC on the association of the OCT to the EEC in the light of the memoranda from the relevant Member States[2] (France, Netherlands and the UK),[3] last year's communication from the Commission[3] and the Commission's official proposal to the Council of December this year on mid-term review. The Council based its work on the two options put forward by the Commission: in certain areas, particularly those connected with EDF management and relations with the EIB, talks would be conducted in tandem with those on the mid-term review of Lomé IV; in other areas, new initiatives specifically tailored to the OCT would continue. The position underlying this two-pronged approach is that while the OCT are not part of the Community (though they are associated with it and thus benefit from the EDF and the same types of development cooperation measures as ACP States), the Community has nevertheless opened its markets to OCT products and now proposes to recognize individual OCT nationals as citizens of the European Union.

957.   At the Cannes European Council,[4] funding from the eighth EDF and EIB for both the OCT and ACP was approved at the same time (→ point 936); the OCT's share was set at 1.28% of total eighth EDF resources. Funds for the OCT over the second five-year period covered by the association decision were increased by 21% overall on the first five years, with the EDF allocation rising 18% and the EIB allocation 40%. The final point of the mid-term review discussed by the Council was the breakdown of EDF resources between programmable grants and the various development instruments.

958.   On 23 January and 27 November the Council reduced the amount of transfers to the Falkland Islands under the export earnings stabilization system introduced by Decision 91/482/EEC for 1993[5] and 1994[6] respectively. Lastly, on 20 September the Council adopted a regulation amending Regulation (EC) No 1827/94 opening and providing for the administration of a

---

[1]   1994 General Report, point 940.
[2]   OJ L 263, 19.9.1991; Twenty-fifth General Report, point 984.
[3]   1994 General Report, point 941.
[4]   Bull. 6-1995, points I.19 and I.58.
[5]   Bull. 1/2-1995, point 1.4.115.
[6]   Bull. 11-1995, point 1.4.114.

tariff quota for rum, tafia and arrack originating in the OCT for the second half of 1995.

Chapter V

Cooperation in the fields of justice and home affairs

Section 1

Priority activities and objectives

959. The work of consolidating the new framework for cooperation established by the Union Treaty continued, and the Council achieved a number of significant results. March, for example, saw the signing of the first convention drawn up under Title VI of the Treaty, relating to simplified extradition, followed in July by three others, one of which concerns Europol, a major component of cooperation between the police forces of the Member States. In November, agreement was reached on an initial joint position within the meaning of Article K.3, concerning the interpretation of the term 'refugee' in Article 1A of the Geneva Convention. And on 25 September the Council adopted Joint Action 95/401/JHA and Decision 95/402/JHA defining the detailed arrangements for the financing by the Community of cooperation activities in the fields of justice and home affairs.[1]

In keeping with a practice established the previous year,[2] matters falling within the scope of cooperation in the fields of justice and home affairs were assigned an important place on the agenda for relations with various countries or regions. This was the case, for example, with the relaunching of the Transatlantic Dialogue (→ point 888) and the Euro-Mediterranean conference in Barcelona (→ point 839). Similarly, the first ministerial meetings took place under the structured dialogue with the associated countries of Central and Eastern Europe and the Baltic States[3] (→ point 814) and with Cyprus and Malta[4] (→ point 843).

---

[1]   OJ L 238, 6.10.1995; Bull. 9-1995, point 1.5.1.
[2]   1994 General Report, point 1074.
[3]   Bull. 6-1995, point 1.4.61; Bull. 9-1995, point 1.4.33.
[4]   Bull 9-1995, point 1.4.39.

However, these advances were not enough to allay the concerns raised by the operation of Title VI and the level of results achieved. In their different ways, Council, Commission and Parliament alike made observations to this effect in their separate reports to the Reflection Group set up to prepare for the Intergovernmental Conference, while the Reflection Group itself confirmed in its own report that the progress made was not commensurate with the challenges to be met (→ point 1026). As in 1994,[1] the European Parliament set out its criticisms in the Resolution adopted on 14 December at the close of its annual debate on the implementation of Title VI of the Treaty on European Union.[2] As for the Commission, its position was reflected in the communication on a possible application of Article K.9 of the Treaty on European Union adopted on 22 November,[3] in which it confirmed its commitment to defend at the Intergovernmental Conference the principle of bringing all fields covered by Article K.1, with the exception of police cooperation and judicial cooperation in criminal matters, within the Community system as such.

---

[1]   OJ C 18, 23.1.1995; 1994 General Report, point 1074.
[2]   OJ C 17, 22.1.1996; Bull. 12-1995.
[3]   COM(95) 566; Bull. 11-1995, point 1.5.1.

Section 2

Asylum, external frontiers and immigration

960. After reaching an agreement on 7 March,[1] the Council formally passed a Resolution on minimum guarantees for asylum procedures on 21 June,[2] confirming a number of principles to ensure that procedures comply with the Geneva Convention of 28 July 1951 on the Status of Refugees and the New York Protocol of 1967. On 23 November it agreed on the principle of a joint position, the first since the entry into force of the Union Treaty, concerning the harmonized application of the definition of the term 'refugee' for the purposes of Article 1A of the 1951 Convention.[3] National administrative bodies responsible for recognizing refugee status are called on to comply with the guidelines approved by the Council when applying the criteria set out in the Convention, without prejudice to the case-law that has been built up in the Member States.

961. As requested by the Cannes European Council,[4] the Council sent the Madrid European Council a report on progress in work on the draft Convention on the crossing of external frontiers. The European Council encouraged it to work for the earliest possible solution of outstanding questions.[5] Having completed work on the two proposals for Regulations on the uniform format for visas and the countries whose nationals must be in possession of a visa when crossing external frontiers (→ *point 3*), the Council proceeded on 23 November to agree on the principle of joint action on airport transit arrangements[6] and to approve a Recommendation on consular cooperation regarding visas.[7]

962. As requested by the Essen European Council,[8] the Council approved on 21 June[9] and passed on 25 September[10] a resolution on burden-sharing with regard to the admission and residence of displaced persons on a temporary basis. On 23 November it went on to adopt conclusions concerning an alert and emergency procedure for the efficient application of the prin-

---

[1]   Bull. 3-1995, point 1.5.1.
[2]   Bull. 6-1995, point 1.5.4.
[3]   Bull. 11-1995, point 1.5.2.
[4]   Bull. 6-1995, points I.20 to I.24.
[5]   Bull. 12-1995.
[6]   Bull. 11-1995, point 1.5.4.
[7]   Bull. 11-1995, point 1.5.5.
[8]   1994 General Report, point 1078.
[9]   Bull. 6-1995, point 1.5.3.
[10] OJ C 262, 7.10.1995; Bull. 9-1995, point 1.5.6.

ciples governing burden-sharing when crisis situations require swift action.[1]

963.   On 23 November the Council approved the principle of a Resolution[2] on the status of third-country nationals residing long-term in the territory of the Member States, whereby persons having been so resident for 10 years would automatically enjoy that status. On 22 December it also adopted a recommendation on harmonization of measures to combat illicit immigration and employment and to improve control measures.[3]

964.   Following up the 1994 recommendation on a standard form of bilateral readmission agreement,[4] the Council adopted a recommendation on 24 July on the principles for drafting Protocols on the implementation of readmission agreements.[5] On 23 November it reached agreement, with the Representatives of the Member States' Governments, on clauses to be considered for insertion in mixed agreements with non-member countries when negotiating instructions are adopted.[6] On 20 December the Council and the representatives of the Member States' governments adopted conclusions of a similar nature on the question of readmission in Community agreements.[3] On 23 November the Council also approved a Decision on monitoring the implementation of its decisions concerning admission of third-country nationals[7] and a recommendation on concerted action and cooperation in carrying out expulsion measures.[8] These were formally adopted on 22 December.[3]

965.   Parliament's resolution of 21 September[9] approved the general approach taken in the Commission communication of 23 February 1994 on immigration and asylum policies[10] and called for rapid presentation of a practical action programme. On 22 September Parliament passed a series of resolutions on instruments approved by the Council in 1994,[11] concerning the admission of third-country nationals to the Member States for the purposes of study[12] and of pursuing activities as self-employed persons,[13] and on the organization and development of the centre for information, discus-

[1]   Bull. 11-1995, point 1.5.3.
[2]   Bull. 11-1995, point 1.5.7.
[3]   Bull. 12-1995.
[4]   1994 General Report, point 1076.
[5]   Bull. 7/8-1995, point 1.5.1.
[6]   Bull. 7/8-1995, point 1.5.9.
[7]   Bull. 11-1995, point 1.5.8.
[8]   Bull. 11-1995, point 1.5.6.
[9]   OJ C 269, 16.10.1995; Bull. 9-1995, point 1.5.2.
[10]   1994 General Report, point 1075.
[11]   1994 General Report, point 1076.
[12]   OJ C 269, 16.10.1995; Bull. 9-1995, point 1.5.3.
[13]   OJ C 269, 16.10.1995; Bull. 9-1995, point 1.5.4.

sion and exchange on the crossing of frontiers and immigration (Cirefi).[1] On 6 April Parliament passed a resolution on the Schengen Agreement and asylum policy.[2]

---

[1]   OJ C 269, 16.10.1995; Bull. 9-1995, point 1.5.5.
[2]   OJ C 109, 1.5.1995; Bull. 4-1995, point 1.5.1.

Section 3

Judicial, customs and police cooperation

966.　On 10 March the Council, as requested by the Essen European Council,[1] adopted Joint Action 95/73/JHA concerning the Europol Drugs Unit (EDU) on the basis of Article K.3 of the Union Treaty.[2] This supersedes the Copenhagen Ministerial Agreement of 2 June 1993[3] and, in addition to encompassing three new Member States, is also extended to three new areas of criminal activity. After general agreement was reached on the specific provisions of the draft on 21 June[4] and the European Council had discussed the matter at Cannes,[5] the Council formally adopted the Act drawing up the Europol Convention, based on Article K.1 of the Union Treaty, on 26 June.[6] The tasks of Europol — the European Police Office — will be to facilitate the gathering, exchange and analysis of information between Member States and thus help to improve cooperation and efficiency in national police services in preventing and combating serious forms of international organized crime. By resolution passed on 19 May,[7] Parliament recalled that it was entitled under Article K.6 to be informed and consulted in good time on the draft Convention.

967.　On 26 July, following political agreement in June[8] and discussion at the Cannes European Council,[5] the Council formally adopted the Act drawing up the Convention on the protection of the Community's financial interests,[9] which it signed the same day (Table III). On 20 December the Commission adopted a proposal for a Council Act (Table III) drawing up a Protocol to amplify the Convention's provisions relating to the liability of bodies corporate, laundering, priority jurisdiction, judicial assistance and cooperation, the establishment of a fraud register and the jurisdiction of the Court of Justice. The Convention itself amplifies the Regulation on the protection of the Community's financial interests *(→ point 1008)*, requiring Member States to establish a specific criminal offence of fraud against the Community's financial interests and providing for convergence in respect of

---

[1]　1994 General Report, point 1085.
[2]　OJ L 62, 20.3.1995; Bull. 3-1995, point 1.5.4.
[3]　Twenty-sixth General Report, points 1068 and 2071.
[4]　Bull. 6-1995, point 1.5.5.
[5]　Bull. 6-1995, points I.20 to I.24.
[6]　OJ C 316, 27.11.1995; Bull. 7/8-1995, point 1.5.2.
[7]　OJ C 151, 19.6.1995; Bull. 5-1995, point 1.5.1.
[8]　Bull. 6-1995, point 1.5.6.
[9]　OJ C 316, 27.11.1995; Bull. 7/8-1995, point 1.5.3.

penalties. Earlier, on 15 March, Parliament passed a resolution[1] on the Commission proposal[2] and on the draft for a joint action put to the Council by the United Kingdom.[3] In December the Council reached agreement on a draft Protocol to this Convention, dealing specifically with fraud against the Community budget involving corruption of European or national civil servants or Members of the European institutions; Parliament is to be consulted pursuant to Article K.6 of the Union Treaty.

968.   On 10 March the Council completed proceedings in hand since 1994[4] by adopting the Act drawing up the Convention on the simplified extradition procedure between the Member States of the European Union,[5] which it signed the same day. This was the first instrument based on Article K.3 and is to facilitate application of the Council of Europe Convention of 1957 in cases where the person to be extradited consents and the requested Member State agrees. On 23 November the Council adopted conclusions[6] taking stock of progress towards adopting a Convention on the improvement of extradition between the Member States, consolidating existing agreements as regards extraditable offences, tax offences, lapse of time and amnesty and giving guidelines for the further examination of questions such as the exclusion of the political nature of offences as grounds for refusing extradition and relaxing the dual criminality rule. On judicial cooperation in criminal matters, on 23 November the Council also passed a resolution on the protection of witnesses in the fight against international organized crime;[7] agreement had been reached on 21 June.[8]

969.   After reaching agreement on 21 June,[9] the Council formally adopted[10] on 26 July the Convention on the use of information technology for customs purpose (customs information system, CIS),[11] signed the same day by the Representatives of the Governments of the Member States. Also on 26 July, the Representatives adopted a Decision to allow the Convention to come into operation once approved, accepted or ratified by eight Member States. The CIS is a computerized information system set up and maintained by the Member States' customs administrations to help prevent, detect and prosecute serious offences against national laws.

---

[1]   OJ C 89, 10.4.1995; Bull. 3-1995, point 1.5.5.
[2]   OJ C 216, 6.8.1994; 1994 General Report, point 1082.
[3]   OJ C 89, 10.4.1995; Bull. 3-1995, point 1.5.6.
[4]   1994 General Report, point 1083.
[5]   OJ C 78, 30.3.1995; Bull. 3-1995, point 1.5.3.
[6]   Bull. 11-1995, point 1.5.12.
[7]   OJ C 327, 7.12.1995; Bull. 11-1995, point 1.5.11.
[8]   Bull. 6-1995, point 1.5.9.
[9]   Bull. 6-1995, point 1.5.8.
[10] OJ C 316, 27.11.1995; Bull. 7/8-1995, point 1.5.4.
[11] Twenty-seventh General Report, point 975; 1994 General Report, point 1084.

970. On 23 November the Council adopted a declaration on terrorism,[1] setting out a number of means of stepping up cooperation between Member States to prevent and combat terrorism through better police and judicial cooperation facilities. Parliament passed resolutions expressing concern at terrorist attacks in Spain[2] and France.[3]

971. On 10 March the Council approved a report on the fight against racism and xenophobia,[4] following an interim report presented in December 1994; this is part of the general strategy which was welcomed by the Cannes European Council (→ *point 13*). It also discussed a draft joint action against racism and xenophobia to secure effective judicial cooperation in relation to offences corresponding to definitions agreed by the Member States.

972. On 23 November the Conference of the Representatives of the Member States opened for signature the Convention on insolvency proceedings,[5] initialled on 25 September.[6] The Convention is based on Article 220 of the EC Treaty and seeks to share the debtor's assets out fairly and treat creditors equally where proceedings take place in one Member State but produce effects in others.

973. On several occasions the Council considered a draft Convention on jurisdiction and enforcement of judgments in matrimonial matters;[7] this was the topic discussed at its first public debate in the justice and home affairs context, held in September. No agreement has yet been reached on the question whether the exercise of parental authority and the custody of children should be within the scope of the Convention.

---

[1] Bull. 11-1995, point 1.5.10.
[2] OJ C 151, 19.6.1995; Bull. 5-1995, point 1.5.2; OJ C 17, 22.1.1996; Bull. 12-1995.
[3] OJ C 269, 16.10.1995; Bull. 9-1995, point 1.5.10.
[4] Bull. 3-1995, point 1.5.9.
[5] Bull. 11-1995, point 1.5.13.
[6] Bull. 9-1995, point 1.5.7.
[7] 1994 General Report, point 1083.

Section 4

The fight against drugs

974.   On 9 March,[1] 2 June,[2] 21 April[3] and 15 June,[4] the Council, the Committee of the Regions and the European Parliament expressed their respective views on the communication from the Commission concerning a European Union action plan to combat drugs (1995-99).[5] The whole was approved by the European Council meeting in Cannes,[6] which instructed a group of experts of the Member States to present it with an analytical report accompanied by proposals for all matters raised by the practical implementation of a strategy encompassing the reduction of supply, the suppression of trafficking and international cooperation. The Madrid European Council[7] approved the experts' report and asked for a programme of activities taking account of the guidelines set out in that report to be submitted by December 1996. It also welcomed the results of the conference on drugs[7] organized by the Commission, the European Parliament and the Council Presidency in Brussels on 7 and 8 December.

975.   On 26 September, a tripartite meeting was held in Brussels between the Ministers of Justice and Home Affairs of the European Union, the Commission and the Ministers of the Andean Group (Bolivia, Colombia, Ecuador, Peru and Venezuela) responsible for combating drugs.[8] At the close of the meeting, a joint communication was adopted advocating an overall and coordinated approach to drug addiction and trafficking. On 18 December the European Community and the same countries signed agreements on the control of drug precursors (Table III).[9] Those agreements had been initialled on 13 November[10] after particularly rapid negotiations, the instructions for which had been adopted by the Council on the Commission's recommendation on 26 September.[11] The Madrid European Council[7] concluded that priority should be given to the creation of a cooperation mechanism between the Union and Latin America and the Caribbean.

---

[1]   Bull. 3-1995, point 1.5.8.
[2]   Bull. 6-1995, point 1.5.10.
[3]   Bull. 4-1995, point 1.5.2.
[4]   OJ C 166,3.7.1995; Bull. 6-1995, point 1.5.11.
[5]   1994 General Report, point 1081.
[6]   Bull. 6-1995, points I.20 to I.24.
[7]   Bull. 12-1995.
[8]   Bull. 9-1995, point 1.5.8.
[9]   COM(95) 585; Bull. 12-1995.
[10] Bull. 11-1995, point 1.5.14.
[11] Bull. 9-1995, point 1.5.9.

Chapter VI

Financing Community activities

Section 1

Priority activities and objectives

976.   *The 1995 budget was the first for the enlarged 15-member European Union. A supplementary and amending budget had to be adopted on 26 April to distribute the amounts required to cover enlargement, which had been entered in the reserve in the 1995 budget adopted in December 1994 (→ point 989).*

On 6 March an interinstitutional declaration was signed by Parliament, the Council and the Commission concerning the incorporation of financial pro- visions into legislative acts.[1]

The June European Council meeting in Cannes[2] took some important financial decisions: as well as confirming the priority which the Essen European Council had given to trans-European transport networks, it determined overall budgets for cooperation with Central and Eastern Europe and the Mediterranean countries for 1995-99, and the amount and financing arrangements for the Eighth European Development Fund.

The question of the classification of expenditure resurfaced in 1995: after Parliament's second reading confirming its 'amendments' covering what both the Council and the Commission considered to be compulsory expenditure, and the decision by Parliament's President declaring the 1995 budget finally adopted, the Council took the view that Parliament's vote and hence its President's decision were in breach of the Treaty and the 1993 Interinstitutional Agreement and on 17 February therefore brought an action before the Court of Justice to have the 1995 budget annulled. In its judg-

---

[1]   OJ C 293, 8.11.1995; Bull. 3-1995, point 1.6.1.
[2]   Bull. 6-1995, point 1.6.1.

ment of 7 December (→ point 1138) the Court considered that, when the President declared the budget adopted, the budgetary procedure had not yet been completed since there was still disagreement between the two arms of the budgetary authority. It therefore declared that the act was illegal and that the 1995 budget was therefore invalid. However, as the financial year was almost over, the Court upheld the invalidated budget in all its aspects until a new budget could be finally adopted, thus avoiding application of the provisional-twelfths arrangements.

As regards the 1996 budget, the ad hoc *conciliation meeting on compulsory expenditure enabled the Council and Parliament to agree on all the EAGGF Guarantee appropriations and remarks. The budget was declared adopted on 21 December. On its second reading of the draft, Parliament adopted a budget which, overall, increased appropriations for commitments by 8.37% and appropriations for payments by 8.55% in relation to the 1995 budget (including supplementary and amending budgets) and which was thus fairly close overall to the proposals made by the Commission in its preliminary draft budget (increases of 8.17% and 8.72% respectively). Parliament's vote reflected new budgetary priorities such as the information campaigns, the European voluntary service and the continuation of the growth and employ-ment initiative, the importance attached to environmental aspects in the implementation of the Structural Funds, the desire for tighter controls on the utilization of appropriations for the trans-European networks and consideration of the decisions adopted at the Cannes European Council to accelerate the policy of cooperation with the Mediterranean countries.*

Further progress was made on the revision of the 1977 Financial Regulation with the adoption of three important regulations in September (→ point 997).

This year also saw the introduction of the important SEM 2000 project (Sound and efficient management): this is a three-phase programme designed to improve the Commission's administrative and financial management. The first phase is concerned with consolidating the existing management frame-work, rationalizing procedures, improving information tools, redefining tasks and the training of staff responsible for financial management. The second phase involves a major reform of financial management culture within Commission departments by acting on internal organization and the regulatory framework. Responsibilities must be defined more precisely and the link between human and financial resources must be tightened. Finally, more effective methods of evaluation, monitoring and budget transparency are called for. A number of recommendations have already been made in connection with financial control, calling for a switch from automatic ex ante *controls to more delegation, systems audits and* ex post *controls. The objective of the third phase will be to strengthen partnership with Member States in the management of Community funds, with particular attention being paid to the reports produced by the Court of Auditors and Parliament's Committee on Budgetary Control, since nearly 80% of expenditure is handled by tens of thousands of national, regional or local officials.*

Section 2

Budgets

General budget

Financial perspective

977.   The 1996 procedure came within the framework of the financial perspective annexed to the Interinstitutional Agreement on budgetary discipline and improvement of the budgetary procedure of 29 October 1993,[1] as adjusted in December 1994,[2] following the enlargement of the Union to include Austria, Finland and Sweden.

978.   Acting under this Agreement, on 22 February the Commission made the technical adjustment of the financial perspective for 1996 on the basis of the most recent macroeconomic forecasts available at the time.[3] The economic parameters applied concerned the 12-member Community from 1992 to 1995 and the 15-member Community from 1995 to 1996. Following this technical adjustment of the financial perspective in line with movements in gross national product and prices, the ceiling on payment appropriations required for 1996 is ECU 81 267 million, leaving a margin of 0.03% of GNP below the own resources ceiling which, subject to completion by the Member States of the procedures for ratifying the Council decision on own resources,[4] stands at 1.22% of GNP.

979.   Under the new collaboration procedures introduced by the Interinstitutional Agreement of 29 October 1993, an interinstitutional trialogue meeting (European Parliament, Council, Commission) was held in Brussels on 4 April.[5] During this trialogue the institutions reached agreement on the adjustment of the financial perspective under paragraph 10 of the Interinstitutional Agreement to take account of the conditions of implementation.[6] The main purpose of this adjustment was to transfer to 1996 and 1997 the commitment appropriations for the Structural Funds which lapsed in 1994. A

---

[1]   OJ C 331, 7.12.1993; Twenty-seventh General Report, points 1078 to 1080.
[2]   1994 General Report, point 1105.
[3]   Bull. 1/2-1995, point 1.5.2.
[4]   Decision 94/728/EC, OJ L 293, 12.11.1994; 1994 General Report, point 1119.
[5]   Bull. 4-1995, point 1.6.1.
[6]   OJ C 126, 22.5.1995.

total of ECU 1 738 million was transferred, half to 1996 and half to 1997. The overall ceiling on payment appropriations was also raised by ECU 935 million for 1996, ECU 696 million for 1997, ECU 434 million for 1998 and ECU 173 million for 1999. These increases cover the payments corresponding to commitment appropriations transferred for the Structural Funds and also take account of the under-utilization of appropriations which emerged in the 1994 budget outturn. With this higher ceiling on payment appropriations, the margin available beneath the own resources ceiling is reduced to 0.02% of GNP as shown in Table 15.

TABLE 15

Financial perspective for 1996 after technical adjustment and adjustment to take account of conditions of implementation — Appropriations for commitments

(million ECU)

	Current prices		1996 prices (as a guide)		
	1995	1996	1997	1998	1999
1. Common agricultural policy	37 994	40 828	41 576	42 344	43 131
2. Structural operations	26 329	29 131	30 827	31 783	33 614
• Structural Funds	24 069	26 579	28 004	28 906	30 790
• Cohesion Fund	2 152	2 444	2 715	2 769	2 824
• EEA financial mechanism	108	108	108	108	0
3. Internal policies	5 060	5 337	5 558	5 789	6 010
4. External action	4 895	5 264	5 576	5 981	6 465
5. Administrative expenditure	4 022	4 191	4 316	4 380	4 445
6. Reserves	1 146	1 152	1 152	1 152	1 152
• Monetary reserve	500	500	500	500	500
• Guarantee reserve	323	326	326	326	326
• Emergency aid reserve	323	326	326	326	326
7. Compensation	1 547	701	212	99	0
8. Total appropriations for commitments	80 943	86 604	89 216	91 528	94 817
9. Total appropriations for payments	77 229	82 223	85 044	87 700	90 449
Payment appropriations as % of GNP[1]	1.20	1.20	1.21	1.22	1.23
Margin (as % of GNP)	0.01	0.02	0.03	0.04	0.04
Own resources ceiling (as % of GNP)	1.21	1.22	1.24	1.26	1.27

[1] For 1995, on the basis of the GNP figure used for the adjustment of the financial perspective following enlargement.

Budget procedure for 1996

Budget

980. The preliminary draft budget for 1996 adopted by the Commission on 26 April[1] fits into the financial perspective framework agreed at the Edinburgh European Council and adjusted following enlargement. It totalled ECU 86 280 million in appropriations for commitments and ECU 81 928 million in appropriations for payments. These amounts, up by 8.1% and 8.6% respectively on 1995, left an overall margin of ECU 292.5 million in appropriations for commitments in relation to the financial perspective. The forecasts for agricultural expenditure for 1996 totalled ECU 41 687 million, up by ECU 4 790 million on the 1995 figure. The main reasons for this significant increase were the change in the dollar/ecu parity (0.89 in supplementary and amending budget No 1/95 and 0.79 in the preliminary draft 1996 budget), completion of implementation of the reform of the CAP and the effects of enlargement. The commitment appropriations earmarked for structural operations totalled ECU 29 131 million (up by 10.64% on 1995). The overall total of appropriations for internal policies (ECU 5 267 million) was up by ECU 214 million (4.2%) on 1995. The heading covers three main areas of expenditure where trends were markedly different. The ECU 3 228 million proposed for research and technological development was up by 7.9% (ECU 236 million) on 1995. The overall increase of ECU 64 million (16.8%) for expenditure on trans-European networks covered two conflicting movements, an increase of ECU 77 million for infrastructure networks and a decrease of ECU 13 million for data transmission networks between administrations. Because of the top priority given to R&TD and the trans-European networks despite the general constraints on the heading, the total amount left for the 'other internal policies' in 1996 was cut appreciably to ECU 1 594 million, down by ECU 87 million on 1995. Despite this general trend, however, some relative priorities retained much the same level of appropriations (education, vocational training and youth, culture and audiovisual industry, energy) or even received an increase (subsidies for the new agencies, information and communication policy). Total spending proposed for external action was ECU 5 157.3 million, an increase of 5.8% on 1995. An emergency aid reserve of ECU 326 million was also included. The priority in external action is to develop cooperation with non-member Mediterranean countries, including the MEDA programme, which was allocated ECU 412 million compared with ECU 173 million in 1995. There was also a substantial increase

---

[1] Bull. 4-1995, point 1.6.4.

for Central and Eastern Europe. The total amounts for food aid and humanitarian aid were at much the same levels as in 1995. Finally ECU 92 million was earmarked to finance operations under the common foreign and security policy. The ceiling on administrative expenditure (heading 5) was raised by 4.2% to ECU 4 191 million in 1996. The preliminary draft budget also contained three reserves (monetary reserve of ECU 500 million for EAGGF Guarantee expenditure, emergency aid reserve of ECU 326 million and loan guarantee reserve of ECU 326 million) and ECU 701 million for compensation due to the new Member States under the accession agreements.

The preliminary draft budget was amended by two letters of amendment, the first one adopted by the Commission on 12 July amending the total of EAGGF Guarantee expenditure[1] and the second sent to the budgetary authority at the Council's request on 31 October[2] with a view to inserting in the Council section a new chapter for interinstitutional cooperation.

981.   The Council established its draft budget (first reading) on 24 July.[1] The overall total of the draft was well down on the Commission's proposals (ECU 86 020 million in commitment appropriations and ECU 81 360 million in payment appropriations). The cuts made in commitment appropriations concerned only headings 3, 4 and 5 and had the effect of raising the total margin still available in relation to the financial perspective to ECU 584 million (instead of the ECU 236 million left unused in the preliminary draft). The payment appropriations were reduced by ECU 655 million. Generally speaking the cuts were the result of a more restrictive assessment of requirements as well as a particularly strict approach as regards legal bases (several headings which did not have a legal basis were given only token entries). The EAGGF Guarantee expenditure entered was at the level of the agricultural guideline, including the letter of amendment (ECU 40 828 million). The Commission's proposals made in the preliminary draft were taken over almost in their entirety, with the exception of a few amendments agreed at the *ad hoc* conciliation meeting on compulsory expenditure. Unlike the dispute which arose last year, this new procedure introduced by the October 1993 Interinstitutional Agreement[3] produced a formal agreement by the two arms of the budgetary authority on all the EAGGF Guarantee appropriations and remarks. The commitment appropriations proposed in the preliminary draft for structural operations were accepted unchanged. The appropriations for internal policies totalled ECU 5 082 million, a reduction of ECU 185 million on the amounts pro-

---

[1]   Bull. 7/8-1995, point 1.6.3.
[2]   Bull. 10-1995, point 1.6.2.
[3]   OJ C 331, 7.12.1993; Twenty-seventh General Report, point 1078.

posed by the Commission and an increase of only 0.57% on the 1995 allocations. The Council maintained the ECU 3 228 million earmarked for research and technological development in the preliminary draft. The overall
increase for the trans-European networks was ECU 18 million, made up of
an increase of ECU 50 million for transport infrastructure (reflecting the
Council's desire to act on the conclusions of the Essen and Cannes European Councils) and a reduction of ECU 32 million for the other networks.
No change was made in the Commission's proposed subsidies for the agencies. The overall reductions of ECU 203 million were thus concentrated on
the other policies covered by the heading, which had already been severely
restricted in the preliminary draft: there were particularly large cuts in the
areas of transport (excluding the networks), education, vocational training
and youth, audiovisual policy and culture, information and communication
operations, other social operations (in particular the programme to combat
poverty and social exclusion), energy (in particular the Thermie II programme), and the environment. The overall allocation for external action
was cut, but the allocations for Central and Eastern Europe and for Mediterranean countries were set at ECU 1 235 million and ECU 900 million respectively (i.e. ECU 200 million more than in the preliminary draft) in accordance with the Cannes European Council conclusions.[1] This left a margin beneath the ceiling for the heading of ECU 160 million. All the institutions (with the exception of Parliament) had the allocations for
administrative expenditure cut by a total of ECU 109 million, thus raising
the unused margin beneath the ceiling for the heading from ECU 59 million
to ECU 168 million.

982.   The draft budget amended by Parliament on first reading on 26 October (ECU 86 517 million for commitments and ECU 81 896 million for
payments) represented an increase of some ECU 500 million in both commitments and payments in relation to the Council's draft.[2] In relation to the
preliminary draft it was up by some ECU 150 million in commitments but
down by some ECU 120 million in payments. The overall margin still available in relation to the financial perspective was ECU 86 million. Agricultural expenditure and commitment appropriations for structural operations
did not change in relation to the Council's draft, which was itself the same
as the preliminary draft. Parliament's concern for the environment was reflected by the addition of a remark calling for an environmental impact assessment for each major project or programme. The appropriations for internal policies totalled ECU 5 324 million, some ECU 57 million more than
was proposed by the Commission. Parliament thus went a long way towards

[1]   Bull. 6-1995, point I.57.
[2]   OJ C 308, 20.11.1995; Bull. 10-1995, point 1.6.2.

restoring the preliminary draft and, in some cases, even exceeded the amounts proposed by the Commission in areas such as education, social policies and health. The appropriations for the fight against poverty and social exclusion and for Thermie II were partly restored. Parliament's clear priorities were information campaigns, employment and growth, and the creation of a European voluntary service. It made cuts on trans-European networks, agriculture, audiovisual policy, culture, industry and statistical policy. The appropriations for the agencies were severely reduced. Parliament restored virtually all the amounts earmarked in the preliminary draft for external action but completely overhauled the budget nomenclature in this area. While it accepted the overall amounts allocated to the PHARE and MEDA programmes for 1994-99 by the Cannes European Council,[1] it reduced the MEDA allocation for 1996 to the level set in the preliminary draft. By redeploying appropriations in this area it was able to allocate ECU 9 million to a new MEDA programme for democracy. A similar redeployment exercise concerning the TACIS appropriations allowed ECU 30 million to be allocated to a new item for cross-border cooperation operations. Parliament also voted a substantial increase in appropriations for NGOs, for cooperation with Latin America and South Africa and the insertion of new items for anti-personnel mine operations and external cooperation action. An allocation of ECU 92.5 million was made for the reconstruction of former Yugoslavia.

983.   At its second reading on 17 November[2] the Council adopted the draft budget with a total of ECU 86 288 million in commitment appropriations and ECU 81 593 million in payment appropriations, an increase of ECU 268 million and ECU 233 million respectively over the Council's first reading. However, the draft budget is still lower than the amounts proposed by the Commission in its preliminary draft and the amounts adopted by Parliament on first reading. The main amendments by Parliament which the Council accepted related to the growth and employment initiative, changes in the research appropriations, the revamped nomenclature for external action, the increase in appropriations for the reconstruction of former Yugoslavia and the reduction of the allocation for fisheries agreements through entry of appropriations in the reserve. However, the Council basically upheld its first reading as regards structural operations, trans-European networks, the audiovisual media, information policy, social operations, the MEDA programme and the common foreign and security policy.

---

[1]   Bull. 6-1995, point I.19.
[2]   Bull. 11-1995, point 1.6.1.

984.   Parliament gave the 1966 draft budget its second reading on 14 December.[1] Parliament mainly upheld the amendments which it had adopted on first reading and which had been refused by the Council in November. The appropriations adopted came to ECU 86 525 million for commitments and ECU 81 888 million for payments, 8.37% and 8.55% up on the 1995 budget, including supplementary and amending budgets. The total margin still available in relation to the financial perspective is ECU 78.5 million — ECU 12.7 million in heading 3, ECU 3.4 million in heading 4 and ECU 62.4 million in heading 5. The main changes in relation to the first reading are in headings 3, 4 and 5. Parliament accepted the agricultural appropriations adopted by the Council on second reading and entered the same volume of appropriations for structural operations as in the first reading, with the entry of a remark on environmental protection. In heading 3 (Internal policies) Parliament agreed to a number of increases in connection with information and high-definition television. It upheld the establishment of a European voluntary civil service as a pilot project, but reduced the amount allocated. Parliament decided not to enter a general reserve for the agencies in heading 3, but the total allocation for them is still ECU 4.1 million lower than the appropriations proposed in the preliminary draft budget. Only the allocation for the Trade Marks Office is at the level initially planned. As regards the trans-European networks, the idea of entering the appropriations for transport infrastructures in a reserve was extended to all the trans-European networks, including IDA. In the case of heading 4 (External action), Parliament upheld the amounts decided for the reconstruction of former Yugoslavia, but agreed that some could be entered in the reserve and be used for operations under the common foreign and security policy or under the EC Treaty. The allocations which the Council adopted for fisheries agreements at its second reading were accepted unchanged. The MEDA appropriations decided at the Cannes European Council can be made available by creating a negative reserve of ECU 200 million.

985.   Table 17 gives a breakdown, by heading of the financial perspective, of the amounts entered at the various stages of the 1996 budget procedure.

986.   The budget was declared adopted by the President of Parliament on 21 December.[1]

---

[1]   Bull. 12-1995.

Own resources

987.   In response to the concern expressed by the budgetary authority for the monitoring of recovery of own resources in cases of fraud or irregularities, the Commission has devised a method for selective financial monitoring of such cases among those reported by the Member States. On 8 September it sent the Council and Parliament an initial report on the methodology of this monitoring and the position as regards recovery of traditional own resources (customs duties and levies) in a sample of 104 cases involving over ECU 0.5 million in the period 1989 to mid-1993.[1] On 17 November, in order to give the Commission a better opportunity to control the flow of information from the Member States on the making available of own resources and to tighten up the measures to combat fraud, the Council adopted a common position on a proposal for a Council Regulation (Table II) amending Regulation (EEC, Euratom) No 1552/89 implementing Decision 88/376/EEC, Euratom on the system of the Communities' own resources.

988.   Foreseeable revenue for 1996 is shown in Table 16.

Implementation of the 1995 budget

Supplementary and amending budgets

989.   A first supplementary and amending budget was proposed by the Commission on 14 February[2] and finally adopted on 26 April.[3] It allocated to the specific headings, in line with requirements identified, the amounts entered in reserve in the 1995 budget to take account of enlargement. It also entered in the budget the savings made in agricultural expenditure and the repayment to the Member States of the VAT and GNP balances for 1994. On 23 November the Commission also presented to the budgetary authority a request for a supplementary and amending budget from the Court of Justice to allow advance financing of some of its expenditure on buildings. The Council rejected this request.

---

[1]   COM(95) 398.
[2]   Bull. 1/2-1995, point 1.5.4.
[3]   OJ C 129, 22.5.1995; Bull. 4-1995, point 1.6.2.

TABLE 16

Budget revenue

(million ECU)

	1995 (forecast outturn)	1996
Agricultural levies	843.8	864.0
Sugar and isoglucose levies	1 313.0	1 317.5
Customs duties	13 878.7	14 281.0
Own resources collection costs	−1 603.5	−1 646.3
VAT own resources	39 648.6	39 792.3
GNP-based own resources	14 442.2	26 711.8
Balance of VAT and GNP own resources from previous years	−790.7	p.m.
Refunds to Member States	3.6	p.m.
Budget balance from previous years	6 589.0	p.m.
Correction	78.1	p.m.
Other revenue	600.0	568.1
Total	74 995.6	81 888.4
	% of GNP	
Maximum own resources which may be assigned to the budget	1 200	1 200
Own resources actually assigned to the budget	1 151	1 198

Outturn of revenue and expenditure

990. The implementation rate for expenditure under the common agricultural policy (heading 1) came to 93.6% of the appropriations. The ECU 2 360 million not spent is mainly accounted for by under-utilization of appropriations for the accompanying measures and for beef/veal. For headings 2, 3 and 4 of the financial perspective the outturn was 93.8% in commitments and 81.8% in payments. The relative under-utilization of payment appropriations as compared to commitment appropriations is largely due to the fact that a number of new research programmes were implemented for the first time in 1995. Under heading 5 virtually all the appropriations for administrative expenditure were used.

Tables 18 and 19 show the 1995 rates of utilization of available appropriations, 93.1% in commitments and 86.9% in payments.

991. In July the Commission presented a communication on the execution of the 1995 budget which served as a basis for a number of debates within both the Council and Parliament. This procedure, which was set up to

TABLE 17

1996 budget — Financial perspective — Provisional figures
(Appropriations for commitments — Parliament's nomenclature)

(1 000 ECU)

	Budget 1995 (1)	Financial perspective 1996 (2)	Preliminary draft budget 1996 (3)	Council (first reading) (4)	Parliament (first reading) (5)	Council (second reading) (6)	Budget 1996 (7)	Difference % (8) = (7)/(1)
1. Common agricultural policy								
Markets (B1-1 to B1-3)	34 807 500.000		38 554 000.000	38 554 000.000	38 554 000.000	38 554 000.000	38 554 000.000	10.76
Accompanying measures (B1-4 and B1-5)	2 089 500.000		2 274 000.000	2 274 000.000	2 274 000.000	2 274 000.000	2 274 000.000	8.83
Total 1	36 897 000.000	40 828 000.000	40 828 000.000	40 828 000.000	40 828 000.000	40 828 000.000	40 828 000.000	10.65
Margin			0.000	0.000	0.000	0.000	0.000	
2. Structural operations								
EAGGF-Guidance (B2-10)	3 566 900.000		3 772 000.000	3 772 000.000	3 772 000.000	3 772 000.000	3 772 000.000	5.75
FIFG (B2-11)	451 230.000		450 350.000	450 350.000	450 350.000	450 350.000	450 350.000	− 0.20
ERDF (B2-12)	10 814 110.000		11 883 700.000	11 883 700.000	11 883 700.000	11 883 700.000	11 883 700.000	9.89
ESF (B2-13)	6 760 910.000		7 145 800.000	7 145 800.000	7 145 800.000	7 145 800.000	7 145 800.000	5.69
Community initiatives (B2-14)	2 224 200.000		3 030 300.000	3 030 300.000	3 030 300.000	3 030 300.000	3 030 300.000	36.24
Transitional measures, innovation schemes and measures to combat fraud (B2-15 and B2-18)	251 650.000		296 850.000	296 850.000	296 850.000	296 850.000	296 850.000	17.96
Cohesion Fund (B2-3)	2 152 000.000		2 444 000.000	2 444 000.000	2 444 000.000	2 444 000.000	2 444 000.000	13.57
EEA financial mechanism (B2-4)	108 000.000		108 000.000	108 000.000	108 000.000	108 000.000	108 000.000	0.00
Structural Funds — Subtotal	24 069 000.000	26 579 000.000	26 579 000.000	26 579 000.000	26 579 000.000	26 579 000.000	26 579 000.000	10.43
Cohesion Fund — Subtotal	2 152 000.000	2 444 000.000	2 444 000.000	2 444 000.000	2 444 000.000	2 444 000.000	2 444 000.000	13.57
EEA financial mechanism — Subtotal	108 000.000	108 000.000	108 000.000	108 000.000	108 000.000	108 000.000	108 000.000	0.00
Total 2	26 329 000.000	29 131 000.000	29 131 000.000	29 131 000.000	29 131 000.000	29 131 000.000	29 131 000.000	10.64
Total margin			0.000	0.000	0.000	0.000	0.000	
3. Internal policies								
Research (B6)	2 991 696.000		3 228 100.000	3 228 100.000	3 183 150.000	3 183 100.000	3 183 150.000	6.40
Other agricultural operations (B2-5)	214 700.000		179 900.000	176 200.000	162 800.000	176 700.000	162 800.000	− 24.17
Other regional operations (B2-6)	51 800.000		22 000.000	20 000.000	36 800.000	36 800.000	36 800.000	− 28.96
Transport (B2-7)	24 500.000		36 000.000	26 700.000	41 000.000	41 000.000	41 000.000	67.35
Fisheries and the sea (B2-9)	28 200.000		35 500.000	35 500.000	35 500.000	35 500.000	35 500.000	25.89
Education, vocational training, youth (B3-1)	368 410.000		364 900.000	354 200.000	406 825.000	360 700.000	396 825.000	7.71
Culture and audiovisual media (B3-2)	141 780.000		140 000.000	118 500.000	114 400.000	118 500.000	119 400.000	− 15.79
Information and communication (B3-3)	67 300.000		69 000.000	41 000.000	108 500.000	41 000.000	113 000.000	67.90
Other social operations (B3-4)	180 373.000		167 200.000	110 770.000	188 860.000	121 670.000	190 460.000	5.59
Energy (B4-1)	63 000.000		62 000.000	21 000.000	68 000.000	36 000.000	68 000.000	7.94
Euratom nuclear safeguards (B4-2)	19 200.000		18 200.000	18 200.000	19 070.000	18 070.000	19 070.000	− 0.68
Environment (B4-3)	144 188.000		139 000.000	125 900.000	131 900.000	140 400.000	133 400.000	− 7.48
Consumer protection (B5-1)	21 250.000		19 100.000	12 800.000	20 050.000	20 050.000	20 050.000	− 5.65
Aid for reconstruction (B5-2)	6 775.000		4 775.000	4 775.000	4 775.000	4 775.000	4 775.000	− 29.52
Internal market (B5-3)	172 780.000		173 200.000	166 630.000	217 550.000	228 550.000	221 300.000	28.08
Industry (B5-4)	120 300.000		120 200.000	116 600.000	115 650.000	116 900.000	115 650.000	− 3.87
Information market (B5-5)	13 930.000		p.m.	p.m.	p.m.	p.m.	p.m.	− 100.00
Statistical information (B5-6)	37 000.000		38 000.000	37 200.000	35 900.000	37 200.000	35 900.000	− 2.97
Trans-European networks (B5-7)	381 000.000		445 000.000	463 000.000	410 000.000	474 000.000	410 000.000	7.61
Cooperation in the field of justice (B5-8)	5 200.000		5 500.000	5 500.000	13 000.000	5 500.000	13 000.000	150.00
Measures to combat fraud (B5-9)	1 500.000		1 500.000	1 500.000	10 175.000	4 175.000	4 175.000	178.33
Research — Subtotal	2 991 696.000		3 228 100.000	3 228 100.000	3 183 150.000	3 183 100.000	3 183 150.000	6.40
Networks — Subtotal	381 000.000		445 000.000	463 000.000	410 000.000	474 000.000	410 000.000	7.61
Other policies — Subtotal	1 682 186.000		1 595 975.000	1 392 975.000	1 730 755.000	1 543 490.000	1 731 105.000	2.91
Total 3	5 054 882.000	5 337 000.000	5 269 075.000	5 084 075.000	5 323 905.000	5 200 590.000	5 324 255.000	5.33
Margin			67 925.000	252 925.000	13 095.000	136 410.000	12 745.000	

TABLE 17 (continued)

(1 000 ECU)

	Budget 1995	Financial perspective 1996	Preliminary draft budget 1996	Council (first reading)	Parliament (first reading)	Council (second reading)	Budget 1996	Difference %
	(1)	(2)	(3)	(4)	(5)	(6)	(7)	(8) = (7)/(1)
4. External action								
EDF (B7-1)	—		—		p.m.		p.m.	
Food aid (B7-20)	591 900.000		540 900.000	529 000.000	540 900.000	529 000.000	530 900.000	− 10.31
Humanitarian aid (B7-21)	326 000.000		379 000.000	362 000.000	379 500.000	362 000.000	379 500.000	16.41
Cooperation with Asia (B7-30)	395 000.000		406 500.000	374 000.000	406 500.000	382 000.000	406 500.000	2.91
Cooperation with Latin America (B7-31)	245 500.000		253 000.000	234 000.000	263 000.000	238 000.000	263 000.000	7.13
Cooperation with southern Africa (B7-32)	140 000.000		140 000.000	135 000.000	150 000.000	135 000.000	150 000.000	7.14
Cooperation — Mediterranean countries (B7-4) [1]	536 900.000		697 000.000	897 000.000	688 000.000	897 000.000	688 000.000	28.14
Cooperation — Central and Eastern Europe (B7-50)	1 153 910.000		1 235 000.000	1 235 000.000	1 231 000.000	1 235 000.000	1 233 500.000	6.90
Cooperation — former Soviet Union (B7-52)	506 850.000		528 000.000	525 000.000	528 000.000	528 000.000	528 000.000	4.17
Cooperation — former Yugoslavia (B7-54)	9 500.000		18 000.000	18 000.000	98 000.000	68 000.000	98 000.000	931.58
Other cooperation measures (B7-6, B7-51, B7-53)	379 433.000		355 733.000	266 450.000	411 983.000	274 450.000	411 983.000	8.58
Human rights and democracy (B7-7)	75 960.000		80 750.000	44 250.000	90 750.000	50 250.000	90 750.000	19.47
International fisheries agreements (B7-80)	280 000.000		290 000.000	290 000.000	263 500.000	280 000.000	280 000.000	0.00
Other external aspects (B7-81 to B7-87)	119 570.000		137 150.000	99 750.000	138 450.000	100 750.000	138 450.000	15.79
CFSP (B8-0)	110 000.000		92 000.000	92 000.000	62 000.000	92 000.000	62 000.000	− 43.64
Total 4 [1]	4 870 523.000	5 264 000.000	5 153 033.000	5 101 450.000	5 251 583.000	5 171 450.000	5 260 583.000	8.01
Margin			110 967.000	162 550.000	12 417.000	92 550.000	3 417.000	
5. Administrative expenditure								
Commission (part A not including pensions)	2 237 820.356		2 350 226.000	2 286 705.349	2 299 752.349	2 277 866.349	2 300 220.349	2.79
Pensions	349 792.000		399 849.000	396 515.000	396 515.000	396 515.000	396 515.000	13.36
Commission — Subtotal	2 587 612.356		2 750 075.000	2 683 220.349	2 696 267.349	2 674 381.349	2 696 735.349	4.22
Other institutions — Subtotal	1 413 620.496		1 383 634.544	1 339 069.494	1 433 324.642	1 429 704.642	1 431 886.642	1.29
Total 5	4 001 232.852	4 191 000.000	4 133 709.544	4 022 289.843	4 129 591.991	4 104 085.991	4 128 621.991	3.18
Margin			57 290.456	168 710.157	61 408.009	86 914.009	62 378.009	
6. Reserves								
Monetary reserve (B1-6)	500 000.000		500 000.000	500 000.000	500 000.000	500 000.000	500 000.000	0.00
Guarantee reserve (B0-23)	323 000.000		326 000.000	326 000.000	326 000.000	326 000.000	326 000.000	0.93
Emergency aid reserve (B7-91)	323 000.000		326 000.000	326 000.000	326 000.000	326 000.000	326 000.000	0.93
Total 6	1 146 000.000	1 152 000.000	1 152 000.000	1 152 000.000	1 152 000.000	1 152 000.000	1 152 000.000	0.52
Margin			0.000	0.000	0.000	0.000	0.000	
7. Compensation								
Compensation (B1-7)	1 547 000.000		701 000.000	701 000.000	701 000.000	701 000.000	701 000.000	− 54.69
Total 7	1 547 000.000	701 000.000	701 000.000	701 000.000	701 000.000	701 000.000	701 000.000	− 54.69
Margin			0.000	0.000	0.000	0.000	0.000	
MEDA — Additional appropriations [1]							200 000.000	∞
Negative reserve (B0-42) [1]							− 200 000.000	∞
Total — appropriations for commitments — Compulsory	40 392 302.000		43 416 420.000	43 412 987.000	43 386 487.000	43 402 987.000	43 402 987.000	7.45
Non-compulsory	39 453 335.852		42 951 397.544	42 606 827.843	43 130 592.991	42 885 138.991	43 122 472.991	9.30
Total compulsory + non-compulsory	79 845 637.852	86 604 000.000	86 367 817.544	86 019 814.843	86 517 079.991	86 288 125.991	86 525 459.991	8.37
Margin			236 182.456	584 185.157	86 920.009	315 874.009	78 540.009	
Total — appropriations for payments — Compulsory	40 371 302.000		43 424 420.000	43 420 987.000	43 404 487.000	43 410 987.000	43 410 987.000	7.53
Non-compulsory	35 067 123.852		38 590 786.544	37 938 672.843	38 491 260.991	38 181 902.991	38 477 453.991	9.73
Total compulsory + non-compulsory	75 438 425.852	82 223 000.000	82 015 206.544	81 359 659.843	81 895 747.991	81 592 889.991	81 888 440.991	8.55
Margin			207 793.456	863 340.157	327 252.009	630 110.009	334 559.009	

[1] Appropriations from the reserve for MEDA (allocation of ECU 200 million) will be counted under heading 4 only after the negative reserve has been absorbed (allocation of − ECU 200 million).

TABLE 18

Utilization of appropriations for commitments (Commission)
at 31 December 1995 by financial perspective subdivision
(figures not final)

(million ECU)

| | Appropriations entered in 1995 budget (including supplementary/ amending budgets) | Appropriations entered in 1995 budget (including supplementary/ amending budgets and transfers) | Additional 1995 appropriations and carryovers from 1994 | Total appropriations available in 1995 | Book commitments entered into in 1995 | | | | | |
| | | | | | Against 1995 appropriations | | Against additional appropriations and carryovers | | Total appropriations available in 1995 | |
					Amount	%	Amount	%	Amount	%
1. Common agricultural policy										
Markets (B1-1 to B1-3)	34 855.500	34 771.100	0.000	34 771.100	33 633.300	96.7	0.000	0.0	33 633.300	96.7
Accompanying measures (B1-4 and B1-5)	2 089.500	2 090.000	0.000	2 090.000	868.400	41.6	0.000	0.0	868.400	41.6
Expenditure associated with accession (B1-7)	950.000			0.000	0.000	0.0	0.000	0.0	0.000	0.0
Total 1	37 895.000	36 861.100	0.000	36 861.100	34 501.700	93.6	0.000	0.0	34 501.700	93.6
2. Structural operations										
EAGGF-Guidance (B2-10)	3 567.100	3 374.100	0.000	3 374.100	3 348.335	99.2	0.000	0.0	3 348.335	99.2
FIFG (B2-11)	451.280	451.280	0.000	451.280	451.230	100.0	0.000	0.0	451 230	100.0
ERDF (B2-12)	10 814.410	10 684.410	0.000	10 684.410	10 566.085	98.9	0.000	0.0	10 566.085	98.9
ESF (B2-13)	6 761.110	6 706.110	4.631	6 710.741	5 120.665	76.4	4.631	100.0	5 125.295	76.4
Community initiatives (B2-14)	2 224.200	2 602.200	313.578	2 915.778	2 357.708	90.6	308.943	98.5	2 666.651	91.5
Structural Funds — miscellaneous (B2-18 and B2-19)	250.900	250.900	20.938	271.838	93.889	37.4	18.027	86.1	111.916	41.2
Other structural operations (B2-2)	0.000	0.000	0.000	0.000	0.000	0.0	0.000	0.0	0.000	0.0
Cohesion Fund (B2-3)	2 152.000	2 152.000	0.000	2 152.000	2 151.972	100.0	0.000	0.0	2 151.972	100.0
EEA financial mechanism (B2-400)	0.000	0.000	0.000	0.000	0.000	0.0	0.000	0.0	0.000	0.0
Expenditure relating to accession (B2-401)	108.000	108.000	0.000	108.000	89.793	83.1	0.000	0.0	89.793	83.1
Total 2	26 329.000	26 329.000	339.147	26 668.147	24 179.675	91.8	331.601	97.8	24 511.276	91.9
3. Internal policies										
Research (B6)	3 033.097	3 078.097	110.275	3 188.372	3 062.806	99.5	54.028	49.0	3 116.834	97.8
Other agricultural operations (B2-5)	216.200	175.900	0.000	175.900	173.941	98.9	0.000	0.0	173.941	98.9
Other regional operations (B2-6)	51.800	51.800	0.000	51.800	51.602	99.6	0.000	0.0	51.602	99.6
Transport (B2-7)	24.500	24.500	0.000	24.500	24.454	99.8	0.000	0.0	24.454	99.8
Fisheries and the sea (B2-9)	28.200	29.200	0.000	29.200	29.199	100.0	0.000	0.0	29.199	100.0
Education, vocational training, youth (B3-1)	373.932	373.932	15.266	389.198	369.442	98.9	15.034	98.5	384.476	98.8
Culture and audiovisual media (B3-2)	142.881	142.881	0.000	142.881	142.428	99.7	0.000	0.0	142.428	99.7
Information and communication (B3-3)	67.300	77.300	0.000	77.300	77.213	99.9	0.000	0.0	77.213	99.9
Other social operations (B3-4)	180.513	179.513	0.000	179.513	172.820	96.3	0.000	0.0	172.820	96.3
Energy (B4-1)	63.000	42.100	0.000	42.100	41.687	99.0	0.000	0.0	41.687	99.0
Euratom nuclear safeguards (B4-2)	19.200	20.400	3.222	23.622	20.389	99.9	3.188	98.9	23.578	99.8
Environment (B4-3)	144.374	146.374	0.244	146.618	143.715	98.2	0.000	0.0	143.715	98.0
Consumer protection (B5-1)	21.250	21.250	0.000	21.250	21.224	99.9	0.000	0.0	21.224	99.9
Aid for reconstruction (B5-2)	6.775	6.775	0.000	6.775	6.054	89.4	0.000	0.0	6.054	89.4
Internal market (B5-3)	173.423	173.923	1.500	175.423	172.951	99.4	1.500	100.0	174.450	99.4
Industry (B5-4)	120.300	118.300	0.249	118.549	117.733	99.5	0.037	14.9	117.770	99.3
Information market (B5-5)	14.182	16.182	0.000	16.182	16.182	100.0	0.000	0.0	16.182	100.0
Statistical information (B5-6)	37.451	39.951	0.000	39.951	39.939	100.0	0.000	0.0	39.939	100.0
Trans-European networks (B5-7)	381.000	381.000	0.159	381.159	358.322	94.0	0.159	100.0	358.481	94.1
Cooperation in the fields of justice and home affairs (B5-8)	5.200	5.200	0.000	5.200	3.829	73.6	0.000	0.0	3.829	73.6
Exploitation of the results of research in the European Union (B5-9)	0.000	0.000	0.000	0.000	0.000	0.0	0.000	0.0	0.000	0.0
Reserve for internal policies (B5-95)	0.000	0.000	0.000	0.000	0.000	0.0	0.000	0.0	0.000	0.0
Total 3	5 104.578	5 104.578	130.915	5 235.493	5 045.927	98.9	73.946	56.5	5 119.873	97.8

TABLE 18 (continued)

(million ECU)

	Appropriations entered in 1995 budget (including supplementary/ amending budgets)	Appropriations entered in 1995 budget (including supplementary/ amending budgets and transfers)	Additional 1995 appropriations and carryovers from 1994	Total appropriations available in 1995	Book commitments entered into in 1995					
					Against 1995 appropriations		Against additional appropriations and carryovers		Total appropriations available in 1995	
					Amount	%	Amount	%	Amount	%
4. External action										
EDF (B7-1)	0.000	0.000	0.000	0.000	0.000	0.0	0.000	0.0	0.000	0.0
Food aid (B7-2)	857.900	1 288.800	0.000	1 288.800	1 288.227	100.0	0.000	0.0	1 288.227	100.0
Cooperation — Latin American and Asian developing countries (B7-3)	700.500	693.840	123.713	817.553	684.151	98.6	123.713	100.0	807.864	98.8
Cooperation — Mediterranean countries (B7-4)	497.400	494.400	0.000	494.400	491.131	99.3	0.000	0.0	491.131	99.3
Other cooperation measures (B7-5)	678.163	668.163	0.818	668.981	660.142	98.8	0.818	100.0	660.960	98.8
Cooperation — Central and Eastern Europe and independent States of former Soviet Union (B7-6)	1 682.360	1 670.020	15.000	1 685.020	1 663.276	99.6	15.000	100.0	1 678.276	99.6
Cooperation — other non-member countries (B7-7)	52.000	67.000	1.400	68.400	67.000	100.0	1.400	100.0	68.400	100.0
External aspects of certain Community policies (B7-8)	294.200	175.200	0.000	175.200	122.294	69.8	0.000	0.0	122.294	69.8
Common foreign and security policy (B8-1)	110.000	95.000	0.000	95.000	84.660	89.1	0.000	0.0	84.660	89.1
Reserve for external policy actions (B7-95)	0.000	0.000	0.000	0.000	0.000	0.0	0.000	0.0	0.000	0.0
Total 4	4 872.523	5 152.423	140.931	5 293.354	5 060.881	98.2	140.931	100.0	5 201.812	98.3
5. Administrative expenditure										
Commission (part A not including pensions)	2 227.994	2 210.125	0.156	2 210.281	2 171.626	98.3	0.142	91.0	2 171.768	98.3
Pensions (A-19)	349.792	369.683	0.000	369.683	366.874	99.2	0.000	0.0	366.874	99.2
Enlargement reserve (A-105)	9.200	7.070	0.000	7.070	0.000	0.0	0.000	0.0	0.000	0.0
Total 5	2 586.986	2 586.878	0.156	2 587.034	2 538.500	98.1	0.142	91.0	2 538.642	98.1
6. Reserves										
Monetary reserve (B1-6)	500.000	500.000	0.000	500.000	0.000	0.0	0.000	0.0	0.000	0.0
Guarantee reserve (B0-2)	323.000	323.000	0.000	323.000	250.800	77.6	0.000	0.0	250.800	77.6
Humanitarian aid reserve (B7-9)	323.000	87.500	0.000	87.500	0.000	0.0	0.000	0.0	0.000	0.0
Total 6	1 146.000	910.500	0.000	910.500	250.800	27.5	0.000	0.0	250.800	27.5
7. Compensation										
Compensation (B0-5)	1 547.000	1 547.000	0.000	1 547.000	1 547.000	100.0	0.000	0.0	1 547.000	100.0
Total 7	1 547.000	1 547.000	0.000	1 547.000	1 547.000	100.0	0.000	0.0	1 547.000	100.0
Grand total	79 481.087	78 491.479	611.149	79 102.628	73 124.483	93.2	546.620	89.4	73 671.103	93.1

TABLE 19

**Utilization of appropriations for payments (Commission)
at 31 December 1995 by financial perspective subdivision
(figures not final)**

(million ECU)

	Appropriations entered in 1995 budget (including supplementary/ amending budgets)	Appropriations entered in 1995 budget (including supplementary/ amending budgets and transfers)	Additional 1995 appropriations and carryovers from 1994	Total appropriations available in 1995	Payments made in 1995					
					Against 1995 appropriations		Against additional appropriations and carryovers		Total appropriations available in 1995	
					Amount	%	Amount	%	Amount	%
1. Common agricultural policy										
Markets (B1-1 to B1-3)	34 855.500	34 771.100	64.268	34 835.368	33 633.300	96.7	46.644	72.6	33 679.944	96.7
Accompanying measures (B1-4 and B1-5)	2 089.500	2 090.000	0.000	2 090.000	868.400	41.6	0.000	0.0	868.400	41.6
Expenditure associated with accession (B1-7)	950.000	0.000	0.000	0.000	0.000	0.0	0.000	0.0	0.000	0.0
Total 1	37 895.000	36 861.100	64.268	36 925.368	34 501.700	93.6	46.644	72.6	34 548.344	93.6
2. Structural operations										
EAGGF-Guidance (B2-10)	2 878.350	2 878.350	56.889	2 935.239	2 530.612	87.9	0.000	0.0	2 530.612	86.2
FIFG (B2-11)	518.140	518.140	0.000	518.140	248.054	47.9	0.000	0.0	248.054	47.9
ERDF (B2-12)	9 627.205	9 627.205	0.000	9 627.205	8 373.620	87.0	0.000	0.0	8 373.620	87.0
ESF (B2-13)	5 642.055	5 642.055	209.500	5 851.555	4 542.610	80.5	191.487	91.4	4 734.097	80.9
Community initiatives (B2-14)	2 107.150	2 107.150	184.360	2 291.510	1 320.062	62.6	17.729	9.6	1 337.791	58.4
Structural Funds — miscellaneous (B2-18 and B2-19)	428.650	428.650	123.060	551.710	199.879	46.6	30.269	24.6	230.147	41.7
Other structural operations (B2-2)	40.000	40.000	66.500	106.500	37.341	93.4	11.170	16.8	48.510	45.5
Cohesion Fund (B2-3)	1 750.000	1 750.000	0.000	1 750.000	1 699.341	97.1	0.000	0.0	1 699.341	97.1
EEA financial mechanism (B2-400)	381.450	381.450	0.000	381.450	0.000	0.0	0.000	0.0	0.000	0.0
Expenditure relating to accession (B2-401)	108.000	108.000	0.000	108.000	89.793	83.1	0.000	0.0	89.793	83.1
Total 2	23 481.000	23 481.000	640.309	24 121.309	19 041.311	81.1	250.654	39.1	19 291.965	80.0
3. Internal policies										
Research (B6)	2 842.349	2 841.349	106.977	2 948.326	2 463.448	86.7	61.280	57.3	2 524.728	85.6
Other agricultural operations (B2-5)	153.450	129.350	0.000	129.350	108.096	83.6	0.000	0.0	108.096	83.6
Other regional operations (B2-6)	55.500	55.500	0.000	55.500	35.648	64.2	0.000	0.0	35.648	64.2
Transport (B2-7)	18.200	18.200	1.265	19.465	18.193	100.0	1.256	99.3	19.449	99.9
Fisheries and the sea (B2-9)	23.130	23.630	0.000	23.630	15.754	66.7	0.000	0.0	15.754	66.7
Education, vocational training, youth (B3-1)	317.626	342.626	15.611	358.237	288.185	84.1	14.662	93.9	302.847	84.5
Culture and audiovisual media (B3-2)	141.759	141.759	0.000	141.759	117.774	83.1	0.000	0.0	117.774	83.1
Information and communication (B3-3)	47.950	47.950	0.000	47.950	39.913	83.2	0.000	0.0	39.913	83.2
Other social operations (B3-4)	152.196	167.296	12.701	179.997	147.079	87.9	11.560	91.0	158.638	88.1
Energy (B4-1)	56.450	43.450	0.000	43.450	33.288	76.6	0.000	0.0	33.288	76.6
Euratom nuclear safeguards (B4-2)	19.750	19.750	1.000	20.750	17.359	87.9	0.000	0.0	17.359	83.7
Environment (B4-3)	120.045	119.045	30.994	150.039	91.153	76.6	0.000	0.0	91.153	60.8
Consumer protection (B5-1)	20.810	20.810	0.750	21.560	17.800	85.5	0.000	0.0	17.800	82.6
Aid for reconstruction (B5-2)	6.775	6.775	0.000	6.775	6.054	89.4	0.000	0.0	6.054	89.4
Internal market (B5-3)	157.934	153.634	0.750	154.384	129.533	84.3	0.750	100.0	130.283	84.4
Industry (B5-4)	79.915	81.215	0.897	82.112	75.885	93.4	0.409	45.6	76.294	92.9
Information market (B5-5)	14.234	14.234	0.000	14.234	11.514	80.9	0.000	0.0	11.514	80.9
Statistical information (B5-6)	32.999	34.499	4.790	39.289	33.737	97.8	4.342	90.6	38.079	96.9
Trans-European networks (B5-7)	261.500	261.500	0.000	261.500	238.709	91.3	0.000	0.0	238.709	91.3
Cooperation in the fields of justice and home affairs (B5-8)	2.600	2.600	0.000	2.600	0.000	0.0	0.000	0.0	0.000	0.0
Exploitation of the results of research in the European Union (B5-9)	0.000	0.000	0.000	0.000	0.000	0.0	0.000	0.0	0.000	0.0
Reserve for internal policies (B5-95)	0.000	0.000	0.000	0.000	0.000	0.0	0.000	0.0	0.000	0.0
Total 3	4 525.173	4 525.173	175.735	4 700.907	3 889.123	85.9	94.258	53.6	3 983.381	84.7

TABLE 19 (continued)

(million ECU)

	Appropriations entered in 1995 budget (including supplementary/ amending budgets)	Appropriations entered in 1995 budget (including supplementary/ amending budgets and transfers)	Additional 1995 appropriations and carryovers from 1994	Total appropriations available in 1995	Payments made in 1995					
					Against 1995 appropriations		Against additional appropriations and carryovers		Total appropriations available in 1995	
					Amount	%	Amount	%	Amount	%
4. External action										
EDF (B7-1)	0,000	0,000	0,000	0,000	0,000	0,0	0,000	0,0	0,000	0,0
Food aid (B7-2)	760,000	1 044,400	186,717	1 231,117	749,350	71,7	181,280	97,1	930,630	75,6
Cooperation — Latin American and Asian developing countries (B7-3)	385,000	450,000	0,478	450,478	435,359	96,7	0,234	49,1	435,594	96,7
Cooperation — Mediterranean countries (B7-4)	421,002	309,252	0,000	309,252	228,982	74,0	0,000	0,0	228,982	74,0
Other cooperation measures (B7-5)	534,183	524,583	0,852	525,435	396,509	75,6	0,426	50,0	396,935	75,5
Cooperation — Central and Eastern Europe and independent States of former Soviet Union (B7-6)	1 336,770	1 287,120	0,000	1 287,120	1 156,958	89,9	0,000	0,0	1 156,958	89,9
Cooperation — other non-member countries (B7-7)	38,996	93,996	0,000	93,996	57,824	61,5	0,000	0,0	57,824	61,5
External aspects of certain Community policies (B7-8)	294,050	270,050	0,000	270,050	166,264	61,6	0,000	0,0	166,264	61,6
Common foreign and security policy (B8-1)	105,000	90,000	0,000	90,000	75,576	84,0	0,000	0,0	75,576	84,0
Reserve for external policy actions (B7-95)	0,000	0,000	0,000	0,000	0,000	0,0	0,000	0,0	0,000	0,0
Total 4	3 875,001	4 069,401	188,047	4 257,448	3 266,822	80,3	181,940	96,8	3 448,762	81,0
5. Administrative expenditure										
Commission (part A not including pensions)	2 227,994	2 210,125	237,019	2 447,144	1 879,891	85,1	203,317	85,8	2 083,208	85,1
Pensions (A-19)	349,792	369,683	0,109	369,792	363,301	98,3	0,109	100,0	363,410	98,3
Enlargement reserve (A-105)	9,200	7,070	0,000	7,070	0,000	0,0	0,000	0,0	0,000	0,0
Total 5	2 586,986	2 586,878	237,128	2 824,006	2 243,192	86,7	203,426	85,8	2 446,618	86,6
6. Reserves										
Monetary reserve (B1-6)	500,000	500,000	0,000	500,000	0,000	0,0	0,000	0,0	0,000	0,0
Guarantee reserve (B0-2)	323,000	323,000	0,000	323,000	250,750	77,6	0,000	0,0	250,750	77,6
Humanitarian aid reserve (B7-9)	323,000	173,000	0,000	173,000	0,000	0,0	0,000	0,0	0,000	0,0
Total 6	1 146,000	996,000	0,000	996,000	250,750	25,2	0,000	0,0	250,750	25,2
7. Compensation										
Compensation (B0-5)	1 547,000	1 547,000	0,000	1 547,000	1 547,000	100,0	0,000	0,0	1 547,000	100,0
Total 7	1 547,000	1 547,000	0,000	1 547,000	1 547,000	100,0	0,000	0,0	1 547,000	100,0
Grand total	75 056,160	74 066,552	1 305,486	75 372,038	64 739,897	87,4	776,922	59,5	65 516,819	86,9

improve the information sent to the budgetary authority and help it in the exercise of its powers of control over the utilization of Community appropriations, led to Parliament's adoption of a resolution on the execution of the 1995 budget on 12 October.[1]

992.   The total budget resources for 1995 came to ECU 74 395.6 million, corresponding to 1.151% of Community GNP. There was also an additional ECU 600 million in miscellaneous revenue. Revenue for 1995 is shown in Table 16.

Discharge procedure

993.   On 21 April 1994 Parliament postponed the discharge in respect of the general budget for 1992.[2] On 5 April it gave the Commission a discharge in respect of the implementation of the general budget in 1992[3] and in 1993,[4] and adopted resolutions containing comments forming an integral part of the decision. It reserved the right to reconsider EAGGF Guarantee expenditure. It also gave the Commission discharge for 1993 in respect of the financial management of the Fifth, Sixth and Seventh EDFs, the ECSC,[5] the Centre for the Development of Vocational Training[6] and the European Foundation for the Improvement of Living and Working Conditions.[7] On 12 October it gave discharge in respect of the implementation of its own budget (1993).[8]

ECSC budget

994.   After taking note of the ECSC Consultative Committee's opinion of 20 July[9] and Parliament's opinion of 26 October[10] on its draft budget[11] the Commission adopted the ECSC operating budget for 1996 on 14 November,[12] reducing the ECSC levy rate for 1996 from 0.21% to 0.19% in anticipation of the expiry of the ECSC Treaty in 2002 (→ point 1019). The budget totals ECU 247 million, of which ECU 87 million is for redeploy-

---

[1]   OJ C 287, 30.10.1995; Bull. 10-1995, point 1.6.1.
[2]   1994 General Report, point 1128.
[3]   OJ L 141, 24.6.1995; OJ C 109, 1.5.1995; Bull. 4-1995, point 1.6.5.
[4]   OJ L 141, 24.6.1995; OJ C 109, 1.5.1995; Bull. 4-1995, point 1.6.6.
[5]   OJ L 141, 24.6.1995; OJ C 109, 1.5.1995; Bull. 4-1995, points 1.6.7 and 1.6.10.
[6]   OJ L 141, 24.6.1995; OJ C 109, 1.5.1995; Bull. 4-1995, point 1.6.8.
[7]   OJ L 141, 24.6.1995; OJ C 109, 1.5.1995; Bull. 4-1995, point 1.6.9.
[8]   OJ C 287, 30.10.1995; Bull. 10-1995, point 1.6.3.
[9]   Bull. 7/8-1995, point 1.6.5.
[10]   OJ C 308, 20.11.1995; Bull. 10-1995, point 1.6.5.
[11]   Bull. 5-1995, point 1.6.3.
[12]   OJ L 283, 25.11.1995; Bull. 11-1995, point 1.6.3.

ment aid, ECU 85 million for aid for research, ECU 40 million for conversion aid, ECU 30 million for social measures connected with the restructuring of the coal industry and ECU 5 million for administrative expenditure.

995. On 9 November[1] the Commission also adopted an amending ECSC operating budget for 1995 after informing the ECSC Consultative Committee on 20 July[2] and obtaining Parliament's opinion on 12 October[3] on its draft.[4]

996. On 21 June the Commission adopted the ECSC financial statements and the outturn of the ECSC operating budget for 1994[5] on which the Court of Auditors had issued its report on 15 June.[6] On 5 April Parliament had adopted a resolution on the Court of Auditors' reports on the 1993 ECSC financial statements and the accounts and financial management of the ECSC.[7]

Financial Regulation

997. On 18 September the Council adopted three new regulations amending the Financial Regulation of 21 December 1977:[8] Regulation (EC, Euratom, ECSC) No 2333/95 was the second part of the first round of amendments (effects of the entry into force of the Treaty on European Union and the Agreement on the European Economic Area, borrowing and lending operations (Table II)); Regulation (EC, Euratom, ECSC) No 2334/95, third round of amendments (treatment of fines, role of financial controller, recovery of debts, adjustment after closure of accounts (Table II)); Regulation (EC, Euratom, ECSC) No 2335/95, fifth round of amendments (new activities of Joint Research Centre (Table II)). These follow the two other sets of amendments already adopted by the Council on 25 July 1994 by Regulation (ECSC, EC, Euratom) No 1923/94 (first part of first round: effects of Maastricht Treaty, in particular Economic and Social Committee, Committee of the Regions and Ombudsman) and on 31 October 1994 by Regulation (ECSC, EC, Euratom) No 2730/94 (second round: follow-up to Edinburgh European Council, in particular reserves for loans and emergency aid).

---

[1] Bull. 11-1995, point 1.6.2.
[2] Bull. 7/8-1995, point 1.6.4.
[3] OJ C 287, 30.10.1995; Bull. 10-1995, point 1.6.4.
[4] Bull. 5-1995, point 1.6.2.
[5] OJ C 244, 21.9.1995; Bull. 6-1995, point 1.6.3.
[6] Bull. 6-1995, point 1.10.25.
[7] OJ C 109, 1.5.1995; Bull. 4-1995, point 1.6.11.
[8] OJ L 356, 31.12.1977, as last amended by Regulation (EC, ECSC, Euratom) No 2730/94, OJ L 293, 12.11.1994.

Following the revision of Regulation (EEC) No 729/70 on the financing of the common agricultural policy, on 2 May the Council adopted an amended proposal for the revision of the Financial Regulation (sixth round (Table II)) to take account of Parliament's amendments on which the Council adopted its common position on 17 November.

A specific amendment (fourth round), which was presented on 21 December 1993 and concerns the way in which the balance for each year is treated in connection with the amendment of Regulation (EEC) No 1552/89 on own resources, was still being discussed in the Council at the end of the year.

The last proposal for amendment (seventh round) connected with the second phase of the project for improving financial management (SEM 2000) (→ point 976) will be presented in early 1996.

998.   On 12 July Parliament passed a resolution calling for the European Development Fund to be incorporated in the general budget and EDF expenditure to be classified as non-compulsory expenditure.[1] On 12 December it passed a resolution on legal bases and maximum amounts (→ point 976).[2]

---

[1]   OJ C 249, 25.9.1995; Bull. 7/8-1995, point 1.6.1.
[2]   OJ C 17, 22.1.1996; Bull. 12-1995.

Section 3

Financial control

999. With a view to greater decentralization of the management and control of Community funds in the Member States, the Financial Controller held further consultations, both bilateral[1] and multilateral, with the supreme authorities responsible for controls at national level. As a result, a protocol was signed with Greece concerning cooperation in on-the-spot inspections of operations financed by the Structural Funds and steps were taken under the protocols signed with Spain, Italy, Luxembourg and France in 1994[2] to coordinate and rationalize inspection programmes. Training seminars for national officials were held in France and Germany.

1000. As part of the increased Community aid to the countries of Central and Eastern Europe under the PHARE programme *(→ point 824)*, a training seminar for Czech officials was held in Prague in April. Fact-finding missions and on-the-spot inspections were carried out in Romania, Poland and the Czech Republic (PHARE) and in Uzbekistan (TACIS *(→ point 869))*.

1001. In order to monitor Community expenditure in international organizations, the Financial Controller, acting on the basis of the Commission communication of November 1993,[3] continued negotiations on the wider introduction of control clauses such as those provided for in the agreement signed with the United Nations in December 1994.

1002. As regards implementation of the Treaty on European Union, Financial Control continued to play an active role in the discussions between the Court of Auditors and the Commission on the statement of assurance *(→ point 1066)*.

1003. In accordance with the Commission Decision of 7 June 1990,[4] the Financial Controller conducted a financial audit of seven Directorates-General or departments and investigated what action had been taken on his recommendations in three Directorates-General and departments audited at an earlier date. A targeted inquiry was also carried out.

---

[1] Meeting with national counterparts in Venice in October.
[2] 1994 General Report, point 1137.
[3] Twenty-seventh General Report, point 1098.
[4] Twenty-fourth General Report, point 1007.

1004.   Improvements to financial management (Sound and efficient management — SEM 2000) are dealt with in Section 1 (Priority activities and objectives) of this chapter *(→ point 976).*

1005.   Financial Control also lent its support to operations to increase awareness of the need to protect the Union's financial interests *(→ point 1008).*

1006.   Lastly, a seminar on customs' role in the verification of Community revenue and expenditure was held in Portugal for officials from the Member States.

Section 4

Action to combat fraud

1007.   In 1995 the Commission continued the fight against fraud along the broad lines which it had defined in 1994 in its new anti-fraud strategy.[1] On 8 February the Commission adopted its 1995 work programme on fraud prevention.[2] Endorsing this programme on 19 June, the Council stressed that fraud must be combated by eliminating the factors which made fraud possible or even attractive and that there was a need for simple and clear Community legislation and for the active cooperation of the Member States.[3]

1008.   Significant progress was made on the protection of the Communities' financial interests. On 18 December the Council adopted a common position on the proposal for a Regulation (Table II) laying down a comprehensive and uniform definition of what constitutes an 'irregularity' adversely affecting the Community budget and establishing a general framework setting out the administrative penalties applicable throughout the Community. Such penalties constitute a specific administrative instrument integrated into the financial support arrangements and are intended to ensure the proper financial management of Community funds. This minimum measure does not exclude the application of national penalties. The Regulation covers revenue and all Community expenditure. Following the agreement reached at the Cannes European Council,[4] a Convention, based on Title VI of the Treaty on European Union, defining the specific concept of fraud against the Communities' financial interests and requiring that it be incorporated into national criminal law, was signed on 26 July *(→ point 967).* On 20 December the Commission adopted a proposal for the establishment of a protocol to the Convention *(→ point 967).* On the same day, it also adopted a proposal for a Council Regulation (Table II) concerning on-the-spot checks and inspections by the Commission for the detection of fraud and irregularities detrimental to the financial interests of the European Communities.

1009.   On the operational side, the establishment of task forces in sensitive areas enabled substantial progress to be made, particularly in the field of cigarette smuggling. The Commission continued activities under the textile

---

[1]   COM(94) 92; 1994 General Report, point 1145.
[2]   COM(95) 23; Bull. 1/2-1995, point 1.5.13.
[3]   Bull. 6-1995, point 1.6.12.
[4]   Bull. 6-1995, point I.21.

anti-fraud initiative (TAFI) (→ *point 774*);[1] on 12 June the Council and the Commission adopted a Joint Declaration on the fight against fraud in trade in textile products between the Community and non-Community countries.[2] On 29 March the Commission adopted a communication on fraud in the customs transit procedures,[3] followed by a Council resolution on 23 November.[4] On 13 December Parliament decided to set up a committee of inquiry into this type of fraud.[5] In its resolution of 25 October, it stressed the need to improve the measures to combat fraud affecting the own resources in the Community budget.[6] On 15 December it also passed a resolution on the fight against corruption in Europe.[7]

The internal organization of the Commission departments responsible for the prevention of fraud against the Community budget underwent considerable changes in 1995, with the assignment of additional staff to this sector,[8] the centralization of all operational activities (in all financial areas) within the Unit for the Coordination of Fraud Prevention (UCLAF) and wider use of data-processing methods to deal with fraud.

1010. The sixth annual report, on the fight against fraud, adopted by the Commission on 29 March, reviews the measures taken in 1994.[9] In that year the number of fraud cases detected by the Member States and by the Commission was substantially higher than in 1993, as were the sums involved, both for own resources (increase of ECU 140 million and 961 cases) and for the EAGGF Guarantee Section (increase of ECU 130 million and 323 cases). The number of cases relating to the Structural Funds and the Cohesion Fund which Member States detected and reported under the Regulations adopted in July 1994[10] increased appreciably, but the exact sums involved could not be identified, the Regulations concerned having been adopted so recently. In these various fields, investigation teams from the Member States and the Commission found clear evidence of the substantial financial impact of certain typical frauds perpetrated by organized criminal networks.

1011. The Essen European Council had asked the Member States to submit reports on the measures they were implementing to combat wasteful-

---

[1]   1994 General Report, point 1046.
[2]   Bull. 6-1995, point 1.4.35.
[3]   COM(95) 108; Bull. 3-1995, point 1.6.9.
[4]   OJ C 327, 7.12.1995; Bull. 11-1995, point 1.6.13.
[5]   Bull. 12-1995.
[6]   OJ C 308, 20.11.1995; Bull. 10-1995, point 1.6.10.
[7]   OJ C 17, 22.1.1996; Bull. 12-1995.
[8]   1994 General Report, point 1145.
[9]   COM(95) 98; Bull. 3-1995, point 1.6.8.
[10] Regulation (EC) No 1681/94 — OJ L 178, 12.7.1994; Regulation (EC) No 1831/94 — OJ L 191, 27.7.1994; 1994 General Report, point 1148.

ness and the misuse of Community resources.[1] On 19 June the Council, having completed a preliminary examination of the reports submitted,[2] was able to assess the progress achieved, particularly as regards cooperation between the Member States and the Community. The reports in question were submitted to the Madrid European Council and served as a basis for the Commission to produce a comparative analysis[3] and a review of the application of Article 209a of the EC Treaty, as requested by the Cannes European Council.[4] This comparative analysis was welcomed in the Council's conclusions of 27 November[5] and by December's European Council in Madrid, which called on the Member States and the institutions to adopt the necessary measures to ensure an equivalent level of protection throughout the Community and in the entire Community budget and the EDF.[6]

---

[1]   Bull. 12-1994, point I.29.
[2]   Bull. 6-1995, point 1.6.13.
[3]   COM(95) 556; Bull. 11-1995, point 1.6.10.
[4]   Bull. 6-1995, point I.21.
[5]   Bull. 11-1995, point 1.6.11.
[6]   Bull. 12-1995.

Section 5

Borrowing and lending operations

1012.   Table 20 shows the loans granted each year from 1993 to 1995. Borrowing operations during the year totalled ECU 860.7 million to which must be added EIB loans *(→ point 82)*, of which ECU 66.1 million was to refinance earlier operations.

TABLE 20

Loans granted

(million ECU)

Instrument	1993	1994	1995
New Community Instrument [1]	—	—	—
EC balance-of-payments loans [1]	4 004.8	—	—
EC medium-term financial assistance to countries of Central Europe and other non-member countries [1]	270.0	245.0	315.0
EC food aid	709.1	156.8	94.1
ECSC	918.3	673.7	402.8
Euratom [1]	—	—	—
EIB (from the Bank's own resources)	19 531.8	21 038.5	21 160.0
of which:			
• loans to countries of the Union [2]	17 724.2	19 660.4	18 602.8
• loans to ACP countries and overseas territories	147.4	222.5	249.7
• loans to Mediterranean countries [2]	679.0	579.0	1 014.5
• loans to Eastern Europe [1]	882.0	357.0	1 005.0
• loans to Asia and Latin America	—	220.0	288.0
Total	25 434.0	22 114.0	21.971.9

[1]   With partial guarantee from the general budget.
[2]   With no guarantee from the general budget.

1013.   The Commission's report on the borrowing and lending activities of the Community in 1994 was adopted on 18 July.[1] The reports on the utilization rate for the NCI in the second half of 1994 and the first half of 1995 were adopted on 18 July[1] and 28 November[2] respectively.

---

[1]   COM(95) 364; Bull. 7/8-1995, point 1.6.7.
[2]   COM(95) 595; Bull. 11-1995, point 1.6.9.

Operations concerning the New Community Instrument

1014. No funds were raised under the NCI. However, the equivalent of ECU 66 million was raised in September to refinance an earlier borrowing in Swiss francs.

Macrofinancial assistance

Balance-of-payments support for the Member States

1015. Under Regulation (EEC) No 1969/88 providing medium-term financial assistance for Member States' balances of payments,[1] and Decision 93/67/EEC granting Italy a loan of ECU 8 billion to be paid in four equal tranches,[2] the fourth tranche became available on 1 February but Italy did not draw it down. This year again Greece did not call in the second tranche of the ECU 2.2 billion loan granted in 1991.[3]

Macrofinancial assistance for non-member countries[4]

1016. In August the Commission paid the first half of the second tranche (ECU 25 million) of the ECU 100 million loan granted to Lithuania in 1992[5] and raised and paid the second tranche (ECU 20 million) of the ECU 45 million loan granted to Moldova in 1994.[6] In November the Commission raised and paid the first tranche (ECU 55 million) of the ECU 125 million loan granted to Romania in June 1994[7] and the first tranche (ECU 100 million) of the ECU 200 million loan granted to Algeria in December 1994.[8] In December the Commission raised ECU 115 million to finance a loan of ECU 85 million granted to Ukraine[9] and the first tranche (ECU 30 million) of the ECU 55 million loan granted to Belarus.[10]

1017. An additional ECU 167 million under the medium-term loan of ECU 1.25 billion granted to the republics of the former Soviet Union in

[1]   OJ L 178, 8.7.1988; Twenty-second General Report, point 256.
[2]   OJ L 22, 30.1.1993; Twenty-seventh General Report, point 1110.
[3]   OJ L 66, 13.3.1990; Twenty-fifth General Report, point 1271.
[4]   See also Chapter III, Section 2 (Economic and monetary policy) *(points 63 et seq.).*
[5]   OJ L 351, 2.12.1992; Twenty-sixth General Report, point 48.
[6]   OJ L 155, 22.6.1994; 1994 General Report, point 1155.
[7]   OJ L 168, 2.7.1994; 1994 General Report, point 66.
[8]   OJ L 366, 31.12.1994; 1994 General Report, point 68.
[9]   Decision 94/940/EC — OJ L 366, 31.12.1994; 1994 General Report, point 67.
[10] Decision 95/132/EC — OJ L 89, 21.4.1995.

1991 to finance imports of foodstuffs and medicines[1] and divided by the Commission in 1993 between the 10 independent States which had signed the loan contract[2] was granted to Georgia, Azerbaijan and Uzbekistan in 1994.[3] The latter two countries used ECU 94.1 million in 1995. A balance of ECU 18 million remains available and may be used until March 1996 as the drawing period has been extended.

Financing ECSC activities

1018.   ECSC loans paid out in 1995 totalled ECU 402.8 million, compared with ECU 673.7 million in 1994. New industrial loans to support restructuring and modernization of iron and steel undertakings (first paragraph of Article 54 of the ECSC Treaty) totalled ECU 42.7 million. The Commission paid out further loans of ECU 17.8 million for new investment in the coal industry. Despite a relative recovery in productive investment, the volume of lending continued to drop in view of the expiry of the ECSC Treaty which is scheduled for 2002. However, the ECSC paid the first loan of around DM 79.7 million to a country in Central and Eastern Europe under the aid for industrial cooperation with that region. Loans totalling ECU 260.2 million for the conversion of coal and steel areas were paid out, mainly to small and medium-sized firms via financial intermediaries. The ECSC continued to look to the capital market for funds, raising a total of ECU 385.6 million, as against ECU 643.9 million in 1994. Finally, the Commission adopted the ECSC financial report for 1994 on 6 September.[4]

1019.   As regards the future of the ECSC's borrowing and lending activities, the ECSC's operations in 1995 were in keeping with the decisions adopted by the Commission in 1994, which provided for a gradual and co-ordinated reduction in the ECSC's financial activities to ensure a smooth transition to the period following expiry of the ECSC Treaty (23 July 2002).[5] On 28 June the ECSC Consultative Committee adopted a memorandum in which it asked to be closely involved in the formulation of the Union's coal and steel policy and in future discussions on aspects relating to the expiry of the ECSC Treaty.[6]

---

[1]   OJ L 362, 31.12.1991; Twenty-fifth General Report, point 78.
[2]   Twenty-seventh General Report, point 1113.
[3]   1994 General Report, point 1156.
[4]   Bull. 9-1995, point 1.6.5.
[5]   OJ C 175, 28.6.1994; COM(94) 269; Decisions 2983/94/ECSC and 2984/94/ECSC — OJ L 315, 8.12.1994; 1994 General Report, point 1160.
[6]   Bull. 6-1995, point 1.6.7.

Financing Euratom activities

1020.   In view of the continuing unfavourable situation in the industry, there were again no loan operations this year. The grand total of loans since such operations began in 1977 is ECU 2.876 billion (at the exchange rates obtaining when contracts were signed). In addition, no projects were financed in 1995 under Decision 94/179/Euratom which authorizes the Commission to contract Euratom borrowings in order to help improve the degree of safety and efficiency of nuclear facilities in Central and Eastern Europe and in the former Soviet Union.[1]

European Investment Bank

1021.   Information relating to the activities of the European Investment Bank appears under 'Economic and monetary policy' in Chapter III *(→ point 76).*

---

[1]   OJ L 84, 29.3.1994; 1994 General Report, point 1162.

Section 6

General budget guarantee for borrowing and lending operations

1022.   The guarantee by the Community budget covers lenders when the Community floats an issue under one of its financial instruments: balance-of-payments facility *(→ point 1015)*, Euratom loans *(→ point 1020)*, New Community Instrument *(→ point 1014)*, medium-term financial assistance for Hungary, the Czech Republic, Slovakia, Bulgaria, Romania, Algeria, Israel, the Baltic States and the independent States of the former Soviet Union. The budget guarantee is also given to the European Investment Bank for the loans it grants from its own resources to the Mediterranean countries (75% guarantee), the countries of Central and Eastern Europe, Latin American countries and South Africa.

1023.   At end-1995, the ceiling for authorized borrowing and lending operations guaranteed by the general budget was ECU 43.332 billion. At 31 December the guarantee was in operation for ECU 10.25 billion of Community borrowing and for ECU 2.864 billion granted by the EIB out of its own resources. The loan made in 1994 by a syndicate of banks to Russia and covered by a 98% guarantee from the Community budget to finance imports of agricultural produce and foodstuffs[1] was repaid in full at 31 December 1995.

1024.   On 31 October 1994 the Council enacted Regulation (EC) No 2728/94 establishing a Guarantee Fund for external actions,[2] to reimburse the Community's creditors in the event of default by the recipient of a loan given or guaranteed by the Community in a non-member country. On 26 July the Commission adopted a communication on the limits imposed by the Fund's machinery.[3] Referring to one of the suggestions made in the communication, its report of 6 September[4] proposed that the cover for EIB operations should be reduced from 100% to 75%. In conclusions adopted on 27 November, the Council called for a study to be made of a new guarantee system.[5] The guarantee was activated after various States of the former Soviet Union which had received loans worth ECU 1.25 billion in 1991 *(→ point 1017)* defaulted on their payments. The amount for which

---

[1]   1994 General Report, point 1165.
[2]   OJ L 293, 12.11.1994; 1994 General Report, point 1133.
[3]   COM(95) 404; Bull. 7/8-1995, point 1.6.6.
[4]   Bull. 9-1995, point 1.10.12.
[5]   Bull. 11-1995, point 1.10.25.

the Community Guarantee Fund was called upon in 1995 and which had not been repaid by 31 December totalled ECU 233.05 million. In 1995 the budget guarantee was again activated[1] for loans granted by the EIB for certain republics of former Yugoslavia. When they failed to make repayments, the Guarantee Fund was called upon for ECU 19.89 million. At 31 December, none of these repayments had been made. The total amount of guarantees activated since 1992 after the republics of former Yugoslavia defaulted on their payments came to ECU 68.2 million.

---

[1]   1994 General Report, point 1167.

Chapter VII

Institutional matters

Section 1

Preparations for 1996 Intergovernmental Conference

1025. As requested by the Corfu European Council,[1] the Community institutions produced their reports on the operation of the Treaty on European Union as input for the Reflection Group set up to prepare the ground for the Intergovernmental Conference *(→ point 1026).*

The Council's report, adopted on 10 April,[2] gives a factual run-down on the operation of the various innovations made by the Treaty on European Union. It makes no value judgments but merely records the facts, and it makes no proposals for subsequent reforms. It underlines that not enough experience has been acquired, the new Treaty having entered into force on 1 November 1993, and that full effect has not yet been given to some of the new provisions so that the exercise is not wholly meaningful and the initial results must be treated with some caution.

The Commission's report was adopted on 10 May.[3] It likewise makes no specific proposals for changes but sets out the general orientation which the Commission will follow during the Treaty review exercise. A more political preface, entitled 'Preparing Europe for the 21st century',[4] sets out the two major challenges that it feels must be taken up — making Europe the business of every citizen and preserving the *acquis communautaire* while making a success of future enlargements. The Commission's examination of the operation of the Treaty focused on the question of whether the intentions of the Treaty's authors had been met as regards democracy and transparency in the Union and the effectiveness and coherence of its policies. The diag-

---

[1]   1994 General Report, point 1176.
[2]   Bull. 4-1995, point 1.9.1.
[3]   Bull. 5-1995, point 1.9.1.
[4]   Reproduced in full in Bull. 5-1995, point 1.9.1.

nosis is variable. The Commission states that on many points the Treaty represents a genuine step forward in the process of European integration and truly adds value. It lays the foundations for economic and monetary union with the prospect of a single currency by the end of the century; it looks beyond the hitherto primarily economic focus of the Community by adding new forms of cooperation on common foreign and security policy and justice and home affairs; and it strengthens the democratic base for Community action, notably by enhancing Parliament's role. However, while emphasizing these advantages, the Commission is constructively critical, aiming at all times to identify areas for improvement so that the Treaty can have the full effect intended. It sets forth inadequacies of different types, some of which may be teething troubles with a still rather new Treaty (citizenship, common foreign and security policy), whereas others flow from failure to apply it properly (the possibility of qualified majority voting in intergovernmental cooperation contexts has not yet been taken up) and yet others are structural in origin (multiplicity and complexity of decision-making procedures; unanimity rule which blocks some new policies and forms of cooperation; the social policy agreement between 14 Member States; the serious deficiencies in the provisions governing justice and home affairs cooperation; problems of definition and overlapping of powers).

In the report adopted on 17 May,[1] the main deficiencies cited by the European Parliament include the lack of openness and full democratic accountability of the Council, the lack of coherence and effectiveness in implementation of the common foreign and security policy and justice and home affairs cooperation, and institutional machinery originally devised for a six-member Community and never adequately reviewed. A number of concrete proposals are made to make the Union operate more efficiently, democratically, transparently and coherently.

Reports were also published by the Court of Justice,[2] the Court of First Instance,[3] the Court of Auditors,[4] the Economic and Social Committee (→ point 1073) and the Committee of the Regions (→ point 1086).

1026. The formal process of preparing for the Intergovernmental Conference began with the inaugural meeting of the Reflection Group at Taormina, Sicily, on 2 June.[5] This was preceded by a ceremony at Messina to commemorate the conference held there at the initiative of Jean Monnet and the Benelux countries in 1955, which relaunched the European integration pro-

---

[1] OJ C 151, 19.6.1995; Bull. 5-1995, point 1.9.2.
[2] Bull. 5-1995, point 1.9.3.
[3] Bull. 5-1995, point 1.9.4.
[4] Bull. 6-1995, point 1.9.4.
[5] Bull. 6-1995, point 1.9.3.

cess following the failure of the European Defence Community in 1954.[1] A solemn interinstitutional declaration was signed,[2] stressing the progress made in European integration since the original six-member Community was established and affirming the desire to make fresh progress, particularly at the 1996 Intergovernmental Conference.

The Reflection Group set up to prepare for the Intergovernmental Conference as decided at the Corfu European Council in June 1994[3] and confirmed at the Cannes European Council,[4] was chaired by Mr Carlos Westendorp, Spanish State Secretary for European Affairs. It comprised the personal representatives of the Member States' Foreign Ministers (one per Member State, with no substitutes allowed), one personal representative of the President of the Commission (Mr Oreja) and two personal representatives of the President of Parliament (Mrs Elisabeth Guigou and Mr Elmar Brok). It held several working meetings and examined five major topics — the principles and objectives of the Conference, the institutional system, the citizen and the Union, the common foreign and security policy, and the instruments available to the Union. An interim report, presented on 5 September, helped to advance the work.[5] The Reflection Group's conclusions were set out in a report presented to the Madrid European Council on 5 December.[6] It identifies the questions to be dealt with by the Conference and, in some cases, suggests solutions.

1027. The Madrid European Council in December[6] warmly welcomed the Reflection Group's report, judging its conclusions, reached after careful consideration of the internal and external challenges facing the Union, a good basis for the work of the Conference. It pointed out that the Intergovernmental Conference would have to look at those provisions of the Treaty on European Union whose review was expressly stipulated in the Treaty, and matters which were earmarked for reassessment by the Brussels and Corfu European Councils, or in interinstitutional agreements, so as to create the political and institutional conditions needed to equip the European Union for present and future needs, particularly the next enlargement. The European Council agreed that the formal review procedure set out in Article N of the Treaty on European Union would be completed as quickly as possible to allow the formal opening of the Conference on 29 March 1996 in Turin. It announced that the Conference would hold regular meetings, at foreign minister level, prepared by a group made up of one representative from each

[1]   Bull. 6-1995, point 1.9.2.
[2]   Reproduced in full in Bull. 6-1995, point 1.9.2.
[3]   1994 General Report, point 1176.
[4]   Bull. 6-1995, point I.28.
[5]   Bull. 9-1995, point 1.9.1.
[6]   Bull. 12-1995.

of the Member States' Foreign Ministers and of the President of the Commission, and that the European Parliament would be closely associated with the work, kept informed of developments and given the opportunity to make its views heard, as it requested in a resolution of 14 December.[1] Furthermore, representatives of the Central and East European countries which have signed Europe Agreements, Malta and Cyprus will be kept informed of the Conference's progress and may express their views at meetings with the Presidency of the European Union. The European Economic Area and Switzerland will also be kept informed.

---

[1]   OJ C 17, 22.1.1996; Bull. 12-1995.

Section 2

Voting in the Council

1028. With the entry into force of the Treaty on European Union on 1 November 1993, qualified-majority voting was extended to a wider range of policy areas. In 1995, the Council acted by qualified majority in 54 cases,[1] confirming the trend that has emerged since entry into force of the Single Act.

1029. On 1 January, in line with the adjustments to the instruments concerning the accession of new Member States necessitated by Norway's decision not to join the Union,[2] the Council adopted a Decision, agreed in December 1994,[3] Decision 95/1/EC, Euratom, ECSC,[4] amending the Decision of 29 March 1994 concerning the taking of decisions by qualified majority by the Council[5] (the original Decision was adopted following the agreement reached at the informal meeting of Foreign Ministers in Ioannina in 1994). The total number of votes in the Council has been increased to 87 and 62 votes are now required for a qualified majority. The Decision also states that, if members of the Council representing a total of 23 to 25 votes indicate their intention to oppose the adoption by the Council of a decision by qualified majority, the Council will do all in its power to reach, within a reasonable time and without prejudicing obligatory time-limits laid down by the Treaties and by secondary law, a satisfactory solution that could be adopted by at least 65 votes.

1030. In conclusions adopted on 29 May[6] the Council reaffirmed its determination to work towards greater transparency of proceedings *(→ points 8 et seq.)* within the guidelines framed by the European Council[7] and in line with the commitments made to Parliament in the October 1993 interinstitutional declaration on democracy, transparency and subsidiarity,[8] without undermining the effectiveness of the decision-making process and restated the principle that the outcome of votes on legislative acts should now be

---

[1]   Adoption of internal legislative instruments only.
[2]   1994 General Report, point 725.
[3]   Bull. 12-1994, point 1.3.12; 1994 General Report, point 727.
[4]   OJ L 1, 1.1.1995; Bull. 1/2-1995, point 1.8.1.
[5]   1994 General Report, point 1170.
[6]   Bull. 5-1995, point 1.9.5.
[7]   Conclusions of the Edinburgh European Council — Bull. 12-1992, point 1.24; Twenty-sixth General Report, point 10.
[8]   Twenty-seventh General Report, point 12.

made public as a matter of course.[1] It also promised to increase the frequency of debates which are broadcast to the public on important matters affecting the interests of the Union or on major new legislative proposals, to ensure that the press and the public are regularly and fully briefed prior to each of its meetings, and to facilitate public access to the minutes of its meetings. This resulted in the Code of Conduct on public access to the minutes and statements in the minutes of the Council acting as legislator adopted by the Council on 2 October, in the interests of further transparency.[2] This Code of Conduct was warmly welcomed by the Madrid European Council in December.[3] Taking note of the Code of Conduct, Parliament adopted a resolution on 12 October calling for such statements to be made only in exceptional cases and only with its prior agreement.[4]

[1] 1994 General Report, point 1171.
[2] Bull. 10-1995, point 1.9.1.
[3] Bull. 12-1995.
[4] OJ C 287, 30.10.1995; Bull. 10-1995, point 1.9.2.

Section 3

Involvement of Parliament in decision-making

1031.   Since the entry into force of the Treaty on European Union, Parliament's involvement in the decision-making process has resulted in particular in the adoption, together with the Council, of a number of instruments covered by the co-decision procedure. Although certain fears had been expressed about its complexity and length, the co-decision procedure has so far operated efficiently. Decisions have been taken within a reasonable time, thanks in particular to the close cooperation between the institutions, which concluded an interinstitutional agreement on the Rules of Procedure of the Conciliation Committee on 21 October 1993. In 1995, 14 instruments were adopted under the co-decision procedure, in six cases following recourse to the Conciliation Committee (under Article 189b of the EC Treaty). At its part-session from 28 February to 2 March, Parliament rejected the joint text prepared by the Conciliation Committee on a proposal for a Directive on the legal protection of biological inventions *(→ point 133)*.

Section 4

Implementing powers conferred on the Commission

1032.   As in the past, the implementing powers conferred on the Commission were subject to procedures involving committees with representatives from the Member States: advisory committees were involved in about 10 cases, management committees in approximately 60 cases and regulatory committees in approximately 30 cases.

Two comments can be made. First, despite the request of the Intergovernmental Conference that prepared the Single European Act, the advisory committee procedure was employed only three times under Article 100a of the EC Treaty,[1] while the Commission proposed it 7 times; the regulatory committee procedure (type IIIb) was employed in about 10 cases. In its report on the functioning of the Treaty on European Union *(→ point 1025)*, the Commission pointed out that it has always refused to propose this type of procedure since it offers no guarantee that a decision will be taken. Furthermore, in some cases, the powers proposed by the Commission were not conferred at all.

1033.   In its resolution of 26 October on committee activities, adopted at the same time as the draft budget for 1996 *(→ points 980 et seq.)*, Parliament stated that the committee procedures should be more transparent. The Commission took this opportunity to show that it was willing to improve the situation, but pointed out that some of the new features which Parliament wanted could require amendment of the Treaties.[2]

1034.   Following the agreement reached at the Interinstitutional Conference of 20 December 1994, comprising a *modus vivendi* concerning the measures taken for the implementation of acts adopted under the co-decision procedure,[3] the Commission began to implement the procedures for informing Parliament in this connection.

---

[1]   Twentieth General Report, point 4.
[2]   OJ C 308, 20.11.1995; Bull. 10-1995, point 1.9.3.
[3]   OJ C 293, 8.11.1995; 1994 General Report, point 1174.

Section 5

Interinstitutional collaboration

1035.   Information on the *modus vivendi* between Parliament, the Council and the Commission concerning the measures taken by the Commission for the implementation of acts adopted under Article 189b of the EC Treaty pending the review of the Treaty on European Union in 1996 appears in Section 4 (Implementing powers conferred on the Commission) of this chapter *(→ point 1034).*

1036.   In a resolution passed on 18 January,[1] Parliament gave its view on the interinstitutional agreement relating to an accelerated procedure for the consolidation of legislation[2] agreed at the Interinstitutional Conference on 20 December 1994. The agreement defines legislative consolidation, which involves repealing the instruments to be consolidated and replacing them by a single instrument, without making any changes of substance, establishes an interinstitutional consultative working party responsible for examining the Commission proposals as quickly as possible and certifying that the proposal does not contain any changes of substance, and spells out an accelerated procedure for its adoption by Parliament and the Council.

1037.   With a view to intensifying interinstitutional cooperation on the basis of mutual trust and adapting the 1990 Code of Conduct to the new institutional context, the Commission and Parliament, agreed on a new Code of Conduct[3] at the Conference of Presidents held on 13 and 14 March. The objectives of the new Code of Conduct are to strengthen the democratic legitimacy of the Union's decision-making process and to improve the exercise of powers by Parliament and the Commission in accordance with the provisions of the Treaty, notably those relating to the interinstitutional balance and the independence of the Commission. The areas covered by the undertakings given by the two institutions include the supply of information to Parliament by the Commission, the choice of legal basis for proposals, the legislative process (including due consideration of the amendments adopted by Parliament at second reading under the cooperation and co-decision procedures and rejection by Parliament of Commission legislative proposals), monitoring of the implementation of Community law, the Commission's implementing powers, legislative programming and inter-

---

[1]   OJ C 43, 20.2.1995; Bull. 1/2-1995, point 1.8.5.
[2]   OJ C 293, 8.11.1995; Bull. 12-1994, point 1.7.1.
[3]   OJ C 89, 10.4.1995; Bull. 3-1995, point 1.9.1.

institutional coordination. The Code of Conduct will be reviewed regularly when the annual legislative programme is drawn up.

1038. An interinstitutional declaration on the incorporation of financial provisions into legislative acts *(→ point 976)* was signed on 6 March. This will make for more effective cooperation in budgetary matters pending reconsideration at the 1996 Intergovernmental Conference.

1039. Lastly, Parliament, Council and Commission Decision 95/167/EC, Euratom, ECSC of 19 April[1] lays down the detailed provisions governing the exercise of Parliament's right of inquiry. The Decision, agreed at the Interinstitutional Conference on 20 December 1994,[2] establishes the *modus operandi* of Parliament's temporary committees of inquiry, with particular reference to the conditions for their establishment, their powers, the basic rules governing hearings and depositions, and access to and use of documents.

---

[1] OJ L 78, 6.4.1995, corrected by OJ L 113, 19.5.1995; Bull. 3-1995, point 1.9.2; Bull. 4-1995, point 1.9.5.
[2] Bull. 12-1994, point 1.7.1; 1994 General Report, point 1191.

Chapter VIII

Institutions

Section 1

Composition and functioning

Parliament

1040.   Following the accession of Austria, Finland and Sweden, Parliament now has 626 Members, of whom 21 are from Austria, 22 from Sweden (directly elected in September) and 16 from Finland. Two Groups — Forza Europa and the European Democratic Alliance — merged to form the Union for Europe Group on 5 July.

At 31 December, the distribution of seats among the political groups was as follows:

Party of European Socialists (PES), chaired by Pauline Green (UK)	217
European People's Party (EPP), chaired by Wilfried Martens (B)	173
European Liberal, Democratic and Reformist Party (ELDR), chaired by Gijs de Vries (NL)	52
Confederal Group of the European United Left (EUL), chaired by Alonso José Puerta Gutiérrez (E)	33
Union for Europe (UFE), chaired by Jean-Claude Pasty (F)	54
Greens, chaired by Claudia Roth (D)	27

European Radical Alliance (ERA),
chaired by Catherine Lalumière (F) 20

Europe of the Nations (EN),
chaired by James Goldsmith (F) 19

Non-affiliated (NI) 31

1041. At the September part-session, Parliament passed a controversial organizational resolution scheduling its part-sessions for 1996; there are to be only 11 part-sessions in Strasbourg (the second October part-session having been dropped) and eight two-day additional part-sessions in Brussels.[1]

1042. At the part-session from 16 to 20 January,[2] Parliament debated and then voted on the confirmation of the new Commission presided by Jacques Santer *(→ point 1053)*, which obtained a large majority. Mr Santer presented the Commission's general policy thrust — an economy with strong job-creating capacity, social and regional solidarity, implementation of the common foreign and security policy, and reinforcement of the Union's status as the leading economic and trading power — and offered a number of ideas on preparations for the 1996 Intergovernmental Conference. The Commission's work programme for 1995 *(→ point 9)* was presented by Mr Santer in February,[3] and Parliament passed a resolution on it at the part-session from 13 to 17 March,[4] while at December's part-session Mr Santer presented the work programme for 1996 *(→ point 9)*, which revolves around four priorities: employment and solidarity, preparations for EMU, strengthening the internal market and enlargement.

1043. Part-sessions throughout the year were dominated by the Union's institutional future but also by the emergence of new geopolitical relationships — pre-accession strategy for Central and Eastern Europe and the new equilibrium in relations with the Mediterranean countries. There were also lively debates on the subject of France's nuclear testing programme at the June to October part-sessions *(→ point 701)*.

On the institutional front, Parliament passed a resolution[5] (288 votes for, 103 against, 76 abstentions) on the operation of the Treaty on European Union in the run-up to the 1996 Intergovernmental Conference *(→ point 1025)*; this was in response to the request from the Corfu European Council

---

[1] Bull. 9-1995, point 1.10.2.
[2] Bull. 1/2-1995, point 1.9.2.
[3] Bull. 1/2-1995, point 1.9.3.
[4] Bull. 3-1995, point 1.10.3.
[5] OJ C 151, 19.6.1995; Bull. 5-1995, point 1.9.2.

in June 1994 and also provided a basis for assessing the work done by the Reflection Group set up to prepare the ground for the Conference. The Ombudsman, Jacob Söderman, was appointed on 12 July (→ *point 7*). At the January part-session, Parliament also passed two resolutions relating to the Decision of Parliament, the Council and the Commission on Parliament's right of inquiry[1] (→ *point 1039*) and the interinstitutional *modus vivendi* on measures for the implementation of instruments adopted by the co-decision procedure (→ *point 1034*). In March a resolution was passed on the revised Code of Conduct. At its November part-session,[2] Parliament, on the initiative of its President, Klaus Hänsch, organized a debate on the state of the Union which was attended by the Commission and the Council. This was the first-ever such debate.

On the external relations front, the prospects of accession by countries of Central and Eastern Europe (→ *point 814*) were debated at the part-session from 3 to 7 April;[3] Mr Santer addressed the additional sitting from 28 February to 2 March[4] on the same subject, when he reminded the House that the basic decision of principle had been taken to envisage Union membership for Cyprus, Malta, the six countries with which the Community had signed Europe Agreements, the Baltic States and subsequently Slovenia. Parliament also passed a resolution on the Euro-Mediterranean partnership in October and a resolution on the results of the Barcelona conference in December (→ *point 839*), following the decisions taken by the Cannes European Council. At the December part-session, it gave its assent to the proposal for a customs union with Turkey (→ *point 844*) and regularly debated the peace process in the Middle East (→ *point 850*), Algeria (→ *point 847*), the war in former Yugoslavia (→ *point 845*) and the situation in Nigeria (→ *point 949*). The conflict between the Union and Canada following the seizure of a Spanish fishing vessel (→ *point 578*) was debated and a resolution passed. October's debate on relations with South Africa (→ *point 953*) revealed a broad consensus on the need for constructive cooperation with that country.[5]

Implementation of economic and monetary union (→ *point 36*) was a regular item on the agenda; the Commission confirmed, both after the Cannes European Council and after the informal summit in Majorca and during the discussions in preparation for the Madrid European Council, that the timetable for the changeover to the single currency was maintained unchanged.

---

[1]   OJ C 43, 20.2.1995; Bull. 1/2-1995, point 1.8.3.
[2]   Bull. 11-1995, point 1.10.1.
[3]   Bull. 4-1995, point 1.10.1.
[4]   Bull. 3-1995, point 1.10.2.
[5]   Bull. 10-1995, point 1.10.1.

In April Parliament unanimously approved the programme proposed by the Commission to encourage the peace process in Ireland (→ point 321). It also passed resolutions on the liberalization of telecommunications infrastructure (→ point 429) and on the G7 Conference on the Information Society (→ point 456).

1044.   Parliament gave the 1996 budget its two readings (→ points 980 et seq.) and the President declared it finally adopted on 21 December.

1045.   At formal sittings, Parliament heard an emotional valedictory address by French President, François Mitterrand,[1] and addresses by Mary Robinson, President of Ireland,[2] Boutros Boutros-Ghali, UN Secretary-General,[3] and Roman Herzog, President of Germany;[4] in January it paid glowing tribute to Jacques Delors upon his relinquishing the Commission Presidency.[1]

1046.   A breakdown of Parliament's work in 1995 is shown in Table 21.

Parliament addressed 4 971 questions to the Commission and the Council — 3 661 written questions (3 217 to the Commission and 444 to the Council), 297 oral questions with a debate (188 to the Commission and 109 to the Council) and 1 013 during question time (691 to the Commission and 322 to the Council).

1047.   At 31 December, the establishment plan of Parliament's Secretariat comprised 3 493 permanent posts and 602 temporary posts.

Council

1048.   Following the accession of Austria, Finland and Sweden and Norway's decision not to accede, the Council adopted a Decision amending the Decision concerning the taking of decisions by qualified majority in the Council (→ point 1029) and, on 1 January, a Decision determining the order in which the office of President of the Council will be held.[5] France was in the chair for the first half of the year and Spain for the second half.

---

[1]   Bull. 1/2-1995, point 1.9.2.
[2]   Bull. 5-1995, point 1.10.3.
[3]   Bull. 11-1995, point 1.10.1.
[4]   Bull. 10-1995, point 1.10.1.
[5]   OJ L 1, 1.1.1995; Bull. 1/2-1995, point 1.8.1.

TABLE 21

Parliamentary proceedings from January to December 1995

Part-session	Consultations (single reading)	Cooperation procedures — First reading	Cooperation procedures — Second reading	Co-decision procedures — First reading	Co-decision procedures — Second reading	Co-decision procedures — Third reading	Assent procedures	Other opinions[7]	Budgetary matters	Recommendations[8] (Rules 46, 90, 92 and 94)	Own-initiative reports and resolutions — Rules 45, 148 and 157 (reports)	Own-initiative reports and resolutions — Rules 37 and 40 (resolutions)	Own-initiative reports and resolutions — Rule 47 (topical and urgent)	Miscellaneous decisions and resolutions[9]
January	7	1	—	—	—	1	—	5	—	—	2	1	10	5
February I	11	2	—	4	—	—	—	3	—	—	—	7	14	1
February II	—	1	3	1	—	3	—	—	1	—	—	3	—	—
March	13	—	—	3	—	—	—	1	1	—	1	8	10	1
April I	10	—	1	3	—	—	—	3	10	—	1	10	13	—
April II	3	1	1	1	—	—	1	—	2	—	—	1	—	—
May	42	4	—	6	5	2	—	3	1	1	3	2	17	2
June I	6	—	1	1	—	1	—	5	—	—	3	4	10	1
June II	1	3	—	1	—	—	—	6	—	—	2	—	—	—
July	4	—	—	3	1	—	—	6	—	1	6	8	16	2
September	17	3	—	4	—	—	—	6	—	—	1	7	19	1
October I	10	—	2	5	7	—	2	2	3	1	1	1	19	—
October II	7	4	2	3	1	—	—	6	5	—	—	8	—	1
November I	6	2	2	—	—	—	8	1	—	—	4	1	14	—
November II	4	5	—	—	5	—	4	4	2	1	1	2	—	1
December	23	—	—	—	—	—	2	6	—	—	—	10	13	2
Total	**164[1]**	**26[2]**	**12[3]**	**35[4]**	**19[5]**	**7[6]**	**17**	**57**	**25**	**4**	**25**	**73**	**155**	**17**

NB: In addition, Parliament adopted one resolution pursuant to Rule 49 of its Rules of Procedure on the legislative programme for 1995, four resolutions concerning the legal basis of a proposal and one resolution pursuant to Rule 61(4) to ask the Commission to maintain a proposal for a directive, rather than replace it with a proposal for a recommendation. On 26 October 1995 Parliament adopted a resolution requesting the Commission to submit a legislative proposal to it in accordance with Article 138b of the EC Treaty and Rule 50 of its Rules of Procedure.

1 Including 91 cases in which Parliament tabled amendments to the Commission proposal and one case in which it rejected it.
2 Including 24 cases in which Parliament tabled amendments to the Commission proposal.
3 Including 11 cases in which Parliament amended the common position of the Council.
4 Including 30 cases in which Parliament tabled amendments to the Commission proposal.
5 Including 15 cases in which Parliament amended the common position of the Council.
6 Including one case in which Parliament rejected the Council text.
7 Mainly opinions on Commission reports or communications.
8 Recommendations relating to the opening of negotiations with third countries, implementation of a common foreign and security policy, or cooperation in the fields of justice and home affairs.
9 Decisions concerning waiver of immunity, amendments to the Rules of Procedure and interinstitutional agreements.

1049.   The European Council met twice formally — in Cannes in June and in Madrid in December — and once informally — in Formentor in September.

The Cannes European Council on 26 and 27 June[1] was devoted in great part to economic and monetary issues and the fight against unemployment. The determination to prepare for the changeover to the single currency no later than 1 January 1999 in strict compliance with the convergence criteria, timetable, procedures and protocols laid down in the Treaty was reaffirmed. On the external relations front, agreement was reached on the financing to 1999 of financial cooperation with Central and Eastern Europe and the Mediterranean countries and the amount and financing of the eighth European Development Fund. While the European Council was meeting, there was also a meeting with Heads of State or Government and Foreign Ministers of the associated countries of Central and Eastern Europe, the Baltic States, Cyprus and Malta devoted mainly to structured dialogue with these countries. On justice and home affairs cooperation, the European Council welcomed the agreement reached on the Europol Convention and agreed to defer the question of the jurisdiction to be conferred on the European Court of Justice to June 1996 at the latest. Agreement was reached on the Convention on the protection of the Community's financial interests and the Convention on the use of information technology for customs purposes. The mandate given to the Reflection Group set up to prepare the 1996 Intergovernmental Conference was confirmed. Resolutions relating to the European Council were passed in Parliament on 13 June[2] and 12 July.[3]

The European Council meeting in Madrid on 15 and 16 December confirmed that 1 January 1999 would be the starting date for the third stage of economic and monetary union and adopted the scenario for the changeover to the single currency, which will be called the Euro. It considered that job creation was the principal social, economic and political objective of the European Union and its Member States and declared its firm intention to continue to make every effort to reduce unemployment and promote equal opportunities. It was pleased with the way in which the procedure for monitoring employment provided for at the Essen European Council, on the basis of a strategy of cooperation between all concerned, had been put into practice and indicated how this process could continue. As regards enlargement in Central and Eastern Europe and the Mediterranean, the European Council reiterated that the accession negotiations with Malta and Cyprus would commence, on the basis of the Commission proposals, six months

[1]   Bull. 6-1995, points I.1 to I.57.
[2]   OJ C 166, 3.7.1995; Bull. 6-1995, point 1.9.6.
[3]   OJ C 249, 25.9.1995; Bull. 7/8-1995, point 1.9.3.

after the conclusion of the 1996 Intergovernmental Conference and that, following the conclusion of the Intergovernmental Conference and in the light of its outcome and of the opinions and reports requested from the Commission, it would, at the earliest opportunity, take the necessary decisions for launching the accession negotiations with the countries of Central and Eastern Europe and hoped that the preliminary stage would coincide with the start of negotiations with Cyprus and Malta. The European Council noted with satisfaction some achievements in the area of external relations in which the European Union had played a decisive role such as the signing in Paris of the Dayton Agreement which puts an end to the war in former Yugoslavia, the new transatlantic agenda and the joint EU-US action plan, the signing of the agreement with Mercosur, the Euro-Mediterranean Barcelona Declaration, the signing of the revised Lomé IV Convention and Parliament's assent to the customs union between the European Union and Turkey. Finally, having welcomed the Reflection Group's report, the European Council decided to inaugurate the Intergovernmental Conference on 29 March 1996 in order to establish the political and institutional conditions for adapting the European Union to present and future needs, particularly with a view to the next enlargement. A meeting also took place with the Heads of State or Government and the Ministers for Foreign Affairs of the associated countries of Central and Eastern Europe, including the Baltic States, as well as Cyprus and Malta, concerning the pre-accession strategy and various issues relating to international policies. Parliament passed a resolution on 14 December on the preparation of the Madrid European Council.[1]

1050.   At its 76 meetings in 1995, the Council adopted 39 directives, 242 regulations and 175 decisions.

1051.   There were 2 445 permanent posts and 19 temporary posts on the Council's establishment plan at the end of the year.

1052.   Questions relating to transparency in Council proceedings and voting are dealt with at Section 2 (Voting in the Council) of Chapter VII (→ point 1028) and Section 3 (Openness, subsidiarity and simplification) of Chapter I (→ points 8 et seq.).

---

[1]   OJ C 17, 22.1.1996; Bull. 12-1995.

Commission

1053. On 23 January, following the confirmation vote in Parliament on 18 January,[1] the Representatives of the Governments of the Member States adopted Decision 95/12/EC, Euratom, ECSC[2] appointing the President (Jacques Santer) and Members of the Commission for a five-year term of office. The oath was sworn at a ceremony in Luxembourg on 24 January.[3] At its first meeting, on 25 January, the Commission distributed responsibilities among its Members;[4] Sir Leon Brittan and Manuel Marín were elected Vice-Presidents on 1 February.[5]

1054. The composition and distribution of responsibilities in the Commission are as follows:[6]

Jacques Santer, President: Secretariat-General, Legal Service, Security Office, Forward Studies Unit, Inspectorate-General, Joint Interpreting and Conference Service, Spokesman's Service, monetary matters (with Mr de Silguy), common foreign and security policy and human rights (with Mr Van den Broek), institutional matters and Intergovernmental Conference (with Mr Oreja);

Sir Leon Brittan, Vice-President: external relations with North America, Australia, New Zealand, Japan, China, Korea, Hong Kong, Macao and Taiwan, common commercial policy, and relations with the OECD and WTO;

Manuel Marín, Vice-President: external relations with the southern Mediterranean countries, the Middle and Near East, Latin America and Asia (except Japan, China, Korea, Hong Kong, Macao and Taiwan), including development aid;

Martin Bangemann: industrial affairs, information and telecommunications technologies;

Karel Van Miert: competition;

Hans van den Broek: external relations with the countries of Central and Eastern Europe, the former Soviet Union, Mongolia, Turkey, Cyprus, Malta and other European countries, common foreign and security policy and human rights (in agreement with the President), and external diplomatic missions;

---

[1] OJ C 43, 20.2.1995; Bull. 1/2-1995, points I.2 and I.6.
[2] OJ L 19, 27.1.1995; Bull. 1/2-1995, point I.3.
[3] Bull. 1/2-1995, point I.4.
[4] Bull. 1/2-1995, point I.6.
[5] Bull. 1/2-1995, point I.5.
[6] Bull. 1/2-1995, point I.6. Biographical information on the Members of the new Commission can be found in Bull. 1/2-1995, point I.7.

João de Deus Pinheiro: external relations with African, Caribbean and Pacific countries and South Africa (including development aid), and Lomé Convention;

Pádraig Flynn: employment and social affairs, and relations with the Economic and Social Committee;

Marcelino Oreja: relations with the European Parliament, relations with the Member States (transparency, communication and information), culture and audiovisual policy, Publications Office, institutional matters and preparations for the 1996 Intergovernmental Conference (in agreement with the President);

Anita Gradin: immigration, justice and home affairs, relations with the Ombudsman, financial control, fraud prevention;

Édith Cresson: science, research and development, Joint Research Centre, human resources, education, training and youth;

Ritt Bjerregaard: environment and nuclear safety;

Monika Wulf-Mathies: regional policies, relations with the Committee of the Regions, and Cohesion Fund (in agreement with Mr Kinnock and Mrs Bjerregaard);

Neil Kinnock: transport (including trans-European networks);

Mario Monti: internal market, financial services and financial integration, customs and taxation;

Franz Fischler: agriculture and rural development;

Emma Bonino: fisheries, consumer policy and European Community Humanitarian Office (ECHO);

Yves-Thibault de Silguy: economic and financial affairs, monetary matters (in agreement with the President), credit and investments, and Statistical Office;

Erkki Liikanen: budget, personnel and administration, translation and in-house computer services;

Christos Papoutsis: energy and Euratom Supply Agency, small and medium-sized enterprises (SMEs), and tourism, distributive trades and cooperatives.

1055.   Information on the Commission's work programme is given in Section 3 (Openness, subsidiarity and simplification) of Chapter I (→ point 9).

1056. On 8 March, the Commission revised certain aspects of its Rules of Procedure regarding the delegation of powers,[1] following the judgment given by the Court of Justice in the 'PVC' case.[2]

1057. The Commission held 46 meetings in the course of the year. It sent the Council 600 proposals, recommendations or draft instruments (71 proposals for directives, 290 proposals for regulations and 236 proposals for decisions, one draft recommendation, one proposal for a recommendation and one draft resolution) and 275 communications, memoranda and reports, as well as the new initiatives, new legislative proposals, measures to stimulate public discussion, programmes and action plans, and further action on measures under way as set out in its 1995 work programme *(→ point 9).* These figures include proposals for routine management instruments (in particular in agriculture, fisheries, customs and commercial policy) and proposals for consolidation of existing legislative instruments.

1058. The Commission's establishment plan for 1995 comprised 15 001 permanent posts (including 1 763 LA posts for the Language Service) and 835 temporary posts (including 23 LA posts) paid out of administrative appropriations; 3 452 permanent posts and 171 temporary posts paid out of research appropriations; 525 permanent posts in the Publications Office; 76 permanent posts at the European Centre for the Development of Vocational Training and 71 at the European Foundation for the Improvement of Living and Working Conditions.

Under the secondment and exchange arrangements between the Commission and the Member States' government departments, 35 Commission officials were seconded to national civil services and international organizations, and the number of national experts coming to work for Commission departments was equivalent to 603 man/years, paid from the administrative budget.

Court of Justice and Court of First Instance

1059. Following the accession of Austria, Finland and Sweden, the European Court of Justice now consists of 15 Judges assisted by nine Advocates-General. On 1 January the Representatives of the Governments of the Member States adopted Decisions 95/4/EC, Euratom, ECSC and 95/8/EC, Euratom, ECSC appointing the Judges and Advocates-General of the Court of

---

[1]   Decision 95/148/EC, Euratom, ECSC — OJ L 97, 29.4.1995; Bull. 3-1995, point 1.10.16.
[2]   Case C-137/92 P *Commission* v *BASF and others* (judgment given on 15 June 1994); 1994 General Report, points 166 and 1286.

Justice, and Decision 95/5/EC, Euratom, ECSC appointing the Members of the Court of First Instance.[1] The new Members of the two Courts were sworn in on 25 January.[2]

1060. On 25 January the composition of the Chambers of the Court of Justice was determined as follows for the period from 25 January to 6 October 1995:[3]

First Chamber: President: Mr Jann; Judges: Mr Joliet, Mr Edward and Mr Sevón;

Second Chamber: President: Mr Schockweiler; Judges: Mr Mancini and Mr Hirsch;

Third Chamber: President: Mr Gulmann; Judges: Mr Moitinho de Almeida and Mr Puissochet;

Fourth Chamber: President: Mr Kapteyn; Judges: Mr Kakouris, Mr Murray and Mr Ragnemalm;

Fifth Chamber: President: Mr Gulmann; Judges: Mr Jann, Mr Joliet, Mr Moitinho de Almeida, Mr Edward, Mr Puissochet and Mr Sevón;

Sixth Chamber: President: Mr Schockweiler; Judges: Mr Kapteyn, Mr Mancini, Mr Kakouris, Mr Murray, Mr Hirsch and Mr Ragnemalm.

Mr Jacobs was appointed First Advocate-General for the same period.

On 13 September, the Representatives of the Governments of the Member States appointed Melchior Wathelet Judge at the Court of Justice to replace Mr Joliet, who died in July, for the period from 18 September 1995 to 6 October 1997.[4]

On 19 September, decisions were adopted on the appointment of the Presidents of the Chambers and the First Advocate-General and the composition of the Chambers for the 1995/96 court year starting on 7 October.[5]

1061. On 25 January, the composition of the Chambers of the Court of First Instance was determined as follows for the 1994/95 court year:[6]

First Chamber: President: Mr da Cruz Vilaça; Judges: Mr Kirschner, Mr Kalogeropoulos and Mrs Tiili;

---

[1] OJ L 1, 1.1.1995; OJ L 17, 25.1.1995; Bull. 1/2-1995, points 1.9.19 and 1.9.23.
[2] OJ C 54, 4.3.1995; Bull. 1/2-1995, points 1.9.20 and 1.9.24.
[3] OJ C 54, 4.3.1995; Bull. 1/2-1995, point 1.9.21.
[4] Decision 95/387/EC, Euratom, ECSC — OJ L 233, 30.9.1995; Bull. 9-1995, point 1.10.9.
[5] OJ C 299, 11.11.1995; Bull. 11-1995, point 1.10.19.
[6] OJ C 54, 4.3.1995; Bull. 1/2-1995, point 1.9.25.

Second Chamber: President: Mr Vesterdorf; Judges: Mr Barrington and Mr Saggio;

Third Chamber: President: Mr Biancarelli; Judges: Mr Azizi, Mr Briët and Mr Bellamy;

Fourth Chamber: President: Mr Lenaerts; Judges: Mr Schintgen, Mr García-Valdecasas and Mrs Lindh;

First Chamber (extended composition): President: Mr da Cruz Vilaça; Judges: Mr Barrington, Mr Saggio, Mr Kirschner, Mr Kalogeropoulos and Mrs Tiili;

Second Chamber (extended composition): President: Mr Vesterdorf; Judges: Mr Barrington, Mr Saggio, Mr Kirschner, Mr Kalogeropoulos and Mrs Tiili;

Third Chamber (extended composition): President: Mr Biancarelli; Judges: Mr Schintgen, Mr Briët, Mr García-Valdecasas, Mr Azizi, Mr Bellamy and Mrs Lindh;

Fourth Chamber (extended composition): President: Mr Lenaerts; Judges: Mr Schintgen, Mr Briët, Mr García-Valdecasas, Mr Azizi, Mr Bellamy and Mrs Lindh.

On 17 July, the Representatives of the Governments of the Member States appointed Mr Bellamy, Mr García-Valdecasas, Mr Kirschner, Mrs Lindh, Mr Potoki and Mr Saggio Judges at the Court of First Instance for the period from 1 September 1995 to 31 August 2001.[1] On 26 July, following the resignation of Mr da Cruz Vilaça, they appointed Mr Gens de Moura Ramos Judge for the period from 18 September 1995 to 31 August 1998.[2] On 18 September, Mr Saggio was elected President of the Court of First Instance for the same period.[3]

On 19 September, decisions were adopted on the composition of the Chambers, the appointment of the Presidents of the Chambers and the allocation of Judges to the Chambers for the 1995/96 court year starting on 1 October.[4]

1062. The Rules of Procedure of the Court of Justice and the Court of First Instance were amended on 21 February[5] to determine the procedure applicable in the event of referrals pursuant to the Agreement on the European

---

[1]   Decision 95/278/EC, Euratom, ECSC — OJ L 172, 22.7.1995; Bull. 7/8-1995, point 1.10.13.
[2]   Decision 95/315/EC, Euratom, ECSC — OJ L 188, 9.8.1995; Bull. 7/8-1995, point 1.10.14.
[3]   OJ C 274, 19.10.1995.
[4]   OJ C 274, 19.10.1995; Bull. 11-1995, point 1.10.20.
[5]   OJ L 44, 28.2.1995; Bull. 1/2-1995, points 1.9.18 and 1.9.22.

Economic Area and the rights of EFTA States and their legal representatives. The Protocol on the Statute of the Court of Justice[1] and the Rules of Procedure of the Court of First Instance[2] were also amended to take account of the specific features of Council Regulation (EC) No 40/94 relating to intellectual property rights.[3]

1063.   In 1995, 409 cases were brought (242 references for preliminary rulings, 48 appeals (including 10 staff cases) and 119 others. Of the 225 judgments given by the Court of Justice, 140 were preliminary rulings, 21 were appeals (including eight staff cases) and 64 were other cases.[4] The Court of First Instance had 260 new cases on its register and gave 165 judgments.

1064.   There were 842 permanent posts and 108 temporary posts on the establishment plan of the Court of Justice and the Court of First Instance at 31 December.

Court of Auditors

1065.   Following the accession of Austria, Finland and Sweden, the membership of the Court of Auditors was expanded from 12 to 15. On 20 February, the Council, after consulting Parliament,[5] appointed three new Members.[6] They are Hubert Weber for the period from 1 March to 20 December 1995 and Jan O. Karlsson and Aunus Olavi Salmi for the period from 1 March 1995 to 9 February 2000. On 29 June, the Council, with the assent of Parliament,[7] appointed Joergen Mohr to the Court of Auditors to replace Ole Warberg, who had resigned.[8] On 19 January, Parliament passed a resolution on the procedure for appointing Members of the Court of Auditors.[9] On 18 December,[10] the Council, after consulting Parliament, renewed the term of three Members of the Court of Auditors (Mr Friedmann, Mr Wiggins and Mr Weber). It also appointed four new Members (Mrs Nikolaou, Mr Bernicot, Mr Colling and Mr Engwirda).

---

[1]   Council Decision 95/208/EC — OJ L 131, 15.6.1995; Bull. 6-1995, point 1.10.22.
[2]   OJ L 172, 22.7.1995; Bull 7/8-1995, point 1.10.12.
[3]   Council Regulation (EC) No 40/94 on the Community trade mark — OJ L 11, 14.1.1995; Twenty-seventh General Report, point 117; 1994 General Report, point 153.
[4]   The Court's judgments are discussed in Chapter IX: 'Community law' (→ points 1126 et seq.).
[5]   OJ C 56, 6.3.1995.
[6]   OJ L 50, 7.3.1995; Bull. 1/2-1995, point 1.9.28.
[7]   OJ C 166, 3.7.1995.
[8]   OJ L 159, 11.7.1995; Bull. 6-1995, point 1.10.23.
[9]   OJ C 43, 20.2.1995; Bull. 1/2-1995, point 1.9.27.
[10] Bull. 12-1995.

1066. On 14 July, following its usual practice, the Court of Auditors adopted the observations that were likely to appear in its annual general report on 1994;[1] these were transmitted to the Commission and the other institutions in accordance with Article 88 of the Financial Regulation. The Court adopted its report on 26 October,[2] and it was published in the Official Journal with the replies from the institutions.[3] However, there was one major innovation this year: the reform of the adversarial procedure before the Commission finalizes its replies to the Court's observations. In order to eliminate the contradictory arguments which each side puts forward and to clarify their respective positions, the Commission and the Court of Auditors agreed to hold a meeting at what was considered the most appropriate time. This procedure worked satisfactorily.

Acting in accordance with Article 188c of the EC Treaty as inserted by the Union Treaty, the Court for the first time issued its statement of assurance concerning the reliability of the accounts and the legality of the underlying transactions. The Court's preliminary observations, which formed part of the special report on which the statement of assurance was based, were sent to the Commission on 15 September. The statement of assurance and the special report expanding each of the points in the statement were adopted by the Court on 26 October[4] and were transmitted to Parliament on 14 November. The Commission finalized its reply on 31 October. The statement of assurance relating to the general budget assesses the reliability of the accounts (they are considered reliable, although some reservations are made in order to improve their information value) and analyses the legality and regularity of the underlying transactions. In the case of commitments, no serious substantial errors were revealed and the few formal errors originate within the Community institutions; however, a large number of errors are noted with respect to payments — some are substantial, and generally produced within the national administrations, and some are formal, resulting from procedural shortcomings. As a result of these findings, the Commission is recommending a substantial increase in cooperation with the Member States as part of the 'Sound and efficient management' (SEM 2000) project (→ *point 976).*

1067. Special Report 1/95, adopted on 12 January,[5] relates to the cohesion financial instrument; Report 2/95, adopted on 26 April,[6] relates to

---

[1] Bull. 7/8-1995, point 1.10.15.
[2] OJ C 303, 14.11.1995; Bull. 10-1995, point 1.10.16.
[3] OJ C 303, 14.11.1995.
[4] Bull. 10-1995, point 1.10.18.
[5] OJ C 59, 8.3.1995; Bull. 1/2-1995, point 1.9.29.
[6] OJ C 285, 28.10.1995; OJ C 167, 3.7.1995; Bull. 4-1995, point 1.10.13.

Stabex; Report 3/95, adopted on 14 September,[1] relates to the common organization of the market in sheepmeat and goatmeat; Report 4/95, adopted on 12 October,[2] relates to EAGGF Guidance Section expenditure in Portugal.

1068.   This year the Court produced six specific reports relating to 1994, concerning the financial statements for the ECSC,[3] JET,[4] the Euratom Supply Agency,[5] the Foundation for the Improvement of Living and Working Conditions,[6] the Centre for Development of Vocational Training[7] and the European Schools.[8] It also produced the 1994 annual report on the ECSC in accordance with Article 45c(5) of the ECSC Treaty, the ECSC statement of assurance in the form of an accounts certification adopted on 29 June and annexed to the financial statements for 1994, and the EDF statement of assurance which, like its equivalent for the general budget, was adopted for the first time.[9] It was transmitted, together with the Commission's replies, to the discharge authorities at the same time as the annual report and the statement of assurance relating to the general budget.

1069.   The Court also delivered opinions[10] on draft Financial Regulations for the European Training Foundation, the European Monitoring Centre for Drugs and Drug Addiction, the Office for Harmonization in the Internal Market, the European Environment Agency and the European Drugs Evaluation Centre. Finally, on 21 September, it issued the opinion requested by Parliament on the decision on the clearance of the 1991 EAGGF Guarantee Section accounts.[11]

1070.   On 31 December, there were 385 permanent posts and 73 temporary posts on the Court's establishment plan.

Economic and Social Committee

1071.   The Committee held 10 plenary sessions and adopted 156 opinions and two information reports. The Committee's opinion was requested on

---

[1]   Bull. 9-1995, point 1.10.11.
[2]   Bull. 10-1995, point 1.10.19.
[3]   Bull. 10-1995, point 1.10.17.
[4]   Bull. 9-1995, point 1.10.10.
[5]   Bull. 4-1995, point 1.10.12.
[6]   Bull. 11-1995, point 1.10.24.
[7]   Bull. 11-1995, point 1.10.23.
[8]   Bull. 11-1995, point 1.10.22.
[9]   Bull. 11-1995, point 1.10.21.
[10]   Bull. 1/2-1995, point 1.9.30; Bull. 10-1995, point 1.10.20.
[11]   Bull. 9-1995, point 1.10.11a.

53 occasions where this was compulsory and 68 times when consultation was optional. The Committee also issued 35 own-initiative opinions, including eight additional opinions.

1072.   The most significant of the opinions on matters referred to the Committee were on the following topics: the 1995 Annual Economic Report (→ point 46), the Green Paper on the single currency (→ point 44), the safeguarding of employees' rights in the event of transfers of undertakings (→ point 609), the fourth action programme on equal opportunities (1996-2000) (→ point 628), health and safety at work (→ point 619), AIDS prevention (→ point 640), the 1994 report on the single market (→ point 100), cross-border transfers (→ point 122), the free movement of doctors (→ point 117), the mutual recognition of qualifications (→ point 117), exercise of the profession of lawyer (→ point 117), food pricing (→ point 105), additives other than colourants and sweeteners (→ point 105), economic growth and the environment (→ point 466), control of shipments of waste (→ point 487), the information society action plan (→ point 419), the Green Paper on provision of telecommunications infrastructure (→ point 429), cable television networks (→ point 429), television without frontiers (→ point 676), MEDIA II (1996-2000) (→ point 677), pluralism and media concentration (→ point 126), the common organization of the market in sugar (→ point 537), the common policy for fruit and vegetables and processed fruit and vegetables (→ point 539), reform of the common organization of the market in wine (→ point 538), European civil aviation (→ point 409), the transport programme (→ point 385), the Green Paper on energy policy (→ point 353), the revision of Community legislation in the energy sector (→ point 352), the Green Paper on tourism (→ point 216), the Competition Policy Report (→ point 139) and the 'Customs 2000' programme (→ point 737).

1073.   Among the own-initiative opinions, the Committee delivered opinions on the World Social Development Summit (→ point 779), the World Women's Conference (→ point 633), cooperation for territorial development (→ point 296), coordination of research policies (→ point 225), the Treaty on the European Energy Charter (→ point 370), consumer protection (→ point 655), the fifth environment programme (→ point 463), direct and indirect taxation (→ point 128), spatial planning in the Mediterranean region, the Euro-Mediterranean partnership (→ point 840) and relations with Russia and Ukraine.

Special mention should be made of the opinion on the 1996 Intergovernmental Conference and the role of the Economic and Social Committee (→ point 1025), which contained proposals for amendments to the Treaty on European Union. It resulted from the Committee's debate on its advisory function, the means for promoting its role most effectively and the strengthening of the links which it feels should be established between the process of integration and the people of Europe.

1074.   Most of the Committee's opinions were in support of the Commission's objectives, although approval in principle was often accompanied by suggestions or reservations, even criticism of the means deployed. Some of the opinions were extremely critical of the Commission's proposals, such as those on the Green Paper on energy policy (→ point 353), European civil aviation (→ point 409), television without frontiers (→ point 676), the fifth report on the reform of the Structural Funds (→ point 296) and reform of the common organization of the wine market (→ point 538).

1075.   Two information reports were drawn up on relations between the European Union and the United States (→ point 899) and an evaluation of the PHARE programme (→ point 827).

1076.   In October, the Committee devoted its plenary session to employment (→ point 608).[1] It adopted a total of six opinions on youth unemployment, local development initiatives, coordination of research policies, the impact of the CAP on employment, working time and the 1995 economic situation and employment in Europe.

1077.   Mr Santer, President of the Commission,[2] Mr Flynn,[3] Mr de Silguy,[4] Mr Van Miert,[5] Mr Papoutsis, Mrs Wulf-Mathies, Mrs Bjerregaard and Mrs Bonino spoke at various meetings of the Committee. Other prominent speakers at plenary sessions included Mr Hänsch, President of the European Parliament,[6] Mr Lamassoure, French Minister with special responsibility for European affairs,[7] Mr Westendorp, Spanish State Secretary for European Affairs,[8] and Mr Griñan, Spanish Minister for Employment and Social Affairs.[8]

---

[1]   Bull. 10-1995, point 1.10.22.
[2]   Bull. 1/2-1995, point 1.9.37.
[3]   Bull. 1/2-1995, point 1.9.37; Bull. 10-1995, point 1.10.22.
[4]   Bull. 3-1995, point 1.10.22.
[5]   Bull. 5-1995, point 1.10.11.
[6]   Bull. 7/8-1995, point 1.10.18.
[7]   Bull. 1/2-1995, point 1.9.34.
[8]   Bull. 9-1995, point 1.10.14.

1078.   There were 135 permanent posts on the Committee's establishment plan at 31 December and 500 in the organizational structure shared with the Committee of the Regions.

Committee of the Regions

1079.   Following enlargement, the Committee now has 222 members, 33 more than in 1994,[1] though the numbers of commissions and subcommissions have remained unchanged (eight and five respectively). The distribution of seats by Member State is now 12 for Belgium, 9 for Denmark, 24 for Germany, 12 for Greece, 21 for Spain, 24 for France, 9 for Ireland, 24 for Italy, 6 for Luxembourg, 12 for the Netherlands, 12 for Austria, 12 for Portugal, 9 for Finland, 12 for Sweden and 24 for the United Kingdom. In addition to the national groups, four political groups have been formed (Party of European Socialists, European People's Party, Liberal and Democratic Group and Alliance for Europe), as has an interregional group (Europe-Mediterranean). Three quarters of the Committee's members are evenly spread among the Socialist and Christian Democrat Groups.

1080.   On 19 April, the Commission adopted a communication on strengthening relations with the Committee of the Regions.[2] Its political resolve focuses on three main targets: matters to be referred to the Committee will be identified when the annual work programme is drawn up, to facilitate the organization and planning of proceedings; active participation in the Committee's proceedings; and regular reports to the Committee on the action taken on its opinions.

1081.   This year, about 40 items of the work programme were selected for referral to the Committee. They went beyond the range of matters on which consultation is compulsory under the EC Treaty, encompassing not only proposals for new legislation but also Green and White Papers upstream of the legislative process. They were selected on the basis of the three criteria adopted by the Commission for consultation: matters within the regulatory or implementation powers of regional or local authorities; proposed measures likely to directly affect the functioning of regional or local authorities; and Community action likely to have a different economic impact in different regions. The Committee received three reports from the Commission on the action taken on its opinions. This move was warmly welcomed by the Committee.

---

[1]   Bull. 1/2-1995, point 1.9.40.
[2]   Bull. 4-1995, point 1.9.3.

1082. At its September plenary session,[1] the Committee had its first opportunity to exchange views with Mr Santer. Mr Santer's address reminded the Committee of its twofold role of enriching the Community debate by bringing regional and local concerns into the equation and at the same time acquainting regional and local bodies more fully with Community policies. Regarding the Committee's future in the context of the 1996 Intergovernmental Conference, Mr Santer argued that it should have an advisory role in relation to Parliament also and that members holding elective office should be appointed to the Committee. Some members did not share Mr Santer's view of the subsidiarity principle as a rule of good conduct, preferring it to be developed into a firmer form of distribution of powers.

1083. Mrs Wulf-Mathies, Member of the Commission responsible for relations with the Committee, regularly attended plenary sessions. After an initial contact at the February session,[2] where she stressed the importance of the Committee's role in the Community debate and in the European integration process generally, she outlined the Commission's orientations on strengthening dialogue with the Committee at the April session.[3] In September, she presented her vision of the information society as a means of developing cohesion, stressing the vital role played by the Member States and regional and local authorities in ensuring that all regions, especially the peripheral regions, enjoyed a fair and profitable share in the benefits of the information society.[1]

1084. On the institutional front, the Committee's relations with Parliament evolved this year. Mr Hänsch, Parliament's President, addressed the July plenary session.[4] He focused on the spirit of complementarity that should inspire relations between the two bodies and on the issues at stake in the run-up to the 1996 Intergovernmental Conference. He especially emphasized the need for the IGC to engender a more transparent and more efficient Union with greater democratic legitimacy. Committee proceedings were also attended by Mr Speciale, Chairman of Parliament's Regional Policy Committee,[2] and Mr Collins, Chairman of its Environment Committee.

---

[1] Bull. 9-1995, point 1.10.17.
[2] Bull. 1/2-1995, point 1.9.40.
[3] Bull. 4-1995, point 1.10.18.
[4] Bull. 7/8-1995, point 1.10.23.

1085. The 38 opinions adopted at the Committee's five plenary sessions[1] related to a variety of Community issues of topical concern. The legislative proposals on which consultation is mandatory under the EC Treaty included the plan of action against drugs *(→ point 974)* and the Raphael programme *(→ point 680).* In response to requests from the Commission or the Council, the Committee considered the initiative for Northern Ireland and the border counties of Ireland *(→ point 321),* cooperation in territorial development (Europe 2000+) *(→ point 296),* energy policy *(→ point 354),* the medium-term social action programme *(→ point 595),* the integrated programme for small businesses and craft industries *(→ point 206)* and the proposal for amendment of the LIFE Regulation *(→ point 470).* On its own initiative the Committee issued opinions on the financial and administrative repercussions of European Union legislation on the regional and local authorities *(→ point 296),* measures to counter the economic and environmental impact of the drought in southern Europe *(→ point 493)* and urban integration in the context of the review of the Union Treaty *(→ point 323).*

1086. At the April plenary session, the Committee, wishing to play an active part in the institutional debate to prepare for the 1996 Intergovernmental Conference, adopted an opinion on institutional reform of the European Union *(→ point 1025).* One of its demands is for an extension of its advisory function, which it would also like to exercise in relation to Parliament. It asks to be raised to institution status and to be given full organizational and budgetary autonomy from the Economic and Social Committee. It wants the role of the regions and local authorities to be mentioned in the Treaty Article on the subsidiarity principle and seeks the capacity for the Committee and those regions with legislative powers to take annulment proceedings and proceedings for failure to act in the Court of Justice. When addressing the November plenary session, Mr Westendorp, Chairman of the Reflection Group *(→ point 1026),* stated that there was opposition within the Group to some of these demands.[2]

ECSC Consultative Committee

1087. The Committee held eight meetings in 1995 (four ordinary and four extraordinary meetings). On 31 March it adopted an amended set of Rules of Procedure to reflect the accession of the three new Member States.

---

[1]   Five in the course of mandatory consultation, 15 at the request of the Council or the Commission, six by means of self-referral and 12 own-initiative opinions.
[2]   Bull. 11-1995, point 1.10.30.

1088.   The Committee was formally consulted by the Commission on the partnership and cooperation agreements with Ukraine, Russia and Belarus (→ point 865),[1] the interim agreement on trade and related measures with Kazakhstan and Kyrgyzstan (→ point 866),[1] Moldova (→ point 866)[2] and Russia (→ point 866),[2] the Europe Agreement with Slovenia (→ point 837),[3] the introduction of dual licensing for imports of certain ECSC products from Bulgaria and Romania,[1] the granting of financial support for steel research projects and pilot and demonstration projects (→ point 265),[1] the adaptation of the Steel Aids Code (→ point 166),[1] the draft Decision amending Decision 93/1970/ECSC,[1] the forward programmes for steel for the second half of 1995 (→ point 183)[4] and for the first half of 1996 (→ point 183),[5] a plan to grant financial support for coal research projects,[2] the administration of certain restrictions on imports of certain steel products from Russia, Ukraine and Kazakhstan,[2] the Commission reports on the Community solid fuels market (→ point 367),[6] the Euro-Mediterranean agreements with Tunisia (→ point 849)[2] and Israel (→ point 851),[5] the interim agreement with Israel (→ point 851),[5] the agreement with Turkey in the ECSC sector (→ point 844),[5] the conclusion of agreements between the ECSC and Russia on trade in steel products (→ point 763),[5] the Treaty on the Energy Charter (→ point 370),[5] adoption of a reserve list of steel research projects[3] and the State aid schemes for Voest Alpine Erzberg GmbH and Irish Steel.[3]

1089.   The Committee also adopted a memorandum on questions related to the expiry of the ECSC Treaty in 2002 (→ point 1019), a resolution on social research (→ point 622), a resolution on the Green Paper on energy policy guidelines (→ point 353) and a resolution on the restriction on exports of scrap imposed by a number of non-member countries.[5] It exchanged views with the Commission on the historical evaluation of technical research and steel research,[1] on cooperation with the countries of Central and Eastern Europe and the former Soviet Union in restructuring their steel industries,[1] on monitoring steel industry aids,[7] on the draft ECSC budget for 1996 (→ point 994),[8] on the draft amending the ECSC budget for 1995 (→ point 995),[8] on the future of programmes for financing coal and steel workers' housing,[3] on the report on the application of the Steel Aids

---

[1]   Bull. 3-1995, point 1.10.25.
[2]   Bull. 7/8-1995, point 1.10.22.
[3]   Bull. 10-1995, point 1.10.26.
[4]   Bull. 6-1995, point 1.10.29.
[5]   Bull. 12-1995.
[6]   Bull. 7/8-1995, point 1.10.22; Bull. 10-1995, point 1.10.26.
[7]   Bull. 6-1995, point 1.10.29; Bull. 12-1995.
[8]   Bull. 7/8-1995, point 1.10.21.

Code in 1994[1] and on exports of steel products from certain third countries to the European Union.[2]

European Monetary Institute

1090. Information on the activities of the European Monetary Institute is given in Section 2 (Economic and monetary policy) of Chapter III *(→ points 70 et seq.).*

---

[1]   Bull. 10-1995, point 1.10.26.
[2]   Bull. 12-1995.

Section 2

Administration and management

Staff policy and Staff Regulations

1091.   The programme for sound and efficient management (SEM 2000) is covered in Section 1 (Priority activities and objectives) of Chapter VI (→ *point 976*).

Staff Regulations

1092.   Following the establishment of the Committee of the Regions and the creation of the post of European Ombudsman (→ *point 7*), the Commission adopted a proposal for a Council Regulation[1] amending Regulation (EEC) No 259/68 laying down the Staff Regulations of Officials and the Conditions of Employment of Other Servants of the European Communities,[2] to make the Staff Regulations fully applicable to them both.

1093.   On 7 July, following the accession of Austria, Finland and Sweden to the European Union, the Commission adopted two proposals for Council Regulations introducing special measures to terminate the service of officials (Table II) and temporary staff (Table II) of the European Communities, in order that the institutions could propose termination-of-service arrangements to a certain number of officials and temporary staff, in the interests of the service, and thus recruit nationals from the three new Member States without increasing the number of posts in the European administration. The conditions relating to age, seniority and remuneration are identical with those laid down in the Regulations adopted at the time of the Spanish and Portuguese accession.[3] The latest Regulations were adopted by the Council on 17 November but only for officials and temporary staff of the European Parliament.[4]

1094.   Most of the decentralized Community agencies now apply the Staff Regulations to their personnel. On 26 July, in the interests of harmonization and economy, the Commission adopted a communication laying down

---

[1]   COM(94) 601; COM(95) 599.
[2]   OJ L 56, 4.3.1968.
[3]   COM(84) 680; Treaty concerning the accession of Spain and Portugal — OJ L 302, 15.11.1985.
[4]   OJ L 335, 13.12.1995.

guidelines for relations between the institutions and the decentralized agencies in matters of staff management. The Commission is to take over certain aspects of staff management at the agencies (salaries, sickness insurance under Article 72 of the Staff Regulations, occupational disease and accident insurance under Article 73, pensions, unemployment allowance and the transfer of pension rights to and from the Community scheme). The European Centre for the Development of Vocational Training (→ point 288) was transferred from Berlin to Thessaloniki once its personnel had been brought within the Staff Regulations and special measures introduced for those unwilling to make the move.

Staff policy

1095.   The Commission continued active implementation of the staff policy formulated in 1991. In March it allocated the additional posts authorized under the 1995 budget (400 conversions of appropriations into posts, including 350 to replace outside staff by regular staff, and 250 new permanent posts).

Research staff

1096.   On 9 June the Commission took a decision to restore a proper balance to the structure of research staff, made necessary by the development of successive framework programmes and by implementation of the specific programmes covered by the fourth R&TD framework programme (→ point 231). The aim is twofold: first, to introduce the principle of flexibility into staff management; and, second, to maintain the excellence and competence of the research personnel and preserve scientific and technical memory by establishing some of the temporary staff paid from the research budget.

Equal opportunities

1097.   Stepping up its drive to achieve equal opportunities for male and female staff, the Commission continued implementation of its second positive action programme (1992-96) on a threefold basis:

- involving the Directorates-General through individual action plans;
- setting specific targets for the overall percentage of female staff in each category; the 14% target for category A in 1995 was exceeded and the 12% target for women in management posts almost achieved; the Commission also adopted guidelines for the recruitment of women in 1995

with a view to increasing their share of management and senior management posts; the trend was also positive in the other categories (except category D);

• increasing staff and management awareness of its equal opportunities policy; seminars for management staff and special training courses were held in several Directorates-General.

Staff training

1098.   Introduced in 1992,[1] the new training policy resulted in the establishment of 20 training plans in 1995, the majority of which are managed on a decentralized basis by the Directorates-General concerned, thereby improving the match between resources and institutional requirements, and in the periodic organization of training sessions for newly recruited administrators and assistant administrators.

Competitions and recruitment

1099.   Since the end of 1994 the Commission has been organizing batch interviews for all candidates on the reserve lists of category A open competitions, thereby facilitating the selection procedure for the Directorates-General and enabling the 300 successful candidates in the A8 competitions organized for the 12 Member States and the 287 successful candidates in the A8 and A7/6 competitions organized for the new Member States in 1995 to meet with representatives from the different Commission departments.

Integration of officials from the three new Member States

1100.   The Commission set about the task of achieving its objectives for the recruitment of officials from the new Member States. The Council adopted a Regulation derogating from the Staff Regulations as regards the conditions for recruitment and appointment,[2] with a view to ensuring a harmonious distribution of Austrian, Finnish and Swedish officials at all levels of the administration, and a Decision was also adopted on their grade and step classification. Both sets of arrangements will remain in force until 31 December 1999. Competitions were launched for all categories of staff so that nationals of the new Member States could be recruited. The 1995 target of 300 posts was virtually met from natural turnover. And the bud-

---

[1]   Twenty-sixth General Report, point 1132.
[2]   COM(95) 496; COM(95) 22; OJ L 66, 24.3.1995.

getary authority also granted 107 new posts, including 36 for Members' offices.

Staff remuneration

1101. In accordance with the salary adjustment method adopted by the Council in December 1991,[1] which is based on the principle of parallel development designed to ensure that the purchasing power of salaries in the Community civil service moves in line with that of salaries in the national civil services, salaries were increased by a moderate 1.1% in December 1995. At the same time the Council renewed the clause whereby any sums overpaid can be recovered if the effect of the retrospective salary adjustment is negative.

Joint Sickness Insurance Scheme

1102. The introduction of a new computerized system has shortened the time needed for the reimbursement of medical expenses. Agreements were signed with four large Brussels hospitals and talks held with a view to the conclusion of national agreements in Luxembourg. With effect from 1 February a new contract between the European Communities and the Royale Belge came into force, covering the financial consequences arising from the insurance obligations laid down in Article 73 of the Staff Regulations (accident and occupational disease).

Pensions

1103. The question of the weightings applicable to pensions was discussed within the Council; the Commission defended the present arrangements, which aim to ensure equivalence of purchasing power between pensioners residing in different countries. Work began on the administration of the pension transfer agreements with Germany, France and Denmark, negotiations with Spain, Portugal and Greece continued, and the Commission also endeavoured to make rapid progress towards similar agreements with Austria, Finland and Sweden.

---

[1] Twenty-fifth General Report, point 1198.

Statute of the European Schools

1104.   The procedure for ratifying the new Convention defining the Statute of the European Schools, signed by the contracting parties on 21 June 1994,[1] continued throughout the year.

Buildings

1105.   In Brussels, negotiations continued with the Belgian authorities on the future of the Berlaymont, in the course of which the Commission confirmed that it is interested in moving back into the building once it has been renovated, provided it is given every guarantee as regards safety, the renovated building meets its requirements, and the financial terms for renting or purchasing the building are approved by the budgetary authority. At the same time, within the framework of the 1993-99 financial perspective, the Commission continued with the restructuring of its building stock with a view to ensuring that quality standards are maintained and that changing requirements, particularly in the wake of enlargement, are met. As part of the same operation the Commission undertook to move into the Charlemagne building towards the end of 1997, once it has been fully renovated.

1106.   In Luxembourg, the lease taken on the Euroforum building provided the space needed to accommodate steadily increasing numbers of staff and to offset loss of the space sublet to Parliament in the BAK building. It will be occupied until renovation of the Jean Monnet building is complete and all Commission staff can be housed in buildings on the Kirchberg Plateau. The Luxembourg Government has also negotiated the construction of a building (to be known as the Joseph Bech building) to help meet the Commission's requirements.

Interinstitutional cooperation

1107.   The Commission conducted an audit of the various areas of administration relevant to interinstitutional cooperation and drew up a specific programme to widen the scope of such cooperation. It also concluded a number of agreements with the decentralized agencies, relieving them of certain aspects of staff management.

---

[1]   OJ L 212, 17.8.1994; 1994 General Report, point 1248.

Data processing

1108. Computerization continued, focusing on the expansion, modernization and integration of the Commission's main administrative systems. Each system comprises an institutional core and a common module for local management within the Directorates-General.

1109. The Commission introduced a pilot server known as 'Europa' (→ *point 658)* so that information on the European Union can be disseminated via the Internet. The same technology will be used to provide Commission staff with information relevant to their work (Europa-plus).

1110. These services were developed on the basis of the infrastructure made available in earlier years, notably personal computers and communications networks. A new system of electronic mail, which is now used increasingly for the transmission of information both inside and outside the Commission, has been set up, complying fully with international standards.

1111. In 1995, to take account of technical progress, guidelines were prepared for the upgrading of office equipment. Within the 'trialogue' framework, the European institutions also decided to cooperate more closely in the data-processing field.

Language services

1112. In 1995 the Translation Service translated 1 094 370 pages, a 9% increase in workload (new languages included) compared with the previous year. Freelance translation now accounts for 231 530 pages, 25% more than in 1994.

1113. To meet the need for translations into the new languages, the Commission introduced a priority system for translations, as it had at the time of earlier enlargements. New translators were recruited as planned, bringing the number of staff translating into Finnish and Swedish to 50 in both cases by the end of 1995. To expedite the translation process, the Service set up temporary translation offices in both Stockholm and Helsinki.

1114. To meet the challenge of using all the Community languages in the context of European integration, the Translation Service continued its training activities and further modernized its working methods and tools. The conversion of the Service's computer environment was completed and a translation workshop was set up to test the new tools, help prepare the relevant invitations to tender and process the tenders received.

1115. The Interinstitutional Committee on Translation set up on 14 March and meeting under the auspices of the Translation Service set priorities for interinstitutional cooperation: the introduction of a common system of statistics; the establishment of a common terminology data bank with a standard entry structure; the issue of joint invitations to tender for new translation tools; the holding of interinstitutional competitions for the recruitment of translators; and the joint operation of a register of freelance translators.

1116. To enable the institutions and agencies which already have a translation service to use the services of the Translation Centre for the bodies of the European Union on a voluntary basis, the Regulation setting up the Centre was amended by Council Regulation (EC) No 2610/95 of 20 October (Table II) to involve the Centre in the process of interinstitutional cooperation and thus increase its political flexibility.

1117. In 1995 the Joint Interpreting and Conference Service (JICS) provided interpreters for 11 162 meetings (2% up on 1994) held by the Commission, the Council, the Economic and Social Committee, the European Investment Bank, and the Committee of the Regions and other new EU agencies. This was the equivalent of 126 978 interpreter/days (3.56% up on 1994). A further 83 Commission conferences were organized by the JICS or in collaboration with it.

1118. The JICS undertook a number of activities following enlargement, such as recruitment campaigns, accelerated training courses for the new languages and the establishment of a new computer instrument for the allocation of conference interpreters.

1119. On account of the shortage of conference interpreters the JICS continued its prospecting and training efforts, maintaining the same quality standard for all languages. It interviewed some 250 interpreters and 250 young graduates for intensive postgraduate conference interpreting courses. Closer consultations were also held with the members of CIUTI (Standing International Conference of the Directors of University Institutes for the Training of Translators and Interpreters). Subsidies were granted for the continuation of training courses for conference interpreters at the University of Minho (Portugal) and the Europa Institut in Hamburg (Germany) and for the setting-up of new courses at the Töi Institute in Stockholm (Sweden) and the Hellenic Centre for European Studies in Athens (Greece).

1120.   Cooperation with non-member countries in the field of interpreter training continued, notably with China and Slovenia. The JICS, working together with other departments, continued to explore every possibility for selecting and recruiting freelance interpreters in the countries of Central and Eastern Europe, particularly the new associated countries.

Chapter IX

Community law

Section 1

Monitoring the application of Community law

1121.   The Commission pursued its activity of monitoring the application of Community law throughout the year. It commenced 1 016 infringement proceedings in 1995, as against 974 in 1994, and issued 192 reasoned opinions (546 in 1994). The Commission referred 72 cases to the Court of Justice (89 in 1994). The breakdown by country of cases referred in 1995 is as follows: Italy 17, Greece 12, Germany 10, Ireland 6, France 6, Spain 6, Belgium 6, Portugal 4, Luxembourg 3, United Kingdom 2, Netherlands, Denmark, Austria, Sweden and Finland 0.

1122.   The large number (1 336) of infringement proceedings terminated in the course of the year bears witness to the effectiveness of the pre-litigation procedure, the aim of which is to remedy the infringement without the need for full contentious proceedings.

1123.   In 1995, the Commission was particularly attentive to the need to cut the time taken to scrutinize cases and give effect to its decisions; there has been a sharp improvement in this respect.

1124.   Detailed information on the infringement proceedings commenced in the course of the year and on progress in transposing directives into national law will be given in the thirteenth report on the application of Community law, to be published in 1996. The Commission adopted the twelfth report, covering 1994, on 7 June.[1] The European Parliament reacted to the eleventh report, covering 1993, by resolution passed on 20 January.[2]

---

[1]   COM(95) 500; OJ C 254, 29.9.1995; Bull. EC 6-1995, point 1.8.1.
[2]   OJ C 43, 20.2.1995; Bull. EC 1/2-1995, point 1.7.1.

Section 2

Decisions by the Court of Justice and the Court of First Instance[1]

1125. Figures concerning the activities of the Court of Justice and the Court of First Instance are given in Tables 22 to 25.

Free movement of goods and customs union

1126. The United Kingdom's Misuse of Drugs Act 1971, which prohibits the importation of diomorphine, a derivative of opium, was the subject of a preliminary ruling by the Court on 28 March. In Case C-324/93 *The Queen* v *Secretary of State for the Home Department*, ex parte: *Evans Medical and Macfarlan Smith*,[2] the Court found that a national prohibition on the importation of narcotic drugs fell within the scope of Article 30 of the EC Treaty. It also made the point, however, that a country's need for reliable supplies of narcotic substances for essential medical purposes could justify, by virtue of Article 36 of the EC Treaty, a restriction on trade provided that the aim was the protection of public health; on the other hand, measures to ensure the survival of a firm did not fall within the scope of the said Article. Replying to an argument based on the existence of an international convention concluded before the Treaty's entry into force and requiring Member States to ensure that narcotic drugs are manufactured and marketed solely for medical purposes, the Court recalled its earlier rulings concerning Article 234 of the EC Treaty. Where an international agreement enabled a Member State to adopt a measure which appeared contrary to Community law but did not oblige it to do so, the Member State should refrain from adopting any such measure. Lastly, the Court held that the need for reliable supplies of a medicine could also be a criterion for consideration under Article 25 of Directive 77/62/EEC on public supply contracts,[3] but that it would have to be clearly specified as such for award purposes.

1127. On 15 June[4] the Commission clarified the concept of 'rules governing sales methods' for certain products, first introduced in *Keck and Mith-*

---

[1]   See also the quarterly analysis of judgments in the *Bulletin of the European Union* — Bull. 4-1995, points 1.8.30 to 1.8.37; Bull. 6-1995, points 1.8.58 to 1.8.65; Bull. 9-1995, points 1.8.43 to 1.8.50; Bull. 12-1995.
[2]   Bull. 4-1995, point 1.8.33.
[3]   OJ C 11, 15.1.1977.
[4]   Case C-391/92, *Commission* v *Greece*: Bull. 6-1995, point 1.8.58.

ouard.[1] The Commission had applied for a declaration to the effect that Greece, by requiring that modified milk for infants be sold only by pharmacies, had failed to fulfil its obligations pursuant to Article 30 of the EC Treaty. The question was whether the Greek legislation constituted rules governing sales methods (consumers had to go to a particular place to buy baby milk) or a measure affecting the access of goods to the relevant market (producers had to rely on pharmacists for the distribution of their products). The Court held that the Greek legislation constituted rules governing sales methods since it was not concerned with the characteristics of the products themselves. Following the line taken in *Keck and Mithouard*, the Court went on to consider whether these rules were discriminatory in law or in fact. It concluded that since the legislation was applicable to all products irrespective of their origin it was not discriminatory. Discrimination could not arise from the mere circumstance (described by the Court as purely factual and incidental) that Greece did not itself produce any processed milk for infants.

1128.   On 11 August[2] the Court ruled for the first time on whether a pecuniary charge not levied by a Member State but arising from a contract between individuals was compatible with Articles 9 and 12 of the EC Treaty. The charge at issue was intended to cover the expenses borne by a private firm, under a contract concluded with its customers, in respect of the tasks performed by the customs and veterinary authorities as providers of public services. The Court first of all upheld the established principle that it would constitute a charge having equivalent effect if businesses engaged in intra-Community trade were obliged to cover the costs of inspections and administrative formalities carried out by customs offices. It held that the nature of the measure requiring traders to pay part of the operating costs of customs services was immaterial. Whether the pecuniary charge was borne by the trader by virtue of a unilateral measure adopted by the authorities or, as in the present case, as a result of a series of private contracts, it still arose directly or indirectly from the failure of the Member State concerned to fulfil its financial obligations under Articles 9 and 12.

Free movement of workers

1129.   Legislation on direct tax normally makes a distinction between the taxing of residents and that of non-residents, who are taxed only on that part of their income which is received in the country concerned but are sometimes refused certain benefits relating, for example, to family circum-

---

[1]   Cases C-267/91 and C-268/91 [1993] ECR I-6097 (Judgment given on 24 November 1993).
[2]   Case C-16/94 *Edouard Dubois et fils and Others* v *Garonor Exploitation*: Bull. 9-1995, point 1.8.44.

stances. In proceedings between a Belgian national, who lived with his family in Belgium but worked in Germany, and the German tax authorities, fundamental questions were raised as to the limits which the rules on the free movement of workers place on the application of national income tax.

On 14 February[1] the Court of Justice found that, although direct taxation did not as such fall within the purview of the Community, the powers retained by the Member States must nevertheless be exercised consistently with Community law, and in particular with the rules governing the free movement of workers, which require the abolition of any discrimination based on nationality between workers from a Member State. The Court had consistently held that the rules on equal treatment prohibited not only overt discrimination but also any form of concealed discrimination which was based on different criteria but had the same effect. In the case in question, the Court held that tax laws under which a distinction was drawn on the basis of residence (in that non-residents were denied certain benefits granted to residents) were liable to operate mainly to the detriment of nationals of other Member States: in the majority of cases non-residents are foreigners. Tax benefits granted only to residents of a Member State could constitute indirect discrimination by reason of nationality, but only where different rules were applied to comparable situations or the same rule was applied to different situations. Where direct taxes are concerned, as the situations of residents and non-residents are not, as a rule, comparable, the Court found that the provisions on the free movement of workers did not in principle preclude the application of national rules under which a non-resident working as an employed person in a Member State was taxed more heavily on his income than a resident in the same employment. The position was different, however, in cases where the non-resident received no significant income in the State of his residence and obtained the major part of his taxable income from an activity performed in the State of employment. The Court held that in such cases there was no objective difference which could justify different treatment: in the case of a non-resident who received the major part of his income and almost all his family income in a Member State other than that of his residence, discrimination arose from the fact that his personal and family circumstances were not taken into account either in the State of residence or in the State of employment. Consequently, the provisions governing the free movement of workers precluded the State of employment from withholding from non-residents the tax relief which it granted to residents under the same circumstances.

---

[1]   Case C-279/93 *Finanzamt Köln-Altstadt* v *Schumacker*: Bull. 1/2-1995, point 1.8.30.

1130.   On 15 December[1] the Court gave judgment on the practical application of the rules adopted by the private associations responsible for the organization of football at European and world levels. On the expiry of his two-year contract with a Belgian club, Mr Bosman, a player of Belgian nationality, tried to conclude a contract with a French club. Under the rules of the Belgian Football Association, however, the player's former club asked his new club to pay a substantial transfer fee, which proved to be too high a price for any club to pay.

The Court held that Article 48 of the EC Treaty applied to the collective rules adopted by private sports associations since the exercise of sport as an economic activity was covered by Community law. It also held that by preventing or deterring nationals of a Member State from leaving their country of origin the transfer rules constituted an obstacle to the free movement of workers and that the arguments put forward to justify such an obstacle were inadmissible. In particular, the rules governing transfers were unlikely to maintain a financial and sporting balance in the football sector since they did not prevent the richest clubs from obtaining the services of the best players on the market. Nor were the rules in question likely to provide encouragement and financing for clubs training young players, particularly the smaller clubs, since there was no guarantee that they would collect such fees and since the amount of the fees bore no relation to the costs actually incurred. The said encouragement and financing could be provided by other means which did not impede the free movement of workers. The Court's judgment did not apply, however, to players being transferred from one club to another within the Member State of which they were nationals or to relations between clubs in Member States of the Community and those in non-member countries.

The Court also held that under Article 48 no rules could require clubs to field, for a given match, only a limited number of professional players who were nationals of other Member States. For the same reasons as mentioned above, the Court rejected the arguments put forward to justify such rules. On the other hand, the nationality requirement was justified in the case of matches between the national teams of different countries. Lastly, it held that since the two sets of rules in question were incompatible with Article 48, there was no need for an interpretation of Articles 85 and 86.

Where transfer fees were concerned, the Court stated that its judgment would take effect only from the date on which it was given, in view of the uncertainty surrounding the compatibility of the said rules with Community law and the overriding need for legal certainty. Any fees for transfers already

---

[1]   Case C-415/93 *Bosman*: Bull. 12-1995.

completed or in progress could not be reimbursed unless judicial proceedings had been initiated before the date of the judgment.

Freedom to provide services

1131.   On 10 May[1] the Court of Justice ruled for the first time on the compatibility with Article 59 of the EC Treaty of a restriction on the freedom to provide services which had been imposed by the Member State where the provider was established. Dutch legislation prohibited 'cold calling' — the practice of approaching potential clients by telephone without their prior written consent to offer them financial services. The Court had to rule whether this prohibition, as applied to telephone calls to clients resident in other Member States, was compatible with Article 59. The Court found that such a restriction was indeed covered by Article 59 but that in this particular case it was justified by the need to uphold the reputation of the financial sector. The Court noted that, although the prohibition applied to the offer of services rather than the services themselves, this did not preclude the application of Article 59, which did not require that there be a specific recipient for the services in the first place. A prohibition of this kind was likely to restrict the freedom to provide cross-frontier services because it deprived traders of a rapid and direct means of advertising and contacting potential customers in other Member States. The interesting aspect of the Court's judgment is the possible justification for such a measure. In the first place the Court held that the protection of consumers in other Member States was not in itself a matter for the Dutch authorities and could not therefore provide grounds for restricting the freedom to provide services. On the other hand, the Court acknowledged that safeguarding the financial sector's reputation might constitute an imperative reason for action in the public interest and might justify restrictions on the freedom to provide financial services. The Court pointed out that individuals, generally caught unawares, were not in a position to ascertain the risks attached to the deals they were offered or to compare the quality and price of the caller's services with competitors' offers. Moreover, the Member State from which the calls were made was in the best position to regulate cold calling. The Court also held that the Dutch prohibition on cold calling was proportionate to the aim pursued, in that it simply prevented the providers of financial services from contacting potential clients without their prior written consent but did not prevent them from contacting existing clients.

---

[1]   Case C-384/93 *Alpine Investments* v *Minister van Financiën*: Bull. 5-1995, point 1.8.59.

Free movement of capital

1132.   In Spain, the export of banknotes is subject to a prior declaration when the amount is in excess of PTA 1 million and subject to prior administrative authorization when the amount is in excess of PTA 5 million. In criminal proceedings against persons who had transported large sums of money without prior authorization the question had been raised as to whether Spanish legislation was compatible with Community law. On 23 February[1] the Court held that, although Article 4 of Directive 88/361/EEC allowed Member States to take all requisite measures to prevent infringements of their laws and regulations, it precluded national legislation making the export of coins, banknotes or bearer cheques conditional on a prior authorization which would have a suspensory effect on such exports. On the other hand, the Directive did permit Member States to make the exports in question subject to a prior declaration, which need not be a mere formality. The Court stated that such a declaration could be required prior to the export transaction so that the national authorities could exercise effective supervision in order to prevent infringements of their laws and regulations, and that appropriate penalties could be imposed. The Court also held that the relevant provisions of Directive 88/361/EEC had direct effect, since the requirement that Member States should abolish all restrictions on movements of capital was precise and unconditional and did not require a specific implementing measure.

1133.   On 14 November[2] the Court clarified important aspects of the rules on the free movement of capital and loans within the Community. The Svensson family, living in Luxembourg, had been refused housing aid by the Luxembourg authorities because, to build their home in Luxembourg, they had contracted a loan with a bank which was not established in the Grand Duchy. The Court found that the relevant provisions of the Luxembourg legislation constituted an obstacle to the free movement of capital in that they were likely to deter the parties concerned from approaching banks established in another Member State. It also held that this legislation represented discrimination against banks established in other Member States and was prohibited by Article 59 of the EC Treaty. The Court rejected the Luxembourg Government's contention that the aid represented 1% of the total Luxembourg budget and that half of the aid was recovered through the taxes which financial bodies established in Luxembourg paid on their profits. It took the view that this argument was purely economic in nature and was not therefore covered by Article 56 of the EC Treaty. Nor could the Lux-

---

[1]   Joined Cases C-358/93 and C-416/93 *Bordessa and Others*: Bull. 4-1995, point 1.8.31.
[2]   Case C-484/93 *Svensson*: Bull. EC 12-1995.

embourg rules be justified on the grounds of consistency in tax arrangements, an argument which the Court had accepted in earlier cases, for in this particular case there was no direct link between the granting of housing aid to borrowers, on the one hand, and the funding of the aid through the tax levied on banks' profits, on the other.

Equal treatment

1134. On 17 October[1] the Court ruled on whether the arrangements which the *Land* Bremen had introduced on 20 November 1990 concerning equality of treatment in the public services were compatible with Directive 76/207/EEC on the implementation of the principle of equal treatment for men and women. Under the arrangements in question, when staff are recruited or assigned to a higher-paid post, women possessing qualifications equivalent to those of their male counterparts must be given priority treatment if they are under-represented in the area concerned. Under-representation exists where women do not account for at least half the staff complement. Article 2(4) of Directive 76/207/EEC states that the Directive is to be without prejudice to measures to promote equal opportunity for men and women, in particular by removing existing inequalities which affect women's opportunities. The aim of the Directive is thus to prohibit any direct or indirect discrimination based on sex. The Court held that national rules giving absolute and unconditional priority to women holding the same qualifications as their male counterparts would entail sex-based discrimination. It then considered whether such discrimination was justified under Article 2(4) of the said Directive. It found that the precise and limited aim of the rules in question was to authorize measures which, although discriminatory in appearance, were in fact designed to eliminate or to reduce existing inequalities. In the strict sense, however, the rules in question constituted a derogation from the individual rights enshrined in Article 2(1) of the Directive. The Court consequently held that it was contrary to Article 2(1) and (4) for any national rules to confer automatic priority on female candidates in areas where women were under-represented, should the male and female candidates eligible for promotion hold the same qualifications.

---

[1] Case C-450/93 *Kalanke* v *Freie Hansestadt Bremen*: Bull. EC 12-1995.

Common commercial policy and external relations

1135.   Opinion 2/92, delivered on 24 March,[1] follows the same line of reasoning as Opinion 1/94 WTO.[2] The Third OECD Council Decision on national treatment lays down a procedure whereby the OECD is to be notified of any measure adopted by member countries which constitutes an exception to or has repercussions on national treatment. The OECD had been informed that the Community would participate in the Third Decision in those areas which fell within its competence. Belgium had raised the question of the legal basis on which the Community's competence was to be exercised. The Court took the view that Article 113 of the EC Treaty did not confer exclusive competence in this field on the Community, since the national treatment rule related not only to the participation of foreign-controlled undertakings in international trade with third countries; it affected internal trade to the same extent, possibly more so. The Court also rejected the argument that the Community's participation could be based on Article 57 and subsidiarily on Article 100a and would consequently entail exclusive external competence on the basis of *AETR* and Opinion 1/76. It took the view that exclusive external competence could be based on the Community's internal powers only if internal legislation had first been adopted, thus reaffirming its restrictive interpretation of the scope of Opinion 1/76.

Institutional matters

1136.   The Court has consistently held that due consultation of Parliament in the cases specified by the Treaty is an essential procedural requirement, non-compliance with which renders the legislation concerned null and void. It has stressed on several occasions that Parliament's effective participation in the legislative process is essential to the institutional balance and an expression of the fundamental democratic principle that the people should participate in the exercise of power through the agency of a representative assembly. The action in question related to Regulation (EEC) No 3917/92, which extended into 1993 the system of generalized preferences applicable in 1992, adding certain new countries to the list of beneficiaries to take account of the collapse of the former Soviet Union and aligning the Community list of least-developed countries on that of the United Nations. The proposal for a Regulation being based on Article 43 of the EC Treaty, which requires Parliament to be consulted, the Council requested Parliament to treat the matter as urgent, applying the procedure laid down by Rule 75 of

---

[1]   Bull. 4-1995, point 1.8.36.
[2]   1994 General Report, point 1285.

its Rules of Procedure. At its final part-session of 1992, however, Parliament failed to deliver an opinion on the Commission's proposal. On 21 December 1992 the Council adopted the Regulation in question without having obtained Parliament's opinion, giving its reasons in the preamble to the Regulation.

On 30 March[1] the Court upheld its earlier judgments on the effective participation of Parliament in the legislative process, emphasizing that consultation required the expression of Parliament's opinion and that this requirement was not met merely by the Council's request for an opinion. The Council was under an obligation to use all the possibilities offered by the Treaty and Parliament's Rules of Procedure to obtain its prior opinion, even in an emergency. On the other hand, the Court stressed that the same duty to cooperate in good faith applied in the context of interinstitutional dialogue as it did in relations between the Member States and the Community institutions. As regards the substance of the application, the Court held that the request made by the Council for the question to be dealt with by urgent procedure was justified in view of the special relationship between the Community and the developing countries and the political and technical difficulties which would result from the sudden discontinuation of generalized tariff preferences. Although Parliament had taken these considerations fully into account and had given corresponding assurances to the Council, it had decided to bring its final part-session of 1992 to a close without debating the proposal in question. The Court found that such behaviour was at odds with its duty to cooperate in good faith with the Council. It consequently held that Parliament could not justifiably bring an action against the Council for disregard of the consultation requirement and that Parliament's application should therefore be dismissed.

1137.   On 19 October[2] the Court of First Instance ruled against the Council's refusal to grant access to documents concerning its deliberations. The conditions for granting such access are laid down in Council Decision 93/731/EC on public access to Council documents, Article 4(2) of which states that 'access to a Council document may be refused in order to protect the confidentiality of the Council's proceedings', whilst Article 4(1) defines four types of circumstance in which access to a Council document should not be granted. The applicant had asked the Council for access to a number of documents including preparatory reports from the Permanent Representatives Committee, minutes, attendance records, voting records and decisions of the Ministers for Justice and Social Affairs and minutes of the deliberations of the Ministers for Agriculture on certain dates. The reason given by

---

[1]   Case C-65/93 *Parliament v Council* supported by the United Kingdom: Bull. 4-1995, point 1.8.37.
[2]   Case T-194/94 *Carvel and Guardian Newspapers v Council*: Bull. EC 12-1995.

the Council for refusing access was that the documents in question were directly concerned with the Council's proceedings and that its Rules of Procedure prevented the contents from being divulged. The Court of First Instance found that the Council was obliged, by virtue of Article 4 of Decision 93/731/EC, to strike a fair balance between the public's need for access to such documents, on the one hand, and the Council's own need to safeguard the confidentiality of its proceedings. From its perusal of the Council's letters refusing access the Court concluded that the Council had not met its obligation to strike a balance between these interests; on the contrary, the terms of the letters in question indicated that the Council felt itself obliged to refuse access to the documents concerned for the simple reason that they related to its proceedings. The Court therefore annulled the Council's implicit decision to refuse the applicant access to the documents in question.

1138.   On 7 December[1] the Court annulled the act of 15 December 1994 whereby the President of the European Parliament had declared the 1995 general budget of the European Union finally adopted. At second reading, Parliament had maintained 131 amendments to the draft 1995 budget because it considered the budgetary headings concerned to be non-compulsory expenditure, which Parliament had the right to amend under Article 203(4) of the EEC Treaty. The Council, on the other hand, took the view that the headings concerned were compulsory expenditure, to which Parliament could only propose modifications at first reading (second subparagraph of Article 203(4) and Article 203(5) and (6) of the Treaty), so that the final decision lay with the Council. The latter had decided in this particular case to reject the amendments put forward by Parliament. The Court noted that expenditure under the budget, as adopted by the President of the Parliament, exceeded the maximum rate of increase fixed pursuant to Article 203(9)of the EC Treaty, although the two institutions had not reached prior agreement on such an increase. Since, therefore, the budgetary procedure had not been concluded when the President of the Parliament declared the budget finally adopted, the Court ruled that the effect of the annulment of the act in question was to render the 1995 budget invalid. As regards the consequences, the Court, acknowledging the need to ensure continuity in the public service, decided that the 1995 budget should continue to have effect in practice until the date on which it was finally adopted. In its judgment the Court did not express a view on whether the expenditure concerned was compulsory or non-compulsory but left it to the institutions concerned to reach agreement on this matter (→ point 976).

---

[1]   Case C-41/95, *Council* v *Parliament*: 1994 General Report, point 1118.

Activities of the Court of Justice and the Court of First Instance

TABLE 22

Cases analysed by subject matter

Court of Justice 1995

	ECSC	Euratom	EC														Privileges and immunities Article 220 Convention	Staff cases	Total
			Free movement of goods	Customs	Agriculture	Fisheries	Right of establishment and freedom to supply services	Free movement of workers and social security	Transport	Competition	State aid	Taxation	Commercial policy and trade protection	Environment	Other and Opinions			
Actions brought (appeals)	3	1 (1)	57	22	65 (3)	5 (1)	34 (1)	54 (2)	5	25 (17)	10 (4)	36	3 (2)	42 (2)	23 (5)	9	15 (10)	409 (48)
Cases not resulting in a judgment (appeals)	2	—	9	—	17	—	10	7	1	4	1	—	—	1	3	—	—	55 (—)
Cases decided (appeals)	—	1	28	13	35 (2)	5 (3)	26	32	7	20 (6)	4	21	2	4	12 (2)	7	8 (8)	225 (21)

TABLE 23

Cases analysed by type (EC Treaty)[1]

Court of Justice 1995[2]

Type of case	93 para. 2	169	173 By governments	173 By Community institutions	173 By individuals	173 Total	175	177	178 and 215	181	185 and 186	278 para. 2	Art. 220 Conventions	Appeals	Total
Actions brought	1	72	22	5	4	31	1	242	—	1	1	—	9	47	406
Cases not resulting in a judgment	—	27	8	2	—	10	—	16	—	—	—	—	—	—	53
Cases decided	3	39	6	5	—	11	—	140	—	1	—	2	7	21	224
• in favour of applicant	3	36	1	2	—	3	—	—	—	1	—	—	—	2	45
• dismissed on the merits	—	2	5	3	—	8	—	—	—	—	—	—	—	19	29
• rejected as inadmissible	—	1	—	—	—	—	—	—	—	—	—	—	—	—	1

Proceedings brought under the following articles of the Treaty

[1] ECSC: 3 actions brought, no judgment in 2 cases.
Euratom: 1 action brought (appeal) and dismissed on the merits.

TABLE 24

Cases analysed by subjext matter

Court of First Instance 1995

	ECSC	Euratom	EC														Privileges and immunities	Staff cases	Total
			Free movement of goods	Customs	Agriculture	Fisheries	Right of establishment and freedom to supply services	Free movement of workers and social security	Transport	Competition	State aid	Taxation	Commercial policy and trade protection	Environment	Other			
Actions brought	3	3	—	2	46	3	3	3	—	74	13	—	11	3	8	1	87	260
Cases not resulting in a judgment	1	—	—	—	66	1	—	1	—	5	1	—	6	—	2	—	19	102
Cases decided	—	3	—	1	14	3	3	4	—	53	10	—	9	1	8	—	65	165

TABLE 25

Cases analysed by type (EC Treaty)[1]

Court of First Instance 1995

	Proceedings brought under the following articles of the Treaty						Total
	173 individuals	175 individuals	178 and 215	179	181	185 and 186	
Actions brought	118	9	30	79	—	18	254
Cases not resulting in a judgment	14	1	64	18	—	4	101
Cases decided	88	1	13	47	—	13	162
• in favour of applicant	41	—	—	16	—	2	59
• dismissed on the merits	35	—	—	19	—	11	74
• rejected as inadmissible	12	1	—	12	—	—	29

[1] ECSC: 3 actions brought; 1 removed from the register.
Euratom: 3 actions brought and al 3 dismissed on the merits.

Section 3

Computerization of Community law

1139. The Office for Official Publications of the European Communities
(→ *point 669)* applied itself essentially to achieving the priority objectives
set by the control bodies[1] of the interinstitutional computerized documentation system on Community law (CELEX),[2] such as speeding up the input
of documents and improving computer applications. The rate at which
Court of Justice texts are fed into CELEX has been accelerated considerably, so that Court decisions are now available within one or two weeks, or
some five months before their official publication in the Court Reports.
Similarly, in 1995 all the existing language versions of CELEX covered over
96% of the legislation in force as at 1 January 1993 (treaties, external relations, secondary legislation and other instruments). The Finnish and Swedish versions of CELEX should be introduced in 1996. Probably the most
significant achievement by the Publications Office was to make available to
all users a simple interface enabling CELEX to be consulted by a 'natural'
procedure similar to that used for traditional legal research.

1140. The reorganization of the CELEX marketing structures is nearing
completion. CELEX is now available through the following channels: Eurobases (accessible to certain users only, through the Euro-Info Centres
(→ *point 211)* and European documentation centres); 16 official gateways
providing standard (paying) users with on-line access to the reference version; 13 servers using CELEX to construct their own database, which they
make available on-line; and six CD-ROM publishers. On the whole, both
the EU institutions and the public at large are now making wider use of
CELEX. Now that the commercial network has been decentralized, it is no
longer possible to estimate with any accuracy the total number of active
CELEX users. In addition to large-scale access through servers and CD-
ROM publishers, however, some 55 000 hours of direct use were recorded
in 1995.

---

[1]   The Interinstitutional CELEX Group and the Council Working Party on Legal Data Processing.
[2]   Twenty-seventh General Report, point 1154.

The year in brief[1]

1995

European Year of Road Safety and Young Drivers

January

1 January

Austria, Finland and Sweden join European Union

France takes over Presidency of Council of European Union *(→ point 1048)*.

23 January

Following Parliament's vote of approval on 18 January, Representatives of Governments of Member States appoint President, Jacques Santer, and Members of European Commission for five-year term *(→ point 1053)*.

Council adopts Regulation adjusting agrimonetary arrangements *(→ point 549)*.

25 January

Commission adopts second part of Green Paper on liberalization of telecommunications infrastructure and cable television networks *(→ point 429)*.

---

[1] This chronological summary does not claim to be exhaustive. For further details, see the passages of this Report cited in the margin.

February

1 February

Europe Association Agreements with Bulgaria, Romania, and Czech and Slovak Republics enter into force *(→ point 819)*.

8 February

Commission adopts work programme for 1995 *(→ point 9)*.

Commission proposes MEDIA II programme *(→ point 677)*.

25 and 26 February

Commission organizes G7 Ministerial Conference on Information Society in Brussels *(→ point 456)*.

March

1 March

Commission adopts communication on level playing-field for direct investment *(→ point 755)*.

6 March

Council adopts negotiating directives for economic and trade cooperation agreement with Croatia *(→ point 845)* and framework trade and cooperation agreement with Republic of Korea *(→ point 919)*.

8 March

Commission adopts communications on implementing Euro-Mediterranean partnership *(→ point 840)*, future of relations between Europe and Japan *(→ point 897)* and follow-up to Essen European Council in the field of employment *(→ point 604)*.

10 March

First Convention on simplified extradition procedure signed under Title VI of Union Treaty; joint action concerning Europol Drugs Unit adopted *(→ points 968 and 966).*

13 and 14 March

Parliament and Council adopt Socrates *(→ point 627)* and Youth for Europe III education programmes *(→ point 280).*

20 March and 21 March

Stability pact in Europe adopted in Paris *(→ point 696).*

22 March

Commission proposes programme for implementing industrial competitiveness initiatives *(→ point 176).*

29 March

Commission adopts Community action programme in the field of cultural heritage (Raphael programme) *(→ point 680).*

Commission proposes recommendations for decisions on negotiation of agreement on trade and cooperation with South Africa and protocol to fourth Lomé Convention covering terms and conditions of South Africa's accession *(→ point 953).*

April

4 April

Financial perspective adopted *(→ point 979).*

Commission adopts Green Paper on role of Union in the field of tourism *(→ point 216).*

Commission adopts proposal for Decision adopting action programme ('Customs 2000'), to reinforce effectiveness of customs controls at Union's external border *(→ point 737)*.

9 April

Liechtenstein ratifies accession to EEA by referendum *(→ point 809)*.

10 April

Council adopts report on functioning of Union Treaty in preparation for 1996 Intergovernmental Conference *(→ point 1025)*.

12 April

Commission adopts proposal for Regulation on financial instrument for environment (LIFE) *(→ point 470)*.

Commission proposes medium-term social action programme (1995-97) *(→ point 595)*.

20 April

Community and Canada sign fisheries agreement *(→ point 578)*.

21 April

Committee of the Regions adopts own-initiative opinion on preparations for 1996 Intergovernmental Conference *(→ point 1025)*.

26 April

Commission adopts recommendation for Decision on negotiation of agreement with United States in the field of civil aviation *(→ point 416)*.

Commission adopts proposal for Regulation on supervision and control of shipments of hazardous waste *(→ point 487)*.

May

2 May

Solemn Joint Declaration signed between European Union and Mexico *(→ point 930)*.

3 and 10 May

Commission adopts White Paper and annex on preparing associated countries of Central and Eastern Europe for integration into European Union internal market *(→ point 816)*.

4 May

Commission adopts proposal for Council Decision establishing Community action programme in field of civil protection *(→ point 489)*.

10 May

Commission amends May 1992 proposal for Directive introducing carbon dioxide tax *(→ point 465)*.

Commission adopts report on operation of Union Treaty for Reflection Group set up to prepare for 1996 Intergovernmental Conference *(→ point 1025)*.

11 May

Treaty on non-proliferation of nuclear weapons extended for unlimited period (joint action under common foreign and security policy) *(→ point 699)*.

17 May

Parliament delivers report on institutional reform in preparation for 1996 Intergovernmental Conference *(→ point 1025)*.

19 May

Court of Justice and Court of First Instance each send reports to Reflection Group set up to prepare for 1996 Intergovernmental Conference *(→ point 1025).*

23 May

Commission proposes multiannual cooperation programme with non-member countries in energy (Synergy) *(→ point 372).*

29 May

Council adopts standard human rights clause to be included in agreements between Community and non-member countries *(→ point 18).*

31 May

Commission adopts Green Paper on practical arrangements for introduction of single currency *(→ point 43).*

Commission adopts communication and draft common position on future strategy for relations with Russia *(→ point 880)* and for relations with Trans-Caucasian republics *(→ point 884).*

June

1 June

Six new R&TD task forces created to stimulate development of technologies to enhance quality of life and industrial competitiveness in Europe *(→ point 226).*

2 June

Council adopts common positions on three Community action programmes on health: combating cancer, AIDS prevention and health promotion *(→ point 637).*

40th anniversary of Messina Conference marked by solemn interinstitutional declaration *(→ point 1026)*.

2 and 3 June

Reflection Group set up to prepare for 1996 Intergovernmental Conference holds inaugural meeting *(→ point 1026)*.

7 June

Commission adopts proposal for Regulation on financial and technical measures to support reform of economic and social structures in Mediterranean non-member countries and territories (MEDA) *(→ point 840)*.

9 June

Commission adopts communication and draft common position on future relations with republics of Central Asia *(→ point 885)*.

12 June

Council approves negotiating directives for new agreement with Jordan *(→ point 853)*.

European Union signs Association Agreements with three Baltic States *(→ point 819)*.

13 June

Commission adopts communication to Council on local development and employment initiatives *(→ point 604)*.

Group of experts, chaired by Bernhard Molitor, set up to find ways of simplifying and streamlining Community legislation presents final report *(→ point 11)*.

15 June

Europe Association Agreement between European Union and Slovenia initialled in Brussels *(→ point 819)*.

Council adopts Regulation establishing system for management of fishing effort in certain Community fishing areas *(→ point 566)*.

17 June

G7 Summit in Halifax ends *(→ point 886)*.

22 June

Romania applies to join European Union *(→ point 815)*.

23 June

Competitiveness Advisory Group (Ciampi Group) presents first report to European Council and Commission President *(→ point 176)*.

26 and 27 June

European Council meets in Cannes *(→ point 1049)*.

27 June

Cannes European Council reaches overall agreement on external financing, including financing arrangements for eighth EDF for ACP States *(→ point 1049)*.

Slovakia applies to join European Union *(→ point 815)*.

28 June

Commission adopts communication on relations with Cuba *(→ point 932)*.

29 June

Council adopts Regulation determining compensation for reductions in agricultural conversion rates of certain currencies *(→ point 549)*.

30 June

Commission approves 'INFO 2000' programme to stimulate development of European multimedia content industry in emerging information society *(→ point 422).*

July

1 July

Spain takes over Presidency of Council of European Union *(→ point 1048).*

5 July

Commission approves communication on long-term policy for relations with China *(→ point 916).*

10 July

Council formally adopts broad economic policy guidelines and recommendations to 12 Member States with excessive public deficits *(→ point 45).*

12 July

Jacob Söderman elected European Union Ombudsman *(→ point 7).*

Commission adopts communication setting out broad lines of five-year programme (1995-2000) for development of common transport policy *(→ point 385).*

Commission proposes three Directives on abolition of controls on persons at internal frontiers *(→ point 2).*

17 July

Interim agreement with Russia *(→ point 880),* Euro-Mediterranean agreement with Tunisia *(→ point 849)* and cooperation agreement with Vietnam *(→ point 915)* signed.

Council adopts decisions on arrangements for structured dialogue with Cyprus and Malta *(→ point 843)*.

19 July

Commission adopts Green Papers on copyright and related rights in information society *(→ point 132)* and on 'utility models' (legal protection of intellectual property) *(→ point 133)*.

26 July

Union Member States sign Europol Convention *(→ point 966)*, Convention on customs information system *(→ point 969)* and Convention for protection of Communities' financial interests *(→ point 967)*.

Commission adopts communication entitled 'Europe and US: the way forward' *(→ point 889)*.

September

4 September

Fourth World Conference on Women opens in Beijing *(→ point 633)*.

18 September

Council adopts Regulation laying down general rules for granting Community financial aid for trans-European networks *(→ point 340)*.

25 September

Member States sign agreement on insolvency procedures *(→ point 972)* and adopt list of non-member countries whose nationals must be in possession of a visa to enter European Union *(→ point 3)*.

October

2 October

Council adopts conclusions on aid to Left Bank and Gaza (→ *point 850*).

4 October

Commission proposes reform of common organization of market in fruit and vegetables (→ *point 539*).

11 October

Commission adopts communication on European strategy for employment (→ *point 605*).

18 October

Commission adopts communication on international cooperation in R&TD (→ *point 254*).

Council formally adopts Directive eliminating restrictions on use of cable television networks (→ *point 430*).

23 October

Commission adopts strategy document on relations with Latin America up to 2000 (→ *point 925*) and recommendation for Decision on draft agreement with Mexico (→ *point 930*).

24 October

Parliament and Council sign Directive on protection of individuals with regard to processing of personal data (→ *point 135*).

26 October

Commission adopts communication on craft trades and small businesses (→ *point 213*).

27 October

Latvia applies to join European Union *(→ point 815).*

30 October

Cooperation agreement with Brazil, signed in 1992, is formally concluded *(→ point 933).*

Council adopts conclusions on European Union action in former Yugoslavia *(→ point 845).*

31 October

Commission adopts report and communication on social protection *(→ point 613).*

Commission communication sets out priorities for consumer policy *(→ point 644).*

November

4 November

Revised Lomé IV Convention and new financial protocol signed *(→ point 936).*

7 November

New Euratom-US agreement on peaceful use of nuclear energy signed *(→ point 378).*

8 November

Commission adopts recommendation for Decision on negotiation of agreement with Chile *(→ point 931).*

13 November

Fisheries agreement with Morocco initialled *(→ point 848)*.

14 November

Commission proposes establishment of European Guarantee Fund for cinema and television production *(→ point 656)*.

16 November

Euro-Mediterranean Association Agreement with Morocco initialled *(→ point 848)*.

17 November

Commission launches programme of integrated management of coastal areas in Europe for sustainable development *(→ point 499)*.

20 November

Association Agreement with Israel *(→ point 851)* and cooperation agreement with Nepal *(→ point 913)* signed.

Council reaches agreement on revision of television without frontiers Directive *(→ point 656)*.

20 November

Council adopts conclusions on future of relations between European Union and Russia *(→ point 880)*.

22 November

Commission adopts communication on cohesion and environment *(→ point 471)*.

23 November

Council adopts first common position in justice and home affairs, concerning harmonized definition of concept of 'refugee' (→ point 960).

Commission adopts report entitled 'Better law-making' for transmission to European Council (→ point 10).

Economic and Social Committee adopts own-initiative opinion on 1996 Intergovernmental Conference (→ point 1025).

28 November

Estonia applies to join European Union (→ point 815).

Barcelona Declaration adopted at end of Euro-Mediterranean Conference (→ point 839).

29 November

Commission sends European Council three papers on enlargement of European Union to include Central and East European countries (→ point 817).

Commission adopts Green Paper on citizens' network (urban transport) (→ point 404) and White Paper on education and training (→ point 266).

Commission adopts recommendation for Decision on renewal of San José dialogue (→ point 927).

30 November

Council adopts prices of fishery products for 1996 (→ point 587).

Parliament gives assent to partnership and cooperation agreements (→ point 865) with Russia, Moldova, Kyrgyzstan, and Ukraine.

December

3 December

European Union and United States sign new transatlantic agenda and joint action plan *(→ point 888)*.

4 December

Council decides to conclude protocols to admit Central and East European countries to Community programmes *(→ point 821)*.

5 December

Reflection Group on Intergovernmental Conference presents final report *(→ point 1026)*.

Council adopts Directive on minimum safety and health requirements for workers *(→ point 620)*.

7 December

Commission presents report for European Council on overall development of assistance to Baltic Sea region *(→ point 818)*.

Council adopts Regulation amending control system applicable to common fisheries policy *(→ point 566)*.

12 December

Lithuania applies to join European Union *(→ point 815)*.

Commission presents its work programme for 1996 to Parliament *(→ point 9)*.

First agreement under Social Protocol signed by social partners *(→ point 598)*.

13 December

Parliament gives assent to European Union-Turkey customs union *(→ point 844)*.

Commission adopts White Paper on energy policy for European Union *(→ point 353)*.

14 December

Dayton peace agreement for former Yugoslavia signed in Paris *(→ point 845)*.

15 December

Mercosur-European Union framework economic and trade cooperation agreement signed *(→ point 926)*.

15 and 16 December

European Council meets in Madrid *(→ point 1049)*.

It confirms introduction of single currency (Euro) on 1 January 1999 and sets 29 March 1996 as starting date for Intergovernmental Conference *(→ point 1049)*.

16 December

Bulgaria applies to join European Union *(→ point 815)*.

18 December

European Union and Andean Pact countries sign agreement on monitoring of drug precursors *(→ point 929)*.

Joint Chile-European Union Declaration on political dialogue signed *(→ point 931)*.

Council reaches agreement on reform of common organization of rice market *(→ point 541)*.

20 and 21 December

European Commission and World Bank organize meeting in Brussels of donor countries and organizations for reconstruction of Bosnia-Herzegovina *(→ point 845)*.

21 December

The 1996 budget is adopted *(→ point 986)*.

22 December

Council adopts fourth action programme on equal opportunities for women and men (1996-2000) *(→ point 628)*.

Annexes

Annex I   —   Table I: Legislation under the co-decision procedure

Annex II   —   Table II: Legislation under the consultation, cooperation and assent procedures

Annex III   —   Table III: Legislation regarding international agreements

Annex I

Table I: Legislation under the co-decision procedure

	Commission proposal	ESC opinion/ COR opinion°	EP first reading	Amended Commission proposal	Common position Council	EP second reading a, b, c, d, e, f[1]	

Citizenship of the Union

Citizens' rights

Right to freedom of movement and right of abode

2	Prop. for a Dir. amending Dir. 68/360/EEC and 73/148/EEC on the abolition of restrictions on movement and residence for nationals of Member States	OJ C 307/18.11.95, COM(95) 348, Bull. 7/8-95/1.1.4					

Community economic and social area

Internal market

Management of the internal market

97	Dec.: information on national measures which derogate from the principle of free movement of goods	OJ C 18/21.1.94, COM(93) 670, Bull. 12-93/1.2.5	OJ C 195/18.7.94, Bull. 4-94/1.2.13	OJ C 128/9.5.94, Bull. 4-94/1.2.13	OJ C 200/22.7.94 COM(94) 250 Bull. 6-94/1.2.17	OJ C 216/21.8.95, Bull. 6-95/1.3.18	OJ C 308/20.11.95, Bull. 10-95/1.3.24 (a)

Free movement of goods

102	Prop. for a Dir. amending Dir. 93/7/EEC on the return of cultural objects removed illegally from a territory	OJ C 6/11.1.96, COM(95) 479, Bull. 10-95/1.3.39					
105	Dir. 95/2/EC: additives other than colours and sweeteners	OJ C 206/13.8.92, COM(92) 255, Bull. 6-92/1.3.22	OJ C 108/19.4.93, Bull. 1/2-93/1.2.12	OJ C 176/28.6.93, Bull. 5-93/1.2.8	OJ C 189/13.7.93, COM(93) 290, Bull. 6-93/1.2.16	OJ C 172/24.6.94, Bull. 3-94/1.2.21	OJ C 341/5.12.94, Bull. 11-94/1.2.15
105	Prop. for a Dec.: maintenance of national laws prohibiting certain additives	OJ C 134/1.6.95, COM(95) 126, Bull. 4-95/1.3.11	OJ C 301/13.11.95, Bull. 9-95/1.3.7				

° Opinion of the Committee of the Regions.
[1] a = adoption [Article 189b(2)(a)]; b = amendments [Article 189b(2)(c) and (d)]; c = declaration of rejection [Article 189b(2)(c)]; d = rejection [Article 189b(2)(c)]; e = EP failure to take a decision within 3 months [Article 189b(2)(b)]; f = amendments following a declaration of rejection; g = agreement on a common draft; h = failure to agree on a common draft.

TABLE I — CO-DECISION   497

Commission opinion (Art. 189b(2)(d))	Conciliation Committee g, h[1] (Art. 189b(4))	Confirmed common position Council (Art. 189b(6))	EP rejection of confirmed common position	EP adoption of common draft (Art. 189b(5))	Adoption by Council	EP signature Council (Art. 191)	Comments	
							Dir. to be amended: 68/360/EEC (OJ L 257/19.10.68), 73/148/EEC (OJ L 172/28.6.73)	2
					Bull. 11-95/1.3.12	Bull. 12-95	Political Agreement: Bull. 6-95/1.3.18	97
							Dir. to be amended: OJ L 74/27.3.93	102
COM(94) 563, Bull. 12-94/1.2.19					Bull. 12-94/1.2.19	OJ L 61/18.3.95, Bull. 1/2-95/1.3.8	Political Agreement on a common position: Bull. 12-93/1.2.13	105
								105

	Commission proposal	ESC opinion/ COR opinion°	EP first reading	Amended Commission proposal	Common position Council	EP second reading a, b, c, d, e, f[1]	
105 Prop. for a Dir. amending Dir. 95/2/EC: food additives other than colours and sweeteners	OJ C 163/29.6.95, COM(95) 177, Bull. 5-95/1.3.15	Bull. 10-95/1.3.36					
105 Prop. for a Dir. amending Dir. 94/35/EC: sweeteners in foodstuffs	COM(95) 482, Bull. 10-95/1.3.37						
105 Prop. for a Reg.: novel foods and novel food ingredients	OJ C 190/29.7.92, COM(92) 295, Bull. 7/8-92/1.3.15	OJ C 108/19.4.93, Bull. 1/2-93/1.2.13	OJ C 315/22.11.93, Bull. 10-93/1.2.13	OJ C 16/19.1.94, COM(93) 631, Bull. 12-93/1.2.10	OJ C 320/30.11.95, Bull. 10-95/1.3.31		
105 Prop. for a Dir. amending Dir. 80/777/EEC: natural mineral waters	OJ C 314/11.11.94, COM(94) 423, Bull. 10-94/1.2.10	OJ C 110/2.5.95, Bull. 1/2-95/1.3.9	OJ C 287/30.10.95, Bull. 10-95/1.3.33	COM(95) 563, Bull. 11-95/1.3.21	Bull. 12-95		
105 Prop. for a Reg.: flavourings	OJ C 1/4.1.94, COM(93) 609, Bull. 12-93/1.2.11	OJ C 195/18.7.94, Bull. 4-94/1.2.27	OJ C 205/25.7.94, Bull. 5-94/1.2.15	OJ C 171/24.6.94, COM(94) 236, Bull. 6-94/1.2.29	Bull. 12-95		
105 Prop. for a Dir. amending Dir. 79/112/EEC: labelling and presentation of foodstuffs*	OJ C 122/14.5.92, COM(91) 536, Bull. 4-92/1.3.8	OJ C 332/16.12.92, Bull. 10-92/1.3.34	OJ C 315/22.11.93, Bull. 10-93/1.2.14	OJ C 118/29.4.94, COM(94) 24, Bull. 4-94/1.2.24	Bull. 6-95/1.3.22	OJ C 308/20.11.95, Bull. 10-95/1.3.32 (b)	
105 Prop. for a Dir. amending Dir. 89/398/EEC: foodstuffs for particular nutritional uses	OJ C 389/31.12.94, COM(94) 600, Bull. 12-94/1.2.20	OJ C 256/2.10.95, Bull. 7/8-95/1.3.16	OJ C 287/30.10.95, Bull. 10-95/1.3.35	COM(95) 586, Bull. 12-95			
105 Prop. for a Dir. amending Dir. 89/398/EEC: foodstuffs intended for particular nutritional uses	OJ C 108/16.4.94, COM(94) 97, Bull. 3-94/1.2.23	OJ C 388/31.12.94, Bull. 7/8-94/1.2.6	OJ C 287/30.10.95, Bull. 10-95/1.3.34	COM(95) 588, Bull. 11-95/1.3.24			
106 Prop. for a Dir. amending for the 16th time Dir. 76/769/EEC (dangerous substances)	OJ C 382/31.12.94, COM(94) 570, Bull. 12-94/1.2.17	OJ C 236/11.9.95, Bull. 5-95/1.3.14bis	OJ C 269/16.10.95, Bull. 9-95/1.3.6	OJ C 12/17.1.96, COM(95) 531, Bull. 10-95/1.3.30			
106 Prop. for a Dir. amending Dir. 67/548/EEC: dangerous substances	COM(95) 636, Bull. 12-95						
106 Prop. for a Dir.: biocidal products	OJ C 239/3.9.93, COM(93) 351, Bull. 7/8-93/1.2.5	OJ C 195/18.7.94, Bull. 4-94/1.2.22			OJ C 261/6.10.95, COM(95) 387, Bull. 7/8-95/1.3.14		
106 Prop. for a Dir.: harmonizing national laws on *in vitro* diagnostic devices	OJ C 172/7.7.95, COM(95) 130, Bull. 4-95/1.3.10	Bull. 10-95/1.3.29					

° Opinion of the Committee of the Regions.
[1] a = adoption [Article 189b(2)(a)]; b = amendments [Article 189b(2)(c) and (d)]; c = declaration of rejection [Article 189b(2)(c)]; d = rejection [Article 189b(2)(c)]; e = EP failure to take a decision within 3 months [Article 189b(2)(b)]; f = amendments following a declaration of rejection; g = agreement on a common draft; h = failure to agree on a common draft.

TABLE I — CO-DECISION **499**

Commission opinion (Art. 189b(2)(d))	Conciliation Committee g, h[1] (Art. 189b(4))	Confirmed common position Council (Art. 189b(6))	EP rejection of confirmed common position	EP adoption of common draft (Art. 189b(5))	Adoption by Council	EP signature Council (Art. 191)	Comments	
							Dir. to be amended: OJ L 61/18.3.95	105
							Dir. to be amended: OJ L 237/10.9.94	105
								105
							Political Agreement on a common position: Bull. 11-95/1.3.21; Dir. to be amended: OJ L 229/30.8.80	105
							Political Agreement on a common position: Bull. 11-95/1.3.22	105
COM(95) 631, Bull. 12-95							Political Agreement on a common position: Bull. 3-95/1.3.10; Dir. to be amended: OJ L 33/8.2.79	105
							Dir. to be amended: OJ L 186/30.6.89	105
								105
							Dir. to be amended: OJ L 262/27.9.76	106
							Dir. to be amended: OJ 196/16.8.67	106
								106
								106

	Commission proposal	ESC opinion/ COR opinion°	EP first reading	Amended Commission proposal	Common position Council	EP second reading a, b, c, d, e, f[1]	
107 Dir. 95/1/EC: maximum speed of two or three-wheel motor vehicles	OJ C 93/13.4.92, COM(91) 497, Bull. 1/2-92/1.3.30	OJ C 313/30.11.92, Bull. 9-92/1.2.17	OJ C 72/15.3.93, Bull. 1/2-93/1.2.2		Bull. 6-93/1.2.7	OJ C 315/22.11.93, Bull. 10-93/1.2.5 (c); OJ C 61/28.2.94, Bull. 1/2-94/1.2.9 (c); OJ C 205/25.7.94, Bull. 5-94/1.2.10 (f)	
107 Prop. for a Dir.: characteristics of two or three-wheel motor vehicles	COM(93) 449, Bull. 11-93/1.2.2	OJ C 195/18.7.94, Bull. 4-94/1.2.14	OJ C 151/19.6.95, Bull. 5-95/1.3.13	COM(95) 493, Bull. 11-95/1.3.17	Bull. 11-95/1.3.17		
107 Dir. 95/28/EC: burning behaviour of materials used in the interior construction of motor vehicles	OJ C 154/19.6.92, COM(92) 201, Bull. 5-92/1.1.15	OJ C 332/16.12.92, Bull. 10-92/1.3.27	OJ C 305/23.11.92, Bull. 10-92/1.3.27		OJ C 384/31.12.94, Bull. 12-94/1.2.9	OJ C 166/3.7.95, Bull. 6-95/1.3.20 (a)	
107 Prop. for a Dir.: resistance of vehicles to head-on collisions	OJ C 396/31.12.94, COM(94) 520, Bull. 12-94/1.2.11	OJ C 256/2.10.95, Bull. 7/8-95/1.3.13	OJ C 249/25.9.95, Bull. 7/8-95/1.3.13	COM(95) 510, Bull. 11-95/1.3.14			
107 Prop. for a Dir.: resistance of vehicles to side impacts	OJ C 396/31.12.94, COM(94) 519, Bull. 12-94/1.2.10	OJ C 256/2.10.95, Bull. 7/8-95/1.3.19	OJ C 249/25.9.95, Bull. 7/8-95/1.3.19	COM(95) 454, Bull. 10-95/1.3.28	OJ C 353/30.12.95, Bull. 11-95/1.3.13		
108 Dir. 95/16/EC: lifts	OJ C 62/11.3.92, COM(92) 35, Bull. 1/2-92/1.3.19	OJ C 287/4.11.92, Bull. 7/8-92/1.3.22	OJ C 305/23.11.92, Bull. 10-92/1.3.29	OJ C 180/2.7.93, COM(93) 240, Bull. 6-93/1.2.9	OJ C 232/20.8.94, Bull. 6-94/1.2.18	OJ C 305/31.10.94, Bull. 9-94/1.2.16 (b)	
108 Prop. for a Dir.: pressure equipment	OJ C 246/9.9.93, COM(93) 319, Bull. 7/8-93/1.2.2	OJ C 52/19.2.94, Bull. 12-93/1.2.8	OJ C 128/9.5.94, Bull. 4-94/1.2.16	OJ C 207/27.7.94, COM(94) 278, Bull. 6-94/1.2.19			
108 Prop. for a Dir. amending Dir. 89/686/EEC: approximation of laws for PPE	OJ C 23/27.1.96, COM(95) 552, Bull. 11-95/1.3.18						
108 Prop. for a Dir.: textile names	OJ C 96/6.4.94, COM(93) 712, Bull. 1/2-94/1.2.13	OJ C 195/18.7.94, Bull. 4-94/1.2.18	OJ C 56/6.3.95, Bull. 1/2-95/1.3.5				
108 Prop. for a Dir.: quantitative analysis methods for binary textile fibre mixtures	OJ C 96/6.4.94, COM(93) 713, Bull. 1/2-94/1.2.12	OJ C 195/18.7.94, Bull. 4-94/1.2.19	OJ C 56/6.3.95, Bull. 1/2-95/1.3.6				
113 Prop. for a Reg.: additional protection regarding plant protection products	OJ C 390/31.12.94, COM(94) 579, Bull. 12-94/1.2.28	OJ C 155/21.6.95, Bull. 4-95/1.3.16	OJ C 166/3.7.95, Bull. 6-95/1.3.34	OJ C 335/13.12.95, COM(95) 456, Bull. 10-95/1.3.43	OJ C 353/30.12.95, Bull. 11-95/1.3.27		

Free movement of persons

117 Prop. for a Dir. amending Dir. 93/16/EEC: free movement of doctors	OJ C 389/31.12.94, COM(94) 626, Bull. 12-94/1.2.30	OJ C 133/31.5.95, Bull. 3-95/1.3.12	OJ C 183/17.7.95, Bull. 6-95/1.3.35	COM(95) 437, Bull. 11-95/1.3.28			

° Opinion of the Committee of the Regions.
[1] a = adoption [Article 189b(2)(a)]; b = amendments [Article 189b(2)(c) and (d)]; c = declaration of rejection [Article 189b(2)(c)]; d = rejection [Article 189b(2)(c)]; e = EP failure to take a decision within 3 months [Article 189b(2)(b)]; f = amendments following a declaration of rejection; g = agreement on a common draft; h = failure to agree on a common draft.

TABLE I — CO-DECISION   501

Commission opinion (Art. 189b(2)(d))	Conciliation Committee g, h[1] (Art. 189b(4))	Confirmed common position Council (Art. 189b(6))	EP rejection of confirmed common position	EP adoption of common draft (Art. 189b(5))	Adoption by Council	EP signature Council (Art. 191)	Comments	
COM(94) 321, Bull. 7/8-94/1.2.3	Bull. 3-94/1.2.10 (h), Bull. 10-94/1.2.7 (h), Bull. 12-94/1.2.8 (g)			OJ C 43/20.2.95, Bull. 1/2-95/1.3.4	Bull. 1/2-95/1.3.4	OJ L 52/8.3.95, Bull. 1/2-95/1.3.4		107
								107
					Bull. 7/8-95/1.3.11	OJ L 281/23.11.95, Bull. 10-95/1.3.26		107
								107
								107
COM(94) 540, Bull. 12-94/1.2.14	Bull. 3-95/1.3.9 (h), Bull. 5-95/1.3.14 (g)			OJ C 166/3.7.95, Bull. 6-95/1.3.21	Bull. 6-95/1.3.21	OJ L 213/7.9.95, Bull. 6-95/1.3.21		108
							Political Agreement on a common position: Bull. 11-95/1.3.19	108
							Dir. to be amended: OJ L 399/30.12.89	108
								108
								108
								113
							Dir. to be amended: OJ L 165/7.7.93	117

	Commission proposal	ESC opinion/ COR opinion°	EP first reading	Amended Commission proposal	Common position Council	EP second reading a, b, c, d, e, f¹	
117 Prop. for a Dir.: exercising the profession of laywer	OJ C 128/24.5.95, COM(94) 572, Bull. 12-94/1.2.29	OJ C 256/2.10.95, Bull. 7/8-95/1.3.19					

Free movement of services

	Commission proposal	ESC opinion/ COR opinion°	EP first reading	Amended Commission proposal	Common position Council	EP second reading a, b, c, d, e, f¹	
119 Dir. 95/26/EC amending Dir. 77/780/EEC, 73/239/EEC, 79/267/EEC, 93/22/EEC, 85/611/ EEC: reinforcement of prudential supervision (financial services)	OJ C 229/25.8.93, COM(93) 363, Bull. 7/8-93/1.2.19	OJ C 52/19.2.94, Bull. 12-93/1.2.36	OJ C 91/28.3.94, Bull. 3-94/1.2.29	COM(94) 170, Bull. 5-94/1.2.18	OJ C 213/3.8.94, Bull. 6-94/1.2.36	OJ C 323/21.11.94, Bull. 10-94/1.2.12 (b)	
120 Prop. for a Dir. amending Dir. 89/647/EEC: contracts for novation and netting agreements	OJ C 142/25.5.94, OJ C 231/20.8.94, COM(94) 105, Bull. 4-94/1.2.38	OJ C 393/31.12.94, Bull. 9-94/1.2.28	OJ C 56/6.3.95, Bull. 1/2-95/1.3.15	OJ C 165/1.7.95, COM(95) 170, Bull. 5-95/1.3.19	OJ C 288/30.10.95, Bull. 9-95/1.3.14	Bull. 12-95 (b)	
121 Prop. for a Dir.: monitoring of insurance companies which are part of a group	OJ C 341/19.12.95, COM(95) 406, Bull. 10-95/1.3.44						
122 Prop. for a Dir.: cross-border money transfers	OJ C 360/17.12.94, COM(94) 436, Bull. 11-94/1.2.21	OJ C 236/11.9.95, Bull. 5-95/1.3.17; OJ C 301/13.11.95, Bull. 9-95/1.3.12	OJ C 151/19.6.95, Bull. 5-95/1.3.17	OJ C 199/3.8.95, COM(95) 264, Bull. 6-95/1.3.38	OJ C 353/30.12.95, Bull. 12-95		
123 Prop. for a Dir.: investor compensation	OJ C 321/27.11.93, COM(93) 381, Bull. 9-93/1.2.17	OJ C 127/7.5.94, Bull. 1/2-94/1.2.27	OJ C 128/9.5.94, Bull. 4-94/1.2.36	OJ C 382/31.12.94, COM(94) 585, Bull. 12-94/1.2.32	OJ C 320/30.11.95, Bull. 10-95/1.3.45		
123 Prop. for a Dir. amending Dir. 93/6/EEC and 93/22/EEC: investment in securities	OJ C 42/22.2.90, COM(89) 629, Bull. 1/2-90/1.1.29; OJ C 50/25.2.92, COM(92) 13, Bull. 1/2-92/1.3.47			OJ C 253/29.9.95, COM(95) 360, Bull. 7/8-95/1.3.21			

° Opinion of the Committee of the Regions.
¹ a = adoption [Article 189b(2)(a)]; b = amendments [Article 189b(2)(c) and (d)]; c = declaration of rejection [Article 189b(2)(c)]; d = rejection [Article 189b(2)(c)]; e = EP failure to take a decision within 3 months [Article 189b(2)(b)]; f = amendments following a declaration of rejection; g = agreement on a common draft; h = failure to agree on a common draft.

TABLE I — CO-DECISION   503

Commission opinion (Art. 189b(2)(d))	Conciliation Committee g, h[1] (Art. 189b(4))	Confirmed common position Council (Art. 189b(6))	EP rejection of confirmed common position	EP adoption of common draft (Art. 189b(5))	Adoption by Council	EP signature Council (Art. 191)	Comments
							117

Commission opinion (Art. 189b(2)(d))	Conciliation Committee g, h[1] (Art. 189b(4))	Confirmed common position Council (Art. 189b(6))	EP rejection of confirmed common position	EP adoption of common draft (Art. 189b(5))	Adoption by Council	EP signature Council (Art. 191)	Comments
COM(94) 549, Bull. 11-94/1.2.22	Bull. 3-95/1.3.14 (g)			OJ C 151/19.6.95, Bull. 5-95/1.3.18	Bull. 6-95/1.3.37	OJ L 168/18.7.95, Bull. 6-95/1.3.37	Amended Directives: **119** 77/780/EEC (OJ L 322/17.12.77), 73/239/EEC (OJ L 228/16.8.73), 79/267/EEC (OJ L 63/13.3.79), 93/22/EEC (OJ L 141/11.6.93), 85/611/EEC (OJ L 375/31.12.85)
							Dir. to be amended: **120** OJ L 386/30.12.89
							121
							Political Agreement **122** on a common position: Bull. 9-95/1.3.12
							Political Agreement **123** on a common position: Bull. 5-95/1.3.16
							Dir. to be amended: **123** OJ L 141/11.6.93

	Commission proposal	ESC opinion/ COR opinion°	EP first reading	Amended Commission proposal	Common position Council	EP second reading a, b, c, d, e, f[1]	

Intellectual and industrial property

	Commission proposal	ESC opinion/ COR opinion°	EP first reading	Amended Commission proposal	Common position Council	EP second reading a, b, c, d, e, f[1]	
132 Prop. for a Dir.: legal protection of databases	OJ C 156/23.6.92, COM(92) 24, Bull. 1/2-92/1.3.14	OJ C 19/25.1.93, Bull. 11-92/1.3.40	OJ C 194/19.7.93, Bull. 6-93/1.2.32	OJ C 308/15.11.93, COM(93) 464, Bull. 10-93/1.2.26	OJ C 288/30.10.95, Bull. 7/8-95/1.3.25	Bull. 12-95 (b)	
132 Prop. for a Dir.: legal protection of designs	OJ C 345/23.12.93, COM(93) 344, Bull. 12-93/1.2.39	OJ C 388/31.12.94, Bull. 7/8-94/1.2.18; OJ C 110/2.5.95, Bull. 1/2-95/1.3.19°	OJ C 287/30.10.95, Bull. 10-95/1.3.50				
133 Prop. for a Reg.: additional protection regarding plant protection products	OJ C 390/31.12.94, COM(94) 579, Bull. 12-94/1.2.28	OJ C 155/21.6.95, Bull. 4-95/1.3.16	OJ C 166/3.7.95, Bull. 6-95/1.3.34	OJ C 335/13.12.95, COM(95) 456, Bull. 10-95/1.3.43	OJ C 353/30.12.95, Bull. 11-95/1.3.27		
133 Prop. for a Dir.: legal protection of biotechnological inventions	OJ C 10/13.1.89, COM(88) 496, Bull. 10-88/2.1.17	OJ C 159/26.6.89, Bull. 4-89/2.1.44	OJ C 305/23.11.92, Bull. 10-92/1.3.44	OJ C 44/16.2.93, COM(92) 589, Bull. 12-92/1.3.50	Bull. 12-93/1.2.40; OJ C 101/9.4.94, Bull. 1/2-94/1.2.36	OJ C 205/25.7.94, Bull. 5-94/1.2.20 (b)	
133 Prop. for a Dir.: legal protection of biotechnological inventions	COM(95) 661, Bull. 12-95						
133 Prop. for a Reg.: Community designs	OJ C 342/23.12.93, COM(93) 342, Bull. 12-93/1.2.39	OJ C 388/31.12.94, Bull. 7/8-94/1.2.18; OJ C 110/2.5.95, Bull. 1/2-95/1.3.19					

Data protection

	Commission proposal	ESC opinion/ COR opinion°	EP first reading	Amended Commission proposal	Common position Council	EP second reading a, b, c, d, e, f[1]	
135 Dir. 95/46/EC: protection of individuals in relation to the processing of personal data	OJ C 277/5.11.90, COM(90) 314, Bull. 7/8-90/1.3.310	OJ C 159/17.6.91, Bull. 4-91/1.2.140	OJ C 94/13.4.92, Bull. 3-92/1.2.214	OJ C 311/27.11.92, COM(92) 422, Bull. 10-92/1.3.177	OJ C 93/13.4.95, Bull. 1/2-95 /1.3.20	OJ C 166/3.7.95, Bull. 6-95/1.3.44 (b)	

Government procurement

	Commission proposal	ESC opinion/ COR opinion°	EP first reading	Amended Commission proposal	Common position Council	EP second reading a, b, c, d, e, f[1]	
136 Prop. for a Dir. amending Dir. 92/50/EEC, 93/36/EEC and 93/37/EEC: award of public procurement contracts	OJ C 138/3.6.95, COM(95) 107, Bull. 3-95/1.3.19	OJ C 256/2.10.95, Bull. 7/8-95/1.3.28					
136 Prop. for a Dir. amending Dir. 93/38/EEC: award of public procurement contracts	OJ C 138/3.6.95, COM(95) 107, Bull. 3-95/1.3.19	OJ C 256/2.10.95, Bull. 7/8-95/1.3.28					

° Opinion of the Committee of the Regions.
[1] a = adoption [Article 189b(2)(a)]; b = amendments [Article 189b(2)(c) and (d)]; c = declaration of rejection [Article 189b(2)(c)]; d = rejection [Article 189b(2)(c)];
e = EP failure to take a decision within 3 months [Article 189b(2)(b)]; f = amendments following a declaration of rejection; g = agreement on a common draft;
h = failure to agree on a common draft.

TABLE I — CO-DECISION 505

Commission opinion (Art. 189b(2)(d))	Conciliation Committee g, h[1] (Art. 189b(4))	Confirmed common position Council (Art. 189b(6))	EP rejection of confirmed common position	EP adoption of common draft (Art. 189b(5))	Adoption by Council	EP signature Council (Art. 191)	Comments
							Political Agreement on a common position: Bull. 6-95/1.3.42 132
							132
							133
COM(94) 245, Bull. 6-94/1.2.38	Bull. 11-94/1.2.26; Bull. 1/2-95/1.3.18 (g)		OJ C 68/20.3.95, Bull. 3-95/1.3.17				133
							133
							133
COM(95) 375, Bull. 7/8-95/1.3.26				Bull. 7/8-95/1.3.26	OJ L 281/23.11.95, Bull. 10-95/1.3.51		Political Agreement on a common position: Bull. 12-94/1.1.3 135
							Dir. to be amended: 92/50/EEC (OJ L 209/24.7.92), 93/36/EEC (OJ L 199/9.8.93), 93/37/EEC (OJ L 199/9.8.93) 136
							Dir. to be amended: OJ L 199/9.8.93 136

	Commission proposal	ESC opinion/ COR opinion°	EP first reading	Amended Commission proposal	Common position Council	EP second reading a, b, c, d, e, f¹	

Enterprise policy, distributive trades, tourism and the cooperative, mutual and non-profit sector

Cooperative, mutual and other associations and foundations

	Commission proposal	ESC opinion/ COR opinion°	EP first reading	Amended Commission proposal	Common position Council	EP second reading	
214 Prop. for a Reg.: Statutes for the European association	OJ C 99/21.4.92, COM(91) 273, Bull. 12-91/1.2.73	OJ C 223/31.8.92, Bull. 5-92/1.1.59	OJ C 42/15.2.93, Bull. 1/2-93/1.2.89	OJ C 236/31.8.93, COM(93) 252, Bull. 7/8-93/1.2.82			
214 Prop. for a Dir.: Statutes for the European association (involvement of employees)	OJ C 99/21.4.92, COM(91) 273, Bull. 12-91/1.2.73	OJ C 223/31.8.92, Bull. 5-92/1.1.59	OJ C 42/15.2.93, Bull. 1/2-93/1.2.89	OJ C 236/31.8.93, COM(93) 252, Bull. 7/8-93/1.2.82			
214 Prop. for a Reg.: Statutes for the European cooperative society	OJ C 99/21.4.92, COM(91) 273, Bull. 12-91/1.2.73	OJ C 223/31.8.92, Bull. 5-92/1.1.59	OJ C 42/15.2.93, Bull. 1/2-93/1.2.89	OJ C 236/31.8.93, COM(93) 252, Bull. 7/8-93/1.2.82			
214 Prop. for a Dir.: Statutes for the European cooperative society (involvement of employees)	OJ C 99/21.4.92, COM(91) 273, Bull. 12-91/1.2.73	OJ C 223/31.8.92, Bull. 5-92/1.1.59	OJ C 42/15.2.93, Bull. 1/2-93/1.2.89	OJ C 236/31.8.93, COM(93) 252, Bull. 7/8-93/1.2.82			
214 Prop. for a Reg.: Statutes for the European mutual society	OJ C 99/21.4.92, COM(91) 273, Bull. 12-91/1.2.73	OJ C 223/31.8.92, Bull. 5-92/1.1.59	OJ C 42/15.2.93, Bull. 1/2-93/1.2.89	OJ C 236/31.8.93, COM(93) 252, Bull. 7/8-93/1.2.82			
214 Prop. for a Dir.: Statutes for the European mutual society (involvement of employees)	OJ C 99/21.4.92, COM(91) 273, Bull. 12-91/1.2.73	OJ C 223/31.8.92, Bull. 5-92/1.1.59	OJ C 42/15.2.93, Bull. 1/2-93/1.2.89	OJ C 236/31.8.93, COM(93) 252, Bull. 7/8-93/1.2.82			

Research and technology

Community R&TD policy

	Commission proposal	ESC opinion/ COR opinion°	EP first reading	Amended Commission proposal	Common position Council	EP second reading	
231 Prop. for a Dec. amending Dec. 94/1110/EC: adaptation of the general framework programme (1994-98) as a result of enlargement	OJ C 142/8.6.95, COM(95) 145, Bull. 4-95/1.3.63	OJ C 256/2.10.95, Bull. 7/8-95/1.3.76	OJ C 249/25.9.95, Bull. 7/8-95/1.3.76		OJ C 353/30.12.95, Bull. 11-95/1.3.76		

Education, vocational training and youth

Priority activities and objectives

	Commission proposal	ESC opinion/ COR opinion°	EP first reading	Amended Commission proposal	Common position Council	EP second reading	
266 Dec. 2493/95/EC: European Year of Continuing Education (1996)	OJ C 287/15.10.94, COM(94) 264, Bull. 9-94/1.2.186	OJ C 397/31.12.94, Bull. 11-94/1.2.202; OJ C 210/14.8.95, Bull. 11-94/1.2.202°	OJ C 89/10.4.95, Bull. 3-95/1.3.68	OJ C 134/1.6.95, COM(95) 124, Bull. 3-95/1.3.68	OJ C 130/29.5.95, Bull. 4-95/1.3.65	OJ C 166/3.7.95, Bull. 6-95/1.3.89 (b)	

° Opinion of the Committee of the Regions.
¹ a = adoption [Article 189b(2)(a)]; b = amendments [Article 189b(2)(c) and (d)]; c = declaration of rejection [Article 189b(2)(c)]; d = rejection [Article 189b(2)(c)]; e = EP failure to take a decision within 3 months [Article 189b(2)(b)]; f = amendments following a declaration of rejection; g = agreement on a common draft; h = failure to agree on a common draft.

TABLE I — CO-DECISION 507

Commission opinion (Art. 189b(2)(d))	Conciliation Committee g, h[1] (Art. 189b(4))	Confirmed common position Council (Art. 189b(6))	EP rejection of confirmed common position	EP adoption of common draft (Art. 189b(5))	Adoption by Council	EP signature Council (Art. 191)	Comments	
								214
								214
								214
								214
								214
								214
							Political Agreement on a common position: Bull. 10-95/1.3.90; Dec. to be amended: OJ L 126/18.5.94	231
COM(95) 316, Bull. 7/8-95/1.3.81					Bull. 7/8-95/1.3.81	OJ L 256/26.10.95, Bull. 10-95/1.3.99	Political Agreement on a common position: Bull. 3-95/1.3.68	266

	Commission proposal	ESC opinion/ COR opinion°	EP first reading	Amended Commission proposal	Common position Council	EP second reading a, b, c, d, e, f[1]	

Cooperation in the field of education

		Commission proposal	ESC opinion/ COR opinion°	EP first reading	Amended Commission proposal	Common position Council	EP second reading a, b, c, d, e, f[1]	
267	Dec. 95/819/EC: Socrates programme	OJ C 66/3.3.94, COM(93) 708, Bull. 1/2-94/1.2.184	OJ C 195/18.7.94, Bull. 4-94/1.2.165; OJ C 217/6.8.94, Bull. 5-94/1.2.137°	OJ C 128/9.5.94, Bull. 4-94/1.2.165	OJ C 164/16.6.94, COM(94) 180, Bull. 5-94/1.2.137	OJ C 244/31.8.94, Bull. 7/8-94/1.2.167	OJ C 323/21.11.94, Bull. 10-94/1.2.113 (b)	

Cooperation in the field of youth

		Commission proposal	ESC opinion/ COR opinion°	EP first reading	Amended Commission proposal	Common position Council	EP second reading a, b, c, d, e, f[1]	
280	Dec. 95/818/EC: Youth for Europe programme III	OJ C 160/11.6.94, COM(93) 523, Bull. 11-93/1.2.81	OJ C 148/30.5.94, Bull. 3-94/1.2.170; OJ C 217/6.8.94, Bull. 5-94/1.2.141°	OJ C 128/9.5.94, Bull. 4-94/1.2.167	OJ C 170/23.6.94, COM(94) 186, Bull. 5-94/1.2.141	OJ C 232/20.8.94, Bull. 7/8-94/1.2.171	OJ C 323/21.11.94, Bull. 10-94/1.2.116 (b)	

Trans-European networks

Transport

		Commission proposal	ESC opinion/ COR opinion°	EP first reading	Amended Commission proposal	Common position Council	EP second reading a, b, c, d, e, f[1]	
341	Prop. for a Dec.: guidelines for the trans-European transport network	OJ C 220/8.8.94, COM(94) 106, Bull. 4-94/1.2.76	OJ C 210/14.8.95, Bull. 9-94/1.2.101°; OJ C 397/31.12.94, Bull. 11-94/1.2.84	OJ C 151/19.6.95, Bull. 5-95/1.3.61	OJ C 97/20.4.95, COM(95) 48, Bull. 1/2-95/1.3.83	OJ C 331/8.12.95, Bull. 9-95/1.3.62	OJ C 17/22.1.96, Bull. 12-95 (b)	

Telematic systems and telecommunications

		Commission proposal	ESC opinion/ COR opinion°	EP first reading	Amended Commission proposal	Common position Council	EP second reading a, b, c, d, e, f[1]	
345	Prop. for a Dec.: trans-European telecommunications networks	OJ C 302/14.11.95, COM(95) 224, Bull. 5-95/1.3.78	Bull. 11-95/1.3.127					
346	Dec. 2717/95/EC: guidelines concerning the development of ISDN as a trans-European network	OJ C 259/23.9.93, COM(93) 347, Bull. 9-93/1.2.66	OJ C 52/19.2.94, Bull. 12-93/1.2.118; OJ C 217/6.8.94, Bull. 5-94/1.2.74°	OJ C 128/9.5.94, Bull. 4-94/1.2.77	OJ C 353/13.12.94, COM(94) 483, Bull. 11-94/1.2.87	OJ C 384/31.12.94, Bull. 12-94/1.2.105	OJ C 166/3.7.95, Bull. 6-95/1.3.112 (b)	
347	Prop. for a Dec.: guidelines for trans-European data-communications networks between administrations	OJ C 105/16.4.93, COM(93) 69, Bull. 3-93/1.2.61	OJ C 249/13.9.93, Bull. 6-93/1.2.101; OJ C 217/6.8.94, Bull. 5-94/1.2.72°	OJ C 341/5.12.94, Bull. 11-94/1.2.85	OJ C 321/1.12.95, COM(95) 446, Bull. 9-95/1.3.65			

° Opinion of the Committee of the Regions.
[1] a = adoption [Article 189b(2)(a)]; b = amendments [Article 189b(2)(c) and (d)]; c = declaration of rejection [Article 189b(2)(c)]; d = rejection [Article 189b(2)(c)];
e = EP failure to take a decision within 3 months [Article 189b(2)(b)]; f = amendments following a declaration of rejection; g = agreement on a common draft;
h = failure to agree on a common draft.

TABLE I — CO-DECISION 509

Commission opinion (Art. 189b(2)(d))	Conciliation Committee g, h¹ (Art. 189b(4))	Confirmed common position Council (Art. 189b(6))	EP rejection of confirmed common position	EP adoption of common draft (Art. 189b(5))	Adoption by Council	EP signature Council (Art. 191)	Comments	
COM(94) 502, Bull.11-94/1.2.204	Bull.12-94/1.2.226; Bull.1/2-95/1.3.67 (g)			OJ C 68/20.3.95, Bull. 3-95/1.3.69	Bull. 1/2-95/1.3.67	OJ L 87/20.4.95, Bull. 3-95/1.3.69	Political Agreement on a common position: Bull. 6-94/1.2.197	267
COM(94) 490, Bull.11-94/1.2.208	Bull.12-94/1.2.230; Bull.1/2-95/1.3.69 (g)			OJ C 68/20.3.95, Bull. 3-95/1.3.71	Bull. 1/2-95/1.3.69	OJ L 87/20.4.95, Bull. 3-95/1.3.71	Political Agreement on a common position: Bull. 6-94/1.2.199	280
							Political Agreement on a common position: Bull. 6-95/1.3.110	341
								345
COM(95) 417, Bull. 9-95/1.3.63					Bull. 10-95/1.3.125	OJ L 282/24.11.95, Bull. 11-95/1.3.106	Political Agreement: Bull. 11-94/1.2.87	346
								347

	Commission proposal	ESC opinion/ COR opinion°	EP first reading	Amended Commission proposal	Common position Council	EP second reading a, b, c, d, e, f[1]	

Energy

349 Prop. for a Dec.: guidelines for the trans-European energy network	OJ C 72/10.3.94, COM(93) 685, Bull. 1/2-94/1.2.88	OJ C 195/18.7.94, Bull. 4-94/1.2.74; OJ C 217/6.8.94, Bull. 5-94/1.2.70°	OJ C 151/19.6.95, Bull. 5-95/1.3.59	OJ C 205/10.8.95, COM(95) 226, Bull. 5-95/1.3.59	OJ C 216/21.8.95, Bull. 6-95/1.3.108	OJ C 308/20.11.95, Bull. 10-95/1.3.123 (b)	

Energy

Internal energy market

361 Prop. for a Dir.: common rules for the internal market in electricity and natural gas	OJ C 65/14.3.92, COM(91) 548, Bull. 1/2-92/1.3.117	OJ C 73/15.3.93, Bull. 1/2-93/1.2.98	OJ C 329/6.12.93, Bull. 11-93/1.2.82	OJ C 123/4.5.94, COM(93) 643, Bull. 12-93/1.2.121			

The information society and telecommunications

Telecommunications policy

431 Prop. for a Dir.: interconnection in telecommunications and open network provision (ONP)	OJ C 313/24.11.95, COM(95) 379, Bull. 7/8-95/1.3.127						
432 Prop. for a Dec.: personal communications via satellite	COM(95) 529, Bull. 11-95/1.3.133						
433 Dir. 95/62/EC: voice telephony in the context of ONP	OJ C 122/18.5.95, COM(94) 689, Bull. 1/2-95/1.3.102	OJ C 236/11.9.95, Bull. 5-95/1.3.83	OJ C 151/19.6.95, Bull. 5-95/1.3.83		OJ C 281/25.10.95, Bull. 7/8-95/1.3.129	OJ C 308/20.11.95, Bull. 10-95/1.3.145 (b)	
433 Prop. for a Dir. amending Dir. 90/387/EEC and 92/44/EEC: competitive environment in telecommunications	COM(95) 543, Bull. 11-95/1.3.130						
434 Prop. for a Dir.: common framework for individual licences	COM(95) 545, Bull. 11-95/1.3.129						
434 Prop. for a Dir.: telecommunications equipment connected to the network	COM(95) 612, Bull. 12-95						

° Opinion of the Committee of the Regions.
[1] a = adoption [Article 189b(2)(a)]; b = amendments [Article 189b(2)(c) and (d)]; c = declaration of rejection [Article 189b(2)(c)]; d = rejection [Article 189b(2)(c)]; e = EP failure to take a decision within 3 months [Article 189b(2)(b)]; f = amendments following a declaration of rejection; g = agreement on a common draft; h = failure to agree on a common draft.

TABLE I — CO-DECISION   511

Commission opinion (Art. 189b(2)(d))	Conciliation Committee g, h[1] (Art. 189b(4))	Confirmed common position Council (Art. 189b(6))	EP rejection of confirmed common position	EP adoption of common draft (Art. 189b(5))	Adoption by Council	EP signature Council (Art. 191)	Comments	
COM(95) 577, Bull.11-95/1.3.103							Political Agreement on a common position: Bull. 6-95/1.3.108	349
								361
								431
								432
COM(95) 575, Bull.11-95/1.3.134				Bull.11-95/1.3.134	OJ L 321/30.12.95, Bull. 12-95		Political Agreement on a common position: Bull. 6-95/1.3.142	433
							Dir. to be amended: 90/387/EEC (OJ L 192/24.7.90) and 92/44/EEC (OJ L 165/19.6.92)	433
								434
							Dir. to be codified: 91/263/EEC (OJ L 128/23.5.91) and 93/97/EEC (OJ L 290/24.11.93)	434

	Commission proposal	ESC opinion/ COR opinion°	EP first reading	Amended Commission proposal	Common position Council	EP second reading a, b, c, d, e, f¹	
435 Prop. for a Dec.: trans-European telecommunications networks	OJ C 302/14.11.95, COM(95) 224, Bull. 5-95/1.3.78	Bull. 11-95/1.3.127					

Advanced television services

453 Dir. 95/47/EC: television standards	OJ C 341/18.2.93, COM(93) 556, Bull. 11-93/1.2.200	OJ C 148/30.5.94, Bull. 3-94/1.2.180	OJ C 128/9.5.94, Bull. 4-94/1.2.180	OJ C 321/18.11.94, COM(94) 455, Bull. 10-94/1.2.134	OJ C 384/31.12.94, Bull. 12-94/1.2.243	OJ C 166/3.7.95, Bull. 6-95/1.3.144 (b)	

Postal services

454 Prop. for a Dir.: common rules for Community postal services	OJ C 313/24.11.95, COM(95) 227, Bull. 7/8-95/1.3.132						

Environment

Industry and the environment

481 Prop. for a Dir.: elimination of PCBs and PCTs	OJ C 319/12.12.88, COM(88) 559, Bull. 10-88/2.1.111	OJ C 139/5.6.89, Bull. 3-89/2.1.112	OJ C 19/28.1.91, Bull. 12-90/1.3.150	OJ C 299/20.11.91, COM(91) 373, Bull. 10-91/1.2.186	Bull. 11-95/1.3.141		
481 Prop. for a Dir.: classification, packaging and labelling of dangerous substances	COM(93) 638, Bull. 12-93/1.2.179	OJ C 133/15.6.94, Bull. 1/2-94/1.2.162	OJ C 61/28.2.94, Bull. 1/2-94/1.2.162; OJ C 56/6.3.95, Bull. 1/2-95/1.3.105	COM(94) 103, Bull. 4-94/1.2.147			

Quality of the environment and natural resources

500 Prop. for a Dir.: approximation of laws against the emission of gas and particulate pollutants	OJ C 328/7.12.95, COM(95) 350, Bull. 9-95/1.3.95		OJ C 308/20.11.95, Bull. 10-95/1.3.158				

° Opinion of the Committee of the Regions.
¹ a = adoption [Article 189b(2)(a)]; b = amendments [Article 189b(2)(c) and (d)]; c = declaration of rejection [Article 189b(2)(c)]; d = rejection [Article 189b(2)(c)]; e = EP failure to take a decision within 3 months [Article 189b(2)(b)]; f = amendments following a declaration of rejection; g = agreement on a common draft; h = failure to agree on a common draft.

TABLE I — CO-DECISION   513

Commission opinion (Art. 189b(2)(d))	Conciliation Committee g, h[1] (Art. 189b(4))	Confirmed common position Council (Art. 189b(6))	EP rejection of confirmed common position	EP adoption of common draft (Art. 189b(5))	Adoption by Council	EP signature Council (Art. 191)	Comments	
								435
COM(95) 319, Bull.7/8-95/1.3.130				Bull.7/8-95/1.3.130		OJ L 281/23.11.95, Bull. 10-95/1.3.146	Political Agreement on a common position: Bull. 11-94/1.2.228	453
								454
							Political Agreement on a common position: Bull. 12-94/1.2.200; Opinion of the EP on the legal basis: OJ C 269/16.10.95, Bull. 9-95/1.3.85	481
								481
								500

	Commission proposal	ESC opinion/ COR opinion °	EP first reading	Amended Commission proposal	Common position Council	EP second reading a, b, c, d, e, f [1]	
500 Prop. for a Dir. amending Dir. 88/77/EEC: pollution by diesel engine emissions	OJ C 389/31.12.94, COM(94) 559, Bull. 12-94/1.2.13	OJ C 155/21.6.95, Bull. 4-95/1.3.8	OJ C 269/16.10.95, Bull. 9-95/1.3.5	COM(95) 461, Bull. 10-95/1.3.27	OJ C 320/30.11.95, Bull. 11-95/1.3.15	Bull. 12-95 (a)	
500 Prop. for a Dir. amending Dir. 70/220/EEC: pollution by motor vehicle emissions	OJ C 390/31.12.94, COM(94) 558, Bull. 12-94/1.2.12	OJ C 155/21.6.95, Bull. 4-95/1.3.7	OJ C 269/16.10.95, Bull. 9-95/1.3.4	COM(95) 540, Bull. 11-95/1.3.16	Bull. 12-95		
502 Dir. 95/27/EC amending Dir. 86/662/EEC: limitation of noise emitted by earthmoving machinery	OJ C 157/9.6.93, COM(93) 154, Bull. 5-93/1.2.104	OJ C 304/10.11.93, Bull. 9-93/1.2.108	OJ C 255/20.9.93, Bull. 7/8-93/1.2.145		OJ C 213/3.8.94, Bull. 6-94/1.2.186	OJ C 341/5.12.94, Bull. 11-94/1.2.192 (b)	

Agricultural policy

Management of the common agricultural policy

	Commission proposal						
538 Prop. for a Reg. amending Reg. (EEC) No 1601/91: wines and aromatized beverages	COM(95) 570, Bull. 11-95/1.3.159						

Public health

Priority activities and objectives

	Commission proposal	ESC opinion/ COR opinion °	EP first reading	Amended Commission proposal	Common position Council	EP second reading	
637 Prop. for a Dec.: action programme for the benefit of public health	OJ C 252/9.9.94, COM(94) 202, Bull. 6-94/1.2.201	OJ C 210/14.8.95, Bull. 11-94/1.2.212°; OJ C 102/24.4.95, Bull. 1/2-95/1.3.165	OJ C 89/10.4.95, Bull. 3-95/1.3.152	OJ C 135/2.6.95, COM(95) 138, Bull. 4-95/1.3.128	OJ C 216/21.8.95, Bull. 6-95/1.3.212	OJ C 308/20.11.95, Bull. 10-95/1.3.227 (b)	
637 Prop. for a Dec.: health data and indicators	OJ C 338/16.12.95, COM(95) 449, Bull. 10-95/1.3.228						

Fight against cancer

	Commission proposal	ESC opinion/ COR opinion °	EP first reading	Amended Commission proposal	Common position Council	EP second reading	
638 Prop. for a Dec.: action plan against cancer (1995-99)	OJ C 139/21.5.94, COM(94) 83, Bull. 3-94/1.2.171	OJ C 393/31.12.94, Bull. 9-94/1.2.189; OJ C 210/14.8.95, Bull. 9-94/1.2.189°	OJ C 68/20.3.95, Bull. 3-95/1.3.153	OJ C 143/9.6.95, COM(95) 131, Bull. 4-95/1.3.129	OJ C 216/21.8.95, Bull. 6-95/1.3.213	OJ C 308/20.11.95, Bull. 10-95/1.3.229 (b)	

° Opinion of the Committee of the Regions.
[1] a = adoption [Article 189b(2)(a)]; b = amendments [Article 189b(2)(c) and (d)]; c = declaration of rejection [Article 189b(2)(c)]; d = rejection [Article 189b(2)(c)]; e = EP failure to take a decision within 3 months [Article 189b(2)(b)]; f = amendments following a declaration of rejection; g = agreement on a common draft; h = failure to agree on a common draft.

TABLE I — CO-DECISION   515

Commission opinion (Art. 189b(2)(d))	Conciliation Committee g, h[1] (Art. 189b(4))	Confirmed common position Council (Art. 189b(6))	EP rejection of confirmed common position	EP adoption of common draft (Art. 189b(5))	Adoption by Council	EP signature Council (Art. 191)	Comments	
					Bull. 12-95		Political Agreement on a common position: Bull. 10-95/1.3.27; Dir. to be amended: OJ L 36/9.2.88	500
							Political Agreement on a common position: Bull. 12-95; Dir. to be amended: OJ L 76/6.4.70	500
COM(94) 655, Bull. 1/2-95/1.3.115	Bull. 3-95/1.3.109			OJ C 151/19.6.95, Bull. 5-95/1.3.94	Bull. 6-95/1.3.157	OJ L 168/18.7.95, Bull. 6-95/1.3.157	Political Agreement on a common position: Bull. 3-94/1.2.155; Amended Dir.: OJ L 384/31.12.86	502
							Reg. to be amended: OJ L 149/14.6.91	538
COM(95) 633, Bull. 11-95/1.3.193								637
								637
COM(95) 634, Bull. 11-95/1.3.197								638

	Commission proposal	ESC opinion/ COR opinion°	EP first reading	Amended Commission proposal	Common position Council	EP second reading a, b, c, d, e, f[1]	

Fight against AIDS and other transmissible diseases

640	Prop. for a Dec.: programme for the prevention of AIDS and other transmissible diseases	OJ C 333/29.11.94, COM(94) 413, Bull. 11-94/1.2.213	OJ C 133/31.5.95, Bull. 3-95/1.3.154; Bull. 4-95/1.3.130°	OJ C 126/22.5.95, Bull. 4-95/1.3.130	COM(95) 209, Bull. 5-95/1.3.133	OJ C 216/21.8.95, Bull. 6-95/1.3.215	OJ C 308/20.11.95, Bull. 10-95/1.3.230 (b)
640	Dec. 1729/95/EC: extension of the action plan 'Europe against AIDS'	COM(93) 453, Bull. 9-93/1.2.140	OJ C 133/16.5.94, Bull. 1/2-94/1.2.188; OJ C 217/6.8.94, Bull. 5-94/1.2.143°	OJ C 20/24.1.94, Bull. 12-93/1.2.258		OJ C 213/3.8.94, Bull. 6-94/1.2.203	OJ C 341/5.12.94, Bull. 11-94/1.2.214

Fight against drug addiction

641	Prop. for a Dec.: programme for the prevention of drug addiction	OJ C 257/14.9.95, COM(94) 223, Bull. 6-94/1.2.206	OJ C 210/14.8.95, Bull. 11-94/1.2.216°; OJ C 110/2.5.95, Bull. 1/2-95/1.3.166	OJ C 269/16.10.95, Bull. 9-95/1.3.133	COM(95) 579, Bull. 11-95/1.3.200	Bull. 12-95	

Consumer policy

Consumer information and education

648	Prop. for a Dir.: indication of prices	OJ C 260/5.10.95, COM(95) 276, Bull. 7/8-95/1.3.196	Bull. 12-95				
648	Dir. 95/58/EC amending Dir. 79/581/EEC and 88/314/EEC: indication of prices	OJ C 377/31.12.94, COM(94) 431, Bull. 12-94/1.2.239	OJ C 155/21.6.95, Bull. 4-95/1.3.131	OJ C 151/19.6.95, Bull. 5-95/1.3.134	OJ C 184/18.7.95, COM(95) 259, Bull. 6-95/1.3.220	OJ C 182/15.7.95, Bull. 6-95/1.3.220	OJ C 269/16.10.95, Bull. 9-95/1.3.134 (a)

Protection of consumers' economic and legal interests

653	Prop. for a Dir.: protection of consumers in respect of contracts negotiated at a distance (distance selling)	OJ C 156/23.6.92, COM(92) 11, Bull.4-92/1.3.179	OJ C 19/25.1.93, Bull. 11-92/1.3.234	OJ C 176/28.6.93, Bull. 5-93/1.2.81	OJ C 308/15.11.93, COM(93) 396, Bull. 10-93/1.2.94	OJ C 288/30.10.95, Bull. 6-95/1.3.222	Bull. 12-95 (b)

° Opinion of the Committee of the Regions.
[1] a = adoption [Article 189b(2)(a)]; b = amendments [Article 189b(2)(c) and (d)]; c = declaration of rejection [Article 189b(2)(c)]; d = rejection [Article 189b(2)(c)]; e = EP failure to take a decision within 3 months [Article 189b(2)(b)]; f = amendments following a declaration of rejection; g = agreement on a common draft; h = failure to agree on a common draft.

TABLE I — CO-DECISION 517

Commission opinion (Art. 189b(2)(d))	Conciliation Committee g, h[1] (Art. 189b(4))	Confirmed common position Council (Art. 189b(6))	EP rejection of confirmed common position	EP adoption of common draft (Art. 189b(5))	Adoption by Council	EP signature Council (Art. 191)	Comments	
COM(95) 632, Bull. 11-95/1.3.198								640
COM(94) 644, Bull. 12-94/1.2.234					Bull. 12-94/1.2.234	OJ L 168/18.7.95, Bull. 6-95/1.3.214		640
							Political Agreement on a common position: Bull. 11-95/1.3.200	641
								648
					Bull. 10-95/1.3.232	OJ L 299/12.12.95, Bull. 11-95/1.3.203	Commission Approval: Bull. 11-94/1.2.222; Dir. to be amended: 79/581/EEC (OJ L 158/26.6.79) and 88/314/EEC (OJ L 142/9.6.88)	648
							Political Agreement on a common position: Bull. 3-95/1.3.155	653

	Commission proposal	ESC opinion/ COR opinion°	EP first reading	Amended Commission proposal	Common position Council	EP second reading a, b, c, d, e, f[1]	
654 Prop. for a Dir. amending Dir. 84/450/EEC: misleading advertising	OJ C 180/11.7.91, COM(91) 147, Bull. 5-91/1.2.64	OJ C 49/24.2.92, Bull. 12-91/1.2.317	OJ C 337/21.12.92, Bull. 11-92/1.3.232				

Information, communication, culture and audiovisual media

Culture

	Commission proposal	ESC opinion/ COR opinion°	EP first reading	Amended Commission proposal	Common position Council	EP second reading a, b, c, d, e, f[1]	
680 Prop. for a Dec.: Raphael programme	COM(95) 110, Bull. 3-95/1.3.156	OJ C 256/2.10.95, Bull. 7/8-95/1.3.202; Bull. 9-95/1.3.135°	OJ C 287/30.10.95, Bull. 10-95/1.3.233				
681 Prop. for a Dec.: Ariane programme	OJ C 324/22.11.94, COM(94) 356, Bull. 7/8-94/1.2.178	Bull. 4-95/1.3.134°	OJ C 109/1.5.95, Bull. 4-95/1.3.134	OJ C 279/25.10.95, COM(95) 374, Bull. 7/8-95/1.3.201			
681 Prop. for a Dec.: Kaleidoscope 2000	OJ C 324/22.11.94, COM(94) 356, Bull. 7/8-94/1.2.178	Bull. 4-95/1.3.133°	OJ C 109/1.5.95, Bull. 4-95/1.3.133	OJ C 278/24.10.95, COM(95) 373, Bull. 7/8-95/1.3.199	OJ C 281/25.10.95, Bull. 7/8-95/1.3.199	OJ C 323/4.12.95, Bull. 11-95/1.3.208	

The European Union's role in the world

Common commercial policy

General matters

	Commission proposal	ESC opinion/ COR opinion°	EP first reading	Amended Commission proposal	Common position Council	EP second reading a, b, c, d, e, f[1]	
737 Prop. for a Dec.: action programme 'Customs 2000'	OJ C 346/23.12.95, COM(95) 119, Bull. 4-95/1.4.30	OJ C 301/13.11.95, Bull. 9-95/1.4.14	OJ C 308/20.11.95, Bull. 10-95/1.4.15	OJ C 327/7.12.95, COM(95) 451, Bull. 10-95/1.4.15; OJ C 23/27.1.96, COM(95) 576, Bull. 11-95/1.4.14	Bull. 12-95		
737 Prop. for a Reg. amending Reg. (EEC) No 2913/92: Community Customs Code	OJ C 260/5.10.95, COM(95) 335, Bull. 7/8-95/1.4.22						

° Opinion of the Committee of the Regions.
[1] a = adoption [Article 189b(2)(a)]; b = amendments [Article 189b(2)(c) and (d)]; c = declaration of rejection [Article 189b(2)(c)]; d = rejection [Article 189b(2)(c)]; e = EP failure to take a decision within 3 months [Article 189b(2)(b)]; f = amendments following a declaration of rejection; g = agreement on a common draft; h = failure to agree on a common draft.

TABLE I — CO-DECISION 519

Commission opinion (Art. 189b(2)(d))	Conciliation Committee g, h[1] (Art. 189b(4))	Confirmed common position Council (Art. 189b(6))	EP rejection of confirmed common position	EP adoption of common draft (Art. 189b(5))	Adoption by Council	EP signature Council (Art. 191)	Comments	
							Political Agreement on a common position: Bull. 11-95/1.3.205; Dir. to be amended: OJ L 250/19.9.84	654
								680
								681
COM(95) 659, Bull. 12-95	Bull. 12-95 (h)						Political Agreement: Bull. 6-95/1.3.224	681
							Political Agreement on a common position: Bull. 11-95/1.4.14	737
							Reg. to be amended: OJ L 302/19.10.92	737

TABLE II — CONSULTATION, COOPERATION, ASSENT   521

Annex II

Table II: Legislation under the consultation, cooperation and assent prodecures

	Commission proposal	ESC opinion/ COR opinion°	EP first°/ sole reading	Amended Commission proposal	Council common position	EP second reading	Re-examined Commission proposal	Adoption by Council	Comments

Citizenship of the Union

Citizens' rights

Right to freedom of movement and right of abode

	Commission proposal	ESC opinion/ COR opinion°	EP first°/ sole reading	Amended Commission proposal	Council common position	EP second reading	Re-examined Commission proposal	Adoption by Council	Comments
2	Prop. for a Dir.: elimination of frontier controls	OJ C 289/31.10.95, COM(95) 347, Bull. 7/8-95/1.1.2							
2	Prop. for a Dir.: right of third-country nationals to travel in the Union	OJ C 306/17.11.95, COM(95) 346, Bull. 7/8-95/1.1.3							
3	Reg. (EC) No 1683/95: uniform format for visas	OJ C 238/26.8.94, COM(94) 287, Bull. 7/8-94/1.1.1		OJ C 43/20.2.95, Bull. 1/2-95/1.1.1					OJ L 164/14.7.95, Bull. 5-95/1.1.1	Political Agreement: Bull. 3-95/1.1.1
3	Reg. (EC) No 2317/95: visas for the citizens of third countries	OJ C 11/15.1.94, COM(93) 684, Bull. 11-93/1.2.20, Bull. 12-93/1.2.30		OJ C 128/9.5.94, Bull. 4-94/1.1.6					OJ L 234/3.10.95, Bull. 9-95/1.1.1	

° = Opinion of the Committee of the Regions.
* = Cooperation procedure used.

	Commission proposal	ESC opinion/ COR opinion°	EP first*/ sole reading	Amended Commission proposal	Council common position	EP second reading	Re-examined Commission proposal	Adoption by Council	Comments

Human rights and fundamental freedoms

Inside the Union

	Commission proposal	ESC opinion/ COR opinion°	EP first*/ sole reading	Amended Commission proposal	Council common position	EP second reading	Re-examined Commission proposal	Adoption by Council	Comments
13	Prop. for a Dec.: designation of 1997 as 'European Year Against Racism'	COM(95) 653, Bull. 12-95							

Community economic and social area

Economic and monetary policy

Growth initiative and financial activities

	Commission proposal	ESC opinion/ COR opinion°	EP first*/ sole reading	Amended Commission proposal	Council common position	EP second reading	Re-examined Commission proposal	Adoption by Council	Comments
65	Dec. 95/132/EC: macro-financial assistance to Belarus	OJ C 82/4.4.95, COM(95) 36, Bull. 1/2-95/1.4.101		OJ C 89/10.4.95, Bull. 3-95/1.4.76				OJ L 89/21.4.95, Bull. 4-95/1.4.84	Political Agreement: Bull. 3-95/1.4.76
65	Dec. 95/442/EC: further macro-financial assistance to Ukraine	OJ C 164/30.6.95, COM(95) 195, Bull. 5-95/1.4.88		OJ C 269/16.10.95, Bull. 9-95/1.4.49				OJ L 258/28.10.95, Bull. 10-95/1.4.91	Council conclusions: Bull. 5-95/1.4.88; Council Agreement: Bull. 6-95/1.4.95

TABLE II — CONSULTATION, COOPERATION, ASSENT   523

Statistical system

Priority activities and objectives

	Commission proposal	ESC opinion/ COR opinion°	EP first*/ sole reading	Amended Commission proposal	Council common position	EP second reading	Re-examined Commission proposal	Adoption by Council	Comments
85	Reg.: harmonized consumer price indices	OJ C 84/6.4.95, COM(94) 674, Bull. 1/2-95/1.6.1	OJ C 236/11.9.95, Bull. 5-95/1.7.2	OJ C 249/25.9.95, Bull. 7/8-95/1.7.1					Bull. 10-95/1.7.1	
85	Prop. for a Reg.: European system of national and regional accounts	COM(94) 593, Bull. 12-94/1.6.1	OJ C 133/31.5.95, Bull. 3-95/1.7.2	OJ C 287/30.10.95, Bull. 10-95/1.7.2						Political Agreement: Bull. 11-95/1.7.1
85	Prop. for a Reg.: Community action in the field of statistics	OJ C 106/14.4.94, COM(94) 78, Bull. 3-94/1.6.1	OJ C 195/18.7.94, Bull. 4-94/1.6.1	OJ C 109/1.5.95, Bull. 4-95/1.7.1						
85	Prop. for a Dec. amending Dec. 91/115/EEC setting up a statistics committee	OJ C 359/16.12.94, COM(94) 452, Bull. 11-94/1.6.1	OJ C 397/31.12.94, Bull. 12-94/1.6.5	OJ C 269/16.10.95, Bull. 9-95/1.7.1						Dec. to be amended: OJ L 59/6.3.91

Design and guidelines

	Commission proposal	ESC opinion/ COR opinion°	EP first*/ sole reading	Amended Commission proposal	Council common position	EP second reading	Re-examined Commission proposal	Adoption by Council	Comments
87	Prop. for a Reg.: air transport statistics	OJ C 325/6.12.95, COM(95) 353, Bull. 9-95/1.7.3	Bull. 11-95/1.7.4							
87	Dir. 95/64/EC: statistical returns in respect of carriage of goods and passengers by sea	OJ C 214/8.8.94, COM(94) 275, Bull. 7/8-94/1.5.1	OJ C 397/31.12.94, Bull. 11-94/1.6.5	OJ C 151/19.6.95, Bull. 5-95/1.7.4					OJ L 320/20.12.95, Bull. 12-95	Political Agreement: Bull. 6-95/1.7.2
88	Dir. 95/57/EC: tourism statistics	OJ C 35/11.2.95, COM(94) 582, Bull. 1/2-95/1.6.2	OJ C 236/11.9.95, Bull. 5-95/1.7.5	OJ C 183/17.7.95, Bull. 6-95/1.7.3					OJ L 291/6.12.95, Bull. 11-95/1.7.3	

° = Opinion of the Committee of the Regions.

* = Cooperation procedure used.

	Commission proposal	ESC opinion/ COR opinion°	EP first*/ sole reading	Amended Commission proposal	Council common position	EP second reading	Re-examined Commission proposal	Adoption by Council	Comments
89	Reg. (EC) No 2744/95: statistics on the structure and distribution of earnings	COM(95) 287, Bull. 6-95/1.7.1							OJ L 287/30.11.95, Bull. 11-95/1.7.2	
90	Prop. for a Dec.: improvement in agricultural statistics	OJ C 336/14.12.95, COM(95) 472, Bull. 10-95/1.7.3								
90	Prop. for a Dir.: milk statistics	OJ C 321/1.12.95, COM(95) 430, Bull. 9-95/1.7.4								
90	Reg. (EC) No 2597/95: catch statistics for areas other than the North Atlantic	OJ C 329/25.11.94, COM(94) 376, Bull. 9-94/1.6.2		OJ C 363/19.12.94, Bull. 10-95/1.6.4					OJ L 270/13.11.95, Bull. 10-95/1.7.4	
90	Prop. for a Reg.: aquaculture statistics	OJ C 327/7.12.95, COM(95) 394, Bull. 9-95/1.7.5								
91	Reg. (EC) 1172/95: statistics on the trading of goods with non-member countries	OJ C 5/7.1.94, COM(93) 476, Bull. 12-93/1.2.56							OJ L 118/25.5.95, Bull. 5-95/1.7.1	

Internal market

Free movement of goods

	Commission proposal	ESC opinion/ COR opinion°	EP first*/ sole reading	Amended Commission proposal	Council common position	EP second reading	Re-examined Commission proposal	Adoption by Council	Comments
102	Prop. for a Reg. amending the annex to Reg. (EEC) No 3911/92: export of cultural goods	OJ C 6/11.1.96, COM(95) 479, Bull. 10-95/1.3.38								
105	Prop. for a Dir. amending Dir. 94/54/EC: labelling of foodstuffs	COM(95) 551, Bull. 11-95/1.3.23								
106	Reg. (EC) No 297/95: fees payable to the European Agency for the Evaluation of Medicinal Products	COM(94) 167, Bull. 5-94/1.2.14		OJ C 43/20.2.95, Bull. 1/2-95/1.3.7	OJ C 84/6.4.95, COM(95) 27, Bull. 1/2-95/1.3.7				OJ L 35/15.2.95, Bull. 1/2-95/1.3.7	Reg. to be amended: OJ L 395/31.12.92 Dir. to be amended: OJ L 300/23.11.94

TABLE II — CONSULTATION, COOPERATION, ASSENT   525

	Commission proposal	ESC opinion/ COR opinion°	EP first*/ sole reading	Amended Commission proposal	Council common position	EP second reading	Re-examined Commission proposal	Adoption by Council	Comments
108	Prop. for a Dir.: cable-operated installations for the carriage of passengers — OJ C 70/8.3.94, COM(93) 646, Bull. 1/2-94/1.2.10	OJ C 388/31.12.94, Bull. 7/8-94/1.2.4	OJ C 109/1.5.95, Bull. 4-95/1.3.9	COM(95) 523, Bull. 11-95/1.3.20					
109	Dir. 95/38/EC amending Dir. 90/642/EEC: maximum levels for pesticide residues in products of plant origin — COM(94) 482							OJ L 197/22.8.95, Bull. 7/8-95/1.3.18	Amended Directive: OJ L 350/14.12.90
109	Dir. 95/39/EC amending Dir. 86/362/EEC and 86/363/EEC: maximum levels for pesticide residues in cereals and foodstuffs of animal origin — COM(94) 482							OJ L 197/22.8.95, Bull. 7/8-95/1.3.18	Amended Directives: OJ L 221/7.8.86
109	Reg. (EC) No 2506/95 amending Reg. (EEC) No 2100/94: plant variety rights — OJ C 117/12.5.95, COM(95) 144, Bull. 4-95/1.3.104	OJ C 236/11.9.95, Bull. 5-95/1.3.95	OJ C 269/16.10.95, Bull. 9-95/1.3.97					OJ L 258/25.10.95, Bull. 10-95/1.3.169	Reg. to be amended: OJ L 227/1.9.94
110	Dir. 95/29/EC amending Dir. 91/628/EEC: protection of animals during transport — OJ C 250/14.9.93, COM(93) 330, Bull. 7/8-93/1.2.9	OJ C 127/7.5.94, Bull. 1/2-94/1.2.19	OJ C 20/24.1.94, Bull. 12-93/1.2.20	COM(94) 252, Bull. 6-94/1.2.31				OJ L 148/30.6.95, Bull. 6-95/1.3.23	Political Agreement: Bull. 6-95/1.3.23; Amended Directive: OJ L 340/11.12.91
110	Dir. 95/23/EC amending Dir. 64/433/EEC: health conditions for the production and marketing of fresh meat — OJ C 224/12.8.94, COM(94) 315, Bull. 7/8-94/1.2.9	OJ C 397/31.12.94, Bull. 11-94/1.2.17	OJ C 109/1.5.95, Bull. 4-95/1.3.12	OJ C 241/16.9.95, COM(95) 270, Bull. 6-95/1.3.24				OJ L 243/11.10.95, Bull. 6-95/1.3.24	Amended Directive: OJ L 121/29.7.64
110	Dir. 95/22/EC amending Dir. 91/67/EEC: animal health conditions governing the placing on the market of aquaculture animals and products — COM(94) 396, Bull. 9-94/1.2.23							OJ L 243/11.10.95, Bull. 6-95/1.3.29	Amended Directive: OJ L 46/19.2.91
110	Dec. 95/408/EC: provisional lists of third country establishments (importation of products of animal origin, fishery products and molluscs) — OJ C 208/28.7.94, COM(94) 241, Bull. 6-94/1.2.33		OJ C 276/3.10.94, Bull. 9-94/1.2.22					OJ L 243/11.10.95, Bull. 6-95/1.3.28	

° = Opinion of the Committee of the Regions.
* = Cooperation procedure used.

	Commission proposal	ESC opinion/ COR opinion°	EP first*/ sole reading	Amended Commission proposal	Council common position	EP second reading	Re-examined Commission proposal	Adoption by Council	Comments
110	Prop. for a Dir. amending Dir. 77/93/EEC: protection against organisms harmful to plants OJ C 192/26.7.95, COM(95) 239, Bull. 6-95/1.3.33		OJ C 269/16.10.95, Bull. 9-95/1.3.11						Dir. to be amended: OJ L 26/31.1.77
110	Prop. for a Dir. amending Dir. 92/17/EEC: protection against certain zoonoses OJ C 13/18.1.96, COM(95) 491, Bull. 10-95/1.3.41								Amended Directive: OJ L 62/15.3.93
110	Dir.: control of diseases affecting bivalve molluscs OJ C 285/13.10.94, COM(94) 401, Bull. 9-94/1.2.24		OJ C 109/1.5.95, Bull. 4-95/1.3.13	OJ C 19/23.1.96				Bull. 12-95	
110	Dir. 95/52/EC amending Dir. 90/675/EEC: veterinary checks on products from third countries OJ C 185/19.7.95, COM(95) 254, Bull. 6-95/1.3.30	OJ C 301/13.11.95, Bull. 9-95/1.3.8	OJ C 269/16.10.95, Bull. 9-95/1.3.8					OJ L 265/8.11.95, Bull. 10-95/1.3.40	Amended Directive: OJ L 373/31.12.90
110	Prop. for a Reg.: certification of animals OJ C 373/29.12.94, COM(94) 561, Bull. 12-94/1.2.23								
111	Dir. amending Dir. 70/524/EEC, 74/63/EEC, 79/373/EEC, 82/471/EEC: animal nutrition (authorizations and approvals regarding certain establishments) OJ C 348/28.12.93, COM(93) 587, Bull. 11-93/1.2.18	OJ C 148/30.5.94, Bull. 3-94/1.2.25	OJ C 91/28.3.94, Bull. 3-94/1.2.25					Bull. 12-95	Political Agreement: Bull. 9-95/1.3.10; amended Directives: 70/524/EEC (OJ L 270/14.12.70), 74/63/EEC (OJ L 38/11.2.74), 79/373/EEC (OJ L 86/6.4.79), 82/471/EEC (OJ L 213/21.7.82)
111	Dir. 95/53/EC: inspections in the field of animal nutrition OJ C 313/19.11.93, COM(93) 510, Bull. 10-93/1.2.20	OJ C 127/7.5.94, Bull. 1/2-94/1.2.25	OJ C 128/9.5.94, Bull. 4-94/1.2.34	OJ C 242/30.8.94, COM(94) 371, Bull. 7/8-94/1.2.13				OJ L 265/8.11.95, Bull. 10-95/1.3.42	
111	Prop. for a Dir. amending Dir. 79/373/EEC: compound feedingstuffs OJ C 238/26.8.94, COM(94) 279, Bull. 7/8-94/1.2.11	OJ C 102/24.4.95, Bull. 1/2-95/1.3.14	OJ C 305/31.10.94, Bull. 9-94/1.2.27						Dir. to be amended: OJ L 86/6.4.79
111	Prop. for a Dir.: ingredients for feedingstuffs OJ C 236/24.8.94, COM(94) 313, Bull. 7/8-94/1.2.10	OJ C 102/24.4.95, Bull. 1/2-95/1.3.13	OJ C 305/31.10.94, Bull. 9-94/1.2.26						

TABLE II — CONSULTATION, COOPERATION, ASSENT   527

Taxation

	Commission proposal	ESC opinion/ COR opinion°	EP first*/ sole reading	Amended Commission proposal	Council common position	EP second reading	Re-examined Commission proposal	Adoption by Council	Comments
129	Dir. 95/7/EC amending Dir. 77/388/EEC: simplification of VAT	OJ C 107/15.4.94, COM(94) 58, Bull. 3-94/1.2.30	OJ C 195/18.7.94, Bull. 4-94/1.2.41	OJ C 205/25.7.94, Bull. 5-94/1.2.19				OJ L 102/5.5.95, Bull. 4-95/1.3.17	Political Agreement: Bull. 3-95/1.3.15; Amended Directive: OJ L 145/13.6.77
129	Prop. for a Dir.: VAT on agricultural products	OJ C 389/31.12.94, COM(94) 584, Bull. 12-94/1.2.37	OJ C 236/11.9.95, Bull. 5-95/1.3.20	OJ C 17/22.1.96, Bull. 12-95					
130	Prop. for a Dir. amending Dir. 77/388/EEC: minimum level for the normal rate of VAT	COM(95) 731, Bull. 12-95							Dir. to be amended: OJ L 145/13.06.77
130	Dir. 95/60/EC: fiscal marking of gas oils	OJ C 15/18.1.94, COM(93) 352, Bull. 12-93/1.2.15	OJ C 133/16.5.94, Bull. 1/2-94/1.2.35	OJ C 128/9.5.94, Bull. 4-94/1.2.42				OJ L 291/6.12.95, Bull. 11-95/1.3.32	
130	Dir. 95/59/EC: taxes on tobacco consumption	COM(94) 355, Bull. 10-94/1.2.16	OJ C 133/31.5.95, Bull. 3-95/1.3.16	OJ C 56/6.3.95, Bull. 1/2-95/1.3.17				OJ L 291/6.12.95, Bull. 11-95/1.3.31	

Government procurement

	Commission proposal	ESC opinion/ COR opinion°	EP first*/ sole reading	Amended Commission proposal	Council common position	EP second reading	Re-examined Commission proposal	Adoption by Council	Comments
136	Reg. (EC) No 1836/95: access to public contracts for tenderers from the United States of America	COM(95) 268, Bull. 6-95/1.3.45							OJ L 183/2.8.95, Bull. 7/8-95/1.3.27

° = Opinion of the Committee of the Regions.
* = Cooperation procedure used.

Industrial policy

Industrial competitiveness

	Commission proposal	ESC opinion/ COR opinion°	EP first*/ sole reading	Amended Commission proposal	Council common position	EP second reading	Re-examined Commission proposal	Adoption by Council	Comments
176 Prop. for a Dec.: Community action programme for industrial competitiveness	COM(95) 87, Bull. 3-95/1.3.59		OJ C 308/20.11.95, Bull. 10-95/1.3.84						

Individual sectors

	Commission proposal	ESC opinion/ COR opinion°	EP first*/ sole reading	Amended Commission proposal	Council common position	EP second reading	Re-examined Commission proposal	Adoption by Council	Comments
192 Reg.: aid to shipbuilding	OJ C 304/15.11.95, COM(95) 410, Bull. 7/8-95/1.3.54	Bull. 11-95/1.3.44	OJ C 339/18.12.95, Bull. 11-95/1.3.44	COM(95) 701, Bull. 12-95				Bull. 12-95	Bull. 12-95

Enterprise policy, distributive trades, tourism and the cooperative, mutual and non-profit sector

Cooperative, mutual and other associations and foundations

	Commission proposal	ESC opinion/ COR opinion°	EP first*/ sole reading	Amended Commission proposal	Council common position	EP second reading	Re-examined Commission proposal	Adoption by Council	Comments
214 Prop. for a Dec.: programme to assist cooperatives, mutual societies, associations and foundations (1994-96)	OJ C 87/24.3.94, COM(93) 650, Bull. 1/2-94/1.2.76	OJ C 388/31.12.94, Bull. 7/8-94/1.2.76	OJ C 89/10.4.95, Bull. 3-95/1.3.64	COM(95) 253, Bull. 6-95/1.3.80					

TABLE II — CONSULTATION, COOPERATION, ASSENT   529

Research and technology

Community R&TD policy

	Commission proposal	ESC opinion/ COR opinion°	EP first*/ sole reading	Amended Commission proposal	Council common position	EP second reading	Re-examined Commission proposal	Adoption by Council	Comments
227 Prop. for a Dec.: additional JRC research programme	COM(95) 549, Bull. 11-95/1.3.75		OJ C 17/22.1.96, Bull. 12-95						
231 Prop. for a Dec.: adaptation of the fourth Euratom framework programme (1994-98) following enlargement	OJ C 142/8.6.95, COM(95) 145, Bull. 4-95/1.3.63	OJ C 256/2.10.95, Bull. 7/8-95/1.3.77	OJ C 249/25.9.95, Bull. 7/8-95/1.3.77						Political Agreement: Bull. 10-95/1.3.91

Implementation of specific programmes of the fourth framework programme

	Commission proposal	ESC opinion/ COR opinion°	EP first*/ sole reading	Amended Commission proposal	Council common position	EP second reading	Re-examined Commission proposal	Adoption by Council	Comments
249 Prop. for a Dec.: amendment of the JET statutes	COM(95) 234, Bull. 6-95/1.3.83	Bull. 10-95/1.3.93							
254 Prop. for a Dec. amending Dec. 94/807/EC: cooperation in research and technological development with third countries and international organizations (1994-98)	COM(95) 539, Bull. 11-95/1.3.74								Dir. to be amended: OJ L 334/22.12.94

° = Opinion of the Committee of the Regions.
* = Cooperation procedure used.

Education, vocational training and youth

European Centre for the Development of Vocational Training (Cedefop)

	Commission proposal	ESC opinion/ COR opinion°	EP first*/ sole reading	Amended Commission proposal	Council common position	EP second reading	Re-examined Commission proposal	Adoption by Council	Comments
288	Reg. (EC) No 251/95 amending Reg. (EEC) No 337/75 establishing a European Centre for the Development of Vocational Training								
	OJ C 74/12.3.94, COM(94) 20, Bull. 1/2-94/1.2.186	OJ C 195/18.7.94, Bull. 4-94/1.2.166	OJ C 128/9.5.94, Bull. 4-94/1.2.166					OJ L 30/9.2.95, Bull. 1/2-95/1.3.68	Amended Reg.: OJ L 39/13.2.75

Economic and social cohesion

Community support frameworks and single programming documents

	Commission proposal	ESC opinion/ COR opinion°	EP first*/ sole reading	Amended Commission proposal	Council common position	EP second reading	Re-examined Commission proposal	Adoption by Council	Comments
313	Reg. (EC) No 2719/95 amending Reg. (EC) No 3699/93: structural assistance								
	OJ C 85/7.4.95, COM(95) 55, Bull. 3-95/1.3.53	OJ C 236/11.9.95, Bull. 5-95/1.3.53	OJ C 269/16.10.95, Bull. 9-95/1.3.55					OJ L 283/25.11.95, Bull. 11-95/1.3.89	Amended Reg.: OJ L 346/31.12.93
313	Reg. (EC) No 1624/95 amending Reg. (EC) No 3699/93: structural assistance in fisheries								
	COM(94) 568, Bull. 12-94	OJ C 236/11.9.95, Bull. 5-95/1.3.52	OJ C 151/19.6.95, Bull. 5-95/1.3.52					OJ L 155/6.7.95, Bull. 6-95/1.3.99	Amended Reg.: OJ L 346/31.12.93
313	Prop. for a Reg. amending Reg. (EC) No 3699/93: structural assistance in fisheries								
	COM(95) 627, Bull. 12-95								Reg. to be amended: OJ L 346/31.12.93

Community initiatives

	Commission proposal	ESC opinion/ COR opinion°	EP first*/ sole reading	Amended Commission proposal	Council common position	EP second reading	Re-examined Commission proposal	Adoption by Council	Comments
319	Reg. (EC) No 852/95: modernization of the textile industry in Portugal								
	OJ C 373/29.12.94, COM(94) 562, Bull. 11-94/1.2.130	OJ C 110/2.5.95, Bull. 1/2-95/1.3.77	OJ C 89/10.4.95, Bull. 3-95/1.3.77					OJ L 86/20.4.95, Bull. 4-95/1.3.78	

		Commission proposal	ESC opinion/ COR opinion°	EP first*/ sole reading	Amended Commission proposal	Council common position	EP second reading	Re-examined Commission proposal	Adoption by Council	Comments

Measures for the most remote regions

Agriculture

331	Reg. (EC) No 2598/95 amending Reg. (EEC) No 3763/91: specific measures for the French overseas departments	OJ C 290/18.10.94, COM(94) 344, Bull. 9-94/1.2.137		OJ C 43/20.2.95, Bull. 1/2-95/1.3.82					OJ L 267/9.11.95, Bull. 10-95/1.3.122	Political Agreement: Bull. 10-95/1.3.122; Amended Reg.: OJ L 356/24.12.91

Fisheries

333	Reg. (EC) No 2337/95: system of compensation for additional costs (fishery products from the Azores, Madeira, the Canary Islands and Guyana)	OJ C 343/6.12.94, COM(94) 473, Bull. 11-94/1.2.178	OJ C 102/24.4.95, Bull. 1/2-95/1.3.152	OJ C 109/1.5.95, Bull. 4-95/1.3.125	OJ C 163/29.6.95, Bull. 5-95/1.3.121				OJ L 236/5.10.95, Bull. 10-95/1.3.208	

Customs, tariff and trade measures

334	Reg. (EC) No 3012/95 amending Reg. (EEC) 1605/92: common customs tariff for the Canary Islands	COM(95) 698, Bull. 12-95							OJ L 314/28.12.95, Bull. 12-95	Reg. to be amended: OJ L 173/27.6.92
334	Prop. for a Reg.: common customs tariff for the Canary Islands (industrial products)	COM(95) 648, Bull. 12-95								

° = Opinion of the Committee of the Regions.
* = Cooperation procedure used.

	Commission proposal	ESC opinion/ COR opinion°	EP first°/ sole reading	Amended Commission proposal	Council common position	EP second reading	Re-examined Commission proposal	Adoption by Council	Comments
335	Prop. for a Reg. amending Reg. (EEC) No 1602/92: exoneration from anti-dumping measures for Canary Island importers	COM(95) 649, Bull. 12-95							Reg. to be amended: OJ L 173/27.6.92
336	Prop. for a Reg.: favourable tariff treatment (Madeira and the Azores)	COM(95) 524, Bull. 11-95/1.3.99							

Trans-European networks
Priority activities and objectives

	Commission proposal	ESC opinion/ COR opinion°	EP first°/ sole reading	Amended Commission proposal	Council common position	EP second reading	Re-examined Commission proposal	Adoption by Council	Comments
340	Reg. (EC) No 2236/95: general rules for financial aid in the field of trans-European networks	OJ C 89/26.3.94, COM(94) 62, Bull. 3-94/1.2.79	OJ C 195/18.7.94, Bull. 4-94/1.2.73; OJ C 217/6.8.94, Bull. 5-94/1.2.69°	OJ C 363/19.12.94, Bull. 11-94/1.2.82*	OJ C 115/9.5.95, COM(95) 32, Bull. 3-95/1.3.89	OJ C 130/29.5.95, Bull. 3-95/1.3.89	OJ C 249/25.9.95, Bull. 7/8-95/1.3.101	COM(95) 428, Bull. 9-95/1.3.61	OJ L 228/23.9.95, Bull. 9-95/1.3.61	Political Agreement on a common position: Bull. 3-95/1.3.89

Transport

	Commission proposal	ESC opinion/ COR opinion°	EP first°/ sole reading	Amended Commission proposal	Council common position	EP second reading	Re-examined Commission proposal	Adoption by Council	Comments
342	Prop. for a Dir.: inter-operability of the high-speed train network	OJ C 134/17.5.94, COM(94) 107, Bull. 4-94/1.2.75	OJ C 210/14.8.95, Bull. 9-94/1.2.100°; OJ C 397/31.12.94, Bull. 1/2-95/1.2.83	OJ C 43/20.2.95, Bull. 1/2-95/1.3.84*	OJ C 203/8.8.95, COM(95) 271, Bull. 6-95/1.3.111	OJ C 356/30.12.95, Bull. 12-95				Political Agreement on a common position: Bull. 6-95/1.3.111

Telematic systems and telecommunications

	Commission proposal	ESC opinion/ COR opinion°	EP first°/ sole reading	Amended Commission proposal	Council common position	EP second reading	Re-examined Commission proposal	Adoption by Council	Comments
347	Dec. 95/468/EC: multiannual programme for the interchange of data between administrations (IDA)	OJ C 105/16.4.93, COM(93) 69, Bull. 3-93/1.2.61	OJ C 249/13.9.93, Bull. 6-93/1.2.101; OJ C 217/6.8.94, Bull. 5-94/1.2.72°	OJ C 341/19.12.94, Bull. 11-94/1.2.86*	OJ C 318/29.11.95, COM(95) 436, Bull. 9-95/1.3.64				OJ L 269/11.11.95, Bull. 11-95/1.3.105	Opinion of the EP on the legal basis: OJ C 269/16.10.95, Bull. 9-95/1.3.64

TABLE II — CONSULTATION, COOPERATION, ASSENT   533

Energy

	Commission proposal	ESC opinion/ COR opinion°	EP first*/ sole reading	Amended Commission proposal	Council common position	EP second reading	Re-examined Commission proposal	Adoption by Council	Comments
349 Prop. for a Dec.: measures for the development of energy networks	OJ C 72/10.3.94, COM(93) 685, Bull. 1/2-94/1.2.88	OJ C 195/18.7.94, Bull. 4-94/1.2.74; OJ C 217/6.8.94, Bull. 5-94/1.2.70°	OJ C 151/19.6.94, Bull. 5-95/1.3.60°	OJ C 205/10.8.95, COM(95) 226, Bull. 5-95/1.3.60	OJ C 216/21.8.95, Bull. 6-95/1.3.109	OJ C 308/20.11.95, Bull. 10-95/1.3.124	COM(95) 594, Bull. 11-95/1.3.104		Political Agreement on a common position: Bull. 6-95/1.3.109

Energy

Priority activities and objectives

	Commission proposal	ESC opinion/ COR opinion°	EP first*/ sole reading	Amended Commission proposal	Council common position	EP second reading	Re-examined Commission proposal	Adoption by Council	Comments
352 Prop. for a Reg.: investment of interest to the Community in petroleum, natural gas and electricity	OJ C 346/23.12.95, COM(95) 118, Bull. 7/8-95/1.3.103	Bull. 10-95/1.3.127	OJ C 17/22.1.96, Bull. 12-95						

Community energy strategy

	Commission proposal	ESC opinion/ COR opinion°	EP first*/ sole reading	Amended Commission proposal	Council common position	EP second reading	Re-examined Commission proposal	Adoption by Council	Comments
355 Prop. for a Reg.: promotion of energy technology ('Thermie-II')	OJ C 158/9.6.94, COM(94) 59, Bull. 4-94/1.2.79	OJ C 393/31.12.94, Bull. 9-94/1.2.104	OJ C 341/5.12.94, Bull. 11-94/1.2.90°	COM(94) 654, Bull. 1/2-95/1.3.87					
357 Prop. for a Dir.: rational planning for gas and electricity	OJ C 1/4.1.96, COM(95) 369, Bull. 9-95/1.3.66								
357 Prop. for a Dir.: energy efficiency for refrigerators, deep freezers and electrical household equipment	OJ C 390/31.12.94, COM(94) 521, Bull. 12-94/1.2.108	OJ C 155/21.6.95, Bull. 4-95/1.3.85	OJ C 308/20.11.95, Bull. 10-95/1.3.129	COM(95) 638, Bull. 12-95					Political Agreement on a common position: Bull. 12-95

° = Opinion of the Committee of the Regions.
* = Cooperation procedure used.

	Commission proposal	ESC opinion/ COR opinion°	EP first*/ sole reading	Amended Commission proposal	Council common position	EP second reading	Re-examined Commission proposal	Adoption by Council	Comments
357	Prop. for a Dec.: SAVE II (energy efficiency) — OJ C 346/23.12.95, COM(95) 225, Bull. 5-95/1.3.63	Bull. 12-95							

Sectoral aspects

	Commission proposal	ESC opinion/ COR opinion°	EP first*/ sole reading	Amended Commission proposal	Council common position	EP second reading	Re-examined Commission proposal	Adoption by Council	Comments
365	Reg. (EC) No 296/95 amending Reg. (EEC) No 1893/79: crude oil imports and deliveries — COM(95) 89, Bull. 9-95/1.3.67							OJ L 310/22.12.95, Bull. 12-95	Amended Reg.: OJ L 220/30.8.79

Relations with third countries

	Commission proposal	ESC opinion/ COR opinion°	EP first*/ sole reading	Amended Commission proposal	Council common position	EP second reading	Re-examined Commission proposal	Adoption by Council	Comments
372	Prop. for a Reg.: Synergy programme — OJ C 310/22.11.95, COM(95) 197, Bull. 5-95/1.3.65								

Transport

Transport and environment

	Commission proposal	ESC opinion/ COR opinion°	EP first*/ sole reading	Amended Commission proposal	Council common position	EP second reading	Re-examined Commission proposal	Adoption by Council	Comments
390	Dir.: officer responsible for the prevention of the risks inherent in the carriage of dangerous goods — OJ C 185/17.7.91, COM(91) 4, Bull. 6-91/1.2.86	OJ C 40/17.2.92, Bull. 11-91/1.2.68	OJ C 150/15.6.92, Bull. 5-92/1.1.72		OJ C 297/10.11.95, Bull. 10-95/1.3.133				Political Agreement on a common position: Bull. 3-95/1.3.93

TABLE II — CONSULTATION, COOPERATION, ASSENT 535

Inland transport

	Commission proposal	ESC opinion°/ COR opinion°	EP first*/ sole reading	Amended Commission proposal	Council common position	EP second reading	Re-examined Commission proposal	Adoption by Council	Comments
392	Dir. 95/18/EC: licensing of railway undertakings	OJ C 24/28.1.94, COM(93) 678, Bull. 12-93/1.2.130	OJ C 393/31.12.94, Bull. 9-94/1.2.110	OJ C 205/25.7.94, Bull. 5-94/1.2.81*	OJ C 225/13.8.94, COM(94) 316, Bull. 7/8-94/1.2.88	OJ C 354/13.12.94, Bull. 11-94/1.2.97	OJ C 89/10.4.95, Bull. 3-95/1.3.95	COM(95) 151, Bull. 5-95/1.3.67	OJ L 143/27.6.95, Bull. 6-95/1.3.122	Political Agreement on a common position: Bull. 9-94/1.2.110
392	Dir. 95/19/EC: distribution of railway infrastructure capacity	OJ C 24/28.1.94, COM(93) 678, Bull. 12-93/1.2.130	OJ C 393/31.12.94, Bull. 9-94/1.2.110	OJ C 205/25.7.94, Bull. 5-94/1.2.81*; OJ C 89/10.4.95, Bull. 3-95/1.3.95*	OJ C 225/13.8.94, COM(94) 316, Bull. 7/8-94/1.2.88	OJ C 354/13.12.94, Bull. 11-94/1.2.97		COM(95) 151, Bull. 5-95/1.3.68	OJ L 143/27.6.95, Bull. 6-95/1.3.123	Political Agreement on a common position: Bull. 9-94/1.2.110
393	Prop. for a Dir. amending Dir. 91/440/EEC: development of the Community's railways	OJ C 321/1.12.95, COM(95) 337, Bull. 7/8-95/1.3.112								Dir. to be amended: OJ L 237/24.8.91
394	Prop. for a Dir.: transport of dangerous goods by rail	OJ C 389/31.12.94, COM(94) 573, Bull. 12-94/1.2.118	OJ C 236/11.9.95, Bull. 5-95/1.3.69	OJ C 249/25.9.95, Bull. 7/8-95/1.3.113*	OJ C 313/24.11.95, COM(95) 424, Bull. 9-95/1.3.70	OJ C 356/30.12.95 Bull. 12-95				Political Agreement on a common position: Bull. 9-95/1.3.70
395	Prop. for a Dir.: vehicles hired without drivers	OJ C 80/1.4.95, COM(95) 2, Bull. 1/2-95/1.3.89	OJ C 236/11.9.95, Bull. 5-95/1.3.71	OJ C 249/25.9.95, Bull. 7/8-95/1.3.116*						
396	Prop. for a Dir.: admission to the occupation of road transport operator	OJ C 286/14.11.90, Bull. 11-90/1.3.189	OJ C 295/22.10.94, Bull. 6-94/1.2.111	OJ C 128/9.5.94, Bull. 4-94/1.2.88*	COM(93) 586, Bull. 12-93/1.2.133	OJ C 356/30.12.95 Bull. 12-95				Dir. to be codified: 74/561/EEC and 74/562/EEC (OJ L 308/19.11.74, 777796/EEC (OJ L 334/24.12.77)
398	Dir. 95/50/EC: uniform procedures for checks on the transport of dangerous goods by road	OJ C 26/29.1.94, COM(93) 665, Bull. 12-93/1.2.131	OJ C 195/18.7.94, Bull. 4-94/1.2.89	OJ C 205/25.7.94, Bull. 5-94/1.2.82*	OJ C 238/26.8.94, COM(94) 340, Bull. 7/8-94/1.2.90	OJ C 354/13.12.94, Bull. 11-94/1.2.100	OJ C 89/10.4.95, Bull. 3-95/1.3.97	COM(95) 289, Bull. 7/8-95/1.3.115	OJ L 249/17.10.95, Bull. 10-95/1.3.134	Political Agreement on a common position: Bull. 11-94/1.2.113
399	Prop. for a Dir. amending Dir. 91/439/EEC: driving licences	COM(95) 166, Bull. 5-95/1.3.70	OJ C 301/13.11.95, Bull. 9-95/1.3.72	OJ C 323/4.12.95, Bull. 11-95/1.3.112*	COM(95) 708, Bull. 12-95					Dir. to be amended: OJ L 237/24.8.91

° = Opinion of the Committee of the Regions.
* = Cooperation procedure used.

	Commission proposal	ESC opinion/ COR opinion°	EP first*/ sole reading	Amended Commission proposal	Council common position	EP second reading	Re-examined Commission proposal	Adoption by Council	Comments
399 Prop. for a Dir.: roadworthiness tests for motor vehicles	COM(95) 415, Bull. 9-95/1.3.73	Bull. 11-95/1.3.114							
399 Prop. for a Reg. amending Reg. (EEC) No 3821/85: tachograph	OJ C 243/31.8.94, COM(94) 323, Bull. 7/8-94/1.2.89	OJ C 110/2.5.95, Bull. 1/2-95/1.3.90	OJ C 249/25.9.95, Bull. 7/8-95/1.3.114*	OJ C 25/31.1.96, COM(95) 550, Bull. 11-95/1.3.113					Reg. to be amended: OJ L 370/31.12.85
400 Prop. for a Dir.: weights and dimensions of road vehicles over 3.5 tonnes	OJ C 38/8.2.94, COM(93) 679, Bull. 12-93/1.2.132	OJ C 295/22.10.94, Bull. 6-94/1.2.109	OJ C 354/13.12.94, Bull. 11-94/1.2.101	OJ C 247/23.9.95, COM(95) 193	OJ C 356/30.12.95, Bull. 12-95				Political Agreement on a common position: Bull. 9-95/1.3.71
402 Prop. for a Dir.: chartering and pricing in the transport of goods by inland waterway	OJ C 318/29.11.95, COM(95) 199, Bull. 5-95/1.3.72	Bull. 11-95/1.3.117							
402 Prop. for a Reg. amending Reg. (EEC) No 1107/70: transport aid	OJ C 318/29.11.95, COM(95) 199, Bull. 5-95/1.3.72	Bull. 11-95/1.3.117							Reg. to be amended: OJ L 130/15.6.70
402 Prop. for a Reg. amending Reg. (EEC) No 1101/89: structural improvements in inland waterway transport	OJ C 318/29.11.95, COM(95) 199, Bull. 5-95/1.3.72	Bull. 11-95/1.3.117							Reg. to be amended: OJ L 116/28.4.89
402 Reg. (EC) No 2819/95 amending Reg. (EEC) No 1101/89: structural improvements in inland waterway transport	OJ C 292/7.11.95, COM(95) 200, Bull. 5-95/1.3.73	OJ C 301/13.11.95, Bull. 9-95/1.3.75	OJ C 287/30.10.95, Bull. 10-95/1.3.139*		Bull. 11-95/1.3.115	OJ C 339/18.12.95, Bull. 11-95/1.3.115		OJ L 292/7.12.95, Bull. 12-95	Amended Reg.: OJ L 116/28.4.89
403 Prop. for a Reg.: common rules applicable to inland waterway transport	OJ C 164/30.6.95, COM(95) 167, Bull. 5-95/1.3.74	OJ C 301/13.11.95, Bull. 9-95/1.3.76	OJ C 323/4.12.95, Bull. 11-95/1.3.116*						
403 Prop. for a Dir.: national boatmasters certificates for inland waterway transport	OJ C 280/6.10.94, COM(94) 359, Bull. 9-94/1.2.117	OJ C 102/24.4.95, Bull. 1/2-95/1.3.91	OJ C 68/20.3.95, Bull. 3-95/1.3.99*	COM(95) 474, Bull. 10-95/1.3.138	OJ C 356/30.12.95, Bull. 12-95				Political Agreement on a common position: Bull. 3-95/1.3.99
405 Prop. for a Reg. amending Reg. 1107/70: transport aid	OJ C 253/29.9.95, COM(95) 377, Bull. 7/8-95/1.3.119	Bull. 11-95/1.3.124							Reg. to be amended: OJ L 130/15.6.70

TABLE II — CONSULTATION, COOPERATION, ASSENT   537

Sea transport

	Commission proposal	ESC opinion/ COR opinion°	EP first*/ sole reading	Amended Commission proposal	Council common position	EP second reading	Re-examined Commission proposal	Adoption by Council	Comments
407	Prop. for a Dir.: marine equipment	OJ C 218/23.8.95, COM(95) 269, Bull. 6-95/1.3.131		OJ C 339/18.12.95, Bull. 11-95/1.3.119*					
407	Reg.: safety of ro-ro passenger vessels	OJ C 298/11.11.95, COM(95) 28, Bull. 1/2-95/1.3.92	OJ C 236/11.9.95, Bull. 5-95/1.3.76	OJ C 166/3.7.95, Bull. 6-95/1.3.130*	OJ C 298/11.11.95, COM(95) 286, Bull. 6-95/1.3.130	OJ C 297/10.11.95, Bull. 9-95/1.3.77	OJ C 339/18.12.95, Bull. 11-95/1.3.118	COM(95) 667, Bull. 12-95	Bull. 12-95	Political Agreement on a common position: Bull. 6-95/1.3.130
407	Dir. 95/21/EC: the enforcement, concerning shipping using Community ports, of international standards	OJ C 107/15.4.94, COM(94) 73, Bull. 3-94/1.2.91	OJ C 393/31.12.94, Bull. 9-94/1.2.118	OJ C 323/21.11.94, Bull. 10-94/1.2.66*	OJ C 347/8.12.94, COM(94) 501, Bull. 11-94/1.2.106	OJ C 93/13.4.95, Bull. 3-95/1.3.100	OJ C 151/19.6.95, Bull. 5-95/1.3.75	COM(95) 301, Bull. 6-95/1.3.129	OJ L 157/7.7.95, Bull. 6-95/1.3.129	Political Agreement: Bull. 11-94/1.2.106

Air transport

	Commission proposal	ESC opinion/ COR opinion°	EP first*/ sole reading	Amended Commission proposal	Council common position	EP second reading	Re-examined Commission proposal	Adoption by Council	Comments
409	Prop. for a Reg.: responsibility of the air carrier	COM(95) 724, Bull. 12-95								
413	Prop. for a Dir.: access to the ground handling market at airports	OJ C 142/8.6.95, COM(94) 590, Bull. 12-94/1.2.124	OJ C 301/13.11.95, Bull. 9-95/1.3.79	OJ C 323/4.12.95, Bull. 11-95/1.3.122*						Political Agreement on a common position: Bull. 12-95

° = Opinion of the Committee of the Regions.
* = Cooperation procedure used.

The information society and telecommunications

The information society

	Commission proposal	ESC opinion/COR opinion°	EP first*/sole reading	Amended Commission proposal	Council common position	EP second reading	Re-examined Commission proposal	Adoption by Council	Comments
422	Prop. for a Dec.: INFO 2000 programme	OJ C 250/26.9.95, COM(95) 149, Bull. 6-95/1.3.143							
427	Prop. for a Dec.: multiannual programme for linguistic diversity in the information society	COM(95) 486, Bull. 11-95/1.3.126							

Telecommunications policy

	Commission proposal	ESC opinion/COR opinion°	EP first*/sole reading	Amended Commission proposal	Council common position	EP second reading	Re-examined Commission proposal	Adoption by Council	Comments
436	Recom. 95/144/EC: information technology security evaluation	COM(92) 298, Bull. 9-92/1.2.150	OJ C 73/15.3.93, Bull. 1/2-93/1.2.206	OJ C 176/28.6.93, Bull. 5-93/1.2.144	COM(94) 37, Bull. 1/2-94/1.1.5				OJ L 93/26.4.95, Bull. 4-95/1.3.96	

Environment

General matters

	Commission proposal	ESC opinion/COR opinion°	EP first*/sole reading	Amended Commission proposal	Council common position	EP second reading	Re-examined Commission proposal	Adoption by Council	Comments
464	Prop. for a Dec.: promotion of environment NGOs	COM(95) 573, Bull. 12-95							
465	Prop. for a Dir.: tax on carbon dioxide emissions and energy	OJ C 196/3.8.92, Bull. 5-95/1.1.114	OJ C 108/19.4.93, Bull. 1/2-93/1.2.162	COM(95) 172, Bull. 5-95/1.3.85					

TABLE II — CONSULTATION, COOPERATION, ASSENT   539

	Commission proposal	ESC opinion/ COR opinion°	EP first*/ sole reading	Amended Commission proposal	Council common position	EP second reading	Re-examined Commission proposal	Adoption by Council	Comments
469	Prop. for a Dir. amending Dir. 85/337/EEC: evaluation of the environmental effects of certain products	COM(93) 575, Bull. 3-94/1.2.144	OJ C 393/31.12.94, Bull. 9-94/1.2.165; OJ C 210/14.8.95, Bull. 11-94/1.2.181	OJ C 287/30.10.95, Bull. 10-95/1.3.152					Political Agreement on a common position: Bull. 12-95; Dir. to be amended: OJ L 175/5.7.85
470	Prop. for a Reg. amending Reg. (EEC) No 1973/92: financial instrument for the environment (LIFE)	OJ C 184/18.7.95, COM(95) 135, Bull. 4-95/1.3.98	Bull. 10-95/1.3.153; Bull. 9-95/1.3.83°	OJ C 323/4.12.95, Bull. 11-95/1.3.138*	Bull. 12-95				Reg. to be amended: OJ L 206/22.7.92

Industry and the environment

	Commission proposal	ESC opinion/ COR opinion°	EP first*/ sole reading	Amended Commission proposal	Council common position	EP second reading	Re-examined Commission proposal	Adoption by Council	Comments
484	Prop. for a Dir.: control of major-accident hazards	OJ C 106/14.4.94, COM(94) 4, Bull. 1/2-94/1.2.161	OJ C 295/22.10.94, Bull. 6-94/1.2.172	OJ C 5/6.3.95, Bull. 1/2-95/1.3.104*	OJ C 238/13.9.95, COM(95) 240, Bull. 6-95/1.3.147				Political Agreement on a common position: Bull. 6-95/1.3.147
484	Prop. for a Dir.: integrated pollution prevention and control	OJ C 311/17.11.93, COM(93) 423, Bull. 9-93/1.2.103	OJ C 195/18.7.94, Bull. 4-94/1.2.146	OJ C 18/23.1.95, Bull. 12-94/1.2.201*	OJ C 165/1.7.95, COM(95) 88, Bull. 5-95/1.3.87	Bull. 11-95/1.3.142			Political Agreement on a common position: Bull. 6-95/1.3.148
487	Prop. for a Reg.: shipments of waste to certain non-OECD countries	COM(94) 678, Bull. 1/2-95/1.3.106							
487	Prop. for a Reg. amending Reg. (EEC) No 259/93: supervision and control of shipments of waste within, into and out of the Community	OJ C 164/30.6.95, COM(95) 143, Bull. 4-95/1.3.100	Bull. 10-95/1.3.155						Reg. to be amended: OJ L 30/6.2.93

° = Opinion of the Committee of the Regions.
* = Cooperation procedure used.

	Commission proposal	ESC opinion°/COR opinion°	EP first*/sole reading	Amended Commission proposal	Council common position	EP second reading	Re-examined Commission proposal	Adoption by Council	Comments
488 Prop. for a Dir.: landfill of waste	OJ C 190/22.7.91, COM(91) 102, EC Bull. 4-91/1.2.134	OJ C 40/17.2.92, Bull. 11-91/1.2.182	OJ C 305/23.11.92, Bull. 10-92/1.3.103*	OJ C 212/5.8.93, COM(93) 275, Bull. 6-93/1.2.161	Bull. 10-95/1.3.154				Political Agreement: Bull. 6-94/1.2.176; EP Consultation on the legal basis: OJ C 151/19.6.95, Bull. 5-95/1.3.88

Civil protection

	Commission proposal	ESC opinion°/COR opinion°	EP first*/sole reading	Amended Commission proposal	Council common position	EP second reading	Re-examined Commission proposal	Adoption by Council	Comments
489 Prop. for a Dec.: civil protection action programme	OJ C 142/8.6.95, COM(95) 155, Bull. 5-95/1.3.89	OJ C 301/13.11.95, Bull. 9-95/1.3.88; Bull. 9-95/1.3.88°							

Quality of the environment and natural resources

	Commission proposal	ESC opinion°/COR opinion°	EP first*/sole reading	Amended Commission proposal	Council common position	EP second reading	Re-examined Commission proposal	Adoption by Council	Comments
492 Prop. for a Dir. amending Dir 80/778/EEC: quality of water intended for human consumption	OJ C 131/30.5.95, COM(94) 612, Bull. 1/2-95/1.3.107	Bull. 9-95/1.3.89°; Bull. 12-95							Dir. to be amended: OJ L 229/30.8.80
496 Prop. for a Reg.: possession of and trade in specimens of species of wild fauna and flora (CITES convention)	OJ C 26/3.2.92, COM(91) 448, Bull. 11-91/1.2.179	OJ C 223/31.8.92, Bull. 5-92/1.1.134	OJ C 194/19.7.93, Bull. 6-93/1.2.168*	COM(93) 599, Bull. 1/2-94/1.2.168					Political Agreement on a common position: Bull. 6-95/1.3.150; Opinion of the EP on the legal basis: Bull. 12-95
497 Reg. (EC) No 3062/95: tropical forests	OJ C 78/19.3.93, COM(93) 53, Bull. 1/2-93/1.2.157	OJ C 249/13.9.93, Bull. 6-93/1.2.166	OJ C 315/22.11.93, Bull. 10-93/1.2.128*	OJ C 201/23.7.94, COM(94) 153, Bull. 6-94/1.2.182	Bull. 11-94/1.2.190; OJ C 160/26.6.95, Bull. 1/2-95/1.3.111	OJ C 166/3.7.95, Bull. 6-95/1.3.151	COM(95) 408, Bull. 9-95/1.3.90	OJ L 327/30.12.95, Bull. 12-95	
498 Prop. for a Reg. amending Reg. (EEC) No 3254/91: leghold traps	COM(95) 737, Bull. 12/95								Reg. to be amended: OJ L 308/9.11.91

TABLE II — CONSULTATION, COOPERATION, ASSENT 541

	Commission proposal	ESC opinion/ COR opinion°	EP first*/ sole reading	Amended Commission proposal	Council common position	EP second reading	Re-examined Commission proposal	Adoption by Council	Comments
501	Prop. for a Dir.: ambient air quality	OJ C 216/6.8.94, COM(94) 109, Bull. 7/8-94/1.2.158	OJ C 110/2.5.95, Bull. 1/2-95/1.3.115	OJ C 166/3.7.95, Bull. 6-95/1.3.155*	OJ C 238/13.9.95, COM(95) 312, Bull. 7/8-95/1.3.142	Bull. 11-95/1.3.145			Political Agreement on a common position: Bull. 6-95/1.3.155
501	Prop. for a Dec.: exchange of information on ambient air pollution	OJ C 281/7.10.94, COM(94) 345, Bull. 9-94/1.2.175	OJ C 110/2.5.95, Bull. 1/2-95/1.3.114	OJ C 166/3.7.95, Bull. 6-95/1.3.156*	COM(95) 468, Bull. 11-95/1.3.146				Political Agreement on a common position: Bull. 10-95/1.3.157

Nuclear safety
Radiation protection

	Commission proposal	ESC opinion/ COR opinion°	EP first*/ sole reading	Amended Commission proposal	Council common position	EP second reading	Re-examined Commission proposal	Adoption by Council	Comments
511	Prop. for a Dir.: health protection against the dangers of ionizing radiation	Bull. 7/8-92/1.3.159	OJ C 108/19.4.93, Bull. 1/2-93/1.2.163	OJ C 128/9.5.94, Bull. 4-94/1.2.153	OJ C 245/9.9.93, COM(93) 349, Bull. 7/8 93/1.2.146; OJ C 224/12.8.94, COM(94) 298, Bull. 7/8-94/1.2.160				
512	Prop. for a Dir. replacing Dir. 84/44/Euratom: protection against ionizing radiation	COM(95) 560, Bull. 11-95/1.3.149							Dir. to be repealed: OJ L 265/5.10.84
512	Reg. (EC) No 686/95 extending Reg. (EEC) No 737/90: importation of agricultural products originating in third countries following the Chernobyl accident	COM(94) 597, Bull. 12-94/1.2.215						OJ L 71/31.3.95, Bull. 3-95/1.3.113	Extended Reg.: OJ L 82/29.3.90

° = Opinion of the Committee of the Regions.
* = Cooperation procedure used.

Agricultural policy

Content of the common agricultural policy

	Commission proposal	ESC opinion/ COR opinion°	EP first*/ sole reading	Amended Commission proposal	Council common position	EP second reading	Re-examined Commission proposal	Adoption by Council	Comments
529 Reg. (EC) Nos 1528/95 to 1551/95: fixing of agricultural prices and related measures (1995-96)	OJ C 99/21.4.95, COM(95) 34, Bull. 1/2-95/1.3.120	OJ C 155/21.6.95, Bull. 4-95/1.3.105	OJ C 151/19.6.94, Bull. 5-95/1.3.97					OJ L 148/30.6.95, Bull. 6-95/1.3.160	Political Agreement: Bull. 6-95/1.3.160
532 Reg. (EC) No 1460/95 amending for the eighth time Reg. (EEC) No 1765/92: support for producers of certain arable crops	OJ C 48/25.2.95, COM(94) 636, Bull. 1/2-95/1.3.122		OJ C 151/19.6.95, Bull. 5-95/1.3.99					OJ L 144/28.6.95, Bull. 6-95/1.3.162	Amended Reg.: OJ L 181/1.7.92
533 Reg. (EC) No 3011/95 amending Reg. (EEC) No 823/87: quality wines	OJ C 15/20.1.96, COM(95) 506, Bull. 10-95/1.3.179		OJ C 17/22.1.96, Bull. 12-95					OJ L 314/28.12.95, Bull. 12-95	Amended Reg.: OJ L 84/27.3.87

Management of the common agricultural policy

	Commission proposal	ESC opinion/ COR opinion°	EP first*/ sole reading	Amended Commission proposal	Council common position	EP second reading	Re-examined Commission proposal	Adoption by Council	Comments
535 Reg. (EC) No 2336/95 amending Reg. (EEC) No 1765/92: compulsory set-aside requirement (1996)	OJ C 253/29.9.95, COM(95) 401, Bull. 7/8-95/1.3.146		OJ C 269/16.10.95, Bull. 9-95/1.3.100					OJ L 236/5.10.95, Bull. 9-95/1.3.100	Amended Reg.: OJ L 81/1.7.92
535 Reg. (EC) No 2989 amending Reg. (EEC) No 1765/92: exceptional set-aside	OJ C 260/5.10.95, COM(95) 401, Bull. 7/8-95/1.3.147		OJ C 308/20.11.95, Bull. 10-95/1.3.174					OJ L 312/23.12.95, Bull. 12-95	Political Agreement: Bull. 11-95/1.3.156; Amended Reg.: OJ L 81/1.7.92
535 Reg. (EC) No 603/95: common organization of the market in dried fodder	OJ C 365/21.12.94, COM(94) 508, Bull. 11-94/1.2.141		OJ C 56/6.3.95, Bull. 1/2-95/1.3.125					OJ L 63/21.3.95, Bull. 1/2-95/1.3.125	
535 Reg. (EC) No 684/95 amending Reg. (EC) No 603/95: COM in dried fodder	OJ C 365/21.12.94, COM(94) 508, Bull. 11-94/1.2.141		OJ C 56/6.3.95, Bull. 1/2-95/1.3.125					OJ L 71/31.3.95, Bull. 3-95/1.3.118	Amended Reg.: OJ L 63/21.3.95

TABLE II — CONSULTATION, COOPERATION, ASSENT   543

	Commission proposal	ESC opinion/ COR opinion°	EP first*/ sole reading	Amended Commission proposal	Council common position	EP second reading	Re-examined Commission proposal	Adoption by Council	Comments
535	Reg. (EC) No 1347/95 amending Reg. (EC) No 603/95: COM in dried fodder	OJ C 79/31.3.95, COM(95) 96, Bull. 3-95/1.3.119	OJ C 236/11.9.95, Bull. 5-95/1.3.102	OJ C 151/19.6.95, Bull. 5-95/1.3.102					OJ L 131/15.6.95, Bull. 6-95/1.3.165	Amended Reg.: OJ L 63/21.3.95
536	Reg. (EC) No 636/95 amending Reg. (EEC) No 2261/84: aid for olive oil production	COM(94) 536, Bull. 11-94/1.2.140							OJ L 67/25.3.95, Bull. 1/2-95/1.3.124	Amended Reg.: OJ L 208/3.8.84
536	Reg. (EC) No 1267/95 amending Reg. (EEC) No 1332/92: table olives	OJ C 82/4.4.95, COM(95) 66, Bull. 3-95/1.3.117		OJ C 126/22.5.95, Bull. 4-95/1.3.108					OJ L 123/3.6.95, Bull. 5-95/1.3.101	Amended Reg.: OJ L 145/27.5.92
537	Reg. (EC) No 1101/95 amending Reg. (EEC) No 1785/81: COM in sugar	OJ C 377/31.12.94, COM(94) 439, Bull. 11-94/1.2.138	OJ C 110/2.5.95, Bull. 1/2-95/1.3.123	OJ C 109/1.5.95, Bull. 4-95/1.3.107					OJ L 110/17.5.95, Bull. 4-95/1.3.107	Political Agreement: Bull. 4-95/1.3.107; Amended Reg.: OJ L 177/1.7.81
538	Prop. for a Reg.: reform of the common organization of the market in wine	OJ C 194/16.7.94, COM(94) 117, Bull. 5-94/1.2.103	OJ C 210/14.8.95, Bull. 11-94/1.2.143°; OJ C 110/2.5.95, Bull. 1/2-95/1.3.129	OJ C 109/1.5.95, Bull. 4-95/1.3.111						
539	Prop. for a Reg.: COM in fruit and vegetables	COM(95) 434, Bull. 10-95/1.3.176	Bull. 12-95							
539	Prop. for a Reg.: COM in processed fruit and vegetables	COM(95) 434, Bull. 10-95/1.3.176	Bull. 12-95							
540	Prop. for a Reg. amending Reg. (EEC) No 404/93 following accession: annual quota for the import of bananas	OJ C 136/3.6.95, COM(95) 115, Bull. 4-95/1.3.110	OJ C 236/11.9.95, Bull. 5-95/1.3.104	OJ C 166/3.7.95, Bull. 6-95/1.3.166						Reg. to be amended: OJ L 47/25.2.93
540	Prop. for a Reg. amending Reg. (EEC) Nos 404/93 (bananas), 1035/72 (fruit and vegetables) and 2658/87 (tariff and statistical nomenclature and Common Customs Tariff)	OJ C 136/3.6.95, COM(95) 114, Bull. 4-95/1.3.109	OJ C 301/13.11.95, Bull. 9-95/1.3.101	OJ C 17/22.1.96, Bull. 12-95						Reg. to be amended: (EEC) Nos 404/93 (OJ L 47/25.2.93), 1035/72 (OJ L 118/20.5.72), 2658/87 (OJ L 256/7.9.87)

° = Opinion of the Committee of the Regions.
* = Cooperation procedure used.

	Commission proposal	ESC opinion/ COR opinion	EP first*/ sole reading	Amended Commission proposal	Council common position	EP second reading	Re-examined Commission proposal	Adoption by Council	Comments
541 Reg. (EC) No 3072/95: COM in rice	COM(95) 331, Bull. 7/8-95/1.3.149	Bull. 11-95/1.3.157	OJ C 17/22.1.96, Bull. 12-95					OJ L 329/30.2.95, Bull. 12-95	Political Agreement: Bull. 12-95
541 Reg. (EC) No 3073/95: standard quality of rice	COM(95) 405, Bull. 7/8-95/1.3.150							OJ L 329/30.2.95, Bull. 12-95	Political Agreement: Bull. 12-95
543 Reg. (EC) No 2284/95: aid to hop producers (1994)	OJ C 235/9.9.95, COM(95) 265, Bull. 6-95/1.3.168		OJ C 269/16.10.95, Bull. 9-95/1.3.102					OJ L 233/30.9.95, Bull. 9-95/1.3.102	
543 Reg. (EC) No 423/95 amending Reg. (EEC) No 2997/87: amount of aid to hop producers for the 1986 harvest	OJ C 177/31.12.94, COM(94) 535, Bull. 12-94/1.2.160		OJ C 56/6.3.95, Bull. 1/2-95/1.3.132					OJ L 45/1.3.95, Bull. 1/2-95/1.3.132	Amended Reg.: OJ L 284/7.10.87
544 Reg. (EC) No 711/95 amending Reg. (EEC) No 2075/92: COM in raw tobacco	COM(94) 555, Bull. 1/2-95/1.3.131		OJ C 89/10.4.95, Bull. 3-95/1.3.123					OJ L 73/1.4.95, Bull. 3-95/1.3.123	Amended Reg.: OJ L 215/30.7.92
544 Prop. for a Reg. amending Reg. (EEC) No 2075/92: COM in raw tobacco and guarantee thresholds (1996-97)	COM(95) 592, Bull. 11-95/1.3.160								Reg. to be amended: OJ L 215/30.7.92
545 Reg. (EC) No 1553/95 amending Reg. (EEC) No 1964/87: aid for cotton (annex to the Act of Accession of Greece)	OJ C 94/14.4.95, COM(95) 35, Bull. 3-95/1.3.122							OJ L 148/30.6.95, Bull. 6-95/1.3.167	Political Agreement: Bull. 6-95/1.3.167; Amended Reg.: OJ L 184/3.7.87
545 Reg. (EC) No 1554/95 amending Reg. (EEC) No 2169/81: aid for cotton	OJ C 94/14.4.95, COM(95) 35, Bull. 3-95/1.3.122	OJ C 236/11.9.95, Bull. 5-95/1.3.105	OJ C 151/19.6.95, Bull. 5-95/1.3.105					OJ L 148/30.6.95, Bull. 6-95/1.3.167	Political Agreement: Bull. 6-95/1.3.167; Amended Reg.: OJ L 211/31.7.81
546 Prop. for a Reg. consolidating Reg. (EEC) No 804/68: COM in milk and milk-based products	COM(95) 598, Bull. 12-95								Codified Reg.: OJ L 148/28.6.68
546 Reg. (EC) No 1288/95: extending to the period 1991-93 the increase adopted for the period 1993-95 for Greece, Italy and Spain (the additional levy system)	OJ C 46/23.2.95, COM(95) 19, Bull. 1/2-95/1.3.133		OJ C 151/19.6.95, Bull. 5-95/1.3.107	OJ C 157/23.6.95, COM(95) 146, Bull. 4-95/1.3.112				OJ L 125/29.5.95, Bull. 5-95/1.3.107	

TABLE II — CONSULTATION, COOPERATION, ASSENT 545

		Commission proposal	ESC opinion/ COR opinion°	EP first*/ sole reading	Amended Commission proposal	Council common position	EP second reading	Re-examined Commission proposal	Adoption by Council	Comments
546	Reg. (EC) No 1552/95 amending Reg. (EEC) No 3950/92: additional levy for milk	OJ C 142/8.6.95, COM(95) 147, Bull. 4-95/1.3.113		OJ C 151/19.6.95, Bull. 5-95/1.3.106					OJ L 148/30.6.95, Bull. 6-95/1.3.169	Political Agreement: Bull. 6-95/1.3.169; Amended Reg.: OJ L 405/31.12.92
547	Reg. (EC) No 424/95 amending Reg. (EEC) No 805/68: deseasonalization premium	OJ C 321/18.11.94, COM(94) 451, Bull. 10-94/1.2.89							OJ L 45/1.3.95, Bull. 1/2-95/1.3.135	Amended Reg.: OJ L 148/28.6.68
547	Reg. (EC) No 1265/95 amending Reg. (EEC) No 3013/89: COM in sheepmeat and goatmeat	OJ C 382/31.12.94, COM(94) 643, Bull. 12-94/1.2.163	OJ C 133/31.5.95, Bull. 3-95/1.3.124	OJ C 89/10.4.95, Bull. 3-95/1.3.124					OJ L 123/3.6.95, Bull. 5-95/1.3.109	Amended Reg.: OJ L 289/7.10.89
547	Prop. for a Reg.: common organization of the market in beef (consolidated text)	COM(94) 467, Bull. 1/2-95/1.2.150	OJ C 56/6.3.95, Bull. 1/2-95/1.3.134							
549	Reg. (EC) No 150/95 amending Reg. (EEC) No 3813/92: unit of account and conversion rate	OJ C 360/17.12.94, COM(94) 498, Bull. 11-94/1.2.135		OJ C 43/20.2.95, Bull. 1/2-95/1.3.121					OJ L 22/31.1.95, Bull. 1/2-95/1.3.121	Amended Reg.: OJ L 387/31.12.92
549	Reg. (EC) No 1527/95: compensation for reductions in the agricultural conversion rates of certain currencies	COM(95) 173, Bull. 5-95/1.3.96							OJ L 148/30.6.95, Bull. 6-95/1.3.161	Political Agreement: Bull. 6-95/1.3.161
549	Reg. (EC) No 2990/95: compensation as a result of the fall in the agricultural conversion rates	COM(95) 637, Bull. 12-95							OJ L 312/23.12.95, Bull. 12-95	
550	Reg. (EC) No 2611/95: national aid in compensation for losses of income caused by monetary movements	OJ C 252/28.9.95, COM(95) 343, Bull. 7/8-95/1.3.145		OJ C 287/30.10.95, Bull. 10-95/1.3.172					OJ L 268/10.11.95, Bull. 10-95/1.3.172	
551	Reg. (EC) No 2535/95 amending Reg. (EEC) No 3730/87: food for the most deprived persons	OJ C 260/5.10.95, COM(95) 371, Bull. 7/8-95/1.3.151		OJ C 287/30.10.95, Bull. 10-95/1.3.182					OJ L 260/31.10.95, Bull. 10-95/1.3.182	Amended Reg.: OJ L 352/15.12.87

° = Opinion of the Committee of the Regions.

* = Cooperation procedure used.

	Commission proposal	ESC opinion/ COR opinion	EP first*/ sole reading	Amended Commission proposal	Council common position	EP second reading	Re-examined Commission proposal	Adoption by Council	Comments
552	Reg. (EC) No 1975/95: supply of agricultural products to Armenia, Azerbaijan, Georgia, Kyrgyzstan and Tadjikistan	COM(95) 395, Bull. 7/8-95/1.4.94						OJ L 191/12.8.95, Bull. 7/8-95/1.4.94	
555	Reg. (EC) No 2801/95 amending Reg. (EEC) No 79/65: network for agricultural accountancy data	OJ C 307/18.11.95, COM(95) 407, Bull. 9-95/1.3.98		OJ C 323/4.12.95, Bull. 11-95/1.3.154					OJ L 291/6.12.95, Bull. 11-95/1.3.154	Amended Reg.: OJ L 109/23.6.65

Financing the common agricultural policy: the EAGGF

	Commission proposal	ESC opinion/ COR opinion	EP first*/ sole reading	Amended Commission proposal	Council common position	EP second reading	Re-examined Commission proposal	Adoption by Council	Comments
560	Reg. (EC) No 1469/95: measures to be taken with certain beneficiaries of the EAGGF Guarantee Section (black list)	OJ C 151/2.6.94, COM(94) 122, Bull. 4-94/1.2.124	OJ C 393/31.12.94, Bull. 9-94/1.2.143	OJ C 56/6.3.95, Bull. 1/2-95/1.3.137	OJ C 171/7.7.95, COM(95) 194, Bull. 5-95/1.3.112				OJ L 145/29.6.95, Bull. 6-95/1.3.171	
561	Reg. (EC) No 1287/95 amending Reg. (EEC) No 729/70: financing of the CAP	OJ C 284/12.10.94, COM(94) 240, Bull. 7/8-94/1.2.138		OJ C 89/10.4.95, Bull. 3-95/1.3.125	OJ C 150/17.6.95, COM(95) 161, Bull. 5-95/1.3.110				OJ L 125/8.6.95, Bull. 5-95/1.3.110	Amended Reg.: OJ L 94/28.4.70
561	Prop. for a Reg.: securities, sureties and guarantees in connection with the CAP	COM(94) 480, Bull. 11-94/1.2.152		OJ C 43/20.2.95, Bull. 1/2-95/1.3.136						

Fisheries

Content of the common fisheries policy

	Commission proposal	ESC opinion/ COR opinion	EP first*/ sole reading	Amended Commission proposal	Council common position	EP second reading	Re-examined Commission proposal	Adoption by Council	Comments
566	Reg. (EC) No 685/95: rules for access to certain fishing areas and re-sources	OJ C 247/3.9.94, COM(94) 308, Bull. 7/8-94/1.2.152	OJ C 397/31.12.94, Bull. 11-94/1.2.163	OJ C 18/23.1.95, Bull. 12-94/1.2.170					OJ L 71/31.3.95, Bull. 3-95/1.3.130	Council Agreement: Bull. 12-94/1.2.170
566	Reg. (EC) No 2027/95: management system for the fishing effort	COM(95) 237, Bull. 6-95/1.3.182							OJ L 199/24.8.95, Bull. 6-95/1.3.182	

TABLE II — CONSULTATION, COOPERATION, ASSENT   547

	Commission proposal	ESC opinion/ COR opinion°	EP first*/ sole reading	Amended Commission proposal	Council common position	EP second reading	Re-examined Commission proposal	Adoption by Council	Comments
566	Reg. (EC) No 2870/95 amending Reg. (EEC) No 2847/93: control system for the CFP — OJ C 188/22.7.95, COM(95) 256, Bull. 6-95/1.3.183	Bull. 10-95/1.3.198	OJ C 269/16.10.95, Bull. 9-95/1.3.106	OJ C 6/11.1.96, COM(95) 476, Bull. 10-95/1.3.198				OJ L 301/14.12.95, Bull. 12-95	Political Agreement: Bull. 10-95/1.3.198; Amended Reg.: OJ L 261/20.10.93
567	Prop. for a Reg.: species to be recorded in the logbook — COM(95) 322, Bull. 7/8-95/1.3.165							Bull. 12-95	
568	Dec.: restructuring the fisheries sector in Sweden and Finland (1995-96) — OJ C 171/7.7.95, COM(95) 198, Bull. 5-95/1.3.114	OJ C 323/4.12.95, Bull. 11-95/1.3.171							

Internal resources and policy on conservation and monitoring

	Commission proposal	ESC opinion/ COR opinion°	EP first*/ sole reading	Amended Commission proposal	Council common position	EP second reading	Re-examined Commission proposal	Adoption by Council	Comments
570	Reg.: ACR (1996) — COM(95) 615, Bull. 12-95							Bull. 12-95	
570	Prop. for a Reg.: further conditions for the inter-annual management of ACRs and quotas — OJ C 382/31.12.94, COM(94) 583, Bull. 12-94/1.2.171		OJ C 249/25.9.95, Bull. 7/8-95/1.3.161						
571	Reg. (EC) No 746/95 amending Reg. (EEC) No 3362/94: ACR and quotas for 1995 — COM(95) 84, Bull. 3-95/1.3.131							OJ L 74/1.4.95, Bull. 3-95/1.3.131	Amended Reg.: OJ L 263/31.12.94
571	Reg. (EC) No 2726/95 amending Reg. (EC) No 3362/94: ACR and quotas for 1995 — COM(95) 480, Bull. 10-95/1.3.201							OJ L 284/28.11.95, Bull. 11-95/1.3.172	Amended Reg.: OJ L 363/31.12.94
571	Reg. (EC) No 2780/95 amending Reg. (EC) No 3362/94: ACR and catch conditions — COM(95) 516, Bull. 11-95/1.3.173							OJ L 289/2.12.95, Bull. 11-95/1.3.173	Amended Reg.: OJ L 363/31.12.94
572	Reg. (EC) No 1173/95 amending for the 16th time Reg. (EEC) No 3094/86 (technical measures for conservation) — OJ C 348/9.12.94, COM(94) 481, Bull. 11-94/1.2.164		OJ C 56/6.3.95, Bull. 1/2-95/1.3.145						OJ L 118/25.5.95, Bull. 5-95/1.3.115	Amended Reg.: OJ L 288/11.10.86

° = Opinion of the Committee of the Regions.
* = Cooperation procedure used.

		Commission proposal	ESC opinion/ COR opinion°	EP first*/ sole reading	Amended Commission proposal	Council common position	EP second reading	Re-examined Commission proposal	Adoption by Council	Comments
572	Reg. (EC) No 1909/95 amending for the 17th time Reg. (EEC) No 3094/86	OJ C 348/9.12.94, COM(94) 481, Bull. 11-94/1.2.164		OJ C 56/6.3.95, Bull. 1/2-95/1.3.145					OJ L 184/3.8.95, Bull. 7/8-95/1.3.162	Amended Reg.: OJ L 363/11.10.86
572	Reg. (EC) No 2251/95 amending for the 18th time Reg. (EEC) No 3094/86	OJ C 180/14.7.95, COM(95) 212, Bull. 5-95/1.3.116		OJ C 249/25.9.95, Bull. 7/8-95/1.3.163					OJ L 230/27.9.95, Bull. 9-95/1.3.107	Amended Reg.: OJ L 288/11.10.86
572	Reg. (EC) No 3071/95 amending for the 19th time Reg. (EEC) No 3094/86 (technical conservation measures)	OJ C 348/9.12.94, COM(94) 481, Bull. 11-94/1.2.164		OJ C 56/6.3.95, Bull. 1/2-95/1.3.145					OJ L 329/30.12.95, Bull. 12-95	Amended Reg.: OJ L 288/11.10.86
572	Prop for a Reg.: technical measures of conservation (fish)	Bull. 6-91/1.2.189			COM(95) 613, Bull. 12-95					
575	Dec. 95/523/EC: control system for the CFP	OJ C 186/20.7.95, COM(95) 243, Bull. 6-95/1.3.184	Bull. 10-95/1.3.199	OJ C 287/30.10.95, Bull. 10-95/1.3.199	COM(95) 515, Bull. 10-95/1.3.199				OJ L 301/14.12.95, Bull. 12-95	Political Agreement: Bull. 10-95/1.3.199

External resources

		Commission proposal	ESC opinion/ COR opinion°	EP first*/ sole reading	Amended Commission proposal	Council common position	EP second reading	Re-examined Commission proposal	Adoption by Council	Comments
579	Reg. (EC) No 3069/95: pilot observer scheme	OJ C 211/15.8.95, COM(95) 266, Bull. 6-95/1.3.192		OJ C 17/22.1.96, Bull. 12-95					OJ L 329/30.12.95, Bull. 12-95	
579	Reg. (EC) No 3070/95: satellite tracking	COM(95) 620, Bull. 12-95		OJ C 17/22.1.96, Bull. 12-95					OJ L 329/30.12.95, Bull. 12-95	
579	Reg. (EC) No 3067/95 amending Reg. (EEC) No 1956/88: joint international inspection	OJ C 20/4.8.95, COM(95) 266, Bull. 6-95/1.3.192		OJ C 17/22.1.96, Bull. 12-95					OJ L 329/30.12.95, Bull. 12-95	
579	Reg. (EC) No 3068/95 amending Reg. (EEC) No 189/92: control measures	OJ C 200/4.8.95, COM(95) 266, Bull. 6-95/1.3.192		OJ C 17/22.1.96, Bull. 12-95					OJ L 329/30.12.95, Bull. 12-95	
579	Prop. for a Reg.: conservation and resource management for 1996 (NAFO area)	COM(95) 717, Bull. 12-95							Bull. 12-95	

TABLE II — CONSULTATION, COOPERATION, ASSENT   549

	Commission proposal	ESC opinion/ COR opinion°	EP first*/ sole reading	Amended Commission proposal	Council common position	EP second reading	Re-examined Commission proposal	Adoption by Council	Comments
583	Reg. (EC) No 749/95 amending Reg. (EC) No 3363/94: catch quotas in the waters around Greenland (1995) COM(95) 104, Bull. 3-95/1.3.134							OJ L 74/1.4.95, Bull. 3-95/1.3.134	Amended Reg.: OJ L 363/31.12.94
583	Reg. (EC) No 751/95 amending Reg. (EC) No 3365/94: catch quotas in the waters around the Faeroe Islands COM(95) 102, Bull. 3-95/1.3.135							OJ L 74/1.4.95, Bull. 3-95/1.3.135	Amended Reg.: OJ L 363/31.12.94
583	Reg. (EC) No 748/95 amending Reg. (EC) No 3377/94: catch quotas in the Norwegian exclusive economic zone and the Jan Mayen zone COM(95) 103, Bull. 3-95/1.3.136							OJ L 74/1.4.95, Bull. 3-95/1.3.136	Amended Reg.: OJ L 363/31.12.94
585	Dec. 95/399/EC: accession of the Community to the Indian Ocean Tuna Commission COM(94) 386, Bull. 9-94/1.2.162		OJ C 109/1.5.95, Bull. 4-95/1.3.123					OJ L 236/5.10.95, Bull. 9-95/1.3.115	
586	Reg. (EC) No 2250/95 amending Reg. (EEC) No 1866/86: conservation of resources in the waters of the Baltic, the Belts and the Sound OJ C 302/14.11.95, COM(95) 70, Bull. 3-95/1.3.137	OJ C 236/11.9.95, Bull. 5-95/1.3.120	OJ C 166/3.7.95, Bull. 6-95/1.3.190	OJ C 302/14.11.95, COM(95) 211, Bull. 5-95/1.3.120				OJ L 230/27.9.95, Bull. 9-95/1.3.112	Amended Reg.: OJ L 162/18.6.86
586	Prop. for a Reg.: control of fishing activities in the waters of the Baltic, the Belts and the Sound OJ C 313/24.11.95, COM(95) 249, Bull. 9-95/1.3.113	Bull. 11-95/1.3.180							
586	Prop. for a Reg. repealing Reg. (EEC) No 2245/85: marine fauna and flora in the Antarctic OJ C 8/13.1.96, COM(95) 475, Bull. 10-95/1.3.207								Reg. to be repealed: OJ L 210/7.8.85

° = Opinion of the Committee of the Regions.
* = Cooperation procedure used.

Market organization

	Commission proposal	ESC opinion°/COR opinion°	EP first*/sole reading	Amended Commission proposal	Council common position	EP second reading	Re-examined Commission proposal	Adoption by Council	Comments
588 Reg. (EC) No 1300/95 amending Reg. (EEC) No 104/76: marketing standards for Nordic shrimps	COM(95) 82, Bull. 3-95/1.3.142							OJ L 126/9.6.95, Bull. 6-95/1.3.195	Amended Reg.: OJ L 20/28.1.76
588 Reg. (EC) No 1099/95 amending Reg. (EC) No 3136/94: guide prices for certain fisheries products (1995)	COM(95) 81, Bull. 3-95/1.3.141							Bull. 4-95/1.3.124; OJ L 126/9.6.95, Bull. 6-95/1.3.194	Amended Reg.: OJ L 332/22.12.94

Employment and social policy

Implementation of the White Paper on social policy

	Commission proposal	ESC opinion°/COR opinion°	EP first*/sole reading	Amended Commission proposal	Council common position	EP second reading	Re-examined Commission proposal	Adoption by Council	Comments
596 Prop. for a Dir.: safeguarding of employees' rights in the event of transfers of undertakings	OJ C 274/1.10.94, COM(94) 300, Bull. 9-94/1.2.182	OJ C 133/31.5.95, Bull. 3-95/1.3.145; Bull. 4-95/1.3.127°							

Employment

	Commission proposal	ESC opinion°/COR opinion°	EP first*/sole reading	Amended Commission proposal	Council common position	EP second reading	Re-examined Commission proposal	Adoption by Council	Comments
609 Prop. for a Dir.: safeguarding of employees' rights in the event of transfers of undertakings	OJ C 274/1.10.94, COM(94) 300, Bull. 9-94/1.2.182	OJ C 133/31.5.95, Bull. 3-95/1.3.145; Bull. 4-95/1.3.127°							

TABLE II — CONSULTATION, COOPERATION, ASSENT   551

Social security

	Commission proposal	ESC opinion/ COR opinion°	EP first*/ sole reading	Amended Commission proposal	Council common position	EP second reading	Re-examined Commission proposal	Adoption by Council	Comments
615	Reg. amending Reg. (EEC) No 1408/71: social security schemes for employed persons, self-employed persons and their families. OJ C 143/26.5.94, COM(94) 135, Bull. 4-94/1.2.157	OJ C 393/31.12.94, Bull. 9-94/1.2.184	OJ C 166/3.7.95, Bull. 6-95/1.3.202	OJ C 242/19.9.95, COM(95) 284, Bull. 6-95/1.3.202				Bull. 12-95	Reg. to be amended: OJ L 149/5.7.71
615	Reg. amending Reg. (EEC) Nos 1408/71 and 574/72: social security for employed persons, self-employed persons and their families. OJ C 260/5.10.95, COM(95) 352, Bull. 7/8-95/1.3.184	Bull. 11-95/1.3.186	OJ C 339/19.12.95, Bull. 11-95/1.3.186					Bull. 12-95	Reg. to be amended: (EEC) Nos 1408/71 (OJ L 149/5.7.71), 574/72 (OJ L 74/27.3.72)

Health and safety

	Commission proposal	ESC opinion/ COR opinion°	EP first*/ sole reading	Amended Commission proposal	Council common position	EP second reading	Re-examined Commission proposal	Adoption by Council	Comments
619	Prop. for a Dec.: non-legislative measures for health and safety at work. OJ C 262/7.10.95, COM(95) 282, Bull. 7/8-95/1.3.182	Bull. 11-95/1.3.188							
620	Prop. for a Dir. amending Dir. 90/394/EEC: protection of workers from exposure to carcinogens at work. OJ C 317/28.11.95, COM(95) 425, Bull. 9-95/1.3.119								Dir. to be amended: OJ L 196/26.7.90
620	Prop. for a Dir.: minimum health and safety requirements for workers at risk from explosive atmospheres. OJ C 332/9.12.95, COM(95) 310, Bull. 9-95/1.3.120								
620	Dir. amending Dir. 89/655/EEC: minimum prescriptions for the use of work equipment. OJ C 104/12.4.94, COM(94) 56, Bull. 3-94/1.2.166	OJ C 397/31.12.94, Bull. 11-94/1.2.201	OJ C 56/6.3.95, Bull. 1/2-95/1.3.158*	OJ C 246/22.9.95, COM(95) 311, Bull. 6-95/1.3.203	OJ C 281/25.10.95, Bull. 7/8-95/1.3.183	OJ C 323/4.12.95, Bull. 11-95/1.3.187	COM(95) 642, Bull. 12-95	Bull. 12-95	Political Agreement on a common position: Bull. 6-95/1.3.203; Dir. to be amended: OJ L 393/31.12.89

° = Opinion of the Committee of the Regions.

* = Cooperation procedure used.

	Commission proposal	ESC opinion/ COR opinion°	EP first*/ sole reading	Amended Commission proposal	Council common position	EP second reading	Re-examined Commission proposal	Adoption by Council	Comments

Equal opportunities

| 628 | Dec.: 4th action programme on equal opportunities for men and women (1996-2000) | OJ C 306/17.11.95, COM(95) 381, Bull. 7/8-95/1.3.187 | Bull. 11-95/1.3.190 | OJ C 323/4.12.95, Bull. 11-95/1.3.190 | COM(95) 602 | | | | Bull. 12-95 | |
| 632 | Prop. for a Dir. amending Dir. 86/378/EEC: equal treatment for men and women in occupational social security schemes | OJ C 218/23.8.95, COM(95) 186, Bull. 5-95/1.3.125 | Bull. 10-95/1.3.222 | | | | | | | Dir. to be amended: OJ L 225/12.8.86 |

Solidarity

Actions for the elderly

| 635 | Prop. for a Dec.: support for elderly persons | OJ C 115/9.5.95, COM(95) 53, Bull. 3-95/1.3.149 | OJ C 236/11.9.95, Bull. 5-95/1.3.127 | OJ C 308/20.11.95, Bull. 10-95/1.3.223 | | | | | | |

Consumer policy

Protection of consumer health and safety

| 650 | Dec. 95/184/EC amending Dec. 3092/94/EC: information on home and leisure accidents | COM(95) 5, Bull. 1/2-95/1.3.168 | | | | | | | OJ L 120/31.5.95, Bull. 5-95/1.3.135 | Amended Dec.: OJ L 331/21.12.94 |

TABLE II — CONSULTATION, COOPERATION, ASSENT 553

Information, communication, culture and audiovisual media

Audiovisual policy

	Commission proposal	ESC opinion°/COR opinion°	EP first*/sole reading	Amended Commission proposal	Council common position	EP second reading	Re-examined Commission proposal	Adoption by Council	Comments
676	Prop. for a Dir. amending Dir. 89/552/EEC: television without frontiers	OJ C 185/19.7.95, COM(95) 86, Bull. 5-95/1.3.139	OJ C 301/13.11.95, Bull. 9-95/1.3.138						Dir. to be amended: OJ L 298/17.10.89
677	Dec.: MEDIA II – training	OJ C 108/29.4.95, COM(94) 523, Bull. 1/2-95/1.3.170		OJ C 166/3.7.95, Bull. 6-95/1.3.227*	COM(95) 523	OJ C 281/25.10.95, Bull. 7/8-95/1.3.207	OJ C 323/4.12.95, Bull. 11-95/1.3.210	COM(95) 725, Bull. 12-95	Bull. 12-95	Political Agreement on a common position: Bull. 6-95/1.3.227; Political Agreement: Bull. 11-95/1.3.210
677	Dec. 95/563/EC: MEDIA II – development and distribution	OJ C 108/29.4.95, COM(94) 523, Bull. 1/2-95/1.3.170	OJ C 256/2.10.95, Bull. 7/8-95/1.3.208	OJ C 166/3.7.95, Bull. 6-95/1.3.228					OJ L 321/30.12.95, Bull. 7/8-95/1.3.208	Political Agreement: Bull. 6-95/1.3.228
677	Prop. for a Dec.: European guarantee fund for cinematographic and television productions	COM(95) 546, Bull. 11-95/1.3.211								

The European Union's role in the world

Common commercial policy

General matters

	Commission proposal	ESC opinion°/COR opinion°	EP first*/sole reading	Amended Commission proposal	Council common position	EP second reading	Re-examined Commission proposal	Adoption by Council	Comments
737	Prop. for a Reg.: transitional customs measures following the accession of Finland and Sweden	COM(95) 4, Bull. 1/2-95/1.4.39			COM(95) 152, Bull. 5-95/1.4.30					

° = Opinion of the Committee of the Regions.
* = Cooperation procedure used.

	Commission proposal	ESC opinion/ COR opinion°	EP first*/ sole reading	Amended Commission proposal	Council common position	EP second reading	Re-examined Commission proposal	Adoption by Council	Comments
738	Reg. (EC) No 837/95 amending Reg. (EC) No 3381/94: control of exports of dual-use goods COM(95) 79, Bull. 3-95/1.4.23							OJ L 90/21.4.95, Bull. 4-95/1.4.31	Amended Reg.: OJ L 367/31.12.94
742	Reg. (EC) No 1251/95 amending Reg. (EC) No 3283/94: protection against dumped imports from non-member countries COM(95) 63, Bull. 3-95/1.4.25							OJ L 122/2.6.95, Bull. 5-95/1.4.32	Amended Reg.: OJ L 349/31.12.94
742	Reg. (EC) No 1252/95 amending Reg. (EC) No 3284/94: protection against subsidized imports from non-member countries COM(95) 61, Bull. 3-95/1.4.25							OJ L 122/2.6.95, Bull. 5-95/1.4.32	Amended Reg.: OJ L 349/31.12.94
742	Reg. (EC) No 355/95 amending Reg. (EC) No 3283/94: protection against dumped imports from non-member countries COM(95) 7, Bull. 1/2-95/1.4.42							OJ L 41/23.2.95, Bull. 1/2-95/1.4.42	Amended Reg.: OJ L 349/31.12.94
742	Reg. repealing Reg. (EC) No 3283/94: protection against dumped imports from non-member countries OJ C 319/30.11.95, COM(95) 363, Bull. 7/8-95/1.4.24		OJ C 17/22.1.96, Bull. 12-95					Bull. 12-95	Reg. repealed: OJ L 349/31.12.94
745	Reg. (EC) No 356/95 amending Reg. (EC) No 3286/94: exercise of the Community's rights under international trade rules COM(95) 8, Bull. 1/2-95/1.4.42							OJ L 41/23.2.95, Bull. 1/2-95/1.4.42	Amended Reg.: OJ L 349/31.12.94
747	Reg. (EC) No 538/95 amending Reg. (EC) No 519/94: rules for imports from certain third countries COM(94) 646, Bull. 12-94/1.3.143							OJ L 55/11.3.95, Bull. 3-95/1.4.36	Amended Reg.: OJ L 66/10.3.94
747	Reg. (EC) No 839/95 amending the list of countries in Annex I to Reg. (EC) No 519/94 COM(95) 14, Bull. 1/2-95/1.4.45							OJ L 85/19.4.95, Bull. 4-95/1.4.50	Amended Reg.: OJ L 67/10.3.94
747	Prop. for a Reg. amending Reg. (EC) No 519/94: extension to ECSC products of the rules governing imports from State-trading countries COM(95) 470								Reg. to be amended: OJ L 66/10.3.94

TABLE II — CONSULTATION, COOPERATION, ASSENT   555

	Commission proposal	ESC opinion°/ COR opinion°	EP first*/ sole reading	Amended Commission proposal	Council common position	EP second reading	Re-examined Commission proposal	Adoption by Council	Comments
748	Prop. for a Reg. amending Reg. (EC) No 3285/94 and (EC) No 519/94: single document for Community surveillance	COM(95) 459, Bull. 10-95/1.4.37							Reg. to be amended: (EC) No 3285/94 (OJ L 349/31.12.94) and (EC) No 519/94 (OJ L 67/10.3.94)
749	Prop. for a Reg. amending Reg. (EC) No 520/94: management of quantitative quotas	COM(95) 460, Bull. 10-95/1.4.38								Reg. to be amended: OJ L 66/10.3.94
751	Dec. 95/133/EC: automatic renewal of certain trade agreements	COM (95) 31, Bull. 1/2-95/1.4.59							OJ L 89/21.4.95, Bull. 4-95/1.4.51	

Individual sectors

	Commission proposal	ESC opinion°/ COR opinion°	EP first*/ sole reading	Amended Commission proposal	Council common position	EP second reading	Re-examined Commission proposal	Adoption by Council	Comments
765	Prop. for a Reg.: adverse price practices in the shipbuilding industry	COM(95) 473, Bull. 10-95/1.4.42	OJ C 13/18.1.96, COM(95) 473,	OJ C 17/22.1.96, Bull. 12-95					
767	Reg.: textile trade with Taiwan	COM(95) 603, Bull. 11-95/1.4.27							Bull. 12-95	
772	Reg. (EC) No 1325/95 amending Reg. (EC) No 517/94: common rules for imports of textile products from certain third countries	COM(94) 633, Bull. 12-94/1.3.145							OJ L 128/13.6.95, Bull. 6-95/1.4.36	Amended Reg.: OJ L 67/10.3.94

° = Opinion of the Committee of the Regions.

* = Cooperation procedure used.

Development policy

General aspects and cooperation with the year 2000 in view

	Commission proposal	ESC opinion/ COR opinion°	EP first*/ sole reading	Amended Commission proposal	Council common position	EP second reading	Re-examined Commission proposal	Adoption by Council	Comments
778	Prop. for a Reg.: aid for population policies in developing countries	OJ C 310/22.11.95, COM(95) 295, Bull. 9-95/1.4.22							
778	Prop. for a Reg.: decentralized co-operation in development	OJ C 250/26.9.95, COM(95) 290, Bull. 7/8-95/1.4.49	OJ C 17/22.1.96, Bull. 12-95*						

Generalized system of preferences

	Commission proposal	ESC opinion/ COR opinion°	EP first*/ sole reading	Amended Commission proposal	Council common position	EP second reading	Re-examined Commission proposal	Adoption by Council	Comments
781	Reg. extending Reg. (EEC) Nos 3833/90, 3835/90, 3900/91, and (EC) No 2651/95 and amending Reg. (EC) No 3282/94: generalized preferences	COM(95) 626, Bull. 12-95						Bull. 12-95	Reg. (EEC) prolonged: OJ L 370/31.12.90, 368/31.12.91, 273/16.11.95, and amended: OJ L 348/31.12.94

Cooperation through the services of the NGOs

	Commission proposal	ESC opinion/ COR opinion°	EP first*/ sole reading	Amended Commission proposal	Council common position	EP second reading	Re-examined Commission proposal	Adoption by Council	Comments
786	Prop. for a Reg.: co-financing operations with NGOs	OJ C 251/27.9.95, COM(95) 292, Bull. 7/8-95/1.4.53	OJ C 17/22.1.96, Bull. 12-95*						

TABLE II — CONSULTATION, COOPERATION, ASSENT   557

'EC Investment Partners' (ECIP) instrument

	Commission proposal	ESC opinion/ COR opinion°	EP first*/ sole reading	Amended Commission proposal	Council common position	EP second reading	Re-examined Commission proposal	Adoption by Council	Comments
788	Prop. for a Reg.: EC Investment Partners (ECIP) — OJ C 287/15.10.94, COM(94) 358, Bull. 7/8-94/1.3.114		OJ C 323/21.11.94, Bull. 10-94/1.3.98*	COM(95) 686	OJ C 160/26.6.95, Bull. 5-95/1.4.49	OJ C 308/20.11.95, Bull. 10-95/1.4.45			

Environmental protection

	Commission proposal	ESC opinion/ COR opinion°	EP first*/ sole reading	Amended Commission proposal	Council common position	EP second reading	Re-examined Commission proposal	Adoption by Council	Comments
789	Prop. for a Reg.: environmental measures in developing countries — COM(95) 294, Bull. 6-95/1.4.42	Bull. 12-95							

North-South cooperation in the fight against drugs

	Commission proposal	ESC opinion/ COR opinion°	EP first*/ sole reading	Amended Commission proposal	Council common position	EP second reading	Re-examined Commission proposal	Adoption by Council	Comments
791	Prop. for a Reg.: North-South co-operation in the campaign against drugs — OJ C 242/19.9.95, COM(95) 296, Bull. 6-95/1.4.46								

North-South cooperation in connection with health and HIV/AIDS

	Commission proposal	ESC opinion/ COR opinion°	EP first*/ sole reading	Amended Commission proposal	Council common position	EP second reading	Re-examined Commission proposal	Adoption by Council	Comments
793	Prop. for a Reg.: campaigns against AIDS in developing countries — OJ C 252/28.9.95, COM(95) 293, Bull. 7/8-95/1.4.52								

° = Opinion of the Committee of the Regions.
* = Cooperation procedure used.

Aid for rehabilitation

	Commission proposal	ESC opinion/ COR opinion°	EP first*/ sole reading	Amended Commission proposal	Council common position	EP second reading	Re-examined Commission proposal	Adoption by Council	Comments
794	Prop. for a Reg.: rehabilitation in developing countries	OJ C 253/9.9.95, COM(95) 291, Bull. 6-95/1.4.49		OJ C 17/22.1.96, Bull. 12-95*						Political Agreement on a common position: Bull. 12/95
794	Prop. for a Reg.: financial support for rehabilitation in southern Africa	COM(95) 175, Bull. 5-95/1.4.110		OJ C 17/22.1.96, Bull. 12-95*						

Food aid

796	Prop. for a Reg.: food aid and food security	OJ C 253/29.9.95, COM(95) 283, Bull. 7/8-95/1.4.56		OJ C 17/22.1.96, Bull. 12-95*						Political Agreement on a common position: Bull. 12/95

Aid to refugees

798	Prop. for a Reg.: aid for uprooted peoples in developing countries in Asia and Latin America	OJ C 237/12.9.95, COM(95) 297, Bull. 6-95/1.4.106								

TABLE II — CONSULTATION, COOPERATION, ASSENT   559

Humanitarian aid

General strategy

	Commission proposal	ESC opinion/ COR opinion°	EP first*/ sole reading	Amended Commission proposal	Council common position	EP second reading	Re-examined Commission proposal	Adoption by Council	Comments
800	Prop. for a Reg.: humanitarian aid	OJ C 180/14.7.95, COM(95) 201, Bull. 5-95/1.4.55		OJ C 339/18.12.95, Bull. 11-95/1.4.36*	COM(95) 721, Bull. 12-95					Political Agreement on a common position Bull. 12-95

Relations with Mediterranean third countries and Middle East countries

Mediterranean third countries

	Commission proposal	ESC opinion/ COR opinion°	EP first*/ sole reading	Amended Commission proposal	Council common position	EP second reading	Re-examined Commission proposal	Adoption by Council	Comments
840	Prop. for a Reg.: financial and technical measures to support reforms in Mediterranean countries (MEDA)	OJ C 232/6.9.95, COM(95) 204, Bull. 6-95/1.4.69		OJ C 17/22.1.96, Bull. 12-95						
844	Prop. for a Reg.: financial cooperation measure for Turkey	OJ C 271/17.10.95, COM(95) 389, Bull. 7/8-95/1.4.77		OJ C 17/22.1.96, Bull. 12-95						
845	Prop. for a Reg. amending Reg. (EEC) No 3906/89: economic aid to Bosnia	COM(95) 728, Bull. 12-95								Reg. to be amended: OJ L 375/23.12.89
845	Reg. (EC) No 2815/95 suspending Reg. (EEC) No 990/93 and repealing Reg. (EC) No 2472/94: Serbia and Montenegro	COM(95) 610, Bull. 11-95/1.4.66							OJ L 297/9.12.95	Suspended Reg.: OJ L 102/28.4.93 and Repealed Reg.: OJ L 272/15.10.94

° = Opinion of the Committee of the Regions.
* = Cooperation procedure used.

	Commission proposal	ESC opinion/ COR opinion°	EP first*/ sole reading	Amended Commission proposal	Council common position	EP second reading	Re-examined Commission proposal	Adoption by Council	Comments
845	Reg. (EC) No 3032/95 amending Reg. (EC) Nos 3355/94, 3356/94 and 3357/94: imports from Bosnia-Herzegovina, Croatia and the FYROM	COM(95) 718, Bull. 12-95						OJ L 316/30.12.95, Bull. 12-95	Amended Reg.: OJ L 353/31.12.94
845	Reg. (EC) No 1366/95 amending Reg. (EEC) No 3906/89: extension of economic aid to Croatia	OJ C 360/17.12.94, COM(94) 526, Bull. 11-94/1.3.41		OJ C 126/22.5.95, Bull. 4-95/1.4.76					OJ L 133/17.6.95, Bull. 6-95/1.4.77	Political Agreement: Bull. 5-95/1.4.71

Relations with the independent States of the former Soviet Union and Mongolia

Assistance to the independent States of the former Soviet Union

	Commission proposal	ESC opinion/ COR opinion°	EP first*/ sole reading	Amended Commission proposal	Council common position	EP second reading	Re-examined Commission proposal	Adoption by Council	Comments
871	Prop. for a Reg.: TACIS	OJ C 134/1.6.95, COM(95) 12, Bull. 1/2-95/1.4.102		OJ C 323/4.12.95					Basic Reg. No 2053/93: OJ L 187/29.7.93

Bilateral relations

	Commission proposal	ESC opinion/ COR opinion°	EP first*/ sole reading	Amended Commission proposal	Council common position	EP second reading	Re-examined Commission proposal	Adoption by Council	Comments
882	Prop. for a Dec.: macro-financial aid to Moldova	COM(95) 533, Bull. 11-95/1.4.85								

Relations with the United States, Japan and the other industrialized countries

Japan

	Commission proposal	ESC opinion/ COR opinion°	EP first*/ sole reading	Amended Commission proposal	Council common position	EP second reading	Re-examined Commission proposal	Adoption by Council	Comments
903	Prop. for a Reg.: promotion of exports to Japan	COM(95) 188, Bull. 5-95/1.4.93								

TABLE II — CONSULTATION, COOPERATION, ASSENT   561

Relations with the African, Caribbean and Pacific (ACP) countries and the overseas countries and territories (OCTs)

Relations with South Africa

	Commission proposal	ESC opinion/ COR opinion°	EP first*/ sole reading	Amended Commission proposal	Council common position	EP second reading	Re-examined Commission proposal	Adoption by Council	Comments
953	Prop. for a Reg.: financial, technical and economic cooperation with South Africa	OJ C 235/9.9.95, COM(95) 174, Bull. 5-95/1.4.111	OJ C 287/30.10.95, Bull. 10-95/1.4.127°		Bull. 12-95				

Relations with overseas countries and territories (OCTs)

	Commission proposal	ESC opinion/ COR opinion°	EP first*/ sole reading	Amended Commission proposal	Council common position	EP second reading	Re-examined Commission proposal	Adoption by Council	Comments
955	Prop. for a Dec.: transitional measures for the ACP countries	COM(95) 355, Bull. 7/8-95/1.5.115							

Financing Community activities

Budgets

Financial control

	Commission proposal	ESC opinion/ COR opinion°	EP first*/ sole reading	Amended Commission proposal	Council common position	EP second reading	Re-examined Commission proposal	Adoption by Council	Comments
997	Reg. (EC, Euratom, ECSC) No 2333/95 amending the Financial Regulation of 21.12.77	OJ C 254/1.10.92, COM(92) 358, Bull. 9-92/1.5.3	OJ C 329/6.12.93, Bull. 11-93/1.6.8	OJ C 56/24.2.94, COM(94) 14, Bull. 1/2-94/1.5.5				OJ L 240/7.10.95, Bull. 9-95/1.6.2	Common position of the Council: Bull. 6-95/1.6.4; Amended Reg.: OJ L 356/31.12.77

° = Opinion of the Committee of the Regions.
* = Cooperation procedure used.

	Commission proposal	ESC opinion/ COR opinion°	EP first*/ sole reading	Amended Commission proposal	Council common position	EP second reading	Re-examined Commission proposal	Adoption by Council	Comments
997	Reg. (EC, Euratom, ECSC) No 2334/95 amending the Financial Regulation of 21.12.77	OJ C 221/17.8.93, COM(93) 328, Bull. 7/8 93/1.5.2, 27th GR/ 1081		OJ C 205/25.7.94, Bull. 5-94/1.4.2	OJ C 225/13.8.94, COM(94) 288, Bull. 7/8-94/1.4.8				OJ L 240/7.10.95, Bull. 9-95/1.6.3	Common position of the Council: Bull. 6-95/1.6.5; Amended Reg.: OJ L 356/31.12.77
997	Reg. (EC, Euratom, ECSC) No 2335/95 amending the Financial Regulation of 21/12/77 (general budget)	OJ C 237/25.8.94, COM(94) 338, Bull. 7/8-94/1.4.6		OJ C 89/10.4.95, Bull. 3-95/1.6.6	OJ C 185/19.7.95, COM(95) 208, Bull. 6-95/1.6.6				OJ L 240/7.10.95, Bull. 9-95/1.6.4	Common position of the Council: Bull. 6-95/1.6.6; Amended Reg.: OJ L 356/31.12.77
997	Reg. (EC) No 1287/95 amending Reg. (EEC) No 729/70: financing of the CAP	OJ C 284/12.10.94, COM(94) 240, Bull. 7/8-94/1.2.138		OJ C 89/10.4.95, Bull. 3-95/1.3.125	OJ C 150/17.6.95, COM(95) 161, Bull. 5-95/1.3.110				OJ L 125/8.6.95, Bull. 5-95/1.3.110	Amended Reg.: OJ L 94/28.4.70

Action to combat fraud

	Commission proposal	ESC opinion/ COR opinion°	EP first*/ sole reading	Amended Commission proposal	Council common position	EP second reading	Re-examined Commission proposal	Adoption by Council	Comments
1008	Reg. (EC, Euratom) No 2988/95: protection of the Communities' financial interests	OJ C 216/6.8.94, COM(94) 214, Bull. 5-94/1.5.11		OJ C 89/10.4.95, Bull. 3-95/1.6.10					OJ L 312/23.12.95, Bull. 12-95	Common position of the Council: Bull. 6-95/1.6.10; EP Opinion on a common position: OJ C 339/18.12.95, Bull. 11-95/1.6.12
1008	Prop. for a Reg. (EC, Euratom): checks and audits (financial interests)	COM(95) 690, Bull. 12-95								

TABLE II — CONSULTATION, COOPERATION, ASSENT   563

Institutions and other bodies

Administration and management

Personnel management and Staff Regulations of officials

	Commission proposal	ESC opinion/ COR opinion°	EP first*/ sole reading	Amended Commission proposal	Council common position	EP second reading	Re-examined Commission proposal	Adoption by Council	Comments
1093 Reg. (EC, Euratom, ECSC) No 2688/95: terminating the service of officials	OJ C 246/22.9.95, COM(95) 327		OJ C 287/30.10.95					OJ L 280/23.11.95	
1093 Reg. (EC, Euratom, ECSC) No 2689/95: terminating the service of officials	OJ C 246/22.9.95, COM(95) 327		OJ C 287/30.10.95					OJ L 280/23.11.95	

Translation and interpreting (The Translation Service and The Joint Interpreting and Conference Service)

	Commission proposal	ESC opinion/ COR opinion°	EP first*/ sole reading	Amended Commission proposal	Council common position	EP second reading	Re-examined Commission proposal	Adoption by Council	Comments
1116 Reg. (EC) No 2610/95 amending Reg. (EC) No 2965/94: EC Translation Centre	OJ C 143/9.6.95, COM(95) 125			COM(95) 125				OJ L 268/10.11.95	Amended Reg.: OJ L 314/7.12.94

° = Opinion of the Committee of the Regions.
° = Cooperation procedure used.

TABLE III — INTERNATIONAL AGREEMENTS   565

Annex III

Table III: Legislation regarding international agreements

	Commission recommendation	Council Decision/ Negotiating Directives	Initials	Signature	Commission proposal/ Conclusion	ESC opinion/ COR opinion°	EP opinion/ EP assent*	Council Regulation (or Decision)/ Conclusion	Comments

Community economic and social area

Internal market

Free movement of goods

	Commission recommendation	Council Decision/ Negotiating Directives	Initials	Signature	Commission proposal/ Conclusion	ESC opinion/ COR opinion°	EP opinion/ EP assent*	Council Regulation (or Decision)/ Conclusion	Comments
102 Draft Unidroit Convention on the return of cultural objects		Bull. 6-95/1.3.19							
114 Draft Agreement with third countries on sanitary and phytosanitary measures		Bull. 1/2-95/1.3.10							

Intellectual and industrial property

	Commission recommendation	Council Decision/ Negotiating Directives	Initials	Signature	Commission proposal/ Conclusion	ESC opinion/ COR opinion°	EP opinion/ EP assent*	Council Regulation (or Decision)/ Conclusion	Comments
134 Draft European Convention on copyright and neighbouring rights	COM(95) 154, Bull. 5-95/1.3.21								

NB: Agreements that do not require consultation of Parliament are not followed by an asterisk.
° Opinion of the Committee of the Regions.
* Agreements requiring Parliament's assent.

Government procurement

	Commission recommendation	Council Decision/ Negotiating Directives	Initials	Signature	Commission proposal/ Conclusion	ESC opinion/ COR opinion°	EP opinion/ EP assent*	Council Regulation (or Decision) Conclusion	Comments
136	Agreement with the United States on government procurement					OJ C 291/19.10.94, COM(94) 251, Bull. 6-94/1.2.42, OJ C 48/25.2.95, COM(95) 18, Bull. 1/2-95/1.3.21		OJ C 151/19.6.95, Bull. 5-95/1.3.22*	Dec. 95/215/EC: OJ L 134/20.6.95, Bull. 5-95/1.3.22	

Competition policy

International aspects

	Commission recommendation	Council Decision/ Negotiating Directives	Initials	Signature	Commission proposal/ Conclusion	ESC opinion/ COR opinion°	EP opinion/ EP assent*	Council Regulation (or Decision) Conclusion	Comments
173	Agreement with the United States on competition					COM(94) 430, Bull. 10-94/1.2.47		OJ C 43/20.2.95, Bull. 1/2-95/1.3.58, OJ C 89/10.4.95, Bull. 3-95/1.3.58	Dec. 95/145/EC, ECSC: OJ L 95/27.4.95, Bull. 4-95/1.3.56	
173	Draft Agreement with Canada on competition	Bull. 10-94/1.2.48	Bull. 1/2-95/1.3.59							

Industrial policy

Individual sectors

	Commission recommendation	Council Decision/ Negotiating Directives	Initials	Signature	Commission proposal/ Conclusion	ESC opinion/ COR opinion°	EP opinion/ EP assent*	Council Regulation (or Decision) Conclusion	Comments
201	Draft Cooperation Agreement with the United States, Japan, Canada, Australia, Norway and Switzerland on intelligent manufacturing systems (IMS)	Bull. 3-95/1.3.66								

TABLE III — INTERNATIONAL AGREEMENTS 567

Research and technology

Implementation of specific programmes of the fourth framework programme

	Commission recommendation	Council Decision/ Negotiating Directives	Initials	Signature	Commission proposal/ Conclusion	ESC opinion/ COR opinion°	EP opinion/ EP assent*	Council Regulation (or Decision) Conclusion	Comments
250	Memorandum of Understanding between the EAEC and Canada (nuclear fusion)	Bull. 11-91/1.2.41		Bull. 7/8-95/1.3.80	COM(94) 343; Bull. 9-94/1.2.97			Council Dec.: Bull. 1/2-95/1.3.66; Commission Dec.: Bull. 6-95/1.3.87	
255	Draft Agreement with Switzerland on participation in the Community's technological research and development programmes	Bull. 6-94/1.2.102	Bull. 10-94/1.3.17						
257	Draft Agreement with Canada on scientific and technical cooperation	Bull. 12-92/1.3.115	Bull. 4-93/1.2.69	Bull. 6-95/1.3.86	OJ C 317/28.11.95, COM(95) 419, Bull. 9-95/1.3.45		OJ C 17/22.1.96, Bull. 12-95		Commission Recommendation for a signature: COM(94) 551, Bull. 12-94/1.2.103
257	Draft Agreement with South Africa on scientific and technical cooperation	Bull. 7/8-95/1.3.79							
257	Draft Agreement with Israel on scientific and technical cooperation		Bull. 9-94/1.2.99						Recommendation for a Commission Dec. concerning the signature: COM(95) 664, Bull. 12/95

° Opinion of the Committee of the Regions.
* Agreements requiring Parliament's assent.

Education, vocational training and youth

Cooperation with non-member countries

	Commission recommendation	Council Decision/ Negotiating Directives	Initials	Signature	Commission proposal/ Conclusion	ESC opinion/ COR opinion[c]	EP opinion/ EP assent[a]	Council Regulation (or Decision) Conclusion	Comments
284 Cooperation Agreement with Cyprus on education, training and youth	Bull. 7/8-95/1.3.84							Dec.: Bull. 12-95	
284 Cooperation Agreement with Malta on education, training and youth	Bull. 7/8-95/1.3.84							Dec.: Bull. 12-95	
285 Cooperation Agreement with the United States on training and higher education	Bull. 9-94/1.2.188	Bull. 11-94/1.2.211			OJ C 231/5.9.95, COM(95) 120, Bull. 4-95/1.3.66		OJ C 287/30.10.95, Bull. 10-95/1.3.105	Dec. 95/487/EC: OJ L 279/22.11.95, Bull. 10-95/1.3.105	
285 Cooperation Agreement with Canada on training and higher education	Bull. 9-94/1.2.188	Bull. 11-94/1.2.211			COM(95) 77, Bull. 7/8-95/1.3.83		OJ C 287/30.10.95, Bull. 10-95/1.3.104	Dec. 95/523/EC: OJ L 300/13.12.95, Bull. 11-95/1.3.80	Political Agreement: Bull. 10-95/1.3.104

Energy

Relations with third countries

	Commission recommendation	Council Decision/ Negotiating Directives	Initials	Signature	Commission proposal/ Conclusion	ESC opinion/ COR opinion[c]	EP opinion/ EP assent[a]	Council Regulation (or Decision) Conclusion	Comments
370 Treaty on the European Energy Charter				Bull. 12-94/1.2.110	OJ C 344/6.12.94, COM(94) 405, Bull. 9-94/1.2.108; COM(94) 557, Bull. 11-94/1.2.93; COM(95) 440, Bull. 9-95/1.3.68		OJ C 18/23.1.95, Bull. 12-94/1.2.110		Opinion of the ECSC Consultative Committee: Bull. 10-94/1.2.61; Council Dec. concerning the provisional application: OJ L 380/31.12.94, Bull. 12-94/1.2.110

TABLE III — INTERNATIONAL AGREEMENTS 569

		Commission recommendation	Council Decision/Negotiating Directives	Initials	Signature	Commission proposal/Conclusion	ESC opinion/COR opinion°	EP opinion/EP assent*	Council Regulation (or Decision) Conclusion	Comments
370	Protocol on energy efficiency	COM(94) 531, Bull. 11-94/1.2.94			Bull. 12-94/1.2.111	COM(95) 440, Bull. 9-95/1.3.69				Dec. concerning the signature: Bull. 11-94/1.2.94
374	Draft Agreement on nuclear cooperation with Kazakhstan	Bull. 7/8-94/1.2.85	Bull. 6-95/1.3.119							
374	Draft Agreement on nuclear cooperation with Ukraine	Bull. 7/8-94/1.2.85	Bull. 6-95/1.3.119							
374	Draft Agreement on nuclear cooperation with Kyrgyzstan	Bull. 7/8-94/1.2.85								
374	Draft Agreement on nuclear cooperation with Tadjikistan	Bull. 7/8-94/1.2.85								
374	Draft Agreement on nuclear cooperation with Uzbekistan	Bull. 7/8-94/1.2.85								
376	Draft Agreement between Euratom and Argentina on the peaceful uses of nuclear energy	Bull. 6-95/1.3.118	Bull. 12-95							
378	Agreement with the United States on the peaceful uses of nuclear energy		Bull. 12-91/1.2.126		Bull. 11-95/1.3.109	COM(95) 171, Bull. 5-95/1.3.66			Bull. 7/8-95/1.3.110	

Transport
International cooperation

		Commission recommendation	Council Decision/Negotiating Directives	Initials	Signature	Commission proposal/Conclusion	ESC opinion/COR opinion°	EP opinion/EP assent*	Council Regulation (or Decision) Conclusion	Comments
415	Draft Agreement with Switzerland on road and air transport	Bull. 9-93/1.2.80, Bull. 1/2-94/1.2.97, Bull. 3-95/1.3.102	Bull. 3-95/1.3.102							

° Opinion of the Committee of the Regions.
* Agreements requiring Parliament's assent.

	Commission recommendation	Council Decision/ Negotiating Directives	Initials	Signature	Commission proposal/ Conclusion	ESC opinion/ COR opinion°	EP opinion/ EP assent°	Council Regulation (or Decision) Conclusion	Comments
416 Draft Agreement with the United States on civil aviation	Bull. 4-95/1.3.92								
417 Draft Transport Agreement with Croatia	Bull. 1/2-95/1.3.95								
417 Transport Agreement with Slovenia	Bull. 10-92/1.3.72	Bull. 10-92/1.3.72	Bull. 1/2-93/1.2.110	Bull. 3-93/1.2.71, Bull. 4-93/1.2.77	OJ C 93/2.4.93, COM(93) 57, Bull. 1/2-93/1.2.110	OJ C 201/26.7.93, Bull. 5-93/1.2.76	OJ C 194/19.7.93, Bull. 6-93/1.2.119	Dec. 93/409/EEC: OJ L 189/29.7.93, Bull. 7/8-93/1.2.108	
417 Additional Protocol to the Transport Agreement with Slovenia		29.6.95							
417 Draft Agreement with the FYROM	Bull. 11-95/1.3.123								
418 Draft Agreement on the occasional transport of travellers (EEC)		Bull. 12-95							
418 Draft Transit Agreement with Hungary, Romania and Bulgaria		Bull. 12-95							

Environment

Quality of the environment and natural resources

	Commission recommendation	Council Decision/ Negotiating Directives	Initials	Signature	Commission proposal/ Conclusion	ESC opinion/ COR opinion°	EP opinion/ EP assent°	Council Regulation (or Decision) Conclusion	Comments
495 Convention on the protection and use of transboundary watercourses and international lakes	Bull. 1/2-92/1.3.155			Bull. 3-92/1.2.131	OJ C 212/5.8.93, COM(93) 271, Bull. 6-93/1.2.163	OJ C 34/2.2.94, Bull. 11-93/1.2.135	OJ C 128/9.4.94, Bull. 4-94/1.2.151	Dec. 95/308/EC: OJ L 186/5.8.95, Bull. 7/8-95/1.3.137	Prop. for a Commission Dec. concerning the signature: COM(92) 70, Bull. 3-92/1.2.131

TABLE III — INTERNATIONAL AGREEMENTS   571

		Commission recommendation	Council Decision/ Negotiating Directives	Initials	Signature	Commission proposal/ Conclusion	ESC opinion/ COR opinion°	EP opinion/ EP assent*	Council Regulation (or Decision) Conclusion	Comments
495	Draft Convention for the protection of the marine environment of the North-East Atlantic		Bull. 7/8-92/1.3.153		Bull. 9-92/1.2.102	OJ C 172/7.7.95, COM(94) 660, Bull. 1/2-95/1.3.110		OJ C 89/10.4.95, Bull. 3-95/1.3.107		Prop. concerning the signature: COM(92) 322, Bull. 7/8-92/1.3.153; Dec. concerning the signature: Bull. 9-92/1.2.102
498	Draft Agreement on the conservation of African and Eurasian migratory waterbirds		Bull. 7/8-95/1.3.141			COM(95) 444				Prop. for a Commission Dec. concerning the signature: COM(95) 444, Bull. 9-95/1.3.93
498	Draft Agreement on the conservation of small cetaceans of the Mediterranean and Black Seas	Bull. 9-95/1.3.94								
498	Draft Convention on the protection of vertebrate animals used for experimental purposes				Bull. 2-87/2.1.94	OJ C 200/5.8.89, COM(89) 302, Bull. 7/8-89/2.1.135; COM(94) 366, Bull. 9-94/1.2.173	OJ C 329/30.12.89, Bull. 10-89/2.1.116	OJ C 291/20.11.89, Bull. 10-89/2.1.116; OJ C 269/16.10.95, Bull. 9-95/1.3.92		
499	Draft revision of the Convention for the protection of the Mediterranean Sea and its Protocols	COM(95) 202, Bull. 5-95/1.3.91	Bull. 6-95/1.3.153		Bull. 6-95/1.3.153					
499	Alpine Convention	Bull. 3-91/1.2.71	Bull. 5-91/1.2.156		Bull. 11-91/1.2.185	OJ C 278/5.10.94, COM(94) 336, Bull. 9-94/1.2.171	Bull. 1/2-95/1.3.112	Bull. 12-94/1.2.208		Council Agreement on the conclusion: Bull. 12-94/1.2.208
503	Draft amendment to the Montreal Protocol (ozone layer)	Bull. 10-95/1.3.159	Bull. 11-95/1.3.147							Political Agreement: Bull. 10-95/1.3.159
505	Draft Protocol to the Convention on biological diversity concerning biosafety	Bull. 9-95/1.3.91	Bull. 10-95/1.3.160							

° Opinion of the Committee of the Regions.
* Agreements requiring Parliament's assent.

	Commission recommendation	Council Decision/ Negotiating Directives	Initials	Signature	Commission proposal/ Conclusion	ESC opinion/ COR opinion°	EP opinion/ EP assent*	Council Regulation (or Decision) Conclusion	Comments

Nuclear safety

International action

516	Agreement between Euratom and Switzerland on the latter's inclusion in the Ecurie arrangements (urgent radiological information exchange)								Commission Dec. concerning the conclusion: Bull. 6-95/1.3.159

Agricultural policy

Content of the common agricultural policy

533	Draft Agreement with New Zealand: trade in wine — Bull. 12-95								

Management of the common agricultural policy

535	Provisional application of the Draft International Cereals Agreement — OJ C 191/25.7.95, COM(95) 183, Bull. 5-95/1.3.113			Bull. 6-95/1.3.181			OJ C 287/30.10.95, Bull. 10-95/1.3.197	Dec. 96/88/EC: OJ L 21/27.1.96, Bull. 12-95	Recommendation concerning the provisional application: OJ C 204/9.8.95, COM(95) 280, Bull. 6-95/1.3.181

TABLE III — INTERNATIONAL AGREEMENTS   573

Fisheries

External resources

	Commission recommendation	Council Decision/ Negotiating Directives	Initials	Signature	Commission proposal/ Conclusion	ESC opinion/ COR opinion°	EP opinion/ EP assent*	Council Regulation (or Decision) Conclusion	Comments
578 Provisional application of the Fisheries Agreement with Canada in the context of the NAFO Convention			Bull. 4-95/1.3.121	Bull. 4-95/1.3.121	OJ C 239/14.9.95, COM(95) 251, Bull. 6-95/1.3.191		OJ C 17/22.1.96, Bull. 12-95	OJ L 327/30.12.95, Bull. 12-95	Commission Prop. concerning the signature and the provisional application: OJ L 308/21.12.95, COM(95) 400, Bull. 4-95/1.3.121
580 Draft Fisheries Agreement with Namibia	Bull. 5-95/1.2.138	Bull. 1/2-95/1.3.148							
580 Draft Fisheries Agreement with South Africa		Bull. 9-95/1.3.108							
580 Draft Fisheries Agreement with Estonia, Latvia, Lithuania, Poland and the Russian Federation		Bull. 12-95							
581 Protocol to the Fisheries Agreement with Guinea (1995)					OJ L 188/22.7.94, COM(94) 138, Bull. 4-94/1.2.134		OJ C 43/20.2.95, Bull. 1/2-95/1.3.146	Reg. (EC) No 2663/95; OJ L 278/21.11.95, Bull. 778-95/1.3.167	
581 Fisheries Protocol with Equatorial Guinea (1994-97)					COM(94) 387, Bull. 9-94/1.2.160		OJ C 56/6.3.95, Bull. 1/2-95/1.3.147	Reg. (EC) No 1892/95: OJ L 180/31.7.95, Bull. 6-95/1.3.188	
581 Fisheries Protocol with Cape Verde (1994-97)					COM(94) 388, Bull. 9-94/1.2.155		OJ C 89/10.4.95, Bull. 3-95/1.3.132	Reg. (EC) No 2028/95: OJ L 199/24.8.95, Bull. 6-95/1.3.185	

° Opinion of the Committee of the Regions.
* Agreements requiring Parliament's assent.

	Commission recommendation	Council Decision/ Negotiating Directives	Initials	Signature	Commission proposal/ Conclusion	ESC opinion/ COR opinion°	EP opinion/ EP assent*	Council Regulation (or Decision) Conclusion	Comments
581 Fisheries Protocol with the Comoros (1994-97)					COM(94) 390, Bull. 9-94/1.2.156		OJ C 89/10.4.95, Bull. 3-95/1.3.133	Reg. (EC) No 1893/95: OJ L 180/31.7.95, Bull. 6-95/1.3.186	
581 Fisheries Protocol with the Côte d'Ivoire (1994-97)					COM(94) 385, Bull. 9-94/1.2.157		OJ C 109/1.5.95, Bull. 4-95/1.3.118	Reg. (EC) No 1894/95: OJ L 180/31.7.95, Bull. 6-95/1.3.187	
581 Fisheries Protocol with Senegal (1994-96)					COM(94) 514, Bull. 11-94/1.2.172		OJ C 151/19.6.95, Bull. 5-95/1.3.117	Reg. (EC) No 1982/95: OJ L 193/16.8.95, Bull. 6-95/1.3.189	
581 Provisional application of the Fisheries Protocol with Senegal (1994-96)					COM(94) 514, Bull. 11-94/1.2.172			Bull. 1/2-95/1.3.149	
581 Provisional implementation of the Fisheries Protocol with Guinea-Bissau (1995-97) and financial compensation					OJ C 327/7.12.95, COM(95) 427, Bull. 9-95/1.3.109			Bull. 11-95/1.3.176	
581 Agreement with Madagascar on the provisional application of the Protocol to the Fisheries Agreement					COM(95) 376, Bull. 7/8-95/1.3.168			OJ L 282/24.11.95, Bull. 11-95/1.3.177	
582 Draft Fisheries Agreement with Morocco	Bull. 10-94/1.2.96	Bull. 11-94/1.2.171	Bull. 11-95/1.3.178		Bull. 11-95/1.3.178, COM(95) 608				Dec. concerning the provisional application: Bull. 11-95/1.3.178

TABLE III — INTERNATIONAL AGREEMENTS   575

The European Union's role in the world

International organizations and conferences

United Nations and specialist organizations

	Commission recommendation	Council Decision/ Negotiating Directives	Initials	Signature	Commission proposal/ Conclusion	ESC opinion/ COR opinion°	EP opinion/ EP assent*	Council Regulation (or Decision) Conclusion	Comments
717 Draft Treaty on Trade Mark Law	Bull. 6-94/1.2.40	Bull. 9-94/1.2.33							Commission Recommendation for a signature: Bull. 3-95/1.3.18; Council Dec. on the signature: Bull. 6-95/1.3.43

World Trade Organization (WTO)

	Commission recommendation	Council Decision/ Negotiating Directives	Initials	Signature	Commission proposal/ Conclusion	ESC opinion/ COR opinion°	EP opinion/ EP assent*	Council Regulation (or Decision) Conclusion	Comments
720 Draft Agreements with the WTO members on services		Bull. 3-95/1.4.14, Bull. 7/8-95/1.4.20						Council approval of WTO services: Bull. 7/8-95/1.4.20	Extension of negotiations: Bull. 6-95/1.4.21

Organization for Economic Cooperation and Development (OECD)

	Commission recommendation	Council Decision/ Negotiating Directives	Initials	Signature	Commission proposal/ Conclusion	ESC opinion/ COR opinion°	EP opinion/ EP assent*	Council Regulation (or Decision) Conclusion	Comments
734 Draft Multilateral Investment Agreement	Bull. 5-95/1.4.19	Bull. 11-95/1.4.12							

° Opinion of the Committee of the Regions.
* Agreements requiring Parliament's assent.

Common commercial policy

General matters

	Commission recommendation	Council Decision/ Negotiating Directives	Initials	Signature	Commission proposal/ Conclusion	ESC opinion/ COR opinion°	EP opinion/ EP assent*	Council Regulation (or Decision) Conclusion	Comments
737 Draft Amendment to the Agreement of 22 July 1972 with Switzerland	Bull. 12-95								
739 Draft Customs Convention on containers used in international transport				Bull. 4-95/1.4.33					Commission Prop. on the signature: COM(95) 33, Bull. 1/2-95/1.4.40
740 Draft Agreement on the harmonization of non-preferential rules of origin	Bull. 1/2-95/1.4.41	Bull. 1/2-95/1.4.41							

Individual sectors

	Commission recommendation	Council Decision/ Negotiating Directives	Initials	Signature	Commission proposal/ Conclusion	ESC opinion/ COR opinion°	EP opinion/ EP assent*	Council Regulation (or Decision) Conclusion	Comments
763 Agreements with Russia and Ukraine on steel products	Bull. 12-93/1.3.93	Bull. 6-94/1.3.86		Bull. 12-95				Adoption by the Commission: Bull. 11-95/1.4.26	
764 Draft Free Trade Agreement with Turkey on ECSC products	Bull. 6-95/1.4.74	Bull. 10-95/1.4.77							Draft Decisions concerning the conclusion: Bull. 6-95/1.4.33; assent of the Council: Bull. 10-95/1.4.39. Political agreement on the guidelines for negotiation: Bull. 10-95/1.4.77; ECSC Consultative Committee: Bull. 12-95; assent of the Council: Bull. 12-95

TABLE III — INTERNATIONAL AGREEMENTS 577

	Commission recommendation	Council Decision/ Negotiating Directives	Initials	Signature	Commission proposal/ Conclusion	ESC opinion/ COR opinion°	EP opinion/ EP assent*	Council Regulation (or Decision) Conclusion	Comments
766 Draft Protocols to the Textile Agreements and Bilateral Arrangements to allow for enlargement	Bull. 9-94/1.3.55	Bull. 10-94/1.3.94							Council Dec. 95/131/EC concerning the provisional application: OJ L 94/26.4.95, Bull. 1/2-95/1.4.61
767 Agreement amending the MFA Agreement with China on textile products			Bull. 1/2-95/1.4.60		COM(95) 109, Bull. 3-95/1.4.38			Dec. 94/440/EC: OJ L 261/31.10.95, Bull. 6-95/1.4.38	
767 Draft Agreement with China on trade in textile products	Bull. 10-95/1.4.41	Bull. 10-95/1.4.41	Bull. 12-95						
767 Draft Agreement amending the Textile Agreement with Vietnam		Bull. 4-95/1.4.53							
769 Draft Textile Agreement with Croatia	Bull. 5-95/1.4.43								
769 Arrangement with Turkey on clothing products	Bull. 11-94/1.3.97	Bull. 11-94/1.3.97						Bull. 9-95/1.4.21	
769 Draft Agreement with the United Arab Emirates on textile products	Bull. 4-94/1.3.86								
770 Agreement with Mongolia on trade in textile products					Bull. 7/8-93/1.3.102			Dec. 95/441/EC: OJ L 261/31.10.95, Bull. 6-95/1.4.39	Dec. 94/277/EC concerning the provisional application of the Agreement: OJ L 123/17.5.94, Bull. 12-93/1.3.96

° Opinion of the Committee of the Regions.
* Agreements requiring Parliament's assent.

Development policy

Aid to refugees

	Commission recommendation	Council Decision/ Negotiating Directives	Initials	Signature	Commission proposal/ Conclusion	ESC opinion/ COR opinion°	EP opinion/ EP assent*	Council Regulation (or Decision) Conclusion	Comments
798 Draft Convention with UNRWA (1996-98)	Bull. 7/8-95/1.4.59	Bull. 10-95/1.4.50							

The European Economic Area and relations with the European Free Trade Association

Relations with the EFTA countries

	Commission recommendation	Council Decision/ Negotiating Directives	Initials	Signature	Commission proposal/ Conclusion	ESC opinion/ COR opinion°	EP opinion/ EP assent*	Council Regulation (or Decision) Conclusion	Comments
811 Draft Protocols with Iceland, Norway and Switzerland amending the trade agreements to allow for enlargement		Bull. 3-95/1.4.50							
811 Draft Additional Protocol to the Agreement with Iceland as a result of enlargement					COM(95) 587, Bull. 11-95/1.4.41				
813 Draft Agreement with Switzerland on the free movement of persons, research, agriculture, conformity evaluation and government procurement		Bull. 10-94/1.3.17							

TABLE III — INTERNATIONAL AGREEMENTS   579

Relations with Central and Eastern Europe and the Baltic States

Europe Agreements and other agreements

	Commission recommendation	Council Decision/ Negotiating Directives	Initials	Signature	Commission proposal/ Conclusion	ESC opinion/ COR opinion°	EP opinion/ EP assent*	Council Regulation (or Decision) Conclusion	Comments
820 Draft Protocols to the Europe Agreements, free trade agreements and agreements setting certain tariff quotas as a result of enlargement		Bull. 6-95/1.4.64							
820 Draft Agreements on adjusting the Europe and Interim Agreements as a result of enlargement and the conclusion of the Uruguay Round	Bull. 11-94/1.3.21	Bull. 3-95/1.4.53, Bull. 12-95							Political Agreement on additional Directives: Bull. 11-95/1.4.50
820 Draft Agreement on amending the Additional Protocols for textile products completing the Europe Agreements		Bull. 6-95/1.4.65							
821 Additional Protocols to the Europe Association Agreements on the opening of Community programmes	Bull. 5-94/1.3.28	Bull. 7/8-94/1.3.31			COM(94) 599, Bull. 12-94/1.3.16		OJ C 323/4.12.95, Bull. 11-95/1.4.53*	EAEC-Commission Dec.: Bull. 6-95/1.4.66; Dec. 95/558 to 562/EC, Euratom: OJ L 317/30.12.95, Bull. 12-95	Council Dec. on the signature: Bull. 4-95/1.4.68

Bilateral relations

	Commission recommendation	Council Decision/ Negotiating Directives	Initials	Signature	Commission proposal/ Conclusion	ESC opinion/ COR opinion°	EP opinion/ EP assent*	Council Regulation (or Decision) Conclusion	Comments
830 Draft Europe Agreement with Latvia	Bull. 10-94/1.3.22	Bull. 11-94/1.3.25	Bull. 4-95/1.4.64	Bull. 6-95/1.4.63	COM(95) 207, Bull. 6-95/1.4.63		OJ C 323/4.12.95, Bull. 11-95/1.4.52*		

° Opinion of the Committee of the Regions.
* Agreements requiring Parliament's assent.

	Commission recommendation	Council Decision/ Negotiating Directives	Initials	Signature	Commission proposal/ Conclusion	ESC opinion/ COR opinion°	EP opinion/ EP assent°	Council Regulation (or Decision) Conclusion	Comments
830 Draft Europe Agreement with Lithuania	Bull. 10-94/1.3.22	Bull. 11-94/1.3.25	Bull. 4-95/1.4.64	Bull. 6-95/1.4.63	COM(95) 207, Bull. 6-95/1.4.63		OJ C 323/4,12.95, Bull. 11-95/1.4.52*		
830 Draft Europe Agreement with Estonia	Bull. 10-94/1.3.22	Bull. 11-94/1.3.25	Bull. 4-95/1.4.64	Bull. 6-95/1.4.63	COM(95) 207, Bull. 6-95/1.4.63		OJ C 323/4,12.95, Bull. 11-95/1.4.52*		
833 Europe Agreement with Bulgaria	Bull. 1/2-92/1.4.7	Bull. 5-92/1.2.12	Bull. 12-92/1.4.11	Bull. 3-93/1.3.8	COM(93) 45, Bull. 1/2-93/1.3.12*		OJ C 315/22.11.93, Bull. 10-93/1.3.12*	Dec. 94/908/ECSC, EC, Euratom: OJ L 358/31.12.94, Bull. 12-94/1.3.22	Council Dec. on the signature: Bull. 3-93/1.3.8; entry into force: Bull. 12-95/1.4.74
834 Europe Agreement with Romania	Bull. 1/2-92/1.4.7	Bull. 5-92/1.2.12	Bull. 11-92/1.4.12	Bull. 1/2-93/1.3.9	COM(92) 511, Bull. 12-92/1.4.14		OJ C 315/22.11.93, Bull. 10-93/1.3.16*	Dec. 94/907/ECSC, EC, Euratom: OJ L 357/31.12.94, Bull. 12-94/1.3.26	Council Dec. on the signature: Bull. 1/2-93/1.3.9; entry into force: Bull. 1/2-95/1.4.75
835 Europe Agreement with the Czech Republic	Bull. 1/2-93/1.3.2	Bull. 4-93/1.3.16	Bull. 6-93/1.3.17	Bull. 10-93/1.3.14	COM(93) 386, Bull. 7/8-93/1.3.13		OJ C 315/22.11.93, Bull. 10-93/1.3.14*	Dec. 94/910/ECSC, EC, Euratom: OJ L 360/31.12.94, Bull. 12-94/1.3.33	ECSC Consultative Committee: Bull. 9-93/1.3.10; Council Dec. on the signature: Bull. 10-93/1.3.14; entry into force: Bull. 1/2-95/1.4.77
836 Europe Agreement with the Slovak Republic	Bull. 1/2-93/1.3.2	Bull. 4-93/1.3.16	Bull. 6-93/1.3.17	Bull. 10-93/1.3.14	COM(93) 386, Bull. 7/8-93/1.3.13		OJ C 315/22.11.93, Bull. 10-93/1.3.14*	Dec. 94/909/ECSC, EC, Euratom: OJ L 359/31.12.94, Bull. 12-94/1.3.30	ECSC Consultative Committee: Bull. 9-93/1.3.10; Council Dec. on the signature: Bull. 10-93/1.3.14; entry into force: Bull. 1/2-95/1.3.76
837 Draft Europe Agreement with Slovenia	Bull. 4-94/1.3.33	Bull. 3-95/1.4.64	Bull. 6-95/1.4.62		COM(95) 341, Bull. 7/8-95/1.4.64				ECSC Consultative Committee: Bull. 10-95/1.4.64
837 Draft Interim Agreement with Slovenia on trade and support measures	Bull. 9-95/1.4.36								

TABLE III — INTERNATIONAL AGREEMENTS 581

Relations with Mediterranean third countries and Middle East countries

Mediterranean third countries

		Commission recommendation	Council Decision/ Negotiating Directives	Initials	Signature	Commission proposal/ Conclusion	ESC opinion/ COR opinion°	EP opinion/ EP assent*	Council Regulation (or Decision) Conclusion	Comments
842	Draft Protocols with Mediterranean third countries on the modification of the EC and ECSC Agreements to allow for enlargement	Bull. 11-94/1.3.38	Bull. 3-95/1.4.60							
843	Draft Financial Protocol with Malta	Bull. 3-94/1.3.56	Bull. 6-94/1.3.39		Bull. 6-95/1.4.73	COM(95) 64, Bull. 4-95/1.4.71				
843	Draft Financial Protocol with Cyprus	Bull. 3-94/1.3.55	Bull. 6-94/1.3.38		Bull. 6-95/1.4.71	COM(95) 65, Bull. 4-95/1.4.70				
845	Draft Agreement on economic and trade cooperation with Croatia	Bull. 1/2-95/1.4.85	Bull. 3-95/1.4.61							
845	Draft Agreement on economic and trade cooperation with the FYROM	Bull. 11-95/1.4.64	Bull. 12-95							
845	Draft Financial Protocol with the FYROM	Bull. 11-95/1.4.65	Bull. 12-95							
848	Draft Euro-Mediterranean Agreement with Morocco	Bull. 12-92/1.4.20, Bull. 6-93/1.3.25	Bull. 12-93/1.3.133	Bull. 11-95/1.4.67		COM(95) 740, Bull. 12-95				
849	Draft Euro-Mediterranean Agreement with Tunisia	Bull. 11-93/1.3.26	Bull. 12-93/1.3.38	Bull. 4-95/1.4.80	Bull. 7/8-95/1.4.84	COM(95) 235, Bull. 5-95/1.4.74		OJ C 17/22.1.96, Bull. 12-95*		Dec. concerning the signature: Bull. 7/8-95/1.4.84; ECSC Consultative Committee: Bull. 7/8-95/1.4.84

° Opinion of the Committee of the Regions.
* Agreements requiring Parliament's assent.

	Commission recommendation	Council Decision/ Negotiating Directives	Initials	Signature	Commission proposal/ Conclusion	ESC opinion/ COR opinion°	EP opinion/ EP assent*	Council Regulation (or Decision) Conclusion	Comments
851 Draft Euro-Mediterranean Agreement with Israel	Bull. 9-93/1.3.24	Bull. 12-93/1.3.31	Bull. 9-95/1.4.45	Bull. 11-95/1.4.69					Council Agreement in principle: Bull. 10-93/1.3.27; ECSC Consultative Committee: Bull. 12-95
851 Agreement with Israel on trade and allied matters					COM(95) 618, Bull. 11-95/1.4.70		OJ C 17/22.1.96, Bull. 12-95	Bull. 12/95	ECSC Consultative Committee: Bull. 12-95
852 Draft Euro-Mediterranean Agreement with Egypt	Bull. 11-94/1.3.44	Bull. 12-94/1.3.67							
853 Draft Euro-Mediterranean Agreement with Jordan	Bull. 5-95/1.4.75	Bull. 6-95/1.4.82							
854 Draft Euro-Mediterranean Agreement with Lebanon	Bull. 10-95/1.4.82	Bull. 10-95/1.4.82							

Middle East countries (Gulf Cooperation Council countries, Iran, Iraq and Yemen)

	Commission recommendation	Council Decision/ Negotiating Directives	Initials	Signature	Commission proposal/ Conclusion	ESC opinion/ COR opinion°	EP opinion/ EP assent*	Council Regulation (or Decision) Conclusion	Comments
860 Agreement amending the Cooperation Agreement with Yemen	Bull. 5-92/1.2.26	Bull. 6-92/1.4.21			OJ C 310/16.11.93, COM(93) 504, Bull. 10-93/1.3.31		OJ C 128/9.5.94, Bull. 4-94/1.3.35	OJ L 57/15.3.95, Bull. 3-95/1.4.69	

TABLE III — INTERNATIONAL AGREEMENTS   583

Relations with the independent States of the former Soviet Union and Mongolia

Bilateral relations

	Commission recommendation	Council Decision/ Negotiating Directives	Initials	Signature	Commission proposal/ Conclusion	ESC opinion/ COR opinion°	EP opinion/ EP assent*	Council Regulation (or Decision) Conclusion	Comments
880 Draft Partnership and Cooperation Agreement with Russia	Bull. 7/8-92/1.4.3, Bull. 3-93/1.3.19	Bull. 10-92/1.4.19, Bull. 4-93/1.3.18		Bull. 6-94/1.3.30	COM(94) 257, Bull. 6-94/1.3.30		OJ C 339/18.12.95, Bull. 11-95/1.4.80*		Council conclusions: Bull. 4-94/1.3.27; ECSC Consultative Committee: Bull. 3-95/1.4.74
880 Interim Agreement with Russia on trade and support measures	Bull. 7/8-94/1.3.45	Bull. 7/8-94/1.3.45	Bull. 12-94/1.3.53	Bull. 7/8-95/1.4.89	COM(95) 332, Bull. 7/8-95/1.4.89			Dec. 95/414/EC. OJ L 247/13.10.95, Bull. 7/8-95/1.4.89	Dec. concerning the signature: Bull. 7/8-95/1.4.89; ECSC Consultative Committee: Bull. 7/8-95/1.4.89
881 Draft Partnership and Cooperation Agreement with Ukraine	Bull. 7/8-92/1.4.3, Bull. 1/2-94/1.3.52	Bull. 10-92/1.4.19, Bull. 3-94/1.3.51	Bull. 3-94/1.3.51	Bull. 6-94/1.3.34	COM(94) 226, Bull. 6-94/1.3.34, COM(95) 137, Bull. 5-95/1.4.87		OJ C 339/18.12.95, Bull. 11-95/1.4.83*		ECSC Consultative Committee: Bull. 3-95/1.4.75
881 Interim Agreement with Ukraine on trade and support measures	Bull. 6-94/1.3.35	Bull. 6-94/1.3.35		Bull. 6-95/1.4.93	COM(94) 341, Bull. 7/8-94/1.3.46		OJ C 308/20.11.95, Bull. 10-95/1.4.90	Dec. 95/541/EC and Dec. 95/542/Euratom, ECSC: OJ L 311/23.12.95, Bull. 12-95	ECSC Consultative Committee: Bull. 12-94/1.3.56
882 Partnership and Cooperation Agreement with Moldova	Bull. 7/8-92/1.4.3	Bull. 10-92/1.4.19, Bull. 7/8-94/1.3.43	Bull. 7/8-94/1.3.43	Bull. 11-94/1.3.35	COM(94) 477, Bull. 11-94/1.3.35, COM(95) 137, Bull. 5-95, 1.4.86		OJ C 339/18.12.95, Bull. 11-95/1.4.77*		ECSC Consultative Committee: Bull. 12-94/1.3.52

° Opinion of the Committee of the Regions.
* Agreements requiring Parliament's assent.

		Commission recommendation	Council Decision/ Negotiating Directives	Initials	Signature	Commission proposal/ Conclusion	ESC opinion/ COR opinion°	EP opinion/ EP assent°	Council Regulation (or Decision) Conclusion	Comments
882	Draft Interim Agreement with Moldova		Bull. 7/8-94/1.3.44		Bull. 10-95/1.4.88	COM(95) 244, Bull. 6-95/1.4.90		OJ C 339/18.12.95, Bull. 11-95/1.4.79		Dec. concerning the signature: Bull. 10-95/1.4.88; ECSC Consultative Committee: Bull. 7/8-95/1.4.90
883	Draft Partnership and Cooperation Agreement with Belarus	Bull. 7/8-92/1.4.3, Bull. 10-94/1.3.31	Bull. 10-92/1.4.19, Bull. 11-94/1.3.33	Bull. 12-94/1.3.48	Bull. 3-95/1.4.70	COM(95) 44, Bull. 1/2-95/1.4.96, COM(95) 137, Bull. 5-95/1.4.83				ECSC Consultative Committee: Bull. 3-95/1.4.70
883	Draft Interim Agreement with Belarus		Bull. 11-94/1.3.34			COM(95) 245				
884	Draft Partnership and Cooperation Agreement with Georgia			Bull. 12-95						
884	Draft Partnership and Cooperation Agreement with Armenia			Bull. 12-95						
884	Draft Partnership and Cooperation Agreement with Azerbaijan			Bull. 12-95						
885	Draft Partnership and Cooperation Agreement with Kazakhstan	Bull. 7/8-92/1.4.3, Bull. 3-93/1.3.19	Bull. 10-92/1.4.19, Bull. 4-93/1.3.18	Bull. 5-94/1.3.35	Bull. 1/2-95/1.4.97	OJ C 319/16.11.94, COM(94) 411, Bull. 10-94/1.3.32, COM(95) 137, Bull. 5-95/1.4.84				Dec. concerning the signature: Bull. 12-94/1.3.49; ECSC Consultative Committee: Bull. 3-95/1.4.71
885	Draft Partnership and Cooperation Agreement with Kyrgyzstan	Bull. 7/8-92/1.4.3, Bull. 3-93/1.3.19	Bull. 10-92/1.4.19	Bull. 5-94/1.3.36	Bull. 1/2-95/1.4.99	OJ C 326/24.11.94, COM(94) 412, Bull. 10-94/1.3.33, COM(95) 137, Bull. 5-95/1.4.85		OJ C 339/18.12.95, Bull. 11-95/1.4.75*		Dec. concerning the signature: Bull. 12-94/1.3.51; ECSC Consultative Committee: Bull. 3-95/1.4.85
885	Draft Interim Agreement with Kazakhstan on trade and support measures	Bull. 7/8-94/1.3.41	Bull. 7/8-94/1.3.41	Bull. 12-94/1.3.50	Bull. 12-95	COM(95) 29, Bull. 1/2-95/1.4.98				ECSC Consultative Committee: Bull. 3-95/1.4.71
885	Draft Interim Agreement with Kyrgyzstan	Bull. 7/8-94/1.3.42	Bull. 7/8-94/1.3.42			COM(95) 49, Bull. 3-95/1.4.72				ECSC Consultative Committee: Bull. 3-95/1.4.72

TABLE III — INTERNATIONAL AGREEMENTS   585

Relations with Asian countries

Bilateral relations

	Commission recommendation	Council Decision/ Negotiating Directives	Initials	Signature	Commission proposal/ Conclusion	ESC opinion/ COR opinion[o]	EP opinion/ EP assent[a]	Council Regulation (or Decision) Conclusion	Comments
913 Draft Framework Agreement with Nepal		Bull. 10-94/1.3.48	Bull. 7/8-95/1.4.99	Bull. 11-95/1.4.92	OJ C 338/16.12.95, COM(95) 488, Bull. 10-95/1.4.99				
914 Cooperation Agreement with Sri Lanka		Bull. 1/2-93/1.3.37	Bull. 12-93/1.3.53	Bull. 7/8-94/1.3.57	OJ C 86/23.3.94, COM(94) 15, Bull. 1/2-94/1.3.74		OJ C 18/23.1.95, Bull. 12-94/1.3.74	Dec. 95/129/EC, OJ L 85/19.4.95, Bull. 3-95/1.4.84	Dec. concerning the signature: Bull. 7/8-94/1.3.57
915 Draft Cooperation Agreement with Vietnam	Bull. 7/6-93/1.3.47	Bull. 10-93/1.3.41	Bull. 5-95/1.4.98	Bull. 7/8-95/1.4.100	OJ C 12/17.1.96, COM(95) 305, Bull. 6-95/1.4.104				Dec. concerning the signature: Bull. 7/8-95/1.4.100
919 Draft Agreement on trade and cooperation with Korea		Bull. 3-95/1.4.81							

Relations with Latin American countries

Relations with regional groupings

	Commission recommendation	Council Decision/ Negotiating Directives	Initials	Signature	Commission proposal/ Conclusion	ESC opinion/ COR opinion[o]	EP opinion/ EP assent[a]	Council Regulation (or Decision) Conclusion	Comments
926 Draft Agreement on commercial and economic cooperation with Mercosur	Bull. 4-95/1.4.88	Bull. 6-95/1.4.108	Bull. 9-95/1.4.55	Bull. 12-95	COM(95) 504				
927 San José Dialogue	COM(95) 600, Bull. 11-95/1.4.96								Dec. concerning the signature: Bull. 11-95/1.4.95

[o] Opinion of the Committee of the Regions.
[a] Agreements requiring Parliament's assent.

Bilateral relations

	Commission recommendation	Council Decision/ Negotiating Directives	Initials	Signature	Commission proposal/ Conclusion	ESC opinion/ COR opinion°	EP opinion/ EP assent^a	Council Regulation (or Decision) Conclusion	Comments
931 Draft Framework Agreement on cooperation with Chile	COM(95) 530, Bull. 11-95/1.4.97								
933 Framework Agreement on cooperation with Brazil	Bull. 1/2-92/1.4.44	Bull. 3-92/1.3.37	Bull. 4-92/1.4.21	Bull. 6-92/1.4.30	OJ C 163/30.6.92, COM(92) 209, Bull. 5-92/1.2.33		OJ C 337/21.12.92, Bull. 11-92/1.4.39	Dec. 95/445/EC: OJ L 262/1.11.95, Bull. 10-95/1.4.106	

Relations with the African, Caribbean and Pacific (ACP) countries and the overseas countries and territories (OCTs)

Relations with the ACP countries

	Commission recommendation	Council Decision/ Negotiating Directives	Initials	Signature	Commission proposal/ Conclusion	ESC opinion/ COR opinion°	EP opinion/ EP assent^a	Council Regulation (or Decision) Conclusion	Comments
936 Fourth Lomé Convention: half-way stage of revision	Bull. 9-93/1.3.44	Bull. 1/2-94/1.3.80		Bull. 11-95/1.4.102	COM(95) 707				
942 Agreement on guaranteed prices for cane sugar (1994-95)					COM(95) 464, Bull. 10-95/1.4.120			Dec. 95/518/EC: OJ L 299/12.12.95, Bull. 11-95/1.4.108	
942 Agreement on the accession of Zambia to Protocol No 8 on ACP sugar					COM(95) 41, Bull. 1/2-95/1.4.112			OJ L 120/31.5.95, Bull. 5-95/1.4.107	
942 Draft Agreement on the price of cane sugar from the ACP countries referred to in Protocol No 8 (1995-96)	Bull. 9-95/1.4.60	Bull. 10-95/1.4.119							
942 Draft Agreement on guaranteed prices for cane sugar (1994-95)	Bull. 11-94/1.3.66								

TABLE III — INTERNATIONAL AGREEMENTS   587

	Commission recommendation	Council Decision/ Negotiating Directives	Initials	Signature	Commission proposal/ Conclusion	ESC opinion/ COR opinion°	EP opinion/ EP assent*	Council Regulation (or Decision) Conclusion	Comments
946 Draft Protocol to the fourth ACP-EC Convention: adjustments as a result of enlargement	COM(94) 416, Bull. 10-94/1.3.58	Bull. 12-94, 1.3.85		Bull. 11-95/1.4.104					

Relations with South Africa

	Commission recommendation	Council Decision/ Negotiating Directives	Initials	Signature	Commission proposal/ Conclusion	ESC opinion/ COR opinion°	EP opinion/ EP assent*	Council Regulation (or Decision) Conclusion	Comments
953 Draft Agreement on trade and co-operation with South Africa and draft Protocol to the Lomé IV Convention	Bull. 3-95/1.4.97	Bull. 6-95/1.4.118							

Cooperation in the fields of justice and home affairs

Judicial, customs and police cooperation

	Commission recommendation	Council Decision/ Negotiating Directives	Initials	Signature	Commission proposal/ Conclusion	ESC opinion/ COR opinion°	EP opinion/ EP assent*	Council Regulation (or Decision) Conclusion	Comments
967 Convention on the protection of the Communities' financial interests				OJ C 316/27.11.95, Bull. 7/8-95/1.5.3	Prop. for an act of the Council laying down an agreement: COM(94) 214, Bull. 6-95/1.4.8		OJ C 89/10.4.95, Bull. 3-95/1.5.5	Formal adoption by the Council: Bull. 7/8-95/1.5.3	Political Agreement: Bull. 6-95/1.5.6
967 Draft Protocol to the Convention on the protection of financial interests					Proposal for an act of the Council: COM(95) 693, Bull. 12-95				

° Opinion of the Committee of the Regions.

* Agreements requiring Parliament's assent.

	Commission recommendation	Council Decision/ Negotiating Directives	Initials	Signature	Commission proposal/ Conclusion	ESC opinion/ COR opinion°	EP opinion/ EP assent*	Council Regulation (or Decision) Conclusion	Comments

Fight against drugs

	Commission recommendation	Council Decision/ Negotiating Directives	Initials	Signature	Commission proposal/ Conclusion	ESC opinion/ COR opinion°	EP opinion/ EP assent*	Council Regulation (or Decision) Conclusion	Comments
975	Agreements with the member States of the OAS on the control of drug precursors	Bull. 9-95/1.5.9	Bull. 11-95/1.5.14	Bull. 12-95	COM(95) 585, Bull. 11-95/1.5.14			Bull. 12-95	

Institutions and other bodies

European Parliament

Secretariat
Centre européen, Plateau du Kirchberg
L-2929 Luxembourg
Tel.: 43 001

Council of the European Union

General Secretariat
Rue de la Loi 175
B-1048 Brussels
Tel.: 285 61 11

European Commission

Rue de la Loi 200
B-1049 Brussels
Tel.: 299 11 11

Court of Justice of the European Communities

Boulevard Konrad Adenauer
L-2925 Luxembourg
Tel.: 43 031

European Court of Auditors

12, rue Alcide De Gasperi
L-1615 Luxembourg
Tel.: 43 981

Economic and Social Committee

Rue Ravenstein 2
B-1000 Brussels
Tel.: 519 90 11

Committee of the Regions

Rue Ravenstein 2
B-1000 Brussels
Tel.: 546 22 11

ECSC Consultative Committee

Bâtiment Jean Monnet
Rue Alcide De Gasperi
L-2920 Luxembourg
Tel.: 430 11

European Investment Bank

100, boulevard Konrad Adenauer
L-2950 Luxembourg
Tel.: 43 791

European Monetary Institute

Postfach 10 20 31
D-60020 Frankfurt am Main
Tel.: 24 00 06 91

List of abbreviations[1]

ACP	African, Caribbean and Pacific countries party to the Lomé Convention
ACTS	Specific R&TD programme in the field of advanced communications technologies and services
APEC	Asia-Pacific Economic Cooperation
APIM	Spanish tax on production and imports (Arbitrio sobre la producción y las importaciones)
Aproma	Association for Soft Commodities, European Economic Community/Africa-Caribbean-Pacific
ASEAN	Association of South-East Asian Nations
BC-Net	Business Cooperation Network
BCC	Business Cooperation Centre
BRITE/EURAM	Specific R&TD programme in the fields of industrial technologies and advanced materials
CAP	Common agricultural policy
Cedefop	European Centre for the Development of Vocational Training
CELEX	Interinstitutional system of computerized documentation on Community law
CEN	European Committee for Standardization
CFSP	Common foreign and security policy
CIS	Commonwealth of Independent States
CIS	Customs information system

---

[1] This list is not exhaustive. It contains the more important acronyms and abbreviations which appear in several places in the Report.

CLEPA	Liaison Committee for the Automotive Equipment and Parts Industry
Coleacp	Liaison Committee for the Promotion of Tropical Fruits and Off-Season Vegetables exported from ACP States
COM	Common organization of the markets
Comett	Community action programme in education and training for technology
Cordis	Community research and development information service
COST	European cooperation on scientific and technical research
CREST	Scientific and Technical Research Committee
CSF	Community support framework (Structural Funds)
EAGGF	European Agricultural Guidance and Guarantee Fund
EBRD	European Bank for Reconstruction and Development
ECE	United Nations Economic Commission for Europe
ECHO	European Community Humanitarian Office
ECIP	European Community Investment Partners
ECO	Economic Cooperation Organization
EDF	European Development Fund
EDI	Electronic data interchange
EEA	European Economic Area
EEIG	European Economic Interest Grouping
EFTA	European Free Trade Association
Ehlass	European home and leisure accident surveillance system
EIB	European Investment Bank
EIC	Euro-Info Centre
EIF	European Investment Fund
EMI	European Monetary Institute
EMS	European Monetary System

EMU	Economic and monetary union
EOQ	European Organization for Quality
EOTC	European Organization for Testing and Certification
Erasmus	European Community action scheme for the mobility of university students
ERDF	European Regional Development Fund
ESA	European Space Agency
ESF	European Social Fund
EURES	European Employment Services
Eurocontrol	European Organization for the Safety of Air Navigation
Europol	European Police Office
Eurostat	Statistical Office of the European Communities
Eurotecnet	Community action programme in the field of training and technological change
FADN	Farm accountancy data network
FAO	Food and Agriculture Organization of the United Nations
FIFG	Financial Instrument for Fisheries Guidance
FORCE	Programme for the development of continuing vocational training
FYROM	Former Yugoslav Republic of Macedonia
GATS	General Agreement on Trade in Services
GATT	General Agreement on Tariffs and Trade
GCC	Gulf Cooperation Council
GDP	Gross domestic product
GNP	Gross national product
GNSS	Global Navigation Satellite System
Helios	Handicapped people in Europe living independently in an open society (Community programme)
IAEA	International Atomic Energy Agency (UN)

IBRD	International Bank for Reconstruction and Development (World Bank) (UN)
ICRC	International Committee of the Red Cross
IDA	Interchange of data between administrations
IGC	Intergovernmental Conference
ILO	International Labour Organization
IMF	International Monetary Fund (UN)
IMO	International Maritime Organization
INTAS	International Association for the Promotion of Cooperation with Scientists from the New Independent States of the former Soviet Union
ISDN	Integrated services digital network
ISPO	Information Society Project Office
ISTC	International Science and Technology Centre
ITER	International Thermonuclear Experimental Reactor
ITU	International Telecommunication Union
JAMA	Japan Automobile Manufacturers' Association
JET	Joint European Torus
JETRO	Japan External Trade Organization
JICS	Joint Interpreting and Conference Service
JRC	Joint Research Centre
LIFE	Financial instrument for the environment
Lingua	Programme to promote foreign language competence in the European Community
MEDIA	Programme to encourage the development of the audio-visual industry
Mercosur	Southern Cone Common Market
MFA	Multifibre Arrangement
MFN	Most-favoured nation
NAFO	North-West Atlantic Fisheries Organization

NATO	North Atlantic Treaty Organization
NCI	New Community Instrument
NGO	Non-governmental organization
NIS	New independent States
NPA	New partnership approach
NPT	Treaty on the non-proliferation of nuclear weapons
OAU	Organization of African Unity
OCTs	Overseas countries and territories
OECD	Organization for Economic Cooperation and Development
ONP	Open network provision
OSCE	Organization for Security and Cooperation in Europe
PACE	Community programme to improve the efficiency of electricity use
PETRA	Programme for the vocational training of young people and their preparation for adult and working life
PHARE	Programme of Community aid for Central and East European countries
PLO	Palestine Liberation Organization
Poseican	Programme of options specific to the remote and insular nature of the Canary Islands
Poseidom	Programme of options specific to the remote and insular nature of the overseas departments
Poseima	Programme of options specific to the remote and insular nature of Madeira and the Azores
R&TD	Research and technological development
SDRs	Special drawing rights (IMF)
SMEs	Small and medium-sized enterprises
SPD	Single programming document (Structural Funds)
Stabex	System for the stabilization of ACP and OCT export earnings

Sysmin	System for the stabilization of export earnings from mining products
TAC	Total allowable catch
TACIS	Programme for technical assistance to the new independent States and Mongolia
TEDIS	Trade electronic data interchange systems (Community programme)
Tempus	Trans-European mobility scheme for university studies
TENs	Trans-European networks
Thermie	European technologies for energy management
TIDE	Technological initiative for disabled and elderly people
TNA	Telematics networks between administrations
TRIPs	Trade-related aspects of intellectual property rights
UCLAF	Unit for the coordination of fraud prevention
UNCED	United Nations Conference on Environment and Development
Unctad	United Nations Conference on Trade and Development
UNDP	United Nations Development Programme
UNEP	United Nations Environment Programme
Unesco	United Nations Educational, Scientific and Cultural Organization
UNHCR	United Nations High Commissioner for Refugees
Unicef	United Nations Children's Fund
UNIDO	United Nations Industrial Development Organization
UNRWA	United Nations Relief and Works Agency for Palestine Refugees in the Near East
UPU	Universal Postal Union
VALUE	Specific programme for the dissemination and utilization of R&TD results
WEU	Western European Union

WFP	World Food Programme (UN)
WHO	World Health Organization (UN)
WIPO	World Intellectual Property Organization (UN)
WTO	World Trade Organization

Publications cited in this Report

General Report on the Activities of the European Union
   (abbr.: General Report), published annually by the Commission

Works published in conjunction with the General Report:

- *The Agricultural Situation in the European Union*
  (abbr.: Agricultural Report), published annually

- *Report on Competition Policy*
  (abbr.: Competition Report), published annually

- *Report on the application of Community law*
  published annually

Bulletin of the European Union
   (abbr.: Bull.), published monthly by the Commission

Supplement to the Bulletin of the European Communities
   (abbr.: Supplement... — Bull.), published at irregular intervals by the
   Commission

   3/93   The future development of the common transport policy

   6/93   Growth, competitiveness, employment — The challenges and
          ways forward into the 21st century — White Paper

   3/94   An industrial competitiveness policy for the European Union

   1/95   Address by Jacques Santer, President of the Commission, to the
          European Parliament on the occasion of the investiture debate of
          the new Commission
          Commission's programme for 1995
          Presentation to the European Parliament by Jacques Santer
          Resolution of the European Parliament on the programme for
          1995

   2/95   Strengthening the Mediterranean policy of the European Union:
          Establishing a Euro-Mediterranean partnership

3/95   The European Union and human rights in the world

Official Journal of the European Communities
Legislation series (abbr.: OJ L)
Information and notices series (abbr.: OJ C)
Supplement on public works and supply contracts (abbr.: OJ S)

Reports of Cases before the Court
(abbr.: ECR), published by the Court of Justice in annual series, parts
appearing at irregular intervals throughout the year

Annual Report of the European Investment Bank

Annual Report of the European Investment Fund

**All the above publications are printed and distributed through
the Office for Official Publications of the European Communities,
L-2985 Luxembourg**

Index[1]

A

ACP States: 81, 689, 798, 936 to 951
Administrations: 438
Advanced television services: 453, 678
Advertising: 654
Aerospace industry: 193, 194, 239
Afghanistan: 700, 784, 807
Africa: 706, 792, 794
Agriculture: see Common agricultural policy
Agrimonetary arrangements: 549, 550
AIDS and other communicable diseases: 640, 792, 793
Air (quality): 501
Air safety: 411
Air traffic: 410
Air transport: 144, 409 to 414, 416, 418, 820
Airports: 170, 413
Albania: 64, 729, 805, 838
Algeria: 66, 704, 784, 847, 1016, 1022
Altener: see Renewable energy sources
Andean Pact: 929, 975
Angola: 689, 695, 706, 784, 804, 950
Antarctic: 584, 586
Anti-dumping: 335, 741 to 744
Anti-subsidy activities: 741 to 744
Areas with exceptionally low population densities: 317, 318
Argentina: 376, 581, 707
Armenia: 552, 805, 874, 884
Arms: 697 to 701
Asia: 81, 377, 689, 708, 767, 788, 798, 807, 910 to 924
Association agreements: 847 to 849, 851 to 853
Atlantic: 495, 584
Audiovisual: 28, 656, 658, 676 to 679
Australia: 201, 371, 416, 522, 753, 905, 906

Austria: 231, 248, 766, 1029
Azerbaijan: 552, 702, 805, 884, 1017

B

Baltic Sea: 584, 586, 818
Baltic States: 172, 418, 689, 805, 830, 1022
Banana trade: 332, 540, 941
Bangladesh: 807
Basic industries (steel, chemicals, raw materials): 166, 183 to 186, 760
Belarus: 65, 805, 874, 883, 1016
Benin: 784
Biomedicine: 244
Biotechnology: 28, 197, 242, 478 to 481, 505
Bolivia: 793, 807, 934, 975
Border controls: 2, 101, 115
Borrowing operations: 58, 82, 1012 to 1024
Bosnia-Herzegovina: 695, 703, 825, 845
Brazil: 376, 776, 933
Broad guidelines of economic policies: 38, 45, 48
Budget discharge procedure: 993
Bulgaria: 418, 762, 777, 815, 833, 1022
Burma: see Myanmar
Burundi: 689, 695, 706, 804, 948

C

Cambodia: 700, 784, 807
Canada: 173, 201, 250, 257, 285, 378, 416, 522, 753, 907, 908
Canary Islands: 337
Cancer: 638, 639
CAP: see Common agricultural policy

---

[1] The figures refer to point numbers in the Report.

Cape Verde: 581, 784
Caribbean: 707, 938, 975
Carriage of dangerous goods: 390, 394, 398
Cedefop: 288 to 290
CEEC: see Central and East European countries
Central Asia: 695, 885
Central and East European countries: 60, 64, 69, 81, 138, 256, 267, 283, 286, 373, 418, 457, 687, 689, 729, 732, 733, 768, 814 to 838, 1000, 1049
Cereals: 535
CFSP: see Common foreign and security policy
Chad: 784
Chechnya: 702
Chemical products: 106, 480
Chemicals: see Basic industries
Chernobyl: 374, 515, 516, 805, 881
Chile: 707, 931
China: 179, 377, 477, 708, 758, 767, 776, 784, 807, 916 to 918
China Sea: 708
Civil protection: 489
Climate: 238
Climatic change: 504
Clothing: 196
Coal: 265, 356, 384
Coastal areas: 499
Cohesion Fund: 78, 326, 327, 354, 471
Colombia: 707, 934, 975
Commission work programme: 8, 9, 1055
Committee procedures: 1032 to 1034
Commodities: 787
Common agricultural policy: 90, 243, 331, 525 to 564, 895, 990
Common agricultural policy (agricultural structures): 307 to 311
Common agricultural policy (reform): 526, 528, 529
Common commercial policy: 91, 188, 737 to 777, 817, 893, 894, 900, 901, 938, 1135
Common Customs Tariff: 334
Common foreign and security policy: 689, 690 to 709
Common foreign and security policy (declarations): 702 to 709
Common organization of markets (CAP): 535 to 547
Common organization of markets (fisheries): 587, 588

Commonwealth of Independent States: see Independent States of the former Soviet Union
Communicable diseases: see AIDS and other communicable diseases
Community initiatives: 319 to 321, 471
Community law: 94 to 96, 137, 1121 to 1140
Community law (computerization): 1139, 1140
Community law (consolidation): 113, 668
Community law (monitoring of application): 1121 to 1124
Community Plant Variety Office: 109
Community support frameworks: 297 to 318
Comoros: 581, 706
Company law: 131
Competition: 139 to 174, 188, 454, 895, 908
Concentrations: 152 to 159
Consumer credit: 652
Consumers: 644 to 655
Controlled thermonuclear fusion: 248 to 251
Convention on the Law of the Sea: 715
Cooperation between businesses: 209
Copyright: 132, 134, 717
Costa Rica: 934
Côte d'Ivoire: 581
Council of Europe: 643, 729 to 732
Court of First Instance: 383, 1061 to 1064
Court of Justice: 1059 to 1064
Craft industry: 206, 212 to 214
Croatia: 417, 703, 769, 825, 845
Crop products: 535 to 545
Cuba: 707, 784, 807, 932
Culture: 88, 102, 224, 656, 680 to 688
Customs: 737, 969
Customs union: 844, 1126 to 1128
Cyprus: 267, 284, 689, 841, 843, 1049
Czech Republic: 418, 762, 835, 1022

D

Dangerous substances: 106
Data protection: 14, 132, 135, 421, 455
Declining industrial areas: 303, 304
Developing countries: 259, 459
Development: 778 to 799, 954

Diplomatic and consular protection: 6
Direct taxation: 128
Disabled people: 445, 634
Dominant positions (abuses of): 151
Drug dependence: see Drugs
Drugs: 641, 642, 791, 974, 975

E

EAGGF
— Guarantee Section: 558 to 562, 981
— Guidance Section: 307, 530, 563, 564
EC Investment Partners (ECIP): 179, 788
ECHO: 800 to 802
Economic   Cooperation   Organization (ECO): 862
Economic and monetary policy: 31 to 84
Economic and social cohesion: 296 to 329
ECSC operating budget: 994 to 996
Ecuador: 707, 807, 935, 975
EDF: see European Development Fund
Education: 266 to 295, 441, 464, 646, 895
EFTA: 104, 282, 809, 811 to 813
Egypt: 705, 769, 852
Elderly people: 445, 635
Electricity: 357, 361, 362, 368
Emergency aid: 339, 636
Employment: 26, 34, 47, 162, 594, 604 to 610, 635, 734, 1049
Energy: 245, 349, 352 to 384, 465, 840
Energy (Community strategy): 353
Energy efficiency: 357
Energy technologies: 355
Enlargement: 320, 667, 689, 766, 772, 946, 1048
Environment: 30, 182, 217, 238 to 240, 309, 351, 359, 389, 446, 462 to 507, 510, 531, 589 to 591, 789, 790, 840, 873
Environment (fifth action programme): 463
Environment (financial instruments): 470, 471
Equal opportunities: 627 to 633, 634, 1134
Equatorial Guinea: 581
Estonia: 580, 583, 815, 830
Ethiopia: 706, 784
Euratom: 249, 380, 510, 517 to 524, 895, 1020, 1022
Euro-Arab Dialogue: 861
Europa (server): 658, 670, 1109
Europe Agreements and other agreements

(Central and East European countries): 819 to 821
European Agency for the Evaluation of Medicinal Products: 106, 198
European Agricultural Guidance and Guarantee Fund: see EAGGF
European Bank for Reconstruction and Development (EBRD): 60 to 62, 736
European citizenship: 1 to 11
European Development Fund (EDF): 936, 937, 946, 955, 957, 998
European Economic Area (EEA): 78, 104, 231, 255, 282, 329, 689, 809, 810
European Energy Charter: 370
European Environment Agency: 507
European Foundation for the Improvement of Living and Working Conditions: 625
European Investment Bank (EIB): 59, 76 to 82, 208, 329, 846, 855, 956, 957, 1021, 1022, 1024
European Investment Fund (EIF): 83, 84
European Monetary Institute (EMI): 41, 44, 70 to 75
European Monetary System (EMS): 51 to 53
European officials: 1091 to 1107
European Ombudsman: 7
European Training Foundation: 286, 287
European University Institute: 291 to 295
Europol: 966
Eurostat: 92
Export arrangements: 750
Export credits: 756
Exports: 757, 903
External borders: 961

F

Falkland Islands: 958
FAO: see United Nations Food and Agriculture Organization
Farm accountancy data network (FADN): 555
Faeroe Islands: 583
Federal Republic of Yugoslavia (Serbia and Montenegro): 695, 845
Financial control: 999 to 1006
Financial Instrument for Fisheries Guidance (FIFG): 313
Financial perspective: 977 to 979

Financial regulations: 997, 998
Financial services: 119 to 125, 145, 720
Financial and technical cooperation: 924, 935
Financing of Community activities: 55 to 57, 76, 208, 221, 300, 322, 327, 558 to 564, 944, 976 to 1024
Finland: 231, 248, 317, 318, 381, 568, 737, 766, 1029
Firms: 140, 147 to 149, 204, 205 to 219
Fisheries: 90, 243, 312, 313, 333, 565 to 593, 907
Fisheries (external aspects): 577 to 586
Fisheries (internal aspects): 570 to 576
Fisheries (orientation): 566 to 569
Food aid: 551, 552, 795 to 797, 877
Foodstuffs: 105
Forests: 497, 506, 531, 532
Framework programme for research 1990-94 (R&TD): 230, 443
Framework programme for research 1994-98 (R&TD): 178, 200, 201, 210, 231 to 233, 436
France: 384
Fraud: 560, 774, 967, 1007 to 1011
Free movement of capital: 127, 1132, 1133
Free movement of goods: 97, 1126 to 1128
Free movement of persons: 2
Free movement of services: 403, 406, 1131
Free movement of workers: 118, 611, 1129, 1130
Fruit and vegetables: 539
Fuels: 367
FYROM: see Macedonia

G

G24: 516, 823
G7: 68, 426, 456, 477, 516, 886, 887
Gabon: 706
Gambia: 706
GATT: see World Trade Organization
Gaza Strip: 705
General budget: 35, 49, 563, 977 to 993
Generalized tariff preferences: 781, 954
Georgia: 552, 805, 874, 884, 1017
Germany: 384
Ghana: 784
Greece: 327, 728, 1015
Greenland: 583

Growth initiative: 54, 77
Guatemala: 707, 784, 807, 934
Guinea-Bissau: 581
Guinea (Republic): 581
Gulf Cooperation Council (GCC): 856

H

Haiti: 707, 784, 804
Health and safety at work: 618 to 621
Higher education: 268, 908
Historical archives of the EC: 672 to 675
HIV: see AIDS and other communicable diseases
Honduras: 793
Hong Kong: 758, 923
Human rights: 12 to 23, 726, 799, 844, 857
Human rights (outside the Union): 15 to 23
Humanitarian aid: 689, 800 to 808
Hungary: 215, 418, 758, 832, 1022

I

Iceland: 255, 267, 491, 584, 809, 811, 812
IDA: see Interchange of data between administrations
Immigration: 963
Import arrangements: 747 to 749
Imports: 903
Independent States of the former Soviet Union: 60, 65, 256, 286, 371, 374, 382, 515, 519, 689, 770, 805, 863 to 885, 1017, 1022, 1024
India: 377, 784, 912
Indian Ocean: 585, 938
Indirect taxation: 129, 130
Industrial competitiveness: 27, 176, 177, 207
Industrial cooperation: 178, 828, 902, 943
Industrial and materials technologies: 236, 237
Industrial property: 133, 717
Industrialized countries: 477, 886 to 909
Industry: 175 to 204, 226, 240, 306
Industry aid: 166
Information: 98, 199, 464, 646 to 649, 656 to 663
Information society: 28, 191, 419 to 461, 895

Information technology: 200 to 203, 235, 440
Inland transport: 414
Inland waterway transport: 402, 403
Innovation and technology transfer: 263
Institutional affairs: 1025 to 1039, 1136 to 1138
Institutions (administration and management): 1091 to 1120
Institutions (composition and functioning): 1040 to 1090
Intellectual property: 132, 262, 428
Interchange of data between administrations (IDA): 451, 452
Intergovernmental Conference 1996: 216, 728, 1025
Interinstitutional cooperation: 1035 to 1039
Internal market: 93 to 138, 188, 425
International Atomic Energy Agency (IAEA): 516, 520, 524
International Monetary Fund (IMF): 67, 716
Internet: 202, 440, 658
Investment: 123, 127, 310, 554, 734, 755, 826, 896
Iran: 857
Iraq: 700, 704, 784, 806, 858
Ireland: 248, 327
Iron and steel: see Basic industries
Israel: 257, 705, 850, 851, 1022
Italy: 1015

J

Japan: 179, 197, 201, 249, 371, 459, 522, 626, 753, 758, 759, 765, 775, 874, 897 to 904
Joint Research Centre (JRC): 227, 700
Jordan: 705, 784, 853
Judicial, customs and police cooperation: see Justice and home affairs
Justice and home affairs: 829, 959 to 975, 1049

K

Kazakhstan: 374, 702, 763, 874
Kenya: 784, 938
Kyrgyzstan: 552, 805, 874

L

Language teaching: 277, 278, 448
Latin America: 81, 179, 376, 460, 687, 689, 707, 788, 793, 798, 807, 925 to 935, 975, 1022
Latvia: 580, 583, 729, 815, 830
Lebanon: 850, 854
Lending operations: 58, 79, 84, 328, 1012 to 1024
Lesotho: 784
Less-developed regions: 301, 302
Liberia: 706, 804
Libraries: 442, 669
Libya: 705
Liechtenstein: 255, 267, 809
Lithuania: 64, 580, 583, 815, 830, 1016
Livestock products: 546, 547
Lomé Convention (implementation): 937
Lomé Convention (review): 936

M

Macedonia (former Yugoslav Republic of): 417, 729, 825, 845
Machinery: 187
Macrofinancial assistance: 63 to 66, 879, 881, 1015 to 1017
Madagascar: 581
Maghreb: 846 to 849
Malawi: 784
Malta: 267, 284, 689, 769, 841, 843, 1049
Marine science and technologies: 241
Maritime industry: 189, 190
Mashreq: 850 to 855
Meat: 547
Media: 126, 630
Mediterranean: 499
Mediterranean third countries: 81, 172, 179, 375, 458, 472, 689, 788, 793, 839 to 855, 1049
Mercosur Group: 926
Mexico: 807, 930
Middle East: 81, 689, 695, 705, 850, 856 to 860
Migrant workers: 615
Milk and milk products: 546
Mobility of researchers: 264
Moldova: 65, 729, 882, 1016
Mongolia: 770

Montenegro: see Federal Republic of Yugoslavia
Morocco: 313, 582, 769, 848
Motor vehicles: 107, 155, 142, 166, 188, 775, 902
Mozambique: 700, 784, 793, 798
Multimedia: 422, 423, 449, 688
Multimodal transport: 405
Mutual recognition of qualifications: 117, 270, 276
Myanmar: 708, 807

N

Namibia: 580, 938
Natural gas: 357, 361, 362, 366
Nepal: 784, 913
New Community Instrument (NCI): 58, 1014, 1022
New Zealand: 416, 533, 753, 909
Nicaragua: 784, 807
Niger: 706
Nigeria: 689, 695, 706, 949
Non-governmental organizations (development): 786
North Korea: 708
North Sea: 495, 591
Northern Ireland: 321
North-West Atlantic Fisheries Organization (NAFO): 578, 579
Norway: 201, 255, 267, 491, 583, 737, 765, 809, 811, 812, 1029
Nuclear energy: 369, 908
Nuclear fission: 246, 247
Nuclear safety: 508 to 516, 517, 875

O

Office for Harmonization in the Internal Market: 133
Office for Official Publications of the European Communities: 667 to 671
Oil: 365
Oman: 859
Open and distance learning: 279
Organization for Economic Cooperation and Development (OECD): 127, 192, 460, 487, 733 to 735, 755, 765

Organization for Security and Cooperation in Europe (OSCE): 696, 724 to 726
Overseas countries and territories (OCTs): 81, 955 to 958
Overseas departments: 338

P

Pact on stability in Europe: 696, 724
Pakistan: 708, 784, 807
Palestine Liberation Organization (PLO): 705
Palestinian Territories: 806, 850
Partnership and cooperation agreements: 865 to 867, 913 to 915, 919, 953
Peru: 707, 793, 807, 934, 975
PHARE: 56, 62, 372, 457, 703, 824 to 827, 845, 1000
Pharmaceutical industry: 197, 198
Philippines: 708, 793, 915
Plant health: 109
Poland: 355, 418, 580, 583, 777, 831
Political dialogue: 891, 892, 899, 909, 917
Pollution: 482, 484, 499 to 501, 531
Portugal: 59, 196, 327, 336, 350, 566
Postal services: 169, 454
Pre-accession strategy: 179, 473, 814, 824
Protocol on social policy: 598 to 602
Public access to the institutions' documents: 8
Public health: 89, 244, 444, 637 to 643, 650, 651, 792, 793
Public procurement: 136

R

Racism: 13, 624, 971
Radiation protection: 509 to 512
Rail transport: 159, 342, 344, 392 to 394
Railway industry: 195
Raw materials: see Basic industries
Refugees: 798
Regional aid: 167
Rehabilitation: 794
Renewable energy sources: 357
Republic of Korea: 459, 733, 765, 776, 919 to 922
Research: 188, 569

Research (dissemination of results): 260 to 262
Research and technological development: 28, 163, 218 to 265, 391
Right of asylum: 960
Right of entry and residence: 2, 116
Right of petition: 7
Right to vote and stand in municipal elections: 4
Rio Conference: 463, 789
Rio Group: 928
Road transport: 343, 388, 395 to 401
Romania: 64, 418, 762, 777, 805, 815, 834, 1016, 1022
Rural areas: 314 to 316, 443
Russia: see Russian Federation
Russian Federation: 215, 249, 374, 519, 522, 580, 695, 702, 727, 729, 758, 763, 805, 874, 880
Rwanda: 706, 784, 804, 948

S

Safety of installations: 513
San José (Conference): 927
São Tomé and Príncipe: 706, 951
Saudi Arabia: 704
SAVE: see Energy efficiency
School education: 269
Scientific and technical cooperation: 254, 257, 851, 878, 895, 908
Senegal: 581
Serbia: see Federal Republic of Yugoslavia
Shipbuilding: 166, 192
Shipping: 141, 406 to 408, 414
Shipping safety: 407
Sierra Leone: 706, 804
Simplification: 11, 27
Singapore: 758
Single programming documents (SPDs): 297 to 318
Slovak Republic: see Slovakia
Slovakia: 418, 513, 762, 815, 836, 1022
Slovenia: 417, 768, 837, 845
Small and medium-sized enterprises (SMEs): 27, 55, 206, 208, 212 to 214, 325, 436
Social dialogue: 603
Social exclusion: 623
Social policy: 89, 594 to 626
Social protection: 408, 412, 613

Social security: 613, 615, 632
Socrates: 267
Solidarity: 634 to 636
Somalia: 706, 784, 804
South Africa: 59, 81, 257, 580, 689, 706, 781, 788, 938, 952 to 954, 1022
South Korea: see Republic of Korea
Spain: 327, 350, 566
Sri Lanka: 708, 914
Stabex: 939
Standardization: 180, 237, 364
State aid: 160 to 165, 220, 468, 553, 554, 593
Statistics: 85 to 92, 217, 406, 688
Steel: 183, 265, 760
Structural Funds: 999
Structured relations: 814, 843
Subsidiarity: 10
Sudan: 706, 784, 804
Sugar Protocol: 942
Supplementary and amending budget: 989
Sustainable development: 789
Sustainable Development Commission (SDC): 475, 713
Swaziland: 784
Sweden: 231, 317, 318, 381, 568, 737, 766, 1029
Switzerland: 104, 201, 415, 811, 813
Syria: 850
Sysmin: 940

T

TACIS: 62, 372, 869 to 876, 1000
TACs and quotas (fisheries): 570, 571
Taiwan: 767, 776
Tadjikistan: 552, 805
Tanzania: 706, 784, 793, 804
Targeted socioeconomic research (1994-98): 253
Technical assistance: 827
Telecommunications: 84, 157, 168, 203, 345, 419
Telecommunications industry: 203
Telematics: 447
Telematics applications: 234, 437
Telematics networks between administrations (TNA): 347, 451, 452
Television: 153, 154, 429, 676

Textiles: 196, 766 to 774, 820, 1009
Thailand: 708, 745, 793
Thermie: see Energy technologies
TNA: see Telematics networks between administrations
Togo: 784
Tourism: 88
Trade agreements: 751 to 754, 811
Trans-European networks: 29, 78, 83, 340 to 351, 386, 435
Trans-Caucasian republics: 695, 884
Translation Service: 1112 to 1120
Transparency: 8, 668, 802, 827, 1052
Transport: 84, 87, 252, 341, 351, 369, 385 to 418, 439
Tunisia: 769, 784, 849
Turkey: 172, 745, 764, 769, 841, 844

U

Uganda: 784, 804
Ukraine: 65, 215, 374, 516, 727, 729, 763, 805, 881, 1016
UN Economic and Social Council: 712
UN: see United Nations and specialized institutions
Unemployment: 305, 604, 1049
United Arab Emirates: 758, 769
United Nations Conference on Trade and Development (Unctad): 782, 938
United Nations Economic Commission for Europe (ECE): 714
United Nations Food and Agriculture Organization (FAO): 785
United Nations Industrial Development Organization (UNIDO): 783
United Nations and specialized institutions: 577, 633, 709, 710 to 717, 780, 791
United States: 136, 173, 197, 201, 249, 257, 285, 378, 416, 459, 522, 689, 720, 737, 753, 765, 874, 888 to 896
Urban areas: 443
Urban transport: 404
Uruguay: 934
Uruguay Round: 723, 771 to 773, 820
USSR (former): see Independent States of the former Soviet Union
Uzbekistan: 1000, 1017

V

VAT: 129
Venezuela: 934, 975
Very remote regions: 330 to 339
Veterinary matters: 110, 112
Vietnam: 767, 915
Visas: 3, 961
Vocational training: 188, 272 to 276, 908
Voting in the Council: 1028 to 1030

W

Waste: 485 to 488, 514, 515
Water quality: 492 to 495
West Bank: 705
Western Economic Summit: see G7
Western European Union (WEU): 698, 727, 728
White Paper (Growth, competitiveness, employment): 24, 48, 197, 206, 466
White Paper (Preparation of the associated countries of Central and Eastern Europe for integration into the internal market): 457, 816
White Paper (Social policy): 595, 596
Wild fauna and flora: 496, 498
Wine: 533, 538
Workers in ECSC industries: 616, 617
World Bank (IBRD): 716
World Food Programme (WFP): 784
World Intellectual Property Organization (WIPO): 717
World Trade Organization (WTO): 460, 689, 718 to 723, 734, 771, 918

Y

Yemen: 784, 860
Young people: 280, 281
Yugoslavia (former): 675, 687, 689, 703, 803, 845, 1024

Z

Zaire: 804, 948